# Windows PowerShell
# Best Practices

Ed Wilson

Published with the authorization of Microsoft Corporation by:

O'Reilly Media, Inc.
1005 Gravenstein Highway North
Sebastopol, California 95472

ISBN: 978-0-7356-6649-8

Second Printing: April 2014

Printed and bound in the United States of America.

Microsoft Press books are available through booksellers and distributors worldwide. If you need support related to this book, email Microsoft Press Book Support at *mspinput@microsoft.com*. Please tell us what you think of this book at *http://www.microsoft.com/learning/booksurvey*.

**Acquisitions and Developmental Editor:** Michael Bolinger
**Production Editor:** Christopher Hearse
**Editorial Production:** nSight, Inc.

**Technical Reviewer:** Brian Wilhite
**Cover Design:** Twist Creative • Seattle
**Cover Composition:** Ellie Volckhausen
**Illustrator:** nSight, Inc.

*This book is dedicated to Teresa. You make each day feel like it is filled with infinite possibilities.*

—ED WILSON

# Contents at a glance

# Contents

---

**What do you think of this book? We want to hear from you!**

Microsoft is interested in hearing your feedback so we can continually improve our
books and learning resources for you. To participate in a brief online survey, please visit:

**www.microsoft.com/learning/booksurvey/**

## Chapter 5   Configuring the script environment   111

## Chapter 6   Avoiding scripting pitfalls   151

## Chapter 11   Handling input and output             339

## Chapter 12   Handling errors             397

## Chapter 18  Logging results                                    531

## Chapter 19  Troubleshooting scripts                            559

**What do you think of this book? We want to hear from you!**

Microsoft is interested in hearing your feedback so we can continually improve our
books and learning resources for you. To participate in a brief online survey, please visit:

**www.microsoft.com/learning/booksurvey/**

# Foreword

In April 2003, Microsoft's Jeffrey Snover gave me an early peek at PowerShell or, as it was known in its beta days, "Monad." I must admit that, while I fell in love with PoSH at first sight, I was just too darned busy with other work to really get my hands dirty with it for another five years, and I soon realized that boy, had I missed a few memos. "Objects in a pipeline? Is that anything like snakes on a plane?" "Hash tables? Can I get mine with a fried egg?"

Yup, there was a lot to learn, and I nearly wore out Google looking up PoSH-y things. Just about every one of those searches, however, seemed to lead me to the same place: the Hey, Scripting Guy! Blog. I quickly noticed that the blog delivered new articles daily, and so I was very surprised to see that the vast majority of those articles were penned by one guy: Ed Wilson. Since then, I've gotten to know Ed personally, and trust me, he's even funnier and more entertaining in person than he is in print, which brings me to this volume.

If you're a Windows admin, learning Windows PowerShell is an essential (as in you need to do this if you want to remain a Windows admin) task. It's not always an easy one, though, and you will often find yourself wishing for the "answers in the back of the book" so to speak. Well, Ed's written that book, and you're holding the latest edition. Work your way through *Windows PowerShell Best Practices*, actually take the time to try out the examples, and soon you, too, will be automating, scripting, and workflow-ing like mad. Happy PowerShelling!

—Mark Minasi, author of the *Mastering Windows Server* books

P.S. In case you don't already know, objects in a pipeline are way cooler than snakes on a plane. Really.

# Introduction

Welcome to *Windows PowerShell Best Practices*, a book that was developed together with the Microsoft Windows PowerShell product group to provide in-depth information about Windows PowerShell and best practices based on real-life experiences with the product in use in different environments. Numerous sidebars are also included that detail experiences from skilled industry professionals such as Enterprise Admins and Windows PowerShell Most Valuable Professionals (MVPs).

The book is largely based on Windows PowerShell 4.0 as it exists on Windows 8.1 and on Windows Server 2012 R2. Because Windows PowerShell introduced Desired State Configuration in Windows PowerShell 4.0, Chapter 23, "Using the Windows PowerShell DSC," must be run on a computer with Windows PowerShell 4.0 installed on it. Nearly all of the material in the other chapters will work without modification on Windows PowerShell 3.0 (on Windows 8 or on Windows Server 2012). A large part of the book also applies to Windows PowerShell 2.0 running on any version of Windows that it installs upon.

## Who is this book for?

Microsoft *Windows PowerShell Best Practices* is for anyone tasked with designing, implementing or managing enterprise products. This includes Active Directory Domain Services, System Center, Exchange, and SharePoint products. In addition, it is designed for anyone who either teaches or trains others on Windows PowerShell or even for the MCSE track of courseware. Lastly, power users who want to automate their desktops will also benefit from the explanations, scenarios, and sample scripts.

## How is this book organized?

This book is organized into four parts:

- Part I: Understanding the basics of Windows PowerShell
- Part II: Planning for scripting
- Part III: Designing the script
- Part IV: Deploying the script

The first part of this book consists of two chapters that focus on the basics of Windows PowerShell capabilities. This portion of the book is a level setting and would be ideal for anyone just learning Windows PowerShell.

The second part of the book discusses identifying scripting opportunities, the scripting environment, and avoiding scripting pitfalls. This part is also ideal for people learning Windows PowerShell, but it is also a great section for admins experienced with the fundamentals of Windows PowerShell but who need to write new scripts.

The third section of the book talks about how you actually design a script—how you plan for inputs and outputs to the script and how you document your scripts. This is a more advanced section, and it is appropriate for advanced students and for people who write scripts that others are expected to utilize.

The last section of the book talks about deploying scripts—how you run them; how you handle versioning; and how you use remote, workflow, and DSC capabilities in your script. This is appropriate for enterprise admins who are firmly entrenched in DevOps.

## System requirements

This book is designed to be used with the following Exchange 2010 software:

- Windows Server 2008 or Windows Server 2008 R2
- 1 GB of RAM
- x64 architecture-based computer with Intel or AMD processor that supports 64 bit
- 1.2 GB of available disk space
- Display monitor capable of 800 × 600 resolution

The following list details the minimum system requirements needed to run the content in the book's companion website:

- Windows XP with the latest service pack installed and the latest updates from Microsoft Update Service
- Display monitor capable of 1024 × 768 resolution
- CD-ROM drive
- Microsoft mouse or compatible pointing device

# The companion website

This book features a companion website that makes available to you additional information such as job aids, quick reference guides, and additional Windows PowerShell resources. These elements are included to help you plan and manage your Windows PowerShell organization and apply the book's recommended best practices. The companion website includes the following:

- **Job Aids**  Additional documents on most of the chapters that help you to collect and structure your work through the book.
- **Quick Reference Guides**  These guides provide an overview of all best practice recommendations in the book as well as a collection of all Internet links referenced in the book.

You can download these files from the companion website, which is located at *http://gallery.technet.microsoft.com/scriptcenter/PowerShell-40-Best-d9e16039*.

# Acknowledgements

A book of this scope does not happen without assistance. First I must thank my wife, Teresa Wilson, aka the Scripting Wife. She not only coordinated the acquisition of sidebars, but she also read the entire book at least three times. My technical reviewer, Microsoft PFE Brian Wilhite, was great at catching things that would have made me look silly. He also made numerous suggestions for improving not only the clarity of the writing, but in some cases the accuracy of the code. Brian absolutely rocks. Luckily, the Windows PowerShell community is very enthusiastic and as a result was receptive for my call for sidebars. The high quality of the sidebars, and the diversity of content was fun to read, and in the end makes for a much better book. If you run across one of the authors of the sidebars, make sure you tell them "hi." Lastly, I want to thank Jeffrey Snover, Ken Hansen and the rest of the Windows PowerShell team. They made an awesome product that just keeps getting better and better each year. Windows PowerShell for the win!

# Support & feedback

The following sections provide information on errata, book support, feedback, and contact information.

## Errata

We have made every effort to ensure the accuracy of this book. If you do find an error, please report it on our Microsoft Press site:

*http://aka.ms/PowershellBestPractices/errata*

You will find additional information and services for your book on its catalog page. If you need additional support, please e-mail Microsoft Press Book Support at *mspinput@ microsoft.com*.

Please note that product support for Microsoft software is not offered through the addresses above.

## We want to hear from you

At Microsoft Press, your satisfaction is our top priority, and your feedback our most valuable asset. Please tell us what you think of this book at:

*http://www.microsoft.com/learning/booksurvey*

The survey is short, and we read every one of your comments and ideas. Thanks in advance for your input!

## Stay in touch

Let us keep the conversation going! We are on Twitter: *http://twitter.com/MicrosoftPress*.

# PART I

# Understanding the basics of Windows PowerShell

# CHAPTER 1

# Survey of Windows PowerShell capabilities

- Understanding Windows PowerShell
- Installing Windows PowerShell
- Deploying Windows PowerShell
- Using command-line utilities
- Security issues with Windows PowerShell
- Working with Windows PowerShell
- Supplying options for cmdlets
- Working with the help options
- Additional resources

## Understanding Windows PowerShell

Perhaps the biggest obstacle for a Windows network administrator in migrating to Windows PowerShell 4.0 is understanding what the PowerShell actually is. In some respects, it is like a replacement for the venerable CMD (command) shell. In fact, on Windows Server 2012 R2 running in core mode, it is possible to replace the CMD shell with Windows PowerShell so that when the server boots up it uses Windows PowerShell as the interface. As shown in the following code example, after Windows PowerShell launches, you can use *cd* to change the working directory and then use *dir* to produce a directory listing in exactly the same way you would perform these tasks from the CMD shell.

```
Windows PowerShell
Copyright (C) 2013 Microsoft Corporation. All rights reserved.

PS C:\Users\ed.IAMMRED> cd c:\
PS C:\> dir

    Directory: C:\

Mode                LastWriteTime     Length Name
----                -------------     ------ ----
d----        9/4/2013  12:06 PM              DCS
d----        9/8/2013   8:32 PM              DemoUser
d----        9/8/2013   6:52 PM              fso
```

```
d----         9/8/2013    9:15 PM              myprocess
d----         8/22/2013  11:22 AM              PerfLogs
d-r--         8/22/2013   3:11 PM              Program Files
d-r--         8/27/2013   8:19 PM              Program Files (x86)
d----         9/8/2013   10:12 PM              ScriptFolder
d----         9/8/2013    7:22 PM              server1Config
d----         9/8/2013   10:46 PM              ServerConfig
d----         9/8/2013    9:22 PM              StartBits
d-r--         8/27/2013   8:06 PM              Users
d----         8/27/2013   7:52 PM              Windows


PS C:\>
```

You can also combine "traditional" CMD interpreter commands with other utilities such as *fsutil*. This is shown here:

```
PS C:\> md c:\test


    Directory: C:\


Mode                LastWriteTime      Length Name
----                -------------      ------ ----
d----         9/9/2013    3:31 PM             test


PS C:\> fsutil file createnew c:\test\mynewfile.txt 1000
File c:\test\mynewfile.txt is created
PS C:\> cd test
PS C:\test> dir


    Directory: C:\test


Mode                LastWriteTime      Length Name
----                -------------      ------ ----
-a---         9/9/2013    3:31 PM        1000 mynewfile.txt


PS C:\test>
```

We have been using Windows PowerShell in an interactive manner. This is one of the primary uses of Windows PowerShell; it is accomplished by opening a Windows PowerShell prompt and typing commands. The commands can be entered one at a time, or they can be grouped together like a batch file. We will look at this later because you need more information to understand it.

**Jason Helmick, Senior Technologist**
*Concentrated Technology*

It's amazing to think that, in a few short years, Windows PowerShell has grown from a couple hundred cmdlets to thousands—covering a wide variety of Microsoft products. This means that there is probably something lurking out in the Windows PowerShell universe that you haven't discovered and which might be very helpful to you. Using the discovery capabilities of Get-Help is the important and practical way to discover cmdlets—but it's not the only way.

The Windows PowerShell community is strong and vibrant, with MVPs, gurus, and aficionados all blogging, tweeting, and using forums to discover, discuss, and share new revelations when solving real-world problems. Getting involved in the community is a great way to extend and expand your Windows PowerShell skills—but again, it's not the only way.

I learn the most about Windows PowerShell when I'm working on a project with other admins who are also using PowerShell. When working with someone else, I've noticed that they might do a particular task differently than me—often in a way I hadn't thought of or using a technique or cmdlet I wasn't familiar with. Let me give you an example that happened to me recently.

I was getting my virtual machines ready for a live presentation, discussing how to get started learning Windows PowerShell. This was a very special presentation, and one that I really didn't want to screw up. In the process of getting my VMs loaded, I needed to check some IP addresses so that my co-host could remotely connect to the VMs, an easy enough task to solve using the Windows native command IPConfig.exe (which of course runs like a dandy in the Windows PowerShell console). I happened to mention this to my co-host for the presentation, saying something like "Let me get you the outside IP address; let me just run IPconfig and...."

My co-host responded before I could start typing with, "Have you used gip?" I was a little stunned—I'd never heard of gip. After noticing my confused look, he smiled and said: "I learn something new about Windows PowerShell almost every day—try it." So I did. It turns out that gip is an alias for Get-NetIPConfiguration, which produces a better-looking and easier-to-read result than the old IPConfig.exe. In fact, because it's a Windows PowerShell cmdlet producing objects, you can use this in amazing ways. I had just learned something new, something that's much better than how I was doing it before, because I was working with someone else using Windows PowerShell. The moral of the story is simple: Work with other admins who are using Windows PowerShell—even side-by-side if possible. You'll pick up new things from each other.

> Oh, who was my co-host who introduced me to something new? It was the inventor of Windows PowerShell, Distinguished Engineer Jeffrey Snover. If he can still learn something new about Windows PowerShell, so can I, and so can you. Work with your friends and share.

## Installing Windows PowerShell

Windows PowerShell 4.0 comes with Windows 8.1 client and Windows Server 2012 R2. You can download the Windows Management Framework 4.0 package containing updated WinRM, WMI, and Windows PowerShell 4.0 from the Microsoft Download center (*Microsoft.Com/Downloads*). The package allows you to install on Windows 7 and Windows Server 2008 R2—both of which must be running at least Service Pack 1 and the Microsoft .NET Framework 4.5. You can also install on Windows 8 and Windows Server 2012.

To prevent frustration during the installation, it makes sense to use a script that checks for the operating system, service pack level, and .NET Framework 4.5. A sample script that will check for the prerequisites is Get-PowerShellRequirements.ps1, which follows.

```
Get-PowerShellRequirements.ps1
Param([string[]]$computer = @($env:computername, "LocalHost"))
 foreach ($c in $computer)
  {
    $o = Get-WmiObject win32_operatingsystem -cn $c
    switch ($o.version)
    {
        {$o.version -gt 6.2} {"$c is Windows 8 or greater"; break}
        {$o.version -gt 6.1}
          {
            If($o.ServicePackMajorVersion -gt 0){$sp = $true}
            If(Get-WmiObject Win32_Product -cn $c |
                where { $_.name -match '.NET Framework 4.5'}) {$net = $true }
            If($sp -AND $net) { "$c meets the requirements for PowerShell 3" ; break}
            ElseIF (!$sp) {"$c needs a service pack"; break}
            ELSEIF (!$net) {"$c needs a .NET Framework upgrade"} ; break}
        {$o.version -lt 6.1} {"$c does not meet standards for PowerShell 3.0"; break}
        Default {"Unable to tell if $c meets the standards for PowerShell 3.0"}
    }

 }
```

# Deploying Windows PowerShell

After Windows PowerShell is downloaded from *http://www.Microsoft.com/downloads*, you can deploy Windows PowerShell to your enterprise by using any of the standard methods you currently use. A few of the methods some customers have used to accomplish Windows PowerShell deployment include the following:

1. Create a Microsoft Systems Center Configuration Manager package, and advertise it to the appropriate Organizational Unit (OU) or collection.

2. Create a Group Policy Object (GPO) in Active Directory Domain Services (AD DS), and link it to the appropriate OU.

3. Approve the update in Software Update Services (SUS).

If you are not deploying to an entire enterprise, perhaps the easiest way to install Windows PowerShell is to download the package and step through the wizard.

> **NOTE** To use a command-line utility in Windows PowerShell, launch Windows PowerShell by using Start | Run | PowerShell. At the PowerShell prompt, type in the command to run.

## Using cmdlets

In addition to using traditional programs and commands from the CMD.exe command interpreter, we can also use the cmdlets (pronounced *commandlets*) that are built into Windows PowerShell. Cmdlets can be created by anyone. The Windows PowerShell team creates the core cmdlets, but many other teams at Microsoft were involved in creating the hundreds of cmdlets shipping with Windows 8. They are like executable programs, but they take advantage of the facilities built into Windows PowerShell, and therefore are easy to write. They are not scripts, which are uncompiled code, because they are built using the services of a special .NET Framework namespace. Windows PowerShell 4.0 comes with about one thousand cmdlets on Windows 8.1. Because additional features and roles are added often, so are additional cmdlets. These cmdlets are designed to assist the network administrator or consultant to leverage the power of Windows PowerShell without having to learn a scripting language. One of the strengths of Windows PowerShell is that cmdlets use a standard naming convention that follows a Verb-Noun pattern, such as *Get-Help*, *Get-EventLog*, or *Get-Process*. The cmdlets using the *get* verb display information about the item on the right side of the dash. The cmdlets that use the *set* verb modify or set information about the item on the right side of the dash. An example of a cmdlet that uses the *set* verb is Set-Service, which can be used to change the *startmode* of a service. All cmdlets use one of the standard verbs. To find all of the standard verbs you can use the Get-Verb cmdlet. In Windows PowerShell 4.0, there are nearly 100 approved verbs.

**David Moravec, Microsoft PowerShell MVP**
*Mainstream Technologies*

One of the nice new features of Windows PowerShell 4.0 is the ability to count file hashes natively with the `Get-FileHash` cmdlet. In the past, if you wanted to count hashes, you had to use the *System.Security.Cryptography.HashAlgorithm* class. It was fine if you used it locally, but when you shared your scripts, you also had to deliver your function, which created hashes. That is not so anymore.

From my experience, the most frequent method for hash creation is *MD5*. It's quick and easy, and every tool can create this type of hash. If you run `Get-FileHash` in its default configuration, you receive the following:

```
PS C:\Users\Makovec> Get-FileHash .\myFile.exe | fl *
Path : C:\Users\Makovec\myFile.exe
Type : System.Security.Cryptography.SHA256Managed
Hash : p/a6HFn9QkCFQWiaQMo8hVILmCHCPMuaNrRn2DKJKVM=
```

You can see that the method used is *SHA256*. You can specify *MD5* by using an *Algorithm* parameter.

```
PS C:\Users\Makovec> Get-FileHash .\myFile.exe -Algorithm MD5 | fl *
Path : C:\Users\Makovec\myFile.exe
Type : System.Security.Cryptography.MD5CryptoServiceProvider
Hash : L1uabH1YgDx/WSR4e2SIgw==
```

Possible values for *Algorithm* are: *SHA1, SHA256, SHA384, SHA512, MACTripleDES, MD5*, and *RIPEMD160*. Unfortunately `Get-FileHash` doesn't accept pipeline input, so you have to use the following method when you have more files to check:

```
PS C:\Users\Makovec> dir myfile* |% { Get-FileHash -FilePath $_.FullName
} | ft Path, Hash -auto
Path                              Hash
----                              ----
C:\Users\Makovec\myFile.exe    p/
a6HFn9QkCFQWiaQMo8hVILmCHCPMuaNrRn2DKJKVM=
C:\Users\Makovec\myFile1.txt
hvEVE3TDmfnYS9HrOweNDTt2YJjXNfPIjKInOKNYp8g=
C:\Users\Makovec\myFile10.txt
MDO1qpQP8CWfY9RFrhJRFXf6tBRUU18QhUBsEBZzTg0=
C:\Users\Makovec\myFile2.txt    PrLYwFUSFV6ffc+pOPk5voQW1DOjPeK/
DY3071VFFCQ=
C:\Users\Makovec\myFile3.txt    VF1QO1uLMVJUWHJCoyQDf6+KCLu9BU5mokUpDhUH5
hY=
```

```
C:\Users\Makovec\myFile4.txt  9ipYmXXKSmRPa/
pxgGZII5HKt6iz8gmuQnSky8DJXeO=
C:\Users\Makovec\myFile5.txt
Pt95mm1rElrON7zPmkZ8ntffRmmbN6q22bnIlgzJaJk=
C:\Users\Makovec\myFile6.txt
dJXh7cLZb2hf87DtJCRrTAjDLhXJolopRBQYNGt7CPc=
C:\Users\Makovec\myFile7.txt  OOAHHQebMbTxQv1QEKYkd63bF8J8jqHHhOzgA4rFG/
A=
C:\Users\Makovec\myFile8.txt  EEXKqgV/KXSesD6x8HVmF/
jZTN4DzyjCEWjRuM5R7dI=
C:\Users\Makovec\myFile9.txt  jdhlfHvSJ5RJSZ62MOc+J5ujM3fMzzWXwDndZ8VOL
4s=
```

If you want to have *MD5* as the default on your computer, you can specify it *$PSDefaultParameterValues*. Be careful—if you modify this in your profile, your script will probably have a different result on other PCs. But for a quick-and-dirty local check, it's OK. Honestly, I added the following two lines to my profile:

```
Set-Alias -Name md5 -Value Get-FileHash
$PSDefaultParameterValues = @{'Get-FileHash:Algorithm'='MD5'}
```

And still the following two lines show the same result:

```
PS C:\Users\Makovec> Get-FileHash .\myFile.exe -Algorithm MD5
PS C:\Users\Makovec> md5 .\myFile.exe


Path                              Type
Hash                                    .


----                              ----
----
C:\Users\Makovec\myFile.exe              System.Security.Cryptography.
MD5Cryp... L1uabH1YgDx/WSR4e2SIgw==
```

# Using command-line utilities

As mentioned earlier, command-line utilities can be used directly within Windows PowerShell. The advantages of using command-line utilities in Windows PowerShell, as opposed to simply running them in the CMD interpreter, are the Windows PowerShell pipelining and format-ting features. Additionally, if you have batch files or CMD files that already utilize existing command-line utilities, they can easily be modified to run within the Windows PowerShell environment.

Use the following steps to run *ipconfig* commands:

1. Start Windows PowerShell by searching on PowerShell from the Windows Start page. The PowerShell prompt will open by default at the root of your Documents folder.

2. Enter the command **ipconfig /all** as follows:

   ```
   PS C:\> ipconfig /all
   ```

3. Pipe the result of `ipconfig` / to a text file. This is illustrated here:

   ```
   PS C:\> ipconfig /all >ipconfig.txt
   ```

4. Use Notepad to view the contents of the text file, as shown here:

   ```
   PS C:\> notepad ipconfig.txt
   ```

Typing a single command into Windows PowerShell is useful, but at times, you might need more than one command to provide troubleshooting information or configuration details to assist with setup issues or performance problems. This is where Windows PowerShell really shines. In the past, one would have to either write a batch file or type the commands manually.

This is seen in the TroubleShoot.bat script that follows.

**TroubleShoot.bat**

```
ipconfig /all >C:\tshoot.txt
route print >>C:\tshoot.txt
hostname >>C:\tshoot.txt
net statistics workstation >>C:\tshoot.txt
```

Of course, if you typed the commands manually, you had to wait for each command to complete before entering the subsequent command. In that case, it was always possible to lose your place in the command sequence or to have to wait for the result of each command. Windows PowerShell eliminates this problem. You can now enter multiple commands on a single line and then leave the computer or perform other tasks while the computer produces the output. No batch file needs to be written to achieve this capability.

> **TIP** Use multiple commands on a single Windows PowerShell line. Type each complete command, and then use a semicolon to separate each command.

# Security issues with Windows PowerShell

As with any tool as versatile as Windows PowerShell, there are bound to be some security concerns. However, security was one of the design goals in the development of Windows PowerShell.

When you launch Windows PowerShell, it opens in your Documents folder; this ensures that you are in a directory where you will have permission to perform certain actions and activities. This is far safer than opening at the root of the drive or even opening in system root.

To change to a directory, you cannot automatically go up to the next level; you must explicitly name the destination of the change directory operation (although you can use the CD .. command to move up one level).

The running of scripts is disabled by default and can be easily managed through group policy. It can also be managed on a per-user and per-session basis.

## Controlling execution of Windows PowerShell cmdlets

Have you ever opened a CMD interpreter prompt, typed in a command, and pressed Enter so that you could see what it does? What if that command happened to be *Format C:\*? Are you sure you want to format your C drive? In this section, we will look at some arguments that can be supplied to cmdlets that allow you to control the way they execute. Although not all cmdlets support these arguments, most of those included with Windows PowerShell do. The three arguments we can use to control execution are -*whatif*, -*confirm*, and *suspend*. *Suspend* is not really an argument that is supplied to a cmdlet but rather an action that you can take at a confirmation prompt, and it is therefore another method of controlling execution.

> **NOTE**  To use -*whatif* in a Windows PowerShell prompt, enter the cmdlet and type the -*whatif* parameter after the cmdlet. This works only for cmdlets that change system state. Therefore, there is no –*whatif* parameter for cmdlets such as Get-Process, which display only information.

Windows PowerShell cmdlets that change system state (such as Set-Service) support a prototype mode that can be entered using the -*whatif* parameter. The implementation of -*whatif* can be decided on by the person developing the cmdlet; however, it is the recommendation of the Windows PowerShell team that developers implement –*whatif* when a cmdlet changes system state. The following command illustrates using –*whatif*:

```
PS C:\> Set-Service -Name bits -StartupType 'manual' -WhatIf
What if: Performing operation "Set-Service" on Target "Background Intelligent Transfer
Service (bits)".
```

# Confirming commands

As we saw in the preceding section, we can use -*whatif* to prototype a cmdlet in Windows PowerShell. This is useful for seeing what a command would do; however, if we want to be prompted before the execution of the command, we can use the -*Confirm* argument. The use of the –*Confirm* parameter is shown here:

```
PS C:\> Get-Process -Name notepad | Stop-Process -Confirm

Confirm
Are you sure you want to perform this action?
Performing operation "Stop-Process" on Target "notepad (4148)".
[Y] Yes  [A] Yes to All  [N] No  [L] No to All  [S] Suspend  [?] Help
(default is "Y"):y
```

# Suspending confirmation of cmdlets

The ability to prompt for confirmation of the execution of a cmdlet is extremely useful and at times can be vital to assisting in maintaining a high level of system uptime. There are times when you have typed in a long command and then remember that you need to do something else first. For such eventualities, you can tell the confirmation you would like to suspend execution of the command. The great thing is that while the executing command suspends, you have access to the Windows PowerShell shell and can therefore run other commands. In the example here, there are several instances of Notepad running. The first uses –*confirm* when stopping Notepad. The first instance stops, and then the command is suspended. This provides a chance to use Get-Process to find out information about the other running processes.

```
PS C:\> 1..5 | % notepad
PS C:\> 1..5 | % {notepad}
PS C:\> Get-Process -Name notepad | Stop-Process -Confirm

Confirm
Are you sure you want to perform this action?
Performing operation "Stop-Process" on Target "notepad (3552)".
[Y] Yes  [A] Yes to All  [N] No  [L] No to All  [S] Suspend  [?] Help
(default is "Y"):y

Confirm
Are you sure you want to perform this action?
Performing operation "Stop-Process" on Target "notepad (5404)".
[Y] Yes  [A] Yes to All  [N] No  [L] No to All  [S] Suspend  [?] Help
(default is "Y"):s
PS C:\>> get-process notepad
```

| Handles | NPM(K) | PM(K) | WS(K) | VM(M) | CPU(s) | Id | ProcessName |
|---------|--------|-------|-------|-------|--------|----|-------------|
| 81 | 9 | 1688 | 11328 | 98 | 0.03 | 5404 | notepad |
| 81 | 9 | 1680 | 11480 | 98 | 0.06 | 6344 | notepad |

```
   81       9     1676      11364       98      0.05   6868 notepad
   81       9     1680      11312       98      0.00   7092 notepad


PS C:\>> exit

Confirm
Are you sure you want to perform this action?
Performing operation "Stop-Process" on Target "notepad (5404)".
[Y] Yes  [A] Yes to All  [N] No  [L] No to All  [S] Suspend  [?] Help
(default is "Y"):a
PS C:\>
```

# Working with Windows PowerShell

Windows PowerShell can be used as a replacement for the CMD interpreter. Its many built-in cmdlets allow for large number of activities. These cmdlets can be used in a stand-alone fashion, or they can be run together as a group.

---

**NOTES FROM THE FIELD**

**Bill Mell, MCSE Infrastructure Manager**
*DAV*

I have been using Windows PowerShell for more than five years. I got my start thanks to Ed Wilson's Windows PowerShell book. It has been invaluable in helping me understand the program's capabilities. Windows PowerShell has been a tremendous help with simplifying what would normally be complex, time-consuming tasks. For example, we use it to pull detailed information, such as service tag and serial number info, about the servers in our environment. We have well over 200 and growing. To obtain this information manually would be a several day or week-long task. With Windows PowerShell, it can be done in a matter of minutes. Another welcome addition to the framework are the Active Directory cmdlets. Over the years, these have allowed me to automate mundane tasks such as creating large numbers of users and groups. What used to take hours/days now takes only minutes. In addition to this, it seems that more and more companies are catching on to the benefits of Windows PowerShell. Two vendors that immediately come to mind are Dell and VMware. The VMware plugin allows me to pull information about RDM volume mappings and the guests they are attached to. To obtain this manually would be quite a time-consuming task. In short, Windows PowerShell is a huge time saver. It allows me to do twice the work in half the time. It has been an incredible addition to my Engineers toolbox, and I could not do my job without it.

# Accessing Windows PowerShell

After Windows PowerShell is installed, it becomes available for immediate use. However, using the Windows flag key on the keyboard and pressing the letter *r* to bring up a *run* command prompt, or "mousing around" and using Start | Run | Windows PowerShell all the time, becomes somewhat less helpful. (It is not quite as big a problem on Windows 8; just type **PowerShell** on the Start screen). On Windows 8.1, I pin both Windows PowerShell and the Windows PowerShell ISE to the Start screen and to the taskbar. On Windows Server 2012 R2 in core mode, I replace the CMD prompt with the Windows PowerShell console. For me, this is ideal. In fact, this was so useful that I wrote a script to do this. This script can be called through a logon script to automatically deploy the shortcut on the desktop. On Windows 8.1, the script adds both the Windows PowerShell ISE and the Windows PowerShell console to the Start screen and the taskbar. On Windows 7, it adds both the Windows PowerShell ISE and the Windows PowerShell Console to the taskbar and to the Start area of the Start menu. The script works only for English. To make it work in other languages, change the value of *$pinToStart* or *$pinToTaskBar* to the equivalent values in the target language.

> **NOTE** Using Windows PowerShell scripts is covered in Chapter 16, "Running scripts." See that chapter for information about how the script works and how to actually run the script.

The following script is called PinToStartAndTaskBar.ps1.

```
PinToStartAndTaskBar.ps1

$pinToStart = "Pin to Start"
$pinToTaskBar = "Pin to Taskbar"
$file = @((Join-Path -Path $PSHOME  -childpath "PowerShell.exe"),
          (Join-Path -Path $PSHOME  -childpath "powershell_ise.exe") )
Foreach($f in $file)
 {$path = Split-Path $f
  $shell=New-Object -com "Shell.Application"
  $folder=$shell.Namespace($path)
  $item = $folder.parsename((Split-Path $f -leaf))
  $verbs = $item.verbs()
  foreach($v in $verbs)
    {if($v.Name.Replace("&","") -match $pinToStart){$v.DoIt()}}
  foreach($v in $verbs)
    {if($v.Name.Replace("&","") -match $pinToTaskBar){$v.DoIt()}} }
```

# Configuring Windows PowerShell

Many items can be configured for Windows PowerShell. These items can be stored in a PSConsole file. To export the Console configuration file, use the `Export-Console` cmdlet, as shown here:

```
PS C:\> Export-Console myconsole
```

The PSConsole file is saved in the current directory by default and has an extension of psc1. The PSConsole file is saved in an XML format. A generic console file is shown here:

```xml
<?xml version="1.0" encoding="utf-8"?>
<PSConsoleFile ConsoleSchemaVersion="1.0">
  <PSVersion>3.0</PSVersion>
  <PSSnapIns />
</PSConsoleFile>
```

---

**NOTES FROM THE FIELD**

**Jeff Truman, Platform Engineer**
*Serve by American Express*

I was pulled into a meeting with very little warning, because of the scripting evangelism that I had been doing at my company. The request for the ad hoc script was an interesting one. We needed to get the latest network device backups and zip them up to provide to a partner. Our internal solution for network config management is SolarWinds Network Configuration Manager. The software does a nightly backup of the running configs of each network device and stores it in a folder on the central server.

That doesn't seem too tough, so let's take a look at the requirements. I log in to the server. I open up the ISE and start digging through the directories, ending up at  Data Drive\ Solarwinds\NCM\Backups. OK, that makes sense. Now what do I see? Over 100 folders with names of network devices. Hmm...OK. I open up the first one, and I see 25+ folders that are named via a date stamp. I open one of these folders, and I see the config I need. Here is the small gotcha to all of this: Not every device is backed up each day. I have no way of knowing what the latest time stamp will be in each recursive directory. For mere mortals, this would seem to be a showstopper, but for us PowerShell Peeps, we scoff and giggle. Here's the code:

```powershell
$Path = "D:\Program Files (x86)\SolarWinds\Orion\NCM\Config-Archive\"
$Folders = Get-ChildItem $Path
$FullFiles
Foreach($Folder in $Folders)
```

```
{
$FF = Get-ChildItem -Path "$Path$Folder" | Sort | Select-object -First 1
$File = Get-ChildItem -Path "$Path$Folder\$FF" | Where-object {$_.Name
-like "*Running*"}
$FullFiles += $File
}
```

**The magic of the script is inside the loop. Of course, I could have done most of this on a single command line via the pipeline, but I wanted to show the steps to the newer scripters in the audience.**

```
$FF = Get-ChildItem -Path "$Path$Folder" | Sort | Select-object -First 1
- This gets the Child Items of the full path, sorts them and then select
the newest timestamp.

$File = Get-ChildItem -Path "$Path$Folder\$FF" | Where-object {$_.Name
-like "*Running*"} - now get the Running config within this folder.
```

# Supplying options for cmdlets

One of the useful features of Windows PowerShell is the standardization of the syntax in working with cmdlets. This vastly simplifies the learning of the new shell and language. Table 1-1 lists the common parameters. Keep in mind that all cmdlets will not implement these parameters. However, if these parameters are used, they will be interpreted in the same manner for all cmdlets because it is the Windows PowerShell engine itself that interprets the parameter.

**TABLE 1-1** Common parameters

| Parameter | Meaning |
| --- | --- |
| -whatif | Instructs the cmdlet to not execute but to tell you what would happen if the cmdlet were to run. |
| -confirm | Instructs the cmdlet to prompt before executing the command. |
| -verbose | Instructs the cmdlet to provide a higher level of detail than a cmdlet not using the verbose parameter. |
| -debug | Instructs the cmdlet to provide debugging information. |
| -ErrorAction | Instructs the cmdlet to perform a certain action when an error occurs. Allowed actions are continue, stop, silentlyContinue, and inquire. |
| -ErrorVariable | Instructs the cmdlet to use a specific variable to hold error information. This is in addition to the standard $error variable. |
| -Outvariable | Instructs the cmdlet to use a specific variable to hold the output information. |
| -OutBuffer | Instructs the cmdlet to hold a certain number of objects before calling the next cmdlet in the pipeline. |

# Working with the help options

One of the first commands to run when opening Windows PowerShell for the first time is the Update-Help cmdlet. This is because Windows PowerShell does not ship **help** files with the product. This does not mean that no **help** presents itself—it does mean that **help** beyond simple syntax display requires an additional download.

A default installation of Windows PowerShell 4.0 contains numerous modules that vary from installation to installation, depending on the operating system features and roles selected. For example, Windows PowerShell 4.0 installed on a Windows 7 workstation contains far fewer modules and cmdlets than are available on a similar Windows 8.1 workstation. However, this does not mean all is chaos, because the essential Windows PowerShell cmdlets—the core cmdlets—remain unchanged from installation to installation. The difference between installations is because additional features and roles often install additional Windows PowerShell modules and cmdlets. (For more information about which roles install which specific modules, consult the role- and feature-specific information at *technet.microsoft.com*.)

## Updating help information

The modular nature of Windows PowerShell requires additional consideration when updating **help**. Simply running Update-Help does not update all of the modules loaded on a particular system. In fact, some modules might not support updatable **help** at all—these generate an error when you attempt to update **help**. The easiest way to ensure that you update all possible **help** is to use both the *module* parameter and the *force* switched parameter. The command to update **help** for all installed modules (that support updatable **help**) is shown here:

```
Update-Help -Module * -Force
```

The result of running the Update-Help cmdlet on a typical Windows 8-based client system is shown in Figure 1-1.

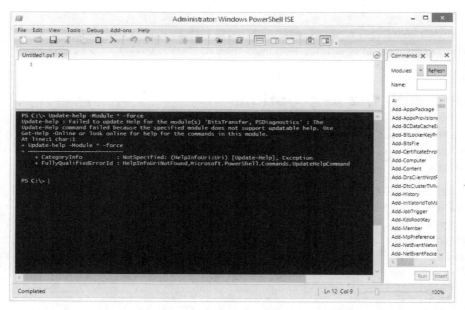

**FIGURE 1-1** Errors appear when attempting to update **help** files that do not support updatable **help**.

One way to update **help** and not receive a screen full of error messages is to run the Update-Help cmdlet and suppress the errors all together, as shown here:

```
Update-Help -Module * -Force -ea 0
```

The problem with this approach is that you can never be certain that you actually received updated **help** for everything you wanted to update. A better approach is to hide the errors during the update process and also to display errors after the update completes. The advantage to this approach is the ability to display cleaner errors. The UpdateHelpTrackErrors.ps1 script illustrates this technique. The first thing that the UpdateHelpTrackErrors.ps1 script does is to empty the error stack by calling the *clear* method. Next it calls the Update-Help module with both the *module* parameter and the *force* switched parameter. In addition, it uses the *ErrorAction* parameter (*ea* is an alias for this parameter) with a value of 0. The value 0 means not to display any errors when the command runs. The script concludes by using a *For* loop to walk through the errors and display the error exceptions. The UpdateHelpTrackErrors.ps1 script appears here.

> **NOTE** For information about writing Windows PowerShell scripts, see Chapter 8, "Designing the script."

```
UpdateHelpTrackErrors.ps1

#requires -version 4.0
#Requires -RunAsAdministrator
Update-Help -Module * -Force -ea 0
For ($i = 0 ; $i -le $error.Count ; $i ++)
  { "'nrror $i" ; $error[$i].exception }
```

When the UpdateHelpTrackErrors script runs, a progress bar displays, indicating the progress as the updatable **help** files update. After the script completes, any errors appear in order. The script and associated errors are shown in Figure 1-2.

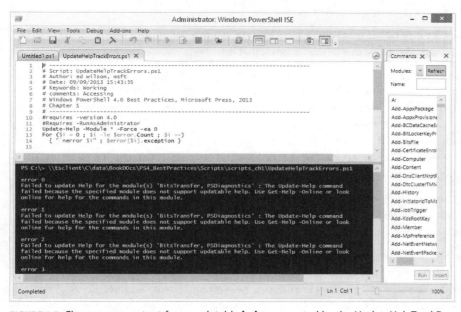

**FIGURE 1-2** Cleaner error output from updatable **help,** generated by the UpdateHelpTrackErrors script.

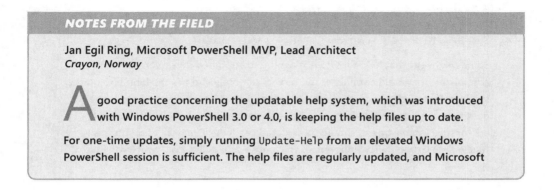

### NOTES FROM THE FIELD

**Jan Egil Ring, Microsoft PowerShell MVP, Lead Architect**
*Crayon, Norway*

A good practice concerning the updatable help system, which was introduced with Windows PowerShell 3.0 or 4.0, is keeping the help files up to date.

For one-time updates, simply running Update-Help from an elevated Windows PowerShell session is sufficient. The help files are regularly updated, and Microsoft has created an RSS-feed where you can stay updated with new releases: *http://sxp.microsoft.com/feeds/msdntn/PowerShellHelpVersions*.

As with other tasks in PowerShell, automation is key. For updating your own computer, you could simply leverage the new *PSScheduledJob* module introduced in Windows PowerShell 3.0 to create a job that will invoke Update-Help—for example, once a week—without you having to remember it.

The following is an example of how to do this:

```
Register-ScheduledJob -Name Update-Help -ScriptBlock {Update-Help
-Module *} -Trigger (New-JobTrigger -DaysOfWeek Monday -Weekly -At 8AM)
-ScheduledJobOption (New-ScheduledJobOption -RequireNetwork)
```

I have a list of things that I configure when I reinstall or configure a new computer for myself, and this is one of the items on that list.

In a corporate environment, there are more things to consider. For example, there is a Group Policy setting called "Set the default source path for Update-Help," which you can read more about here: *http://go.microsoft.com/fwlink/?LinkId=251696*. This setting allows you to download the updated help files from a single computer, while the domain-joined computers download the help files from an internal UNC-path specified by either the Group Policy setting or by using the – *SourcePath* parameter of Update-Help.

One reason for doing this might be that some of the computers on the network are not allowed access to the Internet and thus will need to get the help files from an internal network location.

On the computer managing the download of the help files, you can leverage the Save-Help cmdlet to save the help files to the internal UNC-path. An enhancement made to the Save-Help cmdlet in Windows PowerShell 4.0 makes it possible to download help files for Windows PowerShell modules not installed on the computer running the cmdlet. This can be accomplished by using the –*Module* parameter of Save-Help. This parameter allows wildcards, so the following example will download the help-files for all modules available:

```
Save-Help -Module * -DestinationPath \\server\share
```

Some might say that help files do not need to be updated on servers, because administrators should administer the servers remotely and use the help files on the local computer. Many companies have central management servers used by help desk personnel and administrators. These servers, as well as the client computers for the IT department, should be updated regularly. One way of doing this is to leverage Group Policy Preferences to create a scheduled task, which will invoke

> **Update-Help on a scheduled basis. The following is an example of the path and arguments that can be used for the scheduled task:**
>
> ```
> Path: C:\Windows\System32\WindowsPowerShell\v1.0\powershell.exe
> Arguments: -Command "& {if (($PSVersionTable.PSVersion).Major -ge 3)
> {Update-Help -SourcePath '\\server\share\PowerShell\Help-files'}}"
> ```

## Discovering information in help

Windows PowerShell has a high level of discoverability; that is, to learn how to use PowerShell, you can simply use PowerShell. Online **help** serves an important role in assisting in this discoverability. The **help** system in Windows PowerShell can be entered by several methods. To learn about using Windows PowerShell, use the Get-Help cmdlet as follows:

`Get-Help Get-Help`

This command prints out **help** about the Get-Help cmdlet. The output from this cmdlet is illustrated here:

```
NAME
    Get-Help

SYNOPSIS
    Displays information about Windows PowerShell commands and concepts.


SYNTAX
    Get-Help [[-Name] <String>] [-Category <String>] [-Component <String>] [-Full
    [<SwitchParameter>]] [-Functionality <String>] [-Path <String>] [-Role
    <String>] [<CommonParameters>]

    Get-Help [[-Name] <String>] [-Category <String>] [-Component <String>]
    [-Functionality <String>] [-Path <String>] [-Role <String>] -Detailed
    [<SwitchParameter>] [<CommonParameters>]

    Get-Help [[-Name] <String>] [-Category <String>] [-Component <String>]
    [-Functionality <String>] [-Path <String>] [-Role <String>] -Examples
    [<SwitchParameter>] [<CommonParameters>]

    Get-Help [[-Name] <String>] [-Category <String>] [-Component <String>]
    [-Functionality <String>] [-Path <String>] [-Role <String>] -Online
    [<SwitchParameter>] [<CommonParameters>]

    Get-Help [[-Name] <String>] [-Category <String>] [-Component <String>]
    [-Functionality <String>] [-Path <String>] [-Role <String>] -Parameter <String>
    [<CommonParameters>]
```

```
Get-Help [[-Name] <String>] [-Category <String>] [-Component <String>]
[-Functionality <String>] [-Path <String>] [-Role <String>] -ShowWindow
[<SwitchParameter>] [<CommonParameters>]
```

DESCRIPTION
The **Get-Help** cmdlet displays information about Windows PowerShell concepts and commands, including cmdlets, providers, functions, aliases and scripts.

**Get-Help** gets the **help** content that it displays from **help** files on your computer. Without the **help** files, **Get-Help** displays only basic information about commands. Some Windows PowerShell modules come with **help** files. However, beginning in Windows PowerShell 3.0, the modules that come with Windows PowerShell do not include **help** files. To download or update the **help** files for a module in Windows PowerShell 3.0, use the **Update-Help** cmdlet. You can also view the **help** topics for Windows PowerShell online in the TechNet Library at http://go.microsoft.com/fwlink/?LinkID=107116http://go.microsoft.com/fwlink /?LinkID=107116.

To get **help** for a Windows PowerShell command, type "**Get-Help**" followed by the command name. To get a list of all **help** topics on your system, type "**Get-Help\***".

Conceptual **help** topics in Windows PowerShell begin with "about_", such as "about_Comparison_Operators". To see all "about_" topics, type "**Get-Help** about_\*". To see a particular topic, type "**Get-Help** about_<topic-name>", such as "**Get-Help** about_Comparison_Operators".

You can display the entire **help** topic or use the parameters of the **Get-Help** cmdlet to get selected parts of the topic, such as the syntax, parameters, or examples. You can also use the Online parameter to display an online version of a **help** topic for a command in your Internet browser.

If you type "**Get-Help**" followed by the exact name of a **help** topic, or by a word unique to a **help** topic, **Get-Help** displays the topic contents. If you enter a word or word pattern that appears in several **help** topic titles, **Get-Help** displays a list of the matching titles. If you enter a word that does not appear in any **help** topic titles, **Get-Help** displays a list of topics that include that word in their contents.

In addition to "**Get-Help**", you can also type "**help**" or "man", which displays one screen of text at a time, or "<cmdlet-name> -?", which is identical to **Get-Help** but works only for cmdlets.

For information about the symbols that **Get-Help** displays in the command syntax diagram, see about_Command_Syntaxhttp://go.microsoft.com/fwlink/?LinkID=113215. For information about parameter attributes, such as Required and Position, see about_Parametershttp://go.microsoft.com/fwlink/?LinkID=113243.


RELATED LINKS
Online Version: http://go.microsoft.com/fwlink/?LinkID=113316
**Get-Command**
**Get-Member**
**Get-PSDrive**

```
about_Command_Syntax
about_Comment_Based_Help
about_Parameters
```

REMARKS

```
To see the examples, type: "Get-Help Get-Help -examples".
For more information, type: "Get-Help Get-Help -detailed".
For technical information, type: "Get-Help Get-Help -full".
For online help, type: "Get-Help Get-Help -online"
```

## NOTES FROM THE FIELD

**Sean Kearney, Microsoft PowerShell MVP, Senior Solutions Architect**
*Cistel Technology Inc.*

barely remember my life before using Windows PowerShell, because life with it afterwards has become so wonderful.

My first foray into using this technology showed me not only its ease of use but also its raw power by deleting files by Date and Time. Because of Windows PowerShell, I got to go home early by two hours on a Friday and began singing a song of praise. (That was the beginning of the song that I wrote called *Highway to PowerShell*.)

The song introduced me to Jeffrey Snover, the architect of Windows PowerShell (by way of a blog post that almost scared him). I discovered a community of people within and outside of Microsoft who were incredibly passionate about building on and improving this technology. This community ran their own podcasts, built their own tools, and actively engaged Microsoft to make Windows PowerShell better. This group of people, including Microsoft staff on the Windows PowerShell team, Microsoft MVPs, and other community experts, were part of the inspiration to grow beyond who I was.

It was during this same process, on the PowerScripting Podcast that I first encountered Mr. Ed "Hey Scripting Guy" Wilson. I think I even wrote a small tune about him at the time and gained a friend on that day.

Not soon afterwards, I found myself working for a Fortune 15 Corporation, using Windows PowerShell to migrate Active Directory and Exchange Users. I found that it was the best way to quickly unlock accounts and disable users (as a Single Administrator for a growing division). It also became my tool of choice for quarterly reporting for SOX and daily consistency in user creation. With a single Windows PowerShell script prompting for a user's name, phone extension, and division, I could easily populate six isolated systems and produce a letter for handoff to their manager with credentials and an introduction to our IT environment.

With Windows PowerShell, I gained the power held by VBScript but also the ease of use and the ability to interact and play directly with the command prompt. I now had a tool that would leverage and interact with older systems—a new technology that would help bring console applications and VBScript into newer and more powerful tools.

It was a tool that cost *nothing* to leverage and actually allowed me to get home at a decent hour. I was blown away!

I now work for a Microsoft Gold Partner living in the world of Automation and Systems Center 2012. I am excited each day to go to work. Whenever somebody looks as me and asks, "Can you do this?" I immediately start thinking of how it can be done with Windows PowerShell, because the answers are usually quick and easy. They are simple to repeat.

Thank you, Windows PowerShell and all those involved in its existence. I am forever grateful. You rock!

The good thing about **help** with the Windows PowerShell is that it not only displays **help** about commands, which you would expect, but also has three levels of display: normal, detailed, and full. Additionally, you can obtain **help** about concepts in Windows PowerShell. This last feature is equivalent to having an online instruction manual. To retrieve a listing of all the conceptual **help** articles, use the Get-Help *about\** command as follows:

**Get-Help** about*

Suppose you do not remember the exact name of the cmdlet you want to use, but you remember it was a *get* cmdlet? You can use a wildcard character, such as an asterisk (*), to obtain the name of the cmdlet, as shown here:

**Get-Help** get*

This technique of using a wildcard operator can be extended further. If you remember that the cmdlet was a *get* cmdlet and that it started with the letter *p*, you can use the following syntax to retrieve the desired cmdlet:

**Get-Help** get-p*

However, suppose that you know the exact name of the cmdlet, but you cannot exactly remember the syntax. For this scenario, you can use the *-examples* argument. For example, for the Get-PSDrive cmdlet, you would use Get-Help with the *-examples* argument, as follows:

**Get-Help Get-PSDrive** -examples

To see **help** displayed one page at a time, you can use the help function. The **help** function passes your input to the Get-Help cmdlet and pipelines the resulting information to the more.com utility. This causes output to display one page at a time in the Windows PowerShell console. This is useful if you want to avoid scrolling up and down to see the **help** output.

> **NOTE** Keep in mind that in the Windows PowerShell ISE the pager does not work, and therefore you will see no difference in output from Get-Help or from Help. In the ISE, both Get-Help and Help behave the same way. However, it is likely that if you are using the Windows PowerShell ISE, you will use Show-Command for your help instead of relying on Get-Help.

This formatted output is shown in Figure 1-3.

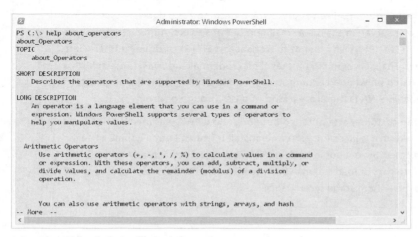

**FIGURE 1-3** Using **help** to display information one page at a time.

Getting tired of typing Get-Help all the time? After all, it is eight characters long, and one of them is a dash. The solution is to create an alias to the Get-Help cmdlet. An *alias* is a shortcut keystroke combination that will launch a program or cmdlet when typed. In creating an alias for the Get-Help cmdlet procedure, we will assign the Get-Help cmdlet to the *gh* key combination as shown here:

```
New-Alias gh Get-Help
```

> **NOTE** To create an alias for a cmdlet, confirm there is not already an alias for the cmdlet by using Get-Alias. Use New-Alias to assign the cmdlet to a unique keystroke combination.

Don Jones, Microsoft PowerShell MVP
*Concentrated Technologies*

I once had a customer who got very eager about Windows PowerShell Web Access (PWA), and installed it on *every one of the servers*. You read that right. *Every server*. They'd contacted me to see whether it was also possible to get PWA running on all of their client computers. "It is," I told them, "but hang on." PWA requires Internet Information Services (IIS), and that's an awful lot of code to be dropping onto every server just to enable a web-based shell console.

What they hadn't quite realized is that PWA is designed as a gateway system. You install it on one server, or maybe a small number of servers. Administrators connect to PWA via HTTPS (PWA isn't meant to work across HTTP), and they authenticate to that server. That server impersonates their credential and uses it to establish a remoting session on whatever computer—client or server—that the administrators want to manage. PWA is therefore a kind of pass-through or proxy.

After I got the customer straightened out about how PWA was meant to be used, they embarked on a quick campaign to uninstall it from all but a couple of servers and dedicated those couple to being PWA servers. They actually set up DNS round-robin to sort of load-balance between the two PWA servers; having two PWA servers also gave them some redundancy.

## Additional resources

- The TechNet Script Center at *http://www.microsoft.com/technet/scriptcenter* contains numerous script examples.
- Detailed information about how to deploy help files by using a scheduled task using Group Policy can be found on Jan Egil Ring's blog at *http://blog.powershell.no /2013/03/09/automatically-update-help-files-for-windows-powershell/*.
- All scripts from this chapter are in the file available from the Script Center Script Repository at *http://gallery.technet.microsoft.com/scriptcenter/PowerShell-40 -Best-d9e16039*.
- The Microsoft Download center at *http://www.microsoft.com/en-us/download/default .aspx* contains many Windows PowerShell-related downloads.

# CHAPTER 2

# Using the CIM cmdlets

- Using the CIM cmdlets to explore Windows Management Instrumentation classes
- Retrieving WMI instances
- Working with Association classes
- Additional resources

## Using the CIM cmdlets to explore WMI classes

The CIM cmdlets support multiple ways of exploring Windows Management Instrumentation (WMI). They work well when working in an interactive fashion. For example, tab expansion increases the namespace when using the CIM cmdlets, thereby permitting you to explore namespaces that might not otherwise be very discoverable. You can even drill down into namespaces by using this technique. All CIM classes support tab expansion of the *namespace* parameter, but to explore WMI classes, you want to use the Get-CimClass cmdlet.

> **NOTE**   The default WMI namespace on all operating systems after Windows NT 4.0 is *Root/Cimv2*. Therefore, all of the CIM cmdlets default to *Root/Cimv2*. The only time you need to change the default WMI namespace (via the *namespace* parameter) is when you need to use a WMI class from a non-default WMI namespace.

## Using the *classname* parameter

Using the Get-CimClass cmdlet, you can use wildcards for the *classname* parameter to enable you to quickly identify potential WMI classes for perusal. You can also use wildcards for the *qualifiername* parameter. In the example appearing here, the Get-CimClass cmdlet looks for WMI classes related to computers.

```
PS C:\> Get-CimClass -ClassName *computer*


    NameSpace: ROOT/CIMV2
```

```
CimClassName                    CimClassMethods       CimClassProperties
------------                    ---------------       ------------------
Win32_ComputerSystemEvent       {}                    {SECURITY_DESCRIPTOR, TIME_
CR...
Win32_ComputerShutdownEvent     {}                    {SECURITY_DESCRIPTOR, TIME_
CR...
CIM_ComputerSystem              {}                    {Caption, Description,
Instal...
CIM_UnitaryComputerSystem       {SetPowerState}       {Caption, Description,
Instal...
Win32_ComputerSystem            {SetPowerState, R...  {Caption, Description,
Instal...
CIM_ComputerSystemResource      {}                    {GroupComponent, PartComponent}
CIM_ComputerSystemMappedIO      {}                    {GroupComponent, PartComponent}
CIM_ComputerSystemDMA           {}                    {GroupComponent, PartComponent}
CIM_ComputerSystemIRQ           {}                    {GroupComponent, PartComponent}
Win32_ComputerSystemProcessor   {}                    {GroupComponent, PartComponent}
CIM_ComputerSystemPackage       {}                    {Antecedent, Dependent}
Win32_ComputerSystemProduct     {}                    {Caption, Description,
Identi...
Win32_NTLogEventComputer        {}                    {Computer, Record}
```

> **NOTE** If you try to use a wildcard for the *classname* parameter of the Get-CimInstance cmdlet, an error returns because the parameter design does not permit wildcard characters.

## NOTES FROM THE FIELD

**Brian Wilhite, Premier Field Engineer (PFE)**
*Microsoft Corporation*

With Windows PowerShell 3.0, Microsoft upped their game by adding the *CimCmdlets* module. There are so many rich features with these new cmdlets, and one of my favorites is the way WMI/CIM classes have become more discoverable within PowerShell. For example, let's say that I need to determine what service pack level my client workstations are on. Before Windows PowerShell 3.0, I would browse the MSDN site trying to find a class that had a property that matched my criteria. Depending on the level of complexity, this could take several minutes and possibly even hours to find. Fast forward to Windows PowerShell 3.0 with the *CimCmdlets* module, and this task becomes quite easy. With the Get-CimClass cmdlet I can "wildcard" search WMI for "ClassNames", "MethodNames",

"PropertyNames" and "QualifierNames". For the example I mentioned here, I would easily search for a "PropertyName" of "*ServicePack*" to find out the classes that match that criteria:

```
Get-CimClass -PropertyName *ServicePack*
```

Normally, this will return two items, the *Win32_OperatingSystem* and *Win32_QuickFixEngineering* WMI classes. Now that I have the classes, I can do one of two things. I can query the class locally to find the property that matches my search criteria, which in this case is great because I have only two classes to parse. But what happens when the query returns quite a few classes? In this case, I would use the following one-liner to parse the data for me:

```
Get-CimClass -PropertyName *ServicePack* |
ForEach-Object {$_ | Select-Object -Property CimClassName, '
@{L="CimClassProperties";E={$_.CimClassProperties.Name -like
"*ServicePack*"}}}
```

This will return the CimClassName that relates to the matched CimClassProperties search criteria. This technique has sped up my WMI property searches because I don't have to search MSDN for a specific class, method, property, and/or qualifier names.

## Finding WMI class methods

If you want to find WMI classes related to processes that contain a method that begins with the letters *term*\*, you use a command similar to the following:

```
PS C:\> Get-CimClass -ClassName *process* -MethodName term*


   NameSpace: ROOT/cimv2

CimClassName                    CimClassMethods        CimClassProperties
------------                    ---------------        ------------------
Win32_Process                   {Create, Terminat...   {Caption, Description,
Instal...
```

To find all WMI classes related to processes that expose any methods, you would use the command appearing here.

```
PS C:\> Get-CimClass -ClassName *process* -MethodName *


   NameSpace: ROOT/cimv2
```

```
CimClassName                    CimClassMethods        CimClassProperties
------------                    ---------------        ------------------
Win32_Process                   {Create, Terminat...   {Caption, Description,
Instal...
CIM_Processor                   {SetPowerState, R...   {Caption, Description,
Instal...
Win32_Processor                 {SetPowerState, R...   {Caption, Description,
Instal...
```

To find any WMI class in the *root/cimv2* WMI namespace that exposes a method called *create,* use the following command:

```
PS C:\> Get-CimClass -ClassName * -MethodName create


    NameSpace: ROOT/cimv2

CimClassName                    CimClassMethods        CimClassProperties
------------                    ---------------        ------------------
Win32_Process                   {Create, Terminat...   {Caption, Description,
Instal...
Win32_ScheduledJob              {Create, Delete}       {Caption, Description,
Instal...
Win32_DfsNode                   {Create}               {Caption, Description,
Instal...
Win32_BaseService               {StartService, St...   {Caption, Description,
Instal...
Win32_SystemDriver              {StartService, St...   {Caption, Description,
Instal...
Win32_Service                   {StartService, St...   {Caption, Description,
Instal...
Win32_TerminalService           {StartService, St...   {Caption, Description,
Instal...
Win32_Share                     {Create, SetShare...   {Caption, Description,
Instal...
Win32_ClusterShare              {Create, SetShare...   {Caption, Description,
Instal...
Win32_ShadowCopy                {Create, Revert}       {Caption, Description,
Instal...
Win32_ShadowStorage             {Create}               {AllocatedSpace, DiffVolume,
...
```

## Filtering classes by qualifier

To find WMI classes that possess a particular qualifier, use the *qualifier* parameter. For example, the following command finds WMI classes that relate to computers and that have the *supportsupdate* WMI qualifier:

```
PS C:\> Get-CimClass -ClassName *computer* -QualifierName *update


    NameSpace: ROOT/cimv2
```

```
CimClassName                    CimClassMethods      CimClassProperties
------------                    ---------------      ------------------
Win32_ComputerSystem            {SetPowerState, R... {Caption, Description,
Instal...
```

The parameters can be combined to produce powerful searches that without using the CIM cmdlets would require rather complicated scripting. For example, the following command finds all WMI classes in the *root/Cimv2* namespace that have the *singleton* qualifier and also expose a method:

```
PS C:\> Get-CimClass -ClassName * -QualifierName singleton -MethodName *


   NameSpace: ROOT/cimv2

CimClassName                    CimClassMethods      CimClassProperties
------------                    ---------------      ------------------
__SystemSecurity                {GetSD, GetSecuri... {}
Win32_OperatingSystem           {Reboot, Shutdown... {Caption, Description,
Instal...
Win32_OfflineFilesCache         {Enable, RenameIt... {Active, Enabled, Location}
```

One qualifier that is important to review is the *deprecated* qualifier. Deprecated WMI classes are not recommended for use because they are being phased out. Using the Get-CimClass cmdlet, it is easy to spot these WMI classes. This technique is shown here:

```
PS C:\> Get-CimClass * -QualifierName deprecated


   NameSpace: ROOT/cimv2

CimClassName                    CimClassMethods      CimClassProperties
------------                    ---------------      ------------------
Win32_PageFile                  {TakeOwnerShip, C... {Caption, Description,
Instal...
Win32_DisplayConfiguration      {}                   {Caption, Description,
Settin...
Win32_DisplayControllerConfigura... {}               {Caption, Description,
Settin...
Win32_VideoConfiguration        {}                   {Caption, Description,
Settin...
Win32_AllocatedResource         {}                   {Antecedent, Dependent}
```

Using this technique, it is easy to find Association classes. (More information about working with WMI Association classes appears in the "Working with Associations" section that follows.) The code that follows finds all of the WMI classes in the *root/cimv2* WMI namespace that relate to sessions. In addition, it looks for the *association* qualifier. Luckily, you can use wildcards for the qualifier names, and therefore the following code uses *assoc\** instead of typing out *association*:

```
PS C:\> Get-CimClass -ClassName *session* -QualifierName assoc*
```

```
NameSpace: ROOT/cimv2


CimClassName                    CimClassMethods     CimClassProperties
------------                    ---------------     ------------------
Win32_SubSession                {}                  {Antecedent, Dependent}
Win32_SessionConnection         {}                  {Antecedent, Dependent}
Win32_LogonSessionMappedDisk    {}                  {Antecedent, Dependent}
Win32_SessionResource           {}                  {Antecedent, Dependent}
Win32_SessionProcess            {}                  {Antecedent, Dependent}
```

One qualifier you should definitely look for is the *dynamic* qualifier, because it is unsupported to query *abstract* WMI classes. Therefore, when looking for WMI classes, you will want to ensure that at some point you run your list through the *dynamic* filter. In the code that follows, three WMI classes return that are related to time:

PS C:\> **Get-CimClass** -ClassName *time

```
NameSpace: ROOT/cimv2


CimClassName            CimClassMethods     CimClassProperties
------------            ---------------     ------------------
Win32_CurrentTime       {}                  {Day, DayOfWeek, Hour,
Millis...
Win32_LocalTime         {}                  {Day, DayOfWeek, Hour,
Millis...
Win32_UTCTime           {}                  {Day, DayOfWeek, Hour,
Millis...
```

By adding the query for the qualifier, the appropriate WMI classes are identified. One class is abstract, and the other two are dynamic classes that could prove to be useful. This code appears here, where first the *dynamic* qualifier is used and secondly where the *abstract* qualifier appears.

PS C:\> **Get-CimClass** -ClassName *time -QualifierName dynamic

```
NameSpace: ROOT/cimv2


CimClassName            CimClassMethods     CimClassProperties
------------            ---------------     ------------------
Win32_LocalTime         {}                  {Day, DayOfWeek, Hour,
Millis...
Win32_UTCTime           {}                  {Day, DayOfWeek, Hour,
Millis...
```

PS C:\> **Get-CimClass** -ClassName *time -QualifierName abstract

```
NameSpace: ROOT/cimv2
```

```
CimClassName                      CimClassMethods        CimClassProperties
------------                      ---------------        ------------------
Win32_CurrentTime                 {}                     {Day, DayOfWeek, Hour,
Millis...
```

# Retrieving WMI instances

To query for WMI data, use the `Get-CimInstance` cmdlet. The easiest way to use the `Get-CimInstance` cmdlet is to query for all properties and all instances of a particular WMI class on the local machine. This is extremely easy to do. The following command illustrates returning BIOS information from the local computer:

```
PS C:\> Get-CimInstance win32_bios
```

```
SMBIOSBIOSVersion : 090004
Manufacturer      : American Megatrends Inc.
Name              : BIOS Date: 03/19/09 22:51:32  Ver: 09.00.04
SerialNumber      : 4429-0046-2083-1237-7579-8937-43
Version           : VRTUAL - 3000919
```

The `Get-CimInstance` cmdlet returns the entire WMI object, but it honors the format*.xml files that Windows PowerShell uses to determine which properties are displayed by default for a particular WMI class. The command appearing here shows the properties available from the *Win32_Bios* WMI class:

```
PS C:\> $b = Get-CimInstance win32_bios
PS C:\> $b.CimClass.CimClassProperties | fw name -Column 3
```

```
Caption             Description             InstallDate
Name                Status                  BuildNumber
CodeSet             IdentificationCode      LanguageEdition
Manufacturer        OtherTargetOS           SerialNumber
SoftwareElementID   SoftwareElementState    TargetOperatingSystem
Version             PrimaryBIOS             BiosCharacteristics
BIOSVersion         CurrentLanguage         InstallableLanguages
ListOfLanguages     ReleaseDate             SMBIOSBIOSVersion
SMBIOSMajorVersion  SMBIOSMinorVersion      SMBIOSPresent
```

## Reduce returned properties and instances

To limit the amount of data returned from a remote connection, reduce the number of properties returned as well as the number of instances. To reduce properties, use the *property* parameter. To reduce the number of returned instances, use the *filter* parameter. The command here uses *gcim,* which is an alias for the `Get-CimInstance` cmdlet. It also abbreviates the *classname* parameter and the *filter* parameter. As seen here, the command returns only the *name* and the *state* from the *bits* service. While the default output shows all of the property names as well as the system properties, only the two selected properties contain data.

```
PS C:\> gcim -clas win32_service -Property name, state -Fil "name = 'bits'"
```

```
Name                      : BITS
Status                    :
ExitCode                  :
DesktopInteract           :
ErrorControl              :
PathName                  :
ServiceType               :
StartMode                 :
Caption                   :
Description               :
InstallDate               :
CreationClassName         :
Started                   :
SystemCreationClassName   :
SystemName                :
AcceptPause               :
AcceptStop                :
DisplayName               :
ServiceSpecificExitCode   :
StartName                 :
State                     : Running
TagId                     :
CheckPoint                :
ProcessId                 :
WaitHint                  :
PSComputerName            :
CimClass                  : root/cimv2:Win32_Service
CimInstanceProperties     : {Caption, Description, InstallDate, Name...}
CimSystemProperties       : Microsoft.Management.Infrastructure.CimSystemProperties
```

## Clean up output from the command

To produce a cleaner output, send the selected data to the Format-Table cmdlet. This is easy to do because *ft* is an alias for the Format-Table cmdlet.

```
PS C:\> gcim -clas win32_service -Property name, state -Fil "name = 'bits'" | ft name,
state
```

```
name                                      state
----                                      -----
BITS                                      Running
```

Make sure to choose properties that you have already selected in the *property* parameter or else they will not display. In the command appearing here, the status property is selected in the Format-Table cmdlet. There is a status property on the *Win32_Service* WMI class, but it was not chosen when the properties were selected.

```
PS C:\> gcim -clas win32_service -Property name, state -Fil "name = 'bits'" | ft name,
state, status

name                      state                     status
----                      -----                     ------
BITS                      Running
```

The Get-CimInstance cmdlet does not accept a wildcard parameter for property names
(neither does the Get-WmiObject cmdlet). One thing that can simplify some of your coding
is to put your property selection into a variable. This permits you to use the same property
names both in the Get-CimInstance cmdlet and in your Format-Table cmdlet (or Format-List
or Select-Object or whatever you are doing after you get your WMI data) without having to
type things twice. This technique is shown here:

```
PS C:\> $property = "name","state","startmode","startname"
PS C:\> gcim -clas win32_service -Pro $property -fil "name = 'bits'" | ft $property -A

name state   startmode startname
---- -----   --------- ---------
BITS Running Manual    LocalSystem
```

# Working with Association classes

In the old-fashioned VBScript days, working with Association classes was extremely complicated. This was unfortunate because WMI Association classes are extremely powerful and
useful. Earlier versions of Windows PowerShell simplified, working with Association classes,
primarily because it simplified working with WMI data in general. However, figuring out how
to utilize the Windows PowerShell advantage was still pretty much an advanced technique.
Luckily, we have the CIM classes (introduced in Windows PowerShell 3.0) that give us the
Get-CimAssociatedInstance cmdlet.

The first thing to do is to retrieve a CIM instance and store it in a variable. In the example shown here, instances of the *Win32_LogonSession* WMI class are retrieved and stored
in the *$logon* variable. Next, the Get-CimAssociatedInstance cmdlet is used to retrieve
instances associated with this class. To see what type of objects will return from the command, the results pipe to the Get-Member cmdlet. As seen here, two WMI classes return: the
*Win32_UserAccount* class and all processes that are related to that user account in the form of
instances of the *Win32_Process* class.

```
PS C:\> $logon = Get-CimInstance win32_logonsession
PS C:\> Get-CimAssociatedInstance $logon | Get-Member


   TypeName: Microsoft.Management.Infrastructure.CimInstance#root/cimv2/Win32_
UserAccount

Name                      MemberType  Definition
----                      ----------  ----------
Clone                     Method      System.Object ICloneable.Clone()
```

```
Dispose                        Method        void Dispose(), void IDisposable.Dispose()
Equals                         Method        bool Equals(System.Object obj)
GetCimSessionComputerName      Method        string GetCimSessionComputerName()
GetCimSessionInstanceId        Method        guid GetCimSessionInstanceId()
GetHashCode                    Method        int GetHashCode()
GetObjectData                  Method        void GetObjectData(System.Runtime.
Serialization....
GetType                        Method        type GetType()
ToString                       Method        string ToString()
AccountType                    Property      uint32 AccountType {get;}
Caption                        Property      string Caption {get;}
Description                    Property      string Description {get;}
Disabled                       Property      bool Disabled {get;set;}
Domain                         Property      string Domain {get;}
FullName                       Property      string FullName {get;set;}
InstallDate                    Property      CimInstance#DateTime InstallDate {get;}
LocalAccount                   Property      bool LocalAccount {get;set;}
Lockout                        Property      bool Lockout {get;set;}
Name                           Property      string Name {get;}
PasswordChangeable             Property      bool PasswordChangeable {get;set;}
PasswordExpires                Property      bool PasswordExpires {get;set;}
PasswordRequired               Property      bool PasswordRequired {get;set;}
PSComputerName                 Property      string PSComputerName {get;}
SID                            Property      string SID {get;}
SIDType                        Property      byte SIDType {get;}
Status                         Property      string Status {get;}
PSStatus                       PropertySet   PSStatus {Status, Caption, PasswordExpires}
```

TypeName: Microsoft.Management.Infrastructure.CimInstance#root/cimv2/Win32_Process

| Name | MemberType | Definition |
| ---- | ---------- | ---------- |
| Handles | AliasProperty | Handles = Handlecount |
| ProcessName | AliasProperty | ProcessName = Name |
| VM | AliasProperty | VM = VirtualSize |
| WS | AliasProperty | WS = WorkingSetSize |
| Clone | Method | System.Object ICloneable.Clone() |
| Dispose | Method | void Dispose(), void IDisposable.Dispose() |
| Equals | Method | bool Equals(System.Object obj) |
| GetCimSessionComputerName | Method | string GetCimSessionComputerName() |
| GetCimSessionInstanceId | Method | guid GetCimSessionInstanceId() |
| GetHashCode | Method | int GetHashCode() |
| GetObjectData | Method | void GetObjectData(System.Runtime. |
| Serializat... | | |
| GetType | Method | type GetType() |
| ToString | Method | string ToString() |
| Caption | Property | string Caption {get;} |
| CommandLine | Property | string CommandLine {get;} |
| CreationClassName | Property | string CreationClassName {get;} |
| CreationDate | Property | CimInstance#DateTime CreationDate {get;} |
| CSCreationClassName | Property | string CSCreationClassName {get;} |
| CSName | Property | string CSName {get;} |
| Description | Property | string Description {get;} |
| ExecutablePath | Property | string ExecutablePath {get;} |

```
ExecutionState          Property        uint16 ExecutionState {get;}
Handle                  Property        string Handle {get;}
HandleCount             Property        uint32 HandleCount {get;}
InstallDate             Property        CimInstance#DateTime InstallDate {get;}
KernelModeTime          Property        uint64 KernelModeTime {get;}
MaximumWorkingSetSize   Property        uint32 MaximumWorkingSetSize {get;}
MinimumWorkingSetSize   Property        uint32 MinimumWorkingSetSize {get;}
Name                    Property        string Name {get;}
OSCreationClassName     Property        string OSCreationClassName {get;}
OSName                  Property        string OSName {get;}
OtherOperationCount     Property        uint64 OtherOperationCount {get;}
OtherTransferCount      Property        uint64 OtherTransferCount {get;}
PageFaults              Property        uint32 PageFaults {get;}
PageFileUsage           Property        uint32 PageFileUsage {get;}
ParentProcessId         Property        uint32 ParentProcessId {get;}
PeakPageFileUsage       Property        uint32 PeakPageFileUsage {get;}
PeakVirtualSize         Property        uint64 PeakVirtualSize {get;}
PeakWorkingSetSize      Property        uint32 PeakWorkingSetSize {get;}
Priority                Property        uint32 Priority {get;}
PrivatePageCount        Property        uint64 PrivatePageCount {get;}
ProcessId               Property        uint32 ProcessId {get;}
PSComputerName          Property        string PSComputerName {get;}
QuotaNonPagedPoolUsage  Property        uint32 QuotaNonPagedPoolUsage {get;}
QuotaPagedPoolUsage     Property        uint32 QuotaPagedPoolUsage {get;}
QuotaPeakNonPagedPoolUsage Property     uint32 QuotaPeakNonPagedPoolUsage {get;}
QuotaPeakPagedPoolUsage Property        uint32 QuotaPeakPagedPoolUsage {get;}
ReadOperationCount      Property        uint64 ReadOperationCount {get;}
ReadTransferCount       Property        uint64 ReadTransferCount {get;}
SessionId               Property        uint32 SessionId {get;}
Status                  Property        string Status {get;}
TerminationDate         Property        CimInstance#DateTime TerminationDate {get;}
ThreadCount             Property        uint32 ThreadCount {get;}
UserModeTime            Property        uint64 UserModeTime {get;}
VirtualSize             Property        uint64 VirtualSize {get;}
WindowsVersion          Property        string WindowsVersion {get;}
WorkingSetSize          Property        uint64 WorkingSetSize {get;}
WriteOperationCount     Property        uint64 WriteOperationCount {get;}
WriteTransferCount      Property        uint64 WriteTransferCount {get;}
Path                    ScriptProperty  System.Object Path {get=$this.ExecutablePath;}
```

When the command runs without piping to the Get-Member object, we see that first the instance of the *Win32_UserAccount* WMI class returns. The output shows the user name, account type, sid, domain, and the caption of the user account. As seen in the output from Get-Member, a lot more information is available, but this is the default display. Following the user account information, the default process information displays the process ID, name, and a bit of performance information related to the processes associated with the user account.

```
PS C:\> $logon = Get-CimInstance win32_logonsession
PS C:\> Get-CimAssociatedInstance $logon

Name        Caption         AccountType     SID              Domain
----        -------         -----------     ---              ------
ed          IAMMRED\ed      512             S-1-5-21-14579... IAMMRED
```

```
ProcessId       : 2780
Name            : taskhostex.exe
HandleCount     : 215
WorkingSetSize  : 8200192
VirtualSize     : 242356224


ProcessId       : 2804
Name            : rdpclip.exe
HandleCount     : 225
WorkingSetSize  : 8175616
VirtualSize     : 89419776


ProcessId       : 2352
Name            : explorer.exe
HandleCount     : 1078
WorkingSetSize  : 65847296
VirtualSize     : 386928640


ProcessId       : 984
Name            : powershell.exe
HandleCount     : 577
WorkingSetSize  : 94527488
VirtualSize     : 690466816


ProcessId       : 296
Name            : conhost.exe
HandleCount     : 54
WorkingSetSize  : 7204864
VirtualSize     : 62164992
```

If you do not want to retrieve both classes from the association query, you can specify the resulting class by name. To do this, use the *resultclassname* parameter from the Get-CimAssociatedInstance cmdlet. In the code that follows, only the *Win32_UserAccount* WMI class returns from the query:

```
PS C:\> $logon = Get-CimInstance win32_logonsession
PS C:\> Get-CimAssociatedInstance $logon -ResultClassName win32_useraccount

Name     Caption          AccountType    SID             Domain
----     -------          -----------    ---             ------
ed       IAMMRED\ed       512            S-1-5-21-14579... IAMMRED
```

When working with the Get-CimAssociatedInstance cmdlet, the *inputobject* you supply must be a single instance. If you supply an object that contains more than one instance of the class, an error raises. This error appears here, where more than one disk is provided to the *inputobject* parameter:

```
PS C:\> $disk = Get-CimInstance win32_logicaldisk
PS C:\> Get-CimAssociatedInstance $disk
Get-CimAssociatedInstance : Cannot convert 'System.Object[]' to the type
```

```
'Microsoft.Management.Infrastructure.CimInstance' required by parameter 'InputObject'.
Specified method is not supported.
At line:1 char:27
+ Get-CimAssociatedInstance $disk
+                           ~~~~~
    + CategoryInfo          : InvalidArgument: (:) [Get-CimAssociatedInstance], Paramete
   rBindingException
    + FullyQualifiedErrorId : CannotConvertArgument,Microsoft.Management.Infrastructure.
   CimCmdlets.GetCimAssociatedInstanceCommand
```

There are two ways to correct this particular error. The first, and the easiest, is to use array indexing. This is shown here:

```
PS C:\> $disk = Get-CimInstance win32_logicaldisk
PS C:\> Get-CimAssociatedInstance $disk[0]
```

| Name | PrimaryOwner Name | Domain | TotalPhysical Memory | Model | Manufacturer |
| ---- | --------------- | ------ | ------------- | ----- | ------------ |
| W8C504 | ed | iammred.net | 2147012608 | Virtual Ma... | Microsoft ... |

```
PS C:\> Get-CimAssociatedInstance $disk[1]
```

| Name | Hidden | Archive | Writeable | LastModified |
| ---- | ------ | ------- | --------- | ------------ |
| c:\ | | | | |

```
NumberOfBlocks   : 265613312
BootPartition    : False
Name             : Disk #0, Partition #1
PrimaryPartition : True
Size             : 135994015744
Index            : 1


Domain               : iammred.net
Manufacturer         : Microsoft Corporation
Model                : Virtual Machine
Name                 : W8C504
PrimaryOwnerName     : ed
TotalPhysicalMemory  : 2147012608
```

Using array indexing is fine when you find yourself in the situation with an *inputobject* parameter that contains an array. However, the results might be a bit inconsistent. A better approach is to ensure that you do not have an array in the first place. To do this, use the *filter* parameter to reduce the number of instances of your WMI class that return. In the code shown here, the filter returns the number of WMI instances to the C drive:

```
PS C:\> $disk = Get-CimInstance win32_logicaldisk -Filter "name = 'c:'"
PS C:\> Get-CimAssociatedInstance $disk
```

```
Name            Hidden          Archive         Writeable       LastModified
----            ------          -------         ---------       ------------
c:\
```

```
NumberOfBlocks    : 265613312
BootPartition     : False
Name              : Disk #0, Partition #1
PrimaryPartition  : True
Size              : 135994015744
Index             : 1
```

```
Domain              : iammred.net
Manufacturer        : Microsoft Corporation
Model               : Virtual Machine
Name                : W8C504
PrimaryOwnerName    : ed
TotalPhysicalMemory : 2147012608
```

An easy way to see the objects returned by the Get-CimAssociatedInstance cmdlet is to pipeline the returned objects to the Get-Member cmdlet and then to select the *typename* property. Because more than one instance of the object can return and clutter the output, it is important to choose *unique* type names. This command is shown here:

```
PS C:\> Get-CimAssociatedInstance $disk | gm | select typename -Unique

TypeName
--------
Microsoft.Management.Infrastructure.CimInstance#root/cimv2/Win32_Directory
Microsoft.Management.Infrastructure.CimInstance#root/cimv2/Win32_DiskPartition
Microsoft.Management.Infrastructure.CimInstance#root/cimv2/Win32_ComputerSystem
```

Armed with this information, it is easy to explore the returned Association classes. This technique is shown here:

```
PS C:\> Get-CimAssociatedInstance $disk -ResultClassName win32_directory

Name            Hidden          Archive         Writeable       LastModified
----            ------          -------         ---------       ------------
c:\
```

```
PS C:\> Get-CimAssociatedInstance $disk -ResultClassName win32_diskpartition

Name            NumberOfBlocks BootPartition PrimaryPartition Size           Index
----            -------------- ------------- ---------------- ----           -----
Disk #0, Part... 265613312      False         True             135994015744  1
```

```
PS C:\> Get-CimAssociatedInstance $disk -ResultClassName win32_Computersystem
```

| Name | PrimaryOwner Name | Domain | TotalPhysical Memory | Model | Manufacturer |
|------|-------------------|--------|----------------------|-------|--------------|
| ---- | ------------ | ------ | -------------- | ----- | ------------ |
| W8C504 | ed | iammred.net | 2147012608 | Virtual Ma... | Microsoft ... |

Keep in mind that the entire WMI class returns and is therefore ripe for further exploration. The easy way to do this is to store the results into a variable and then walk through the data. When you have what interests you, you might decide to display a nicely organized table, such as the following:

```
PS C:\> $dp = Get-CimAssociatedInstance $disk -ResultClassName win32_diskpartition
PS C:\> $dp | FT deviceID, BlockSize, NumberOfBLicks, Size, StartingOffSet -AutoSize


deviceID              BlockSize NumberOfBLicks         Size StartingOffSet
--------              --------- --------------         ---- --------------
Disk #0, Partition #1       512                135994015744      368050176
```

# Additional resources

- The TechNet Script Center at *http://www.microsoft.com/technet/scriptcenter* contains numerous script examples.
- All scripts from this chapter are available via the TechNet Script Center Script Repository at *http://gallery.technet.microsoft.com/scriptcenter/PowerShell-40 -Best-d9e16039*.

# Planning for scripting

# CHAPTER 3

# Using the Active Directory module

- Understanding the Active Directory module
- Using the Active Directory module
- Additional resources

## Understanding the Active Directory module

Microsoft made Active Directory Domain Services (AD DS) Windows PowerShell cmdlets available beginning with Windows Server 2008 R2. You can also download and install the Active Directory Management Gateway Service (ADMGS) that provides a web service interface to Active Directory domains or Active Directory Lightweight Directory Services that are running on the same server as the ADMGS. The ADMGS can run on Windows Server 2003 with Service Pack 2 or on Windows Server 2008. On Windows Server 2008 R2 and above, the ADMGS installs as a role and does not require an additional download. When you have one domain controller running Windows Server 2008 R2 (or later) in your domain, you can use the new cmdlets to manage your AD DS installation. Installing the ADMGS Windows Server 2003 or Windows Server 2008 does not make it possible to load the Active Directory module on those machines, but it does permit you to use the Active Directory module from another machine to manage those servers.

**Ashley McGlone, Senior Premier Field Engineer**
*Microsoft Corporation*

Some of us have been using Active Directory since the release candidates in 1999. Others have gotten started with it recently. But we all have one thing in common. We need to automate tasks across hundreds or thousands of users, computers, groups, OUs, and so on.

Over the years, our tools were basically VBScript with ADSI or canned command-line utilities like CSVDE or DSQUERY. (A few of us even used WMI or ADODB to interface with the directory.) Those legacy scripting techniques faithfully carried us through many implementations and change controls.

But in the autumn of 2009, our tools made a giant leap forward. Windows Server 2008 R2 and the RSAT for Windows 7 introduced the Active Directory PowerShell Module. Wow! What would take 20 lines of VBScript can now be done in a single line of Windows PowerShell.

Here are some great examples of AD PowerShell one-liners:

```
Spreadsheet of stale accounts past 30 days:
Search-ADAccount -AccountInactive -TimeSpan 30 | Export-CSV .\Stale_
Accts.csv

Helpdesk prompt for a user password reset:
Set-ADAccountPassword (Read-Host 'Username') -Reset

Target list of global catalog domain controllers:
(Get-ADForest).GlobalCatalogs
```

In my field experience, I have written some large-scale scripts as well, such as the following:

- Active Directory SID history cleanup and file server ACL migrations
- DNS reorganization and migration to AD-integrated zones
- Security delegation reporting across OUs and GPOs

On the domain controller, this magic is made possible by the Active Directory Web Service (ADWS). The ADWS listens on port 9389 and answers to the Windows PowerShell cmdlets. Whether you're running a quick one-liner or automating across thousands of accounts, this service enables you to read and write directory data with ease.

With each release of Windows Server, the Active Directory module (and now companion modules) grows to support new features. The latest releases offer additional functionality to replace trusty utilities like DCPROMO and REPADMIN. Additionally, the Group Policy module enables further automation of workstation management through Active Directory.

The Active Directory module for Windows PowerShell is no longer new technology. This is a mature product that every administrator needs in their bag of tricks to make the work day go faster. Get started today with one simple Windows PowerShell command: `Import-Module ActiveDirectory`.

# Installing the Active Directory module

The Active Directory module is available beginning with Windows 7 on the client side and with Windows 2008 R2 on servers. To make the cmdlets available on the desktop operating system requires downloading and installing the Remote Server Administration Tools (RSAT).

To install the Active Directory module on either a Windows Server 2012 or Windows Server 2012 R2 machine, you can use the `Add-WindowsFeature` cmdlet because the Active Directory module is directly available to the operating system as an optional Windows feature. Therefore, installation on a server operating system does not require downloading the RSAT tools. To install the RSAT tools for Active Directory, first use the `Get-WindowsFeature` cmdlet to get the rsat-ad-tools, and then pipeline it to the `Add-WindowsFeature` cmdlet. This technique is shown here:

```
Get-WindowsFeature rsat-ad-tools | Add-WindowsFeature
```

The output associated with getting and installing the rsat-ad-tools feature is shown in Figure 3-1.

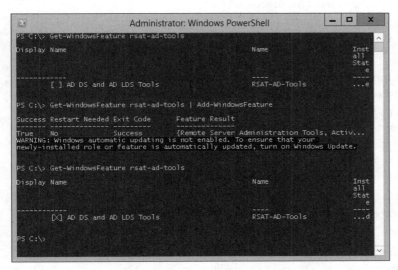

**FIGURE 3-1** Installing the RSAT tools provides access to the Active Directory module.

# Getting started with the Active Directory module

After you have installed the RSAT tools, you will want to verify that the Active Directory is present and that it loads properly. To do this, use the `Get-Module` cmdlet with the *ListAvailable* switch to verify that the *ActiveDirectory* module is present. Here is the command to do this:

```
Get-Module -ListAvailable ActiveDirectory
```

After the *ActiveDirectory* module loads, you can obtain a listing of the Active Directory cmdlets by using the `Get-Command` cmdlet and specifying the *module* parameter. Because Windows PowerShell 4.0 automatically loads modules, you do not need to use the `Import-Module` cmdlet to import the *ActiveDirectory* module if you do not want to do so. This command is shown here:

```
Get-Command -Module ActiveDirectory
```

## Using the Active Directory module

It is not necessary to always load the Active Directory module (or for that matter any module) because Windows PowerShell 3.0 and 4.0 automatically load the module containing a referenced cmdlet. The location searched by Windows PowerShell for modules comes from the environmental variable *PSModulePath*. To view the value of this environmental variable, preface the variable name with the environmental drive. The following command retrieves the default module locations and displays the associated paths:

```
PS C:\> $env:PSModulePath
C:\Users\ed.IAMMRED\Documents\WindowsPowerShell\Modules;C:\Program Files\WindowsPowe
rShell\Modules;C:\Windows\system32\WindowsPowerShell\v1.0\Modules\
```

If you do not want to install the Active Directory module on your client operating systems, all you need to do is to add the rsat-ad-tools feature to at least one server. When installed on the server, use Windows PowerShell remoting to connect to the server hosting the rsat-ad-tools feature from your client workstation. When in the remote session, if the remote server is Windows 8, all you need to do is call one of the Active Directory cmdlets. The *ActiveDirectory* module automatically loads, and the information returns. The following commands illustrate this technique:

```
$credential = get-credential
Enter-PSSession -ComputerName w8Server6 -Credential $credential
Get-ADDomain
```

The technique to use Windows PowerShell remoting to connect to a server that contains the Active Directory module and to automatically load that module while using a cmdlet from that module on Windows PowerShell 4.0 is shown in Figure 3-2.

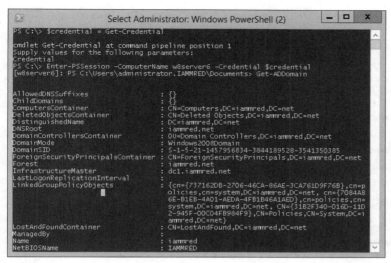

**FIGURE 3-2** Using Windows PowerShell 4.0 remoting to obtain Active Directory information without first loading the module.

**NOTES FROM THE FIELD**

**Brian Wilhite, Premier Field Engineer (PFE)**
*Microsoft Corporation*

Like most Windows administrators, you probably work with Active Directory on a weekly, if not daily, basis. With Windows PowerShell, working with Active Directory is so much easier than it used to be. In fact, I've forgotten how complex structuring ADSI code can be. When installing a fresh copy of Windows, usually after customizing my profile, I will download and install the Remote Server Administration Tools (RSAT), to ensure that I have the *ActiveDirectory* Module for use within Windows PowerShell. From time to time, my manager has asked me to run a query against Active Directory to determine what computers have been enabled for delegation, for compliance reasons, and to possibly execute a task on those systems. So I turn to Windows PowerShell, with the *ActiveDirectory* module, for the answer.

First, you need to determine what Active Directory attributes to filter for. In my case, I'm looking for any computer object that has a value present for the *msDS-AllowedToDelegateTo* attribute or the *TrustedForDelegation* attribute value set to *true*. The Active Directory module has a cmdlet that will allow me to query Active Directory for these attributes and their settings. Consider the following example:

```
Get-ADComputer '
-Filter {msDS-AllowedToDelegateTo -like "*" -or TrustedForDelegation
-eq "True"} '
-Properties TrustedForDelegation, msDS-AllowedToDelegateTo |
Select Name, TrustedForDelegation, msDS-AllowedToDelegateTo
```

This will return any computer object that is trusted for delegation to any service or specific services. Finally, let's assume that you want to take those computers and query the Windows Updates that have been applied to them. You can run the following one-liner, assuming Windows PowerShell remoting is enabled on the targets, to pipe the results into the Invoke-Command cmdlet, launching *Get-HotFix* on the target machine, and storing the results in a variable:

```
$Results = Get-ADComputer '
-Filter {msDS-AllowedToDelegateTo -like "*" -or TrustedForDelegation -eq
"True"} '
-Properties TrustedForDelegation, msDS-AllowedToDelegateTo |
Select Name, TrustedForDelegation, msDS-AllowedToDelegateTo |
ForEach-Object {Invoke-Command -Command {Get-HotFix} -ComputerName
$_.Name}
```

After this runs, which might take a few minutes, given the number of computers, you will have a nice report that you can review. If you wanted to take it a step further, you could take the results variable and pipe it to a CSV file:

```
$Results | Export-Csv -Path C:\Temp\DelegationPatchReport.csv
```

Windows PowerShell with the *ActiveDirectory* module will make a Windows administrator's life easy when given a task big or small.

## Finding the FSMO role holders

To find information about domain controllers and FSMO roles, you do not have to write a Windows PowerShell script; you can do it directly from the Windows PowerShell console or ISE by using the Active Directory cmdlets. The first thing that needs to done, more than likely, is to load the *ActiveDirectory* module into the current Windows PowerShell session. While it is possible to add the import-module command to your Windows PowerShell profile, in general it is not a good idea to load a bunch of modules that you might or might not use on a regular basis. In fact, you can load all the modules at once by piping the results of the Get-Module –*ListAvailable* command to the Import-Module cmdlet. This is shown here:

```
PS C:\> Get-Module -ListAvailable | Import-Module
PS C:\> Get-Module
```

```
ModuleType Name                      ExportedCommands
---------- ----                      ----------------
Script     BasicFunctions           {Get-ComputerInfo, Get-OptimalSize}
Script     ConversionModuleV6        {ConvertTo-Feet, ConvertTo-Miles, ConvertTo-...
Script     PowerShellPack            {New-ByteAnimationUsingKeyFrames, New-TiffBi...
Script     PSCodeGen                 {New-Enum, New-ScriptCmdlet, New-PInvoke}
Script     PSImageTools              {Add-CropFilter, Add-RotateFlipFilter, Add-O...
Script     PSRss                     {Read-Article, New-Feed, Remove-Article, Rem...
Script     PSSystemTools             {Test-32Bit, Get-USB, Get-OSVersion, Get-Mul...
Script     PSUserTools               {Start-ProcessAsAdministrator, Get-CurrentUs...
Script     TaskScheduler             {Remove-Task, Get-ScheduledTask, Stop-Task, ...
Script     WPK                       {Get-DependencyProperty, New-ModelVisual3D, ...
Manifest   ActiveDirectory           {Set-ADOrganizationalUnit, Get-ADDomainContr...
Manifest   AppLocker                 {Get-AppLockerPolicy, Get-AppLockerFileInfor...
Manifest   BitsTransfer              {Start-BitsTransfer, Remove-BitsTransfer, Re...
Manifest   FailoverClusters          {Set-ClusterParameter, Get-ClusterParameter,...
Manifest   GroupPolicy               {Get-GPStarterGPO, Get-GPOReport, Set-GPInhe...
Manifest   NetworkLoadBalancingCl... {Stop-NlbClusterNode, Remove-NlbClusterVip, ...
Script     PSDiagnostics             {Enable-PSTrace, Enable-WSManTrace, Start-Tr...
Manifest   TroubleshootingPack       {Get-TroubleshootingPack, Invoke-Troubleshoo...


PS C:\>
```

After you have loaded the Active Directory module, you will want to use the Get-Command cmdlet to see the cmdlets that are exported by the module. This is shown here:

```
PS C:\> Get-Module -ListAvailable

ModuleType Name                      ExportedCommands
---------- ----                      ----------------
Script     BasicFunctions           {}
Script     ConversionModuleV6        {}
Script     DotNet                    {}
Manifest   FileSystem                {}
Manifest   IsePack                   {}
Manifest   PowerShellPack            {}
Manifest   PSCodeGen                 {}
Manifest   PSImageTools              {}
Manifest   PSRSS                     {}
Manifest   PSSystemTools             {}
Manifest   PSUserTools               {}
Manifest   TaskScheduler             {}
Manifest   WPK                       {}
Manifest   ActiveDirectory           {}
Manifest   AppLocker                 {}
Manifest   BitsTransfer              {}
Manifest   FailoverClusters          {}
Manifest   GroupPolicy               {}
Manifest   NetworkLoadBalancingCl... {}
Manifest   PSDiagnostics             {}
Manifest   TroubleshootingPack       {}


PS C:\> Import-Module active*
```

```
PS C:\> Get-Command -Module active*

CommandType    Name                              Definition
-----------    ----                              ----------
Cmdlet         Add-ADComputerServiceAccount      Add-ADComputerServiceAccount [...
Cmdlet         Add-ADDomainControllerPasswordR... Add-ADDomainControllerPassword...
Cmdlet         Add-ADFineGrainedPasswordPolicy... Add-ADFineGrainedPasswordPolic...
Cmdlet         Add-ADGroupMember                 Add-ADGroupMember [-Identity] ...
Cmdlet         Add-ADPrincipalGroupMembership    Add-ADPrincipalGroupMembership...
Cmdlet         Clear-ADAccountExpiration         Clear-ADAccountExpiration [-Id...
Cmdlet         Disable-ADAccount                 Disable-ADAccount [-Identity] ...
Cmdlet         Disable-ADOptionalFeature         Disable-ADOptionalFeature [-Id...
Cmdlet         Enable-ADAccount                  Enable-ADAccount [-Identity] <...
Cmdlet         Enable-ADOptionalFeature          Enable-ADOptionalFeature [-Ide...
Cmdlet         Get-ADAccountAuthorizationGroup   Get-ADAccountAuthorizationGrou...
Cmdlet         Get-ADAccountResultantPasswordR... Get-ADAccountResultantPassword...
Cmdlet         Get-ADComputer                    Get-ADComputer -Filter <String...
<output truncated>
```

To find a single domain controller, if you are not sure of one in your site, you can use the *discover* switch on the Get-ADDomainController cmdlet. One thing to keep in mind is that the *discover* parameter could return information from the cache. If you want to ensure that a fresh *discover* command is sent, use the *forceDiscover* switch in addition to the *–discover* switch. These techniques are shown here:

```
PS C:\> Get-ADDomainController -Discover


Domain      : NWTraders.Com
Forest      : NWTraders.Com
HostName    : {HyperV.NWTraders.Com}
IPv4Address : 192.168.1.100
IPv6Address :
Name        : HYPERV
Site        : NewBerlinSite




PS C:\> Get-ADDomainController -Discover -ForceDiscover


Domain      : NWTraders.Com
Forest      : NWTraders.Com
HostName    : {HyperV.NWTraders.Com}
IPv4Address : 192.168.1.100
IPv6Address :
Name        : HYPERV
Site        : NewBerlinSite




PS C:\>
```

When using the `Get-ADDomainController` cmdlet, a minimal amount of information returns. If you want to see additional information from the domain controller you discovered, you would need to connect to it by using the *identity* parameter. The value of the *identity* property can be an IP address, GUID, host name, or even a NetBIOS sort of name. This technique is shown here:

```
PS C:\> Get-ADDomainController -Identity hyperv


ComputerObjectDN          : CN=HYPERV,OU=Domain Controllers,DC=NWTraders,DC=Com
DefaultPartition          : DC=NWTraders,DC=Com
Domain                    : NWTraders.Com
Enabled                   : True
Forest                    : NWTraders.Com
HostName                  : HyperV.NWTraders.Com
InvocationId              : 6835f51f-2c77-463f-8775-b3404f2748b2
IPv4Address               : 192.168.1.100
IPv6Address               :
IsGlobalCatalog           : True
IsReadOnly                : False
LdapPort                  : 389
Name                      : HYPERV
NTDSSettingsObjectDN      : CN=NTDS Settings,CN=HYPERV,CN=Servers,CN=NewBerlinSite,
                            CN=Sites,CN=Configuration,DC=NWTraders,DC=Com
OperatingSystem           : Windows Server 2008 R2 Standard
OperatingSystemHotfix     :
OperatingSystemServicePack :
OperatingSystemVersion    : 6.1 (7600)
OperationMasterRoles      : {SchemaMaster, DomainNamingMaster}
Partitions                : {DC=ForestDnsZones,DC=NWTraders,DC=Com, DC=DomainDnsZon
                            es,DC=NWTraders,DC=Com, CN=Schema,CN=Configuration,DC=N
                            WTraders,DC=Com, CN=Configuration,DC=NWTraders,DC=Com...}
ServerObjectDN            : CN=HYPERV,CN=Servers,CN=NewBerlinSite,CN=Sites,CN=Confi
                            guration,DC=NWTraders,DC=Com
ServerObjectGuid          : ab5e2830-a4d6-47f8-b2b4-25757153653c
Site                      : NewBerlinSite
SslPort                   : 636


PS C:\>
```

As shown in the preceding output, the server named Hyperv is a Global Catalog server. It also holds the SchemaMaster and the DomainNamingMaster FSMO roles. It is running Windows Server 2008 R2 Standard edition, which shows that the cmdlet works with down-level versions of the operating system. The `Get-ADDomainController` cmdlet accepts a *filter* parameter that can be used to perform a search and retrieve operation. It uses a special search syntax that is discussed in the online help about files. Unfortunately, it does not accept LDAP syntax.

Luckily, you do not have to learn the special filter syntax, because the Get-ADObject cmdlet will accept a LDAP dialect filter. You can simply pipeline the results of the Get-ADObject cmdlet to the Get-ADDomainController cmdlet. This technique is shown here:

```
PS C:\> Get-ADObject -LDAPFilter "(objectclass=computer)" -searchbase "ou=domain
controllers,dc=nwtraders,dc=com" | Get-ADDomainController
```

```
ComputerObjectDN           : CN=HYPERV,OU=Domain Controllers,DC=NWTraders,DC=Com
DefaultPartition           : DC=NWTraders,DC=Com
Domain                     : NWTraders.Com
Enabled                    : True
Forest                     : NWTraders.Com
HostName                   : HyperV.NWTraders.Com
InvocationId               : 6835f51f-2c77-463f-8775-b3404f2748b2
IPv4Address                : 192.168.1.100
IPv6Address                :
IsGlobalCatalog            : True
IsReadOnly                 : False
LdapPort                   : 389
Name                       : HYPERV
NTDSSettingsObjectDN       : CN=NTDS Settings,CN=HYPERV,CN=Servers,CN=NewBerlinSite,
                             CN=Sites,CN=Configuration,DC=NWTraders,DC=Com
OperatingSystem            : Windows Server 2008 R2 Standard
OperatingSystemHotfix      :
OperatingSystemServicePack :
OperatingSystemVersion     : 6.1 (7600)
OperationMasterRoles       : {SchemaMaster, DomainNamingMaster}
Partitions                 : {DC=ForestDnsZones,DC=NWTraders,DC=Com, DC=DomainDnsZones,
                             DC=NWTraders,DC=Com, CN=Schema,CN=Configuration,DC
                             =NWTraders,DC=Com, CN=Configuration,DC=NWTraders,DC=Com...}
ServerObjectDN             : CN=HYPERV,CN=Servers,CN=NewBerlinSite,CN=Sites,CN=Confi
                             guration,DC=NWTraders,DC=Com
ServerObjectGuid           : ab5e2830-a4d6-47f8-b2b4-25757153653c
Site                       : NewBerlinSite
SslPort                    : 636

ComputerObjectDN           : CN=DC1,OU=Domain Controllers,DC=NWTraders,DC=Com
DefaultPartition           : DC=NWTraders,DC=Com
Domain                     : NWTraders.Com
Enabled                    : True
Forest                     : NWTraders.Com
HostName                   : DC1.NWTraders.Com
InvocationId               : fb324ced-bd3f-4977-ae69-d6763e7e029a
IPv4Address                : 192.168.1.101
IPv6Address                :
IsGlobalCatalog            : True
IsReadOnly                 : False
LdapPort                   : 389
Name                       : DC1
NTDSSettingsObjectDN       : CN=NTDS Settings,CN=DC1,CN=Servers,CN=NewBerlinSite,CN=
                             Sites,CN=Configuration,DC=NWTraders,DC=Com
OperatingSystem            : Windows Serverr 2008 Standard without Hyper-V
```

```
OperatingSystemHotfix       :
OperatingSystemServicePack  : Service Pack 2
OperatingSystemVersion      : 6.0 (6002)
OperationMasterRoles        : {PDCEmulator, RIDMaster, InfrastructureMaster}
Partitions                  : {DC=ForestDnsZones,DC=NWTraders,DC=Com, DC=DomainDnsZones,
                              DC=NWTraders,DC=Com, CN=Schema,CN=Configuration,DC
                              =NWTraders,DC=Com, CN=Configuration,DC=NWTraders,DC=Com...}
ServerObjectDN              : CN=DC1,CN=Servers,CN=NewBerlinSite,CN=Sites,CN=Configur
                              ation,DC=NWTraders,DC=Com
ServerObjectGuid            : 80885b47-5a51-4679-9922-d6f41228f211
Site                        : NewBerlinSite
SslPort                     : 636


PS C:\>
```

If it returns too much information, the Active Directory cmdlets work just like any other Windows PowerShell cmdlet and therefore permit using the pipeline to choose the information you want to display. To obtain only the FSMO information, it comes down to two commands—three commands if you want to include importing the Active Directory module in your count, or four commands if you need to make a remote connection to a domain controller to run the commands. One cool thing about using Windows PowerShell remoting is that you specify the credentials that you need to run the command. If your normal account is a standard user, you use an elevated account only when you require performing actions with elevated rights. If you have already started the Windows PowerShell console with elevated credentials, you can skip typing in credentials when you enter the remote Windows PowerShell session (assuming that the elevated account also has rights on the remote server). The first two commands seen here create a remote session on a remote domain controller and load the *ActiveDirectory* module:

```
Enter-PSSession w8Server6
```

When the Active Directory module loads, you type a one-line command to get the Forest FSMO roles, and you type another one-line command to get the domain FSMO roles. These two commands are shown here:

```
Get-ADForest iammred.net | Format-Table SchemaMaster,DomainNamingMaster
Get-ADDomain iammred.net | format-table PDCEmulator,RIDMaster,InfrastructureMaster
```

That is it—two or three one-line commands, depending on how you want to count. Even at worst case, three one-line commands are much easier to type than 33 lines of code that would be required if you did not have access to the Active Directory module. In addition, the Windows PowerShell code is much easier to read and to understand. The commands and the associated output from the Windows PowerShell commands appear in Figure 3-3.

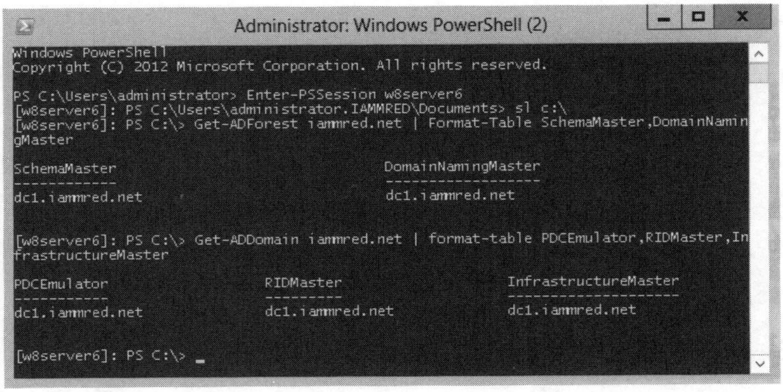

**FIGURE 3-3** Using Windows PowerShell remoting to obtain FSMO information.

## Documenting Active Directory

Using the Microsoft Active Directory Windows PowerShell cmdlets and remoting, you can easily discover information about the forest and the domain. The first thing you need to do is to enter a *PSSession* on the remote computer. To do this you use the `Enter-PSSession` cmdlet. Next, you import the Active Directory module and set the working location to the root of the C drive. The reason for setting the working location to the root of the C drive is to regain valuable command-line space. These commands are shown here:

```
PS C:\Users\Administrator.NWTRADERS> Enter-PSSession dc1
[dc1]: PS C:\Users\Administrator\Documents> Import-Module activedirectory
[dc1]: PS C:\Users\Administrator\Documents> Set-Location c:\
```

After you have connected to the remote domain controller, you can use the `Get-WmiObject` cmdlet to verify the operating system on that computer. This command and associated output are shown here:

```
[dc1]: PS C:\> Get-WmiObject win32_operatingsystem
SystemDirectory : C:\Windows\system32
Organization    :
BuildNumber     : 7601
RegisteredUser  : Windows User
SerialNumber    : 55041-507-0212466-84005
Version         : 6.1.7601
```

Now you want to get information about the forest. To do this, you use the `Get-ADForest` cmdlet. The output from the `Get-ADForest` cmdlet includes lots of great information, such as the Domain Naming Master, Forest Mode, Schema Master, and Domain Controllers. This command and associated output appears here:

```
[dc1]: PS C:\> Get-ADForest
ApplicationPartitions : {DC=DomainDnsZones,DC=nwtraders,DC=com, DC=ForestDnsZones,DC
=nwtraders,DC=com}
CrossForestReferences : {}
```

```
DomainNamingMaster      : DC1.nwtraders.com
Domains                 : {nwtraders.com}
ForestMode              : Windows2008Forest
GlobalCatalogs          : {DC1.nwtraders.com}
Name                    : nwtraders.com
PartitionsContainer     : CN=Partitions,CN=Configuration,DC=nwtraders,DC=com
RootDomain              : nwtraders.com
SchemaMaster            : DC1.nwtraders.com
Sites                   : {Default-First-Site-Name}
SPNSuffixes             : {}
UPNSuffixes             : {}
```

Now, to obtain information about the domain, use the Get-ADDomain cmdlet. The command returns important information such as the location of the default domain controller OU, the PDC emulator, and the RID master. The command and associated output are shown here:

```
[dc1]: PS C:\> Get-ADDomain
AllowedDNSSuffixes                  : {}
ChildDomains                        : {}
ComputersContainer                  : CN=Computers,DC=nwtraders,DC=com
DeletedObjectsContainer             : CN=Deleted Objects,DC=nwtraders,DC=com
DistinguishedName                   : DC=nwtraders,DC=com
DNSRoot                             : nwtraders.com
DomainControllersContainer          : OU=Domain Controllers,DC=nwtraders,DC=com
DomainMode                          : Windows2008Domain
DomainSID                           : S-1-5-21-909705514-2746778377-2082649206
ForeignSecurityPrincipalsContainer  : CN=ForeignSecurityPrincipals,DC=nwtraders,DC=com
Forest                              : nwtraders.com
InfrastructureMaster                : DC1.nwtraders.com
LastLogonReplicationInterval        :
LinkedGroupPolicyObjects            : {CN={31B2F340-016D-11D2-945F-00C04FB984F9},CN
                                      =Policies,CN=System,DC=nwtraders,DC=com}
LostAndFoundContainer               : CN=LostAndFound,DC=nwtraders,DC=com
ManagedBy                           :
Name                                : nwtraders
NetBIOSName                         : NWTRADERS
ObjectClass                         : domainDNS
ObjectGUID                          : 0026d1fc-2e4d-4c35-96ce-b900e9d67e7c
ParentDomain                        :
PDCEmulator                         : DC1.nwtraders.com
QuotasContainer                     : CN=NTDS Quotas,DC=nwtraders,DC=com
ReadOnlyReplicaDirectoryServers     : {}
ReplicaDirectoryServers             : {DC1.nwtraders.com}
RIDMaster                           : DC1.nwtraders.com
SubordinateReferences               : {DC=ForestDnsZones,DC=nwtraders,DC=com,
                                      DC=DomainDnsZones,DC=nwtraders,DC=com,
                                      CN=Configuration,DC=nwtraders,DC=com}
SystemsContainer                    : CN=System,DC=nwtraders,DC=com
UsersContainer                      : CN=Users,DC=nwtraders,DC=com
```

From a security perspective, you should always check the domain password policy. To do this, use the Get-ADDefaultDomainPasswordPolicy cmdlet. Things you want to pay attention to are the use of complex passwords, minimum password length, password age, and password retention. You also need to check the account lockout policy. This policy is especially important to review closely when inheriting a new network. Here is the command and associated output that does that very thing:

```
[dc1]: PS C:\> Get-ADDefaultDomainPasswordPolicy
ComplexityEnabled          : True
DistinguishedName          : DC=nwtraders,DC=com
LockoutDuration            : 00:30:00
LockoutObservationWindow   : 00:30:00
LockoutThreshold           : 0
MaxPasswordAge             : 42.00:00:00
MinPasswordAge             : 1.00:00:00
MinPasswordLength          : 7
objectClass                : {domainDNS}
objectGuid                 : 0026d1fc-2e4d-4c35-96ce-b900e9d67e7c
PasswordHistoryCount       : 24
ReversibleEncryptionEnabled : False
```

The last things to check are the domain controllers themselves. To do this, use the Get-ADDomainController cmdlet. This command returns important information, such as whether the domain controller is read-only, a global catalog server, operations master roles held, and operating system information. Here is the command and associated output:

```
[dc1]: PS C:\> Get-ADDomainController -Identity dc1
ComputerObjectDN          : CN=DC1,OU=Domain Controllers,DC=nwtraders,DC=com
DefaultPartition          : DC=nwtraders,DC=com
Domain                    : nwtraders.com
Enabled                   : True
Forest                    : nwtraders.com
HostName                  : DC1.nwtraders.com
InvocationId              : b51f625f-3f60-44e7-8577-8918f7396c2a
IPv4Address               : 10.0.0.1
IPv6Address               :
IsGlobalCatalog           : True
IsReadOnly                : False
LdapPort                  : 389
Name                      : DC1
NTDSSettingsObjectDN      : CN=NTDS Settings,CN=DC1,CN=Servers,CN=Default-First-Site-Na
me,CN=Sites,CN=Configuration,DC=nwtraders,DC=com
OperatingSystem           : Windows Server 2008 R2 Enterprise
OperatingSystemHotfix     :
OperatingSystemServicePack : Service Pack 1
OperatingSystemVersion    : 6.1 (7601)
OperationMasterRoles      : {SchemaMaster, DomainNamingMaster, PDCEmulator,
                            RIDMaster...}
Partitions                : {DC=ForestDnsZones,DC=nwtraders,DC=com, DC=DomainDnsZones,
                            DC=nwtraders,DC=com, CN=Schema,CN=Configuration,
                            DC=nwtraders,DC=com, CN=Configuration,DC=nwtraders,
                            DC=com...}
ServerObjectDN            : CN=DC1,CN=Servers,CN=Default-First-Site-Name,CN=Sites,
                            CN=Configuration,DC=nwtraders,DC=com
ServerObjectGuid          : 5ae1fd0e-bc2f-42a7-af62-24377114e03d
Site                      : Default-First-Site-Name
SslPort                   : 636
```

To produce a report is as easy as redirecting the output to a text file. These commands gather the information discussed earlier in this section and store the retrieved information in a file named AD_Doc.txt. The commands also illustrate that it is possible to redirect the information to a file stored in a network share.

```
Get-ADForest >> \\dc1\shared\AD_Doc.txt
Get-ADDomain >> \\dc1\shared\AD_Doc.txt
Get-ADDefaultDomainPasswordPolicy >> \\dc1\shared\AD_Doc.txt
Get-ADDomainController -Identity dc1 >>\\dc1\shared\AD_Doc.txt
```

The file as viewed in Notepad appears in Figure 3-4.

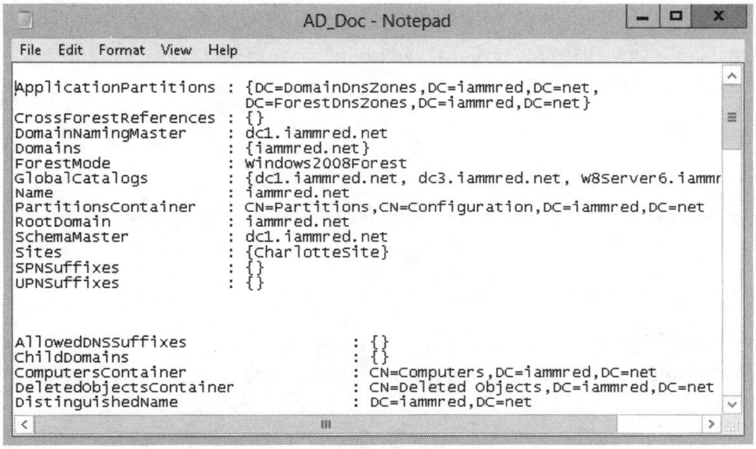

**FIGURE 3-4** Active Directory documentation displayed in Notepad.

# Renaming Active Directory sites

It is easy to rename a site. All you need to do is to right-click the site and select Rename from the action menu. By default, the first site is called Default-First-Site-Name, which is not too illuminating. To work with Active Directory sites, it is necessary to understand that they are a bit strange. First, they reside in the configuration naming context. Connecting to this context by using the Active Directory module is rather simple. Just use the Get-ADRootDSE cmdlet, and then select the *ConfigurationNamingContext* property. First, you have to make a connection to the domain controller and import the Active Directory Module (assuming that you do not have the RSAT tools installed on your client computer). This is shown here:

```
Enter-PSSession -ComputerName dc3 -Credential iammred\administrator
Import-Module activedirectory
```

Here is the code that will retrieve all of the sites. It uses the Get-ADObject cmdlet to search the configuration naming context for objects that have the object class of *site*.

```
Get-ADObject -SearchBase (Get-ADRootDSE).ConfigurationNamingContext -filter "objectclass
-eq 'site'"
```

When you have the site you want to work with, you first change the *DisplayName* attribute. To do this, you pipeline the site object to the `Set-ADObject` cmdlet. The `Set-ADObject` cmdlet allows me to set a variety of attributes on an object. This command is shown here. (This is a single command that is broken into two pieces at the pipeline character.)

```
Get-ADObject -SearchBase (Get-ADRootDSE).ConfigurationNamingContext -filter "objectclass
-eq 'site'" | Set-ADObject -DisplayName CharlotteSite
```

When you have set the *DisplayName* attribute, you decide to rename the object itself. To do this, you use another cmdlet called `Rename-ADObject`. Again, to simplify things, you pipeline the site object to the cmdlet and you assign a new name for the site. This command is shown here. (This is also a one-line command broken at the pipe.)

```
Get-ADObject -SearchBase (Get-ADRootDSE).ConfigurationNamingContext -filter "objectclass
-eq 'site'" | Rename-ADObject -NewName CharlotteSite
```

## Managing users

To create a new Organizational Unit, you use the `New-ADOrganizationalUnit` cmdlet as shown here:

```
New-ADOrganizationalUnit -Name TestOU -Path "dc=nwtraders,dc=com"
```

If you want to create a child Organizational Unit (OU), you use the `New-ADOrganizationalUnit` cmdlet, but in the path, you list the location that will serve as the parent, as shown here:

```
New-ADOrganizationalUnit -Name TestOU1 -Path "ou=TestOU,dc=nwtraders,dc=com"
```

If you want to make several child OUs in the same location, use the up arrow to retrieve the previous command and edit the name of the child. You can use the home key to move to the beginning of the line, the end key to move to the end of the line, and the left and right arrow keys to find your place on the line so that you can edit it. A second child OU is created here:

```
New-ADOrganizationalUnit -Name TestOU2 -Path "ou=TestOU,dc=nwtraders,dc=com"
```

To create a computer account in one of the newly created child Organizational Units, you must type the complete path to the OU that will house the new computer account. The `New-ADComputer` cmdlet is used to create new computer accounts in AD DS. In this example, the TestOU1 OU is a child of the TestOU OU, and therefore, both OUs must appear in the path parameter. Keep in mind that the path that is supplied to the *path* parameter must be contained inside quotation marks, as shown here:

```
New-ADComputer -Name Test -Path "ou=TestOU1,ou=TestOU,dc=nwtraders,dc=com"
```

To create a user account, you use the `New-ADUser` cmdlet as shown here:

```
New-ADUser -Name TestChild -Path "ou=TestOU1,ou=TestOU,dc=nwtraders,dc=com"
```

Because there could be a bit of typing involved that tends to become redundant, you might want to write a script to create the OUs at the same time that the computer and user accounts are created. A sample script that creates OUs, users, and computers is the UseADCmdletsToCreateOuComputerAndUser.ps1 script shown here.

```
UseADCmdletsToCreateOuComputerAndUser.ps1

Import-Module -Name ActiveDirectory
$Name = "ScriptTest"
$DomainName = "dc=nwtraders,dc=com"
$OUPath = "ou={0},{1}" -f $Name, $DomainName

New-ADOrganizationalUnit -Name $Name -Path $DomainName
-ProtectedFromAccidentalDeletion $false

For($you = 0; $you -le 5; $you++)
{
 New-ADOrganizationalUnit -Name $Name$you -Path $OUPath
-ProtectedFromAccidentalDeletion $false
}

For($you = 0 ; $you -le 5; $you++)
{
 New-ADComputer -Name  "TestComputer$you" -Path $OUPath
 New-ADUser -Name "TestUser$you" -Path $OUPath
}
```

The UseADCmdletsToCreateOuComputerAndUser.ps1 script begins by importing the Active Directory module. It then creates the first OU. When testing a script, it is important to disable the deletion protection by using the *ProtectedFromAccidentalDeletion* parameter. This will allow you to easily delete the OU and avoid having to go into the advanced view in Active Directory Users And Computers and changing the protected status on each OU.

After the ScriptTest OU is created, the other OUs, users, and computer accounts can be created inside the new location. It seems obvious that you cannot create a child OU inside the parent OU if the parent has not yet been created, but it is easy to make a logic error like this.

To create a new global security group, use the New-ADGroup Windows PowerShell AD DS cmdlet. The New-ADGroup Windows PowerShell cmdlet requires three parameters: the *name* of the group, a *path* to the location where the group will be stored, and the *groupscope*, which can be global, universal, or domain local. Before running the command shown here, remember that you must import the Active Directory module into your current Windows PowerShell session.

```
New-ADGroup -Name TestGroup -Path "ou=TestOU,dc=nwtraders,dc=com" -groupScope global
```

To create a new universal group, you need to change only the *groupscope* parameter value as shown here:

```
New-ADGroup -Name TestGroup1 -Path "ou=TestOU,dc=nwtraders,dc=com" -groupScope universal
```

To add a user to a group, you must supply values for the *identity* parameter and for the *members* parameter. The value that you use for the identity parameter is the name of the group. You do not need to use the LDAP syntax of *cn=groupname*; you need to supply only the name. Use ADSI Edit to examine the requisite LDAP attributes needed for a group in ADSI Edit.

It is a bit unusual that the *members* parameter is named members and not member because most Windows PowerShell cmdlet parameter names are singular and not plural. The parameters are singular even when they accept an array of values (such as the *computername* parameter). The command to add a new group named TestGroup1 to the UserGroupTest group is shown here:

```
Add-ADGroupMember -Identity TestGroup1 -Members UserGroupTest
```

To remove a user from a group, use the `Remove-ADGroupMember` cmdlet with the name of the user and group. The *identity* and the *members* parameters are required, but the command will not execute without confirmation, as shown here:

```
PS C:\> Remove-ADGroupMember -Identity TestGroup1 -Members UserGroupTest

Confirm
Are you sure you want to perform this action?
Performing operation "Set" on Target "CN=TestGroup1,OU=TestOU,DC=NWTraders,DC=Com".
[Y] Yes  [A] Yes to All  [N] No  [L] No to All  [S] Suspend  [?] Help (default is "Y"):
y
PS C:\>
```

If you are sure that you want to remove the user from the group and that you want to suppress the query, you use the *confirm* parameter and assign the value *$false* to it. The problem is that you will need to supply a colon between the parameter and *$false* value.

> **NOTE** The use of the colon after the *confirm* parameter is not documented, but the technique works on several different cmdlets.

The command is shown here:

```
Remove-ADGroupMember -Identity TestGroup1 -Members UserGroupTest -Confirm:$false
```

You need the ability to suppress the confirmation prompt to be able to use the `Remove-ADGroupMember` cmdlet in a script. The first thing the RemoveUserFromGroup.ps1 script does is load the Active Directory module. When the module is loaded, the `Remove-ADGroupMember` cmdlet is used to remove the user from the group. To suppress the confirmation prompt, the *–confirm:$false* command is used. The RemoveUserFromGroup.ps1 script is shown here.

```
RemoveUserFromGroup.ps1

import-module activedirectory
Remove-ADGroupMember -Identity TestGroup1 -Members UserGroupTest -Confirm:$false
```

# Creating a user

Now create a new user in Active Directory. You will name the user "ed." The command to create a new user is simple; it is New-Aduser and the user name. The command to create a disabled user account in the *users* container in the default domain is shown here:

```
new-aduser -name ed
```

When the preceding command that creates a new user completes, nothing is returned to the Windows PowerShell console. To check to ensure that the user is created, use the Get-Aduser cmdlet to retrieve the user object. This command is shown here:

```
Get-aduser ed
```

When you are certain that your new user is created, you decide to create an organizational unit to store the user account. The command to create a new organizational unit off the root of the domain is shown here:

```
new-ADOrganizationalUnit scripting
```

Just like the previously used New-Aduser cmdlet, nothing returns to the Windows PowerShell console. If you use the Get-ADOrganizationalUnit cmdlet, you must use a different methodology. A simple Get-AdOrganizationalUnit command returns an error; therefore, you use an *LDAPFilter* parameter to find the OU. The command using the *LDAPFilter* parameter to find my newly created OU is shown here:

```
Get-ADOrganizationalUnit -LDAPFilter "(name=scripting)"
```

Now that you have a new user and a new OU, you need to move the user from the *users* container to the newly created *scripting* OU. To do that, you use the Move-ADObject cmdlet. You first get the *distinguishedname* attribute for the scripting OU and store it in a variable called *$oupath*. Next, you use the Move-ADObject cmdlet to move the *ed* user to the new OU. The trick here is that where the Get-AdUser cmdlet can find a user with the name of *ed*, the Move-ADObject cmdlet must have the *distinguishedname* of the *ed* user object to move it. The error that occurs when not supplying the *distinguishedname* appears in the figure that follows. You could use the Get-AdUser cmdlet to retrieve the *distinguishedname* in a similar method as you did with the scripting OU.

The next thing you need to do is to enable the user account. To do this, you need to assign a password to the user account. The password must be a secure string. To do this, you can use the ConvertTo-SecureString cmdlet. By default, warnings display about converting text to a secure string, but these prompts are suppressible by using the *force* parameter. Here is the command you use to create a secure string for a password:

```
$pwd = ConvertTo-SecureString -String "P@ssword1" -AsPlainText -Force
```

Now that you have created a secure string to use for a password for my user account, you call the Set-ADAccountPassword cmdlet to set the password. Because this is a new password, you need to use the *newpassword* parameter. In addition, because you do not have a previous password, you use the *reset* parameter. This command is shown here:

```
Set-ADAccountPassword -Identity ed -NewPassword $pwd -Reset
```

After the account has a password, you can enable the account. To do this, you use the Enable-ADAccount cmdlet and specify the user name to enable. This command is shown here:

```
Enable-ADAccount -Identity ed
```

As with the previous commands, none of the cmdlets return any information. To ensure that you have actually enabled the *ed* user account, you use the Get-ADUser cmdlet. In the output, you are looking for the value of the *enabled* property. The *enabled* property is a Boolean, so expect the value to be true.

## Finding and unlocking AD user accounts

When using the Microsoft Active Directory cmdlets, locating locked out users is a snap. In fact, the Search-ADAccount cmdlet even has a *LockedOut* switch. Use the Search-ADAccount cmdlet with the *LockedOut* parameter. This command is shown here:

```
Search-ADAccount -LockedOut
```

> **NOTE** Many network administrators who spend the majority of their time working with Active Directory import the Active Directory module via their Windows PowerShell profile. This way, they never need to worry about the initial performance hit that occurs due to autoloading the Active Directory module.

The Search-ADAccount command and the associated output are shown here:

```
[w8server6]: PS C:\> Search-ADAccount -LockedOut

AccountExpirationDate :
DistinguishedName     : CN=kimakers,OU=test,DC=iammred,DC=net
Enabled               : True
LastLogonDate         : 1/24/2012 8:40:29 AM
LockedOut             : True
Name                  : kimakers
ObjectClass           : user
ObjectGUID            : d907fa99-cd08-435f-97de-1e99d0eb485d
PasswordExpired       : False
PasswordNeverExpires  : False
```

```
SamAccountName      : kimakers
SID                 : S-1-5-21-1457956834-3844189528-3541350385-1608
UserPrincipalName   : kimakers@iammred.net
```

```
[w8server6]: PS C:\>
```

You can unlock the locked out user account as well—assuming that you have permission. In Figure 3-5, you attempt to unlock the user account with an account that is a normal user, and an error arises.

> **NOTE**  People are often worried about Windows PowerShell from a security perspective. Windows PowerShell is only an application, and therefore a user cannot do anything that they do not have the rights or permission to accomplish. This is a case in point.

If your user account does not have admin rights, you need to start Windows PowerShell with an account that has the ability to unlock a user account. To do this, you right-click the Windows PowerShell icon while holding down the Shift key; this allows you to select Run As Different User from the quick action menu.

When you start Windows PowerShell back up with an account that has rights to unlock users, the Active Directory module needs to load once again. You then check to ensure that you can still locate the locked out user accounts. After you have proven you can do that, you pipeline the results of the Search-ADAccount cmdlet to the Unlock-ADAccount cmdlet. A quick check ensures that you have unlocked all the locked out accounts. The series of commands is shown here:

```
Search-ADAccount –LockedOut
Search-ADAccount –LockedOut | Unlock-ADAccount
Search-ADAccount –LockedOut
```

The commands and associated output are shown in Figure 3-5.

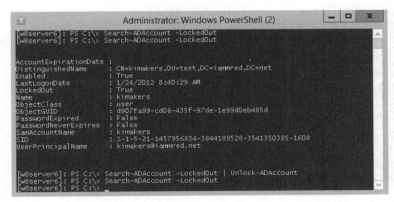

**FIGURE 3-5** Using the Active Directory module to find and to unlock user accounts.

If you do not want to unlock all users, you use the *confirm* parameter from the `Unlock-ADAccount` cmdlet. For example, you first check to see what users are locked out by using the `Search-ADAccount` cmdlet—but you do not want to see everything, only their name. Next, you pipeline the locked out users to the `Unlock-ADAccount` cmdlet with the *confirm* parameter. You are then prompted for each of the three locked out users; choose to unlock the first and third users, but not the second user. You then use the `Search-ADAccount` cmdlet one last time to ensure that the second user is still locked out.

## Finding disabled users

Luckily, by using Windows PowerShell and the Microsoft Active Directory cmdlets, it takes a single line of code to retrieve the disabled users from your domain. The command is shown here. (Keep in mind that running this command automatically imports the Active Directory module into the current Windows PowerShell host.)

```
Get-ADUser -Filter 'enabled -eq $false' -Server dc3
```

Not only is the command a single line of code, but it is also a single line of readable code. You get users from AD DS; you use a filter that looks for the enabled property set to false. You also specify that you want to query a server named dc3 (the name of one of the domain controllers on my network). The command and the associated output appear in Figure 3-6.

**FIGURE 3-6** Finding disabled user accounts.

If you want to work with a specific user, you can use the *identity* parameter. The *identity* parameter accepts several things: distinguishedname, sid, guid, or SamAccountName. Probably the easiest one to use is the SamAccountName. This command and associated output are shown here:

```
PS C:\Users\ed.IAMMRED>    Get-ADUser -Server dc3 -Identity teresa
DistinguishedName : CN=Teresa Wilson,OU=Charlotte,DC=iammred,DC=net
Enabled           : True
GivenName         : Teresa
Name              : Teresa Wilson
ObjectClass       : user
ObjectGUID        : 75f12010-b952-4d3-9b22-3ada7d26eed8
SamAccountName    : Teresa
SID               : S-1-5-21-1457956834-3844189528-3541350385-1104
Surname           : Wilson
UserPrincipalName : Teresa@iammred.net
```

To use the DistinguishedName value for the *identity* parameter, you need to supply it inside a pair of quotation marks—either single or double. This command and associated output are shown here:

```
PS C:\Users\ed.IAMMRED>    Get-ADUser -Server dc3 -Identity 'CN=Teresa Wilson,OU
=Charlotte,DC=iammred,DC=net'
DistinguishedName : CN=Teresa Wilson,OU=Charlotte,DC=iammred,DC=net
Enabled           : True
GivenName         : Teresa
Name              : Teresa Wilson
ObjectClass       : user
ObjectGUID        : 75f12010-b952-4d3-9b22-3ada7d26eed8
SamAccountName    : Teresa
SID               : S-1-5-21-1457956834-3844189528-3541350385-1104
Surname           : Wilson
UserPrincipalName : Teresa@iammred.net
```

It is not necessary to use quotation marks when using the SID for the value of the *identity* parameter. This command and associated output are shown here:

```
PS C:\Users\ed.IAMMRED>    Get-ADUser -Server dc3 -Identity S-1-5-21-1457956834-
3844189528-3541350385-1104

DistinguishedName : CN=Teresa Wilson,OU=Charlotte,DC=iammred,DC=net
Enabled           : True
GivenName         : Teresa
Name              : Teresa Wilson
ObjectClass       : user
ObjectGUID        : 75f12010-b952-4d3-9b22-3ada7d26eed8
SamAccountName    : Teresa
SID               : S-1-5-21-1457956834-3844189528-3541350385-1104
Surname           : Wilson
UserPrincipalName : Teresa@iammred.net
```

Again, you can also use *ObjectGUID* for the *identity* parameter value. It does not require quotation marks either. This command and associated output are shown here:

```
PS C:\Users\ed.IAMMRED>    Get-ADUser -Server dc3 -Identity 75f12010-b952-4d3-9
b22-3ada7d26eed8
DistinguishedName : CN=Teresa Wilson,OU=Charlotte,DC=iammred,DC=net
Enabled           : True
GivenName         : Teresa
Name              : Teresa Wilson
ObjectClass       : user
ObjectGUID        : 75f12010-b952-4d3-9b22-3ada7d26eed8
SamAccountName    : Teresa
SID               : S-1-5-21-1457956834-3844189528-3541350385-1104
Surname           : Wilson
UserPrincipalName : Teresa@iammred.net
```

## Finding unused user accounts

To obtain a listing of all the users in Active Directory, supply a wildcard to the *filter* parameter of the Get-ADUser cmdlet. This technique is shown here:

```
Get-ADUser -Filter *
```

If you want to change the base of the search operations, use the *searchbase* parameter. The *searchbase* parameter accepts an LDAP style of naming. The following command changes the search base to the TestOU:

```
Get-ADUser -Filter * -SearchBase "ou=TestOU,dc=nwtraders,dc=com"
```

When using the Get-ADUser cmdlet, only a certain subset of user properties are displayed (10 properties to be exact). These properties will be displayed when you pipeline the results to Format-List and use a wildcard and the *force* parameter, as shown here:

```
PS C:\> Get-ADUser -Identity bob | format-list -Property * -Force


DistinguishedName : CN=bob,OU=TestOU,DC=NWTraders,DC=Com
Enabled           : True
GivenName         : bob
Name              : bob
ObjectClass       : user
ObjectGUID        : 5cae3acf-f194-4e07-a466-789f9ad5c84a
SamAccountName    : bob
SID               : S-1-5-21-3746122405-834892460-3960030898-3601
Surname           :
UserPrincipalName : bob@NWTraders.Com
PropertyNames     : {DistinguishedName, Enabled, GivenName, Name...}
PropertyCount     : 10



PS C:\>
```

Anyone who knows very much about Active Directory Domain Services (AD DS) knows that there are certainly more than 10 properties associated with a user object. If you try to display a property that is not returned by the Get-ADUser cmdlet, such as the *whenCreated* property, an error is not returned—the value of the property is not returned. This is shown here:

```
PS C:\> Get-ADUser -Identity bob | Format-List -Property name, whenCreated


name          : bob
whencreated :
```

The *whenCreated* property for the user object has a value—it just is not displayed. However, suppose you were looking for users who had never logged on to the system? Suppose you used a query such as the one seen here, and you were going to base a delete operation on the results? The results could be disastrous.

```
PS C:\> Get-ADUser -Filter * | Format-Table -Property name, LastLogonDate

name                             LastLogonDate
----                             -------------
Administrator
Guest
krbtgt
testuser2
ed
SystemMailbox{1f05a927-a261-4eb4-8360-8...
SystemMailbox{e0dc1c29-89c3-4034-b678-e...
FederatedEmail.4c1f4d8b-8179-4148-93bf-...
Test
TestChild
<results truncated>
```

To retrieve a property that is not a member of the default 10 properties, you must select it by using the *property* parameter. The reason that Get-ADUser does not automatically return all properties and their associated values is because of performance reasons on large networks—there is no reason to return a large dataset when a small dataset will perfectly suffice. To display the *name* and the *whenCreated* date for the user named *bob*, the following command can be used:

```
PS C:\> Get-ADUser -Identity bob -Properties whencreated | Format-List -Property name,
whencreated


name          : bob
whencreated : 6/11/2010 8:19:52 AM


PS C:\>
```

To retrieve all of the properties associated with a user object, use the wildcard "*" for the properties parameter value. You would use a command similar to the one shown here:

```
Get-ADUser -Identity kimakers -Properties *
```

Both the command and the results associated with the command to return all user properties are shown in Figure 3-7.

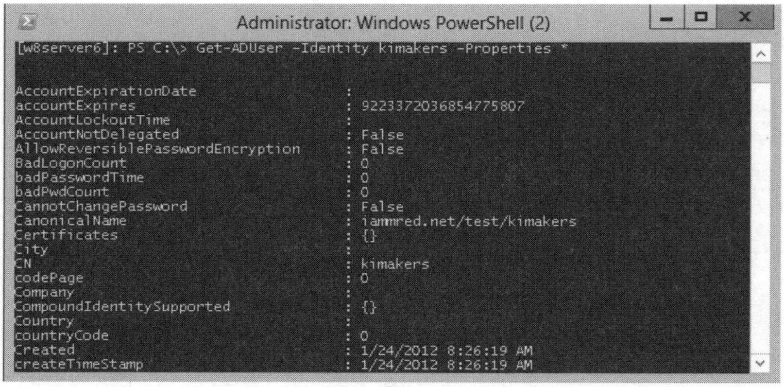

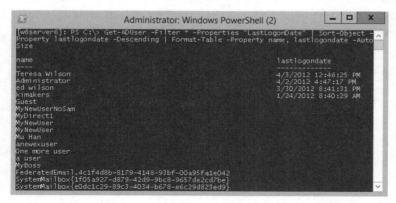

**FIGURE 3-7** Using the Get-ADUser cmdlet to display all user properties.

To produce a listing of all the users and their last logon date, you can use a command similar to the one shown here. This is a single command that might wrap the line, depending on your screen resolution.

```
Get-ADUser -Filter * -Properties "LastLogonDate" |
sort-object -property lastlogondate -descending |
Format-Table -property name, lastlogondate -AutoSize
```

The output produces a nice table. Both the command and the output associated with the command to obtain the time a user last logged on are shown in Figure 3-8.

**FIGURE 3-8** Using the Get-ADUser cmdlet to identify the last logon times for users.

**Jeff Wouters**
*Microsoft PowerShell MVP*

"Write tools, not scripts" is one of my favorite phrases from the Windows PowerShell community. When I had just started to write some Windows PowerShell code, I was (and still am!) crazy about one-liners.

The ease with which the pipeline allows you to connect commands to each other and make them work together were unheard of in the VBS world.

But then I got a customer who wanted me to leave some code with them when I left. So I did, and only one week later, I got a call from that customer, in panic, saying that my script had deleted half their Active Directory!

I asked them to send me the code of the script. After only a few seconds, I noticed that this wasn't my code. There was a whole lot more in there that didn't come from me. So I connected to my home environment and looked in the backup I had made of all the scripts and documentation I had left with the customer, and yes, the script I had left them had a lot less code in there. So someone had changed my script!

Luckily, this customer had the Active Directory Recycle Bin enabled, so restoring the objects in Active Directory wasn't that hard. But for me, this was a wake-up call. Sign your scripts! Or at least make sure that you can verify the integrity of your scripts.

I also found that the person who changed my script, and basically was the cause of the problem, was a member of the service desk at that company. This is where "write tools, not scripts" comes into play.

So I rewrote my script, added a GUI, and signed it. This way, the help desk would have a nice clickable interface, and the script itself would be safe from malicious editors causing all kinds of issues. Because there were a whole bunch of scripts, I've created a module for them called "<CompanyName>Administration." To finish things off, I've introduced them to the concept of a centralized store for their modules.

For me, this was a learning curve, and these days I prefer a six steps approach:

1. Log everything; what it does and who executes it.

2. Support the common parameters, such as *–Whatif* and *-Confirm*.

3. Create an interface for the appropriate user—a command line for people who understand PowerShell and a GUI for those who don't.

4. Sign your script!

5. Group scripts into modules.

6. Use a centralized module repository, preferably with read-only rights for every-one who is not responsible for the modules.

These steps will make your life a whole lot easier when people start messing with your scripts.

## Additional resources

- The TechNet Script Center at *http://www.microsoft.com/technet/scriptcenter* contains numerous script examples.
- All scripts from this chapter are available via the TechNet Script Center Script Repository at *http://gallery.technet.microsoft.com/scriptcenter/PowerShell-40 -Best-d9e16039*.

# CHAPTER 4

# Identifying scripting opportunities

- Automating routine tasks
- Automation interface
- Structured requirements
- Additional resources

## Automating routine tasks

One of the most important tasks when developing a scripting program is to track and coordinate the development endeavors of the scripting team. However, this process is not done in most companies. As a result, much time is wasted developing multiple scripts that perform the same tasks and implement similar functionality.

This is an area in which the judicious application of collaboration tools can play a significant role. One such collaboration tool that can easily be pressed into service is the Microsoft SharePoint Portal product. The discussion forum can be used to track requests for scripts, and the library can be used as a central distribution point for released scripts.

When attempting to identify scripting opportunities, you must know which tasks are ripe for automation and which are not. In general, when making the decision to script or not to script, the most obvious requirement is repeatability. Routine tasks should nearly always be investigated for scripting. However, just because a task is repeatable does not automatically mean that it is rich for automation via scripting. Many repeatable tasks simply cannot be automated via scripting for one reason or another.

Jason Hofferle, IT Specialist

It can be challenging for an IT Professional to keep up with the latest developments in their own specialty, and even more difficult to stay current on Windows PowerShell best practices. By virtue of my enthusiasm for Windows PowerShell, I've filled an informal "scripting guy" role in my organization where I assist other IT staff with learning PowerShell and applying the scripting best practices coming from the PowerShell community.

There is a lot of information about Windows PowerShell available, and more content is being created every day. One useful function of a scripting guy is to help filter this content down to what is specifically useful for your organization. Anyone is free to subscribe to the internal mailing list that I use to distribute information that I think is useful. Maybe there's a specific problem someone is having, the directory administrators are trying to automate a task, or someone is providing some free Windows PowerShell training online. A mailing list becomes a great mechanism for sending out specific articles or examples that are immediately applicable to what your coworkers are doing.

An internal wiki page or SharePoint page is a great way to publicize scripts that are specific to your organization. There are a million generic examples of how to automate certain tasks in Windows PowerShell, but sometimes beginners have a difficult time applying these generic examples to a specific problem. The role of an organization's scripting guy is to bridge this gap and help others see where scripting techniques can save time and effort. After a while, these connections will be seen by others, and they'll start sending *you* tips!

A major strength of Windows PowerShell is the consistency—consistency in the verb-noun naming convention, consistency in parameters, consistency in how objects move through the pipeline, and consistency in how to get help. I'm not an Exchange administrator, or a SQL Server administrator, or a VMware administrator, but I'm able to help our experts because Windows PowerShell best practices are applicable everywhere. I don't have to understand the intricacies of an Exchange deployment to understand how to write a good function or get a script to accept pipeline input. A scripting guy is always open to providing assistance, because it makes the IT organization better as a whole.

Windows PowerShell is a core skill for IT Professionals, but not everyone needs to be an expert. Often, just having one person that can answer a question or provide an example is all that's needed to save hours of frustration. Organizations benefit from having a "scripting guy," and someone reading a book about best practices just might be the right person to fill that role.

# Automation interface

One of the most obvious needs is for some type of automation interface. Automation can be implemented in many ways, such as through a Component Object Model (COM) classic application programming interface (API), Microsoft .NET Framework support, Windows Management Instrumentation (WMI) support, ActiveX Data Object (ADO) support in all of its various versions, and Active Directory Services Interface (ADSI) support, not to mention Windows PowerShell cmdlets or command-line utilities such as NetSH or NetDom. With these various avenues for automation support, identifying the proper means of performing the task can be both time consuming and overwhelming. For example, take the simple task of reading from the registry.

If you want to identify the version of Windows PowerShell that is running on your computer, you can read the *PowerShellVersion* value from the registry. This registry key is shown in Figure 4-1.

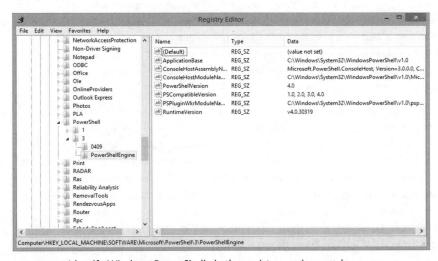

**FIGURE 4-1** Identify Windows PowerShell via the registry version number.

One method for reading from the registry is to use the registry provider from within Windows PowerShell and to read a registry value as you might read a property from a file or folder. To do this, you must use the HKLM PowerShell drive (HKLM in this instance) and follow it with the path to the registry key, which is \SOFTWARE\Microsoft\PowerShell\1\ PowerShellEngine. You can then select the item property in which you are interested, which is *RunTimeVersion* in this example, as shown in the Get-PsVersionRegistry.ps1 script.

```
Get-PsVersionRegistry.ps1

$path = "HKLM:\SOFTWARE\Microsoft\PowerShell\3\PowerShellEngine"
$psv = get-itemproperty -path $path
$psv.PowerShellVersion
```

## Huge paybacks using Windows PowerShell 4.0 automation

Keith Mayer, Senior Technical Evangelist
*Microsoft Corporation*

I've been an IT Professional for over 20 years, and throughout this time, I have worked with lots of enterprise IT organizations. All of the organizations with which I've worked try very hard to ensure standardization of their various deployments to promote reliability and supportability. How do they accomplish this? Why, with Standard Operating Procedure (SOP) documents, of course!

SOP documents can be very detailed, and some SOPs can be hundreds of pages in length. While it's certainly wonderful to have this level of step-by-step instructions documented, SOP documents don't solve one of IT's longest-running challenges: human error. Using an SOP document as the basis for deploying an IT solution often requires extreme diligence in following each of several hundred or, in some cases, thousands of steps exactly. During the deployment, if another IT issue arises, it's quite easy to lose track of your progress and, as a result, accidentally omit certain configuration items or entire steps.

And this is exactly where Windows PowerShell 4.0 and Desired State Configurations can be immediately impactful! As you begin learning and exploring Windows PowerShell 4.0, take the opportunity to review your existing SOP documents. In particular, look for those processes that are tedious to perform and are used over and over again. If you can apply your new Windows PowerShell skills by automating all or a portion of particular processes that are used frequently by your team, you'll likely receive three huge immediate paybacks: (1) You'll save time for your team to focus on other, more strategic tasks—the "fun" stuff in IT; (2) you'll increase reliability and standardization by reducing opportunities for human error; (3) your team will see the business value that Windows PowerShell can provide, and they will be encouraged to join you in learning PowerShell so that they can help to script other processes.

Automating frequently used SOP documents can be a great starting point in your organization to begin applying new Windows PowerShell 4.0 skills. In the past, I've seen many organizations spend tons of cycles brainstorming on how best to begin leveraging Windows PowerShell. Be sure that you don't overlook the opportunity to jumpstart the use of PowerShell on your team to improve existing time-consuming processes that might be right under your nose!

# Using *RegRead* to read the registry

Those of you who are familiar with VBScript might want to create the *WshShell* object and use the *RegRead* method. To do this, you can use the HKLM moniker as a shortcut to refer to the HKEY_LOCAL_MACHINE registry key.

> **NOTE** When used with the *WshShell* object, the HKLM is case sensitive.

You store the path to the Windows PowerShell configuration information in the *$path* variable. Next, you can use the New-Object cmdlet to create an instance of the *WshShell* object. This COM object has the program ID of Wscript.Shell. You can store the returned object in the *$wshShell* variable. After you have the *WshShell* object, you can use the *RegRead* method to read the registry key value, which you can specify by placing the path and value name in an expanding string: "$path\RunTimeVersion". This Get-PsVersionRegRead.ps1 script is shown here.

```
Get-PSVersionRegRead.ps1

$path = "HKLM\SOFTWARE\Microsoft\PowerShell\3\PowerShellEngine"
$WshShell = New-Object -ComObject Wscript.Shell
$WshShell.RegRead("$path\PowerShellVersion")
```

# Using WMI to read the registry

When you want to use WMI to read the registry, you need to use the *stdRegProv* WMI class, which has always been in the *root\default* WMI namespace. Beginning with Windows Vista, you also have an instance of the *stdRegProv* WMI class in the *root\cimv2* namespace (which, incidentally, really is the default namespace). This means that you can use the *stdRegProv* WMI class from either the *root\default* WMI namespace or the *root\cimv2* WMI namespace; it does not matter because it is the same WMI class. Because it does not matter which instance of the class you use, I recommend as a best practice that you use the class from the *root\ default* WMI namespace (as in the Get-PsVersionWmi.ps1 script) to ensure compatibility with older versions of Windows-based operating systems.

WMI uses coded values to determine the registry tree (also known as a *hive*). These coded values are shown in Table 4-1.

**TABLE 4-1** WMI registry tree values

| Name | Value |
| --- | --- |
| HKEY_CLASSES_ROOT | 2147483648 |
| HKEY_CURRENT_USER | 2147483649 |
| HKEY_LOCAL_MACHINE | 2147483650 |
| HKEY_USERS | 2147483651 |
| HKEY_CURRENT_CONFIG | 2147483653 |

You can use the value *2147483650* and assign it to the *$hklm* variable. This value points the WMI query to the HKEY_LOCAL_MACHINE registry tree. You then assign the string SOFTWARE\Microsoft\PowerShell\1\PowerShellEngine to the *$key* variable.

> **NOTE** When using WMI to read the registry, the key is not preceded with a backslash.

You assign the registry property value that you want to read to the *$value* variable. Now you can use the [WMICLASS] type accelerator to obtain an instance of the *stdRegProv* WMI class. You can choose the *root\default* WMI namespace to specify which version of the *stdRegProv* WMI class you want to use. You can also precede the namespace with the name of a computer and read the registry from a remote computer. After you create an instance of the *stdregProv* WMI class, you can use the resulting *System.Management.Management* class to call the *GetStringValue* method. The *GetStringValue* method takes three arguments: the registry key coded value, the registry subkey string, and the property name. Two objects are returned by the method call: the *returnvalue*, which indicates the success or failure of the method call, and the svalue, which is the string value that is stored in the registry property. The complete Get-PsVersionWmi.ps1 script is shown here.

**Get-PsVersionWmi.ps1**

```
$hklm = 2147483650
$key = "SOFTWARE\Microsoft\PowerShell\3\PowerShellEngine"
$value = "PowerShellVersion"
$wmi = [WMICLASS]"root\default:stdRegProv"
($wmi.GetStringValue($hklm,$key,$value)).svalue
```

## Using .NET to read the registry

You can also use the .NET Framework classes to obtain information from the registry. To do this, you can use the *Microsoft.Win32.Registry* .NET Framework class. You can use the *GetValue* static method, which takes three parameters. The first parameter is the registry root and key name; the second parameter is the registry value that you want to read; and the last parameter is the default value of the registry key value. In the Get-PsVersionNet.ps1 script, you can assign the HKEY_LOCAL_MACHINE string value to the *$hklm* variable. Next, you can assign the string representing the remainder of the registry path to the *$key* variable. The registry key property value you want to retrieve is stored in the *$value* variable. You can then use the *Microsoft.Win32.Registry* class plus two colons to signify that you want to use a static method and then use the *GetValue* method with the *$hklm*, *$key*, and *$value* variables passed to it. The Get-PsVersionNet.ps1 script is shown here.

**Get-PsVersionNet.ps1**

```
$hklm = "HKEY_LOCAL_MACHINE"
$key = "SOFTWARE\Microsoft\PowerShell\3\PowerShellEngine"
```

```
$value = "PowerShellVersion"
[Microsoft.Win32.Registry]::GetValue("$hklm\$key",$value,$null)
```

When working with the registry, you can see that there is a Windows PowerShell provider, COM object, WMI class, and .NET Framework class. This plethora of methodologies is one of the strengths of Windows PowerShell, but it is also a significant source of confusion for those who are just learning PowerShell.

So what is the correct way to read the registry? You can never go wrong by using native Windows PowerShell providers and commands. The registry provider in Windows PowerShell is powerful and easy to use from the command line. In addition, because of the remoting features of Windows PowerShell 4.0, the need to remotely access the registry is no longer the key decision factor.

WMI gives you the ability to connect remotely to read the registry. The methodology is very similar to the way that you connect in VBScript; therefore, if you are migrating a script to Windows PowerShell from VBScript, it makes sense to stay with the WMI methodology. The *WshShell* COM object is also a good choice if you are interested in migrating legacy code to Windows PowerShell. The VBScript techniques are very similar and can therefore make a fairly straightforward translation. The .NET Framework classes offer much more flexibility than any of the other techniques explored.

## Using intrinsic Windows PowerShell techniques

Deciding on the best way to retrieve information from computers when working with Windows PowerShell is one of the most basic decisions one has to make prior to scripting. As you have already seen, there are many different ways to read from the registry to obtain information. But in the case of Windows PowerShell, the real question is not how to read the registry but whether or not to read from the registry. This is because there is an automatic variable that displays the version of Windows PowerShell. The variable *$PSVersionTable* is available beginning with Windows PowerShell version 2.0. The variable and output from the variable are shown here:

```
PS C:\> $PSVersionTable

Name                           Value
----                           -----
PSVersion                      4.0
WSManStackVersion              3.0
SerializationVersion           1.1.0.1
CLRVersion                     4.0.30319.33439
BuildVersion                   6.3.9478.0
PSCompatibleVersions           {1.0, 2.0, 3.0, 4.0}
PSRemotingProtocolVersion      2.2
```

Upon discovering an intrinsic Windows PowerShell method to accomplish a particular task, the next problem is how to leverage this method. Because it is unlikely that a network administrator needs to retrieve Windows PowerShell version information from a single computer, the task falls to how best to retrieve the information from a group of remote computers. Two ways of doing this are using a Windows PowerShell workflow or using Windows PowerShell remoting. While this is not exactly a strict dichotomy (because Windows PowerShell workflow uses Windows PowerShell remoting technology), the choice falls to how many remote computers are in the mix.

Using a Windows PowerShell workflow to retrieve Windows PowerShell version information is simple enough. For more information about Windows PowerShell Workflow, see Chapter 22, "Using Windows PowerShell Workflow." The workflow looks similar to a Windows PowerShell function and is called in much the same way. The Get-PSVersionWorkflow.ps1 script appears here.

```
Get-PSVersionWorkflow.ps1

workflow Get-PSVersion
{
 InlineScript {$PSVersionTable.psversion}
}
```

An example of using the Get-PSVersionWorkflow.ps1 script is shown in Figure 4-2.

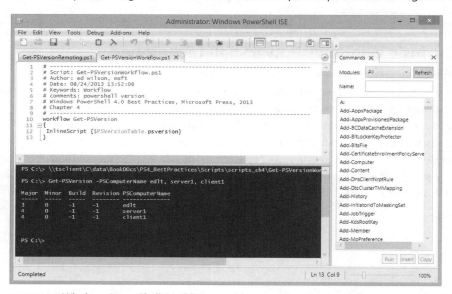

**FIGURE 4-2** Windows PowerShell Workflow provides easy remoting capability.

It is also possible to use Windows PowerShell remoting to execute a command on a remote computer. For more information about Windows PowerShell remoting, see Chapter 21, "Using Windows PowerShell remoting." The easiest way to do this is to use the Invoke-Command cmdlet and use the *$PSVersionTable* automatic variable inside the script block. This technique is shown in Get-PSVersionRemoting.ps1.

---

**Get-PSVersionRemoting.ps1**

```
Invoke-Command -ScriptBlock {$PSVersionTable.PSVersion} -ComputerName edlt, client1,
server1
```

---

An example of calling the `Invoke-Command` cmdlet from within the Windows PowerShell ISE is shown in Figure 4-3.

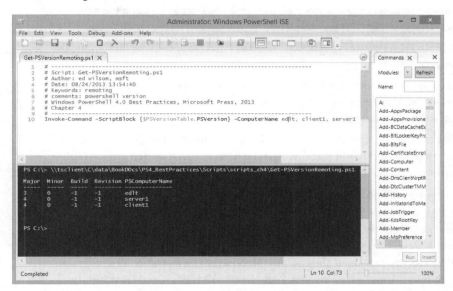

**FIGURE 4-3** Windows PowerShell remoting provides an easy way to obtain information from networked computers.

---

*INSIDE TRACK*

## Working with Windows PowerShell

**Jeffrey Snover, Distinguished Engineer**
*Microsoft Corporation*

Version 4 of Windows PowerShell takes advantage of the rich architecture work we did in version 3, which enables us to deliver at least as much innovation in a much shorter time period. That is why it is hard for me to pick out my favorite feature. If you make me choose just one feature, I'd have to pick remoting, but that's a

---

bit like cheating because there are at least six separate remoting stories, including the following:

- You can remote to existing systems using Remote Procedure Call (RPC) and the Distributed Component Object Model (DCOM) by adding the *–computername* parameter to numerous commands.

- You can do awesome, large-scale WMI remoting by employing a new set of cmdlets that uses semi-synchronous APIs and the *–ThrottleLimit* parameter.

- You can remotely manage raw hardware and UNIX boxes by using the new *WS-Management* (WSMan) cmdlets.

- You can create remote interactive Windows PowerShell sessions on a Windows-based machine.

- You can do fan-out command execution to a large group of machines and get results back immediately, or you can run Windows PowerShell as a background job and collect the results at your leisure.

- You can host Windows PowerShell as an Internet Information Services (IIS) application to support fan-in management scenarios in which service providers offer custom scripting interfaces to individual users across the Internet.

Windows PowerShell remoting provides administrators with much more control over their environment than they ever had before. I can't wait to see what people do with it. I think that most people will perform the classic procedures with our remoting work, such as creating files and folders, making new shares, and working with the registry. Only now, they can do this on a remote machine. These types of procedures are exposed via the Windows PowerShell cmdlets and providers. I also think that a select group of people will look at our remoting capabilities and realize that we have delivered a general-purpose, distributed computing platform—and they will start doing all sorts of crazy and wonderful things with it.

Personally, when I need to work on a remote computer, I like creating PSSessions and then using the `Invoke-Command` cmdlet because it is very fast and flexible. I use this cmdlet whether I need to run a simple command or actually need a remote interactive Windows PowerShell session.

# Structured requirements

When investigating a scripting opportunity, it is important to first analyze the requirements for the script. Several of the items to be examined are listed here:

- Security requirements
- .NET Framework version requirements
- Operating system requirements
- Application requirements
- Module requirements

## Security requirements

Beginning with Windows Vista, the introduction of User Account Control (UAC) has made it easier for users to run programs without having Administrator rights on their computer. While this is a boon for users and corporate security departments, it is somewhat of a headache for network administrators and others who are writing scripts that might require elevated permissions.

Windows PowerShell does not bypass security. If a script attempts to perform an action that the user is not allowed to perform, the script fails.

In Windows PowerShell 4.0, we have improved the detection of security requirements. As shown in Figure 4-4, when a script does not contain the required rights, a failure notification is shown.

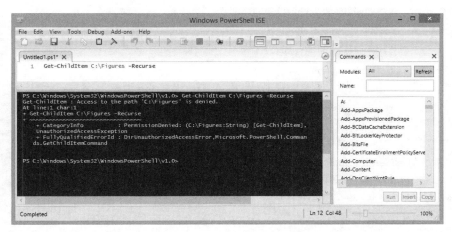

**FIGURE 4-4** When a script does not have permission, it reports an access denied message.

As a best practice, a script should detect the rights it possesses when running and compare them with any requirements the script might need to run properly. An easy way to do this is to use the *#Requires* statement to check for admin rights. The *#Requires* statement is covered in Chapter 12, "Handling errors." The following example uses #*Requires* to check for admin rights:

```
#Requires -RunAsAdministrator
```

To do this, you first need to obtain information about the user, which is covered in the next section.

## Detecting the current user

To provide information about currently logged-on users, you can use the *Security.Principal .WindowsIdentity* .NET Framework class. This class uses the *GetCurrent* method, which returns an instance of a *WindowsIdentity* object that represents the current user. In the following example, the *WindowsIdentity* object is stored in the *$user* variable:

```
$user = [System.Security.Principal.WindowsIdentity]::GetCurrent()
```

The *WindowsIdentity* object contains the properties shown in Table 4-2.

**TABLE 4-2** Properties of the *WindowsIdentity* object

| Name | Definition |
| --- | --- |
| *AuthenticationType* | System.String AuthenticationType {get;} |
| *Groups* | System.Security.Principal.IdentityReferenceCollection Groups {get;} |
| *ImpersonationLevel* | System.Security.Principal.TokenImpersonationLevel ImpersonationLevel {get;} |
| *IsAnonymous* | System.Boolean IsAnonymous {get;} |
| *IsAuthenticated* | System.Boolean IsAuthenticated {get;} |
| *IsGuest* | System.Boolean IsGuest {get;} |
| *IsSystem* | System.Boolean IsSystem {get;} |
| *Name* | System.String Name {get;} |
| *Owner* | System.Security.Principal.SecurityIdentifier Owner {get;} |
| *Token* | System.IntPtr Token {get;} |
| *User* | System.Security.Principal.SecurityIdentifier User {get;} |

After the *WindowsIdentity* object is stored in a variable, you can display the values of all of the properties shown in Table 4-2 by typing the variable at the prompt. You do not need to store the variable, and you can display the data directly as shown in Figure 4-5.

**FIGURE 4-5** Windows PowerShell displays the value of the *WindowsIdentity* object.

While the display shown in Figure 4-5 is somewhat impressive and moderately useful in that it displays the user name and security identifier (SID) of the user, it does not display any information about the user rights to a particular resource or administrator rights in general. There are actually two separate requirements: Does the user have access rights to a resource, and does the user have administrator rights?

To determine the rights of a user to a resource, you must examine the group information. As shown in Table 4-2, the *WindowsIdentity* class has a *Groups* property. You can easily display the contents of the *Groups* property by simply printing the value as shown here:

```
$user = [System.Security.Principal.WindowsIdentity]::GetCurrent()

$user.Groups
```

The problem with this approach is that the resulting collection of groups is not in the most readable format, as shown in Figure 4-6.

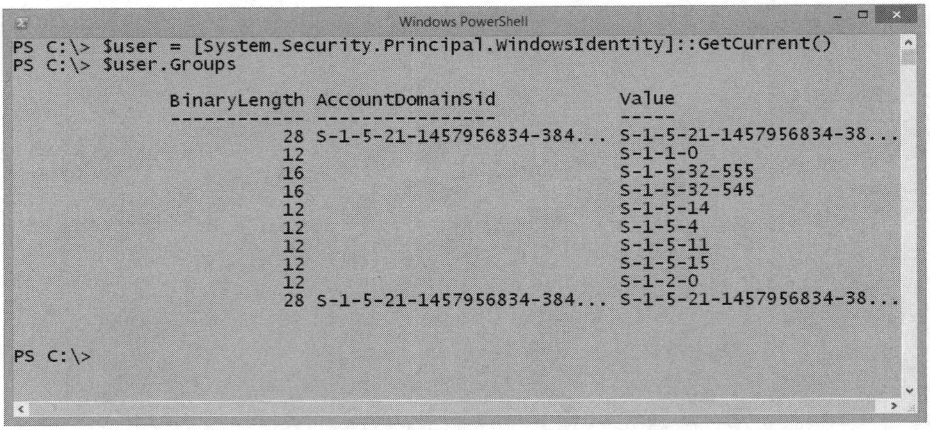

```
Windows PowerShell                                                    _ □ ✕
PS C:\> $user = [System.Security.Principal.WindowsIdentity]::GetCurrent()
PS C:\> $user.Groups

        BinaryLength AccountDomainSid              Value
        ------------ ----------------              -----
                  28 S-1-5-21-1457956834-384...    S-1-5-21-1457956834-38...
                  12                               S-1-1-0
                  16                               S-1-5-32-555
                  16                               S-1-5-32-545
                  12                               S-1-5-14
                  12                               S-1-5-4
                  12                               S-1-5-11
                  12                               S-1-5-15
                  12                               S-1-2-0
                  28 S-1-5-21-1457956834-384...    S-1-5-21-1457956834-38...


PS C:\>
```

**FIGURE 4-6** The *Groups* property of the *WindowsIdentity* class is subilluminating.

You need to convert the group information from a SID into something more recognizable. When you have an actual group name, it is easier to use any of the string manipulation tools provided by Windows PowerShell to determine specific group membership. You can index directly into the collection of *SecurityIdentifiers* that is returned by the *Groups* property. The following code allows you to do this:

```
$user.Groups[0]
```

Of course, there is one problem with this approach. How do you know what group[0] is? If you add the *ToString* method, you get a little bit of assistance as shown here, with the resulting display as well.

```
PS C:\Users\bob> $user.Groups[0].tostring()

S-1-4-21-540299044-341859138-929407116-513
```

At this point, you have succeeded in directly obtaining the SID of the group. In some cases, this can be enough information if you want to match group membership based on SIDs. However, most network administrators do not have this information at their fingertips, so it is necessary to take the output to an additional level of processing.

To change a SID into a noun name, you can use the *Translate* method from the *System .Security.Principal.SecurityIdentifier* .NET Framework class. The members of this class are shown in Table 4-3.

**TABLE 4-3** Members of the *SecurityIdentifier* class

| Name | MemberType | Definition |
|------|-----------|-----------|
| *CompareTo* | Method | System.Int32 CompareTo(SecurityIdentifier sid) |
| *Equals* | Method | System.Boolean Equals(Object o) System.Boolean Equals(SecurityIdentifier sid) |
| *GetBinaryForm* | Method | System.Void GetBinaryForm(Byte[] binaryForm Int32 offset) |

| Name | MemberType | Definition |
|------|-----------|------------|
| GetHashCode | Method | System.Int32 GetHashCode() |
| GetType | Method | System.Type GetType() |
| IsAccountSid | Method | System.Boolean IsAccountSid() |
| IsEqualDomainSid | Method | System.Boolean IsEqualDomainSid(SecurityIdentifier sid) |
| IsValidTargetType | Method | System.Boolean IsValidTargetType(Type targetType) |
| IsWellKnown | Method | System.Boolean IsWellKnown(WellKnownSidType type) |
| ToString | Method | System.String ToString() |
| Translate | Method | System.Security.Principal.IdentityReference Translate(Type targetType) |
| AccountDomainSid | Property | System.Security.Principal.SecurityIdentifier AccountDomainSid {get;} |
| BinaryLength | Property | System.Int32 BinaryLength {get;} |
| Value | Property | System.String Value {get;} |

To translate the SID from a number to a Windows group name, you must specify that you want to translate to the type of *NTAccount* by first creating an instance of an *NTAccount* type. To do this, you use a string that represents the *System.Security.Principal.NTAccount* class and then use the *–as* operator to specify the string as a [type], as shown here:

```
$nt = "System.Security.Principal.NTAccount" -as [type]
```

After you create the *NTAccount* type, you can use it with the *Translate* method as shown here:

```
PS C:\>  $user = [System.Security.Principal.WindowsIdentity]::GetCurrent()
PS C:\> $nt = "System.Security.Principal.NTAccount" -as [type]
PS C:\>  $user.Groups[0].translate($nt)
Value
-----
NWTRADERS\Domain Users
```

This might seem like a bit of work to find out that the currently logged-on user is a member of the Domain Users group. (You would have known that anyway.) But based on the fact that a collection is returned by the *Groups* property, a looping type of cmdlet can be used to provide access to one group at a time. In this example, the ForEach-Object cmdlet is used as shown here:

```
PS C:\>  $user = [System.Security.Principal.WindowsIdentity]::GetCurrent()
PS C:\> $nt = "System.Security.Principal.NTAccount" -as [type]
PS C:\> $user.Groups | ForEach-Object { $_.translate($NT) }
Value
-----
NWTRADERS\Domain Users
Everyone
BUILTIN\Users
```

```
NT AUTHORITY\INTERACTIVE
NT AUTHORITY\Authenticated Users
NT AUTHORITY\This Organization
LOCAL
NWTRADERS\moreBogus
NWTRADERS\bogus
```

When you see that you can obtain the actual names of the groups, there are several ways to search the strings for a group match, such as using the *–contains*, *–like*, or *–match* operators.

## Tradeoff *–Contains*, *–Like*, or *–Match*

When searching a string, you can use at least three different operators: *–contains*, *–like*, and *–match*. The most confusing of the bunch is the *–contains* operator. This is not due to its complexity of use but rather to an attempt at understanding when to use the operator. Perhaps a few examples will help. In the following code, an array of numbers is created and stored in the *$a* variable. Next, the *–contains* operator is used to see whether the array that is stored in the *$a* variable contains the number 1. It does, and *true* is reported. The *–contains* operator is then used to see whether the *$a* array contains the number 6. It does not, and *false* is reported, as shown here:

```
PS C:\> $a = 1,2,3,4,5
PS C:\> $a -contains 1
True
PS C:\> $a -contains 6
False
```

In the next example, the number 12345 is stored in the *$b* variable. The *–contains* method is used to see whether the number stored in *$b* contains the number 4. While the number 4 is indeed present in the number 12345, *–contains* reports back *false*. The number stored in *$b* does not contain 4. Next, the *–contains* method is used to see whether *$b* contains 12345, which it does, and *true* is reported back, as shown here:

```
PS C:\> $b = 12345
PS C:\> $b -contains 4
False
PS C:\> $b -contains 12345
True
```

Suppose the variable *$c* stores the following string: "This is a string". When the *–contains* method is used to look for the string "is", *false* is returned. If the *–contains* method is used to look for the string "This is a string", it returns *true*, as shown here:

```
PS C:\> $c = "This is a string"
PS C:\> $c -contains "is"
False
PS C:\> $c -contains "This is a string"
True
```

For our last example of the *–contains* operator, if *$d* contains an array of strings ("This","is","a","string") when the *–contains* operator is used to look for the value of "is", *true* is returned. When the *–contains* operator looks for "ring", it returns *false,* as shown here:

```
PS C:\> $d = "This","is","a","string"
PS C:\> $d -contains "is"
True
PS C:\> $d -contains "ring"
False
```

The *–contains* operator is used to examine the elements of an array. If the array contains a particular value, the operator returns *true*. If there is not an exact match for the value, the *–contains* operator returns *false*. This process can be an easy way to locate items in an array.

The *–like* operator is used to perform a wildcard search of a string. If the *$a* variable is used to hold the string "This is a string" and the *–like* operator searches for "*ring*", the *–like* operator returns *true,* as shown here:

```
PS C:\> $a = "This is a string"
PS C:\> $a -like "*ring*"
True
```

An interesting use of the *–like* operator is to search the elements of an array. If the *$b* variable is used to hold the array "This","is","a","string" and the *–like* operator searches the array for "*ring*", every match for the wildcard pattern is returned—not just a true/false answer, as shown here:

```
PS C:\> $b = "This","is","a","string"
PS C:\> $b -like "*ring*"
string
```

The *–match* operator is used to perform a regular expression pattern match. When the match is found, *true* is returned. If a match is not found, *false* is returned. If the *$a* variable is assigned the value "This is a string" and the

−*match* operator is used to look for the value of "is", the pattern is a match and *true* is returned, as shown here:

```
PS C:\> $a = "This is a string"
PS C:\> $a -match "is"
True
```

More complex match patterns can be used. The \w character is used with regular expressions to look for any white space, such as a space before or after a letter. When the *$a* variable is used to hold the string "This is a string" and the regular expression pattern [\w a \w] is used, a match will be returned if the letter *a* is found with a space in front and a space behind the letter, as shown here:

```
PS C:\> $a = "This is a string"
PS C:\> $a -match "[\w a \w]"
True
```

What about matching with an array? If the *$c* variable is used to hold the array "This","is","a","string" and the regular expression pattern match, "is", is used, two matches are found. In this example, the actual string that contains the pattern match is returned as shown here. When a match is found, an array of strings is returned, as also shown here:

```
PS C:\> $c = "This","is","a","string"
PS C:\> $c -match "is"
This
is
```

The *Get-MemberOf* function uses the *GetCurrent* static method from the *System.Security .Principal.WindowsIdentity* class to create a *WindowsIdentity* object. After creating an *NTAccount* type, it uses the *Groups* property to obtain a collection of security groups, whereupon it uses the ForEach-Object cmdlet to translate the group from a SID to an *NTAccount* as the groups come across the pipeline. If the group name matches the group that is used when the function is called, it displays a message stating that the user is a member of the group. The Get-MemberOf.ps1 script is shown here.

```
Get-MemberOf.ps1

Function Get-MemberOf
{
 Param ($group)
 $user = [System.Security.Principal.WindowsIdentity]::GetCurrent()
 $nt = "System.Security.Principal.NTAccount" -as [type]
 If( $user.Groups.translate($NT) -match "$group" )
```

```
  { "$($user.name) is a member of a $group group" }
ELSE
  { "$($user.name) is not a member of a $group group" }
}
```

An example of using the *Get-MemberOf* function from the Get-MemberOf.ps1 script is the UseGetMemberOf.ps1 script. This script checks to determine whether the logged-on user has rights to a folder named bogus. The security permission on the bogus folder is shown in Figure 4-7. The bogus group has full control, and no one else has permission.

**FIGURE 4-7** Only the bogus group has permission to access the bogus folder.

The bogus group has one direct member—MyDomainAdmin. It also has two groups that are members: the morebogus group and the useless group. These group memberships are shown in Figure 4-8.

The logged-on user is Bob. As shown in Figure 4-8, Bob does not have direct membership in the bogus group. Bob is a member of the morebogus group, as shown in Figure 4-9.

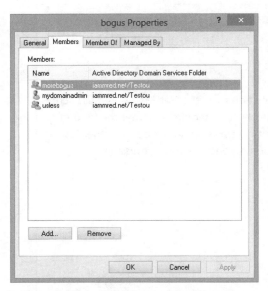

**FIGURE 4-8** The bogus group contains other groups.

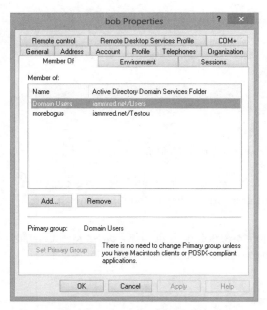

**FIGURE 4-9** Bob is a member of the morebogus group and Domain Users.

In the UseGetMemberOf.ps1 script, first an instance of the *GetCurrent* static method from the *System.Security.Principal.WindowsIdentity* class is created. You will need to store the *WindowsIdentity* object that is returned in a variable.

You next need to create an instance of an *NTAccount* type by using the *–as* operator to cast the string "System.Security.Principal.NTAccount" as a [type]. You will use this type later.

The essential portion of the script uses an *If* statement to evaluate whether the name of the user group is found within the collection of groups. The *Groups* property returns a collection of groups that is contained within the *$users* object. Using Windows PowerShell automatic collection expansion, it is possible to evaluate each group from the collection without using the ForEach-Object cmdlet. Using the *Translate* method that accepts the *NTAccount* type created earlier and assigned to the *$NT* variable, you now have a translated group name and can use the *–match* operator to determine whether the group that is stored in the *$group* variable matches what is in the collection of objects. You can treat this value as if it were a Boolean value by using the *If* statement as shown here:

```
If( $user.Groups.translate($NT) -match "$group" )
```

When a match with the group is found, you need to determine whether the file actually exists by using the Test-Path cmdlet, which receives the path stored in the *$bogusFile* variable. The Test-Path cmdlet returns a Boolean value. Here is the code to check for the existence of the file:

```
If(Test-Path -Path $bogusFile)
```

If the file exists, the script enters the code block, which adds text to the file. To write to the file, you can use the Add-Content cmdlet, which receives the path to the file and the data you want to add. At the end of the line, two special characters are used: backtick r and backtick n. The `r is a return, and the `n is a new line. Together they form a carriage return and line feed that is equivalent to the VBScript vbcrlf keyword. The special characters are shown in Table 4-4.

**TABLE 4-4** Special characters

| Character | Definition |
| --- | --- |
| `0 (number zero) | Null |
| `a | Alert |
| `b | Backspace |
| `f | Form feed |
| `n | New line |
| `r | Carriage return |
| `t | Horizontal tab |
| `v | Vertical tab |
| `r`n | Carriage return line feed |

When the additional text is added to the text file, a message is displayed on the screen and the file is opened in Notepad as shown here:

```
{
 Add-Content -Path $bogusFile -Value "Added bogus content'r'n"
 "Added content to $bogusFile"
 Notepad $bogusFile
} #end if Test-Path
```

If the file does not exist, a message is printed to the screen, as shown here:

```
ELSE
    {
        "Unable to find $bogusFile"
    } #end else
  } #end if user
```

If the user does not belong to a group with rights to the file, the user's name is displayed on the screen with a message regarding the lack of group membership, as shown here:

```
ELSE
   {
    "$($user.name) is not a member of $group"
   }
} #end GetMemberOf
```

The completed UseGetMemberOf.ps1 script is shown here.

```
UseGetMemberOf.ps1

Function Get-MemberOf
{
 Param ([string]$group,
        [string]$path)
 $user = [System.Security.Principal.WindowsIdentity]::GetCurrent()
 $nt = "System.Security.Principal.NTAccount" -as [type]
 If( $user.Groups.translate($NT) -match "$group" )
   { if(Test-Path -Path $path)
       {
           Add-Content -Path $path -Value "Added bogus content'r'n"
           "Added content to $path"
           Notepad $path
       } #end if Test-Path
     ELSE
       { "Unable to find $path"} }
 ELSE
 { "$($user.name) is not a member of a $group group" }
} # end function Get-MemberOf
```

To call the *Get-MemberOf* function, first the function loads into memory. This can be as simple as running the UseGetMemberOf.ps1 script from within the Windows PowerShell

ISE. The following illustrates calling the function to test for membership in a group prior to attempting access to the file:

```
PS C:\> Get-Memberof -group bogus -path 'C:\bogus\bogusfile.txt'
IAMMRED\ed is not a member of a bogus group
```

## Changing the way you write scripts

**Jeffrey Snover, Distinguished Engineer**
*Microsoft Corporation*

Version 2 has changed the way I write functions and scripts. Now, I always write functions that incorporate the version 2 cmdlet features. Before Windows PowerShell 2.0, functions were pale substitutes for cmdlets, but now they are full peers. That's right—you can now write full cmdlets in Windows PowerShell itself. That capability is a game changer. The tiny bit of extra syntax provides an incredible amount of functionality. This is the basis for what we call meta-programming, which is going to change the world. You can mark my words on that.

We can do meta-programming with the `Import-PSSession` cmdlets, in which we inspect the cmdlets on a remote machine and emit local proxies for those functions on the local machine, which makes it appear as if the cmdlets are installed on the local machine. You have tab completion, help, formatting—the whole works. Yet, what happens behind the scenes is that we emit a function with cmdlet semantics that uses the remote machine to do the work. This is very powerful indeed. When people begin to use the `Import-PSSession` cmdlet, it will be like the *2001 Space Odyssey* movie in which the large black monolith appeared, the apes figured out how to use tools, and the evolution toward mankind was initiated.

Even with all of the new command-line features in Windows PowerShell 2.0, I still write scripts. In fact, I am writing more scripts now than during my Windows PowerShell 1.0 days. Why? First and perhaps foremost—joy. It is simply a joy to write a Windows PowerShell script. It's like driving a BMW. This incredible machine goes exactly where you point it and makes you feel powerful and competent. With Windows PowerShell 2.0, you can achieve so much so easily that I tend to write a script, step back to look it, and say, "Wow! That is cool!" Let me be quick to say that I have the same experience when looking at other people's scripts. Lee Holmes, a Senior Software Development Engineer at Microsoft, just sent me a 103-line script that makes me just dizzy with excitement. I simply can't believe what he can do by using 103 lines of code. At the end of the day, it comes down to being effective at your job. Windows PowerShell makes it easy for you to be effective at your job.

# Detecting the user role

It is possible that the Windows PowerShell console that is running does not have Administrator rights. If this is the case, even if the user is in the Administrators role for the computer, the script will fail due to insufficient rights. One way to handle this situation is to launch either the Windows PowerShell console or the Windows PowerShell ISE as an administrator. The way to do this is to right-click the shortcut to the Windows PowerShell console. This produces a task list that offers options to run as an administrator, as shown in Figure 4-10.

**FIGURE 4-10** Right-click the Windows PowerShell console shortcut to bring up a task list to run as an administrator.

You could place the *Test-IsAdmin* function that is contained in the Test-IsAdminFunction .ps1 script into your profile or into any script that requires administrative rights. The Test-IsAdminFunction.ps1 script begins by declaring the *Test-IsAdmin* function, which accepts a single value—a variable named *$isAdmin*. This variable is passed by reference, which means that you will change the value of the *$isAdmin* variable from within the function itself. You can specify that a variable is passed by reference by using the [ref] type constraint on the variable. This type constraint is required in the function declaration line of the code, as well as when you call the function from the main body of the script. The *$isAdmin* variable itself is null when it is passed to the function because it is set to null when it is declared in the main body of the script. The function declaration is shown here:

```
Function Test-IsAdmin(
```

The next action in the *Test-IsAdmin* function is to use the static *GetCurrent* method from the *Security.Principal.WindowsIdentity* .NET Framework class to retrieve an instance of the *WindowsIdentity* class that represents the current user. The returned *WindowsIdentity* object is stored in the *$currentUser* variable, as shown here:

```
$currentUser = [Security.Principal.WindowsIdentity]::getCurrent()
```

Next, the *Test-IsAdmin* function creates an instance of a *WindowsPrincipal* class that represents the current user by passing the *WindowsIdentity* object, which is stored in the *$identity* variable as the constructor to the *Security.Principal.WindowsPrincipal* class. Because a new object is required, the function uses the New-Object cmdlet. The resulting *WindowsPrincipal* object is stored in the *$principal* variable as shown here:

```
$principal = new-object security.Principal.windowsPrincipal $identity
```

Now the static property administrator is used from the *Security.Principal .WindowsBuiltInRole* enumeration. The administrator role enumeration is shown here:

```
[security.principal.WindowsBuiltInRole]::administrator
```

To use the *IsInRole* method from the *WindowsPrincipal* class, you need to give it a *WindowsBuiltInRole* enumeration, which was created in the previous line of code. The result of the *IsInRole* method is a Boolean value, *true* or *false*, which returns directly from the function.

The completed Test-IsAdminFunction.ps1 script is shown here.

```
Test-IsAdmin.ps1

Function Test-IsAdmin
{
 <#
    .Synopsis
        Tests if the user is an administrator
    .Description
        Returns true if a user is an administrator, false if the user is not an
administrator
    .Example
        Test-IsAdministrator
    #>
 $identity = [Security.Principal.WindowsIdentity]::GetCurrent()
 $principal = New-Object Security.Principal.WindowsPrincipal $identity
 $principal.IsInRole([Security.Principal.WindowsBuiltinRole]::Administrator)
}
```

To use the *Test-IsAdmin* function, I call it in an evaluation after it loads into memory. A common way to do this is to use the *If* statement to evaluate the Boolean value returned from the function. This technique is shown here:

```
PS C:\> if (Test-IsAdmin) {"Console has admin rights"}
Console has admin rights
```

The *Security.Principal.WindowsBuiltInRole* .NET Framework enumeration has the following possible values:

- Administrator
- User
- Guest
- PowerUser

- AccountOperator
- SystemOperator
- PrintOperator
- BackupOperator
- Replicator

These enumeration values are documented in reference information contained on the MSDN website. A link to MSDN is included in the "Additional resources" section later in this chapter. However, you do not need to search the documentation if all you want to do is find the enumeration values. You can use Windows PowerShell to provide this information by using the static *GetNames* method from the *System.Enum* .NET Framework class. You place the *Security.Principal.WindowsBuiltInRole* enumeration class name in quotation marks to the method and press Enter to retrieve the names of all of the enumerations contained in the class, as shown here:

```
PS C:\> [enum]::getnames("security.principal.WindowsBuiltInRole")
Administrator
User
Guest
PowerUser
AccountOperator
SystemOperator
PrintOperator
BackupOperator
Replicator
```

The *Enum* class also has the *GetValues* static method, which lists the values of the enumerations instead of the names of the enumerations. This would be a bit boring in this particular case because both the value and the name of the *WindowsBuiltInRole* enumerations are the same things. To find all of the static methods of the *Enum* class, you can use the following line of code (although the only thing I do with the *Enum* class 95 percent of the time is to use it to obtain the names of a particular .NET Framework enumeration):

```
[enum] | Get-Member -Static -MemberType method
```

Because there are no static properties defined in the *Enum* class, you can get away with omitting the *–MemberType* parameter and use the following line of code:

```
[enum] | Get-Member -Static
```

If you do not want to do that much typing, you can use the following from the console:

```
[enum] | gm -s
```

The GetAdminFunction.ps1 script can easily be modified to provide information based on the other roles available in the *Security.Principal.WindowsBuiltInRole* class. The main objective is to replace the hard-coded administrator role name with a variable, as shown here:

```
[security.principal.WindowsBuiltInRole]::$roleName
```

The remaining changes to the script consist of renaming variables and changing the output text slightly. The modified Test-IsInRole.ps1 script is shown here.

```
Test-IsInRole.ps1

Function Test-Isinrole
{
<#
    .Synopsis
        Tests if the user is in a specific role
    .Description
        Returns true if a user is the role, false if the user is not in the role
    .Example
        Test-Isinrole -role Guest
    #>
    Param($roleName)
$identity = [Security.Principal.WindowsIdentity]::GetCurrent()
$principal = New-Object Security.Principal.WindowsPrincipal $identity
$principal.IsInRole([Security.Principal.WindowsBuiltinRole]::$roleName)
}
```

To call the *Test-IsinRole* function after loading it, add a bit of evaluation code around the call and pass one of the permissible enumeration values. This technique is shown here:

```
PS C:\> if (Test-Isinrole -roleName 'guest') {"Console is in role"} ELSE {"Console is
not in role"}
Console is not in role
```

## NOTES FROM THE FIELD

**Jonathan Tyler, IT Pro**

Having originally been a system administrator, I used Windows PowerShell a lot for diagnostics. Since I have moved into the development world, I still use Windows PowerShell for diagnostics; I just use it in a slightly different way.

Because Windows PowerShell is syntactically very close to C#, I like to use PowerShell to test code before I add the code to my C# project. By leveraging Windows PowerShell this way, I find that I can step through the code a line or two at a time to see how the process reacts without having to continually recompile code. This saves me some compiling and testing cycles that I might normally use. This method also allows me to reduce the number of try/catch blocks because I can generally plan ahead for what types of exceptions to look for. This is not foolproof, but it does help the development process.

There are also several scenarios where I use Windows PowerShell in preparing data for my C# projects. The automation that Windows PowerShell provides helps to quickly produce input files or other assets that I need for my C# project. One such way I could prepare a test data file is to quickly generate a CSV file with several hundred entries and create random data for each of the fields.

## .NET Framework version requirements

When working with Windows PowerShell, it's easy access to the .NET Framework while providing flexibility and ease of development also introduces an additional consideration—the version of the .NET Framework that is installed on the computer. There are several ways to detect the version.

To check the version of the .NET Framework system, you can use the static *GetSystemVersion* method from the *System.Runtime.InteropServices.RunTimeEnvironment* .NET Framework class as shown here:

```
[runtime.interopServices.RunTimeEnvironment]::GetSystemVersion()
```

However, when I call this method on my computer, it reports v4.0.30319, which is .NET Framework 4.5. The value returned occurs because of the way the Framework is installed—the service packs are considered to be extensions to the run time.

One way of finding a specific version of the .NET Framework is to check the registry. When the .NET Framework is installed, each version adds a key to the registry. Beginning with .NET Framework 4.5, I need to read the HKEY_LOCAL_MACHINE\SOFTWARE\Microsoft\NET Framework Setup\NDP\v4\Full\Release key value. To do this, I use the Get-ItemProperty cmdlet and the Registry provider, as shown here:

```
PS C:\> (Get-ItemProperty -Path 'HKLM:\SOFTWARE\Microsoft\NET Framework Setup\NDP\
v4\Full').Release
378675
```

The release number of .NET Framework 4.5 is 378389. The release number of .NET Framework 4.5.1 is 378675.

## Determining .NET Framework versions

Luís Canastreiro, Premier Field Engineer
*Microsoft Portugal*

When I write a script that depends on a feature from a particular version of the .NET Framework, such as version 3.5, I always like to include a test to ensure that the required version of the .NET Framework is installed. One basic test is to test the presence of the installation path: %SystemRoot%\Microsoft.NET\Framework\ v3.5. Because this folder does not exist if .NET Framework 3.5 has not been installed on the machine, this check helps me to ensure that the script will run properly.

Since the days of .NET Framework 2.0, a key has been created in the registry for each new version. I like to use this registry key because it can provide additional information, such as when the version was actually installed, the path, the version number, and whether the version has been service pack installed. Figure 4-11 shows the registry key from a machine with .NET Framework version 3.5. This installation has been service pack installed.

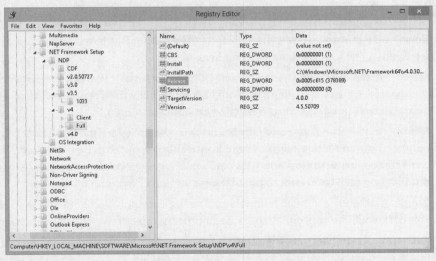

**FIGURE 4-11** The registry provides an easy way to verify .NET Framework version information.

What is a bit confusing is that there is a difference between the Common Language Runtime (CLR) and the .NET Framework. It is quite possible to have a computer with the CLR 2.0 SP2 and .NET Framework 3.5 with SP1. When you install .NET Framework 3.5 SP1, you are upgrading the CLR to version 2.0 SP2. You can consider the .NET

> Framework as a package that includes the CLR plus a set of richly managed libraries for implementing GUIs, using web services, accessing Windows operating system functionality, and so forth, as well as the managed language compilers and tools.

## Operating system requirements

There is a wide range of operating systems on which Windows PowerShell 4.0 can be installed, ranging from Windows 7 on up, and they can all be considered for certain scripts that might rely on the presence of a feature that exists only in particular versions of the operating system.

One way to obtain the operating system version is to use the *OSVersion* static property from the *System.Environment* .NET Framework class, as shown here:

```
PS C:\> [System.Environment]::OSVersion | Format-List


Platform      : Win32NT
ServicePack   :
Version       : 6.3.9478.0
VersionString : Microsoft Windows NT 6.3.9478.0
```

As shown in the preceding code, the version of the operating system is composed of a four-part number. The four parts are detailed here:

- **Major** Assemblies with the same name but different major versions are not interchangeable. For example, this part would be appropriate for a major rewrite of a product in which backward compatibility cannot be assumed.

- **Minor** If the name and major number on two assemblies are the same but the minor number is different, this indicates significant enhancement with the intention of backward compatibility. For example, this part would be appropriate on a point release of a product or a fully backward-compatible new version of a product.

- **Build** A difference in build number represents a recompilation of the same source. This part would be appropriate because of processor, platform, or compiler changes.

- **Revision** Assemblies with the same name, major, and minor version numbers but different revisions are intended to be fully interchangeable. This part would be appropriate to fix a security hole in a previously released assembly.

If you store the results of the *[environment]::OSVersion* static property into a variable, you have an instance of a *System.Version* object returned for the *version* property, as shown here:

```
PS C:\> [System.Environment]::OSVersion | Get-Member -MemberType Properties


   TypeName: System.OperatingSystem
```

```
Name              MemberType Definition
----              ---------- ----------
Platform          Property   System.PlatformID Platform {get;}
ServicePack       Property   string ServicePack {get;}
Version           Property   version Version {get;}
VersionString     Property   string VersionString {get;}
```

The advantage of this approach is that the *System.Version* class allows easy access to each of the different properties of the version number. The *System.Version* class is the object that returns from the *OSVersion.Version* property, as shown here:

```
PS C:\> [System.Environment]::OSVersion.Version | Get-Member -MemberType Properties


   TypeName: System.Version

Name             MemberType Definition
----             ---------- ----------
Build            Property   int Build {get;}
Major            Property   int Major {get;}
MajorRevision    Property   int16 MajorRevision {get;}
Minor            Property   int Minor {get;}
MinorRevision    Property   int16 MinorRevision {get;}
Revision         Property   int Revision {get;}
```

By using this approach, you have the ability to specify that you want the code to run only if it is on a particular version of the operating system. The GetOsVersionFunction.ps1 script illustrates this procedure. The Get-OsVersionFunction.ps1 script begins with the *Get-OsVersion* function. In the function declaration, the input variable is defined as a reference type, which allows the function to return the operating system version information back to the calling portion of the script. The function declaration specifies the name of the function and any input variables, as shown here:

```
Function Get-OsVersion([ref]$os)
```

The code block of the function retrieves the static *OSVersion* property from the *System .Environment* .NET Framework class and assigns it to the *Value* property of the *$os* variable as shown here:

```
$os.value = [environment]::OSVersion
```

Now, to use the *Get-OsVersion* function, you call the function by passing a reference type variable to it. The code here initializes the *$os* variable as null and then passes it to the function.

```
$os = $null
Get-OsVersion([ref]$os)
```

You can then use an *If ... Else* type of statement to evaluate the major version of the operating system. To assist you in evaluating version numbers, you can refer to Table 4-5. You might find it surprising that both Windows Vista and Microsoft Windows Server 2008 have the same version numbers. If you find a match, you can then proceed to the next portion of the script; otherwise, you can exit the script as illustrated here:

```
if($os.version.major -ge 6)
 {
  "Windows Vista or greater detected"
 }
else
{
 "Windows Vista or greater not detected"
 exit
}
```

**TABLE 4-5** Operating system names and versions

| Version Number | Operating System Name |
|---|---|
| 5.1.2600 | Windows XP |
| 5.2.3790 | Windows Server 2003 |
| 6.0.6001 | Windows Vista |
| 6.0.6001 | Windows Server 2008 |
| 6.1.6801 | Windows 7 |
| 6.1.6801 | Windows Server 2008 R2 |
| 6.2.9200 | Windows 8 |
| 6.2.9200 | Windows Server 2012 |
| 6.3.9600 | Windows 8.1 |
| 6.3.9600 | Windows Server 2012 R2 |

The complete Get-OsVersionFunction.ps1 script is shown here.

```
Get-OsVersion.ps1

Function Get-OsVersion
{
 [System.Environment]::OSVersion.Version
}

# *** entry point to script ***

$os = Get-OsVersion
if($os.major -ge 6 -and $os.Minor -ge 2)
 { "Windows 8 or greater detected" }
else
{ "Windows 8 or greater not detected" }
```

The *System.Environment* .NET Framework class does not have any remote features built into it. That is, you cannot give it a string and have it connect to a remote computer to retrieve information. This is not an issue with Windows PowerShell 2.0. You can use the Invoke-Command cmdlet to run the command remotely, as illustrated here:

```
PS C:\> $computers = "berlin","win7"
PS C:\> Invoke-Command -ComputerName $computers -ScriptBlock {[environment]::OSVersion }

PSComputerName      : berlin
RunspaceId          : d23f85ed-3f2b-465b-877a-37dd43125f40
PSShowComputerName  : True
Platform            : Win32NT
ServicePack         : Service Pack 1
Version             : 6.0.6001.65536
VersionString       : Microsoft Windows NT 6.0.6001 Service Pack 1

PSComputerName      : win7
RunspaceId          : 04b1ce80-19e9-4dde-9b8d-8725b032dfff
PSShowComputerName  : True
Platform            : Win32NT
ServicePack         :
Version             : 6.1.6801.0
VersionString       : Microsoft Windows NT 6.1.6801.0
```

**INSIDE TRACK**

## Why write PowerShell scripts?

**Jeffrey Snover, Distinguished Engineer**
*Microsoft Corporation*

I think the scripting community is going to flood the world with script cmdlets because they are incredibly easy to write, share, and debug. You can post them on a blog and improve the world. Not only will people observe your functions, but they will see how you executed the function; some might even give you feedback on your script and teach you something in the process. I have certainly benefited from reading other people's scripts, and numerous people have taught me lessons in response to the scripts I've posted.

I love GUIs, but if you use a GUI all day long, you have sore arms by the end of the day. However, if you write a script, you have an artifact that you can use again and again to increase your productivity and value to your employer (and thus increase your employability and earning potential). You have an artifact that you can share with others and, in sharing, create a debt of gratitude. You have an artifact that people can review and admire and learn from using. You have an artifact that can be analyzed and critiqued and improved. When you script, you participate in a community of people who are learning with each additional script they use.

In Windows PowerShell 1.0, it is difficult to write a script because the functions do not allow you to generate the correct semantics, you cannot provide help for your functions, and it isn't easy to share scripts. With Windows PowerShell 2.0, we added extensions to functions and added modules to solve this scripting problem and make participation in the scripting community simple and easy.

I use both the command-line and the graphical versions of Windows PowerShell, but I no longer use Notepad for writing scripts. The Windows PowerShell ISE is tremendous for creating and debugging scripts.

What do I do with Windows PowerShell? I explore! What I love about Windows PowerShell is its ability to let you explore so many aspects of the system. Windows PowerShell makes it easy and safe to check such things as WMI, .NET, the registry, COM, a file—whatever. If I come across something useful, I write a script and often share it.

If you are just beginning to use Windows PowerShell, I want to tell you this: learn to learn. One of my favorite stories involves a group of novice and expert UNIX administrators who were given a written test, and the experts didn't score much higher than the novices. However, when the groups were put in front of a machine and given a hands-on examination, the experts won easily. What we learned was that even though expert administrators might not necessarily remember more than novices, they are certainly experts at figuring out problems. Focus on learning. Learn how to use the Get-Help and Get-Member cmdlets. Learn how to use the object utilities. Then, start exploring. You'll be amazed at what you can accomplish by combining the basics, which is the point of a compositional system.

There isn't a command named Do My Job. Instead, in Windows PowerShell, there is a toolkit that allows you to combine a few commands together to do your job. You need to learn how to put the pieces together and what the pieces are. Part of the process involves leveraging the community of people who are more than willing to help you with your problems if they can.

## Application requirements

After you ensure that the script has the appropriate security rights and the correct version of the .NET Framework installed on the appropriate version of the operating system, you might still need to determine whether a particular application is running on your target machine. To check for an application, you can use either the Get-Process or Get-Service cmdlet—whichever one is appropriate.

The GetRunningService.ps1 script can be used to determine whether a particular service has been created on a computer and whether the service is running. To check for a service, the script uses an *If ... Else* construction. Inside the *If* statement, the `Get-Service` cmdlet is used to obtain a list of all services that are defined on the current computer. The *–computername* parameter of the `Get-Service` cmdlet can be used to cause the cmdlet to retrieve information from a remote computer. Results from the `Get-Service` cmdlet are pipelined to the `Where-Object` cmdlet, which is used to filter the results. Two criteria are used inside the `Where-Object` cmdlet: the status of the service, which must be running, and the actual name of the service itself. This section of the code is shown here:

```
Get-Service |
Where-Object { $_.status -eq 'running' -AND $_.name -eq $serviceName }
```

If this condition is satisfied, the script enters the code block associated with the *If* statement. In this example, the script prints the fact that the service is running. If the service does not exist or is not running, the script prints a message that the service is not running. Inside these two code blocks is where you place your code that depends on a particular state of a given service. The completed GetRunningService.ps1 script is shown here.

```
GetRunningService.ps1

$serviceName = "ZuneBusEnum"
if(
   Get-Service |
   Where-Object { $_.status -eq 'running' -AND $_.name -eq $serviceName }
  )
 {
  "$serviceName is running"
 } #end if
ELSE
 {
  "$serviceName is not running"
 } #end else
```

At other times, a particular process and not a service must be running. To verify the existence of a process, you can use the `Get-Process` cmdlet. The logic can be simplified because a process exists only if it is running; a compound WHERE clause is not required. The simplified logic is shown here:

```
Get-Process | Where-Object ProcessName -eq $processName
```

The remainder of the GetRunningProcess.ps1 script shown here is similar to the GetRunningService.ps1 script.

```
GetRunningProcess.ps1

$processName = "iexplore"
if(
   Get-Process | Where ProcessName -eq $processName
  )
```

```
{
  "$processName is running"
} #end if
ELSE
{
  "$processName is not running"
} #end else
```

# Module requirements

The extensible nature of Windows PowerShell is one of its greatest features. You can down-load modules from the Internet that come equipped with dozens of free cmdlets. You can also purchase commercial software that solves very real mission-critical problems from major software companies. Both solutions have one thing in common: The cmdlets are delivered housed within modules. There are two requirements: The module must be installed, and it must be loaded. Of course, the loading of the module is a non-issue because Windows PowerShell automatically loads modules that are contained in the *$env:PSModulePath* loca-tion. If a module is stored in a location not within *$env:PSModulePath,* you must also take care of loading the module.

To ensure that a Windows PowerShell module is available, prior to attempting to use cmd-lets from the module, use the *#Requires* directive. The *#Requires* directive must be the first item on a line in a script. It is possible to use multiple *#Requires* directives to ensure that sev-eral requirements are met. To do this, each *#Requires* directive must appear on an individual line. RequiresModule.ps1 illustrates this technique.

```
RequiresModule.ps1

#requires -modules activedirectory
#requires -version 4

Get-aduser -filter *
```

I had been a SharePoint admin for a long time before SharePoint 2010 came around and forced me to learn Windows PowerShell. I had been administrating a large SharePoint 2003 and then a SharePoint 2007 farm and had become pretty handy with SharePoint's command-line utility, stsadm.exe. I didn't need any fancy Windows PowerShell to get my job done. But I saw the writing on the wall, and I begrudgingly, reluctantly, started learning Windows PowerShell. We've all been hit by Windows PowerShell's steep learning curve, and I was no exception.

I struggled in the beginning, but then when I wasn't looking I started figuring it out. I didn't wake up one morning and shout, "I've conquered Windows PowerShell; next, the world!!" but I did notice that I wasn't beating my head against my desk quite as often. Writing a single working line of Windows PowerShell didn't take an hour anymore. Windows PowerShell was training me to do things its way. I was a slower learner, but I was learning.

Now Windows PowerShell and I are BFFs. I always have at least one Windows PowerShell console open, and I find myself seeking out things to do in PowerShell. I initially used Windows PowerShell in SharePoint only because I had to. Now it's happily my go-to tool in all aspects of Windows and other Microsoft software. And I almost never bang my head on my desk anymore. Almost never.

## Additional resources

- The TechNet Script Center at *http://www.microsoft.com/technet/scriptcenter* contains numerous script examples.
- A history of the .NET Framework versions can be found at *http://blogs.msdn.com /dougste/archive/2007/09/06/version-history-of-the-clr-2-0.aspx*.
- You can find help at *http://msdn.microsoft.com/en-us/library/hh925568.aspx* for how to determine which version of the .NET Framework is installed.
- The entry point to the MSDN website is found at *http://msdn.microsoft.com*.
- All scripts from this chapter are available via the TechNet Script Center Script Repository at *http://gallery.technet.microsoft.com/scriptcenter/PowerShell-40 -Best-d9e16039*.

# CHAPTER 5

# Configuring the script environment

- Configuring a profile
- Creating a profile
- Accessing functions in other scripts
- Additional resources

Windows PowerShell 4.0 provides many ways in which the scripting environment can be customized or tailored to individual needs. This capability unlocks tremendous opportunities to change the way in which Windows PowerShell starts, the way it runs, and even the syntax of commonly used functions. However, this flexibility comes at a price: it's possible to customize the scripting environment to such an extent that you do not know what the commands are, how they are used, or even what you should type to find help. In this chapter, you will examine the ways in which leading experts customize their environment and also explore options to assist both power users and corporate IT personnel in obtaining the most functionality from this rich and powerful tool.

## Configuring a profile

By default, there are no profiles when you install Windows PowerShell. You use a profile to configure the Windows PowerShell scripting environment, but you also use it to make working from the PowerShell command line more convenient (or to extend the capability of the Windows PowerShell ISE). The Windows PowerShell profile is a useful place to create and store the following four types of items:

- Aliases
- Functions
- PSDrives
- Variables

# Creating aliases

Aliases are helpful from a usability standpoint. Consider a command, such as `Measure-Object`, that counts and provides statistical information, such as the minimum and maximum values of an object. `Measure-Object` can be a bit cumbersome to type from the command line. Given the relative frequency of its use, `Measure-Object` becomes a good candidate for aliasing.

Prior to creating a new alias, it is a best practice to determine whether there is a suitable alias already created for the cmdlet in question. By default, Windows PowerShell on Windows 8.1 ships with more than 190 predefined aliases for its 271 cmdlets and functions. When you consider that several cmdlets have more than one alias defined, you can see that there is great opportunity for the creation of additional aliases. The GetCmdletsWithMoreThanTwoAliases.ps1 script lists all of the cmdlets with more than one alias defined, as shown here

```
GetCmdletsWithMoreThanTwoAliases.ps1


Get-Alias |
Group-Object -Property definition |
Sort-Object -Property count -Descending |
Where-Object count -gt 2
```

When the GetCmdletsWithMoreThanTwoAliases.ps1script runs, the following appears:

```
Count Name                        Group
----- ----                        -----
    6 Remove-Item                 {del, erase, rd, ri...}
    3 Invoke-WebRequest           {curl, iwr, wget}
    3 Move-Item                   {mi, move, mv}
    3 Get-ChildItem               {dir, gci, ls}
    3 Get-Content                 {cat, gc, type}
    3 Set-Location                {cd, chdir, sl}
    3 Copy-Item                   {copy, cp, cpi}
    3 Get-History                 {ghy, h, history}
```

To see whether an alias for the `Measure-Object` cmdlet exists, you can use the `Get-Alias` cmdlet and the *–definition* parameter as shown here:

```
PS C:\> Get-Alias -Definition measure-object

CommandType     Name                                               ModuleName
-----------     ----                                               ----------
Alias           measure -> Measure-Object
```

If you like the alias *measure*, you can simply begin to use that alias. However, you might decide that the readability of the alias *measure* is hampered by the fact that it saves only two keystrokes. Due to the implementation of the tab expansion feature, all you need to do is type **measure-o** and press the Tab key. In general, when creating personal aliases, I prefer to sacrifice readability for ease of use. My favorite aliases are one- and two-letter aliases. I use one-letter aliases for commands that I frequently use. Remember that one-letter aliases are also the most obscure and they do not always make sense unless you happen to remember why you created the alias in the first place. I use two-letter aliases for most of my other alias needs. The two-letter combination can easily correspond to the verb-noun naming convention; therefore, *mo* is a logical alias for the Measure-Object cmdlet. To ensure the availability of *mo* for Measure-Object, use the Get-Alias cmdlet as shown here:

```
PS C:\> Get-Alias -Name mo
```

## How many two-letter aliases are there?

The two-letter alias namespace is rather large, but how large is it really? You must take every letter in the *a–z* range and pair them with every other letter in the *a–z* range to get the answer. If you are good with math, you already know that there are 676 possible letter combinations. However, if your math skills are a bit rusty, or just for fun, you can write a Windows PowerShell script to figure out the answer. The problem with this approach is that you cannot use the *range* operator (..) to produce a range of letters. The *range* operator works with numbers; 1..10 automatically creates a range of numbers with the values 1 through 10 and can save you a great deal of typing. However, because you have ASCII numeric representations of the letters *a–z*, you can use the *range* operator to create a range of the letters. The ASCII value 97 is the *a* character, and ASCII 122 is *z*. After you determine the numeric range, you can use the ForEach-Object cmdlet and convert each letter to a character by using the [char] type. You can store the resulting array of letters in the *$letters* variable. After doing two loops through the array, you can store the resulting letter combinations in the *$lettercombination* variable, which is constrained as an array by using the [array] type. The Measure-Object cmdlet is used to count the number of possible letter combinations. GetTwoLetterAliasCombinations.ps1 script is shown here.

GetTwoLetterAliasCombinations.ps1

```
$letterCombinations = $null
$asciiNum = 97..122
$letters = $asciiNum | ForEach-Object { [char]$_ }
Foreach ($1letter in $letters)
{
 Foreach ($2letter in $letters)
 {[array]$letterCombinations += "$1letter$2letter"} }
"There are " + ($letterCombinations | Measure-Object).count +
" possible combinations"
"They are listed here: "
$letterCombinations
```

To create a new alias, you can either use the `New-Alias` or `Set-Alias` cmdlet. You can also use the `New-Item` cmdlet and target the alias drive. The problem with the latter technique is that it does not support the *–description* parameter, which allows you to specify additional information about the alias. Another problem with using `New-Item` to create an alias is that more typing is involved. So, as a best practice, I always use either the `New-Alias` or `Set-Alias` cmdlet. In choosing between the two cmdlets, which one should you use when creating a new alias? Before answering that question, I will discuss what the cmdlets are intended to be used for. The `New-Alias` cmdlet obviously creates a new alias. The `Set-Alias` cmdlet is used to modify an existing alias; if an alias does not exist, it creates the alias for you. Therefore, many people use `Set-Alias` to both create and modify an alias. The danger in using the `Set-Alias` cmdlet is that you can inadvertently modify a previously existing alias with no notification. However, if this is your desired behavior, using the `Set-Alias` approach is fine.

A better approach is to use the `New-Alias` cmdlet when creating an alias. `New-Alias` allows you to specify the *–description* parameter and to receive notification if an alias that you are trying to create already exists. To assign a description to an alias when creating it, you can use the *–description* parameter as shown here:

```
New-Alias -Name mo -Value Measure-Object -Description "MrEd Alias"
```

In an enterprise-scripting environment, many companies like to define a corporate set of aliases, which provides for a consistent environment. A network administrator working on one machine can be assured that a particular alias is available. Corporate aliases also help to ensure a predictable and consistent environment. By using the same value for the *–description* parameter of the alias, it is easy to list all corporate aliases. To do this, you can filter the list of aliases by the *–description* parameter as shown here.

```
PS C:\> Get-Alias | where description -eq 'mred alias'
```

```
CommandType     Name                                               ModuleName
-----------     ----                                               ----------
Alias           mo -> Measure-Object
```

When using the *–eq* operator in the code block of the `Where-Object` cmdlet, the filter is case insensitive. If you need a case-sensitive operator, you can use *–ceq*. The "c" is added to all of the operators to form a case-sensitive form of the operator—by default, the operators are case insensitive. As shown here, when using the case-sensitive operator, the filter does not return any aliases.

```
PS C:\> Get-Alias | Where description -ceq 'MrEd Alias'
PS C:\>
```

In addition to specifying the *–description* parameter, many companies also like to use the *–option* parameter to make the alias either read-only or constant. To make the alias read-only, you supply the *read-only* keyword to the *–option* parameter as shown here:

```
New-Alias -Name mo -Value Measure-Object -Description "MrEd Alias" –Option
readonly
```

The advantage of making the alias read-only is that this offers protection against accidental modification or deletion, as shown in Figure 5-1.

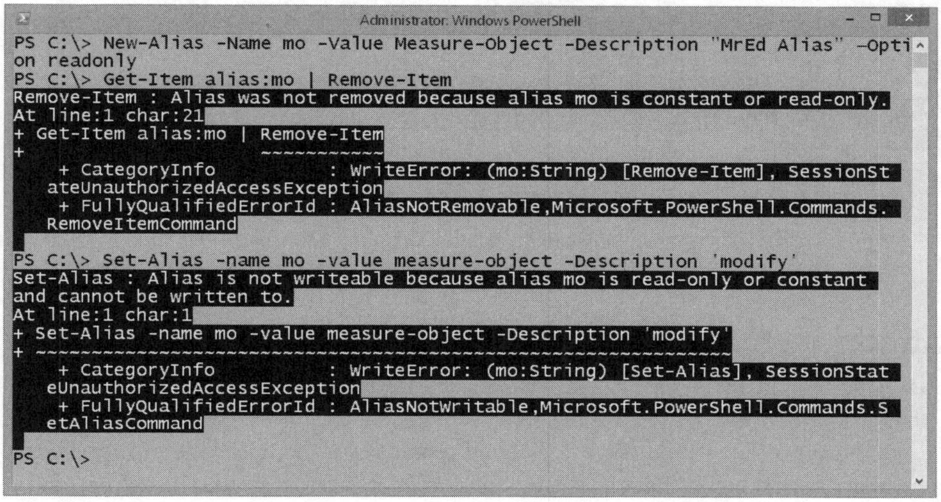

**FIGURE 5-1** Attempts to modify a read-only alias generate an error message.

An additional advantage to making the alias read-only is that the alias can be modified or
deleted if needed. If you want to modify the description, you can use the Set-Alias cmdlet to
specify the name, value the new description, and use the *–force* parameter as shown here:

```
Set-Alias -Name mo -value measure-object -Description "my alias" –Force
```

If you need to delete a read-only cmdlet, you can use the Remove-Item cmdlet and specify
the *–force* parameter as shown here:

```
Remove-Item Alias:\mo -Force
```

To create a constant alias, you can use the *constant* keyword with the *–option* parameter
as shown here:

```
New-Alias -Name mo -Value Measure-Object -Description "MrEd Alias" -Option constant
```

As a best practice, you should not create constant aliases unless you are certain that you
do not need to either modify it or delete it. A constant alias can neither be modified nor
deleted—in effect, they really are constant. The error message is a bit misleading in that it
states that the alias is either read-only or constant, and it suggests attempting to use the *–
force* parameter. The reason that this is misleading is because the error message is displayed
even when the command is run with the *–force* parameter. This error message is shown in
Figure 5-2.

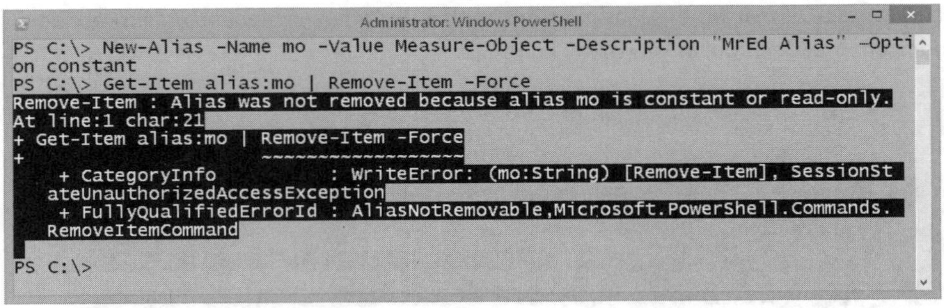

**FIGURE 5-2** An error message is generated when attempting to delete a constant alias.

## Creating functions

Functions provide a nearly endless capability of customization from within Windows PowerShell. The profile is a great place to supply some of this customization. For example, when using the Get-Help cmdlet, suppose that you prefer to see the full article. However, you also know that, in most cases, the article is too long to fit on a single screen. Therefore, you like to pipeline the output to the *more* function, which provides paging control. For example, if you are looking for information about the Get-Process cmdlet, the command is shown here:

```
Get-Help Get-Process -Full | more
```

There is nothing wrong with typing the preceding command; however, even when paired with tab expansion, it is more than 20 keystrokes. It will not take long before you become tired of typing such a command. Therefore, this command is a perfect candidate for a function. When naming functions, it is a best practice to use the verb-noun naming convention because this syntax is familiar to users of Windows PowerShell and because you can take advantage of tab expansion. As shown here, I named our function *Get-MoreHelp*.

```
Get-MoreHelp.ps1

Function Get-MoreHelp()
{
 Get-Help $args[0] -Full |
 more
} #end Get-MoreHelp
```

The *Get-MoreHelp* function begins by using the *Function* keyword to declare the function. After the *Function* keyword, you specify the name of the function, which in this example is *Get-MoreHelp*. The empty parentheses are not required after the function name; parentheses are used to define parameters, and without any parameters, the parentheses are not required. I generally include parentheses as an indicator that a parameter could be specified in the position, as shown here:

```
Function Get-MoreHelp()
```

Following the *Function* keyword, the function opens the code block by using an opening curly bracket. When typing the function, I always open the code block with one curly bracket and, immediately, type the closing curly bracket on the next line. In this way, I never forget to close a code block. As a best practice, I always include a comment indicating that the bottom curly bracket closes the function. End comments are also a tremendous help when it's time to troubleshoot the script because they promote readability and make it easier to understand the delimiters of the function. In addition, if you have a long function that scrolls off of the screen, the end comment, with its repetition of the function name, makes it easier to create the alias for the function, as shown here:

```
{

} #end Get-MoreHelp
```

The *Get-MoreHelp* function uses the *$args* automatic variable to hold the argument that is passed to the function when it is called. Because the Get-Help cmdlet does not accept an array for the *name* parameter, you can use [0] to index into the first element of the *$args* array. If, as is required, there is only one item passed to the function, the item is always element 0 of the array. The function passes the *–full* switched parameter to the Get-Help cmdlet. The resulting help information is passed along the pipeline via the pipe | symbol, as shown here:

```
Get-Help $args[0] -full |
```

## Overriding existing commands

Because it is possible that the *Get-MoreHelp* function could return more than a single screen of textual information, the function pipelines the help information to the *more* function. Because functions are first-class citizens in Windows PowerShell, they have priority over executables and even over native PowerShell cmdlets. Due to this fact, it is easy to modify the behavior of an executable or cmdlet by creating a function with the same name as an existing executable, which is illustrated by the *more* function. More.com is an executable that provides the ability to return information to the screen one page at a time—it has been available since the DOS days. The *more* function is used to modify the behavior of more.com. The content of the *more* function is shown here:

```
param([string[]]$paths)
if($paths)
{
    foreach ($file in $paths)
    {
        Get-Content $file | more.com
    }
}
else
{
    $input | more.com
}
```

By looking at the content of the *more* function, you can see that there has been a useful addition to the functionality of more.com. If you supply a path to the *more* function, it retrieves the content of the file and pipelines the result to the more.com executable, as shown in Figure 5-3.

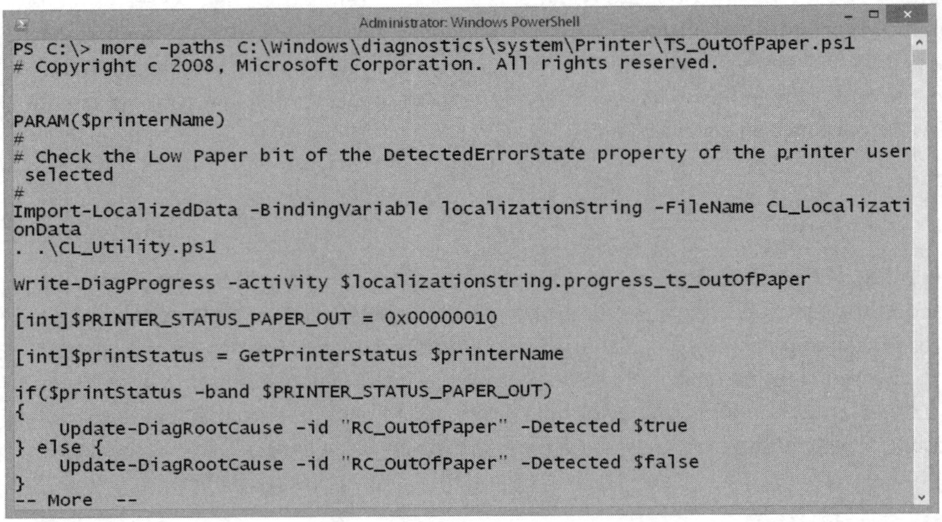

```
Administrator: Windows PowerShell
PS C:\> more -paths C:\Windows\diagnostics\system\Printer\TS_OutofPaper.ps1
# Copyright c 2008, Microsoft Corporation. All rights reserved.


PARAM($printerName)
#
# Check the Low Paper bit of the DetectedErrorState property of the printer user
 selected
#
Import-LocalizedData -BindingVariable localizationString -FileName CL_Localizati
onData
. .\CL_Utility.ps1

Write-DiagProgress -activity $localizationString.progress_ts_outofPaper

[int]$PRINTER_STATUS_PAPER_OUT = 0x00000010

[int]$printStatus = GetPrinterStatus $printerName

if($printStatus -band $PRINTER_STATUS_PAPER_OUT)
{
    Update-DiagRootCause -id "RC_OutofPaper" -Detected $true
} else {
    Update-DiagRootCause -id "RC_OutofPaper" -Detected $false
}
-- More  --
```

**FIGURE 5-3** Passing a path to the *more* function retrieves the content and pipes the results to more.com.

## Aliasing the function

When I create utility functions, I generally like to create an alias to enable quick and easy access to the function. It is possible to create the function and the alias in the same script, but not within the function definition. The problem arises in that, within the function definition, the function has not yet been created; therefore, you cannot create an alias for a function that does not yet exist. However, there is nothing wrong with creating the alias and the function in the same script, as shown here in the Get-MoreHelpWithAlias.ps1 script. Interestingly enough, you can create the alias on a line either before or after the function is declared. The position does not matter.

```
Get-MoreHelpWithAlias.ps1

Function Get-MoreHelp()
{
 Get-Help $args[0] -full |
 more
} #End Get-MoreHelp
New-Alias -name gmh -value Get-MoreHelp -Option allscope
```

## Looping the array

Because the *$args* variable returns an array, you can use *$args to* add the ability to pass two or more pieces of information and receive help for each topic. To do this, you can use the *for* statement to loop through the elements of *$args*. The *for* statement uses three parameters: the beginning, the destination, and the method of travel. In this example, the variable *$i* is used to keep track of the position within the array. The variable *$i* is set equal to 0, and the *−le* operator, less than or equal to, is used to allow the loop to continue for the number of times represented by the number of items in *$args*. As the loop progresses, the value of *$i* is incremented by 1 during each loop by using the *$i++* construction, as shown here:

```
For($i = 0 ;$i -le $args.count ; $i++)
```

One small change is required to the line of code that calls the Get-Help cmdlet. Instead of using *$args*[0], which always retrieves the first element in the array, you can change the 0 to *$i*. As the value of *$i* increases for each loop, the Get-Help cmdlet queries the next item in the array. This modified line of code is shown here:

```
Get-Help $args[$i] -full |
```

The remainder of the *Get-MoreHelp* function is the same as that found in the previous versions discussed earlier. The complete function is shown in the Get-MoreHelp2.ps1 script.

```
Get-MoreHelp2.ps1

Function Get-MoreHelp
{
 # .help Get-MoreHelp Get-Command Get-Process
 For($i = 0 ;$i -le $args.count ; $i++)
 {
  Get-Help $args[$i] -full |
  more
 } #end for
} #end Get-MoreHelp
New-Alias -name gmh -value Get-MoreHelp -Option allscope
```

To run the *Get-MoreHelp* function, you can use the *gmh* alias and supply it one or more cmdlet names to obtain help. This process is shown in Figure 5-4, in which the function code was typed directly into the Windows PowerShell console.

```
Regular PowerShell dude                                          - □ x

PS C:\> gmh Get-Command

NAME
    Get-Command

SYNOPSIS
    Gets all commands.

SYNTAX
    Get-Command [[-ArgumentList] <Object[]>] [-All] [-ListImported] [-Module
    <String[]>] [-Noun <String[]>] [-ParameterName <String[]>] [-ParameterType
    <PSTypeName[]>] [-Syntax] [-TotalCount <Int32>] [-Verb <String[]>]
    [<CommonParameters>]

    Get-Command [[-Name] <String[]>] [[-ArgumentList] <Object[]>] [-All]
    [-CommandType <CommandTypes>] [-ListImported] [-Module <String[]>]
    [-ParameterName <String[]>] [-ParameterType <PSTypeName[]>] [-Syntax]
    [-TotalCount <Int32>] [<CommonParameters>]

DESCRIPTION
    The Get-Command cmdlet gets all commands that are installed on the computer,
    including cmdlets, aliases, functions, workflows, filters, scripts, and
    applications. Get-Command gets the commands from Windows PowerShell modules and
    snap-ins and commands that were imported from other sessions. To get only
    commands that have been imported into the current session, use the ListImported
    parameter.

    Without parameters, a "Get-Command" command gets all of the cmdlets, functions,
    workflows and aliases installed on the computer. A "Get-Command *" command gets
    all types of commands, including all of the non-Windows-PowerShell files in the
    Path environment variable ($env:path), which it lists in the "Application"
    command type.
-- More  --
```

**FIGURE 5-4** You can use an alias for a function to facilitate ease of use.

# Passing multiple parameters

When using a function, it is quite common to want to accept two or more parameters for input, which adds flexibility and usefulness to the function. In Windows PowerShell, there are two choices. The first method of passing parameters is to use the *$args* automatic variable as shown in the preceding section. Another way to pass parameters is to use named parameters. When named parameters are used with a script, they are preceded by the *Param* statement. To use a named parameter within a function, you do not need to use the *Param* statement. You simply supply variables in each position in which you want a parameter. The name of the variable becomes the name of the parameter. There are a few tricks to keep in mind when using both methods of passing multiple parameters. To that end, let's first examine the *$args* variable in a bit more detail.

## Multiple parameters with *$args*

One way to pass two parameters is to use the *$args* automatic variable. When passing two values to the function, you can index into the array to retrieve a specific value. In the *Get-WmiClass* function, two values are passed when calling the function. The first value is used to hold the WMI namespace to search for WMI class names, and the second value is the type of

WMI class for which to search. The *Get-WmiClass* function is useful for locating WMI classes. Use of the *Get-WmiClass* function is shown in Figure 5-5.

**FIGURE 5-5** the *$args* variable can support positional arguments.

The *Get-WmiClass* function begins by retrieving two values from the *$args* variable. The *$args* variable is an automatic variable and is populated with whatever is fed to the function. The element from the first position is stored in the *$ns* variable, and the second element is kept in the *$class* variable, as shown here:

```
$ns = $args[0]
$class = $args[1]
```

The Get-WmiObject cmdlet has a *–list* switched parameter that produces a listing of all WMI classes in the namespace. The namespace used is the one specified in the first position of the command that is used to call the function. The resulting listing of all WMI classes in the particular namespace is shunted to the pipeline as shown here:

```
Get-WmiObject -List -Namespace $ns |
```

To make the list of WMI classes useful, the Where-Object cmdlet is used to filter out the unwanted WMI class names. Inside the code block for the Where-Object cmdlet, the automatic *$_* variable is used to refer to the current item on the pipeline. The *–match* operator allows you to use a regular expression to filter out the list of WMI class names. This line of code is shown here:

```
Where-Object { $_.name -match $class }
```

The complete Get-WmiClass.ps1 script is shown here.

```
Get-WmiClass.ps1

Function Get-WmiClass()
{
 #.Help Get-WmiClass "root\cimv2" "Processor"
 $ns = $args[0]
 $class = $args[1]
 Get-WmiObject -List -Namespace $ns |
 Where-Object { $_.name -match $class }
} #end Get-WmiClass
```

## Multiple named parameters

When you have more than two parameters to supply to a function, it might become confusing to keep track of both the position and the meaning of the parameter. In addition, when using named parameters, you can apply type constraints to prevent basic types of errors that can occur when supplying values from the command line.

In the Get-WmiClass2.ps1 script, the *Get-WmiClass* function is rewritten to take advantage of command-line arguments. The primary change involves moving the *$ns* and *$class* variables inside the parentheses following the name of the function. In addition, because both the namespace and the class names should be strings, you can use the [string] type constraint to prevent the inadvertent entry of an illegal value, such as an integer. Because the revised function is using named parameters, the two lines that parse the *$args* variable are also removed. The Get-WmiClass2.ps1 script file is therefore shorter than the Get-WmiClass.ps1 script, and it has more capability. The first line of the *Get-WmiClass* function is shown here:

```
Function Get-WmiClass([string]$ns, [string]$class)
```

An example of the value of the type constraints is shown in Figure 5-6.

In the first example, the *Get-WmiClass* function is called with the value of *5* for the *–ns* parameter, which violates the [string] type constraint for the *–ns* parameter. The resulting error is "Invalid parameter."

In the second example, shown in Figure 5-6, the *Get-WmiClass* function is called with the value of *root/cimv3* for the *–ns* parameter. Because there is no *root/cimv3* namespace in the WMI hierarchy (at least not yet), the function actually executes. The resulting error comes from WMI, which states the problem as an "invalid namespace." As a best practice, you should always apply type constraints to your function parameters. The rudimentary protection afforded by type constraints easily justifies the minimal effort required to type them in.

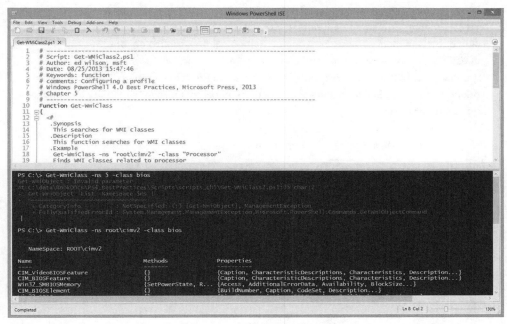

**FIGURE 5-6** Type constraints placed on function parameters cause detailed error messages to display when violated.

To call the *Get-WmiClass* function, you can use the entire parameter name, a shortened unique version of the parameter name, or no parameter at all. Examples demonstrating each way to call the function are shown here. When supplying a parameter, you need to type only enough of the parameter name to ensure that it is unique. As a best practice, you should take this feature into account when naming parameters. If each parameter begins with a unique letter, users of the function can supply single-letter parameter names and still maintain a rudimentary level of readability. For example, in the *Get-WmiClass* function, if you call the namespace *name space* and call the class name simply *name*, you will be required to type the entire word **name** for the *–name* parameter and to type **names** for the namespace. *–Name* and *–namespace* parameters do not shorten very well, as illustrated in the code shown here:

```
Get-WmiClass -ns "root\cimv2" -class "disk"
Get-WmiClass -n root\cimv2 -c disk
Get-WmiClass root\cimv2 disk
```

The complete Get-WmiClass2.ps1 script is shown here.

```
Get-WmiClass2.ps1

Function Get-WmiClass
{
  <#
   .Synopsis
   This searches for WMI classes
   .Description
   This function searches for WMI classes
   .Example
   Get-WmiClass -ns "root\cimv2" -class "Processor"
   Finds WMI classes related to processor
   .Parameter ns
   The namespace
   .Parameter class
   The class
   .Notes
   NAME:  Get-WmiClass
   AUTHOR: ed wilson, msft
   LASTEDIT: 08/25/2013 15:45:16
   KEYWORDS: WMI, Scripting Technique
   HSG:
   .Link
     Http://www.ScriptingGuys.com
 #Requires -Version 2.0
 #>
 Param ([string]$ns, [string]$class)
 Get-WmiObject -List -Namespace $ns |
 Where-Object { $_.name -match $class }
} #end Get-WmiClass
```

You can also create an alias for the function when you define the function. Because the alias was used for the *Get-WmiClass* function, you can use the Get-Alias cmdlet to check for the existence of the chosen alias letter combination of *gwc* (selecting the first letter of each main word in the function name). You can use the following command to see whether the *gwc* alias is available:

```
Get-Alias -Name gwc
```

This is one occasion when you hope to receive an error because it means that your chosen alias can be used. The error is shown in Figure 5-7.

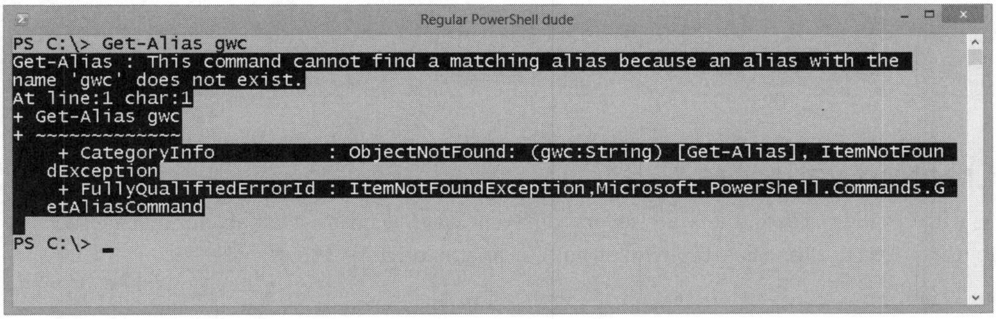

**FIGURE 5-7** An error message means that the queried alias is not in use.

The completed Get-WmiClass2WithAlias.ps1 script is shown here.

```
Get-WmiClass2WithAlias.ps1

Function Get-WmiClass
{
  <#
    .Synopsis
     This searches for WMI classes
    .Description
     This function searches for WMI classes
    .Example
     Get-WmiClass -ns "root\cimv2" -class "Processor"
     Finds WMI classes related to processor
    .Parameter ns
     The namespace
    .Parameter class
     The class
    .Notes
     NAME:  Get-WmiClass
     AUTHOR: ed wilson, msft
     LASTEDIT: 08/25/2013 15:45:16
     KEYWORDS: WMI, Scripting Technique
     HSG:
    .Link
      Http://www.ScriptingGuys.com
```

```
#Requires -Version 2.0
#>
Param ([string]$ns, [string]$class)
Get-WmiObject -List -Namespace $ns |
Where-Object { $_.name -match $class }
} #end Get-WmiClass


New-Alias -Name gwc -Value Get-WmiClass -Description "Mred Alias" '
-Option readonly,allscope
```

## Creating variables

As with creating aliases, there are several different ways to create a variable and assign a value to it. You can use the New-Item cmdlet on the variable drive, as shown here:

```
New-Item -Name temp -Value $env:TEMP -Path variable:
```

You can also use the Set-Item cmdlet to create a variable. The advantage to using Set-Item is that it does not generate an error if the variable already exists. The following example uses Set-Item to create a variable. Keep in mind that the Set-Item cmdlet does not have a *–name* parameter.

```
Set-Item -Value $env:TEMP -Path variable:\temp
```

Neither New-Item nor Set-Item has the ability to specify the *–option* or *–description* parameter. This is an important distinction with variables because you cannot create a constant or a read-only variable without using either Set-Variable or New-Variable. If a variable already exists and you use the Set-Variable cmdlet, the value of the variable is overwritten if it has not been marked read-only or constant. If the variable is marked read-only, you can still modify its value by specifying the *–force* parameter. If the variable is marked as constant, the only way to modify its value is to close the Windows PowerShell console and start over with a new value.

You can also create a variable and assign a value to it at the same time. This technique is often used when the value to be stored in the variable is the result of a calculation, or concatenation. In this example, you decide to create a variable named *$wuLog* to store the path to the Windows Update Log, which is stored in a rather obscure location deep in the user's profile under a folder named AppData. While there is an environmental variable for the local application data folder, the path to the Windows Update Log continues to go on a few levels deeper prior to terminating with the WindowsUpdate.log file. As a best practice, you should use the path cmdlets when building file paths, such as Join-Path, to avoid concatenation errors. By using the environmental *$localappdata* variable and Join-Path with the *–resolve* switched parameter, you also have a formula that stores the path to the Windows Update Log file on any user's computer, which is exactly the type of variable you want to create and store in a user's Windows PowerShell profile. This command is shown here:

```
PS C:\> $wuLog = Join-Path -Path $env:LOCALAPPDATA '
-ChildPath microsoft\windows\windowsupdate.log -Resolve
PS C:\> $wuLog
C:\Users\edwils.NORTHAMERICA\AppData\Local\microsoft\windows\windowsupdate.log
```

When using a variable to hold a computed value, you are not limited to using a direct value assignment. You can use the New-Variable cmdlet to perform exactly the same task.

```
PS C:\> New-Variable -Name wulog -Value (Join-Path -Path $env:LOCALAPPDATA '
-ChildPath microsoft\windows\windowsupdate.log -Resolve)
```

> **NOTE** When using the New-Variable cmdlet to create a variable that holds a computed result, you often need to use parentheses to force the value to be created prior to attempting to assign it to the *-value* parameter. You might see an error message about a missing or invalid parameter. When the New-Variable cmdlet sees a parameter outside of a set of parentheses, it attempts to locate that parameter. An example of such an error is shown in Figure 5-8.

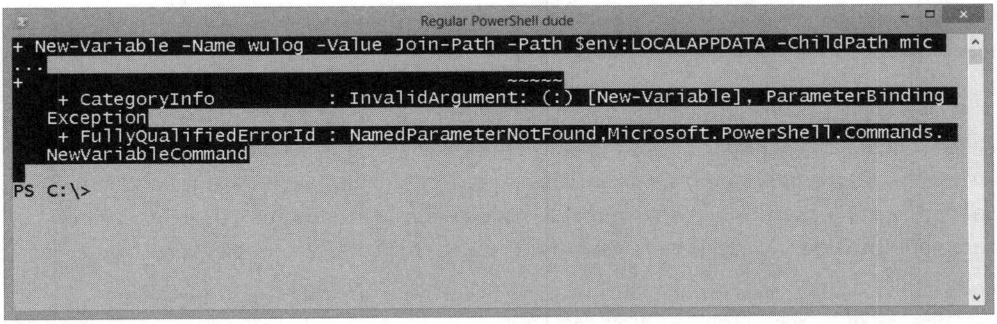

**FIGURE 5-8** An error message due to missing parentheses when creating a new variable.

You can also use automatic variables when creating variables for your profile. A large number of applications place files in the user's Documents directory. While this location is convenient for applications and for users who access documents via a link off the Start menu, it is nearly impossible to locate the Documents folder via the command line.

To facilitate ease of access to the user's Documents folder, you might decide to create a variable that can easily be used to refer to the path. This is another good opportunity to use the Join-Path cmdlet to aid in building the location to the Documents folder. An automatic variable already points to the user's Home directory. The Home directory on my Windows Vista laptop points to the %username% folder under the Users folder, as shown here.

```
PS C:\> $home
C:\Users\edwils.NORTHAMERICA
```

Because the Documents folder resides under this Home directory, as shown in Figure 5-9, you can add to this location and build the path to the Documents directory.

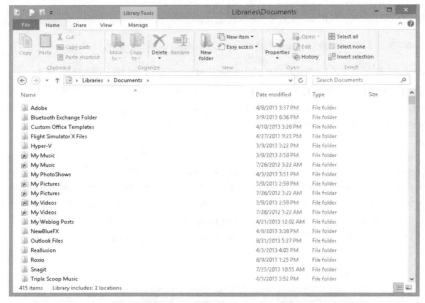

**FIGURE 5-9** The user's Documents folder is the default location for many applications.

By using the New-Variable cmdlet, you can specify the *–value* parameter, which is contained in a set of parentheses so as to resolve the value of the Join-Path command prior to assigning it to the *docs* variable. The variable is read-only, which allows you to modify it if needed, but it is also protected from accidental deletion or modification. The *–description* parameter provides an easy way to keep track of all of the custom variables, as shown here:

```
New-Variable -Name docs -Value (Join-Path -Path $home -ChildPath documents) '
-Option readonly -Description "MrEd Variable"
```

> **IMPORTANT** When I was first learning Windows PowerShell, I was often frustrated when attempting to use the New-Variable, Set-Variable, and Remove-Variable cmdlets. This occurred because a variable is prefixed with the dollar sign when working at the command line, but the *–name* parameter does not use the dollar sign as part of the name of the variable.

You can obtain the path to the Favorites folder when you use the *WshShell* object from VBScript. Because Windows PowerShell provides easy access to Component Object Model (COM) objects, there is no reason to avoid these objects. One way to use this *WshShell* object is to create and use the object in the same line, as shown here:

```
$f = (New-Object -ComObject Wscript.Shell).specialFolders.item("Favorites")
```

From a best practice standpoint, there are at least two problems with the previous syntax. The most obvious issue is that the code is not very readable. Even though this usage is rather common and most developers employ these types of construction, common sense should prevail. It is better to split the command into two lines of code, as shown here:

```
$wshShell = New-Object -ComObject Wscript.Shell
$f = $wshShell.SpecialFolders.Item("Favorites")
```

The additional advantage to the preceding two-line technique is that you now have access to the entire *WshShell* object, which provides access to many useful properties and methods. For example, in addition to resolving the path to the Documents special folder, the *WshSpecialFolders* object (returned by querying the *SpecialFolders* property of the *WshShell* object) can also be used to provide access to the following folders:

- AllUsersDesktop
- AllUsersStartMenu
- AllUsersPrograms
- AllUsersStartup
- Favorites
- Fonts
- NetHood
- PrintHood
- Programs
- Recent
- SendTo
- StartMenu
- Startup
- Templates

Without creating an *intermediate* variable, any of the listed special folders can be resolved to the path, as shown here. If the *$wshShell* object is created in the profile, the values from the SystemFolders property are always available for use within the scripting environment or when working from the command line.

```
$wshShell.SpecialFolders.Item("StartUp")
```

In addition to the ability to easily resolve the special folders, the *WshShell* object also provides a number of other useful properties and methods. Its members are shown in Table 5-1.

**TABLE 5-1** Members of the *WshShell* object

| Name | MemberType | Definition |
| --- | --- | --- |
| AppActivate | Method | bool AppActivate (Variant, Variant) |
| CreateShortcut | Method | IDispatch CreateShortcut (string) |

| Name | MemberType | Definition |
|------|-----------|------------|
| Exec | Method | IWshExec Exec (string) |
| ExpandEnvironmentStrings | Method | string ExpandEnvironmentStrings (string) |
| LogEvent | Method | bool LogEvent (Variant, string, string) |
| Popup | Method | int Popup (string, Variant, Variant, Variant) |
| RegDelete | Method | void RegDelete (string) |
| RegRead | Method | Variant RegRead (string) |
| RegWrite | Method | void RegWrite (string, Variant, Variant) |
| Run | Method | int Run (string, Variant, Variant) |
| SendKeys | Method | void SendKeys (string, Variant) |
| Environment | ParameterizedProperty | IWshEnvironment Environment (Variant) {get} |
| CurrentDirectory | Property | string CurrentDirectory () {get} {set} |
| SpecialFolders | Property | IWshCollection SpecialFolders () {get} |

The *popup* method is useful as well as easy to use. As shown in Figure 5-10, the *popup* method produces a pop-up dialog box.

**FIGURE 5-10** Pop-up message from the *WshShell* object.

To create a pop-up message box, you need to supply only the first value of the method signature. This value is used for the message displayed in the middle of the pop-up box. The second value is a number that controls how long the pop-up box is displayed. The third value is used to change the title of the pop-up box. The last position of the method call controls the button configuration of the pop-up box. If you supply only the first value, you receive a pop-up box with an OK button that displays the message you supply until the user manually clicks either OK or the X to close the box. The signature for the *popup* method is shown in Table 5-2.

**TABLE 5-2** *WshShell popup* method signature

| Return | Object.Method | Text | SecondsToWait | Title | Type |
|--------|--------------|------|---------------|-------|------|
| $returnValue | $wshShell.Popup | "message" | 5 | "title" | 0 |

The title of the box refers to the Windows Script Host, as shown in Figure 5-11.

**FIGURE 5-11** By default, pop-up messages come from the Windows Script Host.

The code that creates the pop-up box in Figure 5-11 is shown here:

```
(New-Object -ComObject wscript.shell).popup("message")
```

One useful feature of the *WshShell.popup* method is its ability to create different button configurations, which provides the ability to interact with the user in a graphical manner. To create a pop-up box that displays the Abort, Retry, and Ignore buttons, you can use the numeric value *2* in the fourth position. Common button configuration values are shown in Table 5-3. To display the pop-up message box until the user clicks one of the buttons, you can place a *0* in the second position (time argument) as shown here:

```
$wshShell.Popup("message",0,"title",2)
```

**TABLE 5-3** *WshShell* pop-up button values and meanings

| Value | Description |
| --- | --- |
| 0 | Show OK button. |
| 1 | Show OK and Cancel buttons. |
| 2 | Show Abort, Retry, and Ignore buttons. |
| 3 | Show Yes, No, and Cancel buttons. |
| 4 | Show Yes and No buttons. |
| 5 | Show Retry and Cancel buttons. |

Of course, the entire reason for displaying different button configurations is to provide an easy way for the user to interact with the script. To interact with the user, you must capture the return code, which is a value assigned to each of the different buttons. The following code produces the pop-up box shown in Figure 5-12. To evaluate the return code from the method, you must capture the return value. Return values from each of the different buttons are shown in Table 5-4. The Retry button is clicked in this example, which stores the value of 4 in the *$return* variable.

```
PS C:\> $rtn = (New-Object -ComObject wscript.shell).popup("message",0,"title",2)
PS C:\> $rtn
```

**FIGURE 5-12** Abort, Retry, Ignore dialog box.

**TABLE 5-4** *WshShell popup* method return values

| Value | Description |
| --- | --- |
| 1 | OK button |
| 2 | Cancel button |
| 3 | Abort button |
| 4 | Retry button |
| 5 | Ignore button |
| 6 | Yes button |
| 7 | No button |

Last, you need to work with the pop-up box icons that can be displayed on any of the different box configurations. As shown in Table 5-5, the icon values seem to have little basis in reality. Additionally, it is a bit odd that the values are added to the button values shown in Table 5-3. To display the Stop Mark icon to an Abort, Retry, Ignore button configuration, you need to add a value of 16 for the Stop Mark icon to the value of 2 for the Abort, Retry, Ignore button display, as shown in the following line of code:

```
$rtn = (New-Object -ComObject wscript.shell).popup("message",0,"title",18)
```

When the code executes, the dialog box shown in Figure 5-13 appears.

**TABLE 5-5** *WshShell popup* method icon values

| Value | Description |
| --- | --- |
| 16 | Show Stop Mark icon. |
| 32 | Show Question Mark icon. |
| 48 | Show Exclamation Mark icon. |
| 64 | Show Information Mark icon. |

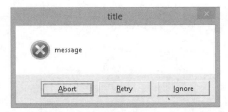

**FIGURE 5-13** Icon values added to the button configuration display different icon types.

## Creating PSDrives

Judicious application in the creation of Windows PowerShell drives can simplify and facilitate the navigation and manipulation of data from the command line. While it is possible to use a variable to hold the path to a long folder and then change the working location to the path of the folder, this action causes you to relinquish much of the command line, as shown in Figure 5-14. Although there is nothing wrong with losing a good deal of the command line, reading long commands that wrap across multiple lines can cause errors.

```
Regular PowerShell dude
PS C:\> $bestPractices = "C:\data\BookDOcs\PS4_BestPractices"
PS C:\> Set-Location $bestPractices
PS C:\data\BookDOcs\PS4_BestPractices>
```

**FIGURE 5-14** Long paths often use up too much of the command line.

One advantage of using a Windows PowerShell drive is that you can choose any location that is supported by the PowerShell provider as the root of the new drive. To create a new Windows PowerShell drive, you can use the `New-PSDrive` cmdlet, give the drive a name, and specify the provider and root location. The code to create a Windows PowerShell drive rooted in the C:\Data\BookDocs\PowerShellBestPractices folder is shown here:

```
New-PSDrive -Name bp -PSProvider filesystem -Root '
C:\data\BookDocs\PS4_BestPractices -Description "MrEd Drive"
```

After you create the Windows PowerShell drive, you can use the `Set-Location` cmdlet to change your working location to the newly created drive. This process allows you to reclaim your command-line real estate, as shown in Figure 5-15.

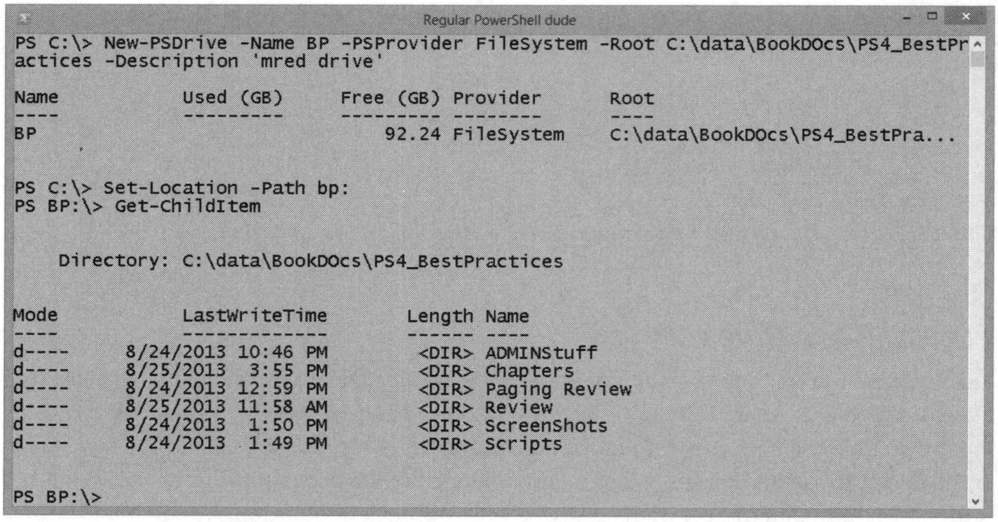

```
PS C:\> New-PSDrive -Name BP -PSProvider FileSystem -Root C:\data\BookDOcs\PS4_BestPr
actices -Description 'mred drive'

Name            Used (GB)    Free (GB) Provider        Root
----            ---------    --------- --------        ----
BP                             92.24 FileSystem      C:\data\BookDOcs\PS4_BestPra...


PS C:\> Set-Location -Path bp:
PS BP:\> Get-ChildItem


    Directory: C:\data\BookDOcs\PS4_BestPractices


Mode            LastWriteTime        Length Name
----            -------------        ------ ----
d----      8/24/2013 10:46 PM       <DIR> ADMINStuff
d----      8/25/2013  3:55 PM       <DIR> Chapters
d----      8/24/2013 12:59 PM       <DIR> Paging Review
d----      8/25/2013 11:58 AM       <DIR> Review
d----      8/24/2013  1:50 PM       <DIR> ScreenShots
d----      8/24/2013  1:49 PM       <DIR> Scripts


PS BP:\>
```

**FIGURE 5-15** A Windows PowerShell drive is a good way to reclaim command-line real estate.

As a best practice, I also prefer to specify the *description* attribute when creating a Windows PowerShell drive. Setting the same *–description* parameter for all Windows PowerShell drives makes it easy to quickly identify the custom drives contained in the current PowerShell environment. Such a command might look like the following:

```
Get-PSDrive | Where-Object { $_.description -eq 'MrEd Drive' }
```

By creating Windows PowerShell drives for your most important data locations, you can easily change the working location by using the Set-Location cmdlet. If you create only a single Windows PowerShell drive that is the heart of all of your data activities, you can even use the Set-Location cmdlet to change the working location to your custom PowerShell drive as part of the profile.

---

### NOTES FROM THE FIELD

## Working with profiles

Hal Rottenberg, Microsoft PowerShell MVP

I put many different elements in my profile. First, I load the Windows PowerShell Community Extensions (PSCX). These cmdlets provide additional functionality and make it easier to work with Windows PowerShell. If you are not familiar with PSCX, you can find the project at *www.codeplex.com/PowerShellCX*.

Next, I create a custom prompt function and add numerous snap-ins. I create several aliases because I've been very happy with the defaults. I have a section that

---

adds paths to *$env:path;* I never use cmd.exe anymore. Therefore, the profile is basically the core location where I maintain the %path%. The path section is also used to set some environment variables, such as *$MaximumHistoryCount*. The *$MaximumHistoryCount* variable determines the size of the command history buffer that defaults to storing 64 of your previously typed commands.

The best part of my profile is that I dot-source numerous functions I have written over the past year or so. These functions are small, reusable bits of code that make my job easier. I also create a few PSDrives. One PSDrive that I find particularly useful is called "scripts." It points to "$(split-path $profile)\scripts", which is where I store all of my function libraries and stand-alone .ps1 files. This folder is also in my path.

I also added a section to my profile that is used to load a variety of .NET assemblies. I do not use this section very often, and in fact, it is currently commented out. However, you might find it to be of interest because it loads some .NET assemblies. For example, one .NET assembly that I used had an ID3 tagging utility (for MP3 files) and one did Jabber/Extensible Messaging and Presence Protocol (XMPP) instant messaging.

The last section of my profile is used to load custom types.

I use Microsoft SkyDrive to ensure that my profile is always available. Sky Drive also serves as a backup of my entire WindowsPowerShell folder (and the aforementioned scripts, too). Other tools, such as Syncplicity (cloud), Foldershare (cloud), or Synctoy (local) can also be used for these purposes.

The coolest thing I have done in my profile is to add a *ScriptProperty* to the *System.Io.FileInfo* object by using Extended Type System (ETS) and .ps1 XML files in Windows PowerShell. This new *ScriptProperty*, named *Pages*, is a script that is invoked whenever the property is accessed. The script uses a little-known feature inside of the *Shell.Application* COM object to grab the number of pages in Microsoft Office Word documents. This script gives me the ability to create the following:

```
dir | ft name, length, pages
```

or even the following:

```
dir | Measure-Object -sum pages
```

Here is my profile code that loads the type (or types, if I were to add more).

```
Get-ChildItem -path $profiledir\ps1xml\*.ps1xml |
ForEach-Object {
    Update-TypeData $_
    write-host "Updating type data:'t$($_.name)"
}
```

**Here are the contents of the .ps1 XML file:**

```xml
<?xml version="1.0" encoding="utf-8" ?>
<Types>
    <Type>
        <Name>System.IO.FileInfo</Name>
        <Members>
            <ScriptProperty>
                <Name>Pages</Name>
                <GetScriptBlock>
                    $shellApp = new-object -com shell.application
                    $myFolder = $shellApp.Namespace($this.Directory.
                    FullName)
                    $fileobj = $myFolder.Items().Item($this.Name)
                    "$($myFolder.GetDetailsOf($fileobj,13))"
                </GetScriptBlock>
            </ScriptProperty>
        </Members>
    </Type>
</Types>
```

I do not use the page number capability very often. The most useful thing I have in my profile is the code to dot-source my function libraries. Note the use of the "scripts" PSDrive and "lib–" file name convention. This code makes it very easy for me to load all of the library files without touching my profile repeatedly, as shown in the following code:

```powershell
Get-ChildItem scripts:\lib-*.ps1 |
ForEach-Object {
  . $_
  write-host "Loading library file:'t$($_.name)"
}
```

I don't worry when my profile is not with me because I believe in cloud technologies. By using SkyDrive, my profile is always available. Because my primary PC is a laptop, I am not terribly concerned about profile issues.

Even though I define some aliases in my profile, I never use aliases in scripts—only at the prompt. A strong editor with cmdlet, parameter, file name, and even argument completion goes an incredibly long way toward making it convenient to produce very readable scripts.

I generally do some basic, simple error checking in my scripts, such as "If param is missing, throw err." However, the scripts that I publish for others usually receive a bit more treatment than that.

What I recommend to a new scripter is this: Download and install PSCX, and use the default profile, which is what I did when I was new to Windows PowerShell. It's very well-constructed and can serve as a great base and inspiration. Here is my personal profile:

```
# comments: $profiledir, Add-PathVariable come with PSCX

$ErrorPreference = "silentlycontinue"


# ----------------------------------------------------------------------------
# Load PSCX
# ----------------------------------------------------------------------------
. "$home\My Documents\WindowsPowerShell\PSCX_Profile.PS1"


# ----------------------------------------------------------------------------
# Load SQL PSX
# ----------------------------------------------------------------------------
# . "$home\My Documents\WindowsPowerShell\Scripts\SQLPSX\LibrarySmo.ps1"


# ----------------------------------------------------------------------------
# Set prompt
# ----------------------------------------------------------------------------


. $profiledir\prompt.ps1


# ----------------------------------------------------------------------------
# Add third-party snapins
# ----------------------------------------------------------------------------


$snapins =
  # "psmsi", # Windows Installer PowerShell Extensions
  "PshX-SAPIEN", # AD cmdlets from Sapien
  #  "GetGPObjectPSSnapIn", # GPO management
   "Quest.ActiveRoles.ADManagement", # more AD stuff
  #  "Microsoft.Office.OneNote",
  "PowerGadgets",
  "VMware.VimAutomation.Core",
  #  "PoshXmpp",
  # "PSMobile",
  #"PoshHttp",
  "NetCmdlets",
  "OpenXml.PowerTools",
  "IronCowPosh"
$snapins | ForEach-Object {
```

```
  if ( Get-PSSnapin -Registered $_ -ErrorAction SilentlyContinue ) {
    Add-PSSnapin $_
  }
}


# --------------------------------------------------------------------------
# Aliases
# --------------------------------------------------------------------------
set-alias grep select-string
set-alias nsl resolve-host
Set-Alias rsps Restart-PowerShell
set-alias which get-command
Set-Alias cvi Connect-VIServer


# --------------------------------------------------------------------------
# V2 modules
# --------------------------------------------------------------------------
# dir $profiledir\modules\*.psm1 | Add-Module


# --------------------------------------------------------------------------
# Setup environment
# --------------------------------------------------------------------------
New-PSDrive -Name Scripts -PSProvider FileSystem -Root '
 $profiledir\scripts
Add-PathVariable Path $profiledir\scripts
Add-PathVariable Path $profiledir
Add-PathVariable Path "C:\Program Files\OpenSSL\bin"
Add-PathVariable Path "C:\Program Files\Reflector"
$MaximumHistoryCount = 4KB


# --------------------------------------------------------------------------
# Load function / filter definition library
# --------------------------------------------------------------------------

Get-ChildItem scripts:\lib-*.ps1 | % {
  . $_
  write-host "Loading library file:'t$($_.name)"
}
write-host


# --------------------------------------------------------------------------
# PS Drives
# --------------------------------------------------------------------------

New-PSDrive -Name Book -PSProvider FileSystem -Root 'C:\Documents and
Settings\hrottenberg\My Documents\MVP-TFM'
```

```
    Write-Host

    # -------------------------------------------------------------------
    # Load .NET assemblies
    # -------------------------------------------------------------------
    #Get-ChildItem $profiledir\Assemblies\*.dll | % {
    # [void][reflection.assembly]::LoadFrom( $_.FullName )
    # write-host "Loading .NET assembly:'t$($_.name)"
    #}
    #Write-Host

    # -------------------------------------------------------------------
    # Load custom types
    # -------------------------------------------------------------------
    Get-ChildItem $profiledir\ps1xml\*.ps1xml | % {
      Update-TypeData $_
      write-host "Updating type data:'t$($_.name)"
    }
    Write-Host
    if ($?) { Write-Host 'There were errors loading your profile.  Check the
    $error object for details.' }
```

# Enabling scripting

When Windows PowerShell is first installed, the script execution policy is set to restricted. When the execution policy is restricted, no scripts are permitted to run. Because a profile is a .ps1 file, it is therefore a script and by default will not run. Five levels of execution policy can be configured in Windows PowerShell by using the Set-ExecutionPolicy cmdlet, and they are listed in Table 5-6. The restricted execution policy can be configured via Group Policy by using the "Turn On Script Execution" Group Policy setting in Active Directory. It can be applied to either the computer object or user object; the computer object setting takes precedence over other settings.

User preferences for the restricted execution policy can be configured by using the Set-ExecutionPolicy cmdlet, but the preferences do not override settings configured by Group Policy. An example of changing the current execution policy to RemoteSigned is shown here. To run the Set-ExecutionPolicy cmdlet, the Windows PowerShell console must be launched with admin rights. To do this, right-click the shortcut to Windows PowerShell and select Run As Administrator. See Chapter 4, "Identifying scripting opportunities," for a discussion about the different ways to handle security issues. If you attempt to run the Set-ExecutionPolicy cmdlet, even when logged on to the computer as the administrator or as a user who is a member of the local administrators group, the error message shown in Figure 5-16 appears if you are using Windows Vista or above.

```
Set-ExecutionPolicy -ExecutionPolicy remotesigned
```

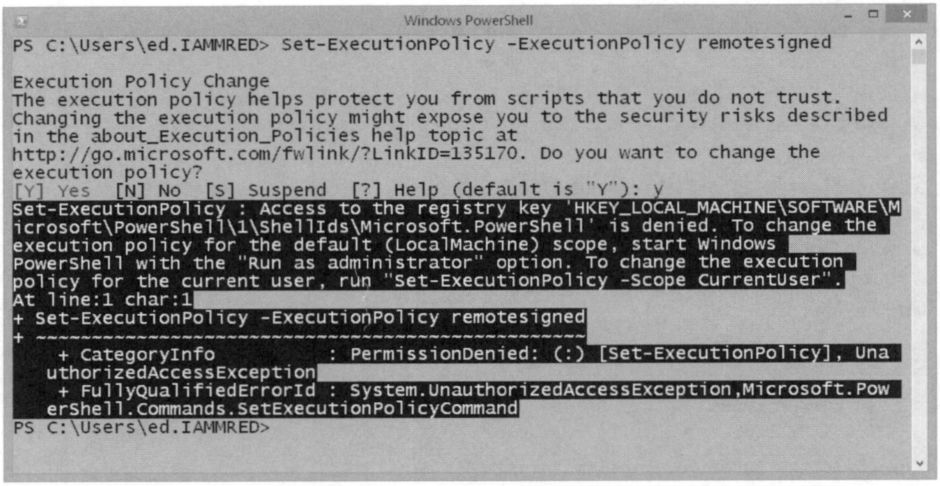

**FIGURE 5-16** Attempts to change the restricted execution policy generate an error message if the Windows PowerShell console is not run as administrator.

The resultant set of restricted execution policy settings can be obtained by using the Get-ExecutionPolicy cmdlet.

**TABLE 5-6** Execution policy level settings

| Level | Meaning |
|---|---|
| Restricted | Does not run scripts or configuration files. |
| AllSigned | All scripts and configuration files must be signed by a trusted publisher. |
| RemoteSigned | All scripts and configuration files downloaded from the Internet must be signed by a trusted publisher. |
| Unrestricted | All scripts and configuration files do run. Scripts downloaded from the Internet prompt for permission prior to running. |
| Bypass | Nothing is blocked, and there are no warnings or prompts. |

In addition to the five restricted execution policy settings, you can also configure the scope of the policy. When you set the scope of the restricted execution policy, it determines how the policy is applied by using three valid values: Process, CurrentUser, and LocalMachine. These values are detailed in Table 5-7.

**TABLE 5-7** Execution policy scope settings

| Scope | Meaning |
|---|---|
| Process | The execution policy affects only the current Windows PowerShell process. |
| CurrentUser | The execution policy affects only the current user. |
| LocalMachine | The execution policy affects all users of the computer. |

# Creating a profile

When Windows PowerShell is first installed, no profiles are installed on the computer. In one respect, you can consider the profile to be similar to the Autoexec.bat file from several years ago. On the one hand, the Autoexec.bat file is simply a batch file in that it executes only batch types of commands. On the other hand, because it is located in the root and has the name Autoexec.bat, it takes on an importance that is greatly out of proportion to a simple batch file because the commands that exist in the file are used to configure all types of activities, including configuring the environment and even launching Windows itself. The Windows PowerShell profile does not launch PowerShell; it is simply a PowerShell script that happens to have a special name and to exist in a special place—or, rather, it happens to have two special names and to exist in four special places! That's right. There are actually four Windows PowerShell profiles, as listed in Table 5-8.

**TABLE 5-8** Windows PowerShell profiles and locations

| Profile | Location |
| --- | --- |
| AllUsersAllHosts | C:\Windows\system32\WindowsPowerShell\v1.0\profile.ps1 |
| AllUsersCurrentHost | C:\Windows\system32\WindowsPowerShell\v1.0\Microsoft.PowerShell_profile.ps1 |
| CurrentUserAllHosts | C:\Users\UserName\Documents\WindowsPowerShell\profile.ps1 |
| CurrentUserCurrentHost | C:\Users\UserName\Documents\WindowsPowerShell\Microsoft.PowerShell_profile.ps1 |

# Choosing the correct profile

Two of the four profiles are used by all Windows PowerShell users on a computer. Anything placed in the All Users profiles is available to any script or any user that runs Windows PowerShell. As a result, you should be rather circumspect about what you place in the All Users profiles. However, the All Users profiles are great locations to configure aliases that you want to make available to all users, variables that you intend to use in a corporate scripting environment, or a Windows PowerShell drive or function. In fact, the items that you decide to mandate as part of the corporate Windows PowerShell environment are best placed in the All Users profiles.

The next question involves which of the two All Users profiles you should use. The AllUsersAllHosts profile applies to all of the users on the computer and to every instance of Windows PowerShell that can run on the computer, including the PowerShell console, the PowerShell Integrated Scripting Environment (ISE), and any other program that can host Windows PowerShell, which can include the Exchange Management Environment, the SQL console, or any application that can host Windows PowerShell. If you are careful with the aliases you create, the variables you assign, the functions you write, and any Windows PowerShell drives that you decide to make, you still need to test them to ensure compatibility.

The AllUsersCurrentHost profile gives you the same ability to modify the Windows PowerShell environment for all users, but it applies only to the console host.

The two Current User profiles are used to modify the Windows PowerShell environment for the current user. The profile that is most often modified by a user to configure personal Windows PowerShell settings is the CurrentUserCurrentHost profile. This profile is referenced by the *$profile* automatic variable. On my computer, the value of the *$profile* variable is shown here:

```
PS C:\> $PROFILE
C:\Users\edwilson\Documents\WindowsPowerShell\Microsoft.PowerShell_profile.ps1
```

On a Windows Vista computer, you can see that the user's Personal folder is in the user's Documents folder. The WindowsPowerShell folder does not exist if no profile is created as shown here, where the Test-Path cmdlet is used to determine whether the parent folder that should contain the Microsoft.Powershell_profile.ps1 file exists. Because no personal profile has yet been created on this laptop, the WindowsPowerShell folder has not been created.

```
PS C:\> Test-path (Split-Path $PROFILE -Parent)
False
```

To create a CurrentUserCurrentHost profile, you can use the New-Item cmdlet as shown here. When using the New-Item cmdlet, you need to specify the *–force* parameter if the folder does not exist and to specify the *itemtype* as file as shown here.

```
New-Item -Path $PROFILE -ItemType file –Force
```

After the profile is created, you can open it in Notepad or in the Windows PowerShell ISE to edit the file. If you choose to edit it in Notepad, it is as simple as typing **notepad** and giving it the *$profile* automatic variable as shown here:

```
Notepad $profile
```

After adding the functions, variables, aliases, and a Windows PowerShell drive, the CurrentUserCurrentHost profile is shown here:

```
CurrentUserCurrentHostProfile.ps1

# *** Functions go here ***

Function Set-Profile()
{
 Notepad $profile
 #MrEd function
}

Function Get-MoreHelp()
{
 #.Help Get-MoreHelp Get-Command
 Get-Help $args[0] -Full |
 more
```

```
  #MrEd function
} #end Get-MoreHelp


Function Get-WmiClass([string]$ns, [string]$class)
{
 #.Help Get-WmiClass -ns "root\cimv2" -class "Processor"
 $ns = $args[0]
 $class = $args[1]
 Get-WmiObject -List -Namespace $ns |
 Where-Object { $_.name -match $class }
  #MrEd function
} #end Get-WmiClass


# *** Aliases go here ***

New-Alias -Name mo -Value Measure-Object -Option allscope '
  -Description "MrEd Alias"
New-Alias -name gmh -value Get-MoreHelp -Option allscope '
  -Description "MrEd Alias"
New-Alias -Name gwc -Value Get-WmiClass -Option readonly,allscope '
  -Description "Mred Alias"


# *** Variables go here ***

New-Variable -Name wulog -Value (Join-Path -Path $env:LOCALAPPDATA '
  -ChildPath microsoft\windows\windowsupdate.log -Resolve) '
  -Option readonly -Description "MrEd Alias"
New-Variable -Name docs -Value (Join-Path -Path $home -ChildPath documents) '
  -Option readonly -Description "MrEd Variable"
New-Variable -name wshShell -value (New-Object -ComObject Wscript.Shell) '
  -Option readonly -Description "MrEd Alias"


# *** PSDrives go here ***

New-PSDrive -Name HKCR -PSProvider registry -Root Hkey_Classes_Root '
  -Description "MrEd PSdrive" | out-null
```

## Creating other profiles

In addition to referencing the CurrentUserCurrentHost profile via the *$profile* variable, you can also reference all of the other profiles by using a dotted notation. To address the AllUsersAllHosts profile, you can use the *$profile* variable, as shown here:

```
PS C:\> $PROFILE.AllUsersAllHosts
C:\Windows\system32\WindowsPowerShell\v1.0\profile.ps1
```

You can also easily create the AllUsersAllHosts profile by using the same technique you used for the CurrentUserCurrentHost profile:

```
New-Item -Path $PROFILE.AllUsersAllHosts -ItemType file -Force
```

One thing to keep in mind is that, on Windows Vista and above, you need to launch the Windows PowerShell console by right-clicking the icon and selecting Run As Administrator from the menu, because the System32 directory is a protected area of the file system. If you do not do this, the error message shown in Figure 5-17 appears.

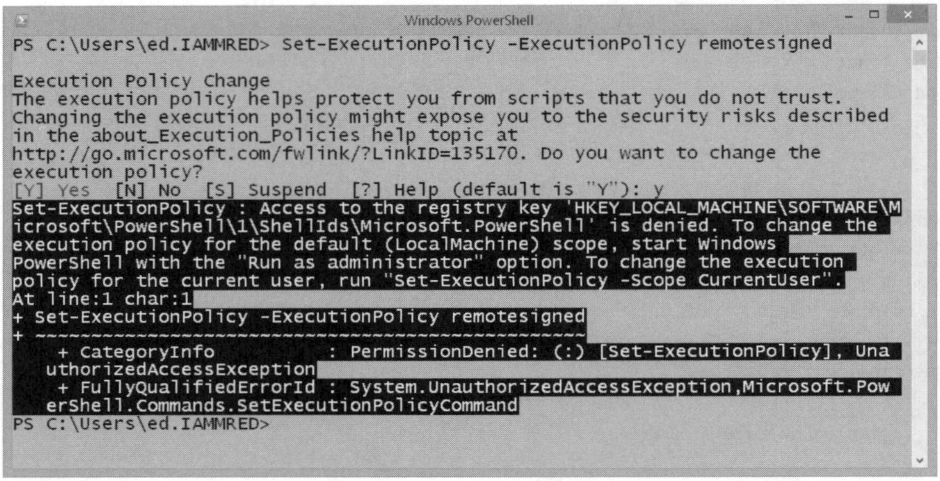

**FIGURE 5-17** Attempts to create the All Users profile fail if Windows PowerShell is not run as an administrator.

To create the AllUsersCurrentHost profile, you again need to start the Windows PowerShell console with admin rights and then use the New-Item cmdlet to create the profile. This command is shown here:

```
New-Item -Path $PROFILE.AllUsersCurrentHost -ItemType file -Force
```

If you want to create the CurrentUserAllHosts profile, you can do so without using admin rights because it is stored in the user's Documents folder. Therefore, a typical user always has the rights to create the CurrentUserAllHosts and CurrentUserCurrentHost profiles. The command to create the CurrentUserAllHosts profile is shown here:

```
New-Item -Path $PROFILE.CurrentUserAllHosts -ItemType file -Force
```

When working with profiles, you should always consider the effect of the application on all of the different profiles. It is possible that items you place in a profile could be overwritten by other profiles, and the effect could very well be cumulative. Therefore, the concept of Resultant Set of Profiles (RSOP) comes into play. The four profiles are applied in the following order. The first profile is the most likely to be overwritten. The profile that is the closest to the user—the CurrentUserCurrentHost profile—is the one with the highest priority:

- All Users, All Hosts
- All Users, Current Host
- Current User, All Hosts
- Current User, Current Host

### Use a standard naming convention to avoid conflict

As a best practice, when creating standard aliases and variables, you should mark them as constant to ensure that they are always available. When creating functions and Windows PowerShell drives, you should use a naming convention that is unlikely to result in naming conflicts. A company that I know uses a company name prefix for their functions, as illustrated here:

```
Function CompanyAITWigitFunction() { do something interesting here }
New-Alias -Name CAWA -Value CompanyAITWigitFunction -Option constant '
-Description "CompanyA IT alias"
```

### How I use my profile

**James Brundage, Owner**
*Start-Automating*

Profiles are an interesting trade-off. The upside of using profiles is that they can give you a consistent and personalized environment that sets up Windows PowerShell to your specifications. The downside of using profiles is that a personalized Windows PowerShell profile is always a little harder to share than a standard PowerShell profile; therefore, the way you write your profile can have a huge impact on how easy it is for others to use.

In my opinion, the ideal profile is simply a series of module imports or dot-sourcing of scripts. Both modules and script files are easy to copy from one computer to another computer, so keeping your profile in this format means that your profile remains clean and easy to understand and the scripts on which your profile depends are easy to share with the outside world. If your profiles are kept as a series of module imports or a dot-sourcing of scripts, you should be able to merely copy a module from one box to another, copy your profile, and be done.

You can also use your profile to make life more convenient. The Windows PowerShell ISE contains an object model that allows you to add tools to the environment, and PowerShell lets you customize the prompt by writing your own prompt function. If I'm adding cool things to the environment, such as a Verb menu, I always put them in my profile.

On this note, the coolest thing that I ever had in my profile was the Verb menu. I built a script to create a menu hierarchy in the ISE so that I could click commands by their verb. (For example, go to the Get menu, and then click "Process" to run Get-Process.) This type of customization is great to use in a profile because it makes life within the scripting environment easier.

I tend to shy away from using aliases in my profile because aliases make my scripts more difficult to share with the world outside of Microsoft (due to the chance that I might forget to de-alias the script before posting it to a blog). Aliases are a fine component to have in a profile if you are not scripting for public consumption, but I usually want an alias to which I can write a function with a small amount of additional effort. I believe that aliases increase the need to place your profile on every computer all of the time. Because I have a blog, I often try to minimize the dependencies of my scripts; therefore, I avoid aliases because they are a superfluous dependency.

My profile is typically short because I keep almost everything in modules. I have several more items in my *$loadedModules* variable, but the following gives you an idea of how my profile looks:

```
$loadedModules = 'DotNet',
    'WPF'
Import-Module $loadedModules –force
```

The DotNet module is very simple. It is merely a file with the .psm1 extension that dot-sources a file with a *Get-Type* function. It is placed in the $env:UserProfile\Documents\WindowsPowerShell\Modules\DotNet folder.

```
MyDotNetmodule

. $psScriptRoot\Get-Type.ps1
Get-Type.ps1:
Function Get-Type() {
    [AppDomain]::CurrentDomain.GetAssemblies() | Foreach-Object {
    $_.GetTypes() }
}
```

The *Get-Type* function is the most useful addition that I ever put into a profile. It outputs all of the types that are currently loaded so that I can search them in Windows PowerShell, such as the following:

```
Get-Type | Where-Object { $_.FullName –like "**File*" }
```

# Accessing functions in other scripts

After you write a large number of functions, you might like to reuse them in other scripts. Code reuse is a great idea. The easiest way to reuse code is to simply copy and paste the function from one script into another script. Suppose that you have a script containing code that performs a conversion from Celsius to Fahrenheit, and you want to use the algorithm to create another script with different capabilities. You can simply write your script and copy the code from your other script. When finished, your script might look like the ConvertToFahrenheit.ps1 script shown here.

```
ConvertToFahrenheit.ps1

Param($Celsius)
Function ConvertToFahrenheit($Celsius)
{
 "$Celsius Celsius equals $((1.8 * $Celsius) + 32) Fahrenheit"
} #end ConvertToFahrenheit
ConvertToFahrenheit($Celsius)
```

Nothing is wrong with this script. It does one thing and does it fairly well. To use the script, you supply a command-line parameter. You do not need to type the entire parameter name when calling the script, as shown here:

```
PS C:\> C:\BestPracticesBook\ConvertToFahrenheit.ps1 -c 24
24 celsius equals 75.2 fahrenheit
```

# Creating a function library

The problem with reusing code occurs when you want to use the function; you need to copy and paste it into the new script. If you want to change the way the function works, you need to find all instances where the function occurs and make the necessary changes. Otherwise, you can end up with many slightly different versions of the function, which can lead to support problems.

What is the solution? One approach is to place all of your functions into a single script, such as the ConversionFunctions.ps1 script shown here.

```
ConversionFunctions.ps1

Function ConvertToMeters($feet)
{
  "$feet feet equals $($feet*.31) meters"
} #end ConvertToMeters
Function ConvertToFeet($meters)
{
 "$meters meters equals $($meters * 3.28) feet"
} #end ConvertToFeet
```

```
Function ConvertToFahrenheit($celsius)
{
 "$celsius celsius equals $((1.8 * $celsius) + 32 ) fahrenheit"
} #end ConvertToFahrenheit
Function ConvertTocelsius($fahrenheit)
{
 "$fahrenheit fahrenheit equals $( (($fahrenheit - 32)/9)*5 ) celsius"
} #end ConvertTocelsius
Function ConvertToMiles($kilometer)
{
  "$kilometer kilometers equals $( ($kilometer *.6211) ) miles"
} #end convertToMiles
Function ConvertToKilometers($miles)
{
  "$miles miles equals $( ($miles * 1.61) ) kilometers"
} #end convertToKilometers
```

## Using an include file

If you need to use one of the conversion functions, you can include it in the script by placing a period in front of the path to the script. When you include the script containing the conversion functions, you now have access to all of the functions and can use them directly as if they were in the actual file itself. The ConvertToFahrenheit_Include.ps1 script illustrates this technique. You can still use the command-line parameter *$celsius* to supply the temperature that you want to convert. You then use the period followed by the path to the script for the include file. Lastly, you can call the function by name and supply it with the value that came into the script via the command line. The revised ConvertToFahrenheit_Include.ps1 script is shown here.

```
ConvertToFahrenheit_Include.ps1

Param($Celsius)
. C:\data\scriptingGuys\ConversionFunctions.ps1
ConvertToFahrenheit($Celsius)
```

You can see that the script is much cleaner and less cluttered, and it is easier to read. Because it is easier to read, the script is easier to understand and is therefore easier to maintain. Of course, there are two downsides to this equation. The first is that the two scripts are now married. A change in one script might affect a change in the other script. However, more importantly, both scripts now must travel together because both now need to have a single working script. This outside dependency can become rather difficult to troubleshoot if you are not expecting it or have not planned for it.

One way to make the script easier to troubleshoot is to use the Test-Path cmdlet to determine whether the include file is present. If the include file is missing, you can generate a message to that effect to alert you to the missing file and simplify the troubleshooting scenario. As a best practice, I always recommend using Test-Path whenever you use the include file scenario. The revised ConvertToFahrenheit_Include2.ps1 script illustrates this technique and is shown here.

```
ConvertToFahrenheit_Include2.ps1

Param($Celsius)
$includeFile = "c:\data\scriptingGuys\ConversionFunctions.ps1"
if(!(test-path -path $includeFile))
  {
   "Unable to find $includeFile"
   Exit
  }
. $includeFile
ConvertToFahrenheit($Celsius)
```

As you can see, this process begins to become a bit ridiculous. You now have a nine-line script to allow you to use a three-line function. You must make the call if you want to use the include file. When writing a more substantial script that uses an include file, the payoff in terms of simplicity and actual code length becomes more evident. In the ConvertUseFunctions.ps1 script, a function named *ParseAction* evaluates the action and value that are supplied from the command line and then calls the appropriate function as shown here in the ConvertUseFunctions.ps1 script.

```
ConvertUseFunctions.ps1

Param($action,$value,[switch]$help)
Function GetHelp()
{
  if($help)
  {
   "choose conversion: M(eters), F(eet) C(elsius),Fa(renheit),Mi(les),K(ilometers) and
value"
   " Convert -a M -v 10 converts 10 meters to feet."
  } #end if help
} #end getHelp
Function GetInclude()
{
 $includeFile = "c:\data\scriptingGuys\ConversionFunctions.ps1"
 if(!(test-path -path $includeFile))
   {
    "Unable to find $includeFile"
    Exit
   }
. $includeFile
} #end GetInclude
```

```
Function ParseAction()
{
 switch ($action)
 {
  "M"  { ConvertToFeet($value) }
  "F"  { ConvertToMeters($value) }
  "C"  { ConvertToFahrenheit($value) }
  "Fa" { ConvertToCelsius($value) }
  "Mi" { ConvertToKilometers($value) }
  "K"  { ConvertToMiles($value) }
  DEFAULT { "Dude illegal value." ; GetHelp ; exit }
 } #end action
} #end ParseAction
# *** Entry Point ***
If($help) { GetHelp ; exit }
if(!$action) { "Missing action" ; GetHelp ; exit }
GetInclude
ParseAction
```

Keep in mind that you need to make a change to the include file. Because you are loading the functions from within a function, the functions are scoped by default into that function's namespace. They are not available from a different function—only from child items. To avoid the inheritance issue, add a script tag to each function when it is created, as shown here:

```
Function Script:ConvertToMeters($feet)
{
  "$feet feet equals $($feet*.31) meters"
} #end ConvertToMeters
```

## Additional resources

- The TechNet Script Center at *http://www.microsoft.com/technet/scriptcenter* contains numerous examples of Windows PowerShell scripts that use include files.

- Windows PowerShell profiles are covered at *http://msdn.microsoft.com/en-us/library /bb613488(VS.85).aspx* in MSDN.

- The script execution policy is covered at *http://msdn.microsoft.com/en-us/library /bb648601(VS.85).aspx* in MSDN.

- All scripts from this chapter are in the file available from the Script Center Script Repository at *http://gallery.technet.microsoft.com/scriptcenter/PowerShell -40-Best-d9e16039*.

# CHAPTER 6

# Avoiding scripting pitfalls

- Lack of cmdlet support
- Complicated constructors
- Version compatibility issues
- Lack of WMI support
- Working with objects and namespaces
- Listing WMI providers
- Working with WMI classes
- Lack of .NET Framework support
- Additional resources

Knowing what you should not script is as important as knowing what you should script. There are times when creating a Windows PowerShell script is not the best approach to a problem due to the lack of support in a particular technology or to project complexity. In this chapter, you will be introduced to some of the red flags that signal danger for a potential script project.

## Lack of cmdlet support

It is no secret that cmdlet support is what makes working with Windows PowerShell so easy. If you need to check the status of the bits service, the easiest method is to use the Get-Service cmdlet as shown here:

```
Get-Service -name bits
```

To find information about the explorer process, you can use the Get-Process cmdlet as shown here:

```
Get-Process -Name explorer
```

If you need to stop a process, you can easily use the Stop-Process cmdlet as shown here:

```
Stop-Process -Name notepad
```

You can even check the status of services on a remote computer by using the *–ComputerName* switch from the `Get-Service` cmdlet as shown here:

```
Get-Service -Name bits -ComputerName vista
```

> **IMPORTANT** If you are working in a cross-domain scenario in which authentication is required, you will not be able to use `Get-Service` or `Get-Process` because those cmdlets do not have a *–credential* parameter. You need to use one of the remoting cmdlets, such as `Invoke-Command`, which allows you to supply an authentication context.

You can check the BIOS information on a local computer and save the information to a comma-separated value (CSV) file with just a few lines of code. An example of such a script is the ExportBiosToCsv.ps1 script.

```
ExportBiosToCsv.ps1

$path = "c:\fso\bios.csv"
Get-CimInstance -ClassName win32_bios |
Select-Object -property name, version |
Export-CSV -path $path –noTypeInformation
```

Without cmdlet support for selecting objects and exporting them to a CSV file format, you might be tempted to use *filesystemobject* from Microsoft VBScript fame. If you take that approach, the script will be twice as long and not nearly as readable. An example of a script using *filesystemobject* is the FSOBiosToCsv.ps1 script.

```
FSOBiosToCsv.ps1

$path = "c:\fso\bios1.csv"
$bios = Get-CimInstance -ClassName win32_bios
$csv = "Name,Version'r'n"
$csv +=$bios.name + "," + $bios.version
$fso = new-object -comobject scripting.filesystemobject
$file = $fso.CreateTextFile($path,$true)
$file.write($csv)
$file.close()
```

Clearly, the ability to use built-in cmdlets is a major strength of Windows PowerShell. One problem with Windows Server 2012 R2 and Windows PowerShell 4.0 is the number of cmdlets that exist, which is similar to the problem experienced by Windows Exchange Server administrators. Because there are so many cmdlets, it is difficult to know where to begin. A quick perusal of the Microsoft Exchange Team's blog and some of the Exchange forums reveals that the problem is not in writing scripts but in finding the one cmdlet of the hundreds of possible candidates that performs the specific task at hand. If you factor in community-developed cmdlets and third-party software company cmdlet offerings, you have a potential environment that encompasses thousands of cmdlets.

Luckily, the Windows PowerShell team has a plan to address this situation—standard naming conventions. The Get-Help, Get-Command, and Get-Member cmdlets were discussed in Chapter 1, "Survey of PowerShell capabilities," but they merit mention here. If you are unaware of a specific cmdlet feature or even the existence of a cmdlet, you are forced to implement a workaround that causes additional work or that might mask hidden mistakes. Given the choice between a cmdlet that is part of the operating system and a create-your-own solution, the pre-existing cmdlet should be used in almost all cases. Therefore, instead of assuming that a cmdlet or feature does not exist, you should spend time using Get-Help, Get-Command, and Get-Member before embarking on a lengthy development effort. In this chapter, you will examine some of the potential pitfalls that can develop when you do not use cmdlets.

# Complicated constructors

If you do not have support from cmdlets when developing an idea for a script, there might be a better way to do something and you should at least consider your alternatives.

In the GetRandomObject.ps1 script, a function named *GetRandomObject* is created. This function takes two input parameters: one named *$in* that holds an array of objects and the other named *$count* that controls how many items are randomly selected from the input object.

The New-Object cmdlet is used to create an instance of the *System.Random* Microsoft .NET Framework class. The new instance of the class is created by using the default constructor (no seed value supplied) and is stored in the *$rnd* variable.

A *for...next* loop is used to loop through the collection—once for each selection desired. The next method of the *System.Random* class is used to choose a random number that resides between the number 1 and the maximum number of items in the input object. The random number is used to locate an item in the array by using the index so that the selection of the item from the input object can take place. The GetRandomObject.ps1 script is shown here.

```
GetRandomObject.ps1

Function GetRandomObject($in,$count)
{
 $rnd = New-Object system.random
 for($i = 1 ; $i -le $count; $i ++)
 {
  $in[$rnd.Next(1,$a.length)]
 } #end for
} #end GetRandomObject

# *** entry point ***
$a = 1,2,3,4,5,6,7,8,9
$count = 3
GetRandomObject -in $a -count $count
```

While there is nothing inherently wrong with the GetRandomObject.ps1 script, you can use the Get-Random cmdlet when working with Windows PowerShell 2.0 (and above) to accomplish essentially the same objective as shown here:

```
$a = 1,2,3,4,5,6,7,8,9
Get-Random -InputObject $a -Count 3
```

Clearly, by using the native Get-Random cmdlet, you can save yourself a great deal of time and trouble.

One advantage of using a cmdlet is that you can trust it will be implemented correctly. At times, .NET Framework classes have rather complicated constructors that are used to govern the way the instance of a class is created. A mistake that is made when passing a value for one of these constructors does not always mean that an error is generated. It is entirely possible that the code will appear to work correctly, and it can therefore be very difficult to spot the problem.

An example of this type of error is shown in the BadGetRandomObject.ps1 script in which an integer is passed to the constructor for the *System.Random* .NET Framework class. The problem is that every time the script is run, the same random number is generated. While this particular bad implementation is rather trivial, it illustrates that the potential exists for logic errors that often require detailed knowledge of the utilized .NET Framework classes to troubleshoot.

---

**BadGetRandomObject.ps1**

```
Function GetRandomObject($in,$count,$seed)
{
 $rnd = New-Object system.random($seed)
 for($i = 1 ; $i -le $count; $i ++)
 {
  $in[$rnd.Next(1,$a.length)]
 } #end for
} #end GetRandomObject

# *** entry point ***
$a = 1,2,3,4,5,6,7,8,9
$count = 3
GetRandomObject -in $a -count $count -seed 5
```

---

The *System.Random* information is contained in MSDN, but it is easy to overlook some small detail because there is so much documentation and some of the classes are very complicated. When the overlooked detail does not cause a run-time error and the script appears to work properly, you have a potentially embarrassing situation at best.

# Version compatibility issues

While the Internet is a great source of information, it can often lead to confusion rather than clarity. When you locate a source of information, it might not be updated to include the current version of the operating system. This update situation is worsening due to a variety of complicating factors such as User Account Control (UAC), Windows Firewall, and other security factors that have so many different configuration settings that it can be unclear whether an apparent failure is due to a change in the operating system or to an actual error in the code. For example, suppose that you decide to use the *WIN32_Volume* Windows Management Instrumentation (WMI) class to determine information about your disk drives. First, you need to realize that the WMI class does not exist on any operating system older than Microsoft Windows Server 2003; it is a bit surprising that the class does not exist on Windows XP. However, when you try the following command on Windows Vista, it generates an error:

```
Get-WmiObject -Class win32_volume -Filter "Name = 'c:\'"
```

The first suspect when dealing with Windows Vista and later versions is user rights. You open the Windows PowerShell console as an administrator and try the code again; it fails. You then wonder whether the error is caused by the differences between expanding quotes and literal quotes. After contemplation, you decide to write the filter to take advantage of literal strings. The problem is that you have to escape the quotes, which involves more work, but it is worth the effort if it works. So you come up with the following code that, unfortunately, also fails when it is run.

```
Get-WmiObject -Class win32_volume -Filter 'Name = ''c:\'''
```

This time, you decide to read the error message. Here is the error that was produced by the previous command:

```
Get-WmiObject : Invalid query
At line:1 char:14
+ Get-WmiObject <<<<  -Class win32_volume -Filter "Name = 'c:\' "
    + CategoryInfo          : InvalidOperation: (:) [Get-WmiObject],
    ManagementException
    + FullyQualifiedErrorId : GetWMIManagementException,
    Microsoft.PowerShell.Commands.GetWmiObjectCommand
```

You focus on the line that says invalid operation and decide that perhaps the backslash is a special character. When this is the problem, you need to escape the backslash; therefore, you decide to use the escape character to make one more attempt. Here is the code you create.

```
Get-WmiObject -Class win32_volume -Filter "Name = 'c:'\' "
```

Even though this is a good idea, the code still does not work and once again generates an error, as shown here:

```
Get-WmiObject : Invalid query
At line:1 char:14
```

```
+ Get-WmiObject <<<<  -Class win32_volume -Filter "Name = 'c:'\' "
  + CategoryInfo          : InvalidOperation: (:) [Get-WmiObject],
  ManagementException
  + FullyQualifiedErrorId : GetWMIManagementException,
  Microsoft.PowerShell.Commands.GetWmiObjectCommand
```

Next, you search to determine whether you have rights to run the query. (I know that you are running the console with Administrator rights, but some processes deny access even to the Administrator, so it is best to check.) The easiest way to check your rights is to perform the WMI query and omit the *–filter* parameter as shown here:

```
Get-WmiObject -Class win32_volume
```

This command runs without generating an error. You might assume that you cannot filter the WMI class at all and decide that the class is a bit weird. You might decide to write a different filter and see whether it will accept the syntax of a new filter, such as the following line of code:

```
Get-WmiObject -Class win32_volume -Filter "DriveLetter = 'c:'"
```

The previous command rewards you with an output similar to the one shown here:

```
PS C:\> Get-WmiObject -Class win32_volume -Filter "DriveLetter = 'c:'"


__GENUS                       : 2
__CLASS                       : Win32_Volume
__SUPERCLASS                  : CIM_StorageVolume
__DYNASTY                     : CIM_ManagedSystemElement
__RELPATH                     : Win32_Volume.DeviceID="\\\\?\\Volume{5a4a2fe5-70
                                f0-11dd-b4ad-806e6f6e6963}\\"
__PROPERTY_COUNT              : 44
__DERIVATION                  : {CIM_StorageVolume, CIM_StorageExtent, CIM_Logic
                                alDevice, CIM_LogicalElement...}
__SERVER                      : MRED1
__NAMESPACE                   : root\cimv2
__PATH                        : \\MRED1\root\cimv2:Win32_Volume.DeviceID="\\\\?\
                                \Volume{5a4a2fe5-70f0-11dd-b4ad-806e6f6e6963}\\"
Access                        :
Automount                     : True
Availability                  :
BlockSize                     : 4096
BootVolume                    : True
Capacity                      : 158391595008
Caption                       : C:\
Compressed                    : False
ConfigManagerErrorCode        :
ConfigManagerUserConfig       :
CreationClassName             :
Description                   :
DeviceID                      : \\?\Volume{5a4a2fe5-70f0-11dd-b4ad-806e6f6e6963}
                                \
DirtyBitSet                   :
DriveLetter                   : C:
```

```
DriveType                     : 3
ErrorCleared                  :
ErrorDescription              :
ErrorMethodology              :
FileSystem                    : NTFS
FreeSpace                     : 23077511168
IndexingEnabled               : True
InstallDate                   :
Label                         :
LastErrorCode                 :
MaximumFileNameLength         : 255
Name                          : C:\
NumberOfBlocks                :
PageFilePresent               : False
PNPDeviceID                   :
PowerManagementCapabilities   :
PowerManagementSupported      :
Purpose                       :
QuotasEnabled                 :
QuotasIncomplete              :
QuotasRebuilding              :
SerialNumber                  : 1893548344
Status                        :
StatusInfo                    :
SupportsDiskQuotas            : True
SupportsFileBasedCompression  : True
SystemCreationClassName       :
SystemName                    : MRED1
SystemVolume                  : False
```

If you return to the error message generated by the earlier queries, the InvalidOperation CategoryInfo field might cause you to reconsider the backslash. Your earlier attempts to escape the backslash were on the right track. The problem revolves around the strange mixture of the WMI Query Language (WQL) syntax and Windows PowerShell syntax. The –*filter* parameter is definitely Windows PowerShell syntax, but you must supply a string that conforms to WQL dialect inside this parameter. This is why you use the equal sign for an operator instead of the Windows PowerShell –*eq* operator when you are inside the quotation marks of the –*filter* parameter. To escape the backslash in the WQL syntax, you must use another backslash as found in C or C++ syntax. The following code filters out the drive based on the name of the drive:

```
Get-WmiObject -Class win32_volume -Filter "Name = 'c:\\'"
```

> **IMPORTANT**   Use of the backslash to escape another backslash is a frustrating factor when using WMI. While our documentation in MSDN is improving, we still have a way to go in this arena. Because this WMI class does not behave as you might expect, I have filed a documentation bug for the *name* property of the *Win32_Volume* class. The result will be an additional note added to the description of the property. I have since found a few more places where the backslash is used as an escape character, and I will file bugs on them as well.

As a best practice, you can write a script to return the WMI information from the *WIN32_Volume* class and hide the escape details from the user. Use the *Get-Volume* function that comes with Windows 8 and above. The function accepts multiple command-line parameters, two of which are –*driveletter* and –*cimsession*. The drive is supplied as a drive letter without a colon. By default, the function returns information from all volumes on the local computer. In the *Get-Volume* function, the –*driveletter* value is a single letter. It does not need to be quoted, nor does it need a colon. The cimsession parameter accepts a computer name or an actual CIM session. The GetVolume.ps1 script is shown here.

**GetVolume.ps1**

```
Get-Volume -DriveLetter 'c' -CimSession client1
```

If you need to work in a cross-domain situation, you need to pass credentials to the remote computer. The *Get-Volume* function does not contain the –*credential* parameter. But because it accepts a CIM session, you can still pass credentials.

To do this, first create a CIM session by using the New-CimSession cmdlet while specifying the credentials and the computer name. Use the CIM session when calling the *Get-Volume* function to make the remote connection and return the information. This technique appears in the GetVolumeWithCredentials.ps1 script shown here.

**GetVolumeWithCredentials.ps1**

```
$cim = New-CimSession -Credential iammred\administrator -ComputerName client1
Get-Volume -CimSession $cim
```

## Choosing the right script methodology

Luis Canastreiro, Premier Field Engineer
*Microsoft Corporation, Portugal*

When I am writing a script, often there are many ways of accomplishing the same task. For example, if I am writing a VBScript, I prefer to use a Component Object Model (COM) object rather than shelling out and calling an external executable, because COM is native to VBScript. The same principle holds when I am writing a Windows PowerShell script. I prefer to use the .NET Framework classes if a Windows PowerShell cmdlet is not available because PowerShell is built on the .NET Framework.

Of course, my number-one preference is to use a cmdlet if it is available to me because a cmdlet will hide the complexity of dealing directly with the .NET Framework. By this I mean that there are some .NET Framework classes that at first glance appear to be simple. However, when you begin to use them, you realize that they contain complicated constructors. If you are not an expert with that particular class, you can make a mistake that will not be realized until after much testing. If a cmdlet offers the required features and if it solves my problem, the cmdlet is my first choice.

For example, there are several ways to read and write to the registry. You can use the *regread* and *regwrite* VBScript methods, the *stdRegProv* WMI class, the .NET Framework classes, or even various command-line utilities to gain access to the registry. My favorite method of working with the registry is to use the Windows PowerShell registry provider and the various `*-item` and `*-itemproperty` cmdlets. These cmdlets are very easy to use, and I need only to open the Windows PowerShell shell to accomplish everything I need to do with these cmdlets.

When I am writing a new script, I always like to create small generic functions, which offer a number of advantages. These functions make it easy for me to test the script while I am in the process of writing it. I need call only the function or functions on which I am working. I can leave the other code unfinished if I need to test it later. The functions are easy to reuse or to improve as time goes by. I run the script by creating a main function whose primary purpose is to initialize the environment and manage the global flow of the script by calling the appropriate functions at the proper time.

# Trapping the operating system version

Given the differences between the various versions of the Windows operating system, it is a best practice to check the version of the operating system prior to executing the script if you know that there could be version compatibility issues. There are several different methods to check version compatibility. In Chapter 4, "Identifying scripting opportunities," you used the *System.Environment* .NET Framework class to check the operating system version in the Get-OsVersion.ps1 script. While it is true that you can use remoting to obtain information from this class remotely, you can also achieve similar results by using the *Win32_OperatingSystem* WMI class. The advantage of this approach is that WMI automatically remotes.

The Get-Version.ps1 script accepts two command-line parameters, *computername* and *credential*. The computername parameter accepts an array of strings for the local or for the remote connections. The credential parameter must be a type of the *PSCredential* class. The easiest way to obtain a credential object is to use the Get-Credential cmdlet. The *Get-Version* function uses the *$PSBoundParameters* automatic variable to SPLAT the supplied parameters to the New-CimSession cmdlet. In this way, if you call the function and do not pass a *Credential* object, no error arises because an empty credential object does not pass to the cmdlet. If you do not pass a credential object, the cmdlet runs and impersonates the logged on user. In the same way, if no value supplies to the *ComputerName* parameter, the function runs against the localhost computer. By using the CIM cmdlets to provide the information from the *Win32_OperatingSystem* management object, the function can make a local connection using alternate credentials—a limitation of WMI since the earliest implementation. The entire *Win32_OperatingSystem* management object returns from the function. The *ProductType* property can be used to distinguish between a workstation and a server. The possible values for the *ProductType* property are shown in Table 6-1.

**TABLE 6-1** *Win32_OperatingSystem ProductType* values and associated meanings

| Value | Meaning |
| --- | --- |
| 1 | Workstation |
| 2 | Domain controller |
| 3 | Server |

After the version of the operating system is detected, you have a choice of how much information to return. For example, the caption property returns a string that identifies the operating system, but if a decision is required, you might be better off evaluating the actual version number. The complete Get-Version.ps1 script is shown here.

```
Get-Version.ps1

Function Get-Version
{
 <#
   .Synopsis
    This returns OS information from local or remote computers
   .Description
    This function returns OS information from local or remote computers
   .Example
    Get-Version -computername client1, server1 -credential (Get-Credential iammred\
administrator)
    Returns OS information from two remote computers using credentials supplied when
run
   .Example
    $cred = Get-Credential iammred\administrator
    Get-Version -computername client1, server1, edlt -credential $cred | select
caption, version
    Returns caption and version from two remote computers using credentials stored in
variable
   .Parameter Computername
    The name of target computer or computers
   .Parameter Credential
    The credentials to use to make the connection
   .Notes
    NAME:  Get-Version
    AUTHOR: ed wilson, msft
    LASTEDIT: 08/26/2013 13:25:38
    KEYWORDS: CIM, OS
    HSG:
   .Link
     Http://www.ScriptingGuys.com
 #Requires -Version 2.0
 #>
 Param([string[]]$computername,
 [System.Management.Automation.PSCredential]$credential)
 $cim = New-CimSession @PSBoundParameters
 Get-CimInstance -CimSession $cim -ClassName Win32_OperatingSystem
}
```

The Get-Version.ps1 script, when run, loads the *Get-Version* function into memory. The entire *Win32_OperatingSystem* management object returns from the function. It is therefore necessary to parse the returned information in the context of your particular application.

**Georges Maheu, Security Premier Field Engineer**
*Microsoft Corporation, Canada*

When I am working with Windows PowerShell, I mostly invest my time writing scripts. However, I will use the console to test syntax or to experiment. The thing to keep in mind is that Windows PowerShell can go from simple (using a cmdlet with no parameters) to complex scripts very quickly. Be careful when writing scripts, because what might seem like a simple script can easily peg a processor. For example, the following script might bring a single CPU computer to 100% CPU utilization: 1..2000 | ForEach-Object {Get-WmiObject win32_bios}; however, the following script will not: 1..2000 | ForEach-Object {Get-WmiObject win32_bios;start-sleep –milli 2}. A poorly written script can bring an old server to its knees.

## Lack of WMI support

Windows Management Instrumentation has been in existence since the days of Microsoft Windows NT 4.0. In the years since its introduction, every new version of Windows has added WMI classes and, at times, additional methods to existing WMI classes. One advantage of WMI is its relatively consistent approach to working with software and hardware. Another advantage of WMI is that it is a well-understood technology, and numerous examples of scripts can be found on the Internet. With improved support for WMI in Windows PowerShell 2.0, the introduction of the CIM cmdlets in Windows PowerShell 3.0, and the expanded support for CIM functions in Windows 8.1 and on Windows Server 2012 R2, there is very little that cannot be accomplished via Windows PowerShell that could be done by using VBScript. In fact, with the CIM-based functions, many configuration tasks can be accomplished with a single line command. Before you look at some of the issues in working with WMI from Windows PowerShell, let's review some basic WMI concepts.

WMI is sometimes referred to as a *hierarchical namespace*—so named because the layers build on one another like a Lightweight Directory Access Protocol (LDAP) directory used in Active Directory or the file system structure on your hard disk drive. Although it is true that WMI is a hierarchical namespace, the term doesn't really convey its richness. The WMI model contains three sections: resources, infrastructure, and consumers, which can be described as follows:

- **WMI resources**   Resources include anything that can be accessed by using WMI: the file system, networked components, event logs, files, folders, disks, Active Directory, and so on.

- **WMI infrastructure**  The infrastructure is composed of three parts: the WMI service, WMI repository, and WMI providers. Of these parts, WMI providers are most important because they provide the means for WMI to gather needed information.

- **WMI consumers**  A consumer "consumes" the data from WMI. A consumer can be a VBScript, an enterprise management software package, or some other tool or utility that executes WMI queries.

# Working with objects and namespaces

Let's return to the idea of a namespace introduced in the last section. You can think of a *namespace* as a way to organize or collect data related to similar items. Visualize an old-fashioned filing cabinet. Each drawer can represent a particular namespace. Inside each drawer are hanging folders that collect information related to a subset of what the drawer actually holds. For example, there is a drawer at home in my filing cabinet that is reserved for information related to my woodworking tools. Inside this particular drawer are hanging folders for my table saw, my planer, my joiner, my dust collector, and so on. In the folder for the table saw is information about the motor, the blades, and the various accessories I purchased for the saw (such as an over-arm blade guard).

The WMI namespace is organized in a similar fashion. The namespaces are the file cabinets. The providers are drawers in the file cabinet. The folders in the drawers of the file cabinet are the WMI classes. These namespaces are shown in Figure 6-1.

**FIGURE 6-1** WMI namespaces on Windows 8.1.

Namespaces contain objects, and these objects contain properties that you can manipulate. Let's use a WMI command to illustrate how the WMI namespace is organized. The Get-WmiObject cmdlet is used to make the connection into the WMI. The class argument is used to specify the *__Namespace* class, and the *namespace* argument is used to specify the level in the WMI namespace hierarchy. The Get-WmiObject line of code is shown here:

```
Get-WmiObject -class __Namespace -namespace root |
Select-Object -property name
```

When the preceding code is run, the following result appears on a Windows Vista computer:

```
name
----
subscription
DEFAULT
MicrosoftDfs
CIMV2
Cli
nap
SECURITY
SecurityCenter2
RSOP
WMI
directory
Policy
ServiceModel
SecurityCenter
Microsoft
aspnet
```

You can use the RecursiveWMINameSpaceListing.ps1 script to get an idea of the number and variety of WMI namespaces that exist on your computer, which is a great way to explore and learn about WMI. The entire contents of the RecursiveWMINameSpaceListing.ps1 script is shown here.

```
RecursiveWMINameSpaceListing.ps1

Function Get-WmiNameSpace($namespace, $computer)
{
 Get-WmiObject -class __NameSpace -computer $computer '
 -namespace $namespace -ErrorAction "SilentlyContinue" |
 Foreach-Object '
 -Process '
   {
     $subns = Join-Path -Path $_.__namespace -ChildPath $_.name
     $subns
     $script:i ++
     Get-WmiNameSpace -namespace $subNS -computer $computer
   }
```

```
} #end Get-WmiNameSpace

# *** Entry Point ***

$script:i = 0
$namespace = "root"
$computer = "LocalHost"
"Obtaining WMI Namespaces from $computer ..."
Get-WmiNameSpace -namespace $namespace -computer $computer
"There are $script:i namespaces on $computer"
```

The output from the RecursiveWMINameSpaceListing.ps1 script is shown here from the same Windows Vista computer that produced the earlier namespace listing. You can see that there is a rather intricate hierarchy of namespaces that exists on a modern operating system.

```
Obtaining WMI Namespaces from LocalHost ...
ROOT\subscription
ROOT\subscription\ms_409
ROOT\DEFAULT
ROOT\DEFAULT\ms_409
ROOT\MicrosoftDfs
ROOT\MicrosoftDfs\ms_409
ROOT\CIMV2
ROOT\CIMV2\Security
ROOT\CIMV2\Security\MicrosoftTpm
ROOT\CIMV2\ms_409
ROOT\CIMV2\TerminalServices
ROOT\CIMV2\TerminalServices\ms_409
ROOT\CIMV2\Applications
ROOT\CIMV2\Applications\Games
ROOT\Cli
ROOT\Cli\MS_409
ROOT\nap
ROOT\SECURITY
ROOT\SecurityCenter2
ROOT\RSOP
ROOT\RSOP\User
ROOT\RSOP\User\S_1_5_21_540299044_341859138_929407116_1133
ROOT\RSOP\User\S_1_5_21_540299044_341859138_929407116_1129
ROOT\RSOP\User\S_1_5_21_540299044_341859138_929407116_1118
ROOT\RSOP\User\S_1_5_21_918056312_2952985149_2686913973_500
ROOT\RSOP\User\S_1_5_21_135816822_1724403450_2350888535_500
ROOT\RSOP\User\ms_409
ROOT\RSOP\User\S_1_5_21_540299044_341859138_929407116_500
ROOT\RSOP\Computer
ROOT\RSOP\Computer\ms_409
ROOT\WMI
ROOT\WMI\ms_409
ROOT\directory
ROOT\directory\LDAP
ROOT\directory\LDAP\ms_409
```

```
ROOT\Policy
ROOT\Policy\ms_409
ROOT\ServiceModel
ROOT\SecurityCenter
ROOT\Microsoft
ROOT\Microsoft\HomeNet
ROOT\aspnet
There are 42 namespaces on LocalHost
```

So, what does all of this mean? It means that, on a Windows Vista-based computer, there are dozens of different namespaces from which you can pull information about your computer. Understanding that the different namespaces exist is the first step to begin navigating in WMI to find the information you need. Often, students and people who are new to Windows PowerShell work on a WMI script to make the script perform a certain action, which is a great way to learn scripting. However, what they often do not know is which namespace they need to connect to so that they can accomplish their task. When I tell them which namespace to work with, they sometimes reply, "It is fine for you, but how do I know that the such and such namespace even exists?" By using the RecursiveWMINameSpaceListing .ps1 script, you can easily generate a list of namespaces installed on a particular machine and, armed with that information, search MSDN to find information about those namespaces. Or, if you like to explore, you can move on to the next section, "Listing WMI providers."

---

### INSIDE TRACK

**Jason Walker, Premier Field Engineer**
*Microsoft Corporation*

Supporting enterprise customers often requires me to come up with solutions to handle large amounts of data. When dealing with large data, errors like 'System .OutOfMemoryException' are commonplace. How do we write our scripts in a way that we don't encounter these errors? I always tell my customers, "Stay away from big objects."

The two most common things I see are storing objects so that they can be displayed all at once and collecting all the objects to be processed before processing the very first one.

Here is an example of storing objects so they are displayed at once:

```
Results = @()
$Servers = Get-Content ServerList.txt


foreach($Server in $Servers)
{
```

```
        $wmi = Get-WmiObject -ComputerName $Server -Class Win32_
OperatingSystem

    $Results += New-Object -TypeName PSObject -Property @{
        ComputerName = $wmi.__Server
        OperatingSystem = $wmi.caption
        }
}


$Results
```

In the preceding example *$Results* is appended to on each iteration of the *foreach* loop. If *$Servers* contains only 10 computer names, this example will work just fine. But if *$Servers* contains 1,000 server names, the script will consume a lot of memory and appear to be very slow because the results will not be displayed until the last server is contacted. The fix for this is very simple: Do away with the *$Results* variable altogether:

```
$Servers = "mail01","mail02","mbx01","mbx02"

foreach($Server in $Servers)
{
    $wmi = Get-WmiObject -ComputerName $Server -Class Win32_
OperatingSystem

    New-Object -TypeName PSObject -Property @{
        ComputerName = $wmi.__Server
        OperatingSystem = $wmi.caption
        }
}
```

Now the script will return results as they are being processed, which makes the script appear faster, and the code will consume very little memory.

Collecting all the objects to be processed before processing the very first one has the same effect as my first example. It will consume lots of memory. I had a customer whose users were reporting NDRs to external recipients. The customer's Exchange admin wanted a script that could add an SMTP address to an external contact to eliminate the NDRs. The script that the admin wrote worked great when running it against one contact at a time. However, the admin wanted to be proactive and run it against all 100,000 contacts in the address book, which consumed all the server's RAM and made it unresponsive. The fix is simple: Write the script to accept input from the pipeline. With input coming in from the pipeline, the input is being processed as it comes in and then disposed of, versus storing all the input in one huge object array. This can be proven in the following simple examples:

```
Example 1: ForEach-Object -InputObject (dir c:\ -Recurse) -Process {$_.
Fullname}
```

```
Example 2:          dir c:\ -Recurse | select Fullname
```

In Example 1, all the file paths have to be collected before they are consumed in the script block. When they are run, there is pause before any results are returned. When Example 2 is run, results are displayed instantly.

To get back to the customer's issue.

Resource intensive:

```
Set-x500Address -Identity (Get-MailContact -ResultSize Unlimited)
```

In the preceding example, all 100,000 contacts need to be collected before the first one can be processed.

Resource efficient:

```
Get-MailContact -ResultSize Unlimted | Set-X500Address
```

When using the pipe, as in the preceding example, the input is being processed as it comes in.

When writing scripts, we need to think about what the code is doing because Windows PowerShell will use a lot of resources if we let it.

## Listing WMI providers

Understanding the namespace assists the network administrator with judiciously applying WMI scripting to his or her network duties. However, as mentioned earlier, to access information via WMI, you must have access to a WMI provider. After the provider is implemented, you can gain access to the information that is made available.

Providers in WMI are all based on a template class or on a system class named __provider. With this information, you can look for instances of the __provider class and obtain a list of all providers that reside in your WMI namespace, which is exactly what the Get-WMIProviders .ps1 script accomplishes.

The Get-WMIProviders.ps1 script begins by assigning the string "root\cimv2" to the $wmiNS variable. This value is used with the Get-WmiObject cmdlet to specify where the WMI query takes place. It should be noted that the WMI *root\cimv2* namespace is the default WMI namespace on every Windows operating system since Microsoft Windows 2000.

The Get-WmiObject cmdlet is used to query WMI. The class provider is used to limit the WMI query to the *__provider* class. The namespace argument tells the Get-WmiObject cmdlet to look only in the *root\cimv2* WMI namespace. The array of objects returned from the *Get-WmiObject* cmdlet is pipelined into the Sort-Object cmdlet, where the listing of objects is alphabetized based on the *name* property. When this process is complete, the reorganized objects are then passed to the Format-List cmdlet, where the name of each provider is printed. The complete Get-WmiProviders.ps1 script is shown here.

```
Get-WmiProviders.ps1

Function Get-WmiProviders(
                          $namespace="root\cimv2",
                          $computer="localhost"
                          )
{
 Get-WmiObject -class __Provider -namespace $namespace '
 -computername $computer |
 Sort-Object -property Name |
 Select-Object -property Name
} #end Get-WmiProviders

Get-WmiProviders
```

# Working with WMI classes

In addition to working with namespaces, the inquisitive network administrator will also want to explore the concept of classes. In WMI parlance, there are core classes, common classes, and dynamic classes. *Core classes* represent managed objects that apply to all areas of management. These classes provide a basic vocabulary for analyzing and describing managed systems. Two examples of core classes are parameters and the *System.Security* class. *Common classes* are extensions to the core classes and represent managed objects that apply to specific management areas. However, common classes are independent of a particular implementation or technology. *CIM_UnitaryComputerSystem* is an example of a common class. Core and common classes are not used as often by network administrators because they serve as templates from which other classes are derived.

Therefore, many of the classes stored in *root\cimv2* are abstract classes and are used as templates. However, a few classes in *root\cimv2* are dynamic classes that are used to retrieve actual information. What is important to remember about *dynamic classes* is that instances of a dynamic class are generated by a provider and are therefore more likely to retrieve "live" data from the system.

To produce a simple listing of WMI classes, you can use the `Get-WmiObject` cmdlet and specify the list argument as shown here:

```
Get-WmiObject -list
```

A partial output from the previous command is shown here:

```
Win32_TSGeneralSetting              Win32_TSPermissionsSetting
Win32_TSClientSetting               Win32_TSEnvironmentSetting
Win32_TSNetworkAdapterListSetting   Win32_TSLogonSetting
Win32_TSSessionSetting              Win32_DisplayConfiguration
Win32_COMSetting                    Win32_ClassicCOMClassSetting
Win32_DCOMApplicationSetting        Win32_MSIResource
Win32_ServiceControl                Win32_Property
```

---

### NOTES FROM THE FIELD

## Working with services

**Clint Huffman, Senior Premier Field Engineer (PFE)**
*Microsoft Corporation*

I travel a great deal, and, unfortunately, the battery life on my laptop isn't spectacular. Therefore, I've spent a fair amount of time discovering which services on my computer are consuming the I/O on my hard drive—most likely the largest consumer of battery power other than my monitor. I identified numerous services that I wouldn't need on a flight, such as antivirus software, Windows Search, the Offline Files service, ReadyBoost, and so on. Because I was stopping and starting these services quite often, I decided to script the services.

WMI is a powerful object model that allows scripting languages, such as VBScript and Windows PowerShell, to perform tasks that were once available only to hardened C++ developers. Furthermore, far less code is needed to perform these tasks, because scripting them makes automation relatively easy.

So, to begin this script, I need to select the correct services. WMI uses a SQL-like syntax named WMI Query Language (WQL); it is not named SQL syntax, because WQL has some odd quirks that are specific to WMI. I want my WQL query to return the Windows services that I identified earlier as users of frequent disk I/O, such as the Offline Files service, the ReadyBoost service, my antivirus services that begin with "Microsoft ForeFront" (Microsoft Forefront Client Security Antimalware Service and Microsoft Forefront Client Security State Assessment Service), and last, my personal file indexer, Windows Search.

```
$WQL = "SELECT Name, State, Caption FROM Win32_Service WHERE Caption LIKE
'Microsoft ForeFront%' OR Name = 'WSearch' OR Caption = 'Offline Files'
OR Caption = 'ReadyBoost'"
Get-WmiObject -Query $WQL
```

In my case, this script returns the following services as follows:

```
Offline Files
ReadyBoost
Microsoft Forefront Client Security Antimalware Service
Microsoft Forefront Client Security State Assessment Service
Windows Search
```

The *Caption* property is the text you see when you bring up Control Panel, Services, and the *name* property is the short name of the service that you might be more familiar with when using the command-line tools "Net Start" and "Net Stop." Finally, the *State* property tells me whether the service is running.

The WHERE clause allows me to limit the information that is returned. For example, if I don't use the WHERE clause, I receive all of the services as objects. This is nice if you want to know what services are on a computer, but it's not helpful when you simply want to shut down a few of them. For more information about WQL, go to "Querying with WQL" at *http://msdn.microsoft.com/en-us/library/aa392902.aspx*.

Because the *Query* parameter always returns a *collection* object, I need to enumerate the *Query* parameter to work with each item individually. This process is similar to receiving a package in the mail in a large cardboard box: before I can use what's inside, I need to open the package. This is the point in the process in which the *Foreach* flow control statement is used. The *Foreach* statement allows me to work with one item at a time (for example, a service), which is similar to taking one item out of the cardboard box at a time. In this case, I have the Get-WmiObject cmdlet's return values go into a variable named *$CollectionOfServices* (my cardboard box). Next, I use the *Foreach* statement to work with each service, whereby the *$Service* variable becomes each service object in turn. The following code is the same as the previous code but with the addition of a *Foreach* loop.

```
$WQL = "SELECT Name, State, Caption FROM Win32_Service WHERE Caption LIKE
'Microsoft ForeFront%' OR Name = 'WSearch' OR Caption = 'Offline Files'
OR Caption = 'ReadyBoost'"
$CollectionOfServices = Get-WmiObject -Query $WQL
Foreach ($Service in $CollectionOfServices)
{
    $Service.Caption
}
```

Now that I can select specific services that I want to shut down, let's actually shut them down. I can do this by using the *StopService()* method as follows:

```
 $WQL = "SELECT Name, State, Caption FROM Win32_Service WHERE Caption
LIKE 'Microsoft ForeFront%' OR Name = 'WSearch' OR Caption = 'Offline
Files' OR Caption = 'ReadyBoost'"
$CollectionOfServices = Get-WmiObject -Query $WQL
Foreach ($Service in $CollectionOfServices)
{
    $Service.Caption
    $Service.StopService()
}
```

If my services don't actually stop, it is most likely because I don't have administrator rights to my customer or, if I am on Windows Vista, I need to run the script in an elevated Windows PowerShell command prompt. To make an elevated Windows PowerShell command prompt, right-click the PowerShell icon, select Run As Administrator, and then try the script again.

Great! My unnecessary services are stopped. However, sometimes the services can be a bit tenacious and start up again the first chance they get. How do I hold them down? By setting them to disabled. How do I do that? By using the *ChangeStartMode()* method with the argument/parameter of "Disabled," as follows:

```
$WQL = "SELECT Name, State, Caption FROM Win32_Service WHERE Caption LIKE
'Microsoft ForeFront%' OR Name = 'WSearch' OR Caption = 'Offline Files'
OR Caption = 'ReadyBoost'"
$CollectionOfServices = Get-WmiObject -Query $WQL
Foreach ($Service in $CollectionOfServices)
{
    $Service.Caption
    $Service.StopService()
    $Service.ChangeStartMode("Disabled")
}
```

Now we're talking! Those pesky services are down for the count.

I've had my fun, my flight is over, and now I need to connect to my corporate network. Corporate policy does not allow me to connect unless my antivirus service is running. No problem. Two slight modifications to the script and the services are running again as follows:

```
$WQL = "SELECT Name, State, Caption FROM Win32_Service WHERE Caption LIKE
'Microsoft ForeFront%' OR Name = 'WSearch' OR Caption = 'Offline Files'
OR Caption = 'ReadyBoost'"
```

```
$CollectionOfServices = Get-WmiObject -Query $WQL
Foreach ($Service in $CollectionOfServices)
{
    $Service.Caption
    $Service.StartService()
    $Service.ChangeStartMode("Automatic")
}
```

I replaced the *StopService()* method with *StartService()* and replaced the argument of the *ChangeStartMode()* method to "Automatic".

You might be thinking that this procedure is all well and good for your laptop battery, but what about doing massive restarts of services? Well, a great modification that you can make to the script is to run it against remote servers. For example, let's assume that you need to restart the services in a farm of 10 Web servers. You can simply modify the script slightly by adding the –*ComputerName* argument.

```
$WQL = "SELECT Name, State, Caption FROM Win32_Service WHERE Caption LIKE
'Microsoft ForeFront%' OR Name = 'WSearch' OR Caption = 'Offline Files'
OR Caption = 'ReadyBoost'"
$CollectionOfServices = Get-WmiObject -Query $WQL -ComputerName
demoserver
Foreach ($Service in $CollectionOfServices)
{
    $Service.Caption
    $Service.StartService()
    $Service.ChangeStartMode("Automatic")
}
```

These scripts have served me well, and I hope they help you too.

## Changing settings

For all of the benefits of using WMI, there are still many frustrating limitations. While WMI is good at retrieving information, it is not always very good at changing that information. The following example illustrates this point. The *Win32_Desktop* WMI class provides information about desktop settings as shown here:

```
PS C:\> Get-WmiObject Win32_Desktop

__GENUS             : 2
__CLASS             : Win32_Desktop
__SUPERCLASS        : CIM_Setting
__DYNASTY           : CIM_Setting
__RELPATH           : Win32_Desktop.Name="NT AUTHORITY\\SYSTEM"
__PROPERTY_COUNT    : 21
```

```
__DERIVATION        : {CIM_Setting}
__SERVER            : MRED1
__NAMESPACE         : root\cimv2
__PATH              : \\MRED1\root\cimv2:Win32_Desktop.Name="NT AUTHORITY\\
                      SYSTEM"
BorderWidth         : 1
Caption             :
CoolSwitch          :
CursorBlinkRate     : 500
Description         :
DragFullWindows     : True
GridGranularity     :
IconSpacing         :
IconTitleFaceName   : Segoe UI
IconTitleSize       : 9
IconTitleWrap       : True
Name                : NT AUTHORITY\SYSTEM
Pattern             : (None)
ScreenSaverActive   : True
ScreenSaverExecutable : C:\Windows\system32\logon.scr
ScreenSaverSecure   : True
ScreenSaverTimeout  : 600
SettingID           :
Wallpaper           :
WallpaperStretched  : False
WallpaperTiled      :
```

As you can see from the properties and values that are returned from the Get-WmiObject cmdlet, much of the information is valuable. Items such as screen saver time-out values and secure screen saver are routine concerns to many network administrators. While it is true that these values can and, in most cases, should be set via Group Policy, there are times when network administrators want the ability to change these values via script. If you use the Get-Member cmdlet to examine the properties of the *Win32_Desktop* WMI class, you are greeted with the following information:

```
PS C:\> Get-WmiObject Win32_Desktop | Get-Member
   TypeName: System.Management.ManagementObject#root\cimv2\Win32_Desktop

Name                MemberType   Definition
----                ----------   ----------
BorderWidth         Property     System.UInt32 BorderWidth {get;set;}
Caption             Property     System.String Caption {get;set;}
CoolSwitch          Property     System.Boolean CoolSwitch {get;set;}
CursorBlinkRate     Property     System.UInt32 CursorBlinkRate {get;set;}
Description         Property     System.String Description {get;set;}
DragFullWindows     Property     System.Boolean DragFullWindows {get;set;}
GridGranularity     Property     System.UInt32 GridGranularity {get;set;}
IconSpacing         Property     System.UInt32 IconSpacing {get;set;}
IconTitleFaceName   Property     System.String IconTitleFaceName {get;set;}
IconTitleSize       Property     System.UInt32 IconTitleSize {get;set;}
IconTitleWrap       Property     System.Boolean IconTitleWrap {get;set;}
Name                Property     System.String Name {get;set;}
Pattern             Property     System.String Pattern {get;set;}
ScreenSaverActive   Property     System.Boolean ScreenSaverActive {get;set;}
```

```
ScreenSaverExecutable  Property         System.String ScreenSaverExecutable {get;...
ScreenSaverSecure      Property         System.Boolean ScreenSaverSecure {get;set;}
ScreenSaverTimeout     Property         System.UInt32 ScreenSaverTimeout {get;set;}
SettingID              Property         System.String SettingID {get;set;}
Wallpaper              Property         System.String Wallpaper {get;set;}
WallpaperStretched     Property         System.Boolean WallpaperStretched {get;set;}
WallpaperTiled         Property         System.Boolean WallpaperTiled {get;set;}
__CLASS                Property         System.String __CLASS {get;set;}
__DERIVATION           Property         System.String[] __DERIVATION {get;set;}
__DYNASTY              Property         System.String __DYNASTY {get;set;}
__GENUS                Property         System.Int32 __GENUS {get;set;}
__NAMESPACE            Property         System.String __NAMESPACE {get;set;}
__PATH                 Property         System.String __PATH {get;set;}
__PROPERTY_COUNT       Property         System.Int32 __PROPERTY_COUNT {get;set;}
__RELPATH              Property         System.String __RELPATH {get;set;}
__SERVER               Property         System.String __SERVER {get;set;}
__SUPERCLASS           Property         System.String __SUPERCLASS {get;set;}
ConvertFromDateTime    ScriptMethod System.Object ConvertFromDateTime();
ConvertToDateTime      ScriptMethod System.Object ConvertToDateTime();
```

When you use the *–filter* parameter to obtain a specific instance of the *Win32_Desktop* WMI class and store it in a variable, you can then directly access the properties of the class. In this example, you need to escape the backslash that is used as a separator between NT Authority and System, as shown here:

```
PS C:\> $desktop = Get-WmiObject Win32_Desktop -Filter '
>> "name = 'NT AUTHORITY\\SYSTEM'"
```

After you have access to a specific instance of the WMI class, you can then assign a new value for the *ScreenSaverTimeout* parameter. As shown here, the value is updated immediately.

```
PS C:\> $Desktop.ScreenSaverTimeout = 300
PS C:\> $Desktop.ScreenSaverTimeout
300
```

However, if you resubmit the WMI query, you see that the *ScreenSaverTimeout* property is not updated. The get:set that is reported by the Get-Member cmdlet is related to the copy of the object that is returned by the WMI query and not to the actual instance of the object represented by the WMI class, as shown here:

```
PS C:\> $desktop = Get-WmiObject Win32_Desktop -Filter '
>> "name = 'NT AUTHORITY\\SYSTEM'"
>>
PS C:\> $Desktop.ScreenSaverTimeout
600
```

## Modifying values through the registry

The Set-SaverTimeout.ps1 script uses three parameters, but only one of them is commonly modified—the timeoutvalue parameter. This parameter configures the screen saver time-out value. Because the *Set-ScreenSaverTimeout* function uses the *[cmdletbinding()]* attribute, you get access to the common parameters such as verbose. Note that nothing further needs to be done to gain access to the common parameters. The `Write-Verbose` cmdlet displays the verbose stream only when calling the function with the *–Verbose* switch. If the *–Verbose* switch does not appear when calling the function, no verbose stream displays. This means that it is possible to use the *Set-ScreenSaverTimeOut* function and display no output–something that is ideal for logon scripts, for example.

Because the function modifies the registry, it is not a bad idea to use a *transaction*. Using a transaction means that the change successfully completes, or else it can be rolled back. Beginning a transaction is easy; use the `Start-Transaction` cmdlet as appears here:

```
Start-Transaction
```

Then, when initiating the change, use the *–UseTransaction* switch. This command appears here:

```
Set-ItemProperty -Path $path -name $name -value $timeOutValue -UseTransaction
```

This particular function does not actually roll back the transaction, but it would be easy enough to do so if required. By using the *–Verbose* switch, the beginning value displays as well as the newly changed value of the *ScreenSaver* time-out value. To see what the new value will be if the transaction is completed, it is necessary to use the *–UseTransaction* switch when using `Get-ItemProperty`. This command appears here:

```
Get-ItemProperty -path $path -name $name -UseTransaction
```

After everything completes successfully, use the `Complete-Transaction` cmdlet, as shown here:

```
Complete-Transaction
```

Calling the function with the *–Verbose* parameter is shown here:

```
Set-ScreenSaverTimeOut -timeOutValue 600 -Verbose
```

When the function runs, the output in Figure 6-2 appears.

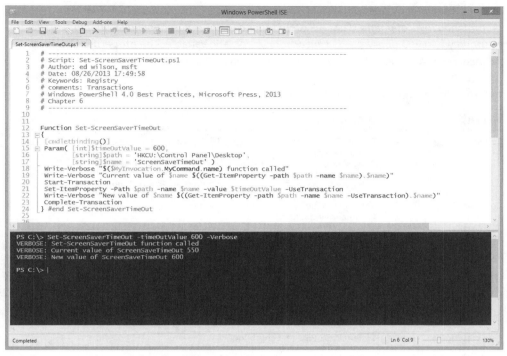

Windows PowerShell ISE

```
File  Edit  View  Tools  Debug  Add-ons  Help

Set-ScreenSaverTimeOut.ps1 ×

  1   # ------------------------------------------------------------------
  2   # Script: Set-ScreenSaverTimeOut.ps1
  3   # Author: ed wilson, msft
  4   # Date: 08/26/2013 17:49:58
  5   # Keywords: Registry
  6   # comments: Transactions
  7   # Windows PowerShell 4.0 Best Practices, Microsoft Press, 2013
  8   # Chapter 6
  9   # ------------------------------------------------------------------
 10
 11
 12   Function Set-ScreenSaverTimeOut
 13 □ {
 14     [cmdletbinding()]
 15 □   Param( [int]$timeOutValue = 600,
 16           [string]$path = 'HKCU:\Control Panel\Desktop',
 17           [string]$name = 'ScreenSaveTimeOut' )
 18     Write-Verbose "$($MyInvocation.MyCommand.name) function called"
 19     Write-Verbose "Current value of $name $((Get-ItemProperty -path $path -name $name).$name)"
 20     Start-Transaction
 21     Set-ItemProperty -Path $path -name $name -value $timeOutValue -UseTransaction
 22     Write-Verbose "New value of $name $((Get-ItemProperty -path $path -name $name -UseTransaction).$name)"
 23     Complete-Transaction
 24   } #end Set-ScreenSaverTimeOut
 25
 26
```

```
PS C:\> Set-ScreenSaverTimeOut -timeOutValue 600 -Verbose
VERBOSE: Set-ScreenSaverTimeOut function called
VERBOSE: Current value of ScreenSaveTimeOut 550
VERBOSE: New value of ScreenSaveTimeOut 600

PS C:\> |
```

Completed                                                    Ln 6 Col 9          130%

**FIGURE 6-2**  Detailed information is easily obtained when the script implements a verbose parameter.

Instead of using Write-Verbose, the function could have used Write-Debug. The Write-Debug cmdlet automatically formats the text with yellow and black colors (this is configurable, however), and it writes text to the console only if you tell it to do so. By default, Write-Debug does not print anything to the console, which means that you do not need to remove the Write-Debug statements prior to deploying the script. The *$DebugPreference* automatic variable is used to control the behavior of the Write-Debug cmdlet. By default, *$DebugPreference* is set to *SilentlyContinue* so that when it encounters a Write-Debug cmdlet, Windows PowerShell either skips over the cmdlet or silently continues to the next line. You can configure the *$DebugPreference* variable with one of four values defined in the *System .Management.Automation.ActionPreference* enumeration class. To see the possible enumeration values, you can either look for them on MSDN or use the *GetNames* static method from the *System.Enum* .NET Framework class as shown here:

```
PS C:\> [enum]::GetNames("System.Management.Automation.ActionPreference")
SilentlyContinue
Stop
Continue
Inquire
```

The Write-Debug cmdlet is used to print the value of the *name* property from the *System .Management.Automation.ScriptInfo* object. The *System.Management.Automation.ScriptInfo* object is obtained by querying the *MyCommand* property of the *System.Management* *.Automation.InvocationInfo* class. A *System.Management.Automation.InvocationInfo* object is returned when you query the *$MyInvocation* automatic variable. The properties of *System* *.Management.Automation.InvocationInfo* are shown in Table 6-2.

**TABLE 6-2** Properties of the *System.Management.Automation.InvocationInfo* class

| Property | Definition |
|---|---|
| BoundParameters | System.Collections.Generic.Dictionary`2[[System.String, mscorlib, Version=2.0.0.0, Culture=neutral, PublicKeyToken=b77a5c561934e089],[System.Object, mscorlib, Version=2.0.0.0, Culture=neutral, PublicKeyToken=b77a5c561934e089]] BoundParameters {get;} |
| CommandOrigin | System.Management.Automation.CommandOrigin CommandOrigin {get;} |
| ExpectingInput | System.Boolean ExpectingInput {get;} |
| InvocationName | System.String InvocationName {get;} |
| Line | System.String Line {get;} |
| MyCommand | System.Management.Automation.CommandInfo MyCommand {get;} |
| OffsetInLine | System.Int32 OffsetInLine {get;} |
| PipelineLength | System.Int32 PipelineLength {get;} |
| PipelinePosition | System.Int32 PipelinePosition {get;} |
| PositionMessage | System.String PositionMessage {get;} |
| ScriptLineNumber | System.Int32 ScriptLineNumber {get;} |
| ScriptName | System.String ScriptName {get;} |
| UnboundArguments | System.Collections.Generic.List`1[[System.Object, mscorlib, Version=2.0.0.0, Culture=neutral, PublicKeyToken=b77a5c561934e089]] UnboundArguments {get;} |

The `Write-Debug` commands can be modified to include any of the properties you deem helpful to aid in troubleshooting. These properties become even more helpful when you are working with the *System.Management.Automation.ScriptInfo* object, whose properties are shown in Table 6-3.

**TABLE 6-3** Properties of the *System.Management.Automation.ScriptInfo* object

| Property | Definition |
|---|---|
| CommandType | System.Management.Automation.CommandTypes CommandType {get;} |
| Definition | System.String Definition {get;} |
| Module | System.Management.Automation.PSModuleInfo Module {get;} |
| ModuleName | System.String ModuleName {get;} |
| Name | System.String Name {get;} |

| Property | Definition |
|---|---|
| Parameters | System.Collections.Generic.Dictionary`2[[System.String, mscorlib,Version=2.0.0.0, Culture=neutral, PublicKeyToken=b77a5c561934e089], [System.Management.Automation.ParameterMetadata, System.Management.Automation, Version=1.0.0.0, Culture=neutral, PublicKeyToken=31bf3856ad364e35]] Parameters {get;} |
| ParameterSets | System.Collections.ObjectModel.ReadOnlyCollection`1 [[System.Management.Automation.CommandParameterSetInfo, System.Management.Automation, Version=1.0.0.0, Culture=neutral, PublicKeyToken=31bf3856ad364e35]] ParameterSets {get;} |
| ScriptBlock | System.Management.Automation.ScriptBlock ScriptBlock {get;} |
| Visibility | System.Management.Automation.SessionStateEntryVisibility Visibility {get;set;} |

The completed Set-SaverTimeOut.ps1 is shown here.

```
Set-SaverTimeOut.ps1

Function Set-ScreenSaverTimeOut
{
 [cmdletbinding()]
 Param( [int]$timeOutValue = 600,
        [string]$path = 'HKCU:\Control Panel\Desktop',
        [string]$name = 'ScreenSaveTimeOut' )
 Write-Verbose "$($MyInvocation.MyCommand.name) function called"
 Write-Verbose "Current value of $name $((Get-ItemProperty -path $path -name
$name).$name)"
 Start-Transaction
 Set-ItemProperty -Path $path -name $name -value $timeOutValue -UseTransaction
 Write-Verbose "New value of $name $((Get-ItemProperty -path $path -name $name
-UseTransaction).$name)"
 Complete-Transaction
} #end Set-ScreenSaverTimeOut
```

# Lack of .NET Framework support

The ability to work with the .NET Framework from within Windows PowerShell is very exciting. Because Windows PowerShell itself is a .NET Framework application, access to the .NET Framework is very direct and natural. At times, the question is not what can be done with .NET Framework classes, but rather what cannot be done. The constructors for some of the .NET Framework classes can be both confusing and complicated. A *constructor* is used to create an instance of a class; in many cases, you must first create an instance of a class prior to using the classes. However, sometimes you do not need a constructor at all, and these methods are called static. There are both static methods and static properties.

# Use of static methods and properties

Static methods and properties are members that are always available. To use a static method, you place the class name in square brackets and separate the method name by two colons. An example is the *tan* method from the *System.Math* class. The *tan* method is used to find the tangent of a number. As shown here, you can use the *tan* static method from the *System .Math* class to find the tangent of a 45-degree angle:

```
PS C:\> [system.math]::tan(45)
1.61977519054386
```

When referring to *System.Math*, the word *system* is used to represent the namespace in which the "*math* class" is found. In most cases, you can drop the word *system* if you want to and the process will work exactly the same. When working at the command line, you might want to save some typing and drop the word *system*, but I consider it to be a best practice to always include the word *system* in a script. If you drop the word *system*, the command looks like the following code:

```
PS C:\> [math]::tan(45)
1.61977519054386
```

You can use the Get-Member cmdlet with the *static* switched parameter to obtain the members of the *System.Math* .NET Framework class. To do this, the command looks like the following example:

```
[math] | Get-Member –static
```

The static members of the *System.Math* class are shown in Table 6-4. These static methods are very important because you can perform most of the functionality from the class by using them. For example, there is no *tan* function built into Windows PowerShell. If you want the tangent of an angle, you must use either the static methods from *System.Math* or write your own tangent function. This occurs by design. To perform these mathematical computations, you need to use the .NET Framework. Rather than being a liability, the .NET Framework is a tremendous asset because it is a mature technology and is well-documented.

**TABLE 6-4** Members of the *System.Math* class

| Name | MemberType | Definition |
|---|---|---|
| Abs | Method | static System.SByte Abs(SByte value) static System.Int16 Abs(Int16 value) static System.Int32 Abs(Int32 value) static System.Int64 Abs(Int64 value) static System.Single Abs(Single value) static System .Double Abs(Double value) static System.Decimal Abs(Decimal value) |
| Acos | Method | static System.Double Acos(Double d) |
| Asin | Method | static System.Double Asin(Double d) |
| Atan | Method | static System.Double Atan(Double d) |
| Atan2 | Method | static System.Double Atan2(Double y Double x) |
| BigMul | Method | static System.Int64 BigMul(Int32 a Int32 b) |

| Name | MemberType | Definition |
| --- | --- | --- |
| Ceiling | Method | static System.Decimal Ceiling(Decimal d) static System.Double Ceiling(Double a) |
| Cos | Method | static System.Double Cos(Double d) |
| Cosh | Method | static System.Double Cosh(Double value) |
| DivRem | Method | static System.Int32 DivRem(Int32 a Int32 b Int32& result) static System.Int64 DivRem(Int64 a Int64 b Int64& result) |
| Equals | Method | static System.Boolean Equals(Object objA Object objB) |
| Exp | Method | static System.Double Exp(Double d) |
| Floor | Method | static System.Decimal Floor(Decimal d) static System.Double Floor(Double d) |
| IEEERemainder | Method | static System.Double IEEERemainder(Double x Double y) |
| Log | Method | static System.Double Log(Double d) static System.Double Log(Double a Double newBase) |
| Log10 | Method | static System.Double Log10(Double d) |
| Max | Method | static System.SByte Max(SByte val1 SByte val2) static System.Byte Max(Byte val1 Byte val2) static System.Int16 Max(Int16 val1 Int16 val2) static System.UInt16 Max(UInt16 val1 UInt16 val2) static System.Int32 Max(Int32 val1 Int32 val2) static System.UInt32 Max(UInt32 val1 UInt32 val2) static System.Int64 Max(Int64 val1 Int64 val2) static System.UInt64 Max(UInt64 val1 UInt64 val2) static System.Single Max(Single val1 Single val2) static System.Double Max(Double val1 Double val2) static System.Decimal Max(Decimal val1 Decimal val2) |
| Min | Method | static System.SByte Min(SByte val1 SByte val2) static System.Byte Min(Byte val1 Byte val2) static System.Int16 Min(Int16 val1 Int16 val2) static System.UInt16 Min(UInt16 val1 UInt16 val2) static System.Int32 Min(Int32 val1 Int32 val2) static System.UInt32 Min(UInt32 val1 UInt32 val2) static System.Int64 Min(Int64 val1 Int64 val2) static System.UInt64 Min(UInt64 val1 UInt64 val2) static System.Single Min(Single val1 Single val2) static System.Double Min(Double val1 Double val2) static System.Decimal Min(Decimal val1 Decimal val2) |
| Pow | Method | static System.Double Pow(Double x Double y) |
| ReferenceEquals | Method | static System.Boolean ReferenceEquals(Object objA Object objB) |
| Round | Method | static System.Double Round(Double a) static System.Double Round(Double value Int32 digits) static System.Double Round(Double value MidpointRounding mode) static System.Double Round(Double value Int32 digits MidpointRounding mode) static System.Decimal Round(Decimal d) static System.Decimal Round(Decimal d Int32 decimals) static System.Decimal Round(Decimal d MidpointRounding mode) static System.Decimal Round(Decimal d Int32 decimals MidpointRounding mode) |

| Name | MemberType | Definition |
|------|------------|------------|
| Sign | Method | static System.Int32 Sign(SByte value) static System.Int32 Sign(Int16 value) static System.Int32 Sign(Int32 value) static System.Int32 Sign(Int64 value) static System.Int32 Sign(Single value) static System.Int32 Sign(Double value) static System.Int32 Sign(Decimal value) |
| Sin | Method | static System.Double Sin(Double a) |
| Sinh | Method | static System.Double Sinh(Double value) |
| Sqrt | Method | static System.Double Sqrt(Double d) |
| Tan | Method | static System.Double Tan(Double a) |
| Tanh | Method | static System.Double Tanh(Double value) |
| Truncate | Method | static System.Decimal Truncate(Decimal d) static System.Double Truncate(Double d) |
| E | Property | static System.Double E {get;} |
| PI | Property | static System.Double PI {get;} |

## Version dependencies

One of the more interesting facets of the .NET Framework is that there always seems to be a new version available, and, of course, between versions there are service packs. While the .NET Framework is included in the operating system, updates to the .NET Framework are unfortunately not included in service packs. It therefore becomes the responsibility of the network administrators to package and deploy updates to the framework. Until the introduction of Windows PowerShell, network administrators were not keen to provide updates, simply because they did not have a vested interest in the deployment of the .NET Framework. This behavior was not due to a lack of interest; in many cases, it was due to a lack of understanding of the .NET Framework. If developers did not request updates to the .NET Framework, it did not get updated.

## Lack of COM support

Many very useful capabilities are packaged as Component Object Model (COM) components. Finding these COM objects is sometimes a matter of luck. Of course, you can always read the MSDN documentation; unfortunately, the articles do not always list the program ID that is required to create the COM object, and this is even true in articles that refer to the scripting interfaces. An example can be found in the Windows Media Player scripting object model. You can work your way through the entire Software Development Kit (SDK) documentation without discovering that the program ID is *wmplayer.ocx* and not *player*, which is used for illustrative purposes. The most natural way to work with a COM object in Windows PowerShell is to use the New-Object cmdlet, specify the *−ComObject* parameter, and give the parameter the program ID. However, if the program ID is not forthcoming, you have a more difficult proposition. You can search the registry and, by doing a bit of detective work, find the program ID.

An example of a COM object whose program ID is hard to find is the object with the *makecab.makecab* program ID. The *makecab.makecab* object is used to make *cabinet files,* which are highly compressed files often used by programmers to deploy software applications. There is no reason why an enterprise network administrator cannot use .cab files to compress log files prior to transferring them across the application. The only problem is that, while the *makecab.makecab* object is present in Windows XP and Windows Server 2003, it has been removed from the operating system beginning with Windows Vista. When working with newer operating systems, a different approach is required.

To make the script easier to use, you must first create some command-line parameters by using the *Param* statement. The *Param* statement must be the first noncommented line in the script. When the script is run from within the Windows PowerShell console or from within a script editor, the command-line parameters are used to control the way in which the script executes. In this way, the script can be run without needing to edit it each time you want to create a .cab file from a different directory. You need only to supply a new value for the *–filepath* parameter, as shown here:

```
CreateCab.ps1 –filepath C:\fso1
```

What is good about command-line parameters is that they use partial parameter completion, which means that you need to supply only enough of the parameter for it to be unique. Therefore, you can use command-line syntax such as the following:

```
CreateCab.ps1 –f c:\fso1 –p c:\fso2\bcab.cab –d
```

The previous syntax searches the c:\fso directory and obtains all of the files. It then creates a cabinet file named bcab.cab in the fso2 folder of the C:\ drive. The syntax also produces debugging information while it is running. Note that the *debug* parameter is a switched parameter because *debug* affects the script only when it is present. This section of the CreateCab.ps1 script is shown here.

```
Param(
        $filepath = "C:\fso",
        $path = "C:\fso\aCab.cab",
        [switch]$debug
    )
```

It is now time to create the *New-Cab* function, which will accept two input parameters. The first is the *–path* parameter, and the second is the *–files* parameter.

```
Function New-Cab($path,$files)
```

You can assign the *makecab.makecab* program ID to a variable named *$makecab,* which makes the script a bit easier to read. This is also a good place to put the first Write-Debug statement.

```
{
 $makecab = "makecab.makecab"
 Write-Debug "Creating Cab path is: $path"
```

You now need to create the COM object:

```
$cab = New-Object -ComObject $makecab
```

A bit of error checking is in order. To do this, you can use the *$?* automatic variable.

```
if(!$?) { $(Throw "unable to create $makecab object")}
```

If no errors occur during the attempt to create the *makecab.makecab* object, you can use the object contained in the *$cab* variable and call the *createcab* method.

```
$cab.CreateCab($path,$false,$false,$false)
```

After you create the .cab file, you need to add files to it by using the *Foreach* statement.

```
Foreach ($file in $files)
  {
  $file = $file.fullname.tostring()
  $fileName = Split-Path -path $file -leaf
```

After you turn the full file name into a string and remove the directory information by using the Split-Path cmdlet, another Write-Debug statement is needed to let the user of the script be informed of progress, as shown here:

```
Write-Debug "Adding from $file"
Write-Debug "File name is $fileName"
```

Next, you need to add a file to the cabinet file.

```
$cab.AddFile($file,$filename)
  }
Write-Debug "Closing cab $path"
```

To close the cabinet file, you can use the *closecab* method.

```
$cab.CloseCab()
} #end New-Cab
```

It is now time to go to the entry point of the script. First, you must determine whether the script is being run in debug mode by looking for the presence of the *$debug* variable. If it is running in debug mode, you must set the value of the *$DebugPreference* variable to *continue*, which allows the Write-Debug statements to be printed on the screen. By default, *$DebugPreference* is set to *SilentlyContinue*, which means that no debug statements are displayed, and Windows PowerShell skips past the Write-Debug command without taking any action, as shown here:

```
if($debug) {$DebugPreference = "continue"}
```

Now you need to obtain a collection of files by using the Get-ChildItem cmdlet.

```
$files = Get-ChildItem -path $filePath | Where-Object { !$_.psiscontainer }
```

After you have a collection of files, you can pass the collection to the *New-Cab* function as shown here:

```
New-Cab -path $path -files $files
```

The completed CreateCab.ps1 script is shown here.

> **NOTE** The CreateCab.ps1 script will not run on Windows Vista and later versions due to lack of support for the *makecab.makecab* COM object. An alternate method of creating .cab files is explored in the "Lack of external application support" section later in the chapter.

```
CreateCab.ps1

Param(
        $filepath = "C:\fso",
        $path = "C:\fso\aCab.cab",
        [switch]$debug
        )
Function New-Cab($path,$files)
{
 $makecab = "makecab.makecab"
 Write-Debug "Creating Cab path is: $path"
 $cab = New-Object -ComObject $makecab
 if(!$?) { $(Throw "unable to create $makecab object")}
 $cab.CreateCab($path,$false,$false,$false)
 Foreach ($file in $files)
  {
   $file = $file.fullname.tostring()
   $fileName = Split-Path -path $file -leaf
   Write-Debug "Adding from $file"
   Write-Debug "File name is $fileName"
   $cab.AddFile($file,$filename)
  }
 Write-Debug "Closing cab $path"
 $cab.CloseCab()
} #end New-Cab

# *** entry point to script ***
if($debug) {$DebugPreference = "continue"}
$files = Get-ChildItem -path $filePath | Where-Object { !$_.psiscontainer }
New-Cab -path $path -files $files
```

You cannot use the *makecab.makecab* object to expand the cabinet file because it does not have an *expand* method. You also cannot use the *makecab.expandcab* object because it does not exist. Because the ability to expand a cabinet file is inherent in the Windows shell, you can use the *shell* object to expand the cabinet file. To access the shell, you can use the *Shell.Application* COM object.

You must first create command-line parameters. This section of the script is very similar to the parameter section of the previous CreateCab.ps1 script. The command-line parameters are shown here:

```
Param(
    $cab = "C:\fso\acab.cab",
    $destination = "C:\fso1",
    [switch]$debug
    )
```

After you create command-line parameters, it is time to create the *ConvertFrom-Cab* function, which will accept two command-line parameters. The first parameter contains the .cab file, and the second parameter contains the destination to expand the files, as shown here:

```
Function ConvertFrom-Cab($cab,$destination)
```

You should now create an instance of the *Shell.Application* object. The *Shell.Application* object is a very powerful object with a number of useful methods. The members of the *Shell .Application* object are shown in Table 6-5.

**TABLE 6-5** Members of the *Shell.Application* object

| Name | MemberType | Definition |
| --- | --- | --- |
| AddToRecent | Method | void AddToRecent (Variant, string) |
| BrowseForFolder | Method | Folder BrowseForFolder (int, string, int, Variant) |
| CanStartStopService | Method | Variant CanStartStopService (string) |
| CascadeWindows | Method | void CascadeWindows () |
| ControlPanelItem | Method | void ControlPanelItem (string) |
| EjectPC | Method | void EjectPC () |
| Explore | Method | void Explore (Variant) |
| ExplorerPolicy | Method | Variant ExplorerPolicy (string) |
| FileRun | Method | void FileRun () |
| FindComputer | Method | void FindComputer () |
| FindFiles | Method | void FindFiles () |
| FindPrinter | Method | void FindPrinter (string, string, string) |
| GetSetting | Method | bool GetSetting (int) |
| GetSystemInformation | Method | Variant GetSystemInformation (string) |
| Help | Method | void Help () |
| IsRestricted | Method | int IsRestricted (string, string) |

| Name | MemberType | Definition |
| --- | --- | --- |
| IsServiceRunning | Method | Variant IsServiceRunning (string) |
| MinimizeAll | Method | void MinimizeAll () |
| NameSpace | Method | Folder NameSpace (Variant) |
| Open | Method | void Open (Variant) |
| RefreshMenu | Method | void RefreshMenu () |
| ServiceStart | Method | Variant ServiceStart (string, Variant) |
| ServiceStop | Method | Variant ServiceStop (string, Variant) |
| SetTime | Method | void SetTime () |
| ShellExecute | Method | void ShellExecute (string, Variant, Variant, Variant, Variant) |
| ShowBrowserBar | Method | Variant ShowBrowserBar (string, Variant) |
| ShutdownWindows | Method | void ShutdownWindows () |
| Suspend | Method | void Suspend () |
| TileHorizontally | Method | void TileHorizontally () |
| TileVertically | Method | void TileVertically () |
| ToggleDesktop | Method | void ToggleDesktop () |
| TrayProperties | Method | void TrayProperties () |
| UndoMinimizeALL | Method | void UndoMinimizeALL () |
| Windows | Method | IDispatch Windows () |
| WindowsSecurity | Method | void WindowsSecurity () |
| WindowSwitcher | Method | void WindowSwitcher () |
| Application | Property | IDispatch Application () {get} |
| Parent | Property | IDispatch Parent () {get} |

Because you want to use the name of the COM object more than once, it is a good practice to assign the program ID of the COM object to a variable. You can then use the string with the New-Object cmdlet and also use it when providing feedback to the user. The line of code that assigns the *Shell.Application* program ID to a string is shown here:

```
{
 $comObject = "Shell.Application"
```

It is now time to provide some feedback to the user. You can do this by using the Write-Debug cmdlet together with a message stating that you are attempting to create the *Shell.Application* object, as shown here:

```
Write-Debug "Creating $comObject"
```

After you provide debug feedback stating that you are going to create the object, you can actually create the object, as shown here:

```
$shell = New-Object -Comobject $comObject
```

Now you want to test for errors by using the *$?* automatic variable. The *$?* automatic variable tells you whether the last command completed successfully. Because *$?* is a Boolean true/false variable, you can use this fact to simplify the coding. You can use the *not* operator, *!*, in conjunction with an *If* statement. If the variable is not true, you can use the *Throw* statement to raise an error and halt execution of the script. This section of the script is shown here:

```
if(!$?) { $(Throw "unable to create $comObject object")}
```

If the script successfully creates the *Shell.Application* object, it is now time to provide more feedback, as shown here:

```
Write-Debug "Creating source cab object for $cab"
```

The next step in the operation is to connect to the .cab file by using the *Namespace* method from the *Shell.Application* object, as shown here. This is another important step in the process, so it makes sense to use another Write-Debug statement as a progress indicator to the user.

```
$sourceCab = $shell.Namespace($cab).items()
Write-Debug "Creating destination folder object for $destination"
```

It is time to connect to the destination folder by using the *Namespace* method as shown here. You also want to use another Write-Debug statement to let the user know the folder to which you actually connected.

```
$DestinationFolder = $shell.Namespace($destination)
Write-Debug "Expanding $cab to $destination"
```

With all of that preparation out of the way, the actual command that is used to expand the cabinet file is somewhat anticlimactic. You can use the *copyhere* method from the *folder* object that is stored in the *$destinationFolder* variable. You give the reference to the .cab file that is stored in the *$sourceCab* variable as the input parameter, as shown here:

```
$DestinationFolder.CopyHere($sourceCab)
}
```

The starting point to the script accomplishes two things. First, it checks for the presence of the *$debug* variable. If found, it then sets *$debugPreference* to *continue* to force the Write-Debug cmdlet to print messages to the console window. Second, it calls the *ConvertFrom-Cab* function and passes the path to the .cab file from the *–cab* command-line parameter and the destination for the expanded files from the *–destination* parameter, as shown here:

```
if($debug) { $debugPreference = "continue" }
ConvertFrom-Cab -cab $cab -destination $destination
```

The completed ExpandCab.ps1 script is shown here.

```
ExpandCab.ps1

Param(
      $cab = "C:\fso\acab.cab",
      $destination = "C:\fso1",
      [switch]$debug
      )
Function ConvertFrom-Cab($cab,$destination)
{
 $comObject = "Shell.Application"
 Write-Debug "Creating $comObject"
 $shell = New-Object -Comobject $comObject
 if(!$?) { $(Throw "unable to create $comObject object")}
 Write-Debug "Creating source cab object for $cab"
 $sourceCab = $shell.Namespace($cab).items()
 Write-Debug "Creating destination folder object for $destination"
 $DestinationFolder = $shell.Namespace($destination)
 Write-Debug "Expanding $cab to $destination"
 $DestinationFolder.CopyHere($sourceCab)
}

# *** entry point ***
if($debug) { $debugPreference = "continue" }
ConvertFrom-Cab -cab $cab -destination $destination
```

## Lack of external application support

Many management features still rely on the use of command-line support; a very common example is NETSH. Another example is the MakeCab.exe utility. The *makecab.makecab* COM object was removed from Windows Vista and later versions. To create a .cab file in Windows Vista and beyond, you need to use the MakeCab.exe utility.

First, you need to create a few command-line parameters as shown here:

```
Param(
      $filepath = "C:\fso",
      $path = "C:\fso1\cabfiles",
      [switch]$debug
      )
```

Then you need to create the *New-DDF* function, which creates a basic .ddf file that is used by the MakeCab.exe program to create the .cab file. The syntax for these types of files is documented in the Microsoft Cabinet SDK on MSDN. When you use the *Function* keyword to create the *New-DDF* function, you can use the Join-Path cmdlet to create the file path to the temporary .ddf file that you will use. You can concatenate the drive, the folder, and the file name together, but this might become a cumbersome and error-prone operation. As a best practice, you should always use the Join-Path cmdlet to build your file paths, as shown here:

```
Function New-DDF($path,$filePath)
{
 $ddfFile = Join-Path -path $filePath -childpath temp.ddf
```

It is time to provide some feedback to the user if the script is run with the –*debug* switch, by using the Write-Debug cmdlet as shown here:

```
Write-Debug "DDF file path is $ddfFile"
```

You now need to create the first portion of the .ddf file by using an expanding here-string. The advantage of a here-string is that it allows you not to worry about escaping special characters. For example, the comment character in a .ddf file is the semicolon, which is a reserved character in Windows PowerShell. If you try to create the .ddf text without the advantage of using the here-string, you then need to escape each of the semicolons to avoid compile-time errors. By using an expanding here-string, you can take advantage of the expansion of variables. A here-string begins with an *at* sign and a quotation mark and ends with a quotation mark and an *at* sign, as shown here:

```
 $ddfHeader =@"
;*** MakeCAB Directive file
;
.OPTION EXPLICIT
.Set CabinetNameTemplate=Cab.*.cab
.set DiskDirectory1=C:\fso1\Cabfiles
.Set MaxDiskSize=CDROM
.Set Cabinet=on
.Set Compress=on
"@
```

You can choose to add more feedback for the user via the Write-Debug cmdlet, as shown here:

```
Write-Debug "Writing ddf file header to $ddfFile"
```

After providing feedback to the user, you come to the section that might cause some problems. The .ddf file must be a pure ASCII file. By default, Windows PowerShell uses Unicode. To ensure that you have an ASCII file, you must use the Out-File cmdlet. You can usually avoid using Out-File by using the file redirection arrows; however, this is not one of those occasions. Here is the syntax.

```
$ddfHeader | Out-File -filepath $ddfFile -force -encoding ASCII
```

You probably want to provide more debug information via the Write-Debug cmdlet before you gather your collection of files via the Get-ChildItem cmdlet, as shown here:

```
Write-Debug "Generating collection of files from $filePath"
Get-ChildItem -path $filePath |
```

It is important to filter out folders from the collection because the MakeCab.exe utility cannot compress folders. To filter folders, use the `Where-Object` cmdlet with a *not* operator stating that the object is not a container, as shown here:

```
Where-Object { !$_.psiscontainer } |
```

After you filter out folders, you need to work with each individual file as it comes across the pipeline by using the `ForEach-Object` cmdlet. Because `ForEach-Object` is a cmdlet as opposed to a language statement, the curly brackets must be on the same line as the `ForEach-Object` cmdlet name. The problem arises in that the curly brackets often get buried within the code. As a best practice, I like to line up the curly brackets unless the command is very short, such as in the previous `Where-Object` command, but this process requires the use of the line continuation character (the backtick). I know some developers who avoid using line continuation, but I personally think that lining up curly brackets is more important because it makes the code easier to read. Here is the beginning of the `ForEach-Object` cmdlet:

```
Foreach-Object `
```

Because the .ddf file used by MakeCab.exe is ASCII text, you need to convert the *FullName* property of the *System.IO.FileInfo* object returned by the `Get-ChildItem` cmdlet to a string. In addition, because you can have files with spaces in their names, it makes sense to ensconce the file *FullName* value in a set of quotation marks, as shown here:

```
{
  '"' + $_.fullname.tostring() + '"'  |
```

You then pipeline the file names to the `Out-File` cmdlet, making sure to specify the ASCII encoding, and use the *–append* switch to avoid overwriting everything else in the text file, as shown here:

```
Out-File -filepath $ddfFile -encoding ASCII -append
}
```

Now you can provide another update to the debug users and call the *New-Cab* function as shown here:

```
Write-Debug "ddf file is created. Calling New-Cab function"
New-Cab($ddfFile)
} #end New-DDF
```

When you enter the *New-Cab* function, you might want to supply some information to the user, as shown here:

```
Function New-Cab($ddfFile)
{
  Write-Debug "Entering the New-Cab function. The DDF File is $ddfFile"
```

If the script is run with the *–debug* switch, you can use the */V* parameter of the MakeCab .exe executable to provide detailed debugging information. If the script is not run with the *–debug* switch, you do not want to clutter the screen with too much information and can therefore rely on the default verbosity of the utility, as shown here:

```
if($debug)
    { makecab /f $ddfFile /V3 }
Else
    { makecab /f $ddfFile }
} #end New-Cab
```

The entry point to the script checks whether the *$debug* variable is present. If it is, the *$debugPreference* automatic variable is set to *continue*, and debugging information is displayed via the Write-Debug cmdlet. After that check is performed, the New-DDF cmdlet is called with the *path* and *filepath* values supplied to the command line, as shown here:

```
if($debug) {$DebugPreference = "continue"}
New-DDF -path $path -filepath $filepath
```

The completed CreateCab2.ps1 script is shown here.

---

**CreateCab2.ps1**

```
Param(
       $filepath = "C:\fso",
       $path = "C:\fso1\cabfiles",
       [switch]$debug
       )
Function New-DDF($path,$filePath)
{
 $ddfFile = Join-Path -path $filePath -childpath temp.ddf
 Write-Debug "DDF file path is $ddfFile"
 $ddfHeader =@"
;*** MakeCAB Directive file
;
.OPTION EXPLICIT
.Set CabinetNameTemplate=Cab.*.cab
.set DiskDirectory1=C:\fso1\Cabfiles
.Set MaxDiskSize=CDROM
.Set Cabinet=on
.Set Compress=on
"@
 Write-Debug "Writing ddf file header to $ddfFile"
 $ddfHeader | Out-File -filepath $ddfFile -force -encoding ASCII
 Write-Debug "Generating collection of files from $filePath"
 Get-ChildItem -path $filePath |
 Where-Object { !$_.psiscontainer } |
 Foreach-Object '
  {
    '"' + $_.fullname.tostring() + '"'  |
   Out-File -filepath $ddfFile -encoding ASCII -append
  }
```

---

```
 Write-Debug "ddf file is created. Calling New-Cab function"
 New-Cab($ddfFile)
} #end New-DDF


Function New-Cab($ddfFile)
{
 Write-Debug "Entering the New-Cab function. The DDF File is $ddfFile"
 if($debug)
    { makecab /f $ddfFile /V3 }
 Else
    { makecab /f $ddfFile }
} #end New-Cab


# *** entry point to script ***
if($debug) {$DebugPreference = "continue"}
New-DDF -path $path -filepath $filepath
```

## Additional resources

- The TechNet Script Center at *http://www.microsoft.com/technet/scriptcenter* has numerous examples of Windows PowerShell scripts that use all of the techniques explored in this chapter.

- Take a look at *Windows PowerShell™ Scripting Guide* (Microsoft Press, 2008) for examples of using WMI and various .NET Framework classes in Windows PowerShell.

- For a good WMI reference, look at *Windows Scripting with WMI Self-Paced Learning Edition* (Microsoft Press, 2005).

- The MSDN reference library has comprehensive product documentation at *http://msdn.microsoft.com/en-us/library/default.aspx* and is the authoritative source for all Microsoft products.

- A series of blog articles discussing Windows PowerShell performance, written by Georges Maheu, Microsoft PFE, is available at *http://gallery.technet.microsoft.com /scriptcenter/Get-on-thousands-of-ef3175c7*.

- All scripts from this chapter are available via the TechNet Script Center Script Repository at *http://gallery.technet.microsoft.com/scriptcenter/PowerShell -40-Best-d9e16039*.

# CHAPTER 7

# Tracking scripting opportunities

- Evaluating the need for the script
- Calculating the benefit from the script
- Script collaboration
- Additional resources

I t is important to track scripting opportunities to ensure that the most profitable scripts are written first. This backlog of scripting opportunities can be an effective tool for managing the scripting efforts of an enterprise. The key is to manage these scripting opportunities properly.

## Evaluating the need for the script

Not everything in Windows PowerShell 4.0 needs to be scripted, which was also true in Windows PowerShell 3.0. When coming from a Microsoft VBScript or Perl background, some people often feel that they must write a script. However, a tremendous amount of work can be accomplished from the command line without the need for writing a script.

One of the more powerful aspects of Windows PowerShell is its ability to use language statements from the command line. The *for* statement provides the ability to control looping operations that require the creation of a script in other languages. To facilitate work from the command line, Windows PowerShell allows you to create incomplete commands on one line and continue them to the next line. When you are finished, you can press the Enter key a second time. The command shown here sends a ping command to each IP address in the range of 192.168.2.1 through 192.168.2.10:

```
PS C:\> for($i = 1 ; $i -le 10 ; $i++)
>> { Test-Connection -Destination 192.168.2.$i -Count 1 -ErrorAction Silentlycontinue
|
>> Format-Table -property Address, statusCode, ResponseTime -AutoSize }
>>

Address     statusCode ResponseTime
-------     ---------- ------------
192.168.2.1          0            1
```

```
Address        statusCode ResponseTime
-------        ---------- ------------
192.168.2.3             0            2
Address        statusCode ResponseTime
-------        ---------- ------------
192.168.2.5             0            0
Address        statusCode ResponseTime
-------        ---------- ------------
192.168.2.10            0           10
```

The preceding command can become quite a bit shorter by taking advantage of a number of economies provided by the Windows PowerShell syntax, such as using aliases, partial parameters, and positional arguments. The shortened version of this command appears here:

```
1..10 | % {Test-Connection 10.1.1.$_ -cou 1 -ea 0 | ft Address, StatusCode, ResponseTime
-au}
```

## Reading a text file

In its most basic form, a Windows PowerShell script is simply a collection of PowerShell commands stored in a file with a specific extension. If you do not want to write a script, you can store a collection of commands as a text file, as shown in Figure 7-1.

**FIGURE 7-1** Text file containing a collection of Windows PowerShell commands.

By using Windows PowerShell, you can easily read the commands.txt text file and execute the commands by using the Get-Content cmdlet to retrieve the commands in the text file. The default parameter for the Get-Content cmdlet is the *path* parameter; when working from the command line, it is not necessary to supply the *path* parameter. The path can be a local path or even a Universal Naming Convention (UNC) path as long as you have rights to read the text file. The best way to use this technique is to pipeline the results to the Invoke-Expression cmdlet. Each command that streams across the pipeline from the Get-Content cmdlet is executed in turn as it arrives to the Invoke-Expression cmdlet, as shown here:

```
Get-Content -Path C:\fso\Commands.txt | Invoke-Expression
```

The results are shown in Figure 7-2.

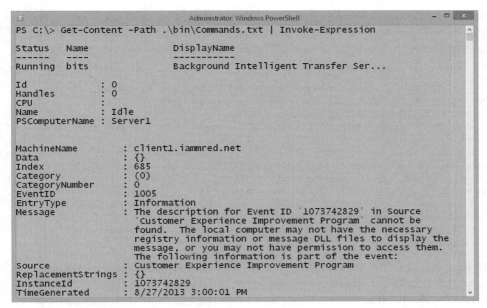

```
PS C:\> Get-Content -Path .\bin\Commands.txt | Invoke-Expression

Status     Name                DisplayName
------     ----                -----------
Running    bits                Background Intelligent Transfer Ser...

Id               : 0
Handles          : 0
CPU              :
Name             : Idle
PSComputerName   : Server1


MachineName        : client1.iammred.net
Data               : {}
Index              : 685
Category           : (0)
CategoryNumber     : 0
EventID            : 1005
EntryType          : Information
Message            : The description for Event ID '1073742829' in Source
                     'Customer Experience Improvement Program' cannot be
                     found.  The local computer may not have the necessary
                     registry information or message DLL files to display the
                     message, or you may not have permission to access them.
                     The following information is part of the event:
Source             : Customer Experience Improvement Program
ReplacementStrings : {}
InstanceId         : 1073742829
TimeGenerated      : 8/27/2013 3:00:01 PM
```

**FIGURE 7-2** Windows PowerShell cmdlets can easily parse a text file and run commands.

When using the Windows PowerShell remoting features against an untrusted domain, it is easy to become confused when using cmdlets such as Get-Content. The *–path* parameter that is used refers to a path that is local to the target computer, not the launching computer. In the example that follows, the *c:\fso\commands.txt* path points to a text file named Commands.txt that must reside in the Fso folder on the C:\ drive of a computer named Sydney in the Woodbridgebank.com domain. If the commands.txt file is not found in that location, the error shown here is emitted.

```
PS C:\> invoke-command -ComputerName sydney.woodbridgebank.com -Credential admin
istrator@woodbridgebank.com -ScriptBlock {get-content -Path C:\fso\Commands.txt
| Invoke-Expression}
Invoke-Command : Cannot find path 'C:\fso\Commands.txt' because it does not
exist.At line:1 char:15
+ invoke-command <<<<  -ComputerName sydney.woodbridgebank.com -Credential
administrator@woodbridgebank.com -ScriptBlock {get-content -Path
C:\fso\Commands.txt | Invoke-Expression}
    + CategoryInfo          : ObjectNotFound: (C:\fso\Commands.txt:String)
    [Get-Content], ItemNotFoundException
    + FullyQualifiedErrorId : PathNotFound,Microsoft.PowerShell.Commands.
GetContentCommand
```

You might think that you can use a UNC path and point to the Commands.txt file on the launching computer. Because the remote domain is untrusted, there is no security context that allows the remote command to access the file system of the local computer. When the command expressed in the *ScriptBlock* parameter is evaluated, it is evaluated in the context of the target computer, which in this case is the Sydney.Woodbridgebank.com computer.

The local computer that is the launching point for the command is Windows 8.NWTraders.com. Because there is no trust relationship between these two domains, no credentials can be supplied to enable the command to run. The results of attempting to run the command are shown here:

```
PS C:\> invoke-command -ComputerName sydney.woodbridgebank.com -Credential
administrator@woodbridgebank.com -ScriptBlock {get-content -Path
'\\Windows 8\fso\Commands.txt' | Invoke-Expression}
Invoke-Command : Cannot find path '\\Windows 8\fso\Commands.txt' because it does
not exist.
At line:1 char:15
+ invoke-command <<<<  -ComputerName sydney.woodbridgebank.com -Credential
administrator@woodbridgebank.com -ScriptBlock {get-content -Path
'\\Windows 8\fso\Commands.txt' | Invoke-Expression}
    + CategoryInfo          : ObjectNotFound: (\\Windows 8\fso\Commands.txt:String)
    [Get-Content],ItemNotFoundException
    + FullyQualifiedErrorId : PathNotFound,Microsoft.PowerShell.Commands.
GetContentCommand
```

What can be confusing is that the Get-Content command works well when run alone. In working on a computer named client1 that has a folder named bin containing a text file named Commands.txt, the command completes successfully when it is ensconced within single quotes, as shown here:

```
PS C:\> Get-Content -Path '\\client1\bin\Commands.txt'
Get-Service -Name bits -ComputerName Windows 8
Get-Process -Name explorer -ComputerName berlin
Get-EventLog -LogName application -Newest 1 -ComputerName berlin,Windows 8
Invoke-Command -ComputerName Berlin { Get-Date }
Get-Date
```

However, this result is expected because the logged-on user has rights to the folder and can therefore use the Get-Content cmdlet to read a UNC path to the Commands.txt file.

You can map a drive on the remote domain and copy the file from your local computer to the appropriate folder on the remote server. You will, of course, be required to open additional ports in the Windows Firewall, which might or might not be an acceptable solution, depending on your network configuration. If you decide to use this route, you can use Windows PowerShell to perform the configuration changes as shown here:

```
PS C:\> Invoke-Command -ComputerName Sydney.WoodBridgeBank.Com -Credential
Administrator@WoodbridgeBank.com -ScriptBlock { netsh advfirewall firewall set rule
group="File and Printer Sharing" new enable=Yes }

Updated 28 rule(s).
Ok.
```

After you enable the firewall exception, you can map a drive by using the GUI, the Net Use command from within Windows PowerShell, or any of the other programmatic methods. After you map the drive, you can copy the Commands.txt file to the remote server by using the Copy-Item cmdlet as shown here:

```
Copy-Item -Path C:\fso\Commands.txt -Destination z:
```

You can now use the Commands.txt file directly in the Windows PowerShell command as shown here:

```
PS C:\> invoke-command -ComputerName Sydney.WoodbridgeBank.com -Credential
administrator@WoodBridgeBank.com -ScriptBlock { Get-Content -Path
C:\fso\Commands.txt | Invoke-Expression }
```

One solution to the dilemma of mapping drives is to use Remote Desktop, which allows you to access local resources if you want to make them available in your session. By selecting Remote Desktop, clicking the Options button, and then selecting the Local Resources tab, you can choose to allow printer connections, Clipboard access, and local drives to be available within the Remote Desktop Protocol (RDP) session. You can access Remote Desktop by going to Start, All Programs, Accessories, and selecting Remote Desktop Connection. If Remote Desktop has not been previously enabled, you are greeted with an access denied message, as shown in Figure 7-3.

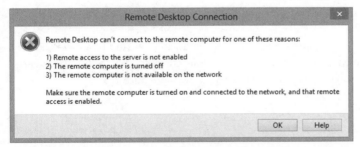

**FIGURE 7-3** Access denied when attempting to connect to Remote Desktop.

To enable Remote Desktop access on Microsoft Windows 2012 and Windows 2012 R2, choose Remote Desktop from within Server Manager in the Local Server node. If you are using Windows 8.1 or the Microsoft Windows 8 operating system, you select Remote Settings from Control Panel, then System And Security, and then System. When the System Properties dialog box appears, choose the Remote Settings as shown in Figure 7-4. Remote Desktop options are shown in the lower half of the dialog box and present three different choices. By default, Remote Desktop connections are not allowed to the local computer. The safest choice is to select Allow Connections Only From Computers Running Remote Desktop With Network Level Authentication. You are also allowed to specify which users are allowed to make the connection. By default, members of the Domain Administrators group are permitted to make connections.

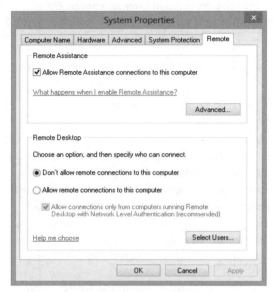

**FIGURE 7-4** Remote Desktop must be enabled.

After you enable Remote Desktop, an exception is automatically created to allow RDP traffic through the Windows Firewall. It is a good idea to double-check to ensure that the exception was permitted. The Windows 8 Firewall exception is shown in Figure 7-5.

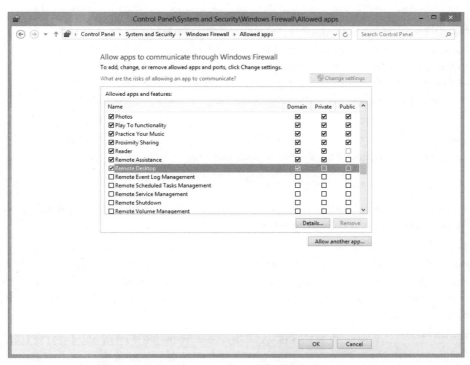

**FIGURE 7-5** Remote Desktop must be permitted through the Windows Firewall.

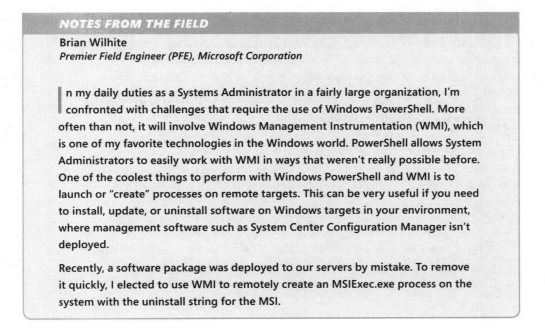

**NOTES FROM THE FIELD**

**Brian Wilhite**
*Premier Field Engineer (PFE), Microsoft Corporation*

In my daily duties as a Systems Administrator in a fairly large organization, I'm confronted with challenges that require the use of Windows PowerShell. More often than not, it will involve Windows Management Instrumentation (WMI), which is one of my favorite technologies in the Windows world. PowerShell allows System Administrators to easily work with WMI in ways that weren't really possible before. One of the coolest things to perform with Windows PowerShell and WMI is to launch or "create" processes on remote targets. This can be very useful if you need to install, update, or uninstall software on Windows targets in your environment, where management software such as System Center Configuration Manager isn't deployed.

Recently, a software package was deployed to our servers by mistake. To remove it quickly, I elected to use WMI to remotely create an MSIExec.exe process on the system with the uninstall string for the MSI.

The "UninstallString" for a specific software product can be found in the registry, commonly observed in the following path, where <SID> is the user's SID that the software was installed with and where <Product GUID> is the product globally unique identifier for the software in question: HKLM\SOFTWARE\Microsoft \Windows\CurrentVersion\Installer\UserData\<SID>\Products\<Product GUID> \InstallProperties.

Next, you'll see the "UninstallString" for the software that I want to remove from our systems. I've removed the Product's GUID to protect the innocent:

```
MsiExec.exe /X{<Product GUID>} /quiet
```

In this case, I know, through testing, that the *quiet* switch will work for the software I want to uninstall; your mileage might vary.

The cmdlet that we will use for this task is `Invoke-WmiMethod`. Also, we will specify the *Create* method of the *Win32_Process* WMI class to create the process on the remote target. Ideally, you'll have Windows PowerShell Remoting enabled in your environment, but if not, don't fret; I'll cover multiple techniques that you can use to perform this task.

The first technique assumes that Windows PowerShell Remoting is enabled on the remote targets. The *$Computers* variable has a collection of "ComputerNames" that we'll use as the target devices:

```
Invoke-Command -ScriptBlock {
    Invoke-WmiMethod -Class Win32_Process '
                     -Name Create '
                     -ArgumentList 'MsiExec.exe /X{<Product GUID>} /
quiet'} '
              -ComputerName $Computers
```

The second technique is used when your remote targets do not have Windows PowerShell Remoting enabled:

```
$Computers | ForEach-Object {
    Invoke-WmiMethod -Class Win32_Process '
                     -Name Create '
                     -ArgumentList 'MsiExec.exe /X{<Product GUID>} /
quiet' '
                     -ComputerName $_}
```

Based on my personal experience, piping computer names to a *ForEach-Object* seems to be more reliable when performing tasks such as this on hundreds if not thousands of targets, in lieu of specifying the entire list of targets to the

> *ComputerName* parameter. Either of the above techniques used should return an
> object that contains a "ReturnValue" and "ProcessId". If the process was created
> successfully, the "ReturnValue" will equal "0". The "0" indicates that the process was
> created successfully; however, it does not signify that the "Uninstall" was successful,
> so querying the event logs on each system would be appropriate to check the status
> of the "Uninstall".

# Export command history

Much administrative work with Windows PowerShell consists of typing a series of commands
at the console. Whether you are editing the registry or stopping various processes and services, the configuration work needs to be replicated to several different servers to ensure a
consistent operating environment. In the past, such duplication of effort required the creation
of scripts. If the commands to be duplicated are a series of commands typed at the console,
you can use the command history mechanism to replace the need for a script by using the
Get-History cmdlet and exporting the commands to an .xml file as shown here:

```
Get-History | Export-Clixml -Path C:\fso\history.xml
```

The result is an .xml file that represents all of the commands typed at the console. The
resulting .xml file is shown in Figure 7-6.

**FIGURE 7-6** Command history .xml file.

After you create a command history .xml file, you can import the commands from the .xml file by using the `Import-Clixml` cmdlet. You pipeline the results of the `Import-Clixml` cmdlet to the `Add-History` cmdlet to add the commands back to the command history. The trick is to use the *–passthru* switch so that the commands go to both the `Add-History` and `ForEach-Object` cmdlets. In the `ForEach-Object` cmdlet, you can use the `Invoke-History` cmdlet to run each command in the history. The commands are shown here, as are the results of running the commands:

```
PS C:\> Import-Clixml -Path C:\fso\history.xml | Add-History -Passthru |
>> ForEach-Object { Invoke-History }
>>
 if(!(test-path -path c:\fso4)) { new-item c:\fso4 -ItemType directory }


    Directory: C:\


Mode                LastWriteTime     Length Name
----                -------------     ------ ----
d----          1/9/2009   12:33 AM           fso4
Get-Command >> C:\fso4\commands.txt
notepad C:\fso4\commands.txt
```

This technique works remotely by using the `Invoke-Command` cmdlet. Keep in mind that the *path* statement is relative to the computer that is the target, not the computer that is executing the command. If you do not keep this in mind, an error appears, such as the one shown in Figure 7-7.

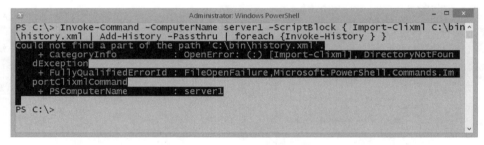

**FIGURE 7-7** An error appears due to the use of local file paths.

If you copy the file to the target machine first and adjust your command line, the import and execute history technique works well. What is good about Windows PowerShell is that you can use a UNC path with the `Copy-Item` cmdlet. This feature actually makes the technique worthwhile because it enables you to easily move a file to a remote computer, as shown here:

```
PS C:\> Copy-Item C:\fso\history.xml \\berlin\c$\fso
PS C:\> Import-Clixml -Path C:\fso\history.xml | Add-History -Passthru | ForEach
-Object { Invoke-History }
 if(!(test-path -path c:\fso4)) { new-item c:\fso4 -ItemType directory }


    Directory: C:\
```

```
Mode            LastWriteTime        Length Name
----            -------------        ------ ----
d----        1/9/2009  12:40 AM             fso4
Get-Command >> C:\fso4\commands.txt
notepad C:\fso4\commands.txt
```

## Fan-out commands

*Fan-out commands* are commands launched from a central computer and run against
a number of remote computers. One way to perform fan-out commands is to use the
Invoke-Command cmdlet, as shown here:

```
PS C:\> Invoke-Command -Computer berlin,Windows 8 -Script '
>> {"$env:computername $(get-date)" }
>>
WINDOWS 8 01/09/2009 08:31:42
BERLIN 01/09/2009 08:31:47
```

You can use fan-out commands by specifying an array of computer names for the
*–computername* parameter for many of the cmdlets. The problem with this approach is
that the results are nearly useless. An example illustrates the issue involved. In the following
command, the Get-Service cmdlet is used to obtain service configuration information from
two computers. The first is a computer named Windows 8, and the second is a server named
Berlin. As you can see from the partial output, the results of the command are merged, and
there is no column that illustrates the computer name to which the result is associated. The
results are rather interesting in that you can quickly look at the service name between two
different computers and easily see divergent configurations. The fan-out command and a
truncated result set are shown here:

```
PS C:\> Get-Service -ComputerName Windows 8, Berlin

Status   Name         DisplayName
------   ----         -----------
Running  1-vmsrvc     Virtual Machine Additions Services ...
Running  1-vmsrvc     Virtual Machine Additions Services ...
Running  AeLookupSvc  Application Experience
Stopped  AeLookupSvc  Application Experience
Stopped  ALG          Application Layer Gateway Service
Stopped  ALG          Application Layer Gateway Service
Stopped  Appinfo      Application Information
Stopped  Appinfo      Application Information
Stopped  AppMgmt      Application Management
Stopped  AppMgmt      Application Management
Stopped  AudioEndpointBu... Windows Audio Endpoint Builder
Stopped  AudioEndpointBu... Windows Audio Endpoint Builder
Stopped  Audiosrv     Windows Audio
Stopped  Audiosrv     Windows Audio
Running  BFE          Base Filtering Engine
Running  BFE          Base Filtering Engine
```

```
Running  BITS                 Background Intelligent Transfer Ser...
Stopped  BITS                 Background Intelligent Transfer Ser...
Stopped  Browser              Computer Browser
Running  Browser              Computer Browser
>>> Results trimmed >>>
```

You can see from the results of the Get-Service cmdlet that the AeLookupSvc service is running on the first computer and is stopped on the second computer. It is a simple matter to use the Get-Service cmdlet to connect to each of the computers and check the status of the service.

```
PS C:\> Get-Service -Name AeLookupSvc -computer Windows 8

Status   Name              DisplayName
------   ----              -----------
Stopped  AeLookupSvc       Application Experience

PS C:\> Get-Service -Name AeLookupSvc -computer Berlin

Status   Name              DisplayName
------   ----              -----------
Running  AeLookupSvc       Application Experience
```

You might think that the first instance of the service name belongs to the computer listed first. As you can see, AeLookupSvc service is running on Berlin but is stopped on Windows 8. This is the same order shown in the original output, but the Windows 8 computer is listed first in the fan-out command. Perhaps this means that the second computer results are listed first and the first computer results are listed second—a Last In First Out (LIFO) operation. However, before assuming this to be the case, you should check another service. In the output from the original fan-out command, the BITS service was listed first as running and second as stopped. To see the status of the BITS service on Berlin and on Windows 8, you can use the following two commands:

```
PS C:\> Get-Service -Name Bits -computer berlin

Status   Name              DisplayName
------   ----              -----------
Stopped  BITS              Background Intelligent Transfer Ser...

PS C:\> Get-Service -Name Bits -computer Windows 8

Status   Name              DisplayName
------   ----              -----------
Running  BITS              Background Intelligent Transfer Ser...
```

You can see that the BITS service is stopped on Berlin and is running on Windows 8. The results of using Get-Service as a fan-out command by supplying an array of computer names to the *–computername* parameter brings back interesting results, but they are meaningless results when you need to check the exact status of a service on a remote computer. As a best practice, you should pipeline the results of the fan-out command to a Format-Table cmdlet and choose the *machineName* property. The value of the *displayName* property is the same value shown in the Services MMC in the Name column. The command and a truncated output are shown here:

```
PS C:\> Get-Service -ComputerName berlin,Windows 8 |
format-table name, status, machinename, displayName -AutoSize
```

```
Name                      Status  MachineName  DisplayName
----                      ------  -----------  -----------
1-vmsrvc                  Running Windows 8    Virtual Machine Additions...
1-vmsrvc                  Running berlin       Virtual Machine Additions...
AeLookupSvc               Running berlin       Application Experience
AeLookupSvc               Stopped Windows 8    Application Experience
ALG                       Stopped berlin       Application Layer Gateway...
ALG                       Stopped Windows 8    Application Layer Gateway...
Appinfo                   Stopped berlin       Application Information
Appinfo                   Stopped Windows 8    Application Information
AppMgmt                   Stopped Windows 8    Application Management
AppMgmt                   Stopped berlin       Application Management
AudioEndpointBuilder      Stopped berlin       Windows Audio Endpoint Bu...
AudioEndpointBuilder      Stopped Windows 8    Windows Audio Endpoint Bu...
Audiosrv                  Stopped berlin       Windows Audio
Audiosrv                  Stopped Windows 8    Windows Audio
BFE                       Running Windows 8    Base Filtering Engine
BFE                       Running berlin       Base Filtering Engine
BITS                      Stopped berlin       Background Intelligent Tr...
BITS                      Running Windows 8    Background Intelligent Tr...
Browser                   Running Windows 8    Computer Browser
Browser                   Stopped berlin       Computer Browser
```

Because the value of the *displayName* property is often quite long, it does not always fit easily within the confines of an 80-column display. If you select *displayName* early in the order of the properties to be selected by the Format-Table cmdlet, you should end up with several columns that are not displayed, as shown here:

```
PS C:\> Get-Service -ComputerName berlin,Windows 8 | format-table name, displayname,
  status, machinename -AutoSize

WARNING: 2 columns do not fit into the display and were removed.
```

```
Name                      DisplayName
----                      -----------
1-vmsrvc                  Virtual Machine Additions Services Application
1-vmsrvc                  Virtual Machine Additions Services Application
AeLookupSvc               Application Experience
AeLookupSvc               Application Experience
```

As you can see, this code defeats the purpose of choosing the *machineName* property in the first place when the *machineName* property is left off because it does not fit on the display. To correct this potential problem, it is a best practice to always choose the property with the longest values to be displayed as the last position in the command. In this way, you allow Windows PowerShell to truncate the property value rather than filling the screen with information that you can easily infer from a truncated display.

The other solution to the problem of the shrinking display output is not to use the *–autosize* parameter of the Format-Table cmdlet. You can use the *Wrap* parameter instead. When the *–Wrap* parameter is used, single-line entries are allowed to wrap and form multiple lines. Depending on the information you are looking for, this output can be either helpful or annoying. Here is an example of using the *–Wrap* parameter:

```
PS C:\> Get-Service -ComputerName berlin,Windows 8 | format-table name, displayname,
 status, machinename -Wrap

Name                 DisplayName                        Status MachineName
----                 -----------                        ------ -----------
1-vmsrvc             Virtual Machine Add               Running Windows 8
                     itions Services App
                     lication
1-vmsrvc             Virtual Machine Add               Running berlin
                     itions Services App
                     lication
AeLookupSvc          Application Experie               Running berlin
                     nce
AeLookupSvc          Application Experie               Stopped Windows 8
                     nce
```

> **NOTE**  At this point in the discussion, you might think that you can solve the problem of the truncated display output by using both the *–autosize* and *–Wrap* parameters. Doing so allows the output to maximize the display real estate (the function of *–autosize*) and also to allow for multiline wrapping (the function of *–Wrap*). This procedure never works, but it does not generate an error. Windows PowerShell gives priority to the *–autosize* parameter and ignores the *–Wrap* parameter; the order in which the two parameters are typed does not matter.

## Query Active Directory

To query Active Directory with Windows PowerShell 1.0, most network administrators feel that they must write a script. To an extent, this belief is a relic of the VBScript days and reflects a reliance on using ActiveX Data Object (ADO) technology to invoke a Lightweight Directory Access Protocol (LDAP) dialect query against Active Directory. While it is possible to use the *System.DirectoryServices.DirectorySearcher* class from a Windows PowerShell line, it is not extremely convenient. While there are third-party cmdlets and providers that make it possible to employ command-line queries against Active Directory, many network administrators are rightfully skeptical about installing unsupported community software on production servers. The other command-line option, using DSQuery.exe, simply does not enter most people's minds. However, with Windows PowerShell 2.0 and later, the command-line situation has changed somewhat. By using the techniques detailed in this section, an IT Pro now has a supportable command-line solution to the problem of performing Active Directory queries.

# Using [ADSISearcher]

Several options are available when querying Active Directory from the Windows PowerShell prompt. One option is to use the [ADSISearcher] type accelerator, which is a shortcut to the *System.DirectoryServices.DirectorySearcher* class. The [ADSISearcher] type accelerator merely saves you a bit of typing; you still need to give [ADSISearcher] the appropriate constructor to actually create an instance of the class. If you do not use [ADSISearcher], you need to use the New-Object cmdlet to create the object. First, you can put the New-Object command inside smooth parentheses to force the creation of the object and then call the *FindAll* method from the *DirectorySearcher* object. The resulting collection of *DirectoryEntry* objects is pipelined to the Select-Object cmdlet where the *path* property is returned, as shown here:

```
PS C:\> (New-Object DirectoryServices.DirectorySearcher "ObjectClass=user").Find
All() | Select path

Path
----
LDAP://CN=Administrator,CN=Users,DC=nwtraders,DC=com
LDAP://CN=Guest,CN=Users,DC=nwtraders,DC=com
LDAP://CN=BERLIN,OU=Domain Controllers,DC=nwtraders,DC=com
LDAP://CN=krbtgt,CN=Users,DC=nwtraders,DC=com
LDAP://CN=WINDOWS 8,CN=Computers,DC=nwtraders,DC=com
LDAP://CN=Windows 8Admin,OU=Students,DC=nwtraders,DC=com
List Truncated -
```

To use the [ADSISearcher] type accelerator, you still need to supply it with an appropriate constructor, which in many cases is the search filter expressed in LDAP search filter syntax. LDAP search filter syntax is defined in RFC 2254 and is represented by Unicode strings. The search filters allow you to specify search criteria in an efficient and effective manner. Some examples of using the LDAP search filter syntax are shown in Table 7-1.

**TABLE 7-1** LDAP search filter examples

| Search Filter | Description |
| --- | --- |
| ObjectClass=Computer | All computer objects |
| ObjectClass=OrganizationalUnit | All organizational unit objects |
| ObjectClass=User | All user objects as well as all computer objects |
| ObjectCategory=User | All user objects |
| (&(ObjectCategory=User)(ObjectClass=Person)) | All user objects |
| L=Berlin | All objects with the location of Berlin |
| Name=*Berlin* | All objects with a name that contains Berlin |
| (&(L=Berlin)(ObjectCategory=OrganizationalUnit)) | All organizational units with the location of Berlin |

| Search Filter | Description |
|---|---|
| (&(ObjectCategory=OrganizationalUnit)(Name=*Berlin*)) | All organizational units with a name that contains Berlin |
| (&(ObjectCategory=OrganizationalUnit)(Name=*Berlin*)(!L=Berlin)) | All organizational units with a name that contains Berlin but does not have a location of Berlin |
| (&(ObjectCategory=OrganizationalUnit)(Name=*Berlin*)(!L=*)) | All organizational units with a name that contains Berlin but does not have any location specified |
| (&(ObjectCategory=OrganizationalUnit)(|(L=Berlin)(L=Charlotte))) | All organizational units with a location of either Berlin or Charlotte |

As shown in the examples in Table 7-1, the search filter can be specified in two ways. The first method is a straightforward assignment filter. The attribute, the operator, and the value constitute the filter, as shown here:

```
PS C:\> ([ADSISearcher]"Name=Charlotte").FindAll() | Select Path

Path
----
LDAP://OU=Charlotte,DC=nwtraders,DC=com
```

The second way to use the LDAP search filter is to combine multiple filters. The operator goes first, followed by filter A and then by filter B. You can combine multiple filters and operators as shown in the syntax examples in Table 7-1. An example of a compound filter is shown here:

```
PS C:\> ([ADSISearcher]"(|(Name=Charlotte)(Name=Atlanta))").FindAll() | Select Path

Path
----
LDAP://OU=Atlanta,DC=nwtraders,DC=com
LDAP://OU=Charlotte,DC=nwtraders,DC=com
```

The operators that you can use for either straightforward assignment filters or compound search filters are listed in Table 7-2.

**TABLE 7-2** LDAP search filter logic operators

| Operator | Description |
|---|---|
| = | Equal to |
| ~= | Approximately equal to |
| <= | Lexicographically less than or equal to |
| >= | Lexicographically greater than or equal to |
| & | AND |
| \| | OR |
| ! | NOT |

Table 7-3 lists special characters. If any of these special characters must appear in a search filter as a literal character, it must be replaced by the escape sequence.

**TABLE 7-3** LDAP search filter special characters

| ASCII Character | Escape Sequence Substitute |
| --- | --- |
| * | \2a |
| ( | \28 |
| ) | \29 |
| \ | \5c |
| NUL | \00 |
| / | \2f |

As shown in Figure 7-8, special characters are allowed in organizational unit names in Active Directory.

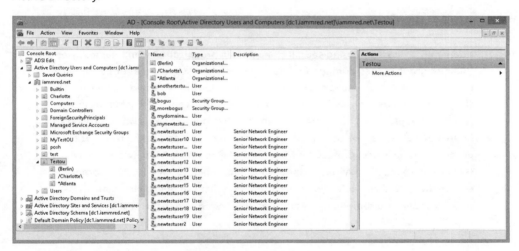

**FIGURE 7-8** Organizational unit names using special characters.

As shown in Figure 7-8, there is an organizational unit named *Atlanta. To retrieve this particular organizational unit, you need to use the \2a character as shown here:

```
PS C:\> ([ADSISearcher]"name=\2aAtlanta").FindAll() | Select Path

Path
----
LDAP://OU=*Atlanta,DC=nwtraders,DC=com
```

To retrieve the organizational unit named (Berlin), you need to use the \28 and \29 escape sequences as documented in Table 7-3 and as shown here:

```
PS C:\> ([ADSISearcher]"name=\28Berlin\29").FindAll() | Select Path
```

```
Path
----
LDAP://OU=(Berlin),DC=nwtraders,DC=com
```

As shown in Figure 7-8, there is also an organizational unit named /Charlotte\. The escape sequence substitute for the forward slash is \2f and for the backward slash is \5c. To retrieve the organizational unit named /Charlotte\ by using the LDAP search filter and the [ADSISearcher] type accelerator, you can use a query that looks like the following:

```
PS C:\> ([ADSISearcher]"name=\2fCharlotte\5c").FindAll() | Select Path

Path
----
LDAP://OU=\/Charlotte\\,DC=nwtraders,DC=com
```

The LDAP search filter special characters and their associated escape sequence substitutes are documented in Table 7-3, earlier in this chapter.

By using the Invoke-Command cmdlet, the [ADSISearcher] can easily be used to query the Active Directory of an untrusted forest or domain. When doing so, it is often important to provide the fully qualified domain name of the computer because it is possible that you might not have complete name resolution when using only the NetBIOS name of the server. It is also best to submit the credentials in a User Principal Name (UPN) fashion. When the command is run, the credential dialog box appears and prompts for the password, which must be typed in. The command is shown here:

```
PS C:\> Invoke-Command -ComputerName Sydney.WoodBridgeBank.Com -Credential '
administrator@WoodBridgeBank.com -ScriptBlock {([ADSISearcher]"L=Berlin").Findall()}
PSComputerName    : sydney.woodbridgebank.com
```

```
RunspaceId          : 112f974a-00aa-417c-8a13-9033a49354bd
PSShowComputerName  : True
Path                : LDAP://OU=Berlin Bank,DC=woodbridgebank,DC=com
Properties          : {ou, dscorepropagationdata, whencreated, name...}
```

## Using Active Directory cmdlets

Active Directory cmdlets are included with Windows Server 2008 R2 and above. They are contained in a module and must first be loaded by using the `Import-Module` cmdlet. Of course, you can simply select the Active Directory Windows PowerShell icon, which starts PowerShell with the Active Directory cmdlets already loaded. It is good that the Active Directory cmdlets are contained in a module because you can use the `Import-Module` cmdlet to add them from a remote computer into a Windows PowerShell session that does not have the cmdlets. To do this, you need to perform the following steps:

1. Establish a remote session to the server running Windows 2008 R2.

2. Import the Active Directory cmdlets by using the `Import-Module` cmdlet.

3. Perform the Active Directory query.

4. Disconnect from the remote session.

5. Remove the remote session.

> **NOTE** When using the `Remove-PSSession` cmdlet with the *–id* parameter, keep in mind that you might not always know what the session ID number actually is. The first session ID is 1, and the second session ID is 2. Windows PowerShell keeps a running tally of all of the sessions. However, you might not be aware of which session ID number you have reached. As a best practice, I always use the `Get-PSSession` cmdlet to obtain a listing of all of the PSSessions on the computer. I also make a habit of removing disconnected sessions that I do not expect to go back to within the near future. This process frees up the resources consumed by the session.

This technique to remove unused sessions is illustrated here:

```
PS C:\> $ps = New-PSSession -ComputerName Sydney.WoodBridgeBank.Com -Credential
administrator@WoodBridgeBank.Com
PS C:\> Enter-PSSession $ps
[sydney.woodbridgebank.com]: PS C:\> Import-Module ActiveDirectory
[sydney.woodbridgebank.com]: PS C:\> Get-ADOrganizationalUnit -Filter "L -eq 'Berlin'"

Name            : Berlin Bank
Country         : DE
PostalCode      :
City            : Berlin
ManagedBy       :
StreetAddress   :
State           : Berlin
ObjectGUID      : dde90f41-128c-4567-9822-00de5a4c96cc
```

```
ObjectClass       : organizationalUnit
DistinguishedName : OU=Berlin Bank,DC=woodbridgebank,DC=com
[sydney.woodbridgebank.com]: PS C:\> Exit-PSSession
PS C:\> Get-PSSession

     Id Name              ComputerName    State    Configuration
     -- ----              ------------    -----    -------------
      1 Session1          sydney.woodb... Broken   Microsoft.PowerShell
PS C:\> Remove-PSSession -Id 1
```

In addition to using the Active Directory filter syntax, which uses Windows PowerShell operators and supports rich type conversions, you can also use the LDAP filter syntax discussed in the previous section. To use the LDAP filter syntax, you can use the *–LDAPFilter* parameter instead of the *–filter* parameter and supply the LDAP search filter expression inside a set of single quotation marks as shown here:

```
PS C:\> Get-ADOrganizationalUnit -LDAPFilter '(L=Berlin)'

Name              : Berlin Bank
Country           : DE
PostalCode        :
City              : Berlin
ManagedBy         :
StreetAddress     :
State             : Berlin
ObjectGUID        : dde90f41-128c-4567-9822-00de5a4c96cc
ObjectClass       : organizationalUnit
DistinguishedName : OU=Berlin Bank,DC=woodbridgebank,DC=com
```

## Just use the command line

Many powerful commands can be executed directly from the command line by using legacy command-line utilities. There is nothing wrong with using these commands, and they are fully supported in Windows PowerShell. The fact that you can use the Get-Command cmdlet to easily search for legacy command-line utilities should be an indicator that Windows PowerShell supports using these commands. To use the Get-Command cmdlet to search for executables, you can use wildcard characters if you are not familiar with the exact name of the program, as shown here:

```
PS C:\> Get-Command ds*

CommandType      Name            Definition
-----------      ----            ----------
Application      ds16gt.dll      C:\Windows\system32\ds16gt.dll
Application      ds32gt.dll      C:\Windows\system32\ds32gt.dll
Application      dsa.msc         C:\Windows\system32\dsa.msc
Application      dsacls.exe      C:\Windows\system32\dsacls.exe
Application      dsadd.exe       C:\Windows\system32\dsadd.exe
Application      dsadmin.dll     C:\Windows\system32\dsadmin.dll
Application      dsauth.dll      C:\Windows\system32\dsauth.dll
Application      dsdbutil.exe    C:\Windows\system32\dsdbutil...
Application      dsdmo.dll       C:\Windows\system32\dsdmo.dll
```

```
Application      dsget.exe          C:\Windows\system32\dsget.exe
Application      dskquota.dll       C:\Windows\system32\dskquota...
Application      dskquoui.dll       C:\Windows\system32\dskquoui...
Application      dsmgmt.exe         C:\Windows\system32\dsmgmt.exe
Application      dsmod.exe          C:\Windows\system32\dsmod.exe
Application      dsmove.exe         C:\Windows\system32\dsmove.exe
Application      dsound.dll         C:\Windows\system32\dsound.dll
Application      dsprop.dll         C:\Windows\system32\dsprop.dll
Application      dsprov.dll         C:\Windows\System32\Wbem\dsp...
Application      dsprov.mof         C:\Windows\System32\Wbem\dsp...
Application      dsquery.dll        C:\Windows\system32\dsquery.dll
Application      dsquery.exe        C:\Windows\system32\dsquery.exe
Application      dsrm.exe           C:\Windows\system32\dsrm.exe
Application      dssec.dat          C:\Windows\system32\dssec.dat
Application      dssec.dll          C:\Windows\system32\dssec.dll
Application      dssenh.dll         C:\Windows\system32\dssenh.dll
Application      dssite.msc         C:\Windows\system32\dssite.msc
Application      dsuiext.dll        C:\Windows\system32\dsuiext.dll
Application      dsuiwiz.dll        C:\Windows\system32\dsuiwiz.dll
Application      dswave.dll         C:\Windows\system32\dswave.dll
```

The previous command returns any valid Windows PowerShell command including functions, cmdlets, and executable files. If you are specifically searching for command-line utilities, you should use the *commandtype* parameter, as shown here:

```
PS C:\> Get-Command -Name ds* -CommandType application

CommandType      Name               Definition
-----------      ----               ----------
Application      ds16gt.dll         C:\Windows\system32\ds16gt.dll
Application      ds32gt.dll         C:\Windows\system32\ds32gt.dll
Application      dsa.msc            C:\Windows\system32\dsa.msc
Application      dsacls.exe         C:\Windows\system32\dsacls.exe
Application      dsadd.exe          C:\Windows\system32\dsadd.exe
Application      dsadmin.dll        C:\Windows\system32\dsadmin.dll
Application      dsauth.dll         C:\Windows\system32\dsauth.dll
Application      dsdbutil.exe       C:\Windows\system32\dsdbutil...
Application      dsdmo.dll          C:\Windows\system32\dsdmo.dll
Application      dsget.exe          C:\Windows\system32\dsget.exe
Application      dskquota.dll       C:\Windows\system32\dskquota...
Application      dskquoui.dll       C:\Windows\system32\dskquoui...
Application      dsmgmt.exe         C:\Windows\system32\dsmgmt.exe
Application      dsmod.exe          C:\Windows\system32\dsmod.exe
Application      dsmove.exe         C:\Windows\system32\dsmove.exe
Application      dsound.dll         C:\Windows\system32\dsound.dll
Application      dsprop.dll         C:\Windows\system32\dsprop.dll
Application      dsprov.dll         C:\Windows\System32\Wbem\dsp...
Application      dsprov.mof         C:\Windows\System32\Wbem\dsp...
Application      dsquery.dll        C:\Windows\system32\dsquery.dll
Application      dsquery.exe        C:\Windows\system32\dsquery.exe
Application      dsrm.exe           C:\Windows\system32\dsrm.exe
Application      dssec.dat          C:\Windows\system32\dssec.dat
Application      dssec.dll          C:\Windows\system32\dssec.dll
Application      dssenh.dll         C:\Windows\system32\dssenh.dll
Application      dssite.msc         C:\Windows\system32\dssite.msc
```

```
Application    dsuiext.dll                 C:\Windows\system32\dsuiext.dll
Application    dsuiwiz.dll                 C:\Windows\system32\dsuiwiz.dll
Application    dswave.dll                  C:\Windows\system32\dswave.dll
```

The ease of use and flexibility of Windows PowerShell created resurgence in the interest of command-line programs. An example is the use of DSQuery.exe, which allows the user to quickly issue a query against Active Directory. With the inclusion of the [ADSISearcher] type accelerator and various Active Directory cmdlets in Windows Server 2008 R2, you might wonder why you should use the DSQuery.exe utility. Here is the syntax to obtain a listing of the organizational units in your domain by using DSQuery.exe:

```
PS C:\> dsquery ou
"OU=Domain Controllers,DC=nwtraders,DC=com"
"OU=Students,DC=nwtraders,DC=com"
"OU=ManagedComputers,DC=nwtraders,DC=com"
"OU=TestOU,DC=nwtraders,DC=com"
```

The syntax to retrieve a listing of the organizational units in your domain by using the [ADSISearcher] type accelerator is as follows:

```
PS C:\> ([ADSISearcher]"objectClass=OrganizationalUnit").findall() | select-Object
-property path

Path
----
LDAP://OU=Domain Controllers,DC=nwtraders,DC=com
LDAP://OU=Students,DC=nwtraders,DC=com
LDAP://OU=ManagedComputers,DC=nwtraders,DC=com
LDAP://OU=TestOU,DC=nwtraders,DC=com
```

The syntax to obtain a listing of organizational units by using the Get-ADOrganizationalUnit cmdlet, which is included in the Active Directory module on Windows Server 2008 R2, is a bit easier to use. When working from the Active Directory Windows PowerShell prompt, you do not always need to specify parameter names. You can also use the alias name (*Select* for Select-Object) if desired. Using an alias name makes the syntax shorter but can lead to problems when it is time to modify the command. Use of the Get-ADOrganizationalUnit cmdlet is shown here:

```
PS C:\> Get-ADOrganizationalUnit -Filter "name -like '*'" | Select DistinguishedName

DistinguishedName
-----------------
OU=Domain Controllers,DC=woodbridgebank,DC=com
OU=Test1,DC=woodbridgebank,DC=com
```

If your only consideration is shortness of syntax, DSQuery.exe obviously wins. However, other considerations might come into play. DSQuery.exe returns a string, while the [ADSISearcher] type accelerator returns a *DirectoryEntry* object. The Get-ADOrganizationalUnit command returns a *Microsoft.ActiveDirectory.Management .ADOrganizationalUnit* object. Depending on what you are trying to do, one type of object might be preferable over another.

Beyond the return type issue, other problems with DSQuery.exe also exist. DSQuery.exe sacrifices power for simplicity, which means that there are only a few attributes that you can use as your search query. If you want to find all of the organizational units in Active Directory that contain the name Berlin in them, you can use the following syntax:

```
dsquery ou -name *berlin*
```

Alternatively, if you want to find all of the organizational units in Active Directory that have a location attribute specified as actually being in Berlin, you need to use either the Active Directory cmdlets or the [ADSISearcher] type accelerator. If you understand what DSQuery .exe can do, there is no problem at all with availing yourself of this easy-to-use tool. You can even pipeline the results from DSQuery.exe into other utilities, such as DSMove.exe. DSMove .exe moves an object to another location in Active Directory, DSMod.exe allows you to change attribute values, and DSrm.exe allows you to delete objects from Active Directory.

**NOTE** As a best practice, I generally prefer to supply full parameter names even when working from the command line in Windows PowerShell. While you can often supply parameters by position, you must remember which parameter is the default parameter as well as remember the order of the parameters of the cmdlet when using more than one parameter. I often try a command multiple times before I retrieve exactly the information I am looking for. When moving from the default parameter to include several modifying parameters, the syntax changes if you do not use parameter names as shown here:

```
PS C:\> Get-Command ds* application
Get-Command : The command could not be retrieved because the
ArgumentList parameter can be specified only when retrieving a single
cmdlet or script.
At line:1 char:12
+ Get-Command <<<< ds* application
+ CategoryInfo : InvalidArgument: (ds16gt.dLL:ApplicationInfo)
[Get-Command], PSArgumentException
+ FullyQualifiedErrorId : CommandArgsOnlyForSingleCmdlet,Microsoft
.PowerShell.Commands.GetCommandCommand
```

# Calculating the benefit from the script

When you consider the time consumed in writing a script, testing the script, and putting the script into change control, a considerable amount of expense can be involved in the development process. Therefore, it is important that IT Pros spend a bit of time assessing the benefit of writing a script before launching a scripting-writing binge. As noted in this chapter, many of the traditional reasons for writing a script are no longer valid with Windows PowerShell. This does not mean that you will never need to write a script, but it does mean that a short command can usually be written that accomplishes a significant amount of work. When considering the question of whether to script or not to script, some of the benefits of a script are discussed in this section.

Jason A. Yoder, MCT
*President, MCTExpert, Inc.*

More often than not, I find myself using Windows PowerShell to empower IT professionals who are accustomed to being treated as an expense, rather than an asset of a business. This no longer needs to be the de facto standard. With Windows PowerShell now in its fourth generation, it is hard to imagine any IT profession who manages a Microsoft server product or domain to justify doing repetitive tasks manually. As a matter of fact, leveraging Windows PowerShell gives the IT professional the ability to quantify their contribution to an organization and demonstrate a high return on their Windows PowerShell investment.

Imagine this: Every time someone in your organization executes a script that you have written, you can have this script send some critical information to a CSV file on a central server. The information passed is simply what script was executed, by whom, the amount of time the script saved the user. Using this information, the IT professional can demonstrate years of increased productivity from the short investment in a few scripts. In some cases, it can be demonstrated that the hiring of additional staff was averted because of the number of hours saved through Windows PowerShell.

In one scenario, I helped a client who had to dedicate a staff member to backing up and clearing security logs for 3 hours every day across a multitude of remote servers. In just 3 hours of development and testing, this client now spends less than 1 hour per year on this task—1095 hours to 1. It does not take a financial wizard to see the potential cost savings. In another case, I had a user who had a weekly task requiring two hours per week to complete utilizing Active Directory and Excel. Leveraging Windows PowerShell, the task is completed automatically, with the final product in her inbox when she walks into the office on Monday morning—104 hours of labor to zero.

The question to ask yourself is not, "What can I do with Windows PowerShell?" The real question is, "What do I *want* to do with Windows PowerShell?" When you answer this question and implement your vision, don't forget to quantify the results. You might just end up looking like an IT rock star and the new company asset.

# Repeatability

When a task needs to be repeated many times, it becomes an obvious candidate for a script (not in all situations, of course). It is quite common for an IT Pro to look at service status information, which is easily obtained by using the Get-Service cmdlet. If you want to check the status of a specific process, you need to use the *Name* parameter, as shown here:

```
PS C:\> Get-Process -Name powershell

Handles  NPM(K)    PM(K)      WS(K) VM(M)   CPU(s)     Id ProcessName
-------  ------    -----      ----- -----   ------     -- -----------
    661       9    42616      46024   202     3.61    880 powershell
```

If you are interested in the latest entry written to the application event log, you need to use two parameters, as shown here:

```
PS C:\> Get-WinEvent -LogName application -MaxEvents 1

TimeCreated          ProviderName                          Id Message
-----------          ------------                          -- -------
1/26/2009 10:47:... VSS                                  8193 Volume Shadow Co...
```

There is little reason to write a script for these cases because the command-line syntax is clear, easy to use, and easily discoverable if you happen to forget the exact syntax. All you need to do is use the Get-Help cmdlet.

If you need to perform a task on a routine basis and it needs to be performed against a group of computers, the task is a candidate for a script. Suppose you need to check the status of the fragmentation on a number of computers. You can probably determine a way to run the command directly from the Windows PowerShell prompt, but the next time you need to check the fragmentation on a number of computers, you will spend another 20 or 30 minutes working to get the syntax just right. Instead, a script named DefragAnalysisReport.ps1 can probably be written in less than one hour. Such a script can use the *Win32_Volume* WMI class, call the *DefragAnalysis* method for each drive on the computer, and write the results to a text file.

In the DefragAnalysisReport.ps1 script, you first need to create an array of computer names and assign them to the *$arycomputer* variable. This procedure can be done either by hard-coding the literal values as shown here or by using the Get-Content cmdlet and reading the values from a text file. Next, you must assign a value for the output path of the defragmentation analysis report. This path is a folder that already exists on the computer that will be running the script; it does not need to exist on the target computer because all of the reports will be stored locally. This section of code is shown here:

```
$arycomputer = "Windows 8","Berlin"
$FilePath = "C:\fso"
```

You now need to walk through the array of computer names that is stored in the *$arycomputer* variable by using the *Foreach* statement, as shown here:

```
Foreach($Computer in $aryComputer)
{
```

You can then use the Get-WmiObject cmdlet to query the *Win32_Volume* WMI class; this class exists on Windows Server 2003 and later versions. As a best practice, if you anticipate running the script on older versions of the Windows operating system, you should add some error handling to detect the operating system version and gracefully move on to the next computer. This technique is discussed in Chapter 6, "Avoiding scripting pitfalls." The WMI query is shown here:

```
Get-WmiObject -Class win32_volume -Filter "DriveType = 3" '
     -ComputerName $computer |
```

The results of the WMI query are pipelined to the ForEach-Object cmdlet. The pipelining technique normally provides performance improvements over storing the results of the query into a variable and then iterating the results through the collection because, as soon as the first object is retrieved, it is passed over the pipeline and the processing continues. The first task to perform when inside the ForEach-Object cmdlet is to print a message that indicates which computer is being tested by using the *–Begin* parameter, as shown here:

```
ForEach-Object '
-Begin { "Testing $computer" } '
```

You can use the *Process* block to perform the actual defrag analysis, which occurs once for each drive. The *DefragAnalysis* method is called for the current object that is on the pipeline; the *$_* variable is an automatic variable that refers to that object. The *DefragAnalysis* method returns both an error report as well as an instance of the *Win32_DefragAnalysis* WMI class. Both are captured in the *$rtn* variable as shown here:

```
-Process {
   "Testing drive $($_.name) for fragmentation. Please wait ..."
   $RTN = $_.DefragAnalysis()
```

To produce the defragmentation report, you can use redirection. A single right-angle arrow (>) overwrites any previously existing reports. Because there is a strong possibility that the server might have more than one drive, it is better to use the double right-angle arrow (>>). The other option when using redirection is to use the Out-File cmdlet, which has the advantage of allowing you to specify what encoding to use with the file. Using the Out-File cmdlet is also more readable than using redirection arrows, so I generally use the Out-File cmdlet when writing a script. The report header section is shown here:

```
"Defrag report for $computer" >> "$FilePath\Defrag$computer.txt"
"Report for Drive $($_.Name)" >> "$FilePath\Defrag$computer.txt"
"Report date: $(Get-Date)" >> "$FilePath\Defrag$computer.txt"
"-------------------------------" >> "$FilePath\Defrag$computer.txt"
```

One of the great features of Windows PowerShell is the way in which it automatically displays the properties and values of an object. VBScript requires more than a dozen lines of code to print the value of each property. As you can see here, the *Win32_DefragAnalysis* management object that is stored in the *DefragAnalysis* property is pipelined to the Format-List cmdlet to remove the system properties of the WMI class. All system properties begin with a double underscore (__), which means that a regular expression pattern that selects properties beginning with the letters *a* through *z* that are followed by one or more characters will remove the system properties. The resulting list of properties and their values are redirected to the file in the location specified by the *$filepath* property, as shown here:

```
    $RTN.DefragAnalysis |
    Format-List -Property [a-z]* >> "$FilePath\Defrag$computer.txt"
} '
```

Last, you can print a message indicating that testing is completed on the computer by using the *End* parameter, as shown here:

```
 -END { "Completed testing $computer" }
} #end foreach computer
```

The completed DefragAnalysisReport.ps1 script is shown here.

**DefragAnalysisReport.ps1**
```
$arycomputer = "Windows 8","Berlin"
$FilePath = "C:\fso"
Foreach($Computer in $aryComputer)
{
 Get-WmiObject -Class win32_volume -Filter "DriveType = 3" '
       -ComputerName $computer |
 ForEach-Object '
 -Begin { "Testing $computer" } '
 -Process {
   "Testing drive $($_.name) for fragmentation. Please wait ..."
    $RTN = $_.DefragAnalysis()
  "Defrag report for $computer" >> "$FilePath\Defrag$computer.txt"
  "Report for Drive $($_.Name)" >> "$FilePath\Defrag$computer.txt"
  "Report date: $(Get-Date)" >> "$FilePath\Defrag$computer.txt"
  "-----------------------------" >> "$FilePath\Defrag$computer.txt"
   $RTN.DefragAnalysis |
   Format-List -Property [a-z]* >> "$FilePath\Defrag$computer.txt"
 } '
 -END { "Completed testing $computer" }
} #end foreach computer
```

Stefan Stranger, Senior Premier Field Engineer
*Microsoft Corporation*

System Center Operations Manager has started to receive their Update Rollups using Windows Update. Because not all my demo/test machines are connected to the Internet, I was looking for a way to find the download links that Operations Manager uses from Windows Update.

Windows Update uses the .cab file at *http://go.microsoft.com/fwlink/?LinkId=76054,* and this .cab file contains a Package.xml file that contains the links where Operations Manager (and other products) download their Windows Update files.

I created a script that downloads the .cab file, extracts the needed files, and parses the .xml file to find the download links to download the Windows Update files, enabling me to update my test/demo environments offline.

The update agent retrieves its information from the wsusscn2.cab archive, which is made available for download by Microsoft at a static URL (*http://go.microsoft.com /fwlink/?linkid=76054*). The Microsoft Baseline Security Analyzer (MBSA) also loads that file to determine whether or not the system is completely patched.

The archive contains a catalog file, called package.xml, in which Microsoft indexes all security updates (and their dependencies) for all operating systems. The download URLs for all updates are also found there, allowing for direct downloading of the individual items from the Microsoft servers.

We first need to download the wsusscn2.cab file by using Windows PowerShell:

```
#Download Windows Update Cab file to search for download links Operations
Manager Cumulative Updates.

$download = "http://go.microsoft.com/fwlink/?LinkId=76054"


# Download cab file
Start-BitsTransfer -Source "http://go.microsoft.com/fwlink/?LinkId=76054"
-Destination "$env:temp\wsussnc2.cab"
```

The next step in the process is to extract the package.xml from the just downloaded wsusscn2.cab file. I used an *Expand-Cab* function, using the Component Object Model.

```
Function Expand-Cab ($SourceFile, $TargetFolder, $Item)
{

    $ShellObject = new-object -com shell.application
```

```
    # Zip File to unzip from:
    $zipfolder = $ShellObject.namespace($sourceFile) # where the .zip is
    $item = $zipfolder.parsename("$Item")         # the item in the zip
    $targetfolder = $ShellObject.namespace("$targetFolder")
    $targetfolder.copyhere($item)


}
```

We can now use this *Expand-Cab* function to extract the wsusscn2.cab file to the user's temp folder:

```
#Expand Package.cab from WSUSsnc2.cab
Expand-Cab -SourceFile "$env:temp\wsussnc2.cab" -TargetFolder "$env:temp"
-Item "Package.cab"
```

When we extract the wsusscn2.cab file, we have a new Package.cab file, which we also need to extract to find the Package.xml file:

```
#Expand Package.xml from Package.cab
Expand-Cab -SourceFile "$env:temp\Package.cab" -TargetFolder "$env:temp"
-Item "Package.xml"
```

The final step in finding the download URLs for the System Center Operations Manager Rollup Updates is to use Windows PowerShell to read the Package.xml file:

```
[xml]$wsusupdate = get-content -path "$env:temp\package.xml"
$urls = $wsusupdate.OfflineSyncPackage.FileLocations.FileLocation
```

And by filtering using the KB article names, we can find the Update Rollup files for each KB article:

```
$KBArticle = "KB2750631"
$urls | ? {$_.Url -like "*$KBArticle*"} | ft -Property Url -wrap
```

And now we use `Start-BitsTransfer` to download the .cab files for this KB article:

```
$urls | ? {$_.Url -like "*KB2750631*"} | select @{L="Source";E={$_.Url}},
@{L="Destination";E={"$env:temp\"+(($_.Url) -split "/")[($_.Url -split
"/").count -1]}} | Start-BitsTransfer
```

# Documentability

A script provides assurance that certain steps have been performed in a consistent manner. This process is important when performing a series of complicated configuration tasks or even when making simple registry changes. The script documents exactly what took place during the configuration change session. If a configuration change is later discovered to have been in error, a Windows PowerShell script provides documentation for the commands that were run, and the same script can usually be easily modified to undo the changes that were made.

In the following example, a new registry key is created in the HKEY_CURRENT_USER hive that is named Scripting; another registry key named Logon is also created. After the two registry keys are created, a property named *ScriptName* with a value of *temp* is created. The resulting registry keys are shown in Figure 7-9, and the following code creates the registry keys:

```
PS C:\> New-Item -Path HKCU:\Scripting\Logon -Force


    Hive: HKEY_CURRENT_USER\Scripting


Name                            Property
----                            --------
Logon


PS C:\> New-ItemProperty -Path HKCU:\Scripting\Logon -Name ScriptName -Value "Temp"


ScriptName   : Temp
PSPath       : Microsoft.PowerShell.Core\Registry::HKEY_CURRENT_USER\Scripting\Logon
PSParentPath : Microsoft.PowerShell.Core\Registry::HKEY_CURRENT_USER\Scripting
PSChildName  : Logon
PSDrive      : HKCU
PSProvider   : Microsoft.PowerShell.Core\Registry
```

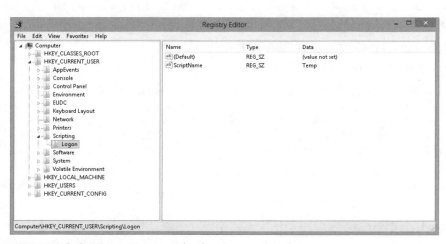

**FIGURE 7-9** *ScriptName* property under the Logon registry key.

If a problem arises during the creation of the registry keys and the associated property values, you must either open the Registry Editor or type an assortment of commands in the Windows PowerShell console. A script is generally easier to modify because you can see all of the code that executed at the same time. The commands that were earlier typed in the Windows PowerShell console are shown in the CreateScriptingRegistryKey.ps1 script.

**CreateScriptingRegistryKey.ps1**

```
New-Item -Path HKCU:\Scripting\Logon -Value "Temp" -Force
New-ItemProperty -Path HKCU:\Scripting\Logon -Name ScriptName -Value "Temp"
```

If a problem arises with the command, it is easy to create a new script based on the first script, which rolls back the changes as shown in the DeleteScriptingRegistryKey.ps1 script. The second line of the script is commented out, and the first line is changed from New-Item to Remove-Item. The *–force* parameter is changed to *Recurse*, and the *value* parameter is not required when using Remove-Item. The modified DeleteScriptingRegistryKey.ps1 script is shown here:

**DeleteScriptingRegistryKey.ps1**

```
Remove-Item -Path HKCU:\Scripting -Recurse
#New-ItemProperty -Path HKCU:\Scripting\Logon -Name ScriptName -Value "Temp"
```

# Adaptability

Depending on the script design, the script can be used to perform other tasks. If a script is written in a modular fashion and takes advantage of functions and command-line arguments, it can be used to perform a variety of tasks. The functions themselves can be imported by dot-sourcing the script into another script. The script itself can also be converted into a module, which can then be imported into the current session by using the Import-Module cmdlet.

As an example of a modular script design, you can look at the SaveWmiInformationAsDocument.ps1 script. The essential functionality of the script is contained as functions that can easily be reused in other scripts.

## Reusing Code

The ability to adapt functions from one script into another script can often justify the time and expense involved in writing the script in the first place. However, code reuse should not always be the first goal of a script writer. Writing a script in a completely modular fashion takes considerably longer than writing a script in a linear fashion. In addition, the investment of time for an undetermined possible future reuse is not always the wisest approach. Writing modular code is a good discipline and generally makes the code easier to read and modify. Both of these design goals are worthwhile endeavors, but potential code reuse alone is not enough reason to justify the extra effort.

The first function in the SaveWmiInformationAsDocument.ps1 script is named the *CreateWordDoc* function, which creates an instance of the *Word.Application* object and stores it in a script-level variable named *$word*. The function next makes the Microsoft Office Word application visible and adds a document to the document collection, as shown here:

```
Function CreateWordDoc()
{
  $script:word = New-Object -ComObject word.application
  $word.visible = $true
  $Script:doc = $word.documents.add()
} #end CreateWordDoc
```

The next function is named *CreateSelection*, and it accepts a string to use in the Office Word document for a heading. To create a Word selection, the script needs an instance of the *Word.Application* object. Because the *$word* variable was created in the script-level scope, it is available inside the *CreateSelection* function. The *selection* object is created by querying the *selection* property. The heading is typed into the Word document by using the *TypeText* method. A blank paragraph is created, and the function ends as shown here:

```
Function CreateSelection($Heading)
{
  $script:selection = $word.selection
  $selection.typeText($Heading)
  $selection.TypeParagraph()
} #end CreateSelection
```

The *GetWmiData* function is used to query a WMI class, convert the output to a string, and write the information into a Word document as a selection, as shown here:

```
Function GetWmiData($WmiClass)
{
 Get-WmiObject -class $wmiClass | Out-String |
 ForEach-Object {$selection.typeText($_)}
} #end GetWmiData
```

When the WMI information is retrieved, it is time to create the file path by using the *CreateFilePath* function so that the Word document can be saved. The function receives the WMI class name via the *$WmiClass* variable. It then uses the substring method from the *System.String* class to remove the first six characters from the WMI class name. The first six characters correspond to "Win32_," which is present in most of the WMI class names. To be more accurate, you need to test for other WMI class name patterns and modify the substring command according to the class name that is actually found. The function then uses the Join-Path cmdlet to build the file path that is to be used when saving the WMI documentation. This function is shown here:

```
Function CreateFilePath($wmiClass)
{
 $script:filename = $wmiClass.substring(6)
 $script:path = Join-Path -Path $folder -childpath $filename
} #end CreateFilePath
```

Next, the Word document needs to be saved. First you must create an instance of the *Microsoft.Office.Interop.Word.WdSaveFormat* enumeration by casting the string representation of the enumeration as a type. This type is also required to be a reference type, so it is cast as a *[ref]*. The *saveas* method from the *Word.Document* object requires both the path and the *saveformat* to be reference types. After the document is saved, the *Word.Application* object can be removed from memory via the *quit* method. The *SaveWordData* function is shown here:

```
Function SaveWordData($path)
{
 [ref]$SaveFormat = "microsoft.office.interop.word.WdSaveFormat" -as [type]
 $doc.saveas([ref]$path, [ref]$saveFormat::wdFormatDocument)
 $word.quit()
} #end SaveWordData
```

The entry point into the script creates some variables and calls the appropriate functions, as shown here:

```
$folder = "C:\fso"
$wmiClass = "Win32_Bios"
$heading = "$wmiClass information:"
CreateWordDoc
CreateSelection($Heading)
GetWmiData($wmiClass)
CreateFilePath($wmiClass)
SaveWordData($path)
```

The completed SaveWmiInformationAsDocument.ps1 script is shown here:

SaveWmiInformationAsDocument.ps1

```
Function CreateWordDoc()
```

```
{
  $script:word = New-Object -ComObject word.application
  $word.visible = $true
  $Script:doc = $word.documents.add()
} #end CreateWordDoc

Function CreateSelection($Heading)
{
  $script:selection = $word.selection
  $selection.typeText($Heading)
  $selection.TypeParagraph()
} #end CreateSelection

Function GetWmiData($WmiClass)
{
 Get-WmiObject -class $wmiClass | Out-String |
 ForEach-Object {$selection.typeText($_)}
} #end GetWmiData

Function CreateFilePath($wmiClass)
{
 $script:filename = $wmiClass.substring(6)
 $script:path = Join-Path -Path $folder -childpath $filename
} #end CreateFilePath

Function SaveWordData($path)
{
 [ref]$SaveFormat = "microsoft.office.interop.word.WdSaveFormat" -as [type]
 $doc.saveas([ref]$path, [ref]$saveFormat::wdFormatDocument)
 $word.quit()
} #end SaveWordData

# *** Entry point ***
$folder = "C:\fso"
$wmiClass = "Win32_Bios"
$heading = "$wmiClass information:"
CreateWordDoc
CreateSelection($Heading)
GetWmiData($wmiClass)
CreateFilePath($wmiClass)
SaveWordData($path)
```

## Tracking scripting opportunities

Chris Bellée, Premier Field Engineer
*Microsoft Corporation, Australia*

often receive requests from customers to create script examples. Often their ideas are good, and I then create a script and file it away for use at a later time, by using Microsoft Notepad, which is quick and easy to use. The plain-text file is compatible with all types of programs, and I do not need to worry about whether I have a specific Microsoft Office application installed. When I am writing a script, I often discover a new technique or technology that causes me to write a quick sample script illustrating the new technique or technology. This is not a very formal technique, but it has the advantage of simplicity.

A database of scripts is a great idea, perhaps easily created in Microsoft Office Access. You can then categorize the scripts by topic as well as by technology and can easily create a report that will point out areas that are lacking certain types of scripts. You can then review the list and fill in the gaps in your script portfolio. You can use this database for storage as well as for lookup and search. One very interesting idea is to create a script builder that is based on generic routines that are stored in a database. Of course, this does not really allow you to track scripting opportunities as much as it allows you to create new scripts based on the storage of your existing ideas. This script builder can be an extension of the Portable Script Center that is available from the Microsoft Script Center.

When I get ready to write a new script, I generally choose Microsoft.NET Framework classes if they are available instead of using an old VBScript function or even WMI classes, because I am more familiar with .NET programming and because I consider this process to be a best practice. The .NET Framework is native to Windows PowerShell, and it is much easier to call Win32 Application Programming Interfaces in Windows PowerShell 2.0. I will use these APIs when a class is not available to me from the .NET library, such as creating network shares and setting permissions on them.

# Script collaboration

While writing scripts can be fun to do and many network administrators seem to enjoy the process, it can also be time consuming. It is therefore important that the process is performed in such a way that it benefits the entire organization. You should understand that there is a difference between learning to script and writing scripts. It is true that network administrators often learn to script by writing scripts, but the two activities should be separated. Learning to script is a training function, and the time invested in learning to script should be tracked as part of the training budget. Writing scripts is an operational expense, and the time invested in writing production scripts should be tracked as an operational expense. If a network administrator takes eight hours to write a script that retrieves the amount of free disk space on a server, that network administrator does not know how to write scripts. Therefore, the eight hours should be tracked as part of the training budget and not as a production expense. It simply is not efficient for a company to have twelve different scripts that all detail the amount of free disk space on a computer.

If people in different departments write the same scripts, the problem of wasted time and effort becomes compounded, which is where collaboration comes into play. Through the use of collaboration tools, scripts can be shared and requested and features can be requested. Specific personnel can be detailed to write specific scripts. The tasks of training and production can be separated, and duplication of time and effort can be avoided.

## Additional resources

- The TechNet Script Center at *http://www.microsoft.com/technet/scriptcenter* contains numerous examples of the LDAP search filter syntax.
- Refer to the Knowledge Base article for information about using the NetSh Advanced Firewall commands at *http://support.microsoft.com/kb/947709.*
- LDAP search filter syntax is documented on MSDN at *http://msdn.microsoft.com/en-us /library/aa746385(VS.85).aspx.*
- All scripts from this chapter are located on the Script Center Script Repository at *http://gallery.technet.microsoft.com/scriptcenter/PowerShell-40-Best-d9e16039.*

# CHAPTER 8

# Designing the script

- Understanding functions
- Using functions to provide ease of code reuse
- Using more than two input parameters
- Using functions to encapsulate business logic
- Using functions to provide ease of modification
- Understanding filters
- Additional resources

Clear-cut guidelines can be used to design scripts and ensure that they are easy to understand, maintain, and troubleshoot. In this chapter, you will examine the reasons for scripting guidelines and view examples of both good and bad code design.

## Understanding functions

In Windows PowerShell 4.0, functions have moved to the forefront as the primary programming element used when writing PowerShell scripts. This is not necessarily due to improvements in functions per se but rather to a combination of factors, including the maturity of Windows PowerShell script writers. In earlier versions of Windows PowerShell, functions were not well understood, perhaps because of a lack of clear documentation as to their use, purpose, and application.

Both subroutines and functions are found in VBScript. According to the classic definitions, a subroutine is used to encapsulate code that can perform such actions as writing to a database or creating a Microsoft Office Word document. A function is used to return a value. An example of the classic VBScript function is one that converts a temperature from Fahrenheit to Celsius. The function receives the value in Fahrenheit and returns the value in Celsius. The classic function always returns a value; if it does not, the subroutine should be used.

To create a function, you begin with the *Function* keyword followed by the name of the function. As a best practice, you should use the Windows PowerShell verb-noun combination when creating functions. Pick the verb from the standard list of Windows PowerShell verbs to make your functions easier to remember. It is a best practice to avoid creating new verbs when there is an existing verb that can easily do the job.

To obtain a better idea of the verb coverage, you can use the `Get-Command` cmdlet and pipe the results to the `Group-Object` cmdlet, as shown here:

```
Get-Command -CommandType cmdlet | Group-Object -Property Verb |
Sort-Object -Property count -Descending
```

When the preceding command is run, the resulting output is displayed in the following list. The command is run on Windows 8.1 and includes only the default cmdlets. As shown in the listing, the verb `Get` is used the most often by the default cmdlets, followed distantly by `Set`, `New`, and `Remove`.

```
Count Name                    Group
----- ----                    -----
   91 Get                     {Get-Acl, Get-Alias, Get-AppLockerFileInformation, Get-
AppLockerPolicy...}
   44 Set                     {Set-Acl, Set-Alias, Set-AppBackgroundTaskResourcePoli
cy, Set-AppLockerPolicy...}
   36 New                     {New-Alias, New-AppLockerPolicy, New-
CertificateNotificationTask, New-CimInstance...}
   26 Remove                  {Remove-AppxPackage, Remove-AppxProvisionedPackage,
Remove-BitsTransfer, Remove-Cert...
   15 Add                     {Add-AppxPackage, Add-AppxProvisionedPackage, Add-
BitsFile, Add-CertificateEnrollmen...
   14 Export                  {Export-Alias, Export-BinaryMiLog, Export-Certificate,
Export-Clixml...}
   12 Disable                 {Disable-AppBackgroundTaskDiagnosticLog, Disable-
ComputerRestore, Disable-JobTrigger...
```

```
  12 Import                   {Import-Alias, Import-BinaryMiLog, Import-Certificate,
Import-Clixml...}
  12 Enable                   {Enable-AppBackgroundTaskDiagnosticLog, Enable-
ComputerRestore, Enable-JobTrigger, E...
  10 Invoke                   {Invoke-CimMethod, Invoke-Command, Invoke-Expression,
Invoke-History...}
   9 Test                     {Test-AppLockerPolicy, Test-Certificate, Test-
ComputerSecureChannel, Test-Connection...
   9 Clear                    {Clear-Content, Clear-EventLog, Clear-History, Clear-
Item...}
   9 Start                    {Start-BitsTransfer, Start-DscConfiguration, Start-
DtcDiagnosticResourceManager, Sta...
   8 Write                    {Write-Debug, Write-Error, Write-EventLog, Write-
Host...}
   7 Out                      {Out-Default, Out-File, Out-GridView, Out-Host...}
   6 Register                 {Register-CimIndicationEvent, Register-EngineEvent,
Register-ObjectEvent, Register-P...
   6 ConvertTo                {ConvertTo-Csv, ConvertTo-Html, ConvertTo-Json,
ConvertTo-SecureString...}
   6 Stop                     {Stop-Computer, Stop-DtcDiagnosticResourceManager, Stop-
Job, Stop-Process...}
   5 Format                   {Format-Custom, Format-List, Format-SecureBootUEFI,
Format-Table...}
   4 ConvertFrom              {ConvertFrom-Csv, ConvertFrom-Json, ConvertFrom-
SecureString, ConvertFrom-StringData}
   4 Update                   {Update-FormatData, Update-Help, Update-List, Update-
TypeData}
   3 Suspend                  {Suspend-BitsTransfer, Suspend-Job, Suspend-Service}
   3 Complete                 {Complete-BitsTransfer, Complete-
DtcDiagnosticTransaction, Complete-Transaction}
   3 Show                     {Show-Command, Show-ControlPanelItem, Show-EventLog}
   3 Select                   {Select-Object, Select-String, Select-Xml}
   3 Rename                   {Rename-Computer, Rename-Item, Rename-ItemProperty}
   3 Resume                   {Resume-BitsTransfer, Resume-Job, Resume-Service}
   3 Receive                  {Receive-DtcDiagnosticTransaction, Receive-Job, Receive-
PSSession}
   3 Wait                     {Wait-Event, Wait-Job, Wait-Process}
   3 Unregister               {Unregister-Event, Unregister-PSSessionConfiguration,
Unregister-ScheduledJob}
   2 Use                      {Use-Transaction, Use-WindowsUnattend}
   2 Copy                     {Copy-Item, Copy-ItemProperty}
   2 Unblock                  {Unblock-File, Unblock-Tpm}
   2 Save                     {Save-Help, Save-WindowsImage}
   2 Restart                  {Restart-Computer, Restart-Service}
   2 Resolve                  {Resolve-DnsName, Resolve-Path}
   2 Split                    {Split-Path, Split-WindowsImage}
   2 Undo                     {Undo-DtcDiagnosticTransaction, Undo-Transaction}
   2 Join                     {Join-DtcDiagnosticResourceManager, Join-Path}
   2 Move                     {Move-Item, Move-ItemProperty}
   2 Measure                  {Measure-Command, Measure-Object}
   2 Disconnect               {Disconnect-PSSession, Disconnect-WSMan}
   2 Send                     {Send-DtcDiagnosticTransaction, Send-MailMessage}
   2 Connect                  {Connect-PSSession, Connect-WSMan}
   1 Where                    {Where-Object}
   1 Pop                      {Pop-Location}
```

```
1 Switch          {Switch-Certificate}
1 Trace           {Trace-Command}
1 Tee             {Tee-Object}
1 Sort            {Sort-Object}
1 Compare         {Compare-Object}
1 Checkpoint      {Checkpoint-Computer}
1 ForEach         {ForEach-Object}
1 Debug           {Debug-Process}
1 Initialize      {Initialize-Tpm}
1 Group           {Group-Object}
1 Enter           {Enter-PSSession}
1 Dismount        {Dismount-WindowsImage}
1 Expand          {Expand-WindowsImage}
1 Exit            {Exit-PSSession}
1 Convert         {Convert-Path}
1 Repair          {Repair-WindowsImage}
1 Confirm         {Confirm-SecureBootUEFI}
1 Restore         {Restore-Computer}
1 Reset           {Reset-ComputerMachinePassword}
1 Mount           {Mount-WindowsImage}
1 Limit           {Limit-EventLog}
1 Read            {Read-Host}
1 Push            {Push-Location}
```

## NOTES FROM THE FIELD

**Juan Carlos Ruiz Lopez, Premier Field Engineer**
*Microsoft Corporation*

Many IT admins are really scared when the terms *development* or *programming* arise. They think, "Well, I'm a system administrator, not a developer." In some countries, they use a nasty definition: "A developer is a cheap engine to convert coffee to code"; so it's usually outside of your plans.

However, sometimes you need to repeat a task. How do you create one thousand users, or move 200 Organizational Units, or restore a hacked web server at midnight, in a hurry, with your boss putting pressure on you, and in an error-free, nerves-free operation?

It is then that you need a script. Windows PowerShell allows you to easily script your tasks. Most of the time, the code that you need is already embedded into cmdlets, so you only have to put the pieces together in the pipeline (or several pipelines).

You are not writing code, just creating scripts. It is something everyone can do, not rocket-science, and it will save you lots of time.

And Windows PowerShell will let you write more and more complicated scripts. In the near future, you'll write into your scripts your own nested loops, calls to .Net objects, and so on. Maybe at that time you'll exchange your Windows PowerShell books on your desktop with the .NET reference, and then you will call that task *pro-gramming* instead of *writing scripts*. Not a bad thing—it simply means that you have learnt something new and that you are more prepared for your job.

In both cases, learn Windows PowerShell when you can do it, not when you must do it, or it will be too late.

And make sure that you script any task that is going to be repeated more than 0 times. Scripts tend to be run often when they are already written.

A function is not required to accept any parameters. In fact, many functions do not require input to perform their job in the script. Let's use an example to illustrate this point. A common task for network administrators is obtaining the operating system version. Script writers often need to do this to ensure that their script uses the correct interface or exits gracefully. It is also quite common that one set of files can be copied to a desktop running one version of the operating system and a different set of files can be copied for another version of the operating system.

The first step in creating a function is to choose a name. Because the function is going to retrieve information, the best verb to use from the listing of cmdlet verbs shown earlier is Get. For the noun portion of the name, it is best to use a term that describes the information that will be obtained. In this example, a noun named OperatingSystemVersion makes sense. An example of such a function is the one shown in the Get-OperatingSystemVersion.ps1 script. The *Get-OperatingSystemVersion* function uses Windows Management Instrumentation (WMI) to obtain the version of the operating system. In this most basic form of the function, you have the *Function* keyword followed by the name of the function as well as a script block containing code that is delimited by curly brackets. This pattern is shown here:

```
Function Function-Name
{
 #insert code here
}
```

In the Get-OperatingSystemVersion.ps1 script, the *Get-OperatingSystemVersion* function is at the top of the script. The script uses the *Function* keyword to define the function followed by the name *Get-OperatingSystemVersion*. The curly brackets are opened, followed by the code. The code uses the Get-WmiObject cmdlet to retrieve an instance of the *Win32_OperatingSystem* WMI class. Because this WMI class returns only a single instance, the properties of the class are directly accessible. The version is the property in question, and parentheses force the evaluation of the code inside them. The returned management object is used to emit the version value, and the curly brackets are used to close the function. The operating system version is returned to the code that calls the function. In this example, a string that writes "This OS is version " is used. A subexpression is used to force evaluation of the function. The version of the operating system is returned to the place from where the function is called, as shown in Get-OperatingSystemVersion.ps1.

```
Get-OperatingSystemVersion.ps1

Function Get-OperatingSystemVersion
{
 (Get-WmiObject -Class Win32_OperatingSystem).Version
} #end Get-OperatingSystemVersion

"This OS is version $(Get-OperatingSystemVersion)"
```

In the earlier listing of cmdlet verbs, the Read-Host cmdlet uses the Read verb to obtain information from the command line. This indicates that the Read verb is not used to describe reading a file. There is no verb named Display, and the Write verb is used in cmdlet names such as Write-Error and Write-Debug, neither of which really conform to the concept of displaying information. If you are writing a function that can read the content of a text file and display statistics about that file, you might call the function *Get-TextStatistics*. This is in keeping with cmdlet names such as Get-Process and Get-Service, which include the concept of emitting their retrieved content within their essential functionality. The *Get-TextStatistics* function accepts a single parameter named *–path*. What is interesting about parameters for functions is that you use a dash when you pass a value to the parameter. You use a variable when you refer to the value inside the function, such as *$path*. To call the *Get-TextStatistics* function, you have a few options. The first is to use the name of the function and put the value in parentheses, as shown here:

```
Get-TextStatistics("C:\fso\mytext.txt")
```

This is a typical way to call the function. This method works when there is a single parameter but does not work when there are two or more parameters. Another way to pass a value to the function is to use the dash and the parameter name as shown here:

```
Get-TextStatistics -path "C:\fso\mytext.txt"
```

You will note from the preceding example that no parentheses are required. You can also use positional arguments when passing a value by omitting the name of the parameter entirely and simply placing the value for the parameter following the call to the function, as illustrated here:

```
Get-TextStatistics "C:\fso\mytext.txt"
```

## Using positional arguments

The use of positional arguments works well when you are working from the command line and want to speed things along by reducing the typing load. This method can be a bit confusing, and I generally tend to avoid it, even when working at the command line. I avoid positional arguments because I often copy my working code from the console directly into a script; as a result, I would need to retype the command a second time to get rid of aliases and unnamed arguments. With the improvements in tab expansion in Windows PowerShell 4.0, I feel that the time saved by using positional or partial arguments does not sufficiently compensate for the time involved in retyping commands when they need to be transferred to scripts. The other reason that I always use named arguments is that they help me to be aware of the exact command syntax.

One additional way to pass a value to a function is to use partial parameter names. All that is required is enough of the parameter name to disambiguate it from other parameters. This means that if you have two parameters that both begin with the letter *p*, you need to supply enough letters of the parameter name to separate it from the other parameter, as illustrated here:

```
Get-TextStatistics -p "C:\fso\mytext.txt"
```

The complete text of the *Get-TextStatistics* function is shown the following Get-TextStatistics.ps1 script.

```
Get-TextStatistics.ps1

Function Get-TextStatistics($path)
{
 Get-Content -path $path |
 Measure-Object -line -character -word
}
```

Between Windows PowerShell 1.0 and PowerShell 4.0, the number of verbs grew from 40 to 98, but between Windows PowerShell 3.0 and 4.0, no new verbs were added. The Windows PowerShell team holds a strict line when it comes to adding new verbs, and the existing approved verbs should be sufficient for all admin tasks.

Upon choosing the verb for your function, you need to choose a noun to describe what the function does. Convention, but no enforced rules, dictate that the noun is singular. In most cases, this convention is followed as strictly as the rule to use approved verbs. For example, the following command lists functions and cmdlets that end in the letter s:

```
Get-Command -CommandType cmdlet, function| where noun -match "s$" | select noun -Unique
```

As appears in the output here, only seven nouns are plural:

```
Noun
----
NetNatExternalAddress
SmbShareAccess
AssignedAccess
NetAdapterQos
NetAdapterRss
NetAdapterQos
NetAdapterRss
AssignedAccess
BCStatus
DAConnectionStatus
DnsClientServerAddress
DtcTransactionsStatistics
LogProperties
MpComputerStatus
NetAdapterQos
NetAdapterRss
NetAdapterStatistics
NetIPAddress
NetNatExternalAddress
SmbShareAccess
StartApps
SupportedClusterSizes
SupportedFileSystems
SmbShareAccess
NetIPAddress
VpnServerAddress
NetIPAddress
NetNatExternalAddress
SmbShareAccess
AssignedAccess
DnsClientServerAddress
LogProperties
NetAdapterQos
NetAdapterRss
NetIPAddress
```

```
SmbShareAccess
Process
Alias
Alias
CimClass
Process
Alias
Alias
Alias
Process
Process
Process
Progress
```

After the function is named, you can create any parameters that the function might require. The parameters are contained within smooth parentheses. In the *Get-TextStatistics* function, the function accepts a single parameter named –*path*. When a function accepts a single parameter, you can pass the value to the function by placing the value for the parameter inside smooth parentheses. This command is shown here:

```
Get-TextLength("C:\fso\test.txt")
```

The "C:\fso\test.txt" path is passed to the *Get-TextStatistics* function via the –*path* parameter. Inside the function, the "C:\fso\text.txt" string is contained in the *$path* variable. The *$path* variable lives only within the confines of the *Get-TextStatistics* function and is not available outside the scope of the function; however, it is available from within child scopes of the *Get-TextStatistics* function. A child scope of *Get-TextStatistics* is one that is created from within the *Get-TextStatistics* function. In the Get-TextStatisticsCallChildFunction.ps1 script, the *Write-Path* function is called from within the *Get-TextStatistics* function, which means that the *Write-Path* function has access to variables created within the *Get-TextStatistics* function. This process involves the concept of variable scope and is an extremely important concept when working with functions. As you use functions to separate the creation of objects, you must always be aware of where the object is created and where you intend to use that object. In the Get-TextStatisticsCallChildFunction.ps1 script, the *$path* variable does not obtain its value until it is passed to the function and therefore lives within the *Get-TextStatistics* function. However, because the *Write-Path* function is called from within the *Get-TextStatistics* function, the *Write-Path* function inherits the variables from that scope. When you call a function from within another function, variables created within the parent function are available to the child function as shown in the Get-TextStatisticsCallChildFunction.ps1 script.

**Get-TextStatisticsCallChildFunction.ps1**

```
Function Get-TextStatistics($path)
{
  Get-Content -path $path |
  Measure-Object -line -character -word
  Write-Path
}
```

```
Function Write-Path()
{
 "Inside Write-Path the '$path variable is equal to $path"
}


Get-TextStatistics("C:\fso\test.txt")
"Outside the Get-TextStatistics function '$path is equal to $path"
```

Inside the *Get-TextStatistics* function, the *$path* variable is used to provide the path to the Get-Content cmdlet. When the *Write-Path* function is called, nothing is passed to it, yet inside the *Write-Path* function, the value of *$path* is maintained. However, outside both of the functions, *$path* does not have any value. The output from running the script is shown here:

```
        Lines            Words          Characters Property
        -----            -----          ---------- --------
          3               41               210
Inside Write-Path the $path variable is equal to C:\fso\test.txt
Outside the Get-TextStatistics function $path is equal to
```

You then need to open and close a script block. The curly bracket (brace) is used to delimit the script block on a function. As a best practice, I always use the *Function* keyword when writing a function and then type in the name, input parameters, and curly brackets for the script block at the same time, as shown here:

```
Function My-Function
{

Param()
 #insert code here
}  #end My-Function
```

In this manner, I do not forget to close the curly brackets. Trying to identify a missing curly bracket within a long script can be somewhat problematic because the error that is presented does not always correspond to the line that is missing the curly bracket. Suppose that the closing curly bracket is left off of the *Get-TextStatistics* function as shown in the Get-TextStatisticsCallChildFunction-DoesNOTWork-MissingClosingBracket.ps1 script. An error is generated as shown here:

```
Missing closing '}' in statement block.
At C:\BestPracticesBook\Get-TextStatisticsCallChildFunction-DoesNOTWork-
MissingClosingBracket.ps1:28 char:1
```

The problem is that the position indicator of the error message points to the first character on line 28. Line 28 happens to be the first blank line after the end of the script. This means that Windows PowerShell scanned the entire script looking for the closing curly bracket. Because the closing curly bracket was not found, Windows PowerShell states that the error is at the end of the script. If you place a closing curly bracket on line 28, the error in this example does go away, but the script does not work. The Get-TextStatisticsCallChildFunction-DoesNOTWork-MissingClosingBracket.ps1 script is shown here with a comment that indicates where the missing closing curly bracket should be placed. One other technique to guard against the missing curly bracket problem is to add a comment to the closing curly bracket of each function.

```
Get-TextStatisticsCallChildFunction-DoesNOTWork-MissingClosingBracket.ps1

Function Get-TextStatistics($path)
{
 Get-Content -path $path |
 Measure-Object -line -character -word
 Write-Path
# Here is where the missing bracket goes

Function Write-Path()
{
 "Inside Write-Path the '$path variable is equal to $path"
}
Get-TextStatistics("C:\fso\test.txt")
Outside the Get-TextStatistics function '$path is equal to $path"
```

I saved typing 29 characters. If I search for text via Windows PowerShell 10 times a day, I save 290 keystrokes, more than 1,000 keystrokes a week, and over 75,000 keystrokes a year.

This is not limited to just Windows PowerShell files. I also set this up to search my C# and XAML files:

```
function fx {dir . -recurse *.xaml}

function fcs {dir . -recurse *.cs}
```

## Using functions to provide ease of code reuse

When scripts are written using well-designed functions, it is easier to reuse them in other scripts and to provide access to these functions from within the Windows PowerShell console. To access these functions, you need to dot-source the containing script. An issue that arises with dot-sourcing scripts to bring in functions is that the script can often contain global variables or other items that you do not want to bring into your current environment.

An example of a good function is the ConvertToMeters.ps1 script. No variables are defined outside the function, and the function itself does not use the Write-Host cmdlet to break up the pipeline. The results of the conversion are returned directly to the calling code. The only problem with the ConvertToMeters.ps1 script is that when it is dot-sourced into the Windows PowerShell console, it runs and returns the data because all executable code in the script is executed. The ConvertToMeters.ps1 script is shown here.

```
ConvertToMeters.ps1

Function Script:ConvertToMeters($feet)
{
  "$feet feet equals $($feet*.31) meters"
} #end ConvertToMeters
$feet = 5
ConvertToMeters -Feet $feet
```

With well-written functions, it is trivial to collect the functions into a single script—you just copy and paste the functions from the original scripts into a new script. When you are done, you have created a Function library.

When pasting your functions into the Function library script, pay attention to the comments at the end of the function. The comments at the closing curly bracket for each function not only point to the closing curly bracket but also provide a visual indicator for the end of each function that can be helpful when you need to troubleshoot a script. An example of such a Function library is the ConversionFunctions.ps1 script, shown here.

```
ConversionFunctions.ps1

Function Script:ConvertToMeters($feet)
{
  "$feet feet equals $($feet*.31) meters"
} #end ConvertToMeters

Function Script:ConvertToFeet($meters)
{
 "$meters meters equals $($meters * 3.28) feet"
} #end ConvertToFeet

Function Script:ConvertToFahrenheit($celsius)
{
 "$celsius celsius equals $((1.8 * $celsius) + 32 ) fahrenheit"
} #end ConvertToFahrenheit

Function Script:ConvertTocelsius($fahrenheit)
{
 "$fahrenheit fahrenheit equals $( (($fahrenheit - 32)/9)*5 ) celsius"
} #end ConvertTocelsius

Function Script:ConvertToMiles($kilometer)
{
  "$kilometer kilometers equals $( ($kilometer *.6211) ) miles"
} #end convertToMiles

Function Script:ConvertToKilometers($miles)
{
  "$miles miles equals $( ($miles * 1.61) ) kilometers"
} #end convertToKilometers
```

One way to use the functions from the ConversionFunctions.ps1 script is to use the dot-sourcing operator to run the script so that the functions from the script are part of the calling scope. To dot-source the script, you can use the dot-source operator (period or dot symbol) followed by the path to the script containing the functions that you want to include in your current scope. When done, you can call the function directly, as shown here:

```
PS C:\> . C:\scripts\ConversionFunctions.ps1
PS C:\> convertToMiles 6
6 kilometers equals 3.7266 miles
```

All of the functions from the dot-sourced script are available to the current session. This can be seen by composing a listing of the function drive, as shown here:

```
PS C:\> dir function: | Where { $_.name -like 'co*'} | Format-Table -Property name,
definition -AutoSize
```

```
Name                    Definition
----                    ----------
ConvertToMeters         param($feet) "$feet feet equals $($feet*.31) meters"...
ConvertToFeet           param($meters) "$meters meters equals $($meters * 3.28) feet"...
ConvertToFahrenheit param($celsius) "$celsius celsius equals $((1.8 * $celsius) + 32 )
fahrenheit"...
ConvertToCelsius        param($fahrenheit) "$fahrenheit fahrenheit equals
$( (($fahrenheit - 32)/9)*5 ) celsius...
ConvertToMiles          param($kilometer) "$kilometer kilometers equals $( ($kilometer
*.6211) ) miles"...
ConvertToKilometers param($miles) "$miles miles equals $( ($miles * 1.61) )
kilometers"...
```

### NOTES FROM THE FIELD

## Understanding functions

**Brandon Shell, Windows PowerShell MVP**

In my mind, functions are, generally speaking, small, single task–based tools (like a flathead screwdriver or hammer). They do one thing, and they do that one thing reliably well. If you take this approach when writing code, you will find it easier to debug and will find yourself writing less code. Why less code? Because you'll find that you are now able to port your functions from one script to another or possibly even in your day-to-day life.

I have three basic guidelines as to when to write a function:

1.  **First guideline:** I find that I am repeating the same code block over and over again. For example, I have a code block that checks several services on a computer. It might make sense to simply write a function to perform the check and then run that function against each server. This process allows me to troubleshoot the code more efficiently.

2.  **Second guideline:** I find that I can use this code in other scripts. For example, if I write a nice recursive parsing block, I might want to reuse that logic in another script.

3.  **Third guideline:** The code is useful outside of this script. This guideline is slightly different from the previous guideline. A good example here is a ping-server function, which is useful both in other scripts and in my day-to-day life.

When writing code, it is generally a good idea to always consider reusing the code. This is paramount when working with functions. The sole purpose of using functions in life is for reuse, so this should be a major consideration when designing your functions. Consider how and where a function will be used, which helps to establish the parameters and defaults (if any) that it should have.

Because we design code for reuse, it is a best practice to be as verbose as possible. The basic rule of thumb is to hard-code nothing; all data should be passed by parameters. Certainly, you can have default values for the parameters, but allow the function call to specify other options without modifying the function. This comes back to the black box approach. You need to consider the effect of every change in the original function and how that change will affect the script as a whole.

In Windows PowerShell version 1.0, I always tried to implement *–verbose* and *–whatif* parameters with my own switches. In version 2.0 and above, this process is handled for you.

When designing functions, think about the looping and processing logic. This logic is generally script specific and should be implemented outside of the function. Ideally, you want to restrict logic to the party that requires the logic. For example, if you have logic to process servers in the script, keep that logic outside of the functions. There is no need to repeatedly implement that logic for each function call. However, if you have logic that is expressly the domain of the function, do not go crazy trying to rip it out just to put in the calling script.

Great functions are born from need but grow from use. As you grow in your understanding, your functions will grow with you. They are like friends who are always there when you need them, but, like friends, they need attention and care. Listed below are some features that functions should have.

### Well-defined parameters

Your function needs to be very clear on what data it expects to generate to produce the data you expect. You accomplish this by establishing very specific parameters (which often includes the data type as well). If you absolutely must have a specific value to process, make sure that the value is received by the function. A great way to accomplish this is by assigning the parameter's default value to (Throw '$ThisParam is required').

### Consistent and expected output

This feature is absolutely critical. You do not want to guess at what type of data will come from the function. You want the data to be what you expect. Design the function so that it returns one or more of a single data type (such as string, DateTime, or Boolean.) Be very cautious not to pollute the data stream with messages written using Write-Output.

### Self-containment

The function should not rely on any variables from the script. If the function needs input from outside, make the outside value a parameter.

## Using two input parameters

To create a function that uses multiple input parameters, you can use the *Function* keyword,
specify the name of the function, use variables for each input parameter inside a *Param* statement, and then define the script block within curly brackets. The pattern is shown here:

```
Function My-Function
{

 Param ($input1, $input2)
 #Insert Code Here
}
```

An example of a function that takes multiple parameters is the *Get-FreeDiskSpace* function
that is shown in the Get-FreeDiskSpace.ps1 script.

The Get-FreeDiskSpace.ps1 script begins with the *Function* keyword, the name of the function, and two input parameters. The input parameters are placed inside smooth parentheses
as shown here:

```
Function Get-FreeDiskSpace

{ Param ($drive,$computer)
```

Inside the curly brackets, the *Get-FreeDiskSpace* function uses the `Get-WmiObject` cmdlet
to query the *Win32_LogicalDisk* WMI class. The *Get-FreeDiskSpace* function connects to the
computer specified in the *–computer* parameter and filters out only the drive that is specified
in the *–drive* parameter. When the function is called, each parameter is specified as *–drive*
and *–computer*. In the function definition, the *$drive* and *$computer* variables are used to
hold the values supplied to the parameters.

After the data from WMI is retrieved, it is stored in the *$driveData* variable. The data that
is stored in the *$driveData* variable is an instance of the *Win32_LogicalDisk* class. This variable
contains a complete instance of the class. The members of this class are shown in Table 8-1.

**TABLE 8-1** Members of the *Win32_LogicalDisk* class

| Name | MemberType | Definition |
| --- | --- | --- |
| Chkdsk | Method | System.Management.ManagementBase-Object Chkdsk(System.Boolean FixErrors, System.Boolean VigorousIndexCheck, System.Boolean SkipFolderCycle, System.Boolean ForceDismount, System.Boolean RecoverBadSectors, System.Boolean OkToRunAtBootUp) |
| Reset | Method | System.Management.ManagementBaseObject Reset() |
| SetPowerState | Method | System.Management.ManagementBaseObject SetPowerState(System.UInt16 PowerState, System.String Time) |
| Access | Property | System.UInt16 Access {get;set;} |
| Availability | Property | System.UInt16 Availability {get;set;} |
| BlockSize | Property | System.UInt64 BlockSize {get;set;} |
| Caption | Property | System.String Caption {get;set;} |
| Compressed | Property | System.Boolean Compressed {get;set;} |
| ConfigManagerErrorCode | Property | System.UInt32 ConfigManagerErrorCode {get;set;} |
| ConfigManagerUserConfig | Property | System.Boolean ConfigManagerUserConfig {get;set;} |
| CreationClassName | Property | System.String CreationClassName {get;set;} |
| Description | Property | System.String Description {get;set;} |
| DeviceID | Property | System.String DeviceID {get;set;} |
| DriveType | Property | System.UInt32 DriveType {get;set;} |
| ErrorCleared | Property | System.Boolean ErrorCleared {get;set;} |
| ErrorDescription | Property | System.String ErrorDescription {get;set;} |
| ErrorMethodology | Property | System.String ErrorMethodology {get;set;} |
| FileSystem | Property | System.String FileSystem {get;set;} |
| FreeSpace | Property | System.UInt64 FreeSpace {get;set;} |
| InstallDate | Property | System.String InstallDate {get;set;} |
| LastErrorCode | Property | System.UInt32 LastErrorCode {get;set;} |
| MaximumComponentLength | Property | System.UInt32 MaximumComponentLength {get;set;} |
| MediaType | Property | System.UInt32 MediaType {get;set;} |
| Name | Property | System.String Name {get;set;} |
| NumberOfBlocks | Property | System.UInt64 NumberOfBlocks {get;set;} |
| PNPDeviceID | Property | System.String PNPDeviceID {get;set;} |
| PowerManagementCapabilities | Property | System.UInt16[] PowerManagementCapabilities {get;set;} |
| PowerManagementSupported | Property | System.Boolean PowerManagementSupported {get;set;} |
| ProviderName | Property | System.String ProviderName {get;set;} |
| Purpose | Property | System.String Purpose {get;set;} |

| Name | MemberType | Definition |
|------|-----------|-----------|
| QuotasDisabled | Property | System.Boolean QuotasDisabled {get;set;} |
| QuotasIncomplete | Property | System.Boolean QuotasIncomplete {get;set;} |
| QuotasRebuilding | Property | System.Boolean QuotasRebuilding {get;set;} |
| Size | Property | System.UInt64 Size {get;set;} |
| Status | Property | System.String Status {get;set;} |
| StatusInfo | Property | System.UInt16 StatusInfo {get;set;} |
| SupportsDiskQuotas | Property | System.Boolean SupportsDiskQuotas {get;set;} |
| SupportsFileBasedCompression | Property | System.Boolean SupportsFileBasedCompression {get;set;} |
| SystemCreationClassName | Property | System.String SystemCreationClassName {get;set;} |
| SystemName | Property | System.String SystemName {get;set;} |
| VolumeDirty | Property | System.Boolean VolumeDirty {get;set;} |
| VolumeName | Property | System.String VolumeName {get;set;} |
| VolumeSerialNumber | Property | System.String VolumeSerialNumber {get;set;} |
| __CLASS | Property | System.String __CLASS {get;set;} |
| __DERIVATION | Property | System.String[] __DERIVATION {get;set;} |
| __DYNASTY | Property | System.String __DYNASTY {get;set;} |
| __GENUS | Property | System.Int32 __GENUS {get;set;} |
| __NAMESPACE | Property | System.String __NAMESPACE {get;set;} |
| __PATH | Property | System.String __PATH {get;set;} |
| __PROPERTY_COUNT | Property | System.Int32 __PROPERTY_COUNT {get;set;} |
| __RELPATH | Property | System.String __RELPATH {get;set;} |
| __SERVER | Property | System.String __SERVER {get;set;} |
| __SUPERCLASS | Property | System.String __SUPERCLASS {get;set;} |
| PSStatus | PropertySet | PSStatus {Status, Availability, DeviceID, StatusInfo} |
| ConvertFromDateTime | ScriptMethod | System.Object ConvertFromDateTime(); |
| ConvertToDateTime | ScriptMethod | System.Object ConvertToDateTime(); |

## Obtaining specific WMI data

While storing the complete instance of the object in the *$driveData* variable is a bit inefficient, in reality the class is rather small, and the ease of using the Get-WmiObject cmdlet is usually worth the wasteful methodology. If performance is a primary consideration, use of the [WMI] type accelerator is a better solution. To obtain the free disk space using this method, you can use the following syntax:

```
([wmi]"Win32_logicalDisk.DeviceID='c:'").FreeSpace
```

To put the preceding command into a usable function, you need to substitute the hard-coded drive letter for a variable. In addition, you also want to modify the class constructor to receive a path to a remote computer. The newly created function is contained in the Get-DiskSpace.ps1 script shown here.

```
Get-DiskSpace.ps1
Function Get-DiskSpace($drive,$computer)
{
 ([wmi]"\\$computer\root\cimv2:Win32_logicalDisk.
DeviceID='$drive'").FreeSpace
}
Get-DiskSpace -drive "C:" -computer "Office"
```

After you make the preceding changes, the code returns the value of the *FreeSpace* property only from the specific drive. If you send the output to the Get-Member cmdlet, you see that you have an integer. This technique is more efficient than storing an entire instance of the *Win32_LogicalDisk* class and then selecting a single value.

After you store the data in the *$driveData* variable, you want to print some information to the user of the script. First, you can print the name of the computer and the drive by placing the variables inside double quotation marks. Double quotes are expanding strings, and variables placed inside double quotes emit their value and not their name, as shown here:

```
"$computer free disk space on drive $drive"
```

Next, you can format the data that is returned by using the Microsoft .NET Framework format strings to specify two decimal places. You need to use a subexpression to prevent unraveling of the WMI object inside the double quotation marks of the expanding string. The subexpression uses the dollar sign and a pair of smooth parentheses to force the evaluation of the expression before returning the data to the string, as shown here:

```
$("{0:n2}" -f ($driveData.FreeSpace/1MB)) MegaBytes
```

```
Get-FreeDiskSpace.ps1

Function Get-FreeDiskSpace($drive,$computer)
{
 $driveData = Get-WmiObject -class win32_LogicalDisk '
 -computername $computer -filter "Name = '$drive'"
"
 $computer free disk space on drive $drive
    $("{0:n2}" -f ($driveData.FreeSpace/1MB)) MegaBytes
"
}

Get-FreeDiskSpace -drive "C:" -computer "Windows 8"
```

## NOTES FROM THE FIELD

**Jason Hofferle**
*IT Specialist*

Many of the resources and discussions about Windows PowerShell are geared towards enterprise IT staff responsible for supporting servers. With entire books written about using Windows PowerShell to manage Exchange, vSphere, and other enterprise technologies, it's easy for end-user support personnel to get the impression that PowerShell isn't something they need to know. The reality is that desktop support and helpdesk staff have just as many reasons to learn Windows PowerShell as a server administrator, and even someone that rarely touches a server should make learning PowerShell a priority.

Remote desktop and similar technologies are extremely helpful for supporting distant users, but there are some simple tasks that can be accomplished more efficiently with Windows PowerShell. Copying a new version of a configuration file, restarting a service, or unlocking an account can all be done much faster from a Windows PowerShell console. While it does initially take more time to learn how to perform a task without pointing and clicking, that time investment will be repaid tenfold the first time that task needs to be performed on multiple computers.

Many organizations utilize some sort of enterprise solution for deploying software, making changes to client systems, and other automated tasks. These tools are great, but sometimes desktop support doesn't have access to utilize them, and even something simple like creating a desktop shortcut for end users gets put on the back-burner by enterprise staff. Because most local IT admins have administrative access to the workstations they're responsible for, something like creating shortcuts is an easy task for Windows PowerShell. Windows PowerShell allows front-line support to develop automated fixes to save themselves time without relying on an enterprise solution.

Not everyone needs to be a Windows PowerShell expert because modules are an easy way to distribute more complex scripts written by advanced PowerShell users. In my VBScript days, it could be an ordeal to write out documentation about how to use a certain script or how to write in-line help for it. With comment-based help and script modules, it's incredibly easy to share automated fixes with others. I maintain a module for my organization that packages some complex tasks into easy-to-use functions with built-in help. This allows beginners just getting started to become immediately effective after understanding some fundamentals like Get-Help. If you become proficient enough with Windows PowerShell to build these tools for others, you get credit for saving everyone's time in addition to your own.

Probably the most important reason to develop Windows PowerShell skills are the career benefits. It's a rare company that doesn't use Microsoft products, and Microsoft products are managed with Windows PowerShell. With the consistency of Windows PowerShell, it's very easy to apply the basic concepts and patterns to anything. Learn Windows PowerShell now, and when you get a position as a Directory Administrator or Exchange Administrator, those PowerShell skills will be immediately useful.

## Using a type constraint

When accepting parameters for a function, it can be important to use a type constraint to ensure that the function receives the correct type of data. To do this, you can place the desired data type alias inside square brackets in front of the input parameter. This action constrains the data type and prevents the entry of an incorrect type of data. Allowable type shortcuts are shown in Table 8-2.

**TABLE 8-2** Data type aliases

| Alias | Type |
| --- | --- |
| [int] | 32-bit signed integer |
| [long] | 64-bit signed integer |
| [string] | Fixed-length string of Unicode characters |
| [char] | Unicode 16-bit character |
| [bool] | True/false value |
| [byte] | 8-bit unsigned integer |
| [double] | Double-precision 64-bit floating point number |

| Alias | Type |
|---|---|
| [decimal] | 128-bit decimal value |
| [single] | Single-precision 32-bit floating point number |
| [array] | Array of values |
| [xml] | Xmldocument object |
| [hashtable] | Hashtable object (similar to a Dictionary object) |

In the *Resolve-ZipCode* function shown in the Resolve-ZipCode.ps1 script, the *–zip* input parameter is constrained to allow only a 32-bit signed integer for input. (Obviously, the [int] type constraint eliminates most of the world's zip codes, but the web service that the script uses resolves only U.S.-based zip codes; therefore, it is a good addition to the function.)

In the *Resolve-ZipCode* function, you can first use a string that points to the Web Services Description Language (WSDL) for the web service. Next, the New-WebServiceProxy cmdlet is used to create a new web service proxy for the ZipCode service. The WSDL for the ZipCode service defines a method named *GetInfoByZip*, which accepts a standard U.S.-based zip code. The results are displayed as a table. The Resolve-ZipCode.ps1 script is shown here.

```
Resolve-ZipCode.ps1

#Requires -Version 4.0
Function Resolve-ZipCode([int]$zip)
{
 $URI = "http://www.webservicex.net/uszip.asmx?WSDL"
 $zipProxy = New-WebServiceProxy -uri $URI -namespace WebServiceProxy -class ZipClass
 $zipProxy.getinfobyzip($zip).table
} #end Get-ZipCode


Resolve-ZipCode 28273
```

When using a type constraint on an input parameter, any deviation from the expected data type generates an error similar to the one shown here:

```
Resolve-ZipCode : Cannot process argument transformation on parameter 'zip'. Cannot
convert value "COW" to type "System
.Int32". Error: "Input string was not in a correct format."
At C:\Users\edwils.NORTHAMERICA\AppData\Local\Temp\tmp3351.tmp.ps1:22 char:16
+ Resolve-ZipCode <<<<  "COW"
    + CategoryInfo          : InvalidData: (:) [Resolve-ZipCode], ParameterBindin...
mationException
    + FullyQualifiedErrorId : ParameterArgumentTransformationError,Resolve-ZipCode
```

Needless to say, such an error can be distracting to users of the function. One way to handle the problem of confusing error messages is to use the *Trap* keyword. In the DemoTrapSystemException.ps1 script, the *My-Test* function uses [int] to constrain the *$myinput* variable to accept only a 32-bit unsigned integer for input. If such an integer is received by the function when it is called, the function returns the string "It worked". If the function receives a string for input, an error is raised similar to the previous one.

Rather than display a raw error message that most users and many IT Pros find confusing, it is a best practice to suppress the display of the error message and to perhaps inform the user that an error condition occurred, providing more meaningful and direct information that the user can then relay to the help desk. Many times, IT departments display such an error message, complete with either a local telephone number for the appropriate help desk or even a link to an internal webpage that provides detailed troubleshooting and self-help corrective steps for the user to take. You can even provide a webpage that hosts a script that the user can run that will fix the problem. This solution is similar to the "Fix it for me" webpages introduced by Microsoft.

When an instance of a *System.SystemException* class is created (when a system exception occurs), the *Trap* statement traps the error rather than allowing the error information to display on the screen. If you query the *$error* variable, you see that the error has in fact occurred and is actually received by the error record. You also have access to the *ErrorRecord* class via the *$_* automatic variable, which means that the error record is passed along the pipeline and thus gives you the ability to build a rich error-handling solution. In this example, the string "error trapped" is displayed, and the *Continue* statement is used to continue the script execution on the next line of code. In this example, the next line of code that is executed is the "After the error" string. When the DemoTrapSystemException.ps1 script is run, the following output is shown:

```
error trapped
After the error
```

The complete DemoTrapSystemException.ps1 script is shown here.

```
DemoTrapSystemException.ps1

Function My-Test([int]$myinput)
{

 "It worked"
} #End my-test function
# *** Entry Point to Script ***

Trap [SystemException] { "error trapped" ; continue }
My-Test -myinput "string"
"After the error"
```

Juan Carlos Ruiz Lopez, Premier Field Engineer
*Microsoft Corporation*

have the habit of starting all my scripts in the same way, no matter how simple they are (because they usually become more complex with time).

First, at the very beginning, I include some comments containing the script name, version, dates, and its purpose. To make this clear, I include a comment, such as the following:

```
# ----------------------------------------------------------------
# Script      : Murgifly.ps1                                     -
# Description : This script is used to murgifly some borogoves…  -
# Author      : JC@company.com                                   -
# Date        : 32-Aug-2013                                      -
# Version     : V 1.0, Now V2 including some feature…            -
# ----------------------------------------------------------------
I also like to add some keywords, as in the following example:
# ----------------------------------------------------------------
# Keywords    : Jabberwocky, borogoves
# ----------------------------------------------------------------
```

Apart from documenting the script for other people (or yourself in the future), all these tags are very useful to find lost scripts. You usually remember some keyword or functionality, but not the script path name, so the following line will find it for sure:

```
Dir -Recurse -Include *.ps1 | Select-String "borog"
```

Now I immediately add some code, such as the following:

```
#requires -Version 4            #
$Error.Clear ()                 #
Set-StrictMode -Version Latest  #
```

The first line reads like a comment, but it is forcing Windows PowerShell to require a minimum version. This way, you guarantee that the script won't fail in the middle of its execution when some new, non-present feature is needed.

The second line will clear the *$Error* array. Being global, you usually prefer to start the script with an empty error collection that does not contain the previous ones.

Finally, the Strict Mode. This should be mandatory in every script (and should be the default, in my opinion...but it is not).

This approach will find many errors in your script and will save you many work hours! It will catch typos, undefined variables, bad calls, non-existing properties, and so on. Take a look at its documentation.

You should create a template file with all these lines, and copy and paste and edit accordingly, every time you need them in a new script. But you can also use the ISE Snippets in Windows PowerShell 4.0. Define a new snippet with these lines, and you'll have them handy, just pressing Ctrl-J. See `Get-Help *snippet* ...y`.

## Using more than two input parameters

When using more than two input parameters, I consider it a best practice to modify the way in which the function is structured. This modification is more of a visual change that makes the function easier to read. In the basic function pattern shown here, the function accepts three input parameters. When considering the default values and type constraints, the parameters that begin to string along are fairly long. Moving the parameters to the inside of the function body highlights the fact that they are input parameters and makes them easier to read, understand, and maintain.

```
Function Function-Name
{
  Param(
        [int]$Parameter1,
        [String]$Parameter2 = "DefaultValue",
        $Parameter3
       )
#Function code goes here
} #end Function-Name
```

An example of a function that uses three input parameters is the *Get-DirectoryListing* function, the complete text of which follows. Due to the type constraints, default values, and parameter names, the function signature can be rather cumbersome to include on a single line, as shown here:

```
Function Get-DirectoryListing (String]$Path,[String]$Extension = "txt",[Switch]$Today)
```

If the number of parameters is increased to four or if a default value for the *–path* parameter is desired, the signature can easily scroll to two lines. Use of the *Param* statement inside the function body also provides the ability to specify input parameters to a function.

Following the *Function* keyword and function name, the *Param* keyword is used to identify the parameters for the function. Each parameter must be separated by a comma, and all parameters must be surrounded with a set of smooth parentheses. If you want to assign a default value for a parameter, such as the string *.txt* value for the *Extension* parameter in the *Get-DirectoryListing* function, you can do a straight value assignment followed by a comma.

In the *Get-DirectoryListing* function, the *Today* parameter is a switched parameter. When it is supplied to the function, only files written to since midnight on the day the script is run are displayed. If the *Today* parameter is not supplied, all files matching the extension in the folder are displayed. The Get-DirectoryListingToday.ps1 script is shown here.

```
Get-DirectoryListingToday.ps1

Function Get-DirectoryListing
{
 Param(
       [String]$Path,
       [String]$Extension = "txt",
       [Switch]$Today
       )
 If($Today)
   {
    Get-ChildItem -Path $path\* -include *.$Extension |
    Where-Object { $_.LastWriteTime -ge (Get-Date).Date }
   }
 ELSE
   {
    Get-ChildItem -Path $path\* -include *.$Extension
   }
} #end Get-DirectoryListing

# *** Entry to script ***
Get-DirectoryListing -p c:\fso -t
```

**IMPORTANT** As a best practice, you should avoid creating functions that have a large number of input parameters because this can cause confusion. When you find yourself creating a large number of input parameters, ask yourself whether there is a better way to achieve your purpose. Using too many input parameters can be an indicator that you do not have a single-purpose function. In the *Get-DirectoryListing* function, I have a switched parameter that filters the files returned by the files written to today. If I write the script for production use instead of writing it simply to demonstrate multiple-function parameters, I create another function named, for example, *Get-FilesByDate*. In this function, I have a *Today* switch and a *Date* parameter to allow a selectable date for the filter. This technique of using multiple parameters allows you to separate data-gathering from the filtering functionality. See the section titled "Using functions to provide ease of modification" later in this chapter for more discussion of this technique.

# Using functions to encapsulate business logic

Script writers need to be concerned with two kinds of logic. The first is program logic, and the second is business logic. *Program logic* is the way the script works, the order in which tasks need to be done, and the requirements of code used in the script. An example of program logic is the requirement to open a connection to a database before querying the database.

*Business logic* is a set of rules that is a requirement of the business but not necessarily a requirement of the program or script. The script can often operate just fine regardless of the particulars of the business rule. If the script is designed properly, it should operate well no matter what is supplied for the business rules.

In the BusinessLogicDemo.ps1 script, a function named *Get-Discount* is used to calculate the discount to be granted to the total amount. Encapsulating the business rules for the discount into a function works well as long as the contract between the function and the calling code does not change. You can drop any type of convoluted discount schedule between the curly brackets of the *Get-Discount* function that the business requests, including database calls to determine on-hand inventory, time of day, day of week, and total sales volume for the month, as well as the buyer's loyalty level and the square root of some random number that is used to determine the instant discount rate.

So, what is the contract with the function? The contract with the *Get-Discount* function states, "If you give me a rate number as a type of *System.Double* and a total as an integer, I will return to you a number that represents the total discount to be applied to the sale." As long as you adhere to that contract, you never need to modify the code.

The *Get-Discount* function begins with the *Function* keyword, the name of the function, and the definition for two input parameters. The first input parameter is the –*rate* parameter, which is constrained to be a *System.Double* class and permits you to supply decimal numbers. The second input parameter is the –*total* parameter, which is constrained to be a *System. Integer* and therefore does not allow decimal numbers. In the script block, the value of the –*total* parameter is multiplied by the value of the –*rate* parameter. The result of this calculation is returned to the pipeline.

The *Get-Discount* function is shown here:

```
Function Get-Discount([double]$rate,[int]$total)
{
  $rate * $total
} #end Get-Discount
```

The entry point to the script assigns values to both the *$total* and *$rate* variables, as shown here:

```
$rate = .05
$total = 100
```

The *$discount* variable is used to hold the result of the calculation from the *Get-Discount* function. When calling the function, it is a best practice to use full parameter names. This practice makes the code easier to read and helps make the code immune to unintended problems if the function signature changes.

```
$discount = Get-Discount -rate $rate -total $total
```

> **IMPORTANT**   The signature of a function is the order and names of the input parameters. If you typically supply values to the signature via positional parameters and the order of the input parameters changes, the code fails or, worse yet, produces inconsistent results. If you typically call functions via partial parameter names and an additional parameter is added, the script fails due to difficulty with the disambiguation process. Obviously, you should take this into account when first writing the script and the function, but the problem can arise months or years later when making modifications to the script or calling the function via another script.

The remainder of the script produces output for the screen. The results of running the script are shown here:

```
Total: 100
Discount: 5
Your Total: 95
```

The complete text of the BusinessLogicDemo.ps1 script is shown here.

```
BusinessLogicDemo.ps1

Function Get-Discount
{


 Param ([double]$rate,[int]$total)
 $rate * $total
} #end Get-Discount

 $rate = .05
$total = 100
$discount = Get-Discount -rate $rate -total $total
"Total: $total"
"Discount: $discount"
"Your Total: $($total-$discount)"
```

Business logic does not have to be related to business purposes. Business logic is anything arbitrary that does not affect the running of the code. In the FindLargeDocs.ps1 script, there are two functions. The first function, named *Get-Doc*, is used to find document files (files with an extension of .doc, .docx, or .dot) in a folder that is passed to the function when it is called. When used with the `Get-ChildItem` cmdlet, the *recurse* switch causes *Get-Doc* to look in the present folder as well as to look within child folders. This is a stand-alone function and has no dependency on other functions.

The LargeFiles piece of code is a filter. A filter is a type of special-purpose function that uses the *Filter* keyword rather than the *Function* keyword when it is created. The complete FindLargeDocs.ps1 script is shown here.

```
FindLargeDocs.ps1

Function Get-Doc
{
 Param ($path)
 Get-ChildItem -Path $path -include *.doc,*.docx,*.dot -recurse
} #end Get-Doc

Filter LargeFiles($size)
{
  $_ | Where-Object length -ge $size
} #end LargeFiles

Get-Doc("C:\FSO") | LargeFiles 1000
```

# Using functions to provide ease of modification

It is a truism that a script is never finished. Something else can always be added to a script: a change that will improve it or additional functionality that someone requests. When a script is written as one long piece of inline code without recourse to functions, it can be rather tedious and error prone during modifications.

An example of an inline script is the InLineGetIPDemo.ps1 script. The first line of code uses the Get-WmiObject cmdlet to retrieve the instances of the *Win32_NetworkAdapterConfiguration* WMI class that IP enabled. The results of this WMI query are stored in the *$IP* variable. This line of code is shown here:

```
$IP = Get-WmiObject -class Win32_NetworkAdapterConfiguration -Filter "IPEnabled = $true"
```

After the WMI information is obtained and stored, the remainder of the script prints information to the screen. The *IPAddress*, *IPSubNet*, and *DNSServerSearchOrder* properties are all stored in an array. This example is interested in only the first IP address and therefore prints element 0, which always exists if the network adapter has an IP address. This section of the script is shown here:

```
"IP Address: " + $IP.IPAddress[0]
"Subnet: " + $IP.IPSubNet[0]
"GateWay: " + $IP.DefaultIPGateway
"DNS Server: " + $IP.DNSServerSearchOrder[0]
"FQDN: " + $IP.DNSHostName + "." + $IP.DNSDomain
```

When the script is run, it produces output similar to the following:

```
IP Address: 192.168.2.5
Subnet: 255.255.255.0
GateWay: 192.168.2.1
DNS Server: 192.168.2.1
FQDN: Windows 8.nwtraders.com
```

The complete InLineGetIPDemo.ps1 script is shown here.

**InLineGetIPDemo.ps1**

```
$IP = Get-WmiObject -class Win32_NetworkAdapterConfiguration -Filter "IPEnabled =
$true"
"IP Address: " + $IP.IPAddress[0]
"Subnet: " + $IP.IPSubNet[0]
"GateWay: " + $IP.DefaultIPGateway
"DNS Server: " + $IP.DNSServerSearchOrder[0]
"FQDN: " + $IP.DNSHostName + "." + $IP.DNSDomain
```

With just a few modifications to the script, a great deal of flexibility can be obtained. The modifications, of course, involve moving the inline code into functions. As a best practice, a function should be narrowly defined and should encapsulate a single purpose. While it is possible to move the entire previous script into a function, you do not have as much flexibility. Two purposes are expressed in the script. The first purpose is obtaining the IP information from WMI, and the second purpose is formatting and displaying the IP information. It is best to separate the gathering and displaying processes from one another because they are logically two different activities.

To convert the InLineGetIPDemo.ps1 script into a script that uses a function, you need only to add the *Function* keyword, give it a name, and surround the original code with a pair of curly brackets. The transformed script is now named GetIPDemoSingleFunction.ps1 and is shown here.

**GetIPDemoSingleFunction.ps1**

```
Function Get-IPDemo
{
 $IP = Get-WmiObject -class Win32_NetworkAdapterConfiguration -Filter "IPEnabled =
$true"
 "IP Address: " + $IP.IPAddress[0]
 "Subnet: " + $IP.IPSubNet[0]
 "GateWay: " + $IP.DefaultIPGateway
 "DNS Server: " + $IP.DNSServerSearchOrder[0]
 "FQDN: " + $IP.DNSHostName + "." + $IP.DNSDomain
} #end Get-IPDemo
```

```
# *** Entry Point To Script ***

Get-IPDemo
```

So, if you go to all of the trouble to transform the inline code into a function, what do you gain? By making this single change, you gain the following benefits:

- Easier to read
- Easier to understand
- Easier to reuse
- Easier to troubleshoot

The script is easier to read because you do not actually need to read each line of code to see what it does. You see a function that obtains the IP address, which is called from outside the function. That is all the script accomplishes.

The script is easier to understand because what you see is a function that obtains the IP address. If you want to know the details of that operation, you read that function. If you are not interested in the details, you can skip that portion of the code.

The script is easier to reuse because you can dot-source the script as shown here. When the script is dot-sourced, all of the executable code in the script is run. As a result, the following output is displayed because each of the scripts prints information:

```
IP Address: 192.168.2.5
Subnet: 255.255.255.0
GateWay: 192.168.2.1
DNS Server: 192.168.2.1
FQDN: Windows 8.nwtraders.com

Windows 8 free disk space on drive C:
    48,767.16 MegaBytes

This OS is version 6.0.6001
```

The DotSourceScripts.ps1 script is shown here. As you can see, this script provides you with a certain level of flexibility to choose the information required, and it also makes it easy to mix and match the required information. If each of the scripts is written in a more standard fashion and the output is standardized, the results will be more impressive. As it is, three lines of code produce an exceptional amount of useful output that can be acceptable in a variety of situations.

**DotSourceScripts.ps1**

```
. C:\BestPracticesBook\GetIPDemoSingleFunction.ps1
. C:\BestPracticesBook\Get-FreeDiskSpace.ps1
. C:\BestPracticesBook\Get-OperatingSystemVersion.ps1
```

The GetIPDemoSingleFunction.ps1 script is easier to troubleshoot in part because it is easier to read and understand. In addition, when a script contains multiple functions, you can test one function at a time, which allows you to isolate a piece of problematic code.

A better way to work with the function is to consider what the function is actually doing. There are two functions in the FunctionGetIPDemo.ps1 script. The first connects to WMI, which returns a management object. The second function formats the output. These are two completely unrelated tasks. The first task gathers data, and the second task presents information. The FunctionGetIPDemo.ps1 script is shown here.

```
Function Get-IPObject
{
 Get-WmiObject -class Win32_NetworkAdapterConfiguration -Filter "IPEnabled = $true"
} #end Get-IPObject

Function Format-IPOutput($IP)
{
 "IP Address: " + $IP.IPAddress[0]
 "Subnet: " + $IP.IPSubNet[0]
 "GateWay: " + $IP.DefaultIPGateway
 "DNS Server: " + $IP.DNSServerSearchOrder[0]
 "FQDN: " + $IP.DNSHostName + "." + $IP.DNSDomain
} #end Format-IPOutput

# *** Entry Point To Script

$ip = Get-IPObject
Format-IPOutput($ip)
```

By separating the data-gathering and presentation activities into different functions, additional flexibility is gained. You can easily modify the *Get-IPObject* function to look for network adapters that are not IP enabled. To do this, you must modify the *–filter* parameter of the Get-WmiObject cmdlet. Because you will most likely be interested only in network adapters that are IP enabled, it makes sense to set the default value of the input parameter to *true*. By default, the behavior of the revised function works exactly as it did prior to modification. The advantage is that you can now use the function and modify the objects returned by it. To do this, you supply *$false* when calling the function, as illustrated in the Get-IPObjectDefaultEnabled.ps1 script.

```
Get-IPObjectDefaultEnabled.ps1

Function Get-IPObject([bool]$IPEnabled = $true)
{
 Get-WmiObject -class Win32_NetworkAdapterConfiguration -Filter "IPEnabled =
$IPEnabled"
```

```
} #end Get-IPObject

Get-IPObject -IPEnabled $False
```

By separating the gathering of information from the presentation of information, you gain flexibility not only in the type of information that is gathered but also in the way the information is displayed. When gathering network adapter configuration information from a network adapter that is not enabled for IP, the results are not as impressive as information from an adapter that is enabled for IP. Therefore, you might decide to create a different display to list only the pertinent information. Because the function that displays information is different than the one that gathers information, a change can easily be made that customizes the information that is most germane. The Begin section of the function is run once during the execution of the function. This is the perfect place to create a header for the output data. The Process section executes once for each item on the pipeline; in this example, it executes for each of the non–IP-enabled network adapters. The Write-Host cmdlet is used to easily write the data out to the Windows PowerShell console. The backtick t ("`t") character is used to produce a tab.

> **NOTE**   The backtick t character (`t) is a string character and, as such, works with cmdlets that accept string input.

The Get-IPObjectDefaultEnabledFormatNonIPOutput.ps1 script is shown here.

**Get-IPObjectDefaultEnabledFormatNonIPOutput.ps1**

```
Function Get-IPObject
{
 Param ([bool]$IPEnabled = $true)
 Get-WmiObject -class Win32_NetworkAdapterConfiguration -Filter "IPEnabled =
$IPEnabled"
} #end Get-IPObject

Function Format-NonIPOutput
{
 Param ($IP)
  Begin { "Index #  Description" }
 Process {
  ForEach ($i in $ip)
  {
   Write-Host $i.Index 't $i.Description
  } #end ForEach
 } #end Process
} #end Format-NonIPOutPut
```

```
$ip = Get-IPObject -IPEnabled $False
Format-NonIPOutput($ip)
```

You can use the *Get-IPObject* function to retrieve the network adapter configuration. The *Format-NonIPOutput* and *Format-IPOutput* functions can then be used to format the displayed output. If you put the functions into a single script, you create the CombinationFormatGetIPDemo.ps1 script shown here.

```
CombinationFormatGetIPDemo.ps1

Function Get-IPObject
{
 Param ([bool]$IPEnabled = $true)
  Get-WmiObject -class Win32_NetworkAdapterConfiguration -Filter "IPEnabled =
$IPEnabled"
} #end Get-IPObject

Function Format-IPOutput
{
 Param ($IP)
 "IP Address: " + $IP.IPAddress[0]
 "Subnet: " + $IP.IPSubNet[0]
 "GateWay: " + $IP.DefaultIPGateway
 "DNS Server: " + $IP.DNSServerSearchOrder[0]
 "FQDN: " + $IP.DNSHostName + "." + $IP.DNSDomain
} #end Format-IPOutput

Function Format-NonIPOutput
{
 Param ($IP)
 Begin { "Index #  Description" }
 Process {
  ForEach ($i in $ip)
  {
   Write-Host $i.Index 't $i.Description
  } #end ForEach
 } #end Process
} #end Format-NonIPOutPut

# *** Entry Point ***
$IPEnabled = $false
$ip = Get-IPObject -IPEnabled $IPEnabled
If($IPEnabled) { Format-IPOutput($ip) }
ELSE { Format-NonIPOutput($ip) }

INSIDE TRACK
```

## Surprising behavior of *return*

**James Craig Burley, Senior Software Development Engineer in Test**
*Microsoft Corporation*

Our team is still coming up to speed on Windows PowerShell, and we recently "discovered" the surprising behavior that "return expr;" does not return the specified expr; to the caller, but merely "appends" expr; to the list of other objects that are already "returned." These other objects are returned because they are uncaptured expressions that are evaluated during execution of the function body.

At first, this struck me as a design flaw in the language because every other language I've used has either required *return* to return a value,[1] used a variable name as a surrogate for the return value,[2] or defaulted to returning the most recently computed expression and optionally allowed a *return* statement to return the value.[3] No other language has built up a list (or array) of computed expressions to which an explicitly returned expression is merely appended!

On second thought, I realize that this behavior is probably unavoidable in the general case, given the intersection of the functions-as-filters feature that I like, with the fact that Windows PowerShell is an interpreted language as illustrated here:

```
function myfunction { 1; 2; 3; invoke-expression $a; }
```

This problem with *return* can perhaps be better appreciated by starting with the *myfunction2* function listed here:

```
function myfunction2 { 1; sleep 1; 2; sleep 1; 3; sleep 1; return
4; }
    foo2
```

When the *myfunction2* function is run, you can see how the results are available dynamically: "1" is written to the console; after a second's delay, "2" is written; and so on, until "4" is written and the function exits.

The only way to avoid having the first three (1, 2, 3) elements "returned" is for Windows PowerShell to recognize the *return* keyword when parsing (before running) the function and to prevent the first elements from being returned

---

[1]  In C: float average(float a, float b) { float c = a * b; return c / 2.0; }.

[2]  In FORTRAN 77: FUNCTION AVERAGE(A,B); C = A*B; AVERAGE=C / 2.0; END.

[3]  In Common Lisp: (defun average (a b) (setf c (* a b)) (/ c 2.0)).

(produced) until the *return* statement or the end of the procedure is hit. Windows PowerShell then either replaces or returns them, respectively.

This scenario potentially leads to problems involving unpredictable control flow and expectations. At run time, until the interpreter knows whether a *return* is going to be executed, Windows PowerShell must save (but not produce) these uncaptured results. When it reaches a point where it is certain to either hit or not hit a *return* statement, it can then discard and stop saving the results or produce all saved results and continue producing new, uncaptured results. Such behavior is fairly surprising when encountered, but most code works as expected.

Yet, what happens when you throw in an Invoke-Expression cmdlet that might (or might not) attempt to expand to include execution of a *return* statement? Now the situation becomes more problematic! In the general case, Windows PowerShell cannot know what will be invoked until it executes that statement. The expression might or might not contain a *return* statement, which will not be determined until just before the Invoke-Expression cmdlet is executed. Therefore, the mere presence of the Invoke-Expression cmdlet or its equivalent amounts to an unpredictable control-flow sequence that might or might not involve executing a *return* statement.

Having Windows PowerShell silently save up instead of produce uncaptured results (but optimize those cases in which no action is necessary) might seem like a temptingly good idea to meet traditional expectations of users of computer languages. But is it really a good idea? Consider what might happen if the code that is executed on prompt delivery of uncaptured results affects the code path and/or variables leading up to the determination as to whether return is executed. For example:

```
function bletch { 1; sleep 1; 2; sleep 1; 3; sleep 1; invoke-

expression $a; }
  $a = "5;"
  bletch | %{ if ($_ -eq 3) { $a = "return 4;" }; $_; }
```

Although this example is certainly contrived, the caller of *bletch* determines, only after seeing the third object produced by *bletch*, that the expression *bletch* is to invoke at the end of the sequence is a *return 4;* statement instead of a *5;* statement.

Because *bletch* cannot reliably predict whether callers (consumers) rely on having uncaptured results or objects streamed to them as they are produced, *bletch* cannot simply withhold, or save up, those uncaptured objects so as to change the state of the system (not just the Windows PowerShell interpreter but also files, registry settings, and so on). *Bletch* must produce/stream the uncaptured results to its consumer right away, as expected.

Therefore, there is also no way for Windows PowerShell to provide a statement that means "wipe the slate clean and then return." Uncaptured results are not being saved; they're being produced (or passed back to the caller, who is the next object in the pipeline). Therefore, the preceding values are already out of the gate by the time Windows PowerShell realizes that there's a *return* statement in the mix. Saving uncaptured results until Windows PowerShell knows whether they are to be produced or flushed defeats one of the primary advantages of using PowerShell—immediacy of results. In addition, saving uncaptured results breaks other code that depends on those results being streamed to determine the next steps for their producer.

Cool architecture thus leads to sometimes astonishing results. Windows PowerShell strikes me as a mix of Lisp-like expressiveness (Lisp-like languages tend to have the return value be the last expression evaluated by the function) and shell-like immediacy (print/produce results as you receive them), resulting in an unexpected and counterintuitive behavior for the *return* expression statement.

One workaround is simply to cast every uncaptured value (that is not to be returned to the caller) to [void]. That is, the function author must simply recognize and constantly be aware of the fact that the function is really a producer of objects and not merely the evaluator of some expression that ultimately returns a single monolithic value.

What if a function already contains a great deal of code that is simply too difficult to recapture in this way? Or what if the author of the function wants to ensure that only the final value is actually returned in case there are still some uncaptured results? The following function illustrates a workable solution.

(Although I'm not convinced that it's exactly correct or as terse as it should be, it seems to work for basic cases.)

```
function return-last { begin { $rtn = @{}; } process { $rtn = $_;
} end { $rtn; } }
```

You can wrap your function's code in another ampersand-prefixed pair of braces and then pipe that into the *Return-Last* function, as shown here:

```
PS C:\> function foo2-last { &{ 1; sleep 1; 2; sleep 1; 3; sleep
1; 4; }|
return-last }
```

```
PS C:\> foo2-last
4
PS C:\>
```

This technique discards all but the last object produced by the function's inner statement body; on termination of that body, this technique returns (produces) the last (final) object it produced.

Or, as Louis Clausen, another Senior Software Development Engineer in Test, pointed out, a simple array-reference wrapper will suffice in lieu of using the *Return-Last* function:

```
 PS C:\Users\jcburley> function foo2-last-quick { @(&{ 1; sleep
1; 2; sleep 1; 3; sleep 1; 4; })[-1] }
 PS C:\Users\jcburley> foo2-last-quick
 4
 PS C:\Users\jcburley>
```

Of course, the caller can wrap the function in a simpler subset environment, as shown here:

```
 PS C:\Users\jcburley> @(foo2)[-1]
 4
 PS C:\Users\jcburley>.
```

# Understanding filters

A *filter* is a special-purpose function that is used to operate on each object in a pipeline and is often used to reduce the number of objects that are passed along the pipeline. Typically, a filter does not use the *–Begin* or *–End* parameters that a function might need to use, so it is often thought of as a function that has only a process block. But then, many functions are written without using the *–Begin* or *–End* parameters, and some filters are written in such a way that they use the *–Begin* or *–End* parameters. The biggest difference between a function and a filter is a bit more subtle. When a function is used inside a pipeline, it actually halts the processing of the pipeline until the first element in the pipeline runs to completion. The function then accepts the input from the first element in the pipeline and begins its processing. When the processing in the function is completed, it then passes the results along to the next element in the script block.

A function runs once for the pipelined data; however, a filter runs once for each piece of data that is passed over the pipeline. The short definition here is that a filter streams data when in a pipeline and a function does not, which can make a big difference in performance. To illustrate this point, you will examine a function and a filter that accomplish the same objectives.

In the MeasureAddOneFilter.ps1 script, an array of 50,000 elements is created by using the 1..50000 syntax. (In Windows PowerShell 1.0, 50,000 was the maximum size of an array created in this manner. In Windows PowerShell 2.0, this ceiling is raised to the maximum size of an [*Int32*] 2146483647. The use of this size is dependent on memory.) This syntax is shown here:

```
PS C:\ > 1..[Int32]::MaxValue
The '..' operator failed: Exception of type 'System.OutOfMemoryException' was thrown..
At line:1 char:4
+ 1.. <<<< 2147483647
    + CategoryInfo          : InvalidOperation: (:) [], RuntimeException
    + FullyQualifiedErrorId : OperatorFailed
```

The array is then pipelined into the *AddOne* filter. The filter prints the "add one filter" string and then adds the number 1 to the current number on the pipeline. The length of time it takes to run the command is then displayed. On my computer, it takes about 2.6 seconds to run the MeasureAddOneFilter.ps1 script.

```
MeasureAddOneFilter.ps1

Filter AddOne
{
 "add one filter"
  $_ + 1
}

Measure-Command { 1..50000 | addOne }
```

The function version is shown next. In a similar fashion as the MeasureAddOneFilter.ps1 script, this version creates an array of 50,000 numbers and pipelines the results to the *AddOne* function. The "Add One Function" string is displayed. An automatic variable named *$input* is created when pipelining input to a function. The *$input* variable is an enumerator and not just a plain array. It has a *MoveNext* method that can be used to move to the next item in the collection. Because *$input* is not a plain array, you cannot index directly into it—*$input*[0] will fail. To retrieve a specific element, you can use the *$input.current* property. It takes 4.3 seconds to run the following script on my computer, which is almost twice as long as running the filter.

```
MeasureAddOneFunction.ps1

Function AddOne
{
  "Add One Function"
  While ($input.moveNext())
   {
      $input.current + 1
   }
}

Measure-Command { 1..50000 | addOne }
```

What makes the filter so much faster than the function in this example? The filter runs once for each item on the pipeline, as shown here:

```
add one filter
2
add one filter
3
add one filter
4
add one filter
5
add one filter
6
```

The DemoAddOneFilter.ps1 script is shown here.

```
DemoAddOneFilter.ps1

Filter AddOne
{
 "add one filter"
  $_ + 1
}


1..5 | addOne
```

The *AddOne* function runs to completion once for all of the items in the pipeline. This approach effectively stops the processing in the middle of the pipeline until all of the elements of the array are created. All of the data is then passed to the function via the *$input* variable at one time. This type of approach does not take advantage of the streaming nature of the pipeline, which in many instances is more memory efficient.

```
Add One Function
2
3
4
5
6
```

The DemoAddOneFunction.ps1 script is shown here.

```
DemoAddOneFunction.ps1

Function AddOne
{
  "Add One Function"
  While ($input.moveNext())
   {
     $input.current + 1
   }
```

```
}

1..5 | addOne
```

To close this performance issue between functions and filters when used in a pipeline, you can write your function in such a manner that it behaves like a filter. To do this, you must explicitly call the process block. When you use the process block, you are also able to use the *$_* automatic variable instead of being restricted to using *$input*. When you do this, the script looks like DemoAddOneR2Function.ps1, the results of which are shown here:

```
add one function r2
2
add one function r2
3
add one function r2
4
add one function r2
5
add one function r2
6
```

The complete DemoAddOneR2Function.ps1 script is shown here.

```
DemoAddOneR2Function.ps1

Function AddOneR2
{
   Process {
   "add one function r2"
   $_ + 1
   }
} #end AddOneR2

1..5 | addOneR2
```

So, what does using an explicit process block do to performance? When run on my computer, it takes about 2.6 seconds, which is virtually the same amount of time that it takes the filter. The MeasureAddOneR2Function.ps1 script is shown here.

```
MeasureAddOneR2Function.ps1

Function AddOneR2
{
   Process {
   "add one function r2"
   $_ + 1
   }
```

```
} #end AddOneR2

Measure-Command {1..50000 | addOneR2 }
```

Another reason for using filters is that they visually stand out and therefore improve readability of the script. The typical pattern for a filter is shown here:

```
Filter FilterName
{
 #insert code here
}
```

The *HasMessage* filter found in the FilterHasMessage.ps1 script begins with the *Filter* keyword and the name of the filter, which is *HasMessage*. Inside the script block (the curly brackets), the *$_* automatic variable is used to provide access to the pipeline. The *$_* variable is sent to the Where-Object cmdlet, which performs the filter. In the calling script, the results of the *HasMessage* filter are sent to the Measure-Object cmdlet, which tells the user how many events in the application log have a message attached to them. The FilterHasMessage.ps1 script is shown here.

**FilterHasMessage.ps1**

```
Filter HasMessage
{
 $_ |
 Where-Object { $_.message }
} #end HasMessage

Get-WinEvent -LogName Application | HasMessage | Measure-Object
```

Just because the Filter has an implicit process block does not prevent you from using the Begin, Process, and End script block explicitly. In the FilterToday.ps1 script, a filter named *IsToday* is created. To make the filter a stand-alone entity with no external dependencies, such as the passing of a date time object to it, the filter needs to obtain the current date. However, if the call to the Get-Date cmdlet is done inside the Process block, the filter continues to work, but the call to Get-Date is made once for each object found in the Input folder. If there are 25 items in the folder, the Get-Date cmdlet is called 25 times. When you want a procedure to occur only once in the processing of the filter, you can place the procedure in a Begin block, which is called only once. The Process block is called once for each item in the pipeline. If you want any postprocessing to take place (such as printing a message stating how many files are found today), the postprocessing is placed in the End block of the filter. The FilterToday.ps1 script is shown here.

**FilterToday.ps1**

```
Filter IsToday
{
```

```
Begin {$dte = (Get-Date).Date}
Process { $_ |
        Where-Object { $_.LastWriteTime -ge $dte }
      }
}


Get-ChildItem -Path C:\fso | IsToday
```

## NOTES FROM THE FIELD

**Mark Tabdilio, Ph.D., Data Mining Scientist**
*Microsoft SQL Server MVP*

As a general pattern, I have found it helpful to first apply the Windows PowerShell interactive command line and build any possible cases for further scripting. As a general practice, I prefer to have fewer rather than more programs: simplicity triumphs complexity. This case study illustrates an example of these principles by using a three-phase process applied to coding the SAS analytics language.

In this story, I followed three independent groups of SAS analytics consultants who had collectively created several thousand SAS program files (saved with a .SAS extension in text format). The client shared justifiable concern at the proliferation of this production code, and I offered a plan. In phase one, I used the Windows PowerShell command line (starting with get-childitem) to audit the entire complexity and organize the results in Excel tables for management. We used these results to organize this code corpus from a high level and define our next objectives.

In phase two, I wrote a series of PowerShell command-line commands (such as select-string) to help identify similar SAS programs. I could keep output or simply read the SAS code. Many of these thousands of files turned out to be versions of the same code, a looser version of source control ("looser" because there was no organized metadata). I did not read thousands of files, but I was able to focus my energy.

Phase three included organizing large groups of code into archives, while identifying the few dozen SAS programs whose logic would be needed for ongoing production use. In this final phase, I was working mostly in SAS to streamline the readability, consolidate similar function, and improve performance. Only at this phase did I justify using more than just single-line Windows PowerShell commands. I applied techniques such as changing file dates and search and replace text within files. I even leveraged the SAS language to create some Windows PowerShell scripts (output to text files from SAS). Using SAS opens the option of leveraging the

SAS/Macro language or content from SAS datasets or catalogs to generate Windows PowerShell script files. Granted, most of the phase-three work required manual editing, but Windows PowerShell helped automate (for example) standardizing SAS *libname* references and updating connection strings to SQL Server.

All three phases resulted in Windows PowerShell code and coding techniques that could be used in future projects. Simple Windows PowerShell command line was sufficient to harness metadata information on thousands of code files in hundreds of directories. More complicated Windows PowerShell scripts were applied selectively to the final group of a few dozen files. This pattern echoes an important message for this book: Use simpler Windows PowerShell in a complex external environment, and more complex PowerShell in simpler subset environment.

## Additional resources

- The TechNet Script Center at *http://www.microsoft.com/technet/scriptcenter* contains numerous examples of using functions in Windows PowerShell.
- The Microsoft Fix It blog at *http://blogs.technet.com/fixit4me/default.aspx* provides numerous examples of self-help webpages.
- Brandon Shell's website at *http://bsonposh.com/* has a variety of Windows PowerShell tips and tricks as well as a good discussion of some of its pitfalls.
- All scripts from this chapter are available via the TechNet Script Center Repository at *http://gallery.technet.microsoft.com/scriptcenter/PowerShell-40-Best-d9e16039*.

# CHAPTER 9

# Designing help for scripts

- Adding help documentation to a script with single-line comments
- Using multiple-line comment tags in Windows PowerShell 4.0
- Using comment-based help
- The 13 rules for writing effective comments
- Additional resources

Although well-written code is easy to understand, easy to maintain, and easy to trouble-shoot, it can still benefit from well-written help documentation. Well-written help documentation can list assumptions that were made when the script was written, such as the existence of a particular folder or the need to run as an administrator. It also documents dependencies, such as relying on a particular version of the Microsoft .NET Framework. Good documentation is a sign of a professional at work because it not only informs the user about how to get the most from your script, but it also explains how users can modify your script or even use your functions in other scripts.

All production scripts should provide some form of help. But what is the best way to provide that help? In this chapter, you will look at proven methods for providing custom help in Windows PowerShell scripts.

When writing help documentation for a script, three tools are available to you. The first tool is the traditional comment that is placed within the script—the single-line comment that is available in Windows PowerShell 1.0. The second tool is the multiple-line comment that is introduced in Windows PowerShell 2.0. The third tool is the comment-based help, which was also introduced in Windows PowerShell 2.0. After describing how to use these tools, we will focus on the 13 rules for writing effective comments.

## Adding help documentation to a script with single-line comments

Single-line comments are a great way to quickly add documentation to a script. They have the advantage of being simple to use and easy to understand. It is a best practice to provide illuminating information about confusing constructions or to add notes for future work items in the script, and they can be used exclusively within your scripting environment. In this section, we will look at using single-line comments to add help documentation to a script.

In the CreateFileNameFromDate.ps1 script, the header section of the script uses the comments section to explain how the script works, what it does, and the limitations of the approach. The CreateFileNameFromDate.ps1 script is shown here:

**CreateFileNameFromDate.ps1**

```
# -------------------------------------------------------------------------
# NAME: CreateFileNameFromDate.ps1
# AUTHOR: ed wilson, Microsoft
# DATE:12/15/2008
#
# KEYWORDS: .NET framework, io.path, get-date
# file, new-item, Standard Date and Time Format Strings
# regular expression, ref, pass by reference
#
# COMMENTS: This script creates an empty text file
# based upon the date-time stamp. Uses format string
# to specify a sortable date. Uses getInvalidFileNameChars
# method to get all the invalid characters that are not allowed
# in a file name. It assumes there is a folder named fso off the
# c:\ drive. If the folder does not exist, the script will fail.
#
# -------------------------------------------------------------------------
Function GetFileName([ref]$fileName)
{
 $invalidChars = [io.path]::GetInvalidFileNamechars()
 $date = Get-Date -format s
 $fileName.value = ($date.ToString() -replace "[$invalidChars]","-") + ".txt"
}

$fileName = $null
GetFileName([ref]$fileName)
new-item -path c:\fso -name $filename -itemtype file
```

In general, you should always provide information about how to use your functions. Each parameter, as well as underlying dependencies, must be explained. In addition to documenting the operation and dependencies of the functions, you should also include information that will be beneficial to those who must maintain the code. You should always assume that the person who maintains your code does not understand what the code actually does, therefore ensuring that the documentation explains everything. In the BackUpFiles.ps1 script, comments are added to both the header and to each function to explain the logic and limitations of the functions, as shown in the BackUpFiles.ps1 script.

**BackUpFiles.ps1**

```
# -----------------------------------------------------------------------
# NAME: BackUpFiles.ps1
# AUTHOR: ed wilson, Microsoft
# DATE: 12/12/2008
#
# KEYWORDS: Filesystem, get-childitem, where-object
# date manipulation, regular expressions
#
# COMMENTS: This script backs up a folder. It will
# back up files that have been modified within the past
# 24 hours. You can change the interval, the destination,
# and the source. It creates a backup folder that is named based upon
# the time the script runs. If the destination folder does not exist, it
# will be created. The destination folder is based upon the time the
# script is run and will look like this: C:\bu\12.12.2008.1.22.51.PM.
# The interval is the age in days of the files to be copied.
#
# -----------------------------------------------------------------------
Function New-BackUpFolder($destinationFolder)
{
 #Receives the path to the destination folder and creates the path to
 #a child folder based upon the date / time. It then calls the New-Backup
 #function while passing the source path, destination path, and interval
 #in days.
 $dte = get-date
 #The following regular expression pattern removes white space, colon,
 #and forward slash from the date and replaces with a period to create the
 #backup folder name.
 $dte = $dte.tostring() -replace "[:\s/]", "."
 $backUpPath = "$destinationFolder" + $dte
 $null = New-Item -path $backUpPath -itemType directory
 New-Backup $dataFolder $backUpPath $backUpInterval
} #end New-BackUpFolder

Function New-Backup($dataFolder,$backUpPath,$backUpInterval)
{
 #Does a recursive copy of all files in the data folder and filters out
 #all files that have been written to within the number of days specified
 #by the interval. Writes copied files to the destination and will create
 #if the destination (including parent path) does not exist. Will overwrite
 #if destination already exists. This is unlikely, however, unless the
 #script is run twice during the same minute.
 "backing up $dataFolder... check $backUppath for your files"
 Get-Childitem -path $dataFolder -recurse |
```

```
Where-Object { $_.LastWriteTime -ge (get-date).addDays(-$backUpInterval) } |
  Foreach-Object { copy-item -path $_.FullName -destination $backUpPath -force }
} #end New-BackUp


# *** entry point to script ***


$backUpInterval = 1
$dataFolder = "C:\fso"
$destinationFolder = "C:\BU\"
New-BackupFolder $destinationFolder
```

## NOTES FROM THE FIELD

### Crafting-inspired cmdlet help

Dean Tsaltas
*Microsoft Scripting Guy Emeritus*

In many ways, writing cmdlet help is no different from writing any other type of help documentation. If you want to do a really good job, you must *"become your user."* This is easier said than done, of course—especially if you are the person who designed and implemented the cmdlets for which you are writing the help. Even though you just created the cmdlets, you can only guess at the mysterious ways in which some of your users will use and abuse your creations. That said, you must give it your all. Rent the original *Karate Kid* and watch it for inspiration. Wax on and wax off before hitting the keyboard. After crafting just the right sentences to convey a concept, remember to ask yourself, "What ambiguity is left in what I just wrote? What can my user possibly still question after reading my text?" Picture yourself explaining the concept to your users, anticipate their questions, and answer them.

For example, suppose that your cmdlet creates some type of file and takes a name or a full path that includes a name as a parameter. Anticipate the questions that users will have about that parameter: how long can it be, are any characters disallowed, how are quotes within quotes handled, will the resultant file include an extension or should I include the appropriate extension in the parameter value? Don't force your users to experiment to answer questions that you can easily anticipate and to which you can quickly provide answers. Help them.

Next, remember that a single example is worth a thousand support calls. You should aim high when it comes to examples. It is a best practice to brainstorm the top tasks that you think your users will be trying to accomplish. At a minimum, you need to include an example for each of those top tasks. After you have established that baseline, you should aim to provide an example that exercises each and every cmdlet parameter set. Even if you simply mine your test cases for bland examples, try to provide your users with a starting point. As you well know, it's much easier to manipulate a working command line and get it to do what you want than it is to start from scratch.

It's important to consider how your users will interact with cmdlet help. They will see it at a command prompt one full screen at a time. Because that first screen is like the "above-the-fold" section of a newspaper, make sure that you handle any really important issues right there in the detailed description. If you need certain privileges to use the cmdlet, let your users know that information up front. If there's an associated provider that might be useful to them, tell your users about it early.

Don't neglect the Related Links section of your help. It's very easy to simply list all of the cmdlets with the same noun, especially when you're in a rush. Yet, are those truly the only cmdlets that are related to the one you're writing about? For example, is there another cmdlet that your users must use to generate an object that your cmdlet can accept as a parameter value? If so, this other cmdlet also deserves a place in the Related Links list. Again, imagine having a discussion with your users. What other help can you suggest that they access? Also include links to this additional help and not just to the help that is obviously related based on cmdlet naming conventions.

My last bit of advice about writing cmdlet help is to write it as early as you can in the development cycle and get it in the hands of some pre-alpha users to start the feedback cycle quickly. The only way to develop excellent cmdlet help (or any other type of technical documentation) is through iterative improvements in response to feedback. Include numerous simple examples in the help as soon as you can. Having someone use a cmdlet with no accompanying help is unlikely to help you understand what information is needed by your users to get the job done. However, providing someone with three examples will certainly elicit a user response as to what the fourth and fifth examples should be.

## Pairing a comment with a closing curly bracket

I once spent an entire train ride in Germany that went from Regensburg to Hamburg (nearly a five-hour trip) troubleshooting a problem with a script that occurred as the train left the central train station in Regensburg. The script was to be used for the *Windows 7 Resource Kit* (Microsoft Press, 2009), and I had a deadline to meet. The problem occurred with an edit that I made to the original script, and I forgot to close the curly bracket. The error was particularly misleading because it pointed to a line in the very long script that was unrelated to the issue at hand. It was on this train ride that I learned the value of adding a comment to closing curly brackets, which is now something that I nearly always do.

Here is the closing curly bracket and associated comment. If you always type comments in the same pattern (for example, #end with no space), they are then easy to spot if you ever decide to write a script to search for them.

```
} #end Get-ieStartPage
```

You now need to create a function to assign new values to the Internet Explorer start pages. You can call the *Set-ieStartPage* function as shown here:

```
Function Set-ieStartPage()
{
```

You must assign some values to a large number of variables. The first four variables are the same ones used in the previous function. (You could have made them script-level variables and saved four lines of code in the overall script, but then the functions would not have been stand-alone pieces of code.) The *$value* variable is used to hold the default home page, and the *$aryvalues* variable holds an array of secondary home page URLs. This section of the code is shown here:

```
$hkcu = 2147483649
$key = "Software\Microsoft\Internet Explorer\Main"
$property = "Start Page"
$property2 = "Secondary Start Pages"
$value = "http://www.microsoft.com/technet/scriptcenter/default.mspx"
$aryValues = "http://social.technet.microsoft.com/Forums/en/ITCG/threads/",
"http://www.microsoft.com/technet/scriptcenter/resources/qanda/all.mspx"
```

After assigning values to variables, you can use the [WMICLASS] type accelerator to create an instance of the *stdRegProv* WMI class. This same line of code is used in the *Get-ieStartPage* function and is shown here:

```
$wmi = [wmiclass]"\\$computer\root\default:stdRegProv"
```

You can now use the *SetStringValue* method to set the value of the string. The *SetStringValue* method takes four values. The first is the numeric value representing the registry hive to which to connect. The next is the string for the registry key. The third position holds the property to modify, and the last is a string representing the new value to assign, as shown here:

```
$rtn = $wmi.SetStringValue($hkcu,$key,$property,$value)
```

Next, you can use the *SetMultiStringValue* method to set the value of a multistring registry key. This method takes an array in the fourth position. The signature of the *SetMultiStringValue* method is similar to the *SetStringValue* signature. The only difference is that the fourth position needs an array of strings and not a single value as shown here:

```
$rtn2 = $wmi.SetMultiStringValue($hkcu,$key,$property2,$aryValues)
```

Now, you can print the value of the *ReturnValue* property. The *ReturnValue* property contains the error code from the method call. A zero means that the method worked (no runs, no errors), and anything else means that there was a problem, as shown here:

```
"Setting $property returned $($rtn.returnvalue)"
"Setting $property2 returned $($rtn2.returnvalue)"
} #end Set-ieStartPage
```

You are now at the entry point to the script. You must first get the starting values and then set them to the new values that you want to configure. If you want to re-query the registry to ensure that the values took effect, you can simply call the *Get-ieStartPage* function again, as shown here:

```
if($get) {Get-ieStartpage}
if($set){Set-ieStartPage}
```

The complete GetSetieStartPage.ps1 script is shown here.

```
GetSetieStartPage.ps1

Param([switch]$get,[switch]$set,$computer="localhost")
$Comment = @"
NAME: GetSetieStartPage.ps1
AUTHOR: ed wilson, Microsoft
DATE: 1/5/2009

KEYWORDS: stdregprov, ie, [wmiclass] type accelerator,
Hey Scripting Guy
COMMENTS: This script uses the [wmiclass] type accelerator
and the stdregprov to get the ie start pages and to set the
ie start pages. Using ie 7 or better you can have multiple
start pages.

"@ #end comment
```

```
Function Get-ieStartPage()
{
$Comment = @"
FUNCTION: Get-ieStartPage
Is used to retrieve the current settings for Internet Explorer 7 and greater.
The value of $hkcu is set to a constant value from the SDK that points
to the Hkey_Current_User. Two methods are used to read
from the registry because the start page is single valued and
the second start page's key is multi-valued.

"@ #end comment
 $hkcu = 2147483649
 $key = "Software\Microsoft\Internet Explorer\Main"
 $property = "Start Page"
 $property2 = "Secondary Start Pages"
 $wmi = [wmiclass]"\\$computer\root\default:stdRegProv"
 ($wmi.GetStringValue($hkcu,$key,$property)).sValue
 ($wmi.GetMultiStringValue($hkcu,$key, $property2)).sValue
} #end Get-ieStartPage

Function Set-ieStartPage()
{
$Comment = @"
FUNCTION: Set-ieStartPage
Allows you to configure one or more home pages for IE 7 and greater.
The $aryValues and the $Value variables hold the various home pages.
Specify the complete URL ex: "http://www.ScriptingGuys.Com." Make sure
to include the quotation marks around each URL.

"@ #end comment
  $hkcu = 2147483649
  $key = "Software\Microsoft\Internet Explorer\Main"
  $property = "Start Page"
  $property2 = "Secondary Start Pages"
  $value = "http://www.microsoft.com/technet/scriptcenter/default.mspx"
  $aryValues = "http://social.technet.microsoft.com/Forums/en/ITCG/threads/",
  "http://www.microsoft.com/technet/scriptcenter/resources/qanda/all.mspx"
  $wmi = [wmiclass]"\\$computer\root\default:stdRegProv"
  $rtn = $wmi.SetStringValue($hkcu,$key,$property,$value)
  $rtn2 = $wmi.SetMultiStringValue($hkcu,$key,$property2,$aryValues)
  "Setting $property returned $($rtn.returnvalue)"
  "Setting $property2 returned $($rtn2.returnvalue)"
} #end Set-ieStartPage
```

```
# *** entry point to script
if($get) {Get-ieStartpage}
if($set){Set-ieStartPage}
```

# Working with temporary folders

You can obtain the path to the temporary folder on the local computer in many different ways, including using the environmental PS drive. This example uses the static *GetTempPath* method from the *System.Io.Path* .NET Framework class. The *GetTempPath* method returns the path to the temporary folder, which is where you will store the newly created text file. You hold the temporary folder path in the *$outputPath* variable as shown here:

```
$outputPath = [io.path]::GetTempPath()
```

You decide to name your new text file after the name of the script. To do this, you need to separate the script name from the path in which the script is stored. You can use the *Split-Path* function to perform this surgery. The *–leaf* parameter instructs the cmdlet to return the script name. If you want the directory path that contains the script, you can use the *–parent* parameter. You put the Split-Path cmdlet inside a pair of parentheses because you want that operation to occur first. When the dollar sign is placed in front of the parentheses, it creates a subexpression that executes the code and then returns the name of the script. You can use .ps1 as the extension for your text file, but that can become a bit confusing because it is the extension for a script. Therefore, you can simply add a .txt extension to the returned file name and place the entire string within a pair of quotation marks.

You can use the Join-Path cmdlet to create a new path to your output file. The new path is composed of the temporary folder that is stored in the *$outputPath* variable and the file name you created using *Split-Path*. You combine these elements by using the Join-Path cmdlet. You can use string manipulation and concatenation to create the new file path, but it is much more reliable to use the Join-Path and Split-Path cmdlets to perform these types of operations. This section of the code is shown here:

```
Join-Path -path $outputPath -child "$(Split-Path $script -leaf).txt"
} #end Get-FileName
```

You need to decide how to handle duplicate files. You can prompt the user by saying that a duplicate file exists, which looks like the code shown here:

```
    $Response = Read-Host -Prompt "$outputFile already exists. Do you wish to delete
it <y / n>?"
    if($Response -eq "y")
      { Remove-Item $outputFile | Out-Null }
    ELSE { "Exiting now." ; exit }
```

You can implement some type of naming algorithm that makes a backup of the duplicate file by renaming it with an .old extension, which looks like the code shown here:

```
if(Test-Path -path "$outputFile.old") { Remove-Item -Path "$outputFile.old" }
Rename-Item -path $outputFile -newname  "$(Split-Path $outputFile -leaf).old"
```

You can also simply delete the previously existing file, which is what I generally choose to do. The action you want to perform goes into the *Remove-OutPutFile* function. You begin the function by using the *Function* keyword, specifying the name of the function, and using the *$outputFile* variable for input to the function as shown here:

```
Function Remove-outputFile($outputFile)
{
```

To determine whether the file exists, you can use the Test-Path cmdlet and supply the string contained in the *$outputFile* variable to the *–path* parameter. The Test-Path cmdlet returns only a *true* or *false* value. When a file is not found, it returns a *false* value, which means that you can use the *If* statement to evaluate the existence of the file. If the file is found, you can perform the action in the script block. If the file is not found, the script block is not executed.  As shown here, the first command does not find the file, and *false* is returned. In the second command, the script block is not executed because the file cannot be located.

```
PS C:\> Test-Path c:\missingfile.txt
False
PS C:\> if(Test-Path c:\missingfile.txt){"found file"}
PS C:\>
```

Inside the *Remove-OutPutFile* function, you can use the *If* statement to determine whether the file referenced by *$outputFile* already exists. If it does, it is deleted by using the Remove-Item cmdlet. The information that is normally returned when a file is deleted is pipelined to the Out-Null cmdlet providing for a silent operation. This portion of the code is shown here:

```
  if(Test-Path -path $outputFile) { Remove-Item $outputFile | Out-Null }

} #end Remove-outputFile
```

After you create the name for the output file and delete any previous output files that might be around, it is time to retrieve the comments from the script. To do this, you can create the *Get-Comments* function and pass it to both the *$script* variable and *$outputFile* variable as shown here:

```
Function Get-Comments($Script,$outputFile)
{
```

## Don't mess with the worker section of the script

If I am going to gather data to pass to a function when writing a script, I generally like to encase the data in the same variable name that will be used both outside and inside the function. One reason for doing this is because it follows one of my best practices for script development: "Don't mess with the worker section of the script." In the *Get-OutPutFile* function, you are "doing work." To change the function in future scripts requires that you edit the string literal value, whereby you run the risk of breaking the code because many methods have complicated constructors. If you are also trying to pass values to the method constructors that require escaping special characters, the risk of making a mistake becomes even worse.

# Using multiple-line comment tags in Windows PowerShell 4.0

Windows PowerShell 4.0 multiple-line comment tags make it easy to comment one or more lines in a script. These comment tags work in a similar fashion to here-strings or HTML tags in that, when you open a comment tag, you must also close the comment tag. In fact, the multiline comment character has been around since Windows PowerShell 2.0, so it is not new technology.

## Creating multiple-line comments with comment tags

The opening tag is the left angle bracket pound sign (<#), and the closing comment tag is the pound sign right angle bracket (#>). The pattern for the use of the multiline comment is shown here:

```
<# Opening comment tag
First line comment
Additional comment lines
#> Closing comment tag
```

The use of the multiline comment is seen in the Demo-MultilineComment.ps1 script.

```
Demo-MultilineComment.ps1

<#
Get-Command
Get-Help
#>
"The above is a multiline comment"
```

When the Demo-MultilineComment.ps1 script is run, the two cmdlets shown inside the comment tags are not run; the only command that runs is the one outside of the comment block, which prints a string in the console window. The output from the Demo-MultilineComment.ps1 script is as follows:

```
The above is a multiline comment
```

Multiline comment tags do not need to be placed on individual lines. It is perfectly permissible to include the commented text on the line that supplies the comment characters. The pattern for the alternate multiline comment tag placement is shown here:

```
<# Opening comment tag First line comment
Additional comment lines #> Closing comment tag
```

The alternate multiline comment tag placement is shown in MultilineDemo2.ps1.

---

**MultilineDemo2.ps1**

```
<# Get-Help
   Get-Command #>
"The above is a multiline comment"
```

---

> **NOTE** As a best practice, I prefer to place multiline comment tags on their own individual lines. This format makes the code much easier to read, and it is easier to see where the comment begins and ends.

## Creating single-line comments with comment tags

You can use the multiline comment syntax to comment a single line of code, with the advantage being that you do not mix your comment characters. You can use a single comment pattern for all of the comments in the script, as shown here:

```
<# Opening comment tag First line comment #> Closing comment tag
```

An example of the single comment pattern in a script is shown in the MultilineDemo3.ps1 script.

---

**MultilineDemo3.ps1**

```
<# This is a single comment #>
"The above is a single comment"
```

---

When using the multiline comment pattern, it is important to keep in mind that anything placed after the end of the closing comment tag is parsed by Windows PowerShell. Only items placed within the multiline comment characters are commented out. However, multiline commenting behavior is completely different from using the pound sign (#) single-line comment character. It is also a foreign concept to users of VBScript who are used to the behavior of the single quote (') comment character in which anything after the character is commented out. A typical-use scenario that generates an error is illustrated in the following example:

```
<# ----------------------------
This example causes an error
#> ----------------------------
```

If you need to highlight your comments in the manner shown in the preceding example, you need only to change the position of the last comment tag by moving it to the end of the line to remove the error. The modified comment is shown here:

```
<# -------------------------------
This example does not cause an error
--------------------------------- #>
```

> **NOTE** No space is required between the pound sign and the following character. I prefer to include the space between the pound sign and the following character as a concession to readability.

The single pound sign (#) is still accepted for commenting, and there is nothing to prohibit its use. To perform a multiline comment using the single pound sign, you simply place a pound sign in front of each line that requires commenting. This pattern has the advantage of familiarity and consistency of behavior. The fact that it is also backward compatible with Windows PowerShell 1.0 is an added bonus.

```
# First commented line
# additional commented line
# last commented line
```

# Using comment-based help

Much of the intensive work of producing help information for your functions is removed when you use the comment-based help. To use the comment-based help, you place the help tags inside the block comment markers when you are writing your script. Writing help information for your function by employing the help tags allows for complete integration with the Get-Help cmdlet, thus providing a seamless user experience for anyone who uses your functions–or your scripts. In fact, it is entirely possible that a Windows PowerShell script would have comment-based help, in addition to the functions contained within the script itself. It is a best practice that functions contained within a Windows PowerShell module contain comment-based help. In addition, help tags promote the custom user-defined function to the same status within Windows PowerShell as native cmdlets. The experience of using a custom user-defined function is no different than using a cmdlet, and to the user, there is indeed no need to distinguish among a custom function that is dot-sourced, loaded via a module, or a native cmdlet. The help function tags and their associated meanings are shown in Table 9-1.

**TABLE 9-1** Function help tags and meanings

| Help Tag name | Help Tag description |
| --- | --- |
| .Synopsis | A very brief description of the function. It begins with a verb and informs the user about what the function does. It does not include the function name or how the function works. The function synopsis tag appears in the SYNOPSIS field of all help views. |
| .Description | Two or three full sentences that briefly list everything that the function can do. It begins with "The <function name> function...." If the function can receive multiple objects or take multiple inputs, use plural nouns in the description. The description tag appears in the DESCRIPTION field of all help views. |
| .Parameter | Brief and thorough. Describes what the function does when the parameter is used and what legal values are set for the parameter. The parameter tag appears in the PARAMETERS field only in the Detailed and Full help views. |
| .Example | Illustrates use of the function with all of its parameters. The first example is the simplest, by showing only the required parameters. The last example is the most complex and should incorporate pipelining if appropriate. The example tag appears only in the EXAMPLES field in the Example, Detailed, and Full help views. |
| .Inputs | Lists the .NET Framework classes of objects that the function accepts as input. There is no limit to the number of input classes that you can list. The inputs tag appears only in the INPUTS field in the Full help view. |
| .Outputs | Lists the .NET Framework classes of objects that the function emits as output. There is no limit to the number of output classes that you can list. The outputs tag appears in the OUTPUTS field only in the Full help view. |
| .Notes | Provides a place to list information that does not fit easily into the other sections. Notes can be special requirements required by the function, as well as author, title, version, and other information. The notes tag appears in the NOTES field only in the Full help view. |
| .Link | Provides links to other help topics and Internet sites of interest. Because these links appear in a command window, they are not direct links. There is no limit to the number of links that you can provide. The link tag appears in the RELATED LINKS field in all help views. |
| .Component | The feature or technology that the function or script uses. Also refers to a related technology or feature. |
| .Role | The user role for the help topic. |
| .Functionality | The intended use of the function or script. |
| .ForwardHelpTargetName | Redirects the help topic for a specific command. Provides ability to redirect to any help topic, including help topics for a function, script, cmdlet, or provider. |
| .ForwardHelpCategory | Specifies the category of the item in the ForwardHelpTargetName. Valid values are: Alias, Cmdlet, HelpFile, Function, Provider, General, FAQ, Glossary, ScriptCommand, ExternalScript, Filter, or All. This tag helps to avoid conflicts when there are multiple commands with the same name. |
| .RemoteHelpRunSpace | Specifies a session that contains the help topic. Accepts a variable containing a PSSession object. This tag is used by the Export-PSSession cmdlet. |
| .ExternalHelp | Used when a function or script uses XML help files. |

You do not need to supply values for all of the help tags. However, as a best practice, you should consider supplying the .synopsis and .example tags because they contain the most critical information needed when instructing someone about how to use the function.

An example of using help tags is shown in the GetWmiClassesFunction1.ps1 script. The help information provided by using the Get-Help cmdlet is exactly the same as the information provided by the GetWmiClassesFunction.ps1 script. The difference occurs with the use of the help tags. There is no longer a need for the switched *–help* parameter due to incorporation of the code with the Get-Help cmdlet. When you no longer need to use a switched *–help* parameter, you also no longer need to test for the existence of the *$help* variable. By avoiding testing for the *$help* variable, your script can become much simpler.

## The benefits of special help tags

Several bonus features are provided by using the special help tags, including the following:

- The name of the function is automatically displayed and is displayed in all help views.

- The syntax of the function is automatically derived from the parameters and is displayed in all help views.

- Detailed parameter information is automatically generated when the *–full* parameter of the Get-Help cmdlet is used.

- Common parameters information is automatically displayed when Get-Help is used with the *–detailed* and *–full* parameters.

In the GetWmiClassesFunction1.ps1 script, the *Get-WmiClasses* function begins the help section with multiline comment block. The multiline comment block special characters begin with the left angle bracket followed by a pound sign (<#) and end with the pound sign followed by the right angle bracket (#>). Everything between the multiline comment characters is considered to be commented out. Two special help tags are included: the .synopsis tag and the .example tag. The other help tags listed in Table 9-1 are not used for this function.

```
<#
 .SYNOPSIS
  Displays a list of WMI Classes based upon a search criteria
 .EXAMPLE
  Get-WmiClasses -class disk -ns root\cimv2"
  This command finds wmi classes that contain the word disk. The
  classes returned are from the root\cimv2 namespace.
#>
```

After the GetWmiClassesFunction1.ps1 script is dot-sourced into the Windows PowerShell console, you can use the Get-Help cmdlet to obtain help information from the

*Get-WmiClasses* function. When the `Get-Help` cmdlet is run with the *–full* parameter, the help display shown in Figure 9-1 appears.

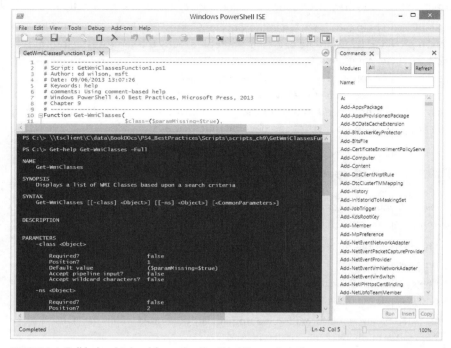

**FIGURE 9-1** Full help obtained from the *Get-WmiClasses* function.

The complete GetWmiClassesFunction1.ps1 script is shown here.

```
GetWmiClassesFunction1.ps1

Function Get-WmiClasses(
                        $class=($paramMissing=$true),
                        $ns="root\cimv2"
                        )
{
<#

    .SYNOPSIS
      Displays a list of WMI Classes based upon a search criteria
    .EXAMPLE
     Get-WmiClasses -class disk -ns root\cimv2"
     This command finds wmi classes that contain the word disk. The
     classes returned are from the root\cimv2 namespace.
#>
  If($local:paramMissing)
    {
      throw "USAGE: Get-WmiClasses -class <class type> -ns <wmi namespace>"
```

```
      } #$local:paramMissing
  "`nClasses in $ns namespace ...."
  Get-WmiObject -namespace $ns -list |
  where-object {
                  $_.name -match $class -and `
                  $_.name -notlike 'cim*'
              }
  # mred function
} #end get-wmiclasses
```

If you intend to use the dot-source method to include functions into your working Windows PowerShell environment and modules, it makes sense to add the directory that contains your scripts to the path. You can add your function storage directory as a permanent change by using the Windows Graphical User Interface (GUI) tools, or you can simply make the addition to your path each time you start Windows PowerShell by making the change via your Windows PowerShell profile. If you decide to add your function directory by using Windows PowerShell commands, you can use the Windows PowerShell environmental drive to access the system path variable and make the change. The code seen here first examines the path and then appends the C:\fso folder to the end of the path. Each directory that is added to the search path is separated by a semicolon. When you append a directory to the path, you must include that semicolon as the first item that is added. You can use the += operator to append a directory to the end of the path. The last command checks the path once again to ensure that the change took place as intended.

```
PS C:\> $env:path
C:\Windows\system32;C:\Windows;C:\Windows\System32\Wbem;C:\Windows\System32
\Windows System Resource Manager\bin;C:\Windows\idmu\common;C:\Windows\system32
\WindowsPowerShell\v1.0\
PS C:\> $env:path += ";C:\fso"
PS C:\> $env:path
C:\Windows\system32;C:\Windows;C:\Windows\System32\Wbem;C:\Windows\System32
\Windows System Resource Manager\bin;C:\Windows\idmu\common;C:\Windows\system32
\WindowsPowerShell\v1.0\;C:\fso
```

A change made to the path via the Windows PowerShell environmental drive is a temporary change that lasts only for the length of the current PowerShell console session. The change takes effect immediately and therefore is a convenient method to quickly alter your current Windows PowerShell environment without making permanent changes to your system environmental settings.

**NOTE**  I personally find the ability to access my scripts from the command line to be extremely useful, and I therefore add my script folder to my path environmental variable via my profile. In this manner, I always have direct access to any of my scripts via a simple dot-sourcing technique. For more information about modifying your Windows PowerShell working environment via the profile, refer to Chapter 5, "Configuring the script environment."

A very powerful feature of modifying the path via the Windows PowerShell environmental drive is that the changes are applied immediately and are at once available to the current Windows PowerShell session. This means that you can add a directory to the path, dot-source a script that contains functions, and use the Get-Help cmdlet to display help information without the requirement of closing and opening Windows PowerShell. When a directory is appended to the search path, you can dot-source scripts from that directory without the need to type the entire path to that directory. The technique of modifying the path, dot-sourcing a directory, and using Get-Help is illustrated here:

```
PS C:\> $env:Path += ";C:\fso"
PS C:\> . GetWmiClassesFunction1.ps1
PS C:\> Get-Help Get-WmiClasses
```

Figure 9-2 displays the results of using the technique of adding a directory to the path, dot-sourcing a script that resides in the newly appended folder, and then calling the Get-Help cmdlet to retrieve information from the newly added functions.

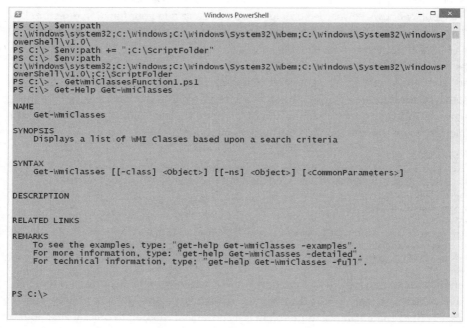

**FIGURE 9-2** By appending to the path, functions can easily be dot-sourced into the current Windows PowerShell environment.

# The 13 rules for writing effective comments

When adding documentation to a script, it is important that you do not introduce errors. If the comments and code do not match, there is a good chance that both are wrong. Make sure that when you modify the script, you also modify your comments. In this way, both the comments and the script refer to the same information.

## Update documentation when a script is updated

It is easy to forget to update comments that refer to the parameters of a function when you add additional parameters to that function. In a similar fashion, it is easy to ignore the information contained inside the header of the script that refers to dependencies or assumptions within the script. Make sure that you treat both the script and the comments with the same level of attention and importance. In the FindDisabledUserAccounts.ps1 script, the comments in the header seem to apply to the script, but they also seem to miss the fact that the script is using the [ADSISearcher] type accelerator. In fact, the script is a modified script that was used to create a specific instance of the *DirectoryServices.DirectorySearcher* .NET Framework class and was recently updated. However, the comments were never updated. This oversight might make a user suspicious as to the accuracy of a perfectly useful script. The FindDisabledUserAccounts.ps1 script is shown here.

```
FindDisabledUserAccounts.ps1

# -----------------------------------------------------------------------
# FindDisabledUserAccounts.ps1
# ed wilson, 3/28/2008
#
# Creates an instance of the DirectoryServices DirectorySearcher .NET
# Framework class to search Active Directory.
# Creates a filter that is LDAP syntax that gets applied to the searcher
# object. If we only look for class of user, then we also end up with
# computer accounts as they are derived from user class. So we do a
# compound query to also retrieve person.
# We then use the findall method and retrieve all users.
# Next we use the properties property and choose item to retrieve the
# distinguished name of each user, and then we use the distinguished name
# to perform a query and retrieve the UAC attribute, and then we do a
# boolean to compare with the value of 2 which is disabled.
#
# -----------------------------------------------------------------------
#Requires -Version 2.0

$filter = "(&(objectClass=user)(objectCategory=person))"
$users = ([adsiSearcher]$Filter).findall()
```

```
foreach($suser in $users)
  {
   "Testing $($suser.properties.item(""distinguishedname""))"
   $user = [adsi]"LDAP://$($suser.properties.item(""distinguishedname""))"

   $uac=$user.psbase.invokeget("useraccountcontrol")
     if($uac -band 0x2)
       { write-host -foregroundcolor red "`t account is disabled" }
     ELSE
       { write-host -foregroundcolor green "`t account is not disabled" }
  } #foreach
```

## Add comments during the development process

When you are writing a script, make sure that you add the comments at the same time that you are doing the initial development. Do not wait until you have completed the script to begin writing your comments. When you make comments after writing the script, it is very easy to leave out details because you are now overly familiar with the script and those items that you looked up in documentation now seem obvious. If you add the comments at the same time that you write the script, you can then refer to these comments as you develop the script to ensure that you maintain a consistent approach. This procedure will help with the consistency of your variable names and writing style. The CheckForPdfAndCreateMarker .ps1 script illustrates this consistency problem. In reviewing the code, it seems that the script checks for PDF files, which also seems rather obvious from the name of the script. However, why is the script prompting to delete the files? What is the marker? The only discernable information is that I wrote the script back in December 2008 for a Hey Scripting Guy! article. Luckily, Hey Scripting Guy! articles explain scripts, so at least some documentation actually exists! The CheckForPdfAndCreateMarker.ps1 script is shown here.

**CheckForPdfAndCreateMarker.ps1**

```
# -------------------------------------------------------------------------------
# CheckForPdfAndCreateMarker.ps1
# ed wilson, msft, 12/11/2008
#
# Hey Scripting Guy! 12/29/2008
# -------------------------------------------------------------------------------
$path = "c:\fso"
$include = "*.pdf"
$name = "nopdf.txt"
if(!(Get-ChildItem -path $path -include $include -Recurse))
  {
```

```
    "No pdf was found in $path. Creating $path\$name marker file."
    New-Item -path $path -name $name -itemtype file -force |
    out-null
  } #end if not Get-Childitem
ELSE
 {
  $response = Read-Host -prompt "PDF files were found. Do you wish to delete <y>
/<n>?"
  if($response -eq "y")
    {
      "PDF files will be deleted."
      Get-ChildItem -path $path -include $include -recurse |
      Remove-Item
    } #end if response
  ELSE
   {
    "PDF files will not be deleted."
   } #end else reponse
} #end else not Get-Childitem
```

# Write for an international audience

When you write comments for your script, you should attempt to write for an international audience. You should always assume that users who are not overly familiar with the idioms of your native language will be reading your comments. In addition, writing for an international audience makes it easier for automated software to localize the script documentation. Key points to keep in mind when writing for an international audience are to use a simple syntax and to use consistent employee standard terminology. Avoid slang, acronyms, and overly familiar language. If possible, have a colleague who is a non-native speaker review the documentation. In the SearchForWordImages.ps1 script, the comments explain what the script does and also its limitations, such as the fact that it was tested using only Microsoft Office Word 2007. The sentences are plainly written and do not use jargon or idioms. The SearchForWordImages.ps1 script is shown here.

```
SearchForWordImages.ps1

# -----------------------------------------------------------------------
# NAME: SearchForWordImages.ps1
# AUTHOR: ed wilson, Microsoft
# DATE: 11/4/2008
#
# KEYWORDS: Word.Application, automation, COM
# Get-Childitem -include, Foreach-Object
#
```

```
# COMMENTS: This script searches a folder for doc and
# docx files, opens them with Word and counts the
# number of images embedded in the file.
# It then prints out the name of each file and the
# number of associated images with the file. This script requires
# Word to be installed. It was tested with Word 2007. The folder must
# exist or the script will fail.
#
# ----------------------------------------------------------------------
#The folder must exist and be followed with a trailing \*
$folder = "c:\fso\*"
$include = "*.doc","*.docx"
$word = new-object -comobject word.application
#Makes the Word application invisible. Set to $true to see the application.
$word.visible = $false
Get-ChildItem -path $folder -include $include |
ForEach-Object `
{
 $doc = $word.documents.open($_.fullname)
 $_.name + " has " + $doc.inlineshapes.count + " images in the file"
}
#If you forget to quit Word, you will end up with multiple copies running
#at the same time.
$word.quit()
```

## Consistent header information

You should include header information at the top of each script. This header information
should be displayed in a consistent manner and should be part of your company's scripting
standards. Typical information to be displayed is the title of the script, author of the script,
date the script was written, version information, and additional comments. Version information does not need to be more extensive than the major and minor versions. This information,
as well as comments about what was added during the revisions, is useful for maintaining
a version control for production scripts. An example of adding comments is shown in the
WriteBiosInfoToWord.ps1 script.

```
WriteBiosInfoToWord.ps1

#==============================================================================
#
# NAME: WriteBiosInfoToWord.ps1
#
# AUTHOR: ed wilson , Microsoft
# DATE  : 10/30/2008
```

```
# EMAIL: Scripter@Microsoft.com
# Version: 1.0
#
# COMMENT: Uses the word.application object to create a new text document
# uses the get-wmiobject cmdlet to query wmi
# uses out-string to remove the "object nature" of the returned information
# uses foreach-object cmdlet to write the data to the word document.
#
# Hey Scripting Guy! 11/11/2008
#=====================================================================

$class = "Win32_Bios"
$path = "C:\fso\bios"

#The wdSaveFormat object must be saved as a reference type.
[ref]$SaveFormat = "microsoft.office.interop.word.WdSaveFormat" -as [type]

$word = New-Object -ComObject word.application
$word.visible = $true
$doc = $word.documents.add()
$selection = $word.selection
$selection.typeText("This is the bios information")
$selection.TypeParagraph()

Get-WmiObject -class $class |
Out-String |
ForEach-Object { $selection.typeText($_) }
$doc.saveas([ref] $path, [ref]$saveFormat::wdFormatDocument)
$word.quit()
```

## Document prerequisites

It is imperative that your comments include information about prerequisites for running the script as well as the implementation of nonstandard programs in the script. For example, if your script requires the use of an external program that is not part of the operating system, you need to include checks within the script to ensure that the program is available when it is called by the script itself. In addition to these checks, you should document the fact that the program is a requirement for running the script. If your script makes assumptions about the existence of certain directories, you should make a note of this fact. Of course, your script should use Test-Path to make sure that the directory exists, but you should still document this step as an important precondition for the script.

An additional consideration is whether or not you create the required directory. If the script requires an input file, you should add a comment that indicates this requirement as well as add a comment to check for the existence of the file prior to actually calling that file. It is also a good idea to add a comment indicating the format of the input file, because one of the most fragile aspects of a script that reads an input file is the actual formatting of that file. The ConvertToFahrenheit_include.ps1 script illustrates adding a note about the requirement of accessing the include file.

```
ConvertToFahrenheit_include.ps1

# ------------------------------------------------------------------------
# NAME: ConvertToFahrenheit_include.ps1
# AUTHOR: ed wilson, Microsoft
# DATE: 9/24/2008
# EMAIL: Scripter@Microsoft.com
# Version 2.0
#   12/1/2008 added test-path check for include file
#             modified the way the include file is called
# KEYWORDS: Converts Celsius to Fahrenheit
#
# COMMENTS: This script converts Celsius to Fahrenheit
# It uses command line parameters and an include file.
# If the ConversionFunctions.ps1 script is not available,
# the script will fail.
#
# ------------------------------------------------------------------------
Param($Celsius)
#The $includeFile variable points to the ConversionFunctions.ps1
#script. Make sure you edit the path to this script.
$includeFile = "c:\data\scriptingGuys\ConversionFunctions.ps1"
if(!(test-path -path $includeFile))
  {
   "Unable to find $includeFile"
   Exit
  }
. $includeFile
ConvertToFahrenheit($Celsius)
```

# Document deficiencies

If the script has a deficiency, it is imperative that this is documented. This deficiency can be as simple as the fact that the script is still in progress, but this fact should be highlighted in the comments section of the header to the script. It is quite common for script writers to begin writing a script, become distracted, and then begin writing a new script, all the while forgetting about the original script in progress. When the original script is later found, someone might begin to use the script and be surprised that it does not work as advertised. For this reason, scripts that are in progress should always be marked accordingly. If you use a keyword, such as *in progress*, you can write a script that will find all of your work-in-progress scripts. In addition to scripts in progress, you should also highlight any limitations of the script. If a script runs on a local computer but will not run on a remote computer, this fact should be added in the comment section of the header. If a script requires an extremely long time to complete the requested action, this information should be noted. If the script generates errors but completes its task successfully, this information should also be noted so that the user can have confidence in the outcome of the script. A note that indicates why the error is generated also increases the confidence of the user in the original writer.

The CmdLineArgumentsTime.ps1 script works but generates errors unless it is used in a certain set of conditions and is called in a specific manner. The comments call out the special conditions, and several in progress tags indicate the future work required by the script. The CmdLineArgumentsTime.ps1 script is shown here.

```
CmdLineArgumentsTime.ps1

# ==========================================================================
#
# NAME: CmdLineArgumentsTime.ps1
# AUTHOR: Ed Wilson , microsoft
# DATE   : 2/19/2009
# EMAIL: Scripter@Microsoft.com
# Version .0
# KEYWORDS: Add-PSSnapin, powergadgets, Get-Date
#
# COMMENT: The $args[0] is unnamed argument that accepts command line input.
# C:\cmdLineArgumentsTime.ps1 23 52
# No commas are used to separate the arguments. Will generate an error if used.
# Requires powergadgets.
# INPROGRESS: Add a help function to script.
# ==========================================================================
#INPROGRESS: change unnamed arguments to a more user friendly method
[int]$inthour = $args[0]
[int]$intMinute = $args[1]
#INPROGRESS: find a better way to check for existence of powergadgets
#This causes errors to be ignored and is used when checking for PowerGadgets
$erroractionpreference = "SilentlyContinue"
#this clears all errors and is used to see if errors are present.
$error.clear()
#This command will generate an error if PowerGadgets are not installed
Get-PSSnapin *powergadgets | Out-Null
#INPROGRESS: Prompt before loading powergadgets
If ($error.count -ne 0)
{Add-PSSnapin powergadgets}

New-TimeSpan -Start (get-date) -end (get-date -Hour $inthour -Minute $intMinute) |
Out-Gauge -Value minutes -Floating -refresh 0:0:30  -mainscale_max 60
```

# Avoid useless information

Inside the code of the script itself, you should avoid comments that provide useless or irrelevant information. Keep in mind that you are writing a script and providing documentation for the script and that such a task calls for technical writing skills, not creative writing skills. While you might be enthralled with your code in general, the user of the script is not interested in how difficult it was to write the script. However, it is useful to explain why you used certain constructions instead of other forms of code writing. This information, along with the explanation, can be useful to people who might modify the script in the future. You should therefore add internal comments only if they will help others to understand how the script actually works. If a comment does not add value, the comment should be omitted. The DemoConsoleBeep.ps1 script contains numerous comments in the body of the script. However, several of them are obvious, and others actually duplicate information from the comments section of the header. There is nothing wrong with writing too many comments, but it can be a bit excessive when a one-line script contains 20 lines of comments, particularly when the script is very simple. The DemoConsoleBeep.ps1 script is shown here.

```
DemoConsoleBeep.ps1

# -----------------------------------------------------------------------
# NAME: DemoConsoleBeep.ps1
# AUTHOR: ed wilson, Microsoft
# DATE: 4/1/2009
#
# KEYWORDS: Beep
#
# COMMENTS: This script demonstrates using the console
# beep. The first parameter is the frequency between
# 37..32767. above 7500 is barely audible. 37 is the lowest
# note it will play.
# The second parameter is the length of time
#
# -----------------------------------------------------------------------
#this construction creates an array of numbers from 37 to 3200
#the % sign is an alias for Foreach-Object
#the $_ is an automatic variable that refers to the current item
#on the pipeline.
#the semicolon causes a new logical line
#the double colon is used to refer to a static method
#the $_ in the method is the number on the pipeline
#the second number is the length of time to play the beep
37..32000 | % { $_ ; [console]::beep($_ , 1) }
```

# Document the reason for the code

While it is true that good code is readable and that a good developer can understand what a script does, some developers might not understand why a script is written in a certain manner or why a script works in a particular fashion. In the DemoConsoleBeep2.ps1 script, extraneous comments have been removed. Essential information about the range that the console beep will accept is included, but the redundant information is deleted. In addition, a version history is added because significant modification to the script was made. The DemoConsoleBeep2.ps1 script is shown here.

```
DemoConsoleBeep2.ps1

# -------------------------------------------------------------------------
# NAME: DemoConsoleBeep2.ps1
# AUTHOR: ed wilson, Microsoft
# DATE: 4/1/2009
# VERSION 2.0
# 4/4/2009 cleaned up comments. Removed use of % alias. Reformatted.
#
# KEYWORDS: Beep
#
# COMMENTS: This script demonstrates using the console
# beep. The first parameter is the frequency. Allowable range is between
# 37..32767. A number above 7500 is barely audible. 37 is the lowest
# note the console beep will play.
# The second parameter is the length of time.
#
# -------------------------------------------------------------------------

37..32000 |
Foreach-Object { $_ ; [console]::beep($_ , 1) }
```

# Use of one-line comments

You should use one-line comments that appear prior to the code that is being commented to explain the specific purpose of variables or constants. You should also use one-line comments to document fixes or workarounds in the code as well as to point to the reference information explaining these fixes or workarounds. Of course, you should strive to write code that is clear enough to not require internal comments. Do not add comments that simply repeat what the code already states. Add comments to illuminate the code but not to elucidate the code. The GetServicesInSvchost.ps1 script uses comments to discuss the logic of mapping the *handle* property from the *Win32_Process* class to the *ProcessID* property from the *Win32_Service*

WMI class to reveal which services are using which instance of the Svchost process. The
GetServicesInSvchost.ps1 script is shown here.

```
GetServicesInSvchost.ps1

# -----------------------------------------------------------------------
# NAME: GetServicesInSvchost.ps1
# AUTHOR: ed wilson, Microsoft
# DATE: 8/21/2008
#
# KEYWORDS: Get-WmiObject, Format-Table,
# Foreach-Object
#
# COMMENTS: This script creates an array of WMI process
# objects and retrieves the handle of each process object.
# According to MSDN the handle is a process identifier. It
# is also the key of the Win32_Process class. The script
# then uses the handle which is the same as the processID
# property from the Win32_service class to retrieve the
# matches.
#
# HSG 8/28/2008
# -----------------------------------------------------------------------

$aryPid = @(Get-WmiObject win32_process -Filter "name='svchost.exe'") |
  Foreach-Object { $_.Handle }

"There are " + $arypid.length + " instances of svchost.exe running"

foreach ($i in $aryPID)
{
 Write-Host "Services running in ProcessID: $i" ;
 Get-WmiObject win32_service -Filter " processID = $i" |
 Format-Table name, state, startMode
}
```

# Avoid end-of-line comments

You should avoid using end-of-line comments. The addition of such comments to your code
has a severely distracting aspect to structured logic blocks and can cause your code to be
more difficult to read and maintain. Some developers try to improve on this situation by
aligning all of the comments at a particular point within the script. While this initially looks
nice, it creates a maintenance nightmare because each time the code is modified, you run
into the potential for a line to run long and push past the alignment point of the comments.
When this occurs, it forces you to move everything over to the new position. After you do

this a few times, you will probably realize the futility of this approach to commenting internal code. One additional danger of using end-of-line comments when working with Windows PowerShell is that, due to the pipelining nature of language, a single command might stretch out over several lines. Each line that ends with a pipeline character continues the command to the next line. A comment character placed after a pipeline character will break the code, as shown here, where the comment is located in the middle of a logical line of code. The following code will not work:

```
Get-Process | #This cmdlet obtains a listing of all processes on the computer
Select-Object –property name
```

A similar situation also arises when using the named parameters of the ForEach-Object cmdlet as shown in the SearchAllComputersInDomain.ps1 script. The backtick (`) character is used for line continuation, which allows placement of the *–Begin*, *–Process*, and *–End* parameters on individual lines. This placement makes the script easier to read and understand. If an end-of-line comment is placed after any of the backtick characters, the script will fail. The SearchAllComputersInDomain.ps1 script is shown here.

```
SearchAllComputersInDomain.ps1

$Filter = "ObjectCategory=computer"
$Searcher = New-Object System.DirectoryServices.DirectorySearcher($Filter)
$Searcher.Findall() |
Foreach-Object `
  -Begin { "Results of $Filter query: " } `
  -Process { $_.properties ; "`r"} `
  -End { [string]$Searcher.FindAll().Count + " $Filter results were found" }
```

## Document nested structures

The previous discussion about end-of-line comments should not be interpreted as dismissing comments that document the placement of closing curly brackets. In general, you should avoid creating deeply nested structures, but sometimes they cannot be avoided. The use of end-of-line comments with closing curly brackets can greatly improve the readability and maintainability of your script. As shown in the Get-MicrosoftUpdates.ps1 script, the closing curly brackets are all tagged.

```
Get-MicrosoftUpdates.ps1

# ---------------------------------------------------------------------------
# NAME: Get-MicrosoftUpdates.ps1
# AUTHOR: ed wilson, Microsoft
# DATE: 2/25/2009
#
# KEYWORDS: Microsoft.Update.Session, com
#
```

```
# COMMENTS: This script lists the Microsoft Updates
# you can select a certain number, or you can choose
# all of the updates.
#
# HSG 3-9-2009
# ------------------------------------------------------------------------
Function Get-MicrosoftUpdates
{
  Param(
        $NumberOfUpdates,
        [switch]$all
       )
  $Session = New-Object -ComObject Microsoft.Update.Session
  $Searcher = $Session.CreateUpdateSearcher()
  if($all)
    {
      $HistoryCount = $Searcher.GetTotalHistoryCount()
      $Searcher.QueryHistory(1,$HistoryCount)
    } #end if all
  Else
    {
      $Searcher.QueryHistory(1,$NumberOfUpdates)
    } #end else
} #end Get-MicrosoftUpdates

# *** entry point to script ***

# lists the latest update
# Get-MicrosoftUpdates -NumberofUpdates 1

# lists All updates
Get-MicrosoftUpdates -all
```

## Use a standard set of keywords

When adding comments that indicate bugs, defects, or work items, you should use a set
of keywords that is consistent across all scripts. This would be a good item to add to your
corporate scripting guidelines. In this way, a script can easily be developed that will search
your code for such work items. If you maintain source control, a comment can be added
when these work items are fixed. Of course, you would also increment the version of the
script with a comment relating to the fix. In the CheckEventLog.ps1 script, the script accepts
two command-line parameters. One parameter is for the event log to query, and the other is
for the number of events to return. If the user selects the security log and is not running the
script as an administrator, an error is generated that is noted in the comment block. Because

this scenario could be a problem, the outline of a function to check for admin rights has been added to the script as well as code to check for the log name. A number of TODO: tags are added to the script to mark the work items. The CheckEventLog.ps1 script is shown here.

```
CheckEventLog.ps1

# -------------------------------------------------------------------
# NAME: CheckEventLog.ps1
# AUTHOR: ed wilson, Microsoft
# DATE: 4/4/2009
#
# KEYWORDS: Get-EventLog, Param, Function
#
# COMMENTS: This accepts two parameters the logname
# and the number of events to retrieve. If no number for
# -max is supplied it retrieves the most recent entry.
# The script fails if the security log is targeted and it is
# not run with admin rights.
# TODO: Add function to check for admin rights if
# the security log is targeted.
# -------------------------------------------------------------------
Param($log,$max)
Function Get-log($log,$max)
{
 Get-EventLog -logname $log -newest $max
} #end Get-Log

#TODO: finish Get-AdminRights function
Function Get-AdminRights
{
#TODO: add code to check for administrative
#TODO: rights. If not running as an admin
#TODO: if possible add code to obtain those rights
} #end Get-AdminRights

If(-not $log) { "You must specify a log name" ; exit}
if(-not $max) { $max = 1 }
#TODO: turn on the if security log check
# If($log -eq "Security") { Get-AdminRights ; exit }
Get-Log -log $log -max $max
```

## Document the strange and bizarre

The last item that should be commented in your documentation is anything that looks strange. If you use a new type of construction that you have not used previously in other scripts, you should add a comment to the effect. A good comment should also indicate the previous coding construction as an explanation. In general, it is not a best practice to use code that looks strange simply to show your dexterity or because it is an elegant solution; rather, you should strive for readable code. However, when you discover a new construction that is cleaner and easier to read, albeit a somewhat novel approach, you should always add a comment to highlight this fact. If the new construction is sufficiently useful, it should be incorporated into your corporate scripting guidelines as a design pattern.

In the GetProcessesDisplayTempFile.ps1 script, a few unexpected items crop up. The first is the *GetTempFileName* static method from the *Io.Path* .NET Framework class. Despite the method's name, *GetTempFileName* creates both a temporary file name and a temporary file. The second technique is much more unusual. When the temporary file is displayed via Notepad, the result of the operation is pipelined to the Out-Null cmdlet. This operation effectively halts the execution of the script until the Notepad application is closed. This "trick" does not conform to expected behavior, but it is a useful design pattern for those wanting to remove temporary files after they have been displayed. As a result, both features of the GetProcessesDisplayTempFile.ps1 script are documented as shown here.

**GetProcessesDisplayTempFile.ps1**

```
# ---------------------------------------------------------------------
# NAME: GetProcessesDisplayTempFile.ps1
# AUTHOR: ed wilson, Microsoft
# DATE: 4/4/2009
# VERSION 1.0
#
# KEYWORDS: [io.path], GetTempFileName, out-null
#
# COMMENTS: This script creates a temporary file,
# obtains a collection of process information and writes
# that to the temporary file. It then displays that file via
# Notepad and then removes the temporary file when
# done.
#
# ---------------------------------------------------------------------
#This both creates the file name as well as the file itself
$tempFile = [io.path]::GetTempFileName()
Get-Process >> $tempFile
#Piping the Notepad filename to the Out-Null cmdlet halts
#the script execution
Notepad $tempFile | Out-Null
#Once the file is closed the temporary file is closed and it is
#removed
Remove-Item $tempFile
```

## Teaching your scripts to communicate

Peter Costantini
*Microsoft Scripting Guy Emeritus*

If code was read only by computers, we could write only 1s and 0s. Even though developers would quickly go blind and insane, a new class of computer science majors graduates every year. Of course, the reality is that code must also be read by humans, and programming languages have been developed to mediate between humans and machines.

If one developer could write, debug, test, maintain, and field support calls for all of the code for an application, it wouldn't be very important whether the programming language was easy for others to understand. A brilliant loner could decide to write in an obscure dialect of Lisp and name the variables and procedures in Esperanto, and that would be fine as long as the code worked.

However, that programming language might not be so fine five years later. By then, the developer's Lisp and Esperanto are a little rusty. Suddenly a call comes in that the now mission-critical application is crashing inexplicably and losing the firm billions of dollars.

"What's a few billion dollars these days? Maybe I'll get a bonus," I hear you muttering under your breath. Anyway, you're not a developer: you're a system engineer who's trying to use scripts to automate some of your routine tasks and to troubleshoot. You thought the whole point of scripting was to let you write quick and dirty code to get a task done in a hurry.

Yes, that is a big benefit of scripting. When you first write a script to solve a problem, you're probably not concerned about producing beautiful-looking, or even comprehensible, code. You just want to make sure that it runs as expected and makes the pain stop.

However, when you decide that the script is a keeper and that you're going to run it as a scheduled task at three every Monday morning, the equation starts to change. At this point, like it or not, you really are a developer. Windows PowerShell is a programming language, albeit a dynamic one, and any code that plays an ongoing role in the functioning of your organization needs to be treated as something more than chewing gum and baling wire.

Furthermore, regardless of your personal relationship with your scripts, you probably work as part of a team, right? Other people on your team might write scripts, too. In any case, these people most likely have to run your scripts and figure out what they do. You can see where I'm going with this. But if it produces a blinding flash of insight, that's all the better for your career and your organization.

The goal is to make your scripts transparent. Your code—and the environment in which it runs—should communicate to your teammates everything they need to know to understand what your script is doing, how to use it successfully, and how to troubleshoot it if problems arise. (Murphy's Law has many scripting corollaries.) Clarity and readability are virtues; terseness and ambiguity are not. Consistent, descriptive variable names and white space do not make the code run any slower, but they can make the script more readable. Begin to look at transparency as an insurance policy against receiving a frantic call on your cell phone when you're lying on a beach in Puerto Vallarta, sipping a margarita.

This is not just a technical and social imperative: it's an economic one as well. IT departments are pushing hard to become strategic assets rather than cost centers. The sprawling skeins of code, scripts, and all that run their operations can earn or lose figures followed by many zeros and make the difference between budget increases and layoffs. Okay, at least this year, adding good documentation to your scripts can make the budget cuts smaller.

## Additional resources

- The TechNet Script Center at *http://www.microsoft.com/technet/scriptcenter* contains numerous examples of Windows PowerShell scripts, as well as some sample documentation templates.
- Refer to "How Can I Delete and Manage PDF Files?" at *http://www.microsoft.com /technet/scriptcenter/resources/qanda/dec08/hey1229.mspx*.
- Refer to "How Can I Create a Microsoft Word Document from WMI Information?" at *http://www.microsoft.com/technet/scriptcenter/resources/qanda/nov08/hey1111.mspx*.
- Refer to *Windows Scripting with WMI: Self-Paced Learning Guide* (Microsoft Press, 2006).
- All scripts from this chapter are available via the TechNet Script Center Script Repository at *http://gallery.technet.microsoft.com/scriptcenter/PowerShell-40 -Best-d9e16039*.

# CHAPTER 10

# Designing modules

- Understanding modules
- Locate and load modules
- Install modules
- Creating a module
- Additional resources

Windows PowerShell modules provide a convenient way to package reusable code. By using modules, it is possible to share them between computers, users, and scripts. The use of these modules solves many of the problems that might confront a new scripter. In this chapter, we begin by understanding what a module is and why you would want to use one, we move to some of the decisions necessitated by modules, and conclude with an example of creating a new module.

## Understanding modules

Windows PowerShell 2.0 introduced the concept of modules. A module is a package that can contain Windows PowerShell cmdlets, aliases, functions, variables, and even providers. In short, a Windows PowerShell module can contain the kinds of things that you might put into your profile, but it can also contain things that Windows PowerShell 1.0 required a developer to incorporate into a PowerShell snap-in. There are several advantages of modules over snap-ins, including the following:

- Anyone who can write a Windows PowerShell script can create a module.
- To install a module you do not need to write a Windows Installer package.
- To install, you do not have to have administrator rights.

These advantages should be of great interest to the IT Pro.

## Locate and load modules

There are three default locations for Windows PowerShell modules. The first location is in the users' home directory, and the second is in the Windows PowerShell home directory. The third default location, introduced in Windows PowerShell 4.0, is in the Program Files

\WindowsPowerShell\Modules directory. The advantage of this new location is that you do not need admin rights to install (such as in the System32 location), and it is not user specific (such as in the user home directory).

The modules directory in the Windows PowerShell home directory always exists, as does the modules directory in the Program Files\WindowsPowerShell location. However, the modules directory in the users' home directory is not present by default. The modules directory will exist in the users' home directory only if it has been created. The creation of the modules directory in the users' home directory does not normally happen until someone has decided to create and to store modules there. A nice feature of the modules directory is that when it exists, it is the first place Windows PowerShell uses when it searches for a module. If the user's modules directory does not exist, the modules directory within the Windows PowerShell home directory is used.

## Listing available modules

Windows PowerShell modules exist in two states: loaded and unloaded. To display a list of all loaded modules, use the Get-Module cmdlet without any parameters. This is shown here:

```
PS C:\> Get-Module

ModuleType   Name                            ExportedCommands
----------   ----                            ----------------
Script       ISE                             {Get-IseSnippet, Import-IseSnippet,
                                             New-IseSnip...
Manifest     Microsoft.PowerShell.Management  {Add-Computer, Add-Content, Checkpoint-
                                             Computer...
Manifest     Microsoft.PowerShell.Utility    {Add-Member, Add-Type, Clear-Variable,
                                             Compare-...
```

If there are multiple modules loaded when the Get-Module cmdlet runs, each module will appear along with its accompanying exported commands on their own individual lines. This is seen here:

```
PS C:\> Get-Module

ModuleType   Name                ExportedCommands
----------   ----                ----------------
Script       GetFreeDiskSpace    Get-FreeDiskSpace
Script       HelloWorld          {Hello-World, Hello-User}
Script       TextFunctions       {New-Line, Get-TextStats}
Manifest     BitsTransfer        {Start-BitsTransfer, Remove-BitsTransfe...
Script       PSDiagnostics       {Enable-PSTrace, Enable-WSManTrace, Sta...


PS C:\>
```

If no modules are loaded, nothing displays to the Windows PowerShell console. No errors appear, nor is there any confirmation that the command actually ran. This situation never occurs on Windows 8 because Windows PowerShell core cmdlets reside in two basic modules:

the *Microsoft.PowerShell.Management* and the *Microsoft.PowerShell.Utility* modules. These two modules always load unless Windows PowerShell launches with the *–noprofile* switch. But even then, the *Microsoft.PowerShell.Management* module loads.

To obtain a listing of all modules that are available on the system but are not loaded, you use the Get-Module cmdlet with the *–ListAvailable* parameter. The Get-Module cmdlet with the *–ListAvailable* parameter lists all modules that are available whether or not the modules are loaded into the Windows PowerShell console. The output appearing here illustrates the default installation of a Windows 8 client system.

> **NOTE** Windows PowerShell 4.0 still installs into the %windir%\system32
> \WindowsPowerShell\v1.0 directory (even on Windows 8.1). The reason for adherence to
> this location is for compatibility with applications that expect this location. A common
> question I receive via the Hey Scripting Guy! blog (*www.scriptingguys.com/blog*) is related
> to this folder name. To determine the version of Windows PowerShell you are running, use
> the *$PSVersionTable* automatic variable.

```
PS C:\> Get-Module -ListAvailable

    Directory: C:\Windows\system32\WindowsPowerShell\v1.0\Modules


ModuleType Name                              ExportedCommands
---------- ----                              ----------------
Manifest   AppLocker                         {Get-AppLockerFileInformation, Get...
Manifest   Appx                              {Add-AppxPackage, Get-AppxPackage,...
Manifest   BitLocker                         {Unlock-BitLocker, Suspend-BitLock...
Manifest   BitsTransfer                      {Add-BitsFile, Complete-BitsTransf...
Manifest   BranchCache                       {Add-BCDataCacheExtension, Clear-B...
Manifest   CimCmdlets                        {Get-CimAssociatedInstance, Get-Ci...
Manifest   DirectAccessClientComponents      {Disable-DAManualEntryPointSelecti...
Script     Dism                              {Add-AppxProvisionedPackage, Add-W...
Manifest   DnsClient                         {Resolve-DnsName, Clear-DnsClientC...
Manifest   International                     {Get-WinDefaultInputMethodOverride...
Manifest   iSCSI                             {Get-IscsiTargetPortal, New-IscsiT...
Script     ISE                               {New-IseSnippet, Import-IseSnippet...
Manifest   Kds                               {Add-KdsRootKey, Get-KdsRootKey, T...
Manifest   Microsoft.PowerShell.Diagnostics  {Get-WinEvent, Get-Counter, Import...
Manifest   Microsoft.PowerShell.Host         {Start-Transcript, Stop-Transcript}
Manifest   Microsoft.PowerShell.Management    {Add-Content, Clear-Content, Clear...
Manifest   Microsoft.PowerShell.Security      {Get-Acl, Set-Acl, Get-PfxCertific...
Manifest   Microsoft.PowerShell.Utility       {Format-List, Format-Custom, Forma...
Manifest   Microsoft.WSMan.Management          {Disable-WSManCredSSP, Enable-WSMa...
Manifest   MMAgent                           {Disable-MMAgent, Enable-MMAgent, ...
Manifest   MsDtc                             {New-DtcDiagnosticTransaction, Com...
Manifest   NetAdapter                        {Disable-NetAdapter, Disable-NetAd...
Manifest   NetConnection                     {Get-NetConnectionProfile, Set-Net...
Manifest   NetLbfo                           {Add-NetLbfoTeamMember, Add-NetLbf...
Manifest   NetQos                            {Get-NetQosPolicy, Set-NetQosPolic...
Manifest   NetSecurity                       {Get-DAPolicyChange, New-NetIPsecA...
```

```
Manifest    NetSwitchTeam                    {New-NetSwitchTeam, Remove-NetSwit...
Manifest    NetTCPIP                         {Get-NetIPAddress, Get-NetIPInterf...
Manifest    NetworkConnectivityStatus        {Get-DAConnectionStatus, Get-NCSIP...
Manifest    NetworkTransition                {Add-NetIPHttpsCertBinding, Disabl...
Manifest    PKI                              {Add-CertificateEnrollmentPolicySe...
Manifest    PrintManagement                  {Add-Printer, Add-PrinterDriver, A...
Script      PSDiagnostics                    {Disable-PSTrace, Disable-PSWSManC...
Binary      PSScheduledJob                   {New-JobTrigger, Add-JobTrigger, R...
Manifest    PSWorkflow                       {New-PSWorkflowExecutionOption, Ne...
Manifest    PSWorkflowUtility                {Invoke-AsWorkflow
Manifest    ScheduledTasks                   {Get-ScheduledTask, Set-ScheduledT...
Manifest    SecureBoot                       {Confirm-SecureBootUEFI, Set-Secur...
Manifest    SmbShare                         {Get-SmbShare, Remove-SmbShare, Se...
Manifest    SmbWitness                       {Get-SmbWitnessClient, Move-SmbWit...
Manifest    Storage                          {Add-InitiatorIdToMaskingSet, Add-...
Manifest    TroubleshootingPack              {Get-TroubleshootingPack, Invoke-T...
Manifest    TrustedPlatformModule            {Get-Tpm, Initialize-Tpm, Clear-Tp...
Manifest    VpnClient                        {Add-VpnConnection, Set-VpnConnect...
Manifest    Wdac                             {Get-OdbcDriver, Set-OdbcDriver, G...
Manifest    WindowsDeveloperLicense          {Get-WindowsDeveloperLicense, Show...
Script      WindowsErrorReporting            {Enable-WindowsErrorReporting, Dis....
```

## NOTES FROM THE FIELD

**Keith Hill**
*Microsoft Windows PowerShell MVP*

One of my favorite features in Windows PowerShell is modules. Modules make it easier for people to package and deploy their reusable functionality, and they make it easier for end users to install and use that functionality.

When I set out to write a script, I can usually tell pretty quickly whether it will be a simple script or a module. Here are a few of the telltale signs for going with a module:

- **The required functionality will expose multiple commands.** Modules are great in this scenario because you can export some functions and not others—for example, private helper functions.

- **You need to create PowerShell commands around a non-Windows PowerShell resource.** Modules are great in this scenario because you can keep a private variable to manage the resource lifetime, which doesn't pollute the user's global session state. And with module auto-loading, the user can use your new commands with no need to dot-source a script first.

- **You know that you will reuse the functionality in multiple scripts—that is, you know it will be library code.** Modules are great for reusable libraries because they provide encapsulation of data and behavior, control over what is exported for the public API, and easy load and unload capability, which are all desirable traits in any form of library code.

I still write simple script (.ps1) script files when the script does a single task. I also occasionally find myself converting a simple ps1 script to a module when I need to add additional commands. In this regard, my modules tend to reflect a cluster of commands (or verbs) around some core noun—for example, `Enable-NetGearSwitchPort`, `Disable-NetGearSwitchPort`, or `Get-NetGearSwitchPort`.

For a software developer, Windows PowerShell remoting has turned out to be handier than I thought it would be at first. We run nightly regression tests on many different PCs. I have found it tremendously useful to gather event log warnings and errors from all these PCs via a script that uses "fan-out" remoting. It saves me a lot of time because I don't have to manually RDP to each machine and comb through its event log.

As a C# developer who has developed many binary cmdlets for PSCX, it is somewhat odd that these days I spend less time writing cmdlets in C# and much more time in the Windows PowerShell Integrated Scripting Environment (ISE) writing advanced functions. One significant advantage that advanced functions have over binary cmdlets is help documentation. With an advanced function, you simply add some documentation comments and Windows PowerShell takes care of the rest. In PSCX, for our binary cmdlets, we have to deal in MAML (XML) files and, trust me, it isn't much fun. In fact, a good bit of the new functionality in PSCX has been implemented via advanced functions. I drop back to binary cmdlets only when performance is an issue or the underlying .NET (or native) API is easier to use from C#.

I still live in the Windows PowerShell console for day-to-day activities—for example, running commands and experimenting with one-liners. However, if I need to create, edit, test, or debug a script, I use the Windows PowerShell ISE.

As a software developer, I use Windows PowerShell as a tool for daily productivity needs such as searching source code, managing source code files, and managing errant processes. I also use Windows PowerShell to script our product's build process and nightly regression tests.

If I were talking to a new adopter, I would say stick with it. Windows PowerShell, like other "powerful but complex" tools, has a somewhat steep learning curve. However, if you can get over the hump, your persistence will pay big dividends on the back end. Also, don't thrash for too long–there are abundant (and passionate) Windows PowerShell gurus available to answer your questions. There is a great bunch of PowerShell experts on StackOverflow that can help you at *http://stackoverflow.com /questions/tagged/powershell*. Be sure to first search previously answered questions; it is likely that your question has already been asked and answered.

# Loading modules

When you have identified a module that you want to load, you use the `Import-Module` cmdlet to load the module into the current Windows PowerShell session. This appears here:

```
PS C:\> Import-Module -Name NetConnection
PS C:\>
```

If the module exists, the `Import-Module` cmdlet completes without displaying any information. If the module is already loaded, no error message displays. This behavior appears here where you use the up arrow to retrieve the previous command and press enter to execute the command. The `Import-Module` command runs three times, but no errors appear.

```
PS C:\> Import-Module -Name NetConnection
PS C:\> Import-Module -Name NetConnection
PS C:\> Import-Module -Name NetConnection
PS C:\>
```

After you import the module, you might want to use the `Get-Module` cmdlet to quickly see the functions exposed by the module. It is not necessary to type the complete module name. You can use wildcards, or you can even use tab expansion to expand the module name. The wildcard technique is shown here:

```
PS C:\> Get-Module net*

ModuleType Name                    ExportedCommands
---------- ----                    ----------------
Manifest   netconnection           {Get-NetConnectionProfile, Set-Net...
```

As seen in the preceding example, the *netconnection* module exports two commands: the *Get-NetConnectionProfile* function and some other command that is probably *Set-NetConnectionProfile*. The one problem with using the `Get-Module` cmdlet is that it truncates the *ExportedCommands* property. The easy solution to this problem is to pipeline the resulting *PSModuleInfo* object to the `Select-Object` cmdlet and expand the ExportedCommands property. This technique is shown here:

```
PS C:\> Get-Module net* | select -expand *comm*

Key                                Value
---                                -----
Get-NetConnectionProfile           Get-NetConnectionProfile
Set-NetConnectionProfile           Set-NetConnectionProfile
```

When loading modules that have long names, you are not limited to typing the entire module name. You can use wildcards or tab expansion to complete the module name. When using wildcards to load modules, it is a best practice to type a significant portion of the module name so that you match only a single module from the list of modules that are available to you. If you do not match a single module, an error generates. This error occurs here because net* matches multiple modules:

```
PS C:\> Import-Module net*
Import-Module : The specified module 'net*' was not loaded because no valid module
```

```
file was found in any module directory.
At line:1 char:1
+ Import-Module net*
+ ~~~~~~~~~~~~~~~~~~
    + CategoryInfo          : ResourceUnavailable: (net*:String) [Import-Module],
  FileNotFoundException
    + FullyQualifiedErrorId : Modules_ModuleNotFound,Microsoft.PowerShell.Commands
  .ImportModuleCommand
```

**IMPORTANT**  In Windows PowerShell 2.0, if a wildcard pattern matches more than one module name, the first matched module loads with the remaining matches ignored. This leads to inconsistent and unpredictable results. Therefore, Windows PowerShell 3.0 changes this behavior to generate an error when a wildcard pattern matches more than one module name.

If you want to load all of the modules that are available on your system, you can use the Get-Module cmdlet with the –*ListAvailable* parameter and pipeline the resulting PSModuleInfo objects to the Import-Module cmdlet. This is shown here:

```
PS C:\> Get-Module -ListAvailable | Import-Module
PS C:\>
```

If you have a module that uses a verb that is not on the allowed verb list, a warning message displays when you import the module. The functions in the module still work, and the module will work, but the warning displays to remind you to check the authorized verb list. This behavior is shown here:

```
PS C:\> Import-Module HelloUser
WARNING: The names of some imported commands from the module 'HelloUser' include
unapproved verbs that might make them less discoverable. To find the commands with
unapproved verbs, run the Import-Module command again with the Verbose parameter.
For a list of approved verbs, type Get-Verb.
PS C:\> hello-user
hello administrator
```

To obtain more information about which unapproved verbs are being used, you use the –*Verbose* parameter of the Import-Module. This command is shown here:

```
PS C:\> Import-Module HelloUser -Verbose
```

The results of the Import-Module –*Verbose* command are seen in Figure 10-1.

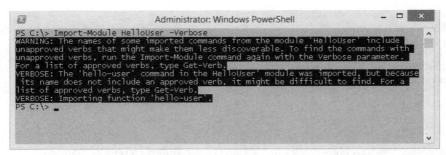

**FIGURE 10-1** The *–Verbose* parameter of `Import-Module` displays information about each function as well as illegal verb names. The *hello* verb used in `Hello-User` is not an approved verb.

In this section, the concept of locating and loading modules was discussed. Modules are listed by using the ListAvailable switched parameter with the `Get-Module` cmdlet. Modules are loaded via the `Import-Module` cmdlet.

---

**NOTES FROM THE FIELD**

**Jim Christopher, Microsoft PowerShell MVP**
*Independent Software Developer, Code Owls LLC*

"You just replaced three years worth of software tooling in an afternoon."

A client said these exact words to me just a few months ago, and it is perhaps the best compliment I can provide for building tools with PowerShell. Software developers have a predisposition to create solutions around well-defined usage patterns. They create and explore use cases to capture these patterns and drive their application designs. These are good things, and they should be done because they produce a higher-quality experience for the *end-user*.

The tooling around the application—the bits that leverage the instrumentation data, the pieces used by support engineers to deal with issues—needs to meet the needs of an entirely different class of user, one I like to think of as the *mastermind*. While rigid paths work well for the end-user, the mastermind needs a lot of flexibility to get their work done. End-users follow paths; masterminds need the ability to blaze their own.

In the case of my client, all of their existing tools worked off the assumption that masterminds should use a management website. This caused a slow tooling cycle: Every support path required the attention of a web developer; the addition of a GUI layer resulted in more opportunities for bugs; and the infrastructure necessary to deploy and maintain a working management website required its own layer of tools. This unresponsiveness translated into customers whose needs couldn't be met, and unhappy customers take their money elsewhere.

So one afternoon I created a PowerShell module around their management needs. Instead of clicking on a User tab in a website, engineers can now use a `Get-User` cmdlet. Instead of finding and updating one resource at a time, engineers could now do this in bulk. While the client's quote is correct–this module effectively replaced all of their previous tooling–there were far more interesting results from this project. First, morale increased significantly in the support and development teams. Support could be proactive with their solutions now; they could leverage their knowledge of the system to solve problems; in short, they now had the ability to do what they were hired to do. With this success, development was happy to focus on product features instead of on the immediate needs of support. Second, the average incident resolution time decreased from days to minutes. Not only did the engineers now have the proper tools to respond in a timely manner, but they also had a newfound ability to save and share their solutions to recurring problems in the form of scripts.

I consider that a pretty amazing return for a few hours of effort.

That's why Windows PowerShell is just a great choice for tooling up: it puts the power and decision-making in the hands of those masterminds who need it to do their job, and it does so with minimal fuss and effort.

# Install modules

One of the features of modules is that they can be installed without elevated rights. Because each user has a modules folder in their %userprofile% directory that they have rights to use, the installation of a module does not require Administrator rights. An additional feature of modules is that they do not require a specialized installer. The files associated with a module can be copied by using the XCopy utility, or they can be copied by using Windows PowerShell cmdlets.

# Creating a modules folder

The users' modules folder does not exist by default. To avoid confusion, you might decide to create the modules directory in the users' profile prior to deploying modules, or you might simply create a module installer script that checks for the existence of the users' modules folder, creates the folder if it does not exist, and then copies the modules. One thing to remember when directly accessing the users' module directory is that the modules folder is in a different location depending on the version of the operating system. On Windows XP and Windows Server 2003, the users' module folder is in the My Documents folder; on Windows Vista and later, the users' module folder is in the Documents folder.

In the Copy-Modules.ps1 script that follows, you solve the problem of different module folder locations by using a function, *Get-OperatingSystemVersion*, which retrieves the major version number of the operating system. The *Get-OperatingSystemVersion* function is shown here:

```
Function Get-OperatingSystemVersion
{
 (Get-WmiObject -Class Win32_OperatingSystem).Version
} #end Get-OperatingSystemVersion
```

The *Test-ModulePath* function uses the major version number of the operating system. If the major version number of the operating system is greater than 6, the operating system is at least Windows Vista and will therefore use the Documents folder in the path to the modules. If the major version number of the operating system is not greater than 6, the script will use the My Documents folder for the module location. When the version of the operating system is determined and the path to the module location is ascertained, it is time to determine whether or not the module folders exist. The best tool for the job of checking for the existence of folders is the Test-Path cmdlet. The Test-Path cmdlet returns a Boolean value. As you are interested only in the absence of the folder, you can use the *–not* operator as shown here in the completed *Test-ModulePath* function:

```
Function Test-ModulePath
{
 $VistaPath = "$env:userProfile\documents\WindowsPowerShell\Modules"
 $XPPath =  "$env:Userprofile\my documents\WindowsPowerShell\Modules"
 if ([int](Get-OperatingSystemVersion).substring(0,1) -ge 6)
    {
       if(-not(Test-Path -path $VistaPath))
         {
           New-Item -Path $VistaPath -itemtype directory | Out-Null
         } #end if
    } #end if
 Else
    {
       if(-not(Test-Path -path $XPPath))
         {
           New-Item -path $XPPath -itemtype directory | Out-Null
         } #end if
    } #end else
} #end Test-ModulePath
```

Upon creating the users' modules folder, it is time to create a child folder to hold the new module. A module installs into a folder that has the same name as the module itself. The name of the module is the file name that contains the module, minus the .psm1 extension. This location is shown in Figure 10-2.

**FIGURE 10-2** Modules are placed in the users' modules directory.

In the *Copy-Module* function from the Copy-Modules.ps1 script, the first action retrieves the value of the *PSModulePath* environmental variable. Because there are two locations where modules can be stored, the *PSModulePath* environmental variable contains the path to both locations. The *PSModulePath* variable is not stored as an array; it is stored as a string. The value contained in *PSModulePath* appears here:

```
PS C:\> $env:PSModulePath
C:\Users\administrator\Documents\WindowsPowerShell\Modules;C:\Windows\system32\
WindowsPowerShell\
v1.0\Modules\
```

If you attempt to index into the data stored in the PSModulePath environmental variable, you will retrieve one letter at a time. This is shown here:

```
PS C:\> $env:psmodulePath[0]
C
PS C:\> $env:psmodulePath[1]
:
PS C:\> $env:psmodulePath[2]
\
PS C:\> $env:psmodulePath[3]
U
```

Attempting to retrieve the path to the users' module location one letter at a time would be problematic at best and error prone at worst. Because the data is a string, you can use string methods to manipulate the two paths. To break a string into a usable array, you use the *split* method from the *System.String* class. You need to pass only a single value to the *split* method—the character upon which to split. Because the value stored in the *PSModulePath* variable is a string, you can access the *split* method directly. This technique is shown here:

```
PS C:\> $env:PSModulePath.Split(";")
C:\Users\administrator\Documents\WindowsPowerShell\Modules
C:\Windows\system32\WindowsPowerShell\v1.0\Modules\
```

You can see from the preceding output that the first string displayed is the path to the users' modules folder, and the second path is the path to the system modules folder. Because the *split* method turns a string into an array, it means that you can now index into the array and retrieve the path to the users' modules folder by using the [0] syntax. You do not need to use an intermediate variable to store the returned array of paths if you do not want to do so. You can index into the returned array directly. If you were to use the intermediate variable to hold the returned array and then index into the array, the code would resemble the following:

```
PS C:\> $aryPaths = $env:PSModulePath.Split(";")
PS C:\> $aryPaths[0]
C:\Users\administrator\Documents\WindowsPowerShell\Modules
```

Because the array is immediately available after the *split* method has been called, you directly retrieve the users' modules path. This is shown here:

```
PS C:\> $env:PSModulePath.Split(";")[0]

C:\Users\administrator\Documents\WindowsPowerShell\Modules
```

## Working with the *$modulePath* variable

The path that will be used to store the module is stored in the *$modulePath* variable. This path includes the path to the users' modules folder plus a child folder that is the same name as the module itself. To create the new path, it is a best practice to use the Join-Path cmdlet instead of doing string concatenation and attempting to build manually the path to the new folder. The Join-Path cmdlet will put together a parent path and a child path to create a new path. This is shown here:

```
$ModulePath = Join-Path -path $userPath '
            -childpath (Get-Item -path $name).basename
```

Windows PowerShell adds a script property called *basename* to the *System.Io.FileInfo* class. This makes it easy to retrieve the name of a file without the file extension. Prior to Windows PowerShell 2.0, it was common to use the *split* method or some other string manipulation technique to remote the extension from the file name. Use of the *basename* property is shown here:

```
PS C:\> (Get-Item -Path C:\fso\HelloWorld.psm1).basename
HelloWorld
```

The last step is to create the subdirectory that will hold the module and to copy the module files into the directory. To avoid cluttering the display with the returned information from the `New-Item` and the `Copy-Item` cmdlets, the results are pipelined to the `Out-Null` cmdlet. This is shown here:

```
New-Item -path $modulePath -itemtype directory | Out-Null
Copy-Item -path $name -destination $ModulePath | Out-Null
```

The entry point to the Copy-Modules.ps1 script calls the *Test-ModulePath* function to determine whether the users' modules folder exists. It then uses the `Get-ChildItem` cmdlet to retrieve a listing of all the module files in a particular folder. The *–Recurse* parameter is used to retrieve all the module files in the path. The resulting *FileInfo* objects are pipelined to the `ForEach-Object` cmdlet. The *fullname* property of each *FileInfo* object is passed to the *Copy-Module* function. This is shown here:

```
Test-ModulePath
Get-ChildItem -Path C:\fso -Include *.psm1,*.psd1 -Recurse |
ForEach-Object { Copy-Module -name $_.fullName }
```

The complete Copy-Modules.ps1 script is shown here.

```
Copy-Modules.ps1

Function Get-OperatingSystemVersion
{
 (Get-WmiObject -Class Win32_OperatingSystem).Version
} #end Get-OperatingSystemVersion

Function Test-ModulePath
{
 $VistaPath = "$env:userProfile\documents\WindowsPowerShell\Modules"
 $XPPath =  "$env:Userprofile\my documents\WindowsPowerShell\Modules"
 if ([int](Get-OperatingSystemVersion).substring(0,1) -ge 6)
   {
     if(-not(Test-Path -path $VistaPath))
       {
          New-Item -Path $VistaPath -itemtype directory | Out-Null
       } #end if
   } #end if
 Else
   {
     if(-not(Test-Path -path $XPPath))
       {
          New-Item -path $XPPath -itemtype directory | Out-Null
       } #end if
   } #end else
} #end Test-ModulePath

Function Copy-Module([string]$name)
{
```

```
$UserPath = $env:PSModulePath.split(";")[0]
$ModulePath = Join-Path -path $userPath '
              -childpath (Get-Item -path $name).basename
New-Item -path $modulePath -itemtype directory | Out-Null
Copy-Item -path $name -destination $ModulePath | Out-Null
}


# *** Entry Point to Script ***
Test-ModulePath
Get-ChildItem -Path C:\fso -Include *.psm1,*.psd1 -Recurse |
ForEach-Object { Copy-Module -name $_.fullName }
```

**NOTE** You must enable script support to use user-created script modules. Script support does not need to be enabled in Windows PowerShell to use the system modules. However, to run the Copy-Modules.ps1 to install modules to the users, profile, you would need script support. To enable scripting support in Windows PowerShell, you use the Set-Execution-Policy cmdlet.

## Creating a module drive

An easy way to work with modules is to create a couple of Windows PowerShell drives by using the *filesystem* provider. Because the modules live in a location that is not easily navigated to from the command line, and because *$PSModulePath* returns a string that contains the path to both the users' and the system modules folders, it makes sense to provide an easier way to work with the modules location.

To create a Windows PowerShell drive for the user module location, you use the New-PSDrive cmdlet, specify a name such as *mymods*, use the *filesystem* provider, and obtain the root location from the *$PSModulePath* environmental variable by using the *split* method from the .NET Framework string class. For the users' modules folder, you use the first element from the returned array. This is shown here:

```
PS C:\> New-PSDrive -Name mymods -PSProvider filesystem -Root ($env:PSModulePath
.Split(";")[0])
```

| Name   | Used (GB) | Free (GB) | Provider   | Root                        |
| ----   | --------- | --------- | --------   | ----                        |
| mymods |           | 116.50    | FileSystem | C:\Users\administrator\Docum... |

The command to create a Windows PowerShell drive for the system module location is the same as the one used to create a Windows PowerShell drive for the user module location. The exception is specifying a different name, such as *sysmods*, and choosing the second element from the array obtained via the *split* method from the *$PSModulePath* variable. This command is shown here:

```
PS C:\> New-PSDrive -Name sysmods -PSProvider filesystem -Root ($env:PSModulePath
.Split(";")[1])

Name            Used (GB)     Free (GB) Provider     Root
----            ---------     --------- --------     ----
sysmods                        116.50 FileSystem     C:\Windows\system32\WindowsP...
```

You can also write a script that creates Windows PowerShell drives for each of the two module locations. To do this, you first create an array of names for the Windows PowerShell drives. You then use a *for* statement to walk through the array of Windows PowerShell drive names, and then you call the New-PSDrive cmdlet. Because you are running the commands inside a script, the new PowerShell drives, by default, would live within the script scope. When the script ends, the script scope goes away. This means that the Windows PowerShell drives would not be available when the script ended—which would defeat your purposes in creating them in the first place. To combat this scoping issue, you need to create the Windows PowerShell drives within the Global scope, which means that they will be available in the Windows PowerShell console when the script has finished running. To avoid displaying confirmation messages when creating the Windows PowerShell drives, you pipe the results to the Out-Null cmdlet.

In the New-ModulesDrive.ps1 script, we create another function. This function displays global *filesystem* Windows PowerShell drives. When the script runs, call the *New-ModuleDrives* function. Follow by calling the *Get-FileSystemDrives* function. The complete *New-ModulesDrive* function is shown here.

```
New-ModulesDrive.ps1

Function New-ModuleDrives
{
<#
    .SYNOPSIS
    Creates two PSDrives: myMods and sysMods
    .EXAMPLE
    New-ModuleDrives
    Creates two PSDrives: myMods and sysMods. These correspond
    to the users' modules folder and the system modules folder respectively.
#>
$driveNames = "myMods","sysMods"

For($i = 0 ; $i -le 1 ; $i++)
{
  New-PSDrive -name $driveNames[$i] -PSProvider filesystem '
  -Root ($env:PSModulePath.split(";")[$i]) -scope Global |
  Out-Null
```

```
    } #end For
} #end New-ModuleDrives


Function Get-FileSystemDrives
{
<#
    .SYNOPSIS
    Displays global PS Drives that use the Filesystem provider
    .EXAMPLE
    Get-FileSystemDrives
    Displays global PS Drives that use the Filesystem provider
#>
 Get-PSDrive -PSProvider FileSystem -scope Global
} #end Get-FileSystemDrives


# *** EntryPoint to Script ***
New-ModuleDrives
Get-FileSystemDrives
```

This section covered the concept of installing modules. Before installing modules, create a special modules folder in the user's profile. A script was developed that will perform this action. The use of a *$modulePath* variable was examined. The section concluded with a script that creates a Windows PowerShell drive to provide easy access to installed modules.

## Checking for module dependencies

One problem with using modules is that you now have a dependency on external code, and this means that a script that uses the module must have the module installed or else the script will fail. If you control the environment, taking an external dependency is not a bad thing; if you do not control the environment, an external dependency can be a disaster.

Because of the potential for problems, Windows PowerShell 3.0 adds additional capability to the *#requires* statement. The *#requires* statement now checks for Windows PowerShell version, modules, snap-ins, and even module and snap-in version numbers. Unfortunately, use of *#requires* works only in a script, not in a function, cmdlet, or snap-in. Figure 10-3 illustrates using the *#requires* statement to ensure the presence of a specific module prior to script execution. The script requires a module named *bogus* that does not exist. Because the *bogus* module does not exist, an error occurs.

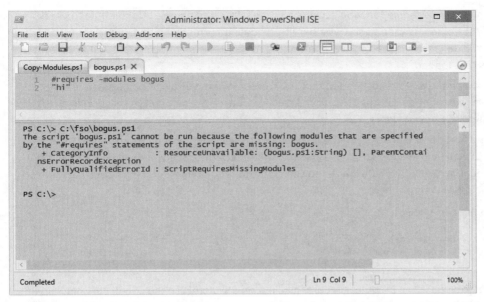

**FIGURE 10-3** Use the *#requires* statement to prevent execution of a script when a required module does not exist.

Because you cannot use the *#requires* statement inside a function, you might want to use the *Get-MyModule* function to determine whether a module exists or is already loaded. The complete *Get-MyModule* function is shown here:

```
Get-MyModule.ps1

Function Get-MyModule
{
 Param([string]$name)
 if(-not(Get-Module -name $name))
   {
    if(Get-Module -ListAvailable |
        Where-Object { $_.name -eq $name })
      {
        Import-Module -Name $name
        $true
      } #end if module available then import
   else { $false } #module not available
   } #end if not module
 else { $true } #module already loaded

} #end function get-MyModule

get-mymodule -name "bitsTransfer"
```

The *Get-MyModule* function accepts a single string–the name of the module to check. The *if* statement is used to see whether the module is currently loaded. If it is not loaded, the Get-Module cmdlet is used to see whether the module exists on the system. If it does exist, the module is loaded.

If the module is already loaded into the current Windows PowerShell session, the *Get-MyModule* function returns *$true* to the calling code. Let's examine the function in a bit more detail to see how it works.

The first thing you do is use the *if* statement to see whether the module is not loaded into the current session. To do this, use the *–not* operator to see whether the module is not loaded. Use the Get-Module cmdlet to search for the required module by name. This section of the script is shown here:

```
Function Get-MyModule
{
 Param([string]$name)
 if(-not(Get-Module -name $name))
   {
```

To obtain a list of modules that are installed on a system, use the Get-Module cmdlet with the *–ListAvailable* switch. Unfortunately, there is no way to filter the results, and this necessitates pipelining the results to the Where-Object cmdlet to see whether the required cmdlet is installed on the system. If the module exists on the system, the function uses the Import-Module cmdlet to import the module, and it returns *$true* to the calling code. This section of the script is shown here:

```
if(Get-Module -ListAvailable |
      Where-Object { $_.name -eq $name })
      {
       Import-Module -Name $name
       $true
      } #end if module available then import
```

The last two things to do in the function is to handle two other cases. If the module is not available, the Where-Object cmdlet will not find anything. This triggers the first *else* clause, where *$false* is returned to the calling code. If the module is already loaded, the second *else* clause returns *$true* to the script. This section of the script is shown here:

```
   else { $false } #module not available
   } #end if not module
 else { $true } #module already loaded

} #end function get-MyModule
```

A simple use of the *Get-MyModule* function is to call the function and pass the name of a module to it. This example is actually seen in the last line of the Get-MyModule.ps1 script:

```
get-mymodule -name "bitsTransfer"
```

When called in this manner, the *Get-MyModule* function will load the *bitstransfer* module if it exists on your system and if it is not already loaded. If the module is already loaded or if it is loaded by the function, *$true* is returned to the script. If the module does not exist, *$false* is returned. The use of the *Get-MyModule* function appears in Figure 10-4.

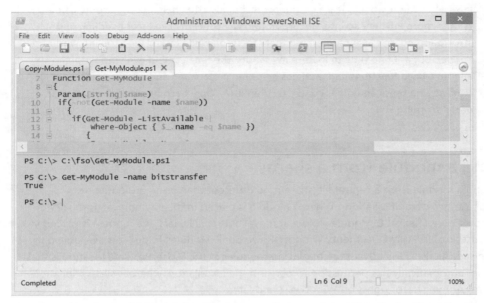

**FIGURE 10-4** Use the *Get-MyModule* function to ensure that a module exists prior to attempting to load it.

A better use of the *Get-MyModule* function is to use it as a prerequisite check for a function that uses a particular module. Your syntax might look something like this:

```
If(Get-MyModule -name "bitsTransfer") { call your bits code here }
ELSE { "Bits module is not installed on this system." ; exit }
```

by transforming the most useful ones so that I can share them with my coworkers. Inevitably, this is where I learn invaluable techniques that help me to become a better and more efficient scripter. Incorporating key concepts like error handling and error trapping isn't likely something that I focus on while tasked with solving world hunger, but as I find time to mature my scripts, the time I spend evolving scripts into advanced functions and modules helps me understand and become more familiar with these and other concepts. Ultimately, they become more characteristic of my scripting style.

## Using a module from a share

Utilizing a module from a central file share is no different than using a module from one of the two default locations. When a module is placed in the %windir%\System32\ WindowsPowerShell\v1.0\Modules folder, it is available to all users. If a module is placed in the %UserProfile%\My Documents\WindowsPowerShell\Modules folder, it is available only to the specific user. The advantage of placing modules in the %UserProfile% location is that the user automatically has permission to perform the installation, whereas system location requires Administrator rights on Windows 7 and later.

Speaking of installation of Windows PowerShell modules, in many cases the installation of a Windows PowerShell module is no more complicated than placing the *.psm1 file in a folder in default user location–the key point is that the folder that is created under the \Modules folder must have the same name as the module itself. When you install a module on a local computer, use the Copy-Modules.ps1 script to simplify the process of creating and naming the folders.

When copying a Windows PowerShell module to a network shared location, follow the same rules; make sure that the folder that contains the module is the same name as the module name.

You need to keep in mind a couple of things. The first thing is that a Windows PowerShell module is basically a script (in our particular application) and that the Script Execution policy must be set so that script execution is permitted. If the script execution policy is set to the default level of *restricted,* an error will be generated (even if the logged on user is an Administrator). Fortunately, the error that is returned informs one of that fact. Even if the execution policy is set to *restricted* on a particular machine, you can always run a Windows PowerShell script (or module) if you start Windows PowerShell with the *bypass* option. The command to do this is shown here:

```
powershell -executionpolicy bypass
```

One of the really cool uses of a shared module is to permit centralization of Windows PowerShell Profiles for networked users. To do this, the profile on the local computer would simply import the shared module. In this way, you need to modify only one module in one location to permit updates for all the users on the network.

## Creating a module

The first thing you will probably want to do is to create a module. You can create a module in the Windows PowerShell ISE. The easiest way to create a module is to use functions that you have previously written. One of the first things to do is to locate the functions that you want to store in the module. You can copy them directly into the Windows PowerShell ISE. This technique appears in Figure 10-5.

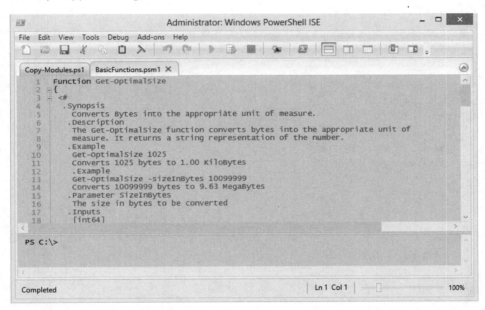

**FIGURE 10-5** Using the Windows PowerShell ISE makes creating a new module as easy as copying and pasting existing functions into a new file.

After you have copied your functions into the new module, save it with the .psm1 extension. A BasicFunctions.psm1 module is shown here.

```
BasicFunctions.psm1

Function Get-OptimalSize
{
 <#
   .Synopsis
     Converts Bytes into the appropriate unit of measure.
   .Description
```

```
     The Get-OptimalSize function converts bytes into the appropriate unit of
     measure. It returns a string representation of the number.
    .Example
     Get-OptimalSize 1025
     Converts 1025 bytes to 1.00 KiloBytes
    .Example
     Get-OptimalSize -sizeInBytes 10099999
     Converts 10099999 bytes to 9.63 MegaBytes
    .Parameter SizeInBytes
     The size in bytes to be converted
    .Inputs
     [int64]
    .OutPuts
     [string]
    .Notes
     NAME:  Get-OptimalSize
     AUTHOR: Ed Wilson
     LASTEDIT: 6/30/2012
     KEYWORDS: Scripting Techniques, Modules
    .Link
      Http://www.ScriptingGuys.com
 #Requires -Version 2.0
 #>
[CmdletBinding()]
param(
       [Parameter(Mandatory = $true,Position = 0,valueFromPipeline=$true)]
       [int64]
       $sizeInBytes
) #end param
 Switch ($sizeInBytes)
  {
   {$sizeInBytes -ge 1TB} {"{0:n2}" -f  ($sizeInBytes/1TB) + " TeraBytes";break}
   {$sizeInBytes -ge 1GB} {"{0:n2}" -f  ($sizeInBytes/1GB) + " GigaBytes";break}
   {$sizeInBytes -ge 1MB} {"{0:n2}" -f  ($sizeInBytes/1MB) + " MegaBytes";break}
   {$sizeInBytes -ge 1KB} {"{0:n2}" -f  ($sizeInBytes/1KB) + " KiloBytes";break}
   Default { "{0:n2}" -f $sizeInBytes + " Bytes" }
  } #end switch
  $sizeInBytes = $null
} #end Function Get-OptimalSize

Function Get-ComputerInfo
{
<#
 .Synopsis
   Retrieves basic information about a computer.
```

```
   .Description
   The Get-ComputerInfo cmdlet retrieves basic information such as
   computer name, domain name, and currently logged on user from
   a local or remote computer.
   .Example
   Get-ComputerInfo
   Returns computer name, domain name and currently logged on user
   from local computer.
   .Example
   Get-ComputerInfo -computer berlin
   Returns computer name, domain name and currently logged on user
   from remote computer named berlin.
   .Parameter Computer
   Name of remote computer to retrieve information from
   .Inputs
   [string]
   .OutPuts
   [object]
   .Notes
   NAME:  Get-ComputerInfo
   AUTHOR: Ed Wilson
   LASTEDIT: 6/30/2012
   KEYWORDS: Desktop mgmt, basic information
   .Link
    Http://www.ScriptingGuys.com
#Requires -Version 2.0
#>
Param([string]$computer=$env:COMPUTERNAME)
$wmi = Get-WmiObject -Class win32_computersystem -ComputerName $computer
$pcinfo = New-Object psobject -Property @{"host" = $wmi.DNSHostname
          "domain" = $wmi.Domain
          "user" = $wmi.Username}
$pcInfo
} #end function Get-ComputerInfo
```

You can control what is exported from the module by creating a manifest. If you place related functions that you will more than likely want to use together, you can avoid creating a manifest. In the BasicFunctions.psm1 module, there are two functions: one that converts numbers from bytes to a more easily understood numeric unit, and another function that returns basic computer information.

The *Get-ComputerInfo* function returns a custom object that contains information about the user, computer name, and computer domain. After you have created and saved the module, you will need to install the module. You can do this manually by navigating to the module directory, creating a folder for the module, and placing a copy of the module in the folder. I prefer to use the Copy-Modules.ps1 script discussed earlier in this chapter.

When the module has been copied to its own directory (installed), you can use the Import-Module cmdlet to import it into the current Windows PowerShell session. If you are not sure of the name of the module, you can use the Get-Module cmdlet with the *–ListAvailable* switch, as shown here:

```
PS C:\> Get-Module -ListAvailable

    Directory: C:\Users\administrator\Documents\WindowsPowerShell\Modules

ModuleType Name                                ExportedCommands
---------- ----                                ----------------
Script     BasicFunctions                      {Get-OptimalSize, Get-ComputerInfo}
Script     ConversionModuleV6                  {ConvertTo-MetersPerSecond, Conver...
Script     HelloUser                           hello-user


    Directory: C:\Windows\system32\WindowsPowerShell\v1.0\Modules


ModuleType Name                                ExportedCommands
---------- ----                                ----------------
Manifest   AppLocker                           {Get-AppLockerFileInformation, Get...
Manifest   Appx                                {Add-AppxPackage, Get-AppxPackage,...
Manifest   BitLocker                           {Unlock-BitLocker, Suspend-BitLock...
Manifest   BitsTransfer                        {Add-BitsFile, Complete-BitsTransf...
Manifest   BranchCache                         {Add-BCDataCacheExtension, Clear-B...
Manifest   CimCmdlets                          {Get-CimAssociatedInstance, Get-Ci...
Manifest   DirectAccessClientComponents        {Disable-DAManualEntryPointSelecti...
Script     Dism                                {Add-AppxProvisionedPackage, Add-W...
Manifest   DnsClient                           {Resolve-DnsName, Clear-DnsClientC...
Manifest   International                       {Get-WinDefaultInputMethodOverride...
Manifest   iSCSI                               {Get-IscsiTargetPortal, New-IscsiT...
Script     ISE                                 {New-IseSnippet, Import-IseSnippet...
Manifest   Kds                                 {Add-KdsRootKey, Get-KdsRootKey, T...
Manifest   Microsoft.PowerShell.Diagnostics    {Get-WinEvent, Get-Counter, Import...
Manifest   Microsoft.PowerShell.Host           {Start-Transcript, Stop-Transcript}
Manifest   Microsoft.PowerShell.Management      {Add-Content, Clear-Content, Clear...
Manifest   Microsoft.PowerShell.Security       {Get-Acl, Set-Acl, Get-PfxCertific...
Manifest   Microsoft.PowerShell.Utility        {Format-List, Format-Custom, Forma...
Manifest   Microsoft.WSMan.Management           {Disable-WSManCredSSP, Enable-WSMa...
Manifest   MMAgent                             {Disable-MMAgent, Enable-MMAgent, ...
Manifest   MsDtc                               {New-DtcDiagnosticTransaction, Com...
Manifest   NetAdapter                          {Disable-NetAdapter, Disable-NetAd...
Manifest   NetConnection                       {Get-NetConnectionProfile, Set-Net...
Manifest   NetLbfo                             {Add-NetLbfoTeamMember, Add-NetLbf...
Manifest   NetQos                              {Get-NetQosPolicy, Set-NetQosPolic...
Manifest   NetSecurity                         {Get-DAPolicyChange, New-NetIPsecA...
Manifest   NetSwitchTeam                       {New-NetSwitchTeam, Remove-NetSwit...
Manifest   NetTCPIP                            {Get-NetIPAddress, Get-NetIPInterf...
Manifest   NetworkConnectivityStatus           {Get-DAConnectionStatus, Get-NCSIP...
Manifest   NetworkTransition                   {Add-NetIPHttpsCertBinding, Disabl...
Manifest   PKI                                 {Add-CertificateEnrollmentPolicySe...
```

```
Manifest    PrintManagement             {Add-Printer, Add-PrinterDriver, A...
Script      PSDiagnostics               {Disable-PSTrace, Disable-PSWSManC...
Binary      PSScheduledJob              {New-JobTrigger, Add-JobTrigger, R...
Manifest    PSWorkflow                  {New-PSWorkflowExecutionOption, Ne...
Manifest    PSWorkflowUtility           {Invoke-AsWorkflow
Manifest    ScheduledTasks              {Get-ScheduledTask, Set-ScheduledT...
Manifest    SecureBoot                  {Confirm-SecureBootUEFI, Set-Secur...
Manifest    SmbShare                    {Get-SmbShare, Remove-SmbShare, Se...
Manifest    SmbWitness                  {Get-SmbWitnessClient, Move-SmbWit...
Manifest    Storage                     {Add-InitiatorIdToMaskingSet, Add-...
Manifest    TroubleshootingPack         {Get-TroubleshootingPack, Invoke-T...
Manifest    TrustedPlatformModule       {Get-Tpm, Initialize-Tpm, Clear-Tp...
Manifest    VpnClient                   {Add-VpnConnection, Set-VpnConnect...
Manifest    Wdac                        {Get-OdbcDriver, Set-OdbcDriver, G...
Manifest    WindowsDeveloperLicense     {Get-WindowsDeveloperLicense, Show...
Script      WindowsErrorReporting       {Enable-WindowsErrorReporting, Dis...
```

When you have imported the module, you can use the Get-Command cmdlet with the
—*module* parameter to see what commands are exported by the module, as shown here:

```
PS C:\> Import-Module basicfunctions
PS C:\> Get-Command -Module basic*

CommandType     Name                                              ModuleName
-----------     ----                                              ----------
Function        Get-ComputerInfo                                  basicfunctions
Function        Get-OptimalSize                                   basicfunctions
```

After you have added the functions from the module, you can use them directly from the
Windows PowerShell prompt. Using the *Get-ComputerInfo* function is illustrated here:

```
PS C:\> Get-ComputerInfo

host                                    domain                                  user
----                                    ------                                  ----
mred1                                   NWTraders.Com
NWTRADERS\ed


PS C:\> (Get-ComputerInfo).user
NWTRADERS\ed
PS C:\> (Get-ComputerInfo).host
mred1
PS C:\> Get-ComputerInfo -computer win8-pc | Format-Table -AutoSize

host     domain        user
----     ------        ----
win8-PC NWTraders.Com NWTRADERS\Administrator


PS C:\>
```

Because the *help* tags were used when creating the functions, you can use the Get-Help
cmdlet to obtain information about using the function. In this manner, the function that

was created in the module behaves exactly like a regular Windows PowerShell cmdlet. This includes tab expansion.

```
PS C:\> Get-Help Get-ComputerInfo

NAME
    Get-ComputerInfo

SYNOPSIS
    Retrieves basic information about a computer.


SYNTAX
    Get-ComputerInfo [[-computer] <String>] [<CommonParameters>]


DESCRIPTION
    The Get-ComputerInfo cmdlet retrieves basic information such as
    computer name, domain name, and currently logged on user from
    a local or remote computer.


RELATED LINKS
    Http://www.ScriptingGuys.com
    #Requires -Version 2.0

REMARKS
    To see the examples, type: "Get-Help Get-ComputerInfo -examples".
    For more information, type: "Get-Help Get-ComputerInfo -detailed".
    For technical information, type: "Get-Help Get-ComputerInfo -full".



PS C:\> Get-Help Get-ComputerInfo -Examples

NAME
    Get-ComputerInfo

SYNOPSIS
    Retrieves basic information about a computer.

    ------------------------- EXAMPLE 1 -------------------------

    C:\PS>Get-ComputerInfo


    Returns computer name, domain name and currently logged on user
    from local computer.
```

```
------------------------ EXAMPLE 2 ------------------------

C:\PS>Get-ComputerInfo -computer berlin


Returns computer name, domain name and currently logged on user
from remote computer named berlin.
```

PS C:\>

The *Get-OptimalSize* function can even receive input from the pipeline, as shown here:

```
PS C:\> (Get-WmiObject win32_volume -Filter "driveletter = 'c:'").freespace
26513960960
PS C:\> (Get-WmiObject win32_volume -Filter "driveletter = 'c:'").freespace | Get-
OptimalSize
24.69 GigaBytes
PS C:\>
```

---

**NOTES FROM THE FIELD**

### Windows PowerShell MVP
Boe Prox
*Senior Windows Administrator*

In most organizations, routine maintenance of a server to install various patches is at the mercy of a specific time range in which to accomplish this task. Depending on the size of an environment, this could potentially take several hours and require many people to assist with the patching of the servers. Usually this requires those people logging in to each system and manually installing a patch.

Enter Windows PowerShell. Windows PowerShell is not just about cmdlets and one-liners. You can leverage the .Net library and throw in inline code to create tools (command-line or GUI) that others can use with little to no effort.

My goal with writing PoshPAIG (PowerShell Patch Audit/Install GUI), available at *https://PoshPAIG.codeplex.com*, was to create a utility that would decrease the time an administrator would take to patch their environment given the limited time allotted to do so. Because the command-line aspect would potentially scare off some people, I went with a GUI approach that would make it easy for anyone to pick up and use. The scope of writing the code was large, and the goals were simple at the time but continue to evolve to meet the requirements of the community.

The code behind it is a mix of XAML (for the UI), .Net (building runspaces to handle multithreading), VBScript (legacy systems where Windows PowerShell might not be installed), COM objects (used for patch auditing), third-party executables (installing patches remotely), and, of course, Windows PowerShell itself to glue everything together as well as to provide existing cmdlets to handle various tasks.

Working on this project did prove to be a challenge in a number of ways, such as how to handle asynchronous operations so that multiple systems can be patched at the same time, and even some user interface-related features that are generally taken for granted such as sorting columns. This seemingly simple operation had to be coded into the user interface to allow a click on the column header to sort the rows.

Using sites such as MSDN allowed me to dig deeper into various aspects of .NET classes and XAML to better leverage the code and to improve usability.

The end result is over 3000 lines of code and multiple scripts that handle various operations of the utility to include some of the following:

- Auditing patches on systems
- Installing patches on systems
- Rebooting servers
- Generating reports of patches (audited and/or installed)

The end result is a GUI that utilizes a mix of techniques, languages, and user interface elements that anyone can use to manage their updates on multiple systems to gather patch information, install patches, and ensure that all of the servers in an environment have been not only updated but also can accomplish this task much quicker, especially in large environments!

## Additional resources

- The TechNet Script Center at *http://www.microsoft.com/technet/scriptcenter* contains numerous script examples.
- All scripts from this chapter are in the file available from the Script Center Script Repository at *http://gallery.technet.microsoft.com/scriptcenter/PowerShell-40 -Best-d9e16039.*

# CHAPTER 11

# Handling input and output

- Choosing the best input method
- Prompting for input
- Choosing the best output method
- Additional resources

There are few scripts that neither receive input nor produce output. These are primarily scripts that run a series of commands in a preconfigured, batch-oriented manner. Most scripts written by IT professionals require either input or output, and most scripts need both. Clearly, for maximum flexibility, scripts must receive input. To maximize utility, most scripts have to produce output.

The form of input and the manner of output are part of the design process and therefore are the purview of the scriptwriter. Traditional input takes the following forms:

- Read from the command line
- Read from a text file
- Read from a database
- Read from a spreadsheet
- Read from the registry
- Read from Active Directory Domain Services

It is common for output to follow the mode of input, but it is not a requirement. The scriptwriter should not be limited by only one model of design. Consider the following scenarios:

- A script receives input from a text file and displays data to the screen.
- A script receives input from a database and writes data back to the database but also provides confirmation of the transaction to the screen.
- A script receives input from the command line and writes data to the registry.
- A script receives input from a spreadsheet, writes to a database, records diagnostic information to a text file, and creates an event in the event log that records the exit code from the script.
- A script receives input from the command line and writes data to a text file but also displays the same data to the screen.

For input and output, the possibilities are varied and the potential combinations are many. Choosing the best input method and output destination is not always an exact science, and often the best solution might be dependent on external factors such as limitations of network infrastructure, ease of use, or speed of development. As a best practice, you should choose the input method that facilitates the intended use of the script. We will look at the strengths and potential uses of the various input and output methods in the following section.

## Choosing the best input method

The selection of the best input method is the one that works for you. When it comes to best practices for input methods, it's possible to feel like the final answer is always a compromise. It might seem that using a Microsoft Office Excel spreadsheet is always the best answer because it is readily available and easy to use, but this ease of use comes with added complexity to your script. You might feel that a text file is the easiest choice because the Get-Content cmdlet makes it easy to read from a text file. Yet using and maintaining a text file comes with a maintenance cost that you might prefer to avoid. For ease of maintenance, you might be inclined to attempt to read data from Active Directory because you know the values you receive will always be up to date, but this approach adds additional complexity to the script and will not work if Active Directory is not available. In the end, your final selection will always be a compromise between usability, understandability, maintainability, and manageability. Let's begin the discussion by examining the easiest approach to receiving input—reading from the command line.

## Reading from the command line

Reading from the command line is a traditional way to provide input to a script. It has the advantage of simplicity, which means it is easy to implement and reduces development time. If you want the ability to alter the script behavior at run time and you plan to run the script in an interactive fashion, accepting input from the command line might be the best solution for you.

Accepting input from the command line can be simple to implement. The biggest limitation of command-line input is the requirement for user intervention. You can circumvent the requirement of user interaction by assigning default values to the command-line parameters and by selecting default actions for script behavior.

### Using the *$args* automatic variable

There are several ways to receive command-line input in a script. The simplest method is to use command-line arguments. When a Windows PowerShell script is run, an automatic variable, *$args*, is created. The *$args* variable will hold values supplied to the script when it is started.

```
Get-Bios.ps1

Get-WmiObject -Class Win32_Bios -computername $args
```

The Get-Bios.ps1 script starts when you call the script and supply the name of the target computer. Because *$args* automatically accepts a string for the input, you do not need to place the name of the target computer in quotation marks.

```
PS bp:\> .\Get-Bios.ps1 localhost
```

While the script is running, the value you supplied from the command is present on the Windows PowerShell variable drive. You can determine the value that was supplied to the script by querying the Windows PowerShell variable drive for the *$args* variable as shown here:

```
Get-Item -path variable:args
```

The result of running the previous preceding query is shown here:

```
PSPath        : Microsoft.PowerShell.Core\Variable::args
PSDrive       : Variable
PSProvider    : Microsoft.PowerShell.Core\Variable
PSIsContainer : False
Name          : args
Description   :
Value         : {localhost}
Visibility    : Public
Module        :
ModuleName    :
Options       : None
Attributes    : {}
```

Even though accessing the value of *$args* via the Windows PowerShell variable drive provides a significant amount of information, it is easier to use the Get-Variable cmdlet:

```
Get-Variable args
```

---

**LESSONS LEARNED**

### The dollar sign is not part of the variable name

When using the Get-Variable cmdlet, you do not supply a dollar sign in front of the variable name. This is extremely confusing and frustrating to beginners who assume that all variables begin with a dollar sign. While it is true that variables begin with a dollar sign, the dollar sign is not technically part of the variable name. The dollar sign is used to indicate that a particular string is to be used as a variable, but the name of the variable does not include the dollar sign. Therefore,

Get-Variable will always fail when the variable is supplied with a dollar sign preceding the variable name. An error message is shown here:

```
PS bp:\> Get-Variable $args
Get-Variable : Cannot find a variable with name 'localhost'.
At C:\Users\edwils.NORTHAMERICA\AppData\Local\Temp\tmp994A.tmp.ps1:17
char:13
+ Get-Variable <<<< $args
    + CategoryInfo          : ObjectNotFound: (localhost:String)
[Get-Variable], ItemNotFoundException
    + FullyQualifiedErrorId : VariableNotFound,Microsoft.PowerShell
.Commands.GetVariableCommand
```

If you examine the error message, it states that it cannot find a variable with the name localhost. This provides a clue as to what is happening under the covers. The Get-Variable cmdlet is translating the *$args* variable into the value contained within the *$args* variable and is then looking for a variable that possesses that name. This process of substituting the value of *$args* instead of looking for the *$args* variable itself can lead to unpredictable results and cause hours of frustrating troubleshooting. Suppose that you have the following code.

```
$localhost = "my computer"
Get-WmiObject -Class Win32_Bios -computername $args
Get-Variable $args
```

When the script is started as shown here, you do not receive an error. Instead, you receive the following output on your display:

```
PS bp:\> .\Get-Bios.ps1 localhost
SMBIOSBIOSVersion : 7LETB7WW (2.17 )
Manufacturer      : LENOVO
Name              : Ver 1.00PARTTBLx
SerialNumber      : L3L4518
Version           : LENOVO - 2170
Name         : localhost
Description :
Value        : my computer
Visibility   : Public
Module       :
ModuleName   :
Options      : None
Attributes   : {}
```

Of course, most of the time you are querying the variable drive only for diagnostic purposes—exactly the situation when the cloud of confusion is at its most devastating.

## Supplying multiple values to *$args*

If you need to supply multiple values via the command line and attempt to do so by using the *$args* automatic variable, you will be greeted with the following error message that warns of a type mismatch. The error does not use the term *type mismatch*, but this is what is meant by the error. It states that you are attempting to supply an object array to a string and that the *–computername* parameter requires a string for its input.

```
Get-WmiObject : Cannot convert 'System.Object[]' to the type 'System.String' required by
parameter 'ComputerName'. Specified method is not supported.
At C:\Users\edwils.NORTHAMERICA\AppData\Local\Temp\tmp774.tmp.ps1:18 char:47
+ Get-WmiObject -Class win32_bios -computername <<<< $args
    + CategoryInfo          : InvalidArgument: (:) [Get-WmiObject],
ParameterBindingException
    + FullyQualifiedErrorId : CannotConvertArgument,Microsoft.PowerShell.Commands
.GetWmiObjectCommand
```

The error is not caused by the array. The error is caused because the *$args* automatic variable arrives as a *System.Object* array. The Get-WmiObject cmdlet will accept an array of computer names to the *–computername* parameter. This is shown in the following script in which an array of computer names is supplied directly to the *–computername* parameter and BIOS information is retrieved via the *Win32_Bios* Windows Management Instrumentation (WMI) class:

```
PS C:\> Get-WmiObject -Class Win32_Bios -computername localhost,loopback
SMBIOSBIOSVersion : 7LETB7WW (2.17 )
Manufacturer      : LENOVO
Name              : Ver 1.00PARTTBLx
SerialNumber      : L3L4518
Version           : LENOVO - 2170

SMBIOSBIOSVersion : 7LETB7WW (2.17 )
Manufacturer      : LENOVO
Name              : Ver 1.00PARTTBLx
SerialNumber      : L3L4518
Version           : LENOVO - 2170
```

There are a few ways to solve this issue. The first is to index into the array and force the retrieval of the computer names as shown in Get-BiosArray1.ps1.

---

**Get-BiosArray1.ps1**

```
Get-WmiObject -Class Win32_Bios -computername $args[0]
```

---

The technique of indexing directly into the *$args* automatic variable works well. Although it looks like it will retrieve only the first item in the array, *$args* in fact retrieves both items. Because Windows PowerShell automatically handles the transition between a single item and multiple items in an array, the technique of indexing into element 0 of the array works whether one or more items are supplied. The issue of the way in which the Windows PowerShell *$args* automatic variable handles an array of information is shown in the StringArgs.ps1 script.

When the StringArgs1.ps1 script is run with the array "string1","String2" supplied from the command line, the entire array is displayed in $args[0] and nothing is displayed for $args[1].

```
PS C:\> StingArgs.ps1 "string1","String2"
The value of arg0 string1 String2 the value of arg1
PS C:\>
```

A better way to handle an array that is supplied to the *$args* automatic variable is to use the Foreach-Object cmdlet and pipeline the array to the Get-WmiObject cmdlet as shown in Get-BiosArray2.ps1.

```
Get-BiosArray2.ps1

$args | Foreach-Object {
Get-WmiObject -Class Win32_Bios -computername $_
}
```

When the Get-BiosArray2.ps1 script is started with an array of computer names from the Windows PowerShell prompt, the following output is displayed:

```
PS C:\> Get-BiosArray2.ps1 localhost,loopback
SMBIOSBIOSVersion : 7LETB7WW (2.17 )
Manufacturer      : LENOVO
Name              : Ver 1.00PARTTBLx
SerialNumber      : L3L4518
Version           : LENOVO - 2170

SMBIOSBIOSVersion : 7LETB7WW (2.17 )
Manufacturer      : LENOVO
Name              : Ver 1.00PARTTBLx
SerialNumber      : L3L4518
Version           : LENOVO - 2170
```

There are two advantages to using the Foreach-Object cmdlet. The first is readability of the code, because spelling out Foreach-Object meets the principle of least shock. When people read the code and see that the script accepts an array for input via the *$args* variable, they are not surprised to see the script using the Foreach-Object cmdlet to walk through the array. Another advantage is that the script will work when a single value is supplied for the input.

Unfortunately, if the same approach is tried with the StringArgsArray.ps1 script, the value of the *$args* array is repeated twice. The StringArgsArray1.ps1 script is shown here.

```
StringArgsArray1.ps1

$args | Foreach-Object {
'The value of arg0 ' + $_ + ' the value of arg1 ' + $_
}
```

When the StringArgsArray1.ps1 script is started, the results shown here are displayed:

```
PS C:\> StingArgsArray1.ps1 "string1","String2"
The value of arg0 string1 String2 the value of arg1 string1 String2
PS C:\>
```

If you examine the output from the StringArgsArray1.ps1 script, you see that both elements of the *$args* array are displayed. If you modify the StringArgsArray1.ps1 script so that
you index into the array that is contained in the *$_* automatic variable (which represents the
current item on the pipeline), you can retrieve both items from the array. The revised script is
named StringArgsArray2.ps1.

---

**StringArgsArray2.ps1**

```
$args | Foreach-Object {
'The value of arg0 ' + $_[0] + ' the value of arg1 ' + $_[1]
}
```

---

When the script is run, the correct information is displayed.

```
PS C:\> StingArgsArray1.ps1 "string1","String2
The value of arg0 string1 the value of arg1 String2
PS C:\>
```

A more common problem when using the *$args* automatic variable is not the need to
handle multiple items from the command line but the need to handle the situation when the
person running the script does not supply any values from the command line. If you run the
Get-Bios.ps1 script and do not supply a value from the command line, an error is generated
by the Get-WmiObject cmdlet.

```
Get-WmiObject : Cannot validate argument on parameter 'ComputerName'. The argument is
null, empty, or an element of the argument collection contains a null value. Supply a
collection that does not contain any null values and then try the command again.
At C:\Users\edwils.NORTHAMERICA\AppData\Local\Temp\tmpF8E3.tmp.ps1:16 char:46
+ Get-WmiObject -Class Win32_Bios -computername <<<< $args
    + CategoryInfo          : InvalidData: (:) [Get-WmiObject],
ParameterBindingValidationException
    + FullyQualifiedErrorId : ParameterArgumentValidationError,Microsoft.PowerShell
.Commands.GetWmiObjectCommand
```

There are two ways to handle the missing data exception, and both methods involve
inspecting the *count* property from *$args*. In the first example, if the *count* property value is
equal to 0, you display a message and exit the script as shown here:

---

**Get-BiosArgsCheck1.ps1**

```
If($args.count -eq 0)
  {
    Write-Host -foregroundcolor Cyan "Please supply computer name"
    Exit
  } #end if
Get-WmiObject -Class Win32_Bios -computername $args
```

---

You can simplify the amount of typing involved in creating a custom error message by using the *Throw* statement to raise an error, which automatically displays the output in red. This allows you to skip using the Write-Host cmdlet to display text in a color other than white. In the Get-BiosArgsCheck2.ps1 script, the *Throw* statement is used to raise an error. The string following the *Throw* statement is the message that is displayed on the screen. The script is further optimized by using the *not (!)* operator to determine whether the *$args* automatic variable has a count, which treats the *$args.count* as if it were a Boolean value. If the count is 0, the *(!$args.count)* expression is evaluated to *false* and the *Throw* statement is entered. The use of the *Throw* statement is shown in the Get-BiosArgsCheck2.ps1 script.

```
Get-BiosArgsCheck2.ps1

If(!$args.count)
  {
   Throw "Please supply computer name"
  } #end if
Get-WmiObject -Class Win32_Bios -computername $args
```

You should keep in mind that when you use the *Throw* statement, it generates an error. This error is populated on the *$error* object and is a *RuntimeException* class in this particular example. As a best practice, you should avoid using the *Throw* statement unless an action actually causes an error. A user omitting a parameter does not really produce an error. You have already trapped the error that would have been created as a result of not checking the *count* property of the *$args* variable.

```
PS C:\Program Files\MrEdSoftware\MrEdScriptEditor> $error
Please supply computer name
At C:\Users\edwils.NORTHAMERICA\AppData\Local\Temp\tmp72FE.tmp.ps1:17 char:9
+     Throw <<<<  "Please supply computer name"
    + CategoryInfo          : OperationStopped: (Please supply computer name:String) [],
RuntimeException
    + FullyQualifiedErrorId : Please supply computer name
```

You can use the *Trap* statement to catch a parameter binding error. If a user starts the script without supplying a computer name for the command-line argument, an error is raised. The particular error that is raised is an instance of the Microsoft .NET Framework *ParameterBindingException* class, which is located in the *System.Management.Automation* namespace. This specific error is raised when there is a problem binding the parameters that are supplied to the script. Other errors involving WMI, such as an invalid WMI class name, do not involve parameter binding and therefore do not raise the *ParameterBindingException* exception.

The advantage of using the *Trap* statement to look for a very specific error is that you can then tailor your messages to the exact problem the user encountered. Instead of glibly replying that there is a problem with the script, you can provide a specific suggestion tailored to the exact error condition that is encountered. You can have multiple *Traps* in your script if you need to do so. Your script traps the error, displays a message, and exits the script gracefully.

An error is still generated on the *$error* object but is not displayed to the user. An example of using the *Trap* statement to display an error message when the script is run without supplying a value for *$args* is shown in the Get-BiosArgsTrap1.ps1 script.

```
Get-BiosArgsTrap1.ps1

Trap [System.Management.Automation.ParameterBindingException]
  {
     Write-Host -foregroundcolor cyan "Supply a computer name"
     Exit
  }

Get-WmiObject -Class Win32_Bios -computername $args
```

If a *ParameterBindingException* error is encountered when the Get-BiosArgsTrap1.ps1 script is started, the script will trap the error. The output displayed from the Get-BiosArgsTrap1.ps1 script is shown here:

```
PS C:\> Get-BiosArgsTrap1.ps1
Supply a computer name
PS C:\>
```

If any other error occurs when the script runs, the error associated with that particular error condition is displayed.

You can also use *Try/Catch/Finally* to attempt an action in the *try* portion of the construction. The error you will trap goes into the *catch* portion, and the action you will perform when all is completed goes into the *finally* section.

An example of using *Try/Catch/Finally* is shown in the GetBiosTryCatchFinally.ps1 script. In the *try* section of the construction, you use the Get-WmiObject cmdlet to retrieve BIOS information from the *Win32_Bios* WMI class. The target computer is supplied from the command line via the *$args* automatic variable, and this is the command that is attempted. If a *System.Management.Automation.ParameterBindingException* error is raised, it will be caught via the *catch* portion of the *Try/Catch/Finally* construction. When the parameter exception is raised, the code that runs is the Write-Host cmdlet. The string "Please enter computer name" displays on the screen in the cyan color. The code that is in the *finally* portion of *Try/Catch/Finally* always runs, and therefore the 'Cleaning up the $error object' string will be displayed to the screen in white text even if no error is raised. The error object will also be cleared, even if there are no errors to be cleared. The complete text of the GetBiosTryCatchFinally.ps1 script is shown here.

```
GetBiosTryCatchFinally.ps1

Try
   { Get-WmiObject -class Win32_Bios -computer $args }
Catch [System.Management.Automation.ParameterBindingException]
   { Write-Host -foregroundcolor cyan "Please enter computer name" }
```

```
Finally
    { 'Cleaning up the $error object' ; $error.clear() }
```

# Using the *Param* statement

Using the *$args* automatic variable is a quick and easy method to receive input to your script from the command line. As shown in the "Using the *$args* automatic variable" section, this simplicity is not without cost. The cost is flexibility. While the *$args* automatic variable works great for retrieving single values, it does not work as well when multiple parameters must be supplied. In addition, there is no way to make switched parameters when using the *$args* automatic variable.

The *Param* statement lets you create named arguments and switched arguments. To use the *Param* statement to create a named argument, you use the *Param* keyword, open a set of parentheses, and specify your parameter name as follows:

```
Param($computer)
```

To specify a default value for the parameter, you use the *Param* keyword, specify the parameter name inside a set of parentheses, and use the *equality* operator to assign a value.

```
Param($computer = "localhost")
```

The *Param* statement must be the first noncommented line in the script. If you try to use the *Param* statement in another position, you will receive an error. In the example shown here, you actually receive the error but the script still runs.

```
BadParam.ps1

Write-Host "Param not in first position"
Param($computer = "localhost")
Get-WmiObject -Class Win32_Bios -computername $computer
```

The error states that *Param* is not recognized as a cmdlet, function, script file, or operable program. This error is shown in Figure 11-1.

The Get-BiosParam.ps1 script illustrates using the *Param* keyword to create a named argument and to assign a default value for the *$computer* variable. The Get-WmiObject cmdlet uses the *Win32_Bios* WMI class to return BIOS information to the display from the computer that is specified in the *$computer* variable, which is either a computer name that was typed when the Get-BiosParam.ps1 script was run or the localhost computer.

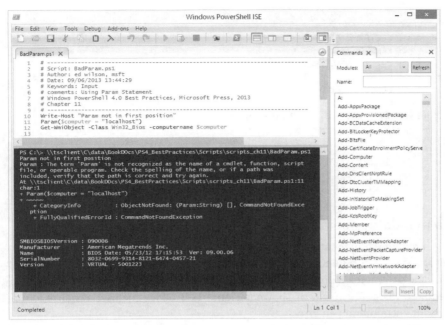

**FIGURE 11-1** When the *Param* statement does not appear in the first noncommented line, an error is raised.

There are three different ways in which the *–computer* parameter can be supplied from the command line, as follows:

- Type the entire parameter name.
- Type a partial parameter name. You must type enough of the parameter name to uniquely identify the parameter.
- Omit the parameter name and rely on position.

These three different methods of using command-line parameters are illustrated here with the Get-BiosParam.ps1 script:

```
PS C:\> Get-BiosParam.ps1 -computer loopback

SMBIOSBIOSVersion : 7LETB7WW (2.17 )
Manufacturer      : LENOVO
Name              : Ver 1.00PARTTBLx
SerialNumber      : L3L4518
Version           : LENOVO - 2170


PS C:\> Get-BiosParam.ps1 -c loopback

SMBIOSBIOSVersion : 7LETB7WW (2.17 )
Manufacturer      : LENOVO
Name              : Ver 1.00PARTTBLx
SerialNumber      : L3L4518
Version           : LENOVO - 2170
```

```
PS C:\> Get-BiosParam.ps1 loopback

SMBIOSBIOSVersion : 7LETB7WW (2.17 )
Manufacturer      : LENOVO
Name              : Ver 1.00PARTTBLx
SerialNumber      : L3L4518
Version           : LENOVO - 2170
```

The complete Get-BiosParam.ps1 script is shown here.

---

**Get-BiosParam.ps1**

```
Param($computer = "localhost")
Get-WmiObject -Class Win32_Bios -computername $computer
```

---

## Creating a mandatory parameter

You can make a parameter mandatory by using a parameter binding tag and setting the value of the *mandatory* attribute to *$true*. When the *mandatory* attribute is used to modify the command-line parameter, a prompt is displayed whenever the script is run without supplying the required value. This behavior, shown in Figure 11-2, allows the user a chance to run the script without encountering an error.

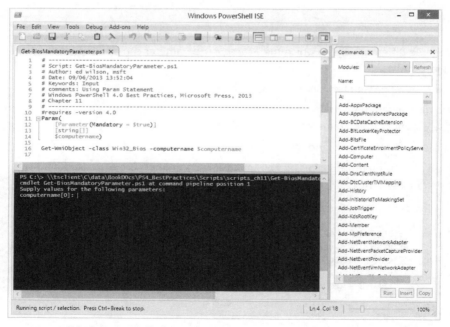

**FIGURE 11-2** Windows PowerShell prompts for missing values when the *mandatory* attribute is used with a command-line parameter.

Parameter statement tags are a powerful feature of Windows PowerShell, and their use prevents interoperability with earlier versions of PowerShell. In the Get-BiosMandatoryParameter.ps1 script, the *#requires –version 4.0* statement prevents the script from attempting to start in an earlier Windows PowerShell environment. The *Param* statement is used to create the command-line parameters. The *[Parameter(Mandatory = $true)]* statement makes the *–computername* parameter a mandatory parameter. The *[string[]]* statement converts the *–computername* parameter into an array. When the Get-BiosMandatoryParameter.ps1 script runs without any parameters supplied, it will prompt for multiple values for the *–computername* parameter until the Enter key is pressed twice. If you want to accept only a single value for the *–computername* parameter, you should leave out the *[]*, as shown here:

```
Param(
    [Parameter(Mandatory = $true)]
    [string]
    $computername)
```

When a value is supplied for the *–computername* parameter from the command line, it is converted into a string if possible because of the *[string[]]* type constraint that is placed in the parameter definition. This is, of course, the same as the *–computername* parameter from the Get-WmiObject cmdlet, which also accepts an array of strings. For example, if you attempt to constrain the input as an integer, an invalid parameter error is generated.

```
PS bp:\> .\Get-BiosMandatoryParameter.ps1 [int]12
Get-WmiObject : Invalid parameter
At C:\data\BookDocs\PowerShellBestPractices\Scripts\chapter12\Get-BiosMandatory
Parameter.ps1:20 char:14
+ Get-WmiObject <<<<  -class Win32_Bios -computername $computername
    + CategoryInfo: InvalidOperation: (:) [Get-WmiObject], ManagementException
    + FullyQualifiedErrorId : GetWMIManagementException,Microsoft.PowerShell
.Commands.GetWmiObjectCommand
```

The complete Get-BiosMandatoryParameter.ps1 script is shown here.

---

**Get-BiosMandatoryParameter.ps1**

```
#requires -version 4.0
Param(
    [Parameter(Mandatory = $true)]
    [string[]]
    $computername)

Get-WmiObject -class Win32_Bios -computername $computername
```

---

Gary Siepser, Premier Field Engineer
*Microsoft Corporation*

A few years ago, when I set out to start writing more reusable code and more advanced functions, I wanted to mimic the behavior of cmdlets I love, such as Stop-Process. What I love about that cmdlet is that you can pipe process objects to, as well as take advantage of, the *-InputObject* parameter directly. I love the flexibility the cmdlet provides through quality parameter design.

When I set out to write my own Export-Excel function (I know there are several out there already; this was some time ago), I had to really dig into how to code this parameter behavior. Using the *Begin-Process-End* structure of functions was clearly the way to go, but I was left with some design choices.

In the Process block, you can leverage *$_* to access the current pipeline object, but by leveraging the *[Parameter]* attribute, you can also map pipeline input directly into parameters. I definitely wanted to use parameter mapping to allow richer and multiple parameter creation using pipeline input.

The next design choice for my *–InputObject* parameter was what object type to use when strong-typing. This was to be the main parameter to receive the objects to be exported into the body of the Excel file. After some testing, I realized that I wanted to allow any type of object to be pipelined and that I would simply export whatever properties were present on the objects. I decided to use *[Object]* to allow for any type of object. To handle multiple instances of the passed objects and to work with parameter pipeline input, the type I finally settled on for the parameter was *[Object[]]*.

The last challenge that I faced was the difference in behavior between pipelining and passing the objects as a named parameter. The Process block runs like a *Foreach* loop when the objects are pipelined; it runs once for each object instance in the pipe. Unfortunately, when passing the same objects as a parameter argument, the Process block runs only once. This is reflective of Windows PowerShell behavior when passing an array through the pipe: The array is unrolled, and the multiple objects are received by the parameter and cause the Process block to run accordingly. When passing the array as an argument, the parameter receives only the single array object instead of multiple objects.

The solution to this last problem was to simply wrap the contents of the Process block into a *Foreach* loop. If the objects are pipelined, the *Foreach* loop enumerates only the single object and everything still runs fine. If the objects are passed as an argument, thus a single array object, the *Foreach* loop unwraps and repeats the code block much as the Process block does for the pipeline. While at first it seemed a bit counter-intuitive to have to add in a loop within the looping nature of the Process block, it all worked out in the end.

# Using parameter attributes

The Get-BiosMandatoryParameter.ps1 script uses the *mandatory* parameter attribute argument to ensure that the *–computername* parameter has a value supplied for it. There are several other parameter attribute arguments that can be used to modify the default behavior of the parameter attribute of the *Param* keyword. The available parameter attribute arguments are shown in Table 11-1.

**TABLE 11-1** Parameter attribute arguments

| Argument Name | Description |
| --- | --- |
| *Mandatory* | The *Mandatory* argument indicates that the parameter is required when the function is run. If this argument is not specified, the parameter is an optional parameter.<br>**Example:**<br>[parameter(*Mandatory=$true*)] |
| *Position* | The *Position* argument specifies the position of the parameter. If this argument is not specified, the parameter name or its alias must be explicitly specified when the parameter is set. Also, if none of the parameters of a function have positions, the Windows PowerShell run time assigns positions to each parameter based on the order in which the parameters are received.<br>**Example:**<br>[parameter(*Position=0*)] |
| *ParameterSetName* | The *ParameterSetName* argument specifies the parameter set to which a parameter belongs. If no parameter set is specified, the parameter belongs to all of the parameter sets defined by the function. This behavior means that each parameter set must have one unique parameter that is not a member of any other parameter set.<br>**Example:**<br>[parameter(*Mandatory=$true,*<br>  *ParameterSetName = "CN"*)] |
| *ValueFromPipeline* | The *ValueFromPipeline* argument specifies that the parameter accepts input from a pipeline object. Specify this argument if the cmdlet accesses the complete object and not just a property of the object.<br>**Example:**<br>[parameter(*Mandatory=$true,*<br>  *ValueFromPipeline=$true*)] |
| *ValueFromPipelineByPropertyName* | The *ValueFromPipelineByPropertyName* argument specifies that the parameter accepts input from a property of a pipeline object.<br>**Example:**<br>[parameter(*Mandatory=$true,*<br>  *ValueFromPipelineByPropertyName=$true*)] |
| *ValueFromRemainingArguments* | The *ValueFromRemainingArguments* argument specifies that the parameter accepts all of the remaining arguments that are not bound to the parameters of the function.<br>**Example:**<br>[parameter(*Mandatory=$true,*<br>  *ValueFromRemainingArguments=$true*)] |

| Argument Name | Description |
|---|---|
| *HelpMessage* | The *HelpMessage* argument specifies a message that contains a short description of the parameter.<br>**Example:**<br>[parameter(*Mandatory=$true, HelpMessage=*"An array of computer names.")] |
| *Alias* | The *Alias* argument establishes an alternate name for the parameter. This is useful when parameter names are excessively long.<br>**Example:**<br>[parameter(Mandatory=$true)]<br>[alias("CN","MachineName")]<br>[String[]]<br>$ComputerName |

## Creating a parameter alias

The *alias* attribute of the *Param* statement can be used to make working from the command line easier. The *alias* attribute typically follows the *parameter* attribute to create an alternative to typing a long parameter name from the command line. Although partial parameter completion can be used, enough of the parameter must be typed to disambiguate it from other parameters that are defined. Consider the following *Param* statement that is used to create two parameters:

```
Param($computername, $computerIPaddress)
```

In this example, you need to type *computern* and *computeri* before the parameters are unique. In a case such as this, a parameter alias is useful. You can see how a parameter alias is used by referring to the Get-BiosMandatoryParameterWithAlias.ps1 script.

```
Get-BiosMandatoryParameterWithAlias.ps1

#requires -version 4.0
Param(
    [Parameter(Mandatory = $true)]
    [alias("CN")]
    [string[]]
    $computername)

Get-WmiObject -class Win32_Bios -computername $computername
```

**Jaap Brasser**
*Technical Consultant*

For me, the great thing about Windows PowerShell is the incremental upgrades that are included with every new release. My personal favorite in Windows PowerShell 4.0 is the addition of the common parameter *PipelineVariable*. In previous Windows PowerShell versions, only the default variable *$_* (or in PowerShell 3.0, *$PSItem*), was available when piping objects through the pipeline. By using the *PipelineVariable* parameter, a specific variable can be assigned, and this is one of the nice improvements in Windows PowerShell 4.0.

The utility of *PipelineVariable* is that it provides an easy and reproducible method of improving readability in my scripts. First, the parameter itself can be used with any cmdlet and can either be used by using its full notation, *−PipelineVariable*, or its alias, *−pv*.

An easy example of how this can be utilized in a script is as follows. In this example, I will enumerate the folders that are in the C:\Users path and assign the *UserFolder* variable to each folder:

```
Get-ChildItem -Directory -Path C:\Users -PipelineVariable UserFolder
```

The first thing to note is that the dollar sign is not included in the variable name, similar to creating a variable using the `New-Variable` cmdlet. When executing this cmdlet, the output is identical to the cmdlet executed without the *PipelineVariable* parameter. The added benefit becomes apparent when this code expands to contain another two *ForEach* statements. Take a look at the following code:

```
Get-ChildItem -Directory -Path C:\Users -PipelineVariable UserFolder |

ForEach-Object -PipelineVariable Access -Process {

    $UserFolder.GetAccessControl().Access

} |

ForEach-Object -Process {

    [pscustomobject]@{

        Folder = $UserFolder.FullName

        User = $Access.IdentityReference
```

```
            AccessRights = $Access.FileSystemRights,
$Access.AccessControlType


    }


}
```

In this example, the results from the initial `Get-ChildItem` cmdlet are piped into a *ForEach-Object* loop, and for each folder, the access rights are retrieved and stored in the *$Access* variable. The result of this is then piped to another *ForEach* loop, which in turn creates custom objects that contain the values we would like to retrieve. We can access the desired properties by using the variables defined by using–*PipelineVariable*.

Another thing to note is that these variables are available only within the scope of this pipeline. After the pipeline completes, no variables remain. We can verify this by running *Test-Path* to verify the existence of a variable:

```
Test-Path -Path Variable:UserFolder
```

When I am using Windows PowerShell, I always feel as though I am collecting bits and pieces to put in my toolkit. *PipelineVariable* is my recent favorite because it allows for an easy and reproducible method of assigning variables in a pipeline. By utilizing this, it becomes easier to see what a variable contains and allows for easier nesting of multiple *ForEach-Object* statements.

## Validating parameter input

It is more efficient to catch problems with your script by inspecting the parameters than it is to wait until the script is launched and then do parameter checking. In Windows PowerShell 4.0, there are a number of validation attributes that can be specified. Validation attributes inspect command-line parameters to ensure that they conform to certain rules. If you need to ensure that the value of a command-line parameter is within a specified range in previous versions of Windows PowerShell, it is common to write a function and to call that function upon entering the script, as illustrated in the CheckNumberRange.ps1 script.

The *Check-Number* function in the CheckNumberRange.ps1 script ensures that the value of the *number* parameter is greater than 1 and less than or equal to 5. If *number* is within the 1 to 5 range, the *Check-Number* function returns the *true* value to the script; otherwise, it returns *false*. The *Set-Number* function multiplies the value of the *number* parameter by 2. The entry point of the script uses the *If* statement to call the *Check-Number* function. If the *Check-Number* function returns *true*, it calls the *Set-Number* function; otherwise, it displays a message stating that the value of the *$number* variable is out of bounds. The complete CheckNumberRange.ps1 script is shown here.

```
CheckNumberRange.ps1

Param($number)

Function Check-Number($number)
{
 if($number -ge 1 -And $number -le 5)
  {  $true }
 Else
  { $false }
} #end check-number

Function Set-Number($number)
{
 $number * 2
} #end Set-Number

# *** Start of script ***
If(Check-Number($number))
  { Set-Number($number) }
Else
  { '$number is out of bounds' }
```

You might prefer to continue to write your own custom boundary-checking functions. A custom function might also be required if there are complicated rules that you need to enforce.

Basic boundary checking, such as that performed by the *Check-Number* function in the CheckNumberRange.ps1 script, can be accomplished in Windows PowerShell 4.0 by using one of the parameter validation attributes listed in Table 11-2, later in this chapter. The parameter validation attribute that checks the range value of a parameter is named *ValidateRange*, and its use is shown in the ValidateRange.ps1 script. In the *Param* statement, the *[ValidateRange(1,5)]* parameter attribute is used to ensure that the value supplied for the *number* parameter falls within the range of 1 to 5. If it does, the ValidateRange.ps1 script starts at the entry point to the script, which calls the *Set-Number* function. The ValidateRange.ps1 script and the CheckNumberRange.ps1 script both accomplish the same thing—they multiply an input number by 2 if that number is within the range of 1 to 5. The ValidateRange.ps1 script is shown here.

```
ValidateRange.ps1

#requires -version 4.0
Param(
      [ValidateRange(1,5)]
      $number
     )
```

```
Function Set-Number($number)
{
 $number * 2
} #end Set-Number

# *** Entry point to script ***
Set-Number($number)
```

As a best practice, you should use parameter validation attributes to inspect parameter values rather than writing your own functions to accomplish the same thing. Some of the main reasons for using parameter validation attributes are as follows:

- Reduces the complexity of your code
- Ensures that your script behaves like the core Windows PowerShell cmdlets
- Helps users of your script know how to run your script
- Promotes syntax discoverability via the Get-Help cmdlet

The most powerful parameter validation attribute is the *ValidatePattern* attribute. By using the *ValidatePattern* parameter validation attribute, you can check input to see whether it conforms to a regular expression pattern. A regular expression pattern can range from a basic pattern match that looks for a specific combination of letters within a computer name to more complex regular expression patterns. A basic pattern match is shown in the PingComputers.ps1 script.

In the PingVComputers.ps1 script, the *ValidatePattern* parameter validation attribute is used to ensure that the string supplied for the *–computername* parameter contains the letters *DC* somewhere in the name of the computer. Valid values would include *DC*, *DCcomputer*, and even *myDCcomputer*. The requirement for a match is that the letters *DC* must appear in the string and must appear in exact order. The *Param* statement is used to allow the use of command-line parameters. The *ValidatePattern* parameter validation attribute sets the regular expression pattern that is used to validate command-line input. The *alias* attribute is used to configure an alternate name for the *–computername* parameter. The *Param* statement is shown here:

```
Param(
     [ValidatePattern("DC")]
     [alias("CN")]
     $computername
 )
```

The *New-TestConnection* function uses the Test-Connection cmdlet to send a specially configured ping packet to the destination computer listed in the *–computername* parameter. The buffer size of the ping packet is reduced from the default of 32 bytes to 16 bytes, and the number of packets is reduced from the default of 4 to 2. The result is that the *New-TestConnection* function will return the status of the destination more quickly, use less network bandwidth, and complete more quickly than the standard Test-Connection cmdlet. The complete PingComputers.ps1 script is shown here.

```
PingComputers.ps1

#requires -version 4.0
Param(
     [ValidatePattern("DC")]
     [alias("CN")]
     $computername
 )


Function New-TestConnection($computername)
{
 Test-connection -computername $computername -buffersize 16 -count 2
} #end new-testconnection

# *** Entry Point to script
New-TestConnection($computername)
```

More complicated regular expression patterns can also be used with the *ValidatePattern* parameter validation attribute. In the PingIpAddress.ps1 script, a regular expression is used to ensure that a string representing an IP address is entered. The pattern used limits input by requiring 1 to 3 numbers followed by a period, then 1 to 3 numbers followed by a period, then 1 to 3 numbers followed by a period, and then an additional 1 to 3 numbers. This pattern accepts a string such as 127.0.0.1 (a valid IP address), but it also accepts 999.999.999.999 (which is not a valid IP address). The regular expression pattern is shown here:

"\d{1,3}\.\d{1,3}\.\d{1,3}\.\d{1,3}"

In the PingIpAddress.ps1 script, the *Param* statement creates the command-line parameters. The *parameter* attribute is used to make the parameter mandatory and to specify a help message, which is available in case the script is run without typing the parameter value. The *ValidatePattern* attribute holds the regular expression pattern that is used to validate the data supplied to the script via the *–computername* parameter. An alias, *IP*, is created to allow the script to run without the need to type the *–computername* parameter name. The complete PingIpAddress.ps1 script is shown here.

```
PingIpAddress.ps1

#requires -version 2.0
Param(
     [Parameter(Mandatory=$true,
                HelpMessage="Enter a valid IP address")]
     [ValidatePattern("\d{1,3}\.\d{1,3}\.\d{1,3}\.\d{1,3}")]
     [alias("IP")]
     $computername
 )
```

```
Function New-TestConnection($computername)
{
 Test-connection -computername $computername -buffersize 16 -count 2
} #end new-testconnection


# *** Entry Point to script
New-TestConnection($computername)
```

The parameter validation attributes are shown in Table 11-2.

**TABLE 11-2** Parameter validation attributes

| Attribute name | Description |
| --- | --- |
| AllowNull | The AllowNull attribute allows the argument of a mandatory cmdlet parameter to be set to null.<br>**Example:**<br>[AllowNull()] |
| AllowEmptyString | The AllowEmptyString attribute allows an empty string as the argument of a mandatory cmdlet parameter.<br>**Example:**<br>[AllowEmptyString()] |
| AllowEmptyCollection | The AllowEmptyCollection attribute allows an empty collection as the argument of a mandatory parameter.<br>**Example:**<br>[AllowEmptyCollection()] |
| ValidateCount | The ValidateCount attribute specifies the minimum and maximum number of arguments that the parameter can accept.<br>**Example:**<br>[ValidateCount(1,5)] |
| ValidateLength | The ValidateLength attribute specifies the minimum and maximum length of the parameter argument.<br>**Example:**<br>[ValidateLength(1,10)] |
| ValidatePattern | The ValidatePattern attribute specifies a regular expression that validates the pattern of the parameter argument.<br>**Example:**<br>[ValidatePattern("[0-9][0-9][0-9]")] |
| ValidateRange | The ValidateRange attribute specifies the minimum and maximum values of the parameter argument.<br>**Example:**<br>[ValidateRange(0,10)] |
| ValidateScript | The ValidateScript attribute specifies a script that is used to validate the parameter argument. The Windows PowerShell run time generates an error if the script result is false or if the script throws an exception.<br>**Example:**<br>[ValidateScript({$_ -lt 4})] |

| Attribute name | Description |
|---|---|
| ValidateSet | The ValidateSet attribute specifies a set of valid values for the argument of the parameter. The Windows PowerShell run time generates an error if the parameter argument does not match a value in the set.<br>**Example:**<br>[ValidateSet("Steve", "Mary", "Carl")] |
| ValidateNotNull | The ValidateNotNull attribute specifies that the argument of the parameter cannot be set to null.<br>**Example:**<br>[ValidateNotNull()] |
| ValidateNotNullOrEmpty | The ValidateNotNullOrEmpty attribute specifies that the argument of the parameter cannot be set to null or cannot be empty.<br>**Example:**<br>[ValidateNotNullOrEmpty()] |

## Using multiple parameter arguments

To use multiple parameter arguments, the *alias* attribute, and parameter validation attributes at the same time with the *Param* statement, you must keep the following rules in mind:

- Parameter arguments go inside parentheses and modify the *parameter* attribute of the *Param* statement.
- Each parameter argument is separated by a comma.
- The *parameter* attribute goes inside square brackets (just like all other parameter attributes).
- Each *parameter* attribute should be on its own line.
- *Parameter* attributes are not separated by commas.
- The command-line parameter begins with a dollar sign and is followed by a comma, unless it is the last command-line parameter defined, in which case it is followed by the closing parenthesis from the *Param* statement.
- You are allowed to have an unlimited number of *parameter* attributes and parameter validation attributes.

The MultiplyNumbersCheckParameters.ps1 script illustrates the use of multiple parameter attributes. It begins with the *#requires –version 4.0* tag that is used to ensure that the script does not attempt to start on a computer running Windows PowerShell 1.0. The *Param* statement creates the command-line parameters for the script. The *parameter* attribute is used to make the *FirstNumber* parameter mandatory, assign it to the first position, and set a help message for the parameter. The *alias* attribute is used to create an alias for the *FirstNumber* parameter. The *ValidateRange* parameter validation attribute is used to ensure that the command-line *FirstNumber* parameter has a value that falls within the range of 1 to 10.

The *FirstNumber* parameter is followed by a comma, and the *parameter* attribute is used to make the *lastnumber* parameter mandatory, occupy position 1, and assign a help message for the *lastnumber* parameter. The *alias* attribute creates an alias of *ln* for the *lastnumber* parameter. The type constraint [*int16*] is used to ensure that the value of the *lastnumber* parameter is a 16-bit integer, which limits its value to 32767. The *ValidateNotNullOrEmpty* validation attribute is used to ensure that the *lastnumber* parameter is neither null nor empty. The *param* section ends by creating the *lastnumber* parameter and closing out the parentheses.

> **NOTE** An easy way to determine the capacity of certain system types is to use the static *Maxvalue* property. To obtain the maximum value of an *int32,* you can access it by using a double colon, as in *[int32]::Maxvalue.*

After all of the work to create the parameters, the code itself is somewhat anti-climactic: It multiplies the two command-line parameters together. The completed MultiplyNumbersCheckParameters.ps1 script is shown here.

```
MultiplyNumbersCheckParameters.ps1

#requires -version 4.0
Param(
            [Parameter(mandatory=$true,
                            Position=0,
                            HelpMessage="A number between 1 and 10")]
            [alias("fn")]
            [ValidateRange(1,10)]
            $FirstNumber,
            [Parameter(mandatory=$true,
                            Position=1,
                            HelpMessage="Not null or empty")]
            [alias("ln")]
            [int16]
            [ValidateNotNullOrEmpty()]
            $LastNumber
)

$FirstNumber*$LastNumber
```

## Working with passwords as input

In an ideal world, you would never need to supply passwords or make passwords available to a script. Scripts would run by using impersonation and would detect whether you had rights to access data. If you had the rights, you gained access; if you did not have the rights, you would not be able to connect. To some extent, this is exactly what happens when working with a script. Issues surrounding the use of passwords come up in the following scenarios:

- Accessing information from an untrusted domain
- Accessing information from legacy databases that do not use integrated security

- Accessing information from stand-alone workstations or servers that are not joined to a domain
- Allowing a user who has no rights to run a script with alternative credentials that perform actions that the user would not otherwise have permission to accomplish

There are several approaches to handling the password issue, including the following:

- Store the password in the script.
- Store the password in a text file.
- Store the password in the registry.
- Store the password in Active Directory.
- Prompt for the password.

## Store the password in the script

The simplest approach to handling the password problem is to store the password in the script. However, obvious concerns arise with storing the password in the script—the first of which is that the password is shown in the script in plain text, and anyone who has access to the script has access to the password.

Two things can be done to limit exposure to the password. One is to use NTFS File System (NTFS) permissions to protect the file from people who do not need to know the password. The other is to use Encrypting File System (EFS) to encrypt the script. Because Windows PowerShell is a .NET Framework application, it has the ability to use the security classes to use your EFS certificate to automatically decrypt the script and to run the encrypted script, which VBScript cannot do. Encrypted VBScripts will not run. In the QueryComputersUseCredentials .ps1 script, the *ADO* class is used to query a resource domain named nwtraders.com. The user that performs the query is named LondonAdmin, and the password is Password1. These values are stored in variables and are passed to the *ADO* connection object via the *password* and *user id* properties. The script then retrieves all of the computer objects from the nwtraders .com domain. The QueryComputersUseCredentials.ps1 script is shown here.

```
QueryComputersUseCredentials.ps1

$strBase = "<LDAP://dc=nwtraders,dc=msft>"
$strFilter = "(objectCategory=computer)"
$strAttributes = "name"
$strScope = "subtree"
$strQuery = "$strBase;$strFilter;$strAttributes;$strScope"
$strUser = "nwtraders\LondonAdmin"
$strPwd = "Password1"


$objConnection = New-Object -comObject "ADODB.Connection"
$objConnection.provider = "ADsDSOObject"
$objConnection.properties.item("user ID") = $strUser
$objConnection.properties.item("Password") = $strPwd
```

```
$objConnection.open("modifiedConnection")
$objCommand = New-Object -comObject "ADODB.Command"

$objCommand.ActiveConnection = $objConnection
$objCommand.CommandText = $strQuery
$objRecordSet = $objCommand.Execute()

Do
{
    $objRecordSet.Fields.item("name") |Select-Object Name,Value
    $objRecordSet.MoveNext()
}
Until ($objRecordSet.eof)

$objConnection.Close()
```

## Store the password in a text file

Perhaps one step above storing the password in the script is to store the password in a text file, which has the advantage of not being directly accessible from within the script. By placing the password in a different file, you can configure different security on the password file than the security configured on the script file itself. This might be a good solution for those who need the ability to read the script but not the ability to run the script. Another advantage of this approach is that it allows you to use the same script to work in different security contexts. One example is when a script is written by network administrators from one domain and then shared with network administrators in a different domain context. This is a common practice when a company is composed of multiple business units, each of which has its own separate infrastructure.

```
QueryComputersUseCredentialsFromText.ps1

$strBase = "<LDAP://dc=nwtraders,dc=msft>"
$strFilter = "(objectCategory=computer)"
$strAttributes = "name"
$strScope = "subtree"
$strQuery = "$strBase;$strFilter;$strAttributes;$strScope"
$strUser = "nwtraders\LondonAdmin"
$strPwd = Get-Content -path "C:\fso\password.txt"

$objConnection = New-Object -comObject "ADODB.Connection"
$objConnection.provider = "ADsDSOObject"
$objConnection.properties.item("user ID") = $strUser
$objConnection.properties.item("Password") = $strPwd
$objConnection.open("modifiedConnection")
```

```
$objCommand = New-Object -comObject "ADODB.Command"

$objCommand.ActiveConnection = $objConnection
$objCommand.CommandText = $strQuery
$objRecordSet = $objCommand.Execute()

Do
{
    $objRecordSet.Fields.item("name") |Select-Object Name,Value
    $objRecordSet.MoveNext()
}
Until ($objRecordSet.eof)

$objConnection.Close()
```

## Store the password in the registry

With the ease of registry access inherent in Windows PowerShell, storing a password in the registry might make sense in some cases. Because you can set security on a registry key, you might want to store a password in the registry. The registry key can be created in a separate process. When the script is run, it accesses the registry for the password that is required for remote access.

```
QueryComputersUseCredentialsFromRegistry.ps1

$strBase = "<LDAP://dc=nwtraders,dc=msft>"
$strFilter = "(objectCategory=computer)"
$strAttributes = "name"
$strScope = "subtree"
$strQuery = "$strBase;$strFilter;$strAttributes;$strScope"
$strUser = "nwtraders\administrator"
$strPwd = (Get-ItemProperty HKCU:\Software\ForScripting\CompatPassword).password

$objConnection = New-Object -comObject "ADODB.Connection"
$objConnection.provider = "ADsDSOObject"
$objConnection.properties.item("user ID") = $strUser
$objConnection.properties.item("Password") = $strPwd
$objConnection.open("modifiedConnection")
$objCommand = New-Object -comObject "ADODB.Command"

$objCommand.ActiveConnection = $objConnection
$objCommand.CommandText = $strQuery
$objRecordSet = $objCommand.Execute()
```

```
Do
{
    $objRecordSet.Fields.item("name") |Select-Object Name,Value
    $objRecordSet.MoveNext()
}
Until ($objRecordSet.eof)

$objConnection.Close()
```

## Store the password in Active Directory Domain Services

It is relatively easy to extend the schema to create an attribute within which you can store a password that is used for certain scripts. This option provides a central location that is accessible from anywhere within the domain.

**NOTE** If you are uncomfortable with adding an attribute to the Active Directory schema, you can use one of the configurable attributes instead of creating your own attributes. In any case, you should ensure that you use a valid object identifier (OID) number and test your changes in a test environment before deploying the changes to your live production network.

```
QueryComputersUseCredentialsFromADDS.ps1

$strBase = "<LDAP://dc=nwtraders,dc=msft>"
$strFilter = "(objectCategory=computer)"
$strAttributes = "name"
$strScope = "subtree"
$strQuery = "$strBase;$strFilter;$strAttributes;$strScope"
$strUser = "nwtraders\testUser"
$strPwd = ([adsi]"LDAP://cn=testUser,ou=myusers,dc=nwtraders,dc=com").compatPassword

$objConnection = New-Object -comObject "ADODB.Connection"
$objConnection.provider = "ADsDSOObject"
$objConnection.properties.item("user ID") = $strUser
$objConnection.properties.item("Password") = $strPwd
$objConnection.open("modifiedConnection")
$objCommand = New-Object -comObject "ADODB.Command"

$objCommand.ActiveConnection = $objConnection
$objCommand.CommandText = $strQuery
$objRecordSet = $objCommand.Execute()
```

```
Do
{
    $objRecordSet.Fields.item("name") |Select-Object Name,Value
    $objRecordSet.MoveNext()
}
Until ($objRecordSet.eof)

$objConnection.Close()
```

## Prompt for the password

The best approach is to have the script prompt you when it needs a password. There are a number of advantages to this method. The biggest advantage is that it removes your concern about storage of the password because it is not stored in the script, a file, the registry, or another location. The next advantage of having the script prompt for the password is that it reduces maintenance requirements. If a password changes on a regular basis and is stored in a text file, the file contents must be updated each time the password changes. Using a prompt makes troubleshooting the script easier. When a script must access a password from a remote location, connectivity issues and remote permissions must be considered if a script fails to execute properly. Of course, if the script contains robust error checking, the script is easier to troubleshoot; however, this introduces an additional level of complexity that can potentially increase the maintenance cost of the script. The easiest way to prompt for a password is to use the Read-Host cmdlet.

```
QueryComputersPromptForPassword.ps1

$strBase = "<LDAP://dc=nwtraders,dc=com>"
$strFilter = "(objectCategory=computer)"
$strAttributes = "name"
$strScope = "subtree"
$strQuery = "$strBase;$strFilter;$strAttributes;$strScope"
$strUser = "nwtraders\administrator"
$strPwd = Read-Host -prompt "Enter password to Connect to AD"

$objConnection = New-Object -comObject "ADODB.Connection"
$objConnection.provider = "ADsDSOObject"
$objConnection.properties.item("user ID") = $strUser
$objConnection.properties.item("Password") = $strPwd
$objConnection.open("modifiedConnection")
$objCommand = New-Object -comObject "ADODB.Command"

$objCommand.ActiveConnection = $objConnection
$objCommand.CommandText = $strQuery
$objRecordSet = $objCommand.Execute()
```

```
Do
{
    $objRecordSet.Fields.item("name") |Select-Object Name,Value
    $objRecordSet.MoveNext()
}
Until ($objRecordSet.eof)

$objConnection.Close()
```

If the cmdlet supports a *PSCredential* object, you can use the *AsSecureString* parameter from the Read-Host cmdlet. A secure string is used for text that should be kept confidential. The text is encrypted for privacy when it is used and is deleted from computer memory when it is no longer needed. The password is never revealed as plain text. The *System.Security* .*SecureString* .NET Framework class is invisible to the Component Object Model (COM) and therefore cannot be used with classic COM interfaces.

**ReadHostSecureStringQueryWmi.ps1**

```
$user = "Nwtraders\administrator"
$password = Read-Host -prompt "Enter your password" -asSecureString
$credential = new-object system.management.automation.PSCredential $user,$password
Get-WmiObject -class Win32_Bios -computername berlin -credential $credential
```

When working with a secure string, it is also possible to store the hash of the password in a text file. The advantage of this technique is that it allows you to use the password with the *PSCredential* object, but it gives you the flexibility of not having to manually enter the password each time the script is run. In addition, it allows you to give the script to another user who does not know the password for the account.

To do this, you use the Read-Host cmdlet and specify the *AsSecureString* parameter. In the following example, the encrypted password is stored in a *$pwd* variable:

```
PS C:\> $pwd = Read-Host -Prompt "Enter your password" -AsSecureString
Enter your password: *********
```

If you use the *ToString* method from the *SecureString* object, the only thing that is relayed back to the Windows PowerShell console is an instance of a *System.Security.SecureString* class as shown here. If you attempt to store the output from the *ToString* method in a text file, the only words that the text file will contain are "System.Security.SecureString."

```
PS C:\> $PWD.ToString()
System.Security.SecureString
```

To be able to store the secure string in a text file, you need to use the ConvertFrom-SecureString cmdlet. As illustrated here, ConvertFrom-SecureString reveals the hash of the password:

```
PS C:\> $PWD | ConvertFrom-SecureString
01000000d08c9ddf0115d1118c7a00c04fc297eb01000000151046ea8f869541a129ff10c91b850
e0000000002000000000003660000a800000010000000aa2caba61452ffd5f973901a5dbd0e8100
00000004800000a0000000100000003172c749434dfac3262616d15dea4d1018000000916d60d59
0d381bff1225663c6b4dcab536fca5920077cb414000000e92d30f80b9fbf337c1a8e5d99f50f11
8fae2d3b
```

You can write this password hash to a text file by using a pair of redirection arrows.

```
PS C:\> $PWD | ConvertFrom-SecureString >> C:\fso\passwordHash.txt
```

The passwordHash.txt file now contains the exact information that was previously displayed on the screen. This is no longer a *System.Security.SecureString* class but is instead a string that represents the hash of a *SecureString* class. To convert the hash back to a secure string, you need to use the ConvertTo-SecureString cmdlet.

```
PS C:\> ConvertTo-SecureString (Get-Content C:\fso\passwordHash.txt)
System.Security.SecureString
```

> **NOTE** Keep in mind that you want to convert the contents of the passwordHash.
> txt file to a secure string and not the path to the passwordHash.txt file. The first time I
> attempted this operation, I used the following command: ConvertTo-SecureString C:\fso
> \passwordHash.txt, which does not work. I then realized that I was trying to encrypt the
> path to the file and not the contents of the file.

A more efficient way to create the password hash text file is to use pipelining and thus avoid the intermediate variable as shown here. When the command is run, it prompts for the password.

```
PS C:\> Read-Host -Prompt "Enter your password" -AsSecureString |
>> ConvertFrom-SecureString >> C:\fso\passwordHash.txt
```

To use this password hash text file in a script, you can use a script like the one shown here.

```
UsePasswordHashFile.ps1

$user = "Nwtraders\administrator"
$password = ConvertTo-SecureString -String (Get-content C:\fso\passwordHash.txt)
$credential = new-object system.management.automation.PSCredential $user,$password
Get-WmiObject -class Win32_Bios -computername berlin -credential $credential
```

## Importing and exporting credentials

Lee Holmes, Senior Software Developer Engineer and author of *Windows PowerShell Cookbook*
*Microsoft Corporation*

One question that comes up fairly often when dealing with Windows PowerShell scripts is how to properly handle user names and passwords. The solution is to use the `Get-Credential` cmdlet to create a *PSCredential* object. A *PSCredential* object ensures that your password stays protected in memory, unlike cmdlets that accept a straight user name/password combination.

If a parameter accepts a *PSCredential* object, Windows PowerShell supports several types of input, such as the following:

- **Empty** If you supply no input to a mandatory *–credential* parameter, Windows PowerShell prompts you for the user name and password.

- **String** If you supply a string to the *–credential* parameter, Windows PowerShell treats it as a user name and prompts you for the password.

- **Credential** If you supply a credential object to the *–credential* parameter, Windows PowerShell accepts it as is.

This is great for interactive use, but what if you want to write an automated script for a cmdlet that accepts a *–credential* parameter? The solution lies in passing a preconstructed *PSCredential* object. This solution is covered by recipe 18.12 in the *Windows PowerShell Cookbook*, which is excerpted here.

The first step for storing a password on disk is usually a manual one. Given a credential that you have stored in the *$credential* variable, you can safely export its password to password.txt using the following commands.

- In Windows PowerShell version 4, use the `Export-CliXml` and `Import-CliXml` cmdlets to import and export credentials.

- In Windows PowerShell version 2, use the `ConvertFrom-SecureString` and `ConvertTo-SecureString` cmdlets.

The first step for storing a password on disk is usually a manual one. There is nothing mandatory about the file name, but we'll use a convention to name the file CurrentScript.ps1.credential. Given a credential that you've stored in the *$credential* variable, you can safely use the `Export-CliXml` cmdlet to save the credential to disk. Replace CurrentScript with the name of the script that will be loading it:

```
PS > $credPath = Join-Path (Split-Path $profile) CurrentScript.ps1
.credential
```

```
PS > $credential | Export-CliXml $credPath
```

In Windows PowerShell version 2, you must use the ConvertFrom-SecureString cmdlet:

```
PS > $credPath = Join-Path (Split-Path $profile) CurrentScript.ps1
.credential
```

```
PS > $credential.Password | ConvertFrom-SecureString | Set-Content
$credPath
```

In the script that you want to run automatically, add the following commands for Windows PowerShell version 4:

```
$credPath = Join-Path (Split-Path $profile) CurrentScript.ps1.credential
```

```
$credential = Import-CliXml $credPath
```

In Windows PowerShell version 2, you must manually create a *PSCredential* object, using the password imported by the ConvertTo-SecureString cmdlet. Whereas the Export-CliXml cmdlet keeps track of the credential user name automatically, this alternate approach needs to keep track of it by hand:

```
$credPath = Join-Path (Split-Path $profile) CurrentScript.ps1.credential
```

```
$password = Get-Content $credPath | ConvertTo-SecureString
```

```
$credential = New-Object System.Management.Automation.PsCredential `

    "CachedUser",$password
```

These commands create a new credential object (for the *CachedUser* user) and store that object in the *$credential* variable.

When reading the Solution, you might at first be wary of storing a password on disk. While it is natural (and prudent) to be cautious of littering your hard drive with sensitive information, the Export-CliXml cmdlet encrypts credential objects by using the Windows standard Data Protection API. This ensures that only your user account can properly decrypt its contents. Similarly, the ConvertFrom-SecureString cmdlet also encrypts the password that you provide.

While keeping a password secure is an important security feature, you might sometimes want to store a password (or other sensitive information) on disk so that other accounts have access to it. This is often the case with scripts run by service accounts or scripts designed to be transferred between computers. The ConvertFrom-SecureString and ConvertTo-SecureString cmdlets support this by letting you specify an encryption key.

> When used with a hard-coded encryption key, this technique no longer acts as a security measure. If a user can access the content of your automated script, that user has access to the encryption key. If the user has access to the encryption key, the user has access to the data you were trying to protect.
>
> Although the Solution stores the password in the directory that contains your profile, you could also load it from the same location as your script.

## Working with connection strings as input

When working with different types of data sources, such as a Microsoft Office Access database or a password-protected Microsoft Office Word document or Office Excel spreadsheet, you are often required to supply a means to pass the credentials to the resource because these types of data sources cannot use impersonation. The methods for passing the password have already been explored and can easily be adapted to these types of data sources. Because access to these data sources are COM-based, you cannot use the .NET Framework *System.Security.SecureString* class to pass credentials. This also means that you cannot use the Get-Credential cmdlet due to its reliance on the *SecureString* class to encrypt the password.

As a best practice when working with connection strings to data sources, you should use variables to hold each portion of the connection string. This makes it easier to update the various components of the connection string, as well as adding additional flexibility to change the input methodology without a major rewrite of the script. An example is shown here.

```
OpenPasswordProtectedExcel.ps1

$filename = "C:\fso\TestNumbersProtected.xls"
$updatelinks = 3
$readonly = $false
$format = 5
$password = "password"
$excel = New-Object -comobject Excel.Application
$excel.visible = $true
$excel.workbooks.open($fileName,$updatelinks,$readonly,$format,$password) |
Out-Null
```

When the *password* parameter is available via a parameter, it is trivial to revise the script to accept the input via the command line. In the OpenPasswordProtectedWord.ps1 script, both the file name and the password are moved to command-line parameters. The logic used to open the password-protected Office Word document is moved into a function, and both command-line values are marked as mandatory. The use of the *Parameter* tag is a feature that requires at least Windows PowerShell 2.0, and the *#requires –version 2.0* statement is used.

```
OpenPasswordProtectedWord.ps1

#requires -version 2.0
Param(
  [Parameter(Mandatory=$true)]
  [string]$fileName,
  [Parameter(Mandatory=$true)]
  [string]$password
)
Function Open-PasswordProtectedDocument($filename,$password)
{
 $Conversion= $false
 $readOnly = $false
 $addRecentFiles = $false
 $doc = New-Object -Comobject Word.Application
 $doc.visible = $true
 $doc.documents.open($filename,$Conversion,$readOnly,$addRecentFiles,$password) |
 out-null
} #end function Open-PasswordProtectedDocument

# *** Entry Point to Script ***

Open-PasswordProtectedDocument -filename $filename -password $password
```

# Prompting for input

From the preceding discussion, you might surmise that if you can use the Read-Host cmdlet to prompt for a password, you can also use the Read-Host cmdlet prior to performing a specific action—and you would be correct. Two primary cases require input from the user. The first case requires the user to supply information to allow the script to complete. This technique is often used when the script can perform multiple actions. The input received from the user determines the way the script will run.

The second case that requires input from the user is more basic. It is a prompt for approval to continue. You might want to use this technique prior to deleting a file or performing an action that might tie up the resources of the computer for a significant period of time. Both of these scenarios are discussed here.

Scripts often require information from the user to customize the information that is returned to the user. In the ReadHostQueryDrive.ps1 script, the Read-Host cmdlet is used to prompt the user to enter the drive letter that will be used to request volume information from WMI. The *Switch* statement is used to evaluate the value that is typed in response to the prompt. The ReadHostQueryDrive.ps1 script is shown here.

```
ReadHostQueryDrive.ps1

$response = Read-Host "Type drive letter to query <c: / d:>"

Switch -regex($response) {
  "C" { Get-WmiObject -class Win32_Volume -filter "driveletter = 'c:'" }
  "D" { Get-WmiObject -class Win32_Volume -filter "driveletter = 'd:'" }
} #end switch
```

A more elegant approach to requesting information from the user is to use the *$host*
*.ui.PromptForChoice* class to handle the prompting. The *PromptForChoice* class uses the
choices created by the *System.Management.Automation.Host.ChoiceDescription* class. When
creating the choice descriptions, each choice is preceded by the ampersand and stored in an
array. Because it is an array, each value has a numeric value that begins counting with 0, as
shown in the PromptForChoice.ps1 script.

```
PromptForChoice.ps1

$caption = "No Disk"
$message = "There is no disk in the drive. Please insert a disk into drive D:"
$choices = [System.Management.Automation.Host.ChoiceDescription[]] `
@("&Cancel", "&Try Again", "&Ignore")
[int]$defaultChoice = 2
$choiceRTN = $host.ui.PromptForChoice($caption,$message, $choices,$defaultChoice)

switch($choiceRTN)
{
  0     { "cancelling ..." }
  1     { "Try Again ..." }
  2     { "ignoring ..." }
}
```

# Choosing the best output method

There are at least as many output methods available to the scriptwriter in Windows
PowerShell 4.0 as there are input methods. If all of the output methods were added up, the
list would probably be much greater than the number of input methods. In this section, you
will look at outputting to the screen, to a file, and to email.

Shane Hoey
*Microsoft PowerShell MVP*

I t's been a few years since I first started to learn Windows PowerShell, and for me, the benefit of using PowerShell is that I get a deeper understanding of the product I'm working with.

Today I specialize in Microsoft Lync, and the Windows PowerShell skills I learned in the early days still have as much value now as they did back then. The only difference is that many of these skills have now become habits.

One of my all-time favorite tricks with Windows PowerShell is also one of the easiest things to do. As an Integrator, I can be at different customer sites every few weeks, and remembering how I have configured their Lync dial plans, for example, can be a challenge after a few months. By using Export-Clixml, I can run a few Windows PowerShell commands and quickly export the entire configuration of a Lync server to an XML file.

Let's look at this a bit closer. Except for these examples, rather than use Lync, we are going to use the Get-Service cmdlet instead. First, we pipe the output object of the Get-Service cmdlet to the Export-Clixml cmdlet, which will store the object(s) in an XML file.

```
Get-Service | Export-Clixml -Path c:\scripts\services.xml
```

After I've exported all the objects to XML, I can then use Import-Clixml at a later date. This is really handy for comparisons and documentation purposes. However, the problem is that customers are not as excited as I am to have XML files. So I decided to create a few Windows PowerShell scripts to help me with the documentation process.

I've been writing and improving a script that saves the current state of a Lync environment and then creates a Word document for me. The cool thing about the script is that because I export the object(s) using Export-Clixml, I can update the documentation at any time, and I can compare changes in the configuration over time by comparing the xml files.

Now the fun bit—first we create a new Word document. We need to do this only once, because we will reuse it every time we run the script. Here are the steps:

1.  Create a new Word document.

2.  Create a heading called "My Services."

3.  Create a paragraph with some descriptive text.

4. Create a "Rich Text Content Control," and after you create the control, make sure that you edit the properties and make the title of the control "RichTextContent1." If you cannot find Rich Text Content Controls, you will need to make sure that the Developer toolbar is visible in Word.

5. Save the document as *c:\Scripts\PoshDoc.docx*.

Now it's time to create a PDF document, so let's use the XML file we exported earlier to generate the content in the document:

```
$service = import-clixml -path .\services.xml

$word = new-object -ComObject Word.Application

$worddoc = $Word.Documents.Add("C:\Scripts\PoshDoc.docx")

$word.Visible = $true

($worddoc.Content.ContentControls | where title –eq "RichTextContent1").
range.text =  foreach ($item in ($service | where {$_.status -match
"running"})){$item.DisplayName + "`r"}

$wdFormatPDF = [Ref]17

$worddoc.SaveAs([ref]"C:\Scripts\PoshDoc.pdf",$wdFormatPDF)
```

Now we have created a PDF document; it's as simple as that. Sure, it needs more formatting and a few more content controls, but those lines of script will hopefully give you a few ideas for using Windows PowerShell and Word to write some future documentation.

## Output to the screen

When a cmdlet is used, it automatically outputs to the screen. This is one of the features that makes Windows PowerShell easy to work with from the PowerShell prompt. When you use the Get-Process cmdlet, it automatically displays output to the screen.

In many cases, you do not have to do anything more complicated than run the cmdlet. When you do, you are automatically rewarded with a nicely formatted output that is displayed to the screen as shown in Figure 11-3.

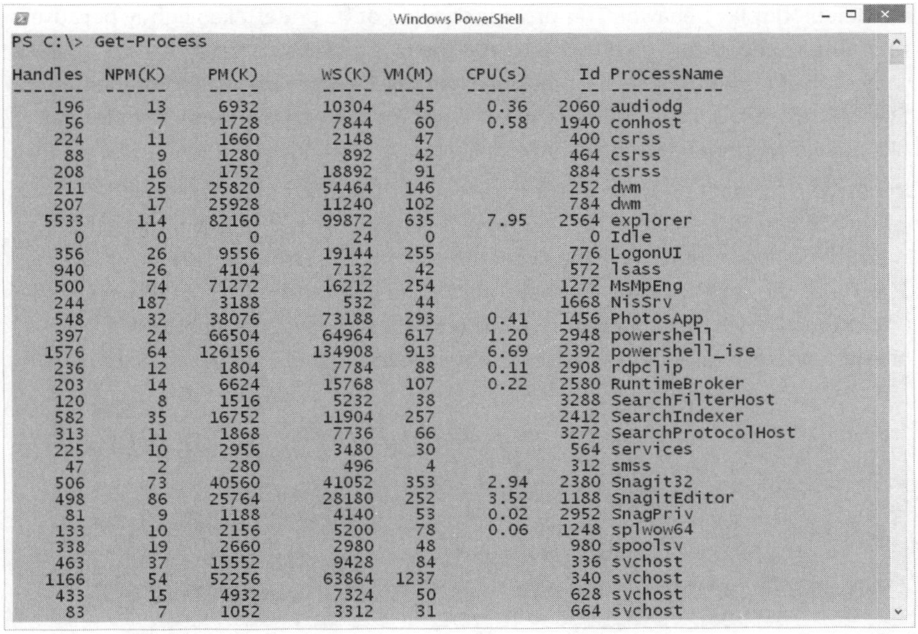

```
Windows PowerShell
PS C:\> Get-Process

Handles  NPM(K)    PM(K)      WS(K) VM(M)   CPU(s)     Id ProcessName
-------  ------    -----      ----- -----   ------     -- -----------
    196      13     6932      10304    45     0.36   2060 audiodg
     56       7     1728       7844    60     0.58   1940 conhost
    224      11     1660       2148    47             400 csrss
     88       9     1280        892    42             464 csrss
    208      16     1752      18892    91             884 csrss
    211      25    25820      54464   146             252 dwm
    207      17    25928      11240   102             784 dwm
   5533     114    82160      99872   635     7.95   2564 explorer
      0       0        0         24     0               0 Idle
    356      26     9556      19144   255             776 LogonUI
    940      26     4104       7132    42             572 lsass
    500      74    71272      16212   254            1272 MsMpEng
    244     187     3188        532    44            1668 NisSrv
    548      32    38076      73188   293     0.41   1456 PhotosApp
    397      24    66504      64964   617     1.20   2948 powershell
   1576      64   126156     134908   913     6.69   2392 powershell_ise
    236      12     1804       7784    88     0.11   2908 rdpclip
    203      14     6624      15768   107     0.22   2580 RuntimeBroker
    120       8     1516       5232    38            3288 SearchFilterHost
    582      35    16752      11904   257            2412 SearchIndexer
    313      11     1868       7736    66            3272 SearchProtocolHost
    225      10     2956       3480    30             564 services
     47       2      280        496     4             312 smss
    506      73    40560      41052   353     2.94   2380 Snagit32
    498      86    25764      28180   252     3.52   1188 SnagitEditor
     81       9     1188       4140    53     0.02   2952 SnagPriv
    133      10     2156       5200    78     0.06   1248 splwow64
    338      19     2660       2980    48             980 spoolsv
    463      37    15552       9428    84             336 svchost
   1166      54    52256      63864  1237             340 svchost
    433      15     4932       7324    50             628 svchost
     83       7     1052       3312    31             664 svchost
```

**FIGURE 11-3** Output from the `Get-Process` cmdlet is automatically displayed to the Windows PowerShell console.

The reason the output is nicely formatted is that the Windows PowerShell team created several format.ps1xml files that are used to control the way in which different objects are formatted when they are displayed. These XML files are located in the Windows PowerShell install directory. Luckily, there is an automatic variable, *$pshome*, that can be used to refer to the Windows PowerShell install directory. To obtain a listing of all of the format.ps1xml files that are installed on your computer, you use the `Get-ChildItem` cmdlet and specify a path that will retrieve any file with the name format in it. Pipeline the resulting *FileInfo* objects to the `Select-Object` cmdlet, and choose the *name* property.

```
PS C:\> Get-ChildItem -Path $pshome/*format* | Select-Object -Property name

Name
----
certificate.format.ps1xml
dotnettypes.format.ps1xml
filesystem.format.ps1xml
help.format.ps1xml
powershellcore.format.ps1xml
powershelltrace.format.ps1xml
registry.format.ps1xml
```

These format.ps1xml files are used by the Windows PowerShell Extended Type System to determine how to display objects. This system is required because most objects do not know how to display themselves. Because the format files are XML files, it is possible to edit them to change the default display behavior. This process should not be undertaken lightly because the files are rather complicated. If you want to edit the files, make sure that you have a good backup copy of the files before you start making changes. Direct manipulation of the format .ps1xml files can result in unexpected behavior. It is also possible to write your own format .ps1xml file, but such a project can be very complicated.

The dotnettypes.format.ps1xml file is used to control the output that is displayed by a number of the cmdlets (for example, Get-Process, Get-Service, Get-EventLog) that return .NET Framework objects. A portion of the dotnettypes.format.ps1xml file is shown in Figure 11-4. This is the section of the file that controls the output from the Get-Process cmdlet. Under the *<TableHeaders>* section, each column heading is specified by the <TableColumnHeader> tag. Under the <TableColumnHeader>, there are additional nodes.

```
PS C:\> Get-Content C:\Windows\System32\WindowsPowerShell\v1.0\DotNetTypes.format.ps1
xml
<?xml version="1.0" encoding="utf-8" ?>
<!-- *********************************************************************
These sample files contain formatting information used by the Windows
PowerShell engine. Do not edit or change the contents of this file
directly. Please see the Windows PowerShell documentation or type
Get-Help Update-FormatData for more information.

Copyright (c) Microsoft Corporation.  All rights reserved.

THIS SAMPLE CODE AND INFORMATION IS PROVIDED "AS IS" WITHOUT WARRANTY
OF ANY KIND,WHETHER EXPRESSED OR IMPLIED, INCLUDING BUT NOT LIMITED TO
THE IMPLIED WARRANTIES OF MERCHANTABILITY AND/OR FITNESS FOR A PARTICULAR
PURPOSE. IF THIS CODE AND INFORMATION IS MODIFIED, THE ENTIRE RISK OF USE
OR RESULTS IN CONNECTION WITH THE USE OF THIS CODE AND INFORMATION
REMAINS WITH THE USER.
********************************************************************* -->

<Configuration>
    <ViewDefinitions>
        <View>
            <Name>System.CodeDom.Compiler.CompilerError</Name>
            <ViewSelectedBy>
                <TypeName>System.CodeDom.Compiler.CompilerError</TypeName>
            </ViewSelectedBy>
            <ListControl>
                <ListEntries>
                    <ListEntry>
                        <ListItems>
                            <ListItem>
                                <PropertyName>ErrorText</PropertyName>
                            </ListItem>
                            <ListItem>
                                <PropertyName>Line</PropertyName>
                            </ListItem>
```

**FIGURE 11-4** The dotnettypes.format.ps1xml file controls the display of cmdlet data.

To display information to the console, you do not need to worry about formatting XML files. You can rely on the defaults and allow Windows PowerShell to make the decision for you. To display a string, you place the string in quotation marks to display it to the console, as shown here:

```
PS C:\> "this string is displayed to the console"
this string is displayed to the console
PS C:\>
```

The important thing to keep in mind is that when the string is emitted to the console it retains its type—that is, it is still a string.

```
PS C:\> "this string is displayed to the console" | Get-Member
   TypeName: System.String

Name                MemberType            Definition
----                ----------            ----------
Clone               Method                System.Object Clone()
CompareTo           Method                int CompareTo(System.Object value), i...
Contains            Method                bool Contains(string value)
CopyTo              Method                System.Void CopyTo(int sourceIndex, c...
EndsWith            Method                bool EndsWith(string value), bool End...
Equals              Method                bool Equals(System.Object obj), bool ...
GetEnumerator       Method                System.CharEnumerator GetEnumerator()
GetHashCode         Method                int GetHashCode()
GetType             Method                type GetType()
GetTypeCode         Method                System.TypeCode GetTypeCode()
IndexOf             Method                int IndexOf(char value), int IndexOf(...
IndexOfAny          Method                int IndexOfAny(char[] anyOf), int Ind...
Insert              Method                string Insert(int startIndex, string ...
IsNormalized        Method                bool IsNormalized(), bool IsNormalize...
LastIndexOf         Method                int LastIndexOf(char value), int Last...
LastIndexOfAny      Method                int LastIndexOfAny(char[] anyOf), int...
Normalize           Method                string Normalize(), string Normalize(...
PadLeft             Method                string PadLeft(int totalWidth), strin...
PadRight            Method                string PadRight(int totalWidth), stri...
Remove              Method                string Remove(int startIndex, int cou...
Replace             Method                string Replace(char oldChar, char new...
Split               Method                string[] Split(Params char[] separato...
StartsWith          Method                bool StartsWith(string value), bool S...
Substring           Method                string Substring(int startIndex), str...
ToCharArray         Method                char[] ToCharArray(), char[] ToCharAr...
ToLower             Method                string ToLower(), string ToLower(Syst...
ToLowerInvariant    Method                string ToLowerInvariant()
ToString            Method                string ToString(), string ToString(Sy...
ToUpper             Method                string ToUpper(), string ToUpper(Syst...
ToUpperInvariant    Method                string ToUpperInvariant()
Trim                Method                string Trim(Params char[] trimChars),...
TrimEnd             Method                string TrimEnd(Params char[] trimChars)
TrimStart           Method                string TrimStart(Params char[] trimCh...
Chars               ParameterizedProperty char Chars(int index) {get;}
Length              Property              System.Int32 Length {get;}
```

If you use one of the out-* cmdlets, such as Out-Host or Out-Default, you destroy the object-oriented nature of the string. That is, the output is no longer an instance of a *System .String* .NET Framework class.

```
PS C:\> "this string is displayed to the console" | Out-Host | Get-Member
this string is displayed to the console
Get-Member : No object has been specified to the get-member cmdlet.
At line:1 char:66
+ "this string is displayed to the console" | Out-Host | Get-Member <<<<
    + CategoryInfo          : CloseError: (:) [Get-Member], InvalidOperationException
    + FullyQualifiedErrorId : NoObjectInGetMember,Microsoft.PowerShell.Commands
    .GetMemberCommand

PS C:\>
```

As a best practice, you should avoid using the Out-Host or Out-Default cmdlet unless there is a reason to use it, because you lose your object after you send the output to the Out-* cmdlet. The only reason for using Out-Host is to use the *–paging* parameter.

```
PS C:\> Get-WmiObject -Class Win32_process | Out-Host –Paging
```

```
__GENUS                     : 2
__CLASS                     : Win32_Process
__SUPERCLASS                : CIM_Process
__DYNASTY                   : CIM_ManagedSystemElement
__RELPATH                   : Win32_Process.Handle="0"
__PROPERTY_COUNT            : 45
__DERIVATION                : {CIM_Process, CIM_LogicalElement, CIM_ManagedSystemElement}
__SERVER                    : VISTA
__NAMESPACE                 : root\cimv2
__PATH                      : \\VISTA\root\cimv2:Win32_Process.Handle="0"
Caption                     : System Idle Process
CommandLine                 :
CreationClassName           : Win32_Process
CreationDate                :
CSCreationClassName         : Win32_ComputerSystem
CSName                      : VISTA
Description                 : System Idle Process
ExecutablePath              :
ExecutionState              :
Handle                      : 0
HandleCount                 : 0
InstallDate                 :
KernelModeTime              : 151488730096
MaximumWorkingSetSize       :
MinimumWorkingSetSize       :
Name                        : System Idle Process
OSCreationClassName         : Win32_OperatingSystem
OSName                      : Microsoftr Windows VistaT Business |C:\Windows|\Device
                              \Harddisk0\Partition1
OtherOperationCount         : 0
OtherTransferCount          : 0
PageFaults                  : 0
PageFileUsage               : 0
ParentProcessId             : 0
PeakPageFileUsage           : 0
PeakVirtualSize             : 0
PeakWorkingSetSize          : 0
Priority                    : 0
PrivatePageCount            : 0
<SPACE> next page; <CR> next line; Q quit
```

If you are not using the *–paging* parameter, there is no advantage to using the Out-Host cmdlet. From a display perspective, the following commands are identical:

```
Get-Process
Get-Process | Out-Host
Get-Process | Out-Default
```

In fact, Out-Default and Out-Host do the same thing on most systems because, by default, the Out-Host cmdlet is the default outputter. The only reason to use the Out-Default cmdlet is if you anticipate changing the default outputter and do not want to rewrite the script. By using Out-Default, the output from the script will always go to the default outputter, which might or might not be the host.

---

### NOTES FROM THE FIELD

**Mark Minasi**
*Microsoft Directory Services MVP*

Twenty-one years ago, Microsoft released its first TCP/IP stack. Code-named "Wolverine," it was a beta implementation that ran on Windows for Workgroups 3.11. After it was installed, I found that it included an amazingly useful, concise command-line tool named "ipconfig," and nary a week goes by that I don't make use of that now-old acquaintance.

Hmmm...perhaps that last sentence overstates the warmth of our relationship in the past half-decade or so. Like some of my old friends, ipconfig has *changed* over the years and, sadly, not always for the better. It's gotten a bit thicker around the waist and, to be honest, just a mite dotty. Its youthful conciseness has been diluted a bit, because I do not know and do not care what a DHCP DUID or a DHCP IAID is. And all of those tunnel adapters? Don't get me started. I still remember the first time I typed "ipconfig /all" on a beta Windows Vista-based machine in 2006. As I watched in horror, my old friend ipconfig produced so much output that it—please, make sure that there are no young children in the room before reading this sentence—*scrolled off the screen*. In that moment, there was a great disturbance in the Force, as if millions of IT pros simultaneously cried out in pain.

For years, I've jokingly suggested that Microsoft provide a "/noEXTRAS" parameter on ipconfig, but my entreaties have apparently fallen on deaf ears. For the last few years, I've kept telling myself that sometime soon I'll dust off my C++ skills, crack the books on Win32's network-related APIs, and create a new ipconfig, but I never seemed to find the time.

Then came Windows 8 and its thousand-plus new Windows PowerShell cmdlets, a few dozen of which relate to IP networking status and configuration. So, on a crisp autumn Saturday in 2012, I set out exploring the new net-related cmdlets and the wealth of information that they provided. Like Scrooge McDuck capering in a vault filled with his cash, I cackled as one cmdlet after another yielded more and more information.

However, my giddy intoxication from this embarrassment of networking riches was soon tempered, as my troubled old friend ipconfig came to mind. In that moment,

I heard a voice behind me say, "We have the technology. We can rebuild him... better." Of course, it just was my housemate watching a rerun of the *Six Million Dollar Man*, but it inspired me to spend a few hours first figuring out which cmdlets provided the various bits and pieces of useful network data that ipconfig delivers, and then I looked up how to build a cmdlet. The result was Get-Ipinfo. (You can find it at *http://www.minasi.com/newsletters/nws1210.htm*.) While it might not be the most beautiful, well-written cmdlet in the world, hey, it works, and it took me hours, not months, to build.

As Robert Kennedy might have said if he were a Windows PowerShell techie, "There are those who look at the limitations of some Windows administration tools and ask, 'why?' I dream of better tools built quickly and easily and ask, 'why not?'"

And so should *you*. Learn Windows PowerShell, and reap the harvest!

## Output to file

If you want to display information to the screen, you run the command. By default, the command will emit the information to the console, as shown here:

```
PS C:\> Get-WmiObject -Class Win32_Bios

SMBIOSBIOSVersion : A01
Manufacturer      : Dell Computer Corporation
Name              : Default System BIOS
SerialNumber      : 9HQ1S21
Version           : DELL   - 6

PS C:\>
```

If you want to store the information in a text file, you can use the redirection arrow.

```
PS C:\> Get-WmiObject -Class Win32_Bios >c:\fso\bios.txt
PS C:\>
```

The problem is that there is no confirmation message stating that the command completed successfully, nor is there any idea of what is contained in the text file. Although you can use the Out-File cmdlet, as shown here, there is no feedback from the command:

```
PS C:\> Get-WmiObject -Class Win32_Bios | Out-File -FilePath C:\fso\bios.txt
PS C:\>
```

You can use the Get-Content cmdlet to inspect the contents of the file to ensure that it has the information you require. The thing to keep in mind is that you are not piping the information from the Out-File cmdlet to the Get-Content cmdlet. The semicolon is used to indicate that you are beginning a new command. The semicolon is the equivalent of typing the command on a new line in a script.

```
PS C:\> Get-WmiObject -Class Win32_Bios | Out-File -FilePath C:\fso\bios.txt ;
Get-Content -Path C:\fso\bios.txt

SMBIOSBIOSVersion : A01
Manufacturer      : Dell Computer Corporation
Name              : Default System BIOS
SerialNumber      : 9HQ1S21
Version           : DELL   - 6
```

Because you have already seen that using the redirection arrow is the same as using the Out-File cmdlet, for your purposes here, you can revise the command to use the redirection arrows. You can also shorten the command a bit by using the alias *cat* instead of the lengthier Get-Content cmdlet name.

```
PS C:\> Get-WmiObject -Class Win32_Bios > C:\fso\bios.txt ; cat C:\fso\bios.txt

SMBIOSBIOSVersion : A01
Manufacturer      : Dell Computer Corporation
Name              : Default System BIOS
SerialNumber      : 9HQ1S21
Version           : DELL   - 6
```

By using an alias for the Get-WmiObject cmdlet and omitting the –*class* parameter name, you can shorten the command quite a bit.

```
PS C:\> gwmi Win32_Bios > C:\fso\bios.txt ; cat C:\fso\bios.txt

SMBIOSBIOSVersion : A01
Manufacturer      : Dell Computer Corporation
Name              : Default System BIOS
SerialNumber      : 9HQ1S21
Version           : DELL   - 6
```

## Splitting the output to both the screen and the file

Now you have a shorter command that you can use to feed the content from the command to a text file for storage and then display the information on the console. While this is a workable solution, it is easier to use a cmdlet if it can essentially do the same thing. As it turns out, there is a cmdlet that will split the output from a cmdlet and direct it to both the screen and to a file, and this cmdlet is named Tee-Object. Most of the time, you will split the output from your command line to a file and to the console. To do this, you can use the –*filepath* parameter and specify the full path to the file. As shown here, the Tee-Object cmdlet supports a number of additional switches and parameters, and three different parameter sets:

```
Tee-Object [-FilePath] <string> [-InputObject <psobject>] [-Append] [<CommonParameters>]

Tee-Object -LiteralPath <string> [-InputObject <psobject>] [<CommonParameters>]

Tee-Object -Variable <string> [-InputObject <psobject>] [<CommonParameters>]
```

To return to the example, you can replace the redirection arrow (or the Out-File cmdlet) and the Get-Content cmdlet (*cat* alias) with the Tee-Object cmdlet. The revised code is shown here:

```
Get-WmiObject -Class Win32_Bios | Tee-Object -FilePath c:\fso\bios.txt
```

When you run the command, you receive the output shown in Figure 11-5.

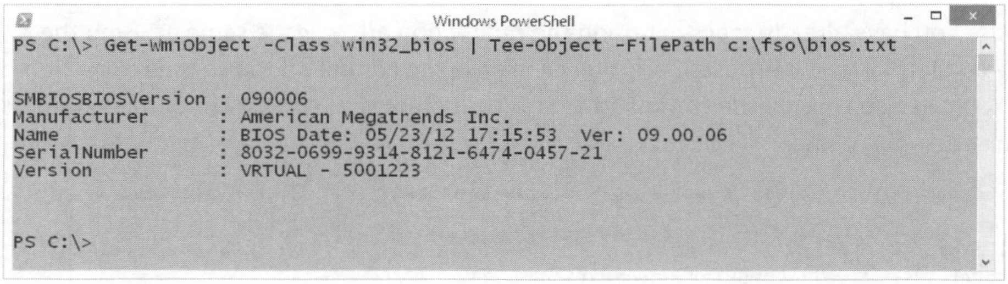

**FIGURE 11-5** The Tee-Object cmdlet splits output between the text file and the Windows PowerShell console.

One thing to keep in mind when using the Tee-Object cmdlet is that it always overwrites the previous text file if the file already exists. However, if the file does not exist, the Tee-Object cmdlet creates the file but does not create the folder. If you attempt to use the Tee-Object cmdlet to write to a folder that does not exist, an error will be received that warns of a missing path.

```
PS C:\> Get-WmiObject -class Win32_Bios | Tee-Object -FilePath C:\fso5\bios.txt
out-file : Could not find a part of the path 'C:\fso5\bios.txt'.
PS C:\>
```

You can also use the Tee-Object cmdlet to hold the output of a command in a variable. This offers a convenient way to save the information for use later in the script. The following code shows you how to save the results of a command in a variable and then display them later without using the Tee-Object cmdlet:

```
PS C:\> $bios = Get-WmiObject -class Win32_Bios
PS C:\> $bios

SMBIOSBIOSVersion : A01
Manufacturer      : Dell Computer Corporation
Name              : Default System BIOS
SerialNumber      : 9HQ1S21
Version           : DELL   - 6

PS C:\>
```

The syntax for the Tee-Object cmdlet when it is used to store the results of a pipeline in a variable is shown here:

```
Tee-Object [-InputObject <PSObject>] -Variable <String> [-Verbose] [-Debug]
[-ErrorAction <ActionPreference>] [-ErrorVariable <String>] [-OutVariable <String>]
[-OutBuffer <Int32>]
```

To store the results of your `Get-WmiObject –Class Win32_Bios` command in a variable named *$bios*, you can use the following command:

```
PS C:\> Get-WmiObject -class Win32_Bios | Tee-Object -Variable bios

SMBIOSBIOSVersion : A01
Manufacturer      : Dell Computer Corporation
Name              : Default System BIOS
SerialNumber      : 9HQ1S21
Version           : DELL   - 6
```

One thing to keep in mind when using the *variable* parameter with the `Tee-Object` cmdlet is that you do not need to use a dollar sign in front of the variable name. This makes the behavior of the cmdlet the same as the behavior when using the `New-Variable` cmdlet.

To see the contents of the *$bios* variable, you type **$bios** on the command line in the Windows PowerShell console as shown here:

```
PS C:\> $bios

SMBIOSBIOSVersion : A01
Manufacturer      : Dell Computer Corporation
Name              : Default System BIOS
SerialNumber      : 9HQ1S21
Version           : DELL   - 6

PS C:\>
```

One of the best features of the `Tee-Object` cmdlet is that it also passes the object through the pipeline. This means that you are not stuck with the default display of information that is returned by the preceding command, such as the `Get-WmiObject` cmdlet. You can store the object in the *$bios* variable and then choose to display only the *name* property.

```
PS C:\> Get-WmiObject -class Win32_Bios | Tee-Object -Variable bios |
select name

name
----
Default System BIOS
```

To retrieve the object from the variable, you once again type the variable **$bios** on the command line or use it elsewhere in your script.

```
PS C:\> $bios

SMBIOSBIOSVersion : A01
Manufacturer      : Dell Computer Corporation
Name              : Default System BIOS
SerialNumber      : 9HQ1S21
Version           : DELL   - 6
```

You are not limited to using the `Tee-Object` cmdlet with Windows PowerShell cmdlets. You can use `Tee-Object` with ordinary command-line utilities as shown here, where the results of the ping command are displayed to the console and stored in the *$ping* variable.

```
PS C:\> ping berlin | Tee-Object -Variable ping
Pinging Berlin.nwtraders.com [192.168.2.1] with 32 bytes of data:
Reply from 192.168.2.1: bytes=32 time=11ms TTL=128
Reply from 192.168.2.1: bytes=32 time=1ms TTL=128
Reply from 192.168.2.1: bytes=32 time=1ms TTL=128
Reply from 192.168.2.1: bytes=32 time=1ms TTL=128
Ping statistics for 192.168.2.1:
    Packets: Sent = 4, Received = 4, Lost = 0 (0% loss),
Approximate round trip times in milli-seconds:
    Minimum = 1ms, Maximum = 11ms, Average = 3ms
PS C:\>
```

The advantage of this technique is that you can now use the Select-String cmdlet to search the contents of the variable and quickly find the information that you need. If you are most interested in only the number of packets that were sent and received, you can pipe the data that is stored in the *$ping* variable to the Select-String cmdlet.

```
PS C:\> $ping | Select-String packet
    Packets: Sent = 4, Received = 4, Lost = 0 (0% loss),
PS C:\>
```

## NOTES FROM THE FIELD

### Working with output

**Dave Schwinn, Senior Consultant**
*Full Service Networking*

In Windows PowerShell 4.0, there are many options when dealing with output from a script or even when working from the Windows PowerShell command shell. For example, I can easily output to a text file, a database, the screen, to HTML, XML, or a comma-separated variable (CSV) file. The choice depends on what I intend to do with the data after I obtain it.

One of the things I really enjoy doing is exporting XML from a command. I will run a command, export it to XML in a file, and then display the contents of that XML on the screen. Although this can be a hassle, the XML formatting makes it easy for me to see relationships between different data elements.

On an average day, it seems that I usually format data to the screen as a table. This view is extremely useful for allowing me to quickly work my way through a long list of related items. You can consider the table view in terms of the Get-Process or the Get-Service cmdlets, which produce a table list by default. For example, consider the WMI *Win32_LogicalDisk* class. I can quickly use the following command to provide exactly the information I need:

```
PS C:\> Get-WmiObject Win32_LogicalDisk |
Format-Table name, size, freespace -AutoSize
```

```
name            size   freespace
----            ----   ---------
C:   158391595008 15872155648
E:
S:     1647308800  1554030592
```

If I send information to a printer, I like to use the `ConvertTo-Html` cmdlet because it allows me to specify details that make for a professional-looking report. However, I will often output to another cmdlet and continue using the command line.

I can also use Microsoft Visual Studio to host Windows PowerShell commands. I often write commands in a Visual Studio project that calls Windows PowerShell to retrieve the data for me and then return it to my application. It is easier for me to use Windows PowerShell to retrieve the WMI objects and for me to consume the data returned by PowerShell in my application than it is for me to call the WMI classes directly from the .NET Framework. I then output the data as a dataset and parse the columns of data for my application.

I use the `Export-CSV` cmdlet quite frequently because I can easily open the file in Excel, which allows me to do advanced data manipulation as well as create charts and reports for various presentations. Because I work for a Microsoft solutions provider, our company has a large number of customers who use a licensing model from Microsoft whereby they basically lease the software from Microsoft. Therefore, these customers always have the right to upgrade to the latest software whenever they want to do so, and they can easily budget for their software expenses. The problem is that they must let Microsoft know how many seats of the software they are using each month. I use Windows PowerShell to query a customer's Microsoft Exchange Server by using the `Get-Mailbox` cmdlet, which gives me a listing of all of the mailboxes used on the server. I then export the list to a CSV file and pipeline it to the `Send-MailMessage` cmdlet. The report goes directly to the purchasing representative so that he can open it in Excel and determine how many seats the client must pay for that month. This type of easy automation simply was not available before Windows PowerShell, and it is the ease of formatting output that makes it all possible.

## Output to email

It is a common request to be able to send information from a script to an email recipient. In the past, this generally meant writing a complicated function and hoping that all of the details were put together correctly to enable this functionality to work properly. It was easier to do before spammers caused security concerns about sending email from scripts. Email viruses have added additional layers of authentication and made the process much more confusing.

Beginning with Windows PowerShell 2.0, the Send-MailMessage cmdlet can be used to simplify the task of sending email from a script. In some cases, this cmdlet works without any additional configuration on your network. At other times, you need to grant the user account that is being used to run the script permission to send email from the script.

## Output from functions

When a function is called, it returns data to the calling code. This behavior is often not understood well by people who come to Windows PowerShell from other scripting languages. When you run the AddOne.ps1 script, the number 6 is displayed to the console. What is confusing is that data is returned from the line of code that calls the function and not from within the function itself, which is different behavior than might be expected. Most of the time, when two numbers are added together, the data is returned from the line that performs the work.

```
PS C:\> $int = 5
PS C:\> $int + 1
6
PS C:\>
```

It is therefore reasonable to expect that the number 6 is coming from inside the *AddOne* function and not from outside the function. The AddOne.ps1 script including the *AddOne* function is shown here.

```
AddOne.ps1

Function AddOne($int)
{
 $int + 1
}


AddOne(5)
```

To illustrate where the data comes from, you can modify the script to store the result of calling the function to a variable. You can then use the Get-Member cmdlet to display the information that is returned, as shown in AddOne1.ps1.

```
AddOne1.ps1

Function AddOne($int)
{
 $int + 1
}

$number = AddOne(5)
```

```
$number | get-member
'Display the value of $number: ' + $number
```

When the AddOne1.ps1 script is run, you can see that the information is returned to the code that calls the function. In the first line after the function call, the object stored in the *$number* variable is shown to be a *System.Int32* object. Following the Get-Member command, the value stored in the *$number* variable is shown to be equal to 6. The value 5 is not displayed from within the *AddOne* function.

```
TypeName: System.Int32

Name           MemberType Definition
----           ---------- ----------
CompareTo      Method     System.Int32 CompareTo(Object value), System.Int32 Co...
Equals         Method     System.Boolean Equals(Object obj), System.Boolean Equ...
GetHashCode    Method     System.Int32 GetHashCode()
GetType        Method     System.Type GetType()
GetTypeCode    Method     System.TypeCode GetTypeCode()
ToString       Method     System.String ToString(), System.String ToString(Stri...
Display the value of $number: 6
```

When you use a cmdlet such as Write-Host from inside the function, you then circumvent the return process that is inherent in the design of the function. The use of Write-Host from within a function is illustrated in AddOne2.ps1.

```
AddOne2.ps1

Function AddOne($int)
{
 Write-Host $int + 1
}


$number = AddOne(5)
$number | get-member
'Display the value of $number: ' + $number
```

When the script is run, you will notice that nothing is returned from inside the function. The *$number* variable no longer contains an object.

```
5 + 1
Get-Member : No object has been specified to get-member.
At C:\Documents and Settings\ed\Local Settings\Temp\tmp6.tmp.ps1:9 char:21
+ $number | get-member <<<<
Display the value of $number:
```

## Avoid populating the global variable

In addition to using cmdlets, such as Write-Host, from within a function to circumvent the output from a function, it is also possible to store the results of a function to a variable. The problem with storing results from the function to a variable within the function is that when a variable is created within a function, it is not available outside of the function as shown in AddOne3.ps1.

```
AddOne3.ps1

Function AddOne($int)
{
 $number =  $int + 1
}


$number = AddOne(5)
$number | get-member
'Display the value of $number: ' + $number
```

When the AddOne3.ps1 script is run, there is no object in the *$number* variable because the variable is not available outside of the *AddOne* function.

```
Get-Member : No object has been specified to get-member.
At C:\Documents and Settings\ed\Local Settings\Temp\tmp9.tmp.ps1:9 char:21
+ $number | get-member <<<<
Display the value of $number:
```

One technique that is sometimes used to provide the value of the variable from within the function to the calling script is to add a scope to the variable, as shown in the AddOne4.ps1 script.

```
AddOne4.ps1

Function AddOne($int)
{
 $global:number =  $int + 1
}

AddOne(5)
$global:number | get-member
'Display the value of $global:number: ' + $global:number
```

A potential problem exists when adding a variable to the global scope—the variable continues to exist after the script has exited. As long as the Windows PowerShell console is open and until you explicitly remove the global variable, it continues to be available. This means that the variable will be available in other scripts and will always be available within the console. This might not be a problem, but it can cause scripts that use the same variable names to operate in an erratic fashion. One way to determine whether the variable persists is to check the variable drive.

```
   TypeName: System.Int32

Name          MemberType Definition
----          ---------- ----------
CompareTo     Method     System.Int32 CompareTo(Object value), System.Int32 Co...
Equals        Method     System.Boolean Equals(Object obj), System.Boolean Equ...
GetHashCode   Method     System.Int32 GetHashCode()
GetType       Method     System.Type GetType()
GetTypeCode   Method     System.TypeCode GetTypeCode()
ToString      Method     System.String ToString(), System.String ToString(Stri...
Display the value of $global:number: 6

PS C:\data\PowerShellBestPractices\Scripts\Chapter12> Get-Item Variable:\number

Name                     Value
----                     -----
number                   6
```

It is possible to remove the global variable in the last line of the script by using the Remove-Variable cmdlet, but a better approach is to use the Script-level scope instead of the Global-level scope. The Script-level variable is available inside and outside the function while the script is running. When the script has completed, the variable is removed. The use of the Script-level scope is shown in the AddOne5.ps1 script.

```
AddOne5.ps1

Function AddOne($int)
{
 $script:number =  $int + 1
}


AddOne(5)
$script:number | get-member
'Display the value of $script:number: ' + $script:number
```

When the AddOne5.ps1 script runs, the value of the *$number* variable is available outside of the function. When the script has completed its run, an error is returned when the Get-Item cmdlet is used to attempt to retrieve the value of the variable.

```
   TypeName: System.Int32

Name          MemberType Definition
----          ---------- ----------
CompareTo     Method     System.Int32 CompareTo(Object value), System.Int32 Co...
Equals        Method     System.Boolean Equals(Object obj), System.Boolean Equ...
GetHashCode   Method     System.Int32 GetHashCode()
GetType       Method     System.Type GetType()
GetTypeCode   Method     System.TypeCode GetTypeCode()
```

```
ToString     Method      System.String ToString(), System.String ToString(Stri...
Display the value of $script:number: 6

PS C:\data\PowerShellBestPractices\Scripts\Chapter12> Get-Item variable:number
Get-Item : Cannot find path 'number' because it does not exist.
At line:1 char:9
+ Get-Item  <<<< variable:number
```

## Using a namespace in the global variable

One way to protect your Windows PowerShell console from inadvertent pollution from global variables that are created within scripts is to add a namespace tag to the variable. This process still allows you to use a global variable if required, but it also reduces variable naming conflicts. To create a global variable in a separate namespace, you can use a dollar sign, a pair of curly brackets, and the global scope tag. The separate namespace follows the colon. Finally, the variable itself is separated by a period from the namespace.

```
${Global:AddOne6.number} =  $int + 1
```

To reference the value that is stored in a global variable within a separate namespace, you can use the dollar sign, curly brackets, and the dotted notation for the namespace/variable name. You do not need to add the global tag.

```
${AddOne6.number}
```

An example of using a global variable in a separate namespace is shown in the AddOne6 .ps1 script.

```
AddOne6.ps1

Function AddOne($int)
{
 ${Global:AddOne6.number} =  $int + 1
}


AddOne(5)
${AddOne6.number} | get-member
'Display the value of ${AddOne6.number}: ' + ${AddOne6.number}
```

When the AddOne6.ps1 script runs, the variable can be accessed after the script runs by including the namespace and the variable name in a dotted notation.

```
   TypeName: System.Int32

Name        MemberType Definition
----        ---------- ----------
CompareTo   Method     System.Int32 CompareTo(Object value), System.Int32 Co...
Equals      Method     System.Boolean Equals(Object obj), System.Boolean Equ...
GetHashCode Method     System.Int32 GetHashCode()
GetType     Method     System.Type GetType()
GetTypeCode Method     System.TypeCode GetTypeCode()
```

```
ToString    Method    System.String ToString(), System.String ToString(Stri...
Display the value of ${AddOne6.number}: 6

PS C:\data\PowerShellBestPractices\Scripts\Chapter12> Get-Item Variable:\AddOne6.number

Name                      Value
----                      -----
AddOne6.number            6
```

## Windows PowerShell requires a new way of thinking

**Richard Norman, Senior Premier Field Engineer**
*Microsoft Corporation*

As a premier field engineer for Microsoft, I spend a lot of time talking to customers about working with Windows PowerShell. I tell them that the number one rule when working with Windows PowerShell is: You must change some of your thinking. This is especially true for people who are migrating to Windows PowerShell from VBScript.

With Windows PowerShell, you obtain all new possibilities along with the old capabilities. The underlying premise of Windows PowerShell is the fact that you are working with objects. These objects have properties and methods that can be exploited in ways that VBScript cannot. Previously, you dealt with results only as text. To accomplish anything more, you needed to use other tools to parse and manipulate the results. With Windows PowerShell, you receive more than just a text representation because you are working with objects that you can manipulate in new ways. You can continue to use text parsing if that is what you are accustomed to doing, but this reduces your possibilities. The next step in your thinking is to start taking advantage of the properties of the objects. For example, you can obtain a list of files that were modified within the last week by using the object properties, as shown here:

```
dir | where-object {$_.lastwritetime –ge (get-date).adddays(-7)})
```

You should also stop thinking that the pipeline is operating on a list (called an array) of objects on the command line. You are sending these objects in a series through to the next command, and the next, and the next, and so on. This list of objects is key to understanding how Windows PowerShell works. Using the objects in your scripts reveals much of the power behind all of the cmdlets. Due to the way in which Windows PowerShell operates on objects, it can process items lazily. This means that while one command is processing, Windows PowerShell can begin processing results before the first command is finished. This procedure typically happens so fast that you aren't aware of it, but it is a process that can come in handy for larger files and lists.

Finally, remember that you can use the Windows PowerShell interpreted string to your advantage. When you use quote marks or double quotes ("..."), Windows PowerShell can interpret any variable within the quotes. (Variables begin with a dollar sign.) This process allows you to go beyond the old ideas of using string concatenation and to instead use your variables directly within any string and script output.

The assumption that Windows PowerShell is just like other scripting languages will get you in trouble. While you can write a Windows PowerShell script code in a similar fashion to VBScript, there are differences in how you should write the script. For example, if you want to filter based on the date or some other factor, VBScript is limited and requires quite a few lines of script. In Windows PowerShell, the filtering can be accomplished in one line, as shown here:

```
dir | where-object {$_.lastwritetime -ge (get-date).adddays(-14)}
```

Another example involves something as simple as converting a time stamp in Domain Name System (DNS) into a usable date and time. Using VBScript can lead to several calculations and functions. Because of the concept of Windows PowerShell objects, you can break the conversion of the date down to a single line of code, as shown here:

```
get-date "1/1/1601 12:00 am GMT").addhours($timestamp)
```

Because Windows PowerShell is strongly object-based, you end up simplifying some things at the expense of complicating a few others. Some functions from VBScript have direct equivalents, while others become slightly more complex in the Windows PowerShell world, such as the CMD.exe `DIR /a:d` command. This command returns a list of folders in the current directory. In Windows PowerShell, a similar command looks like the following: `DIR | Where-Object {$_.PSISContainer}`. The command is a little longer, but the power you receive in other areas more than compensates for some of these shortcomings in verboseness.

Also, procedures that you commonly perform, such as using the *CLS* command in CMD.exe, are now an entirely new function named *Clear-Host* in Windows PowerShell. I will leave this function to the reader to investigate. However, the implementation of this function is clearly more complex than the older *CLS* command.

I often hear that Windows PowerShell is bringing the power that developers have with the .NET Framework to the command line for administrators. Sometimes that power can take some getting used to. For example, it is very easy to do DNS lookups using the .NET Framework (`[system.net.dns]::Resolve($address)`). What is special about this scenario is that the result is not simply text to parse but an object that can be manipulated.

You can use simple strings to show a vast number of methods that are available to parse and manipulate the strings, such as "a string" | Get-Member. The technique of using the underlying .NET Framework classes and methods also works with many other objects, such as dates, IP addresses, and Uniform Resource Identifiers (URIs). You can now use and manipulate all of these items through Windows PowerShell that were previously available only in the .NET Framework. Even user interface and web-based .NET libraries are available to you.

When working with XML, I can now take the string and transform it into an XML document instead of doing other parsing. For example, the following code creates an XML document from a string that can be written to a file or that can be parsed or searched by using an *XPath* or *XQuery* statement.

```
$dom=[xml]"<doc><item1>value1</item1><item1>value2</item1><item1>value3
<item2>subvalue1</item2></item1></doc>"
$dom.doc
$dom | get-member
```

I can take a regular expression and, in two lines of Windows PowerShell script, determine whether a string matches that expression. By using one more line, I can list all of the matches. The ability of Windows PowerShell to use and create regular expressions is very powerful.

```
$regex=[regex]"^((6\.((1\.((98\.(10|[0-9]))|((9[0-7]|[1-8]?
[0-9])\..*)))|(0\..*)))|([0-5]\..*))$"
$regex.ismatch("6.0.84.18")
```

# Additional resources

- The TechNet Script Center at *http://www.microsoft.com/technet/scriptcenter* contains numerous examples of handling input from Windows PowerShell scripts.
- All scripts from this chapter are available via the TechNet Script Center Script Repository at *http://gallery.technet.microsoft.com/scriptcenter/PowerShell -40-Best-d9e16039*.

# CHAPTER 12

# Handling errors

- Handling missing parameters
- Limiting choices
- Handling missing rights
- Handling missing WMI providers
- Incorrect data types
- Out of bounds errors
- Additional resources

When it comes to handling errors in your script, you need to understand how the script will be used. The way that a script will be used is sometimes called the *use case scenario*, and it describes how the user will interact with the script.

If the use case scenario is simple, the user might not need to do anything more than type the name of the script inside the Windows PowerShell console. A script such as Get-Bios.ps1 can get by without much need for any error handling because there are no inputs to the script. The script is called, it runs, and it displays information that should always be readily available because the *Win32_Bios* Windows Management Instrumentation (WMI) class is present in all versions of Windows since Microsoft Windows 2000.

```
Get-Bios.ps1

Get-WmiObject -class Win32_Bios
```

However, if the use case scenario is complicated, the requirements for handling potential errors increase. Most scripts used in enterprise environments allow the user of the script to enter parameters from the command line. Very few scripts actually require the user to open the script in a script editor and manually change variable assignments. Instead, the user types in values from the command line, which opens up all types of potential sources for error. The most common error occurs when the user of the script does not supply a value for something basic, such as the target computer name. What happens when the user types in the name of a computer that is turned off or that does not exist in the network? Suppose you have a script that does performance monitoring on a remote computer and you allow the user of the script to select the monitor interval. What happens if the user chooses to read the performance counters every .1 second? This can have an adverse impact on the performance of the computer that is being tested. What about a script that attempts to read from a WMI class that does not exist on the remote computer? How does the script handle that error condition? There are some tried and true methods for dealing with each of these potential error conditions, and in this chapter, we will examine each of these scenarios.

# Handling missing parameters

When you examine the Get-Bios.ps1 script, you can see that it does not receive any input from the command line. Although this is a good way to avoid user errors in your script, it is not always practical. When your script accepts command-line input, you are opening the door for all types of potential problems. Depending on the way in which you accept command-line input, you might need to test the input data to ensure that it corresponds to the type of input that the script is expecting. Because the Get-Bios.ps1 script does not accept command-line input, you therefore avoid most potential sources of errors.

## Creating a default value for the parameter

There are two ways to assign default values for a command-line parameter. You can assign the default value in the *Param* declaration statement, or you can assign the value in the script itself. Given a choice between the two, I generally feel it is a best practice to assign the default value in the *Param* statement because it makes the script easier to read.

### Detecting the missing value and assigning it in the script

In the Get-BiosInformation.ps1 script, the *–computername* command-line parameter is created to allow the script to target both local and remote computers. If the script is run without a value for the *–computername* parameter, the Get-WmiObject cmdlet fails because it requires a value for the *–computername* parameter. To solve the problem of the missing parameter, the Get-BiosInformation.ps1 script checks for the presence of the *$computerName* variable. If this variable is missing, it was not created via the command-line parameter, and the script therefore assigns a value to the *$computerName* variable. Here is the line of code that populates the value of the *$computerName* variable:

```
If(-not($computerName)) { $computerName = $env:computerName }
```

The complete Get-BiosInformation.ps1 script is shown here.

```
Get-BiosInformation.ps1

Param(
  [string]$computerName
) #end param

Function Get-BiosInformation($computerName)
```

```
{
 Get-WmiObject -class Win32_Bios -computername $computername
} #end function Get-BiosInformation
# *** Entry Point To Script ***
If(-not($computerName)) { $computerName = $env:computerName }
Get-BiosInformation -computername $computername
```

## Assigning the value in the *Param* statement

To assign a default value in the *Param* statement, use the equality operator following the parameter name and assign the value to the parameter, as shown here:

```
Param(
  [string]$computerName = $env:computername
) #end param
```

The advantage of assigning the default value for the parameter in the *Param* statement is that the script is easier to read. Because the parameter declaration and the default parameter are in the same place, you can immediately see which parameters have default values and which do not. The second advantage that arises from assigning a default value in the *Param* statement is that the script is easier to write. Notice that no *If* statement is used to check for the existence of the *$computerName* variable. The complete Get-BiosInformationDefaultParam.ps1 script is shown here.

```
Get-BiosInformationDefaultParam.ps1

Param(
  [string]$computerName = $env:computername
) #end param

Function Get-BiosInformation($computerName)
{
 Get-WmiObject -class Win32_Bios -computername $computername
} #end function Get-BiosInformation
# *** Entry Point To Script ***

Get-BiosInformation -computername $computername
```

# Making the parameter mandatory

The best way to handle an error is to ensure that the error does not occur in the first place. In Windows PowerShell 2.0 and higher versions, you can mark a parameter as mandatory. The advantage of marking a parameter as mandatory is that it requires the user of the script to supply a value for the parameter. If you do not want the user of the script to be able to run the script without making a particular selection, you want to make the parameter mandatory. To make a parameter mandatory, use the *mandatory* parameter attribute, as follows:

```
Param(
    [Parameter(Mandatory=$true)]
    [string]$drive,
    [string]$computerName = $env:computerName
) #end param
```

The complete MandatoryParameter.ps1 script is shown here.

```
MandatoryParameter.ps1

#Requires –version 4.0
Param(
    [Parameter(Mandatory=$true)]
    [string]$drive,
    [string]$computerName = $env:computerName
) #end param


Function Get-DiskInformation($computerName,$drive)
{
 Get-WmiObject –class Win32_volume –computername $computername '
-filter "DriveLetter = '$drive'"
} #end function Get-DiskInformation
# *** Entry Point To Script ***

 Get-DiskInformation –computername $computerName –drive $drive
```

When a script with a mandatory parameter is run without supplying a value for the parameter, an error is not generated. Instead, Windows PowerShell prompts for the required parameter value:

```
PS C:\bp> .\MandatoryParameter.ps1

cmdlet MandatoryParameter.ps1 at command pipeline position 1
Supply values for the following parameters:
drive:
```

## Limiting choices

Depending on the design of the script, there are several things that you can do to decrease the amount of error checking required. If you have a limited number of choices that you want to display to the user, you can use the *PromptForChoice* method. If you want to limit the selection to computers that are currently running, you can ping the computer prior to attempting to connect. If you want to limit the choice to a subset of computers or properties, you can parse a text file and use the *–contains* operator. In this section, you will examine each of these techniques for limiting the permissible input values from the command line.

## Using *PromptForChoice* to Limit Selections

If you use the *PromptForChoice* method of soliciting input from the user, the user has a limited number of options from which to choose. You completely eliminate the problem of bad input. The user prompt from the *PromptForChoice* method is shown in Figure 12-1.

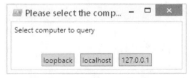

**FIGURE 12-1** The *PromptForChoice* method presents a selectable menu to the user.

The use of the *PromptForChoice* method is illustrated in the Get-ChoiceFunction.ps1 script. In the *Get-Choice* function, the *$caption* variable and the *$message* variable hold the caption and the message that is used by *PromptForChoice*. The choices that are offered are instances of the Microsoft .NET Framework *ChoiceDescription* class. When you create the *ChoiceDescription* class, you also supply an array with the choices that will appear, as shown here:

```
$choices = [System.Management.Automation.Host.ChoiceDescription[]] '
 @("&loopback", "local&host", "&127.0.0.1")
```

Next, you need to select a number that will be used to represent the default choice. When you begin counting, keep in mind that the *ChoiceDescription* class is an array, and the first option is numbered 0. Next, you call the *PromptForChoice* method and display the options:

```
[int]$defaultChoice = 0
$choiceRTN = $host.ui.PromptForChoice($caption,$message,$choices,$defaultChoice)
```

Because the *PromptForChoice* method returns an integer, you can use the *If* statement to evaluate the value of the *$choiceRTN* variable. The syntax of the *Switch* statement is more compact and is actually a better choice for this application. The *Switch* statement from the *Get-Choice* function is shown here:

```
switch($choiceRTN)
 {
  0    { "loopback"  }
  1    { "localhost"  }
  2    { "127.0.0.1"  }
 }
```

When you call the *Get-Choice* function, it returns the computer that was identified by the *PromptForChoice* method. You place the method call in a set of parentheses to force it to be evaluated before the rest of the command.

```
Get-WmiObject -class win32_bios -computername (Get-Choice)
```

This solution to the problem of bad input works well when your help desk personnel are working with a limited number of computers. The other caveat to this approach is that you do not want to change the choices on a regular basis. You want a stable list of computers to avoid creating a maintenance nightmare for yourself. The complete Get-ChoiceFunction.ps1 script is shown here.

```
Get-ChoiceFunction.ps1

Function Get-Choice
{
 $caption = "Please select the computer to query"
 $message = "Select computer to query"
 $choices = [System.Management.Automation.Host.ChoiceDescription[]] '
 @("&loopback", "local&host", "&127.0.0.1")
 [int]$defaultChoice = 0
 $choiceRTN = $host.ui.PromptForChoice($caption,$message, $choices,$defaultChoice)

 switch($choiceRTN)
 {
  0    { "loopback"  }
  1    { "localhost"  }
  2    { "127.0.0.1"  }
 }
} #end Get-Choice function

Get-WmiObject -class win32_bios -computername (Get-Choice)
```

## Using ping to identify accessible computers

If you have more than a few computers that need to be accessible or if you do not have a stable list of computers that you will be working with, one solution to the problem of trying to connect to nonexistent computers is to ping the computer prior to attempting to make the WMI connection.

You can use the *Win32_PingStatus* WMI class to send a ping to a computer. The best way to use the *Win32_PingStatus* WMI class is to create a function that pings the target computer. Because you are interested in a quick reply, the *Test-ComputerPath* function sends one ping only. The *Test-ComputerPath* function accepts a single input, which is the name or IP address of the target computer. To help control the information that is passed to the function, the *$computer* parameter uses a *string* type constraint to ensure that the input to the function is a string. The *Test-ComputerPath* function is shown here:

```
Function Test-ComputerPath([string]$computer)
{
 Get-WmiObject -class win32_pingstatus -filter "address = '$computer'"
} #end Test-ComputerPath
```

A subset of the *Win32_PingStatus* object is returned to the calling code and is shown here:

```
Source        Destination     IPV4Address       IPV6Address
------        -----------     -----------       -----------
EDLT          dc1             192.168.0.101
```

In the Test-ComputerPath.ps1 script, the *statusCode* property from the *Win32_PingStatus* object is evaluated. If the value is 0, the ping was successful. If the *statusCode* property is null or is equal to some other number, the ping was not successful. Because the *Win32_PingStatus* object is returned to the calling script, you can retrieve the *statusCode* property directly and use the equality operator to see whether it is equal to 0.

```
if( (Test-ComputerPath -computer $computer).statusCode -eq 0 )
```

If the *statusCode* property is equal to 0, the Test-ComputerPath.ps1 script uses the Get-WmiObject cmdlet to retrieve the BIOS information from the *Win32_Bios* WMI class.

```
Get-WmiObject -class Win32_Bios -computer $computer
```

If the target computer is unable to be reached, the Test-ComputerPath.ps1 script displays a message to the Windows PowerShell console stating that the target computer is unreachable.

```
Else
 {
  "Unable to reach $computer computer"
 }
```

The complete Test-ComputerPath.ps1 script is shown here.

```
Test-ComputerPath.ps1

Param([string]$computer = "localhost")


Function Test-ComputerPath([string]$computer)
{
 Get-WmiObject -class win32_pingstatus -filter "address = '$computer'"
} #end Test-ComputerPath


# *** Entry Point to Script ***

if( (Test-ComputerPath -computer $computer).statusCode -eq 0 )
 {
   Get-WmiObject -class Win32_Bios -computer $computer
 }
Else
 {
   "Unable to reach $computer computer"
 }
```

# Using the *-contains* Operator to examine the contents of an array

To verify input that is received from the command line, you can use the *-contains* operator to examine the contents of an array of possible values. This technique is illustrated here with an array of three values that is created and stored in the *$noun* variable. The *-contains* operator is then used to see whether the array contains "hairy-nosed wombat." Because the *$noun* variable does not have an array element that is equal to the string "hairy-nosed wombat," the *-contains* operator returns *False*.

```
PS C:\> $noun = "cat","dog","rabbit"
PS C:\> $noun -contains "hairy-nosed wombat"
False
PS C:\>
```

If an array contains a match, the *-contains* operator returns *True*.

```
PS C:\> $noun = "cat","dog","rabbit"
PS C:\> $noun -contains "rabbit"
True
PS C:\>
```

The *-contains* operator returns *True* only when there is an exact match. Partial matches return *False*.

```
PS C:\> $noun = "cat","dog","rabbit"
PS C:\> $noun -contains "bit"
False
PS C:\>
```

The *-contains* operator is case-insensitive. Therefore, it returns *True* when matched regardless of case.

```
PS C:\> $noun = "cat","dog","rabbit"
PS C:\> $noun -contains "Rabbit"
True
PS C:\>
```

If you need to perform a case-sensitive match, you can use the case-sensitive version of the *-contains* operator, *-ccontains*. It returns *True* only if the case of the string matches the value contained in the array, as shown here:

```
PS C:\> $noun = "cat","dog","rabbit"
PS C:\> $noun -ccontains "Rabbit"
False
PS C:\> $noun -ccontains "rabbit"
True
PS C:\>
```

In the Get-AllowedComputer.ps1 script, a single command-line parameter is created that is used to hold the name of the target computer for the WMI query. The *-computer* parameter is a string, and it receives the default value from the environmental drive. This is a good technique because it ensures that the script has the name of the local computer, which can then be used in producing a report of the results. If you set the value of the *–computer* parameter to *LocalHost*, you never know which computer the results belong to.

```
Param([string]$computer = $env:computername)
```

The *Get-AllowedComputer* function is used to create an array of permitted computer names and to check the value of the *$computer* variable to see whether it is present. If the value of the *$computer* variable is present in the array, the *Get-AllowedComputer* function returns *True*. If the value is missing from the array, the *Get-AllowedComputer* function returns *False*. The array of computer names is created by using the Get-Content cmdlet to read a text file that contains a listing of computer names. The text file, servers.txt, is a plain ASCII text file that has a list of computer names on individual lines, as shown in Figure 12-2.

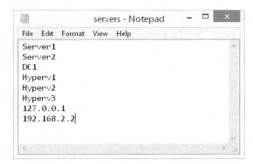

**FIGURE 12-2** A text file with computer names and addresses is an easy way to work with allowed computers.

A text file of computer names is easier to maintain than a hard-coded array that is embedded into the script. In addition, the text file can be placed on a central share and used by many different scripts. The *Get-AllowedComputer* function is shown here:

```
Function Get-AllowedComputer([string]$computer)
{
 $servers = Get-Content -path c:\fso\servers.txt
 $servers -contains $computer
} #end Get-AllowedComputer function
```

Because the *Get-AllowedComputer* function returns a Boolean value (true/false), it can be used directly in an *If* statement to determine whether the value that is supplied for the *$computer* variable is on the permitted list. If the *Get-AllowedComputer* function returns *True*, the Get-WmiObject cmdlet is used to query for BIOS information from the target computer.

```
if(Get-AllowedComputer -computer $computer)
  {
    Get-WmiObject -class Win32_Bios -Computer $computer
  }
```

However, if the value of the *$computer* variable is not found in the *$servers* array, a string stating that the computer is not an allowed computer is displayed.

```
Else
 {
  "$computer is not an allowed computer"
 }
```

The complete Get-AllowedComputer.ps1 script is shown here.

```
Get-AllowedComputer.ps1

Param([string]$computer = $env:computername)


Function Get-AllowedComputer([string]$computer)
{
 $servers = Get-Content -path c:\fso\servers.txt
 $servers -contains $computer
} #end Get-AllowedComputer function


# *** Entry point to Script ***

if(Get-AllowedComputer -computer $computer)
 {
   Get-WmiObject -class Win32_Bios -computer $computer
 }
Else
 {
   "$computer is not an allowed computer"
 }
```

## Using the −*contains* operator to test for properties

You are not limited to testing only for specified computer names in the *Get-AllowedComputer* function. To test for other properties, all you need to do is add additional information to the text file, as shown in Figure 12-3.

Only a few modifications are required to turn the Get-AllowedComputer.ps1 script into the Get-AllowedComputerAndProperty.ps1 script. The first modification is to add an additional command-line parameter to allow the user to choose which property to display.

```
Param([string]$computer = $env:computername,[string]$property="name")
```

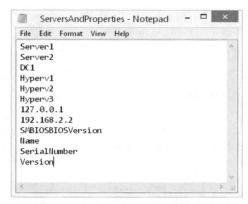

**FIGURE 12-3** A text file with server names and properties adds flexibility to the script.

Next, the signature to the *Get-AllowedComputer* function is changed to permit passing of the property name. Instead of directly returning the results of the *–contains* operator, the returned values are stored in variables. The *Get-AllowedComputer* function first checks to see whether the *$servers* array contains the computer name. It then checks to see whether the *$servers* array contains the property name. Each of the resulting values is stored in variables. The two variables are then added together, and the result is returned to the calling code. When two Boolean values are added together, only the *true* and *true* case is equal to *True*.

```
PS C:\> $true -and $false
False
PS C:\> $true -and $true
True
PS C:\> $false -and $false
False
PS C:\>
```

The revised *Get-AllowedComputer* function is shown here:

```
Function Get-AllowedComputer([string]$computer, [string]$property)
{
 $servers = Get-Content -path c:\fso\serversAndProperties.txt
 $s = $servers -contains $computer
 $p = $servers -contains $property
 Return $s -and $p
} #end Get-AllowedComputer function
```

The *If* statement is used to determine whether both the computer value and the property value are contained in the allowed list of servers and properties. If the *Get-AllowedComputer* function returns true, the Get-WmiObject cmdlet is used to display the chosen property value from the selected computer.

```
if(Get-AllowedComputer -computer $computer -property $property)
 {
   Get-WmiObject -class Win32_Bios -Computer $computer |
   Select-Object -property $property
 }
```

If the computer value and the property value are not on the permitted list, the Get-AllowedComputerAndProperty.ps1 script displays a message stating that there is a non-permitted value.

```
Else
 {
  "Either $computer is not an allowed computer, 'r'nor $property is not an allowed
property"
 }
```

The complete Get-AllowedComputerAndProperty.ps1 script is shown here.

```
Get-AllowedComputerAndProperty.ps1

Param([string]$computer = $env:computername,[string]$property="name")


Function Get-AllowedComputer([string]$computer, [string]$property)
{
 $servers = Get-Content -path c:\fso\serversAndProperties.txt
 $s = $servers -contains $computer
 $p = $servers -contains $property
 Return $s -and $p
} #end Get-AllowedComputer function

# *** Entry point to Script ***

if(Get-AllowedComputer -computer $computer -property $property)
 {
   Get-WmiObject -class Win32_Bios -computer $computer |
   Select-Object -property $property
 }
Else
 {
   "Either $computer is not an allowed computer, 'r'nor $property is not an allowed
property"
 }
```

# Handling missing rights

Another source of potential errors is a script that requires elevated permissions to work correctly. Beginning with Windows Vista, the operating system makes it much easier to run and to allow the user to work without requiring constant access to administrative rights. As a result, more users and network administrators are no longer running their computers with a user account that is a member of the local Administrators group. The User Account Control (UAC) feature makes it easy to provide elevated rights for interactive programs, but Windows PowerShell and other scripting languages are not UAC aware and therefore do not prompt when elevated rights are required to perform a specific activity. Thus, it is incumbent on the scriptwriter to take rights into account when writing scripts. However, the Get-Bios.ps1 script does not use a WMI class that requires elevated rights. As the script is currently written, anyone who is a member of the local Users group—and that includes everyone who is logged on interactively—has permission to run the Get-Bios.ps1 script. Therefore, testing for rights and permissions prior to making an attempt to obtain information from the *Win32_Bios* WMI class is not required.

**Gary Siepser, Senior Premier Field Engineer / PowerShell Technology Lead**
*Microsoft Corporation*

A fun project that a colleague and I have been working on is integrating the Kinect for Windows and Windows PowerShell. The project has really taught me a lot about using an API, coding more like a developer, and translating C# source code in Windows PowerShell script (not as fun as it sounds).

One topic I have had to learn more about is resource management—specifically, freeing up resources when you don't need them anymore. When using the Kinect API, after the Kinect sensor is started and the various data streams are enabled, I found that a constant 20% of my CPU was being used because of the software calculations being performed on the PC to interpret and prepare the Kinect camera data for use through the API. The USB bus that the Kinect was plugged into was also very busy with data, and when the Kinect was started, it was locked up and unavailable to other Kinect-enabled applications (like Windows PowerShell scripts in other windows). Often, in Windows PowerShell, I open a window for a long period of a time, occasionally running scripts, functions, and so on. I realized pretty quickly that I needed to ensure at all costs that the moment my script or function was done evaluating Kinect data, I needed to stop the Kinect sensor to free up and unlock those resources.

Stopping the Kinect and freeing up the resources was quite easy with the API, through a simple method call. At first I simply included the method call at the end of the code. The real problem arose during the development cycle. I was regularly encountering errors or terminating my scripts before completion (using either Ctrl+C or the Stop button in the ISE). Therefore, the clean-up code that stopped the Kinect would execute because I terminated the script early. This was a real problem, leaving resources locked and CPU time being burned for no reason.

I soon learned about an aspect of the *Try/Catch/Finally* error handling structure in Windows PowerShell that was the perfect solution for this situation. Windows PowerShell respects the *Finally* block and will ensure that it gets run even if the code is terminated while still in the *Try* or *Catch* block. Incorporating the Kinect

*Stop* method into a *Finally* block turned out to be one of the best additions to my code. When the code was completed, and during real use, it would come in handy, but during development it was especially handy for repeated terminations and subsequent runs of the code.

While *Try/Catch/Finally* is a nice structure for handling terminating errors and is very commonly used by developers, I personally think that the nearly guaranteed execution of the *Finally* block is invaluable. After I converted my code over to using this structure, I saw that no matter how my code terminated, on its own or because of a manual break (like Ctrl+C), I saw the Kinect *Stop* method being executed, and my resources were successfully cleaned up every time.

## Attempting and failing

One way to handle missing rights is to attempt the action and then fail. This action generates an error. Windows PowerShell has two types of errors: terminating and non-terminating. Terminating errors, as the name implies, will stop a script dead in its tracks. Non-terminating errors will output to the screen and the script will continue. Terminating errors are generally more serious than non-terminating errors. Normally, you receive a terminating error when you try to use .NET class or a Component Object Model (COM) object from within Windows PowerShell, you try to use a command that doesn't exist, or you do not provide all of the required parameters to a command. A good script handles the errors that it expects and reports unexpected errors to the user. Because any good scripting language must provide decent error handling, Windows PowerShell has several ways to approach the problem. The old way is the *Trap* statement, which can sometimes be problematic. The new way (for Windows PowerShell) is to use *Try/Catch/Finally*.

n Windows PowerShell 1.0, there was one and only one way to handle terminating errors: through the *Trap* statement. The *Trap* statement comes at the end of your script and lets you swallow all of the errors in the script (or all of the errors of a specific type). Most Windows PowerShell 1.0 scripts that handle errors end up looking something like the following code:

```
Do-Something
….    Do-SomethingElse
trap {
  "Something Bad Happened"
}
```

Unfortunately, the *Trap* statement is a little strange. First and foremost, it is a concept that is unfamiliar to most scripters or developers. Second, *Trap* statements don't actually allow you to easily trap errors within a few lines of code. Therefore, if you write a *Trap* statement because you expect errors in your script and you call some other script that also hits errors, the *Trap* statement can end up swallowing both sets of errors and leave you mystified as to why your script doesn't work.

People who are familiar with C# or JavaScript will probably be familiar with *Try/Catch/Finally*. In Windows PowerShell 2.0, we introduced *Try/Catch/Finally* to address some of the pain points surrounding error handling in PowerShell 1.0.

A try block identifies a section of code that can handle errors. A try block will attempt to execute the script within it; if any terminating errors are encountered, the nearest catch block catches the errors. Try and catch must be paired together (you can have one and only one catch for each try, and Windows PowerShell does not allow a try without a catch), but you can also add a finally block for good measure. A finally block will run whether you have errors or not, so it's a great place to put any cleanup code.

The following is a complete example:

```
try {
    throw "Houston, We Have a Problem"
}
catch {
    Write-Error $_
    try {
        Test-System
    }
    catch [Management.Automation.CommandNotFoundException] {
        "Where's the $($_.TargetObject) command?"
    }

}
finally {
    "byebye"
}
```

In this example, the first error ("Houston, We Have a Problem") is swallowed by the catch block and is written out with the Write-Error cmdlet. This turns my terminating error into a non-terminating error so that my script can continue. Inside of that catch block is another try/catch block that runs a diagnostic command (Test-System). If Test-System writes out any errors, I want to see them. However, I want to ask the user where the command is located if and only if it's not found, so I create a catch block that catches only *CommandNotFoundExceptions* (the type of exception I see when the command is missing). The finally block is run whether there is an error or not, so I always see a polite *byebye* whenever I run the script.

Quietly reinterpreting errors is one of the handiest things you can do with try/catch blocks. I personally like to be able to see all of the errors that I hit while running a script, but I also do not like users of my scripts to see red errors. (It's bad for their ulcers.) Therefore, I often place something like the following in my script:

```
try {
}
catch {
    Write-Debug ($_|Out-String)
}
```

This try/catch block puts my error in the *Debug* stream (which is hidden by default but which I can turn on with *$DebugPreference* = *"Continue")*. The result is that my scripts almost never show an error to my user, but I obtain a view that shows me all of the errors in my script.

## Checking for rights and exiting gracefully

The best way to handle insufficient rights is to check for the rights and then exit gracefully. What are some of the things that can go wrong with a simple script, such as the Get-Bios .ps1 script that was examined earlier in the chapter? Well, the Get-Bios.ps1 script can fail if the Windows PowerShell script execution policy is set to Restricted. When the script execution policy is set to Restricted, Windows PowerShell scripts will not run. The problem with a restricted execution policy is that, because Windows PowerShell scripts do not run, you cannot write code to detect the restricted script execution policy. Because the script execution policy is stored in the registry, you can write a VBScript script that will query and set the policy prior to launching the Windows PowerShell script, but that is not the best way to manage the problem. The best way to manage the script execution policy is to use Group Policy to set the policy to the appropriate level for your network. On a stand-alone computer, you can set the execution policy by opening Windows PowerShell as an administrator and using the `Set-ExecutionPolicy` cmdlet. In most cases, the RemoteSigned setting is appropriate. You then see the following command:

```
PS C:\> Set-ExecutionPolicy remotesigned
PS C:\>
```

The script execution policy is generally dealt with once, and then no more problems are associated with it. In addition, the error message that is associated with the script execution policy is relatively clear in that it tells you that script execution is disabled on the system. It also refers you to a help article that explains the various settings.

```
File C:\Documents and Settings\ed\Local Settings\Temp\tmp2A7.tmp.ps1 cannot be
loaded because the execution of scripts is disabled on this system. Please see
"get-help about_signing" for more details.
At line:1 char:66
+ C:\Documents' and' Settings\ed\Local' Settings\Temp\tmp2A7.tmp.ps1 <<<<
```

## Using *#Requires*

In Windows PowerShell 4.0, the *#Requires* statement is expanded to permit additional pre-run checks. Keep in mind that a *#Requires* statement is not for use in functions, cmdlets, or snap-ins, but can appear in any script. The rules for its use are as follows:

- The *#Requires* statement must be the first item on a line in a script.
- The *#Requires* statement can appear on any line number in the script.
- A script can contain more than one *#Requires* statement.
- If a script contains more than one *#Requires* statement, each statement must appear on its own line.

Table 12-1 enumerates the available parameters for the *#Requires* statement.

**TABLE 12-1** Parameter values used by *#Requires*

| Parameter | Meaning and Example |
|---|---|
| Version | The minimal version of Windows PowerShell<br>Example:<br>`#Requires –Version 4.0` |
| PSSnapin | The name of a required snap-in.<br>Example:<br>`#Requires –PSSnapin mysnapin` |
| Modules | Modules required by the script.<br>Example:<br>`#Requires –Modules ActiveDirectory` |
| ShellID | Name of a specifically required shell.<br>Example:<br>`#Requires –ShellID Microsoft.PowerShell` |
| RunAsAdministrator | Script can run only with admin rights.<br>Example:<br>`#Requires –RunAsAdministrator` |

## Require Administrator rights

In previous versions of Windows PowerShell, requiring Administrator rights for a script involved writing a special function, such as the *Test-IsAdmin* function in Test-IsAdminFunction.ps1.

```
Test-IsAdminFunction.ps1

Function Test-IsAdmin
{
 <#
    .Synopsis
        Tests if the user is an administrator
    .Description
        Returns true if a user is an administrator, false if the user is not an
administrator
    .Example
        Test-IsAdmin
    #>
 $identity = [Security.Principal.WindowsIdentity]::GetCurrent()
 $principal = New-Object Security.Principal.WindowsPrincipal $identity
 $principal.IsInRole([Security.Principal.WindowsBuiltinRole]::Administrator)
}
```

Use of the *Test-IsAdmin* function generally takes the form of loading the function into memory (via the script) and then using an *if* statement. Such an *if* statement appears here:

```
if(-not (Test-IsAdmin)) {"you must have admin rights to run the script"}
```

Windows PowerShell 4.0 simplifies this task greatly by providing the *#Requires –RunAsAdministrator* statement and parameter. A good case for using this technique occurs when using a cmdlet from the Hyper-V module (use of which requires Administrator rights). When run without Administrator rights, the cmdlets do not return an error–they return nothing. This leads to confusion and can even cause an inexperienced administrator to ruin a perfectly good script in a vain attempt to debug it. An example of using this technique appears in get-VM.ps1.

```
get-VM.ps1

#Requires -Version 4.0
#Requires -RunAsAdministrator
#Requires -Modules Hyper-V


Import-Module Hyper-V
Get-VM
```

When a script containing *#Requires –RunAsAdministrator* runs without Administrator rights, a detailed error appears.

## Requiring specific modules

Windows PowerShell 4.0 makes it easy to require specific modules prior to execution. In fact, specific versions of the modules can be specified. To require a specific module version, use a hashtable with the ModuleName and the ModuleVersion as key elements. The RequireModuleVersion.ps1 script illustrates this technique.

```
RequireModuleVersion.ps1

#Requires -version 4.0
#Requires -RunAsAdministrator
#Requires -modules ScheduledTasks, @{ModuleName='StartScreen';ModuleVersion='1.0.0.0'}
Import-Module StartScreen
Get-StartApps
Get-ScheduledTask
```

# Handling missing WMI providers

About the only thing that can actually go wrong with the Get-Bios.ps1 script is if the WMI provider that supplies the *Win32_Bios* WMI class information is corrupted or missing. To check for the existence of the appropriate WMI provider, you need to know the name of the provider for the WMI class. To check for the name, you can use the Windows Management Instrumentation Tester (WbemTest) that is included as part of the WMI installation. If WMI is installed on a computer, it has Wbemtest.exe. Because WbemTest resides in the system folders, you can launch it directly from within the Windows PowerShell console by typing the name of the executable.

```
PS C:\> wbemtest
PS C:\>
```

When WbemTest appears, the first thing you need to do is connect to the appropriate WMI namespace by pressing the Connect button. In most cases, the appropriate namespace is the *root\cimv2* namespace. Beginning in Windows Vista, *root\cimv2* is the default WMI namespace for WbemTest. On earlier versions of Windows, the default WbemTest namespace is *root\default*. Change or accept the namespace as appropriate, and click the Connect button. The display changes to a series of buttons, many of which appear to have cryptic names and functionality. To obtain information about the provider for a WMI class, you need to open the class. Click the Open Class button, and type the name of the WMI class in the Get Class Name dialog box. You are looking for the provider name for the *Win32_Bios* WMI class so that is the name that is entered in the text box of the Get Class Name dialog box. When you click OK, the Object Editor For *Win32_Bios* WMI class appears, as shown in Figure 12-4. The first section of the Object Editor For *Win32_Bios* lists the qualifiers. Provider is one of the qualifiers. WbemTest tells you that the provider for *Win32_Bios* is CIMWin32.

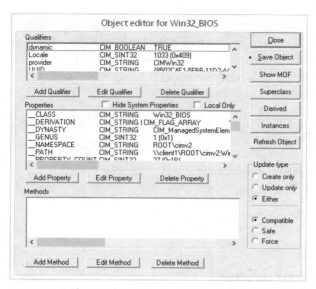

FIGURE 12-4 The Windows Management Instrumentation Tester displays WMI class provider information.

Armed with the name of the WMI provider, you can use the Get-WmiObject cmdlet to determine whether the provider is installed on the computer. To do this, you can query for instances of the __*provider* WMI class. All WMI classes that begin with a double underscore are system classes. The __*provider* WMI class is the class from which all WMI providers are derived. By limiting the query to providers with the name of CIMWin32, you can determine whether the provider is installed on the system.

```
PS C:\> Get-WmiObject -Class __provider -filter "name = 'cimwin32'"
__GENUS                         : 2
__CLASS                         : __Win32Provider
__SUPERCLASS                    : __Provider
__DYNASTY                       : __SystemClass
__RELPATH                       : __Win32Provider.Name="CIMWin32"
__PROPERTY_COUNT                : 24
__DERIVATION                    : {__Provider, __SystemClass}
__SERVER                        : OFFICE
__NAMESPACE                     : ROOT\cimv2
__PATH                          : \\OFFICE\ROOT\cimv2:__Win32Provider.Name="CIMWin32"
ClientLoadableCLSID             :
CLSID                           : {d63a5850-8f16-11cf-9f47-00aa00bf345c}
Concurrency                     :
DefaultMachineName              :
Enabled                         :
HostingModel                    : NetworkServiceHost
ImpersonationLevel              : 1
InitializationReentrancy        : 0
InitializationTimeoutInterval   :
InitializeAsAdminFirst          :
Name                            : CIMWin32
OperationTimeoutInterval        :
```

```
PerLocaleInitialization        : False
PerUserInitialization          : False
Pure                           : True
SecurityDescriptor             :
SupportsExplicitShutdown       :
SupportsExtendedStatus         :
SupportsQuotas                 :
SupportsSendStatus             :
SupportsShutdown               :
SupportsThrottling             :
UnloadTimeout                  :
Version                        :

PS C:\>
```

For the purposes of determining whether the provider exists, you do not need all of the information to be returned to the script. It is easier to treat the query as if it returned a Boolean value by using the *If* statement. If the provider exists, you can perform the query.

```
If(Get-WmiObject -Class __provider -filter "name = 'cimwin32'")
 {
  Get-WmiObject -class Win32_bios
 }
```

If the CIMWin32 WMI provider does not exist, you display a message stating that the provider is missing.

```
Else
 {
  "Unable to query Win32_Bios because the provider is missing"
 }
```

The completed CheckProviderThenQuery.ps1 script is shown here.

```
CheckProviderThenQuery.ps1

If(Get-WmiObject -Class __provider -filter "name = 'cimwin32'")
 {
   Get-WmiObject -class Win32_bios
 }
Else
 {
   "Unable to query Win32_Bios because the provider is missing"
 }
```

A better approach to find out whether a WMI class is available is to check for the existence of the provider. In the case of the *Win32_Product* WMI class, the class is supplied by the MSIProv WMI provider. In this section, we create the *Get-WmiProvider* function that can be used to detect the presence of any WMI provider that is installed on the system.

The *Get-WmiProvider* function contains one parameter, the name of the provider. Because the function uses the *[cmdletbinding()]* attribute when the *Get-WmiProvider* function is called with the *–verbose* switched parameter, detailed status information is displayed to the console. The *–verbose* information provides the user of the script with information that can be useful from a troubleshooting perspective.

After the function is declared, the first thing that you need to do is look for the WMI provider. To do this, the `Get-WmiObject` cmdlet is used to query for all instances of the __*provider* WMI system class. In most cases, they are not of much interest to IT pros, yet familiarity with them can often provide powerful tools to the scripter who takes the time to examine them. All WMI providers are derived from the __*provider* WMI class. This is similar to the way in which all WMI namespaces are derived from the __*Namespace* WMI class. The properties of the __*provider* class are shown in Table 12-2.

**TABLE 12-2** Properties of the __*provider* WMI class

| Property Name | Property Type |
| --- | --- |
| ClientLoadableCLSID | System.String |
| CLSID | System.String |
| Concurrency | System.Int32 |
| DefaultMachineName | System.String |
| Enabled | System.Boolean |
| HostingModel | System.String |
| ImpersonationLevel | System.Int32 |
| InitializationReentrancy | System.Int32 |
| InitializationTimeoutInterval | System.String |
| InitializeAsAdminFirst | System.Boolean |
| Name | System.String |
| OperationTimeoutInterval | System.String |
| PerLocaleInitialization | System.Boolean |
| PerUserInitialization | System.Boolean |
| Pure | System.Boolean |
| SecurityDescriptor | System.String |
| SupportsExplicitShutdown | System.Boolean |
| SupportsExtendedStatus | System.Boolean |
| SupportsQuotas | System.Boolean |
| SupportsSendStatus | System.Boolean |
| SupportsShutdown | System.Boolean |

| Property Name | Property Type |
| --- | --- |
| SupportsThrottling | System.Boolean |
| UnloadTimeout | System.String |
| Version | System.UInt32 |
| __CLASS | System.String |
| __DERIVATION | System.String[] |
| __DYNASTY | System.String |
| __GENUS | System.Int32 |
| __NAMESPACE | System.String |
| __PATH | System.String |
| __PROPERTY_COUNT | System.Int32 |
| __RELPATH | System.String |
| __SERVER | System.String |
| __SUPERCLASS | System.String |

The *-filter* parameter of the `Get-WmiObject` cmdlet is used to return the provider that is specified in the *$providerName* variable. If you do not know the name of the appropriate WMI provider, you need to search for it by using WbemTest. You can start this program by typing the name of the executable inside your Windows PowerShell console.

When the WbemTest appears, the first thing you need to do is connect to the appropriate WMI namespace by clicking the Connect button. In most cases, the appropriate namespace is the *root\cimv2* namespace. Change or accept the namespace as appropriate, and click the Connect button. Click the Open Class button, and type the name of the WMI class in the Enter Target Class Name text box of the Get Class Name dialog box. You are looking for the provider name for the *Win32_Product* WMI class, and that is the name that is entered in the text box. When you click OK, the Object Editor For *Win32_Product* WMI class appears. The first section of the Object Editor For *Win32_Product* lists the qualifiers. Provider is one of the qualifiers. WbemTest tells you that the provider for *Win32_Product* is MSIProv.

You assign the name of the WMI provider to the *$providerName* variable.

```
$providerName = "MSIProv"
```

The resulting object is stored in the *$provider* variable.

```
$provider = Get-WmiObject -Class __provider -filter "name = '$providerName'"
```

If the provider is not found, there is no value in the *$provider* variable. Therefore, you can determine whether the *$provider* variable is null. If the *$provider* variable is not equal to null, the *CLSID* property of the provider is retrieved. The class ID of the WMI provider is stored in the *CLSID* property.

```
If($provider -ne $null)
  {
    $clsID = $provider.CLSID
```

If the function is run with the *–verbose* parameter, the *$verbosePreference* variable is set to *Continue*. When the value of *$verbosePreference* is equal to *Continue*, the `Write-Verbose` cmdlet displays information to the console. However, if the value of the *$verbosePreference* variable is equal to *SilentlyContinue*, the `Write-Verbose` cmdlet does not emit anything. The *[cmdletbinding()]* attribute does this automatically and therefore makes it easy to implement tracing features in a function without creating extensive test conditions. When the function is called with the *–verbose* parameter, the class ID of the provider is displayed.

```
Write-Verbose "$providerName WMI provider found. CLSID is $($CLSID)"
}
```

If the WMI provider is not found, the function returns false to the calling code.

```
Else
  {
    Return $false
  }
```

Next, the function checks the registry to ensure that the WMI provider is properly registered with the Distributed Component Object Model (DCOM). Once again, the `Write-Verbose` cmdlet is used to provide feedback on the status of the provider check.

```
Write-Verbose "Checking for proper registry registration ..."
```

To search the registry for the WMI provider registration, the Windows PowerShell registry provider is used. By default, there is no Windows PowerShell drive for the HKEY_Classes_Root registry hive. However, you cannot take it for granted that someone has not created such a drive in their Windows PowerShell profile. To avoid a potential error that might arise when creating a Windows PowerShell drive for the HKEY_Classes_Root hive, the `Test-Path` cmdlet is used to check whether an HKCR drive exists. If the HKCR drive does exist, it will be used, and the `Write-Verbose` cmdlet is used to print a status message stating that the HKCR drive is found and that the search is commencing for the class ID of the WMI provider.

```
If(Test-Path -path HKCR:)
  {
    Write-Verbose "HKCR: drive found. Testing for $clsID"
```

To detect whether the WMI provider is registered with DCOM, check whether the class ID of the WMI provider is present in the CLSID section of HKEY_Classes_Root. The best way to check for the presence of the registry key is to use the `Test-Path` cmdlet.

```
Test-path -path (Join-Path -path HKCR:\CLSID -childpath $clsID)
}
```

However, if there is no HKCR drive on the computer, you can create one. You can search for the existence of a drive that is rooted in HKEY_Classes_Root and, if you find it, use the Windows PowerShell drive in your query. To discover whether there are any Windows PowerShell drives rooted in HKEY_Classes_Root, use the Get-PSDrive cmdlet.

```
Get-PSDrive | Where-Object { $_.root -match "classes" } |
Select-Object name
```

To be honest, Get-PSDrive is more trouble than it is worth. There is nothing wrong with having multiple Windows PowerShell drives mapped to the same resource. Therefore, if there is no HKCR drive, the Write-Verbose cmdlet is used to print a message stating that the drive does not exist and will be created.

```
Else
  {
    Write-Verbose "HKCR: drive not found. Creating same."
```

To create a new Windows PowerShell drive, use the New-PSDrive cmdlet to specify the name and root location of the Windows PowerShell drive. Because this drive is going to be a registry drive, you can use the registry provider. When a Windows PowerShell drive is created, it displays feedback to the Windows PowerShell console.

```
PS C:\AutoDoc> New-PSDrive -Name HKCR -PSProvider registry -Root HKEYClasses_Root
```

| Name | Provider | Root | CurrentLocation |
| ---- | -------- | ---- | --------------- |
| HKCR | Registry | Hkey_Classes_Root | |

The feedback from creating the registry drive can be distracting. To remove the feedback, you can pipeline the results to the Out-Null cmdlet.

```
New-PSDrive -Name HKCR -PSProvider registry -Root HKEY_Classes_Root | Out-Null
```

After the Windows PowerShell registry drive is created, it is time to look for the existence of the WMI provider class ID. But first, you can use the Write-Verbose cmdlet to provide feedback about this step of the operation.

```
Write-Verbose "Testing for $clsID"
```

The Test-Path cmdlet is used to check for the existence of the WMI provider class ID. To build the path to the registry key, the Join-Path cmdlet is used. The parent path is the HKCR registry drive CLSID hive, and the child path is the WMI provider class ID that is stored in the *clsID* variable.

```
Test-path -path (Join-Path -path HKCR:\CLSID -childpath $clsID)
```

After the Test-Path cmdlet is used to check for the existence of the WMI provider class ID, the Write-Verbose cmdlet is used to display a message stating that the test is complete.

```
Write-Verbose "Test complete."
```

It is a best practice to not make permanent modifications to the Windows PowerShell environment in a script. Therefore, you want to remove the Windows PowerShell drive if it was created in the script. The Write-Verbose cmdlet is employed to provide a status update, and the Remove-PSDrive cmdlet is used to remove the HKCR registry drive. To avoid cluttering the Windows PowerShell console, the result of removing the HKCR registry drive is pipelined to the Out-Null cmdlet.

```
Write-Verbose "Removing HKCR: drive."
Remove-PSDrive -Name HKCR | Out-Null
}
```

The entry point to the script assigns a value to the *$providerName* variable.

```
$providerName = "MSIProv"
```

The *Get-WmiProvider* function is called, and it passes both the WMI provider name that is stored in the *$providerName* variable and the *–verbose* switched parameter. The *If* statement is used because the *Get-WmiProvider* function returns a Boolean value: true or false.

```
if(Get-WmiProvider -providerName $providerName  -verbose )
```

If the return from the *Get-WmiProvider* function is true, the WMI class supported by the WMI provider is queried by using the Get-WMiObject cmdlet.

```
{
  Get-WmiObject -class win32_product
}
```

If the WMI provider is not found, a message stating that the WMI provider is not found is displayed to the console.

```
else
  {
  "$providerName provider not found"
  }
```

The complete Get-WmiProviderFunction.ps1 script is shown here.

```
Get-WmiProviderFunction.ps1

Function Get-WmiProvider
{
 [cmdletbinding()]
 Param ([string]$providerName)
 $provider =  Get-WmiObject -Class __provider -filter "name = '$providerName'"
 If($provider -ne $null)
   {
    $clsID = $provider.clsID
    Write-Verbose "$providerName WMI provider found. CLSID is $($CLSID)"
   }
 Else
   {
```

```
      Return $false
   }
   Write-Verbose "Checking for proper registry registration ..."
   If(Test-Path -path HKCR:)
      {
         Write-Verbose "HKCR: drive found. Testing for $clsID"
         Test-path -path (Join-Path -path HKCR:\CLSID -childpath $CLSID)
      }
   Else
      {
         Write-Verbose "HKCR: drive not found. Creating same."
         New-PSDrive -Name HKCR -PSProvider registry -Root HKEY_Classes_Root | Out-Null
         Write-Verbose "Testing for $clsID"
         Test-path -path (Join-Path -path HKCR:\CLSID -childpath $CLSID)
         Write-Verbose "Test complete."
         Write-Verbose "Removing HKCR: drive."
         Remove-PSDrive -Name HKCR | Out-Null
      }
} #end Get-WmiProvider function

# *** Entry Point to Script ***
$providerName = "msiprov"

 if(Get-WmiProvider -providerName $providerName  -verbose )
   {
     Get-WmiObject -class win32_product
   }
else
   {
     "$providerName provider not found"
   }
```

## Incorrect data types

There are two approaches to ensure that your users enter only allowed values for the
script parameters. The first approach is to offer only a limited number of values. The
second approach allows the user to enter any value for the parameter. It is then determined whether that value is valid before it is passed along to the remainder of the script.
In the Get-ValidWmiClassFunction.ps1 script, a function named *Get-ValidWmiClass* is
used to determine whether the value that is supplied to the script is a legitimate WMI
class name. In particular, the *Get-ValidWmiClass* function is used to determine whether
the string that is passed via the *–class* parameter can be cast to a valid instance of the
*System.Management.ManagementClass* .NET Framework class. The purpose of using

the [WMICLASS] type accelerator is to convert a string into an instance of the *System* *.Management.ManagementClass* class. As shown here, when you assign a string value to a variable, the variable becomes an instance of the *System.String* class. The *GetType* method is used to display information about the type of object that is contained in a variable.

```
PS C:\> $class = "win32_bio"
PS C:\> $class.GetType()

IsPublic IsSerial Name                                    BaseType
-------- -------- ----                                    --------
True     True     String                                  System.Object
```

To convert the string to a WMI class, you can use the [WMICLASS] type accelerator. The string value must contain the name of a legitimate WMI class. If the WMI class you are trying to create on the computer does not exist, an error is generated.

```
PS C:\> $class = "win32_bio"
PS C:\> [wmiclass]$class
Cannot convert value "win32_bio" to type "System.Management.ManagementClass".
Error: "Not found "
At line:1 char:16
+ [wmiclass]$class <<<<
```

The Get-ValidWmiClassFunction.ps1 script begins by creating two command-line parameters. The first is the *−computer* parameter that is used to allow the script to run on a local or remote computer. The second parameter is the *−class* parameter that is used to provide the name of the WMI class that will be queried by the script. The third parameter is used to allow the script to inspect other WMI namespaces. All three parameters are strings.

```
Param (
    [string]$computer = $env:computername,
    [string]$class,
    [string]$namespace = "root\cimv2"
) #end param
```

The *Get-ValidWmiClass* function is used to determine whether the value supplied for the *−class* parameter is a valid WMI class on the particular computer. This is important because certain versions of the operating system contain unique WMI classes. For example, Windows XP contains a WMI class named *NetDiagnostics* that does not exist on any other version of Windows. Windows XP does not contain the *Win32_Volume* WMI class, but Windows Server 2003 and newer versions do have this class. Therefore, checking for the existence of a WMI class on a remote computer is a good practice to ensure that the script will run in an expeditious manner.

First, the *Get-ValidWmiClass* function retrieves the current value for the *$errorActionPreference* variable. There are four possible values for this variable. The possible enumeration values are *SilentlyContinue*, *Stop*, *Continue*, and *Inquire*. The error-handling behavior of Windows PowerShell is governed by these enumeration values. If the value of *$errorActionPreference* is set to *SilentlyContinue*, any error that occurs will be skipped and the script will attempt to execute the next line of code in the script. The behavior is similar to using the VBScript setting *On Error Resume Next*. Normally, you do not want to use this setting because it can make troubleshooting scripts very difficult. It can also make the behavior of a script unpredictable and even lead to devastating consequences.

Consider the case in which you write a script that first creates a new directory on a remote server. Next, the script copies all of the files from a directory on your local computer to the remote server. Last, it deletes the directory and all of the files from the local computer. Now, you enable *$errorActionPreference = SilentlyContinue* and you run the script. The first command fails because the remote server is not available. The second command fails because it cannot copy the files, but the third command completes successfully—and you have just deleted all of the files you wanted to back up instead of actually backing up the files. Hopefully, you have a recent backup of your critical data. If you set *$errorActionPreference* to *SilentlyContinue*, you must handle errors that arise during the course of running the script.

In the *Get-ValidWmiClass* function, the old *$errorActionPreference* setting is retrieved and stored in the *$oldErrorActionPreference* variable. Next, the *$errorActionPreference* variable is set to *SilentlyContinue* because it is entirely possible that errors will be generated while in the process of checking for a valid WMI class name. Then the error stack is cleared of errors. The following three lines of code illustrate this process:

```
$oldErrorActionPreference = $errorActionPreference
$errorActionPreference = "SilentlyContinue"
$Error.Clear()
```

The value stored in the *$class* variable is used with the [WMICLASS] type accelerator to attempt to create a *System.Management.ManagementClass* object from the string. Because you need to run this script on a remote computer as well as on a local computer, the value in the *$computer* variable is used to provide a complete path to the potential management object. When concatenating the variables to make the path to the WMI class, a trailing colon causes problems with the *$namespace* variable. To work around this problem, a subexpression is used to force evaluation of the variable before attempting to concatenate the remainder of the string. The subexpression consists of a leading dollar sign and a pair of parentheses.

```
[WMICLASS]"\\$computer\$($namespace):$class" | out-null
```

To determine whether the conversion from string to *ManagementClass* is successful, the error record is checked. Because the error record was cleared earlier, any error that appears indicates that the command failed. If an error exists, the *Get-ValidWmiClass* function returns false to the calling code. If no error exists, the *Get-ValidWmiClass* function returns true.

```
If($error.count) { Return $false } Else { Return $true }
```

The last thing to do in the *Get-ValidWmiClass* function is to clean up the error environment. First, the error record is cleared, and then the value of the *$errorActionPreference* variable is set back to the original value.

```
$Error.Clear()
$errorActionPreference =  $oldErrorActionPreference
```

The next function in the Get-ValidWmiClassFunction.ps1 script is the *Get-WmiInformation* function. This function accepts the values from the *$computer*, *$class*, and *$namespace* variables and passes them to the Get-WmiObject cmdlet. The resulting *ManagementObject* is pipelined to the Format-List cmdlet, and all properties that begin with the letters *a* through *z* are displayed.

```
Function Get-WmiInformation ([string]$computer, [string]$class, [string]$namespace)
{
  Get-WmiObject -class $class -computername $computer -namespace $namespace|
  Format-List -property [a-z]*
} # end Get-WmiInformation function
```

The entry point to the script calls the *Get-ValidWmiClass* function; if it returns true, the script next calls the *Get-WmiInformation* function. However, if the *Get-ValidWmiClass* function returns false, a message is displayed that details the class name, namespace, and computer name. This information can be used for troubleshooting any difficulty in obtaining the WMI information.

```
If(Get-ValidWmiClass -computer $computer -class $class -namespace $namespace)
  {
    Get-WmiInformation -computer $computer -class $class -namespace $namespace
  }
Else
 {
   "$class is not a valid wmi class in the $namespace namespace on $computer"
 }
```

The complete Get-ValidWmiClassFunction.ps1 script is shown here.

```
Get-ValidWmiClassFunction.ps1

Param (
    [string]$computer = $env:computername,
    [string]$class,
    [string]$namespace = "root\cimv2"
) #end param

Function Get-ValidWmiClass([string]$computer, [string]$class, [string]$namespace)
{
 $oldErrorActionPreference = $errorActionPreference
 $errorActionPreference = "SilentlyContinue"
 $Error.Clear()
 [wmiclass]"\\$computer\$($namespace):$class" | out-null
 If($error.count) { Return $false } Else { Return $true }
 $Error.Clear()
 $errorActionPreference =  $oldErrorActionPreference
} # end Get-ValidWmiClass function

Function Get-WmiInformation ([string]$computer, [string]$class, [string]$namespace)
{
```

```
  Get-WmiObject -class $class -computername $computer -namespace $namespace|
  Format-List -property [a-z]*
} # end Get-WmiInformation function


# *** Entry point to script ***


If(Get-ValidWmiClass -computer $computer -class $class -namespace $namespace)
  {
    Get-WmiInformation -computer $computer -class $class -namespace $namespace
  }
Else
  {
    "$class is not a valid wmi class in the $namespace namespace on $computer"
  }
```

**NOTES FROM THE FIELD**

### Learning to use the Windows PowerShell error-handling mechanisms

**Bill Stewart, Network Administrator**
*Moderator for Official Scripting Guys Forum*

I have written many Windows Script Host (WSH) scripts using VBScript over the years, and error handling is one of the weakest features of VBScript. For example, if a line of VBScript code throws an error, it always terminates the script unless you use the *On Error Resume Next* statement to disable the default error handler. However, the *On Error Resume Next* statement can have unforeseen consequences because it causes the VBScript interpreter to skip all subsequent lines containing errors. I cannot count the number of times I have seen questions about VBScript problems in online forums because the script's author put the *On Error Resume Next* statement at the top of the script without understanding how the VBScript error handler works.

In contrast, the Windows PowerShell error-handling mechanisms are much more flexible and powerful than those of VBScript. Because Windows PowerShell distinguishes between terminating and non-terminating errors, handling errors in Windows PowerShell code can be more complex than in VBScript. However, after I understood the difference between terminating and non-terminating errors, it was easier to write error-handling code in Windows PowerShell scripts.

First, I usually handle non-terminating errors by setting the *$errorActionPreference* variable (or the *–ErrorAction* parameter of a cmdlet) to *SilentlyContinue* and then test the *$?* variable.

```
get-item "C:\FileDoesNotExist.txt" -erroraction SilentlyContinue
if (-not $?) {
  write-host ("Exception: " + $Error[0].Exception.GetType().FullName)
  write-host $Error[0].Exception.Message
}
```

Second, I handle terminating errors using the Windows PowerShell *Try* and *Catch* statements.

```
try {
  $searcher = [WMISearcher] "select * from Win32_NonExistentClass"
  $searcher.Get()
}
catch [System.Management.Automation.RuntimeException] {
  write-host ("Exception: " + $_.Exception.GetType().FullName)
  write-host $_.Exception.Message
}
```

Windows PowerShell 1.0 provided only the *Trap* statement to catch terminating errors, but the *Try* and *Catch* statements are clearer and easier to use.

One thing that initially confused me is that catch blocks handle only terminating errors. That is, you cannot use a catch block to handle non-terminating errors unless the *$errorActionPreference* variable (or the *–ErrorAction* parameter of a cmdlet) is set to *Stop*.

```
try {
  get-item "C:\FileDoesNotExist.txt" -ErrorAction Stop
}
catch {
  write-host ("Exception: " + $_.Exception.GetType().FullName)
  write-host $_.Exception.Message
}
```

If you omit the *–ErrorAction* parameter from this example, the Get-Item cmdlet throws a non-terminating error and the catch block is ignored.

> However, there is one caveat to handling non-terminating errors using *Try/Catch*.
> If you set *$errorActionPreference* to *Stop* and handle the error in a catch block, the
> exception object's message contains the following introductory text: "Command
> execution stopped because the preference variable "errorActionPreference" or com-
> mon parameter is set to Stop." If you don't mind this introductory text in the excep-
> tion message (for example, if you're not writing the exception message anywhere),
> this method works fine. Yet because I usually output the exception message, I prefer
> to set *$errorActionPreference* to *SilentlyContinue* and test the *$?* variable instead.

# Out of bounds errors

When receiving input from a user, an allowed value is limited to a specified range of values.
If the allowable range is small, it might be best to present the user with a prompt that allows
selection from a few choices, as shown in the "Limiting choices" section earlier in this chapter.
However, when the allowable range of values is large, limiting the choices through a menu-
type system is not practical. This is where bounds checking comes into play.

## Using a boundary checking function

One technique used to perform boundary checking is to use a function that determines
whether the supplied value is permissible. One way to create a boundary checking function
is to have the script create a hash table of permissible values. You can then use the *–contains*
method to determine whether the value supplied from the command line is permissible. If
the value is present in the hash table, the *–contains* method returns true. If the value is not
present, it returns false. The *Check-AllowedValue* function is used to gather a hash table of
volumes that reside on the target computer. This hash table is then used to verify that the volume requested from the *–drive* command-line parameter is actually present on the computer.
The *Check-AllowedValue* function returns a Boolean true/false value to the calling code in the
main body of the script. The complete *Check-AllowedValue* function is shown here:

```
Function Check-AllowedValue($drive, $computerName)
{
 Get-WmiObject -class Win32_Volume -computername $computerName|
 ForEach-Object { $drives += @{ $_.DriveLetter = $_.DriveLetter } }
 $drives.contains($drive)
} #end function Check-AllowedValue
```

Because the *Check-AllowedValue* function returns a Boolean value, an *If* statement is used
to determine whether the value supplied to the *–drive* parameter is permissible. If the drive
letter is found in the *$drives* hash table that is created in the *Check-AllowedValue* function,

the *Get-DiskInformation* function is called. If the *–drive* parameter value is not found in the hash table, a warning message is displayed to the Windows PowerShell console, and the script exits. The complete GetDrivesCheckAllowedValue.ps1 script is shown here.

```
GetDrivesCheckAllowedValue.ps1

Param(
   [Parameter(Mandatory=$true)]
   [string]$drive,
   [string]$computerName = $env:computerName
) #end param

Function Check-AllowedValue($drive, $computerName)
{
 Get-WmiObject -class Win32_Volume -computername $computerName|
 ForEach-Object { $drives += $_.DriveLetter }
 $drives.contains($drive)
} #end function Check-AllowedValue

Function Get-DiskInformation($computerName,$drive)
{
 Get-WmiObject -class Win32_volume -computername $computername -filter "DriveLetter =
'$drive'"
} #end function Get-DiskInformation
# *** Entry Point To Script ***

if(Check-AllowedValue -drive $drive -computername $computerName)
  {
    Get-DiskInformation -computername $computerName -drive $drive
  }
else
  {
   Write-Host -foregroundcolor yellow "$drive is not an allowed value:"
  }
```

## Placing limits on the parameter

In Windows PowerShell 2.0 and newer versions, you can place limits directly on the parameter in the *Param* section of the script. This technique works well when you are working with a limited set of allowable values. The *ValidateRange* parameter attribute creates a numeric range of allowable values, but it can also create a range of letters. Using this technique, you can greatly simplify the GetDrivesCheckAllowedValue.ps1 script by creating an allowable range of drive letters. The *Param* statement is shown here:

```
Param(
    [Parameter(Mandatory=$true)]
    [ValidateRange("c","f")]
    [string]$drive,
    [string]$computerName = $env:computerName
) #end param
```

Because you can control the permissible drive letters from the command line, you increase the simplicity and readability of the script by not having the requirement to create a separate function to validate the allowed values. One additional change is required in the GetDrivesValidRange.ps1 script, and that is to concatenate a colon at the end of the drive letter. In the GetDrivesCheckAllowedValue.ps1 script, you could include the drive letter and the colon from the command line; however, this technique does not work with the *ValidateRange* attribute. The trick to concatenating the colon to the drive letter is that it needs to be escaped.

```
-filter "DriveLetter = '$drive':'"
```

The complete GetDrivesValidRange.ps1 script is shown here.

```
GetDrivesValidRange.ps1

Param(
    [Parameter(Mandatory=$true)]
    [ValidateRange("c","f")]
    [string]$drive,
    [string]$computerName = $env:computerName
) #end param

Function Get-DiskInformation($computerName,$drive)
{
 Get-WmiObject -class Win32_volume -computername $computername `
 -filter "DriveLetter = '$drive':'"
} #end function Get-DiskInformation
# *** Entry Point To Script ***

Get-DiskInformation -computername $computerName -drive $drive
```

# Additional resources

- The TechNet Script Center at *http://www.microsoft.com/technet/scriptcenter* contains numerous examples of Windows PowerShell scripts that perform error handling.
- All scripts from this chapter are available via the TechNet Script Center Script Repository at *http://gallery.technet.microsoft.com/scriptcenter/PowerShell-40 -Best-d9e16039.*

# CHAPTER 13

# Testing scripts

- Using basic syntax checking techniques
- Conducting performance testing of scripts
- Using standard parameters
- Using *Start-Transcript* to produce a log
- Advanced script testing
- Additional resources

If you take the time to write a script, you should take a few additional minutes to test the script. How do you know what to test in the script? For many IT professionals, testing a script is nothing more than running the script and looking for errors. If the script runs without errors, the script is considered to be a good script. As you will learn in this chapter, there is more to testing a script than determining whether it runs without errors. When testing your scripts, it is a best practice to check the basic syntax of the script. You should also measure the performance of the script to ensure that the script will meet the demands of your specific environment. If a script accepts command-line parameters, you should also test the script to see how it handles various types of input.

## Using basic syntax checking techniques

Basic syntax checking can be done by running the script and looking for errors. If you have several scripts to check, it makes sense to write a script that will perform basic syntax checking for you. Test-ScriptHarness.ps1 searches a folder for all .ps1 scripts, executes each script while checking for errors, and records the length of time it takes for each script to run. The Test-ScriptHarness.ps1 script writes the results to a text file and then displays the report.

First, the Test-ScriptHarness.ps1 script determines whether the script is running inside a virtual machine. A script that is going to execute a large number of Windows PowerShell scripts can potentially cause a significant amount of damage to your workstation, depending on the actions that the scripts are performing. For example, if one of the scripts kicks off an automated installation of Windows 8, you can potentially wipe out all of your data and end up with a fresh installation of Windows 8. If you run the script inside a virtual machine on Hyper-V with undo disks enabled, you are minimizing the potential disruption that the scripts can cause.

Because the *Win32_ComputerSystem* Windows Management Instrumentation (WMI) class returns a single instance, you can directly access the properties of the class. This means that you do not need to work through a collection of instances of the class to retrieve the model property value. On Hyper-V, the model is reported as "virtual machine." If the model is not reported as "virtual machine," the script displays a prompt asking whether you want to run the script. This prompt is created by using the Read-Host cmdlet. If you type **n** in reply to the prompt, the script will exit. Any other response to the Read-Host prompt permits the script to run.

```
if((Get-WmiObject Win32_ComputerSystem).model -ne "virtual machine")
  {
    $response = Read-Host -prompt "This script is best run in a VM.
    Do you wish to continue? <y / n>"
    if ($response -eq "n") { exit }
  }
```

The path to search for Windows PowerShell scripts is stored in the *$path* variable. Depending on how you plan to run the Test-ScriptHarness.ps1 script, you might want to change the variable to a command-line parameter.

```
$path = "C:\bp"
```

The *GetTempFileName* static method from the *System.Io.Path* Microsoft .NET Framework class is used to create a temporary file name in the Users temporary directory. The path to this temporary file name is stored in the *$report* directory. An example of a temporary file name is shown here:

```
C:\Users\administrator.NWTRADERS.000\AppData\Local\Temp\tmpC484.tmp
```

Because the file name is randomly generated each time the *GetTempFileName* method is called, it is stored in the *$report* variable for use later in the script.

```
$report = [io.path]::GetTempFileName()
```

The Get-ChildItem cmdlet shown here is used to produce a listing of all .ps1 files in the folder referenced by the *$path* variable. The *–recurse* parameter is required to permit the Get-ChildItem cmdlet to retrieve all .ps1 files in the folder. The results from the Get-ChildItem cmdlet are pipelined to the ForEach-Object cmdlet.

```
Get-ChildItem -Path $path -Include *.ps1 -Recurse |
```

The ForEach-Object cmdlet uses the *–Begin* parameter to perform an action once for all items that enter the pipeline. In this example, the starting time of the script processing is stored in the *$stime* variable. (The *$stime* variable is used instead of *$startTime* because *$startTime* will be used later.) The value of the *$errorActionPreference* automatic variable is set to *SilentlyContinue*, indicating that errors are not to be displayed and the script should continue processing when an error is encountered. A status message is written to the *$report* file that indicates the beginning of script testing and the time it commenced.

```
ForEach-Object -Begin '
  {
```

```
$stime = Get-Date
$ErrorActionPreference = "SilentlyContinue"
"Testing ps1 scripts in $path $stime" |
   Out-File -append -FilePath $report
```

The *–Process* parameter occurs once for each object that comes through the pipeline. The first thing that is done inside the Process block is to clear all errors from the error stack to ensure that any errors that do occur are specific to the particular script that is being tested. A new time is written to the *$startTime* variable, and this time stamp will be used to calculate how long it takes the specific script to run. An entry is written to the report that indicates the name of the script and the starting time from the *$startTime* variable. The name of the script is obtained from the *$_* automatic variable, which refers to the current object on the pipeline. All of the output from this section is then pipelined to the Out-File cmdlet with the *–append* parameter, to tell the script to add to the *$report* file instead of overwriting the file.

```
} -Process '
{
$error.Clear()
$startTime = Get-Date
"  Begin Testing $_ at $startTime" |
   Out-File -append -FilePath $report
```

It is now time to run the script that is on the pipeline. To execute the script, you use the Invoke-Expression cmdlet with the *–command* parameter and provide it with the *$_* automatic variable.

```
Invoke-Expression -Command $_
```

When the script completes running, you should retrieve the time that the script completed. The end time of the script is then pipelined to the Out-File cmdlet with the *–append* parameter.

```
$endTime = Get-Date
"  End testing $_ at $endTime." |
   Out-File -append -FilePath $report
```

To continue with the report, the number of errors on the error stack is obtained and written to the *$report* file. Because the *$error* automatic variable contains an object, a subexpression is used (a dollar sign and a set of parentheses surround the *$error* variable) to force the evaluation of the *count* property from the *$error* object. This value is then sent down the pipeline to the Out-File cmdlet.

```
"    Script generated $($error.Count) errors" |
   Out-File -append -FilePath $report
```

The *DateTime* object that is stored in the *$startTime* variable is subtracted from the *DateTime* object that is stored in the *$endTime* variable. Once again, a subexpression is used to force the evaluation of this operation. If you do not use a subexpression inside the expanding string double quotation marks, you need to use concatenation to combine the string and the *DateTime* objects. The time that is created by subtracting the starting time from the ending time is pipelined to the Out-File cmdlet for inclusion in the report. When this is done, the process block of the ForEach-Object cmdlet is completed.

```
"    Elasped time: $($endTime - $startTime)" |
   Out-File -append -FilePath $report
} -end '
```

After the last script has run, the ending time is stored in the *$etime* variable. The value of the *$errorActionPreference* variable is set back to the default value of *Continue,* and the ending time is written to the report.

```
{
 $etime = Get-Date
 $ErrorActionPreference = "Continue"
 "Completed testing all scripts in $path $etime" |
   Out-File -append -FilePath $report
```

Last, you must record the total running time for all script testing. To do this, the start time recorded in the *$stime* variable is subtracted from the time stored in the *$etime* variable. A subexpression is used to force the evaluation of the total elapsed time. The total time is pipelined to the Out-File cmdlet and the entire report is displayed in Notepad.

```
 "Testing took $($etime - $stime)" |
   Out-File -append -FilePath $report
}
Notepad $report
```

The complete Test-ScriptHarness.ps1 script is shown here.

---

**Test-ScriptHarness.ps1**

```
if((Get-WmiObject win32_computersystem).model -ne "virtual machine")
 {
   $response = Read-Host -prompt "This script is best run in a VM.
   Do you wish to continue? <y / n>"
   if ($response -eq "n") { exit }
 }
$path = "C:\ScriptFolder"
$report = [io.path]::GetTempFileName()
Get-ChildItem -Path $path -Include *.ps1 -Recurse |
ForEach-Object -Begin '
 {
  $stime = Get-Date
  $ErrorActionPreference = "SilentlyContinue"
  "Testing ps1 scripts in $path $stime" |
    Out-File -append -FilePath $report
 } -Process '
 {
  $error.Clear()
  $startTime = Get-Date
```

```
   "  Begin Testing $_ at $startTime" |
     Out-File -append -FilePath $report
   Invoke-Expression -Command $_
   $endTime = Get-Date
   "  End testing $_ at $endTime." |
     Out-File -append -FilePath $report
   "     Script generated $($error.Count) errors" |
     Out-File -append -FilePath $report
   "     Elasped time: $($endTime - $startTime)" |
     Out-File -append -FilePath $report
 } -end '
 {
  $etime = Get-Date
  $ErrorActionPreference = "Continue"
  "Completed testing all scripts in $path $etime" |
    Out-File -append -FilePath $report
  "Testing took $($etime - $stime)" |
    Out-File -append -FilePath $report
 }

 Notepad $report
```

Figure 13-1 shows the report that is produced.

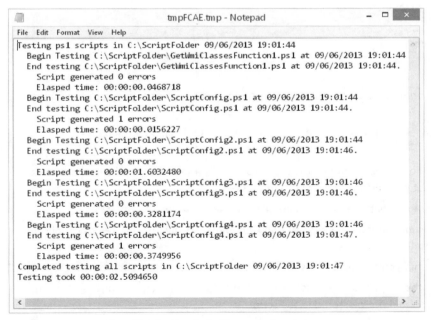

**FIGURE 13-1** Log produced by the Test-ScriptHarness.ps1 script.

# Looking for errors

A systematic script-testing methodology is probably not going to directly save time, and it more than likely will add time during the prerelease phase of your script. However, because you will experience fewer unexplained errors as a result of poorly written scripts, you will likely save time over the lifetime of the script.

One of the simplest ways to test a script is to run the script. However, before you run the script, you should examine it for obvious errors and clues to its functionality. Pay attention to each section of the script. Individual sections are listed here, with details about the types of items you should examine. You should make these checks prior to running the script.

In the *Param* section, focus on the following things:

- The command-line parameters begin with the *param* keyword.
- Each command-line parameter is separated by a comma.
- The last parameter is not followed by a comma.
- The parentheses should open and close.
- Make sure that the *Param* statement is the first noncommented line in the script.
- Look for mandatory parameters and default values of parameters.

A correctly formed *Param* statement is shown here:

```
Param(
    [string]$computer=$env:computerName,
    [switch]$disk,
    [switch]$processor,
    [switch]$memory,
    [switch]$network,
    [switch]$video,
    [switch]$all
) #end param
```

In the *Function* section, there are many different items on which to focus, including the following:

- The function begins by using the *function* keyword followed by the name of the function.
- The function name should follow the Verb-Noun pattern, which follows the same naming format of Windows PowerShell cmdlets.
- Input parameters to the function are placed inside a set of parentheses.
- Each *function* parameter is separated by a comma. The last parameter is not followed by a comma.
- Each opening curly bracket must have a corresponding closing curly bracket.
- How are the functions called from within the script? If a function is not used in the script, it should not be stored in the script.

- Pay particular attention to the function parameters. What types of parameters do the functions require?

A correctly formed function section is shown here:

```
Function Get-Disk($computer)
{
 Get-WmiObject -class Win32_LogicalDisk -computername $computer
} #end Get-Disk
```

You are now at the entry point to the script. The entry point of the script is the first code that is executed when the script runs (following the *Param* statement). This code is extremely important because it governs what the script will actually do. Consider the following questions:

- What does the entry point code actually do?
- What variables are initialized? Are the variables released at the end of the script?
- What constants are declared? In what scope are the constants created?
- What objects are created? What methods and properties are exposed by the new objects?
- What are the default actions? What happens when the script is run without using any command-line parameters?
- Does the script expose any help?
- Does the help provide any examples of using the script?
- What type of output does the script produce? Does it output to the screen, a text file, a database, email, or some other location?
- Is the output location from the script accessible to the workstation that runs the script?

**INSIDE TRACK**

### Testing with Windows PowerShell

**James Brundage and Ibrahim Abdul Rahim, Software Development Engineers**
*Microsoft Corporation*

The key point to remember about testing software in Windows PowerShell is that it is the same general task as automating the operating system with Windows PowerShell. To test software, you must get the operating system into a good working state. (For example, you might launch programs or change registry keys.) You can then automate an action instead of doing it manually, and you can verify the result by looking at what the action does to the operating system.

Because automated software testing and systems automation use so many of the same tools, the first thing to keep in mind as a tester is to leverage the examples that you find from scripters or C# developers. Windows PowerShell can easily work with all of the objects from C# (using the New-Object cmdlet) and VBScript (using the New-Object *–ComObject* parameter).

Another point to keep in mind when considering testing with Windows PowerShell is the need for a framework. Usually, software tests are automated within a testing framework. The testing framework runs a chunk of code with some parameters and writes the results to one or more logs. When you write a Windows PowerShell function, you also have a chunk of code with parameters and, within that code, a function that you can write to several logs (Output, Error, Verbose, Debug, Warning, and Progress Logs or the Event Log). Because Windows PowerShell already contains everything you need for a good framework, including an Integrated Scripting Environment (ISE), I tend to use PowerShell as my framework rather than another testing framework.

The final point to keep in mind when testing in Windows PowerShell is the importance of interactivity. The key to testing in Windows PowerShell is to interact with Application Programming Interfaces (APIs), webpages, and user interfaces by trying them in short scripts and then turning those short scripts into common libraries and automated tests. I recommend using the command pane of the Windows PowerShell ISE to adjust your interaction and then copy working commands into the scripting pane to create tests.

## Running the script

After you examine the script in sufficient detail, it is time to run the script. Before running the script for the first time, consider the possible impact of running the script on your computer. (The best place to test new scripts is in a virtual machine with undo disks enabled.) Consider the following questions:

- Do you have any unsaved work?
- Have you closed all unnecessary programs?
- Is the script that you are working on saved?
- Is the script that you are working on backed up to an external drive? (If the script completely wipes out your computer, you will have a record of what the script actually did to your computer.)
- Do you have a previously working version of the script? (If the changes to the script are radical, you might have trouble backing out the changes in case of a disaster.)
- Do you have a recent backup of your workstation?

When you run the Get-ComputerWmiInformation.ps1 script, you will notice that there is no output and no feedback from the script: no errors, no output, no feedback, and no help.

You will need to determine how the script runs by examining the command-line parameters and the entry point to the script. Nearly all of the command-line parameters are switched parameters and have names such as *–disk*, *–processor*, *–memory*, and one named *–all*. From this bit of information, you might surmise that the script retrieves information about computer hardware. From the name of the script, Get-ComputerWmiInformation.ps1, you might determine that the script uses WMI to obtain information.

The entry point to the script calls the *Get-CommandLineOptions* function. An examination of the *Get-CommandLineOptions* function reveals that it tests for each of the command-line parameters and calls the appropriate function. Because there is no default behavior, the script ends without notice when it is run without any command-line parameters. The *Get-CommandLineOptions* function is shown here:

```
Function Get-CommandLineOptions
{

if($all)
  {
    Get-Disk($computer)
    Get-Processor($computer)
    Get-Memory($computer)
    Get-Network($computer)
    Get-Video($computer)
     exit
  } #end all

if($disk)
  {
    Get-Disk($computer)
  } #end disk

if($processor)
  {
    Get-Processor($computer)
  } #end processor

if($memory)
  {
    Get-Memory($computer)
  } #end memory

if($network)
  {
    Get-Network($computer)
  } #end network

if($video)
  {
    Get-Video($computer)
  } #end video
} #end function Get-CommandLineOptions
```

## Documenting what you did

Make sure that you document how the script was tested. The version of the operating system, service pack level, and installed hotfixes all impact the way a script will run. Document all software that is installed on the computer, including management clients (such as Microsoft System Center Operations Manager Management Packs). If you run the script from within a script editor or directly from the command line of the Windows PowerShell console, it should be noted. If you are running on a 64-bit version of the operating system, you should test the script in both 32-bit and 64-bit Windows PowerShell. The script should be run elevated with Administrator rights and with normal user rights.

The Get-ComputerWmiInformation.ps1 script is shown here.

```
Get-ComputerWmiInformation.ps1

Param(
    [string]$computer=$env:computerName,
    [switch]$disk,
    [switch]$processor,
    [switch]$memory,
    [switch]$network,
    [switch]$video,
    [switch]$all
) #end param


Function Get-Disk($computer)
{
 Get-WmiObject -class Win32_LogicalDisk -computername $computer
} #end Get-Disk


Function Get-Processor($computer)
```

```
{
 Get-WmiObject -class Win32_Processor -computername $computer
} #end Get-Processor

Function Get-Memory($computer)
{
 Get-WmiObject -class Win32_PhysicalMemory -computername $computer
} #end Get-Processor

Function Get-Network($computer)
{
 Get-WmiObject -class Win32_NetworkAdapter -computername $computer
} #end Get-Processor

Function Get-Video($computer)
{
 Get-WmiObject -class Win32_VideoController -computername $computer
} #end Get-Processor

Function Get-CommandLineOptions
{

if($all)
  {
    Get-Disk($computer)
    Get-Processor($computer)
    Get-Memory($computer)
    Get-Network($computer)
    Get-Video($computer)
     exit
  } #end all

if($disk)
  {
    Get-Disk($computer)
  } #end disk

if($processor)
  {
    Get-Processor($computer)
  } #end processor

if($memory)
  {
    Get-Memory($computer)
```

```
    } #end memory

if($network)
  {
    Get-Network($computer)
  } #end network

if($video)
  {
    Get-Video($computer)
  } #end video
} #end function Get-CommandLineOptions

# *** Entry Point to Script ***

Get-CommandLineOptions
```

## Conducting performance testing of scripts

A common mistake that some people make is to use Windows PowerShell as if it were another scripting language. When you use certain constructions, such as the ones that read the contents of a file and store the results in a variable, and then iterate through the contents of the file by using a *Foreach* statement, the performance will generally be substandard. This type of store and forward construction is shown here:

```
$a = Get-Content -Path c:\fso\myfile.txt
Foreach ($i in $a)
{
 Write-Host $i
}
```

The previous construction can easily be written in Microsoft Visual Basic, VBScript, or a dozen other languages because the design pattern is exactly the same. However, for optimal performance and ease of development, it is best to take advantage of the native features of Windows PowerShell. For example, the previous code can be written as shown here:

```
Get-Content -Path c:\fso\myfile.txt
```

One of the more powerful features of Windows PowerShell is the pipeline, and when you do not take advantage of the pipeline, you are setting yourself up for disappointing results. The Windows PowerShell pipeline does not need to read the entire contents of the file before processing it. Additionally, when working with large files, you reduce the amount of memory that is required because you do not need to store the contents of the file in a variable. Due to the asynchronous nature of the pipeline and the reduced memory footprint of the operation, it is a Windows PowerShell best practice to engage the pipeline whenever it makes sense in your code.

Because you know that the Windows PowerShell pipeline is more efficient, it seems logical to always use it in your script. However, this is simply not the case. For certain types of operations, such as those that process small files and do not require large amounts of memory, the store and forward approach previously shown can actually be more efficient. The key to determining the best approach to writing a script is to test two different versions of the script and see which one is the fastest. In this section, we will look at different versions of a script to determine which one is the fastest.

## Using the store and forward approach

The Get-ModifiedFiles.ps1 script is used to count the number of files that were modified in a folder within a specified period of time. The *param* keyword is used to create two command-line parameters. The first parameter is the *–path* parameter that specifies the folder to search. The second parameter is the *-days* parameter that is used to create the starting date for counting modified files.

```
Param(
     $path = "C:\data",
     $days = 30
) #end param
```

The starting date needs to be a *DateTime* object. The Get-Date cmdlet creates an instance of a *DateTime* object, which exposes the *AddDays* method. By using a negative number for the number of days to be added to the current *DateTime* object, a point in time from the past is created. By default, the script creates a *DateModified* object 30 days in the past.

```
$dteModified = (Get-Date).AddDays(-$days)
```

The Get-ChildItem cmdlet is used to obtain a collection of all files and folders in the path that are specified by the *$path* variable. The *–recurse* switched parameter is used to tell the Get-ChildItem cmdlet to burrow down into all of the subfolders. This collection of files and folders is stored in the *$files* variable.

```
$files = Get-ChildItem -path $path –recurse
```

To walk through the collection of files and folders, the *Foreach* statement is used. The variable *$file* is used as the enumerator that keeps track of the current position in the collection. The collection of files and folders is stored in the *$files* variable. Inside the *foreach* loop, the *If* statement is used to evaluate the *DateTime* object that is retrieved from the *LastWriteTime* property of the file object. If the value stored in the *LastWriteTime* property is greater than or equal to the *DateTime* value stored in the *$dteModified* variable, the value of the *$changedFiles* variable is incremented by one.

```
Foreach($file in $files)
{
  if($file.LastWriteTime -ge $dteModified)
    { $changedFiles ++ }
}
```

The last step initiated by the Get-ModifiedFiles.ps1 script is to display a message to the user stating how many modified files are found. The following command is used to display the confirmation message to the user.

```
"The $path has $changedFiles modified files since $dteModified"
```

The complete Get-ModifiedFiles.ps1 script is shown here.

**Get-ModifiedFiles.ps1**

```
Param(
    $path = "D:",
    $days = 30
) #end param
$dteModified= (Get-Date).AddDays(-$days)
$files = Get-ChildItem -path $path -recurse

Foreach($file in $files)
{
  if($file.LastWriteTime -ge $dteModified)
    { $changedFiles ++ }
}

"The $path has $changedFiles modified files since $dteModified"
```

When the Get-ModifiedFiles.ps1 script is run, it takes a bit of time to return on my computer. This is understandable because the D drive on my computer consumes approximately 60 GB of disk space and contains nearly 30,000 files and 4,000 folders. It therefore does not seem to be a horrible performance considering what the script is actually doing.

## Using the Windows PowerShell pipeline

The Get-ModifiedFiles.ps1 script can be changed to take advantage of the Windows PowerShell pipeline. The *Param* statement and the creation of the *DateTime* object contained in the *$dteModified* variable are exactly the same. The first change comes when the results of the Get-ChildItem cmdlet are pipelined to the next command instead of being stored in the *$files* variable. This results in two performance improvements. The first improvement is that subsequent sections of the script can begin work almost immediately. When the results of the Get-ChildItem cmdlet are stored in a variable, all 30,000 files and 4,000 folders in the previous example must be enumerated before any additional processing can begin. In addition, because the variable is stored in memory, it is conceivable that the computer might run out of memory before it finishes enumerating all of the files and folders from an extremely large drive. The change to the pipeline is shown here:

```
Get-ChildItem -path $path -recurse |
```

Instead of using the *Foreach* statement, the Get-ModifiedFilesUsePipeline.ps1 script uses the ForEach-Object cmdlet. The ForEach-Object cmdlet is designed to accept pipelined input and is more flexible than the *Foreach* language statement. The default parameter for the ForEach-Object cmdlet is the *–Process* parameter. As each object comes through the pipeline, the *$_* automatic variable is used to reference it. Here the *$_* automatic variable is acting in a similar fashion to the *$file* variable from the Get-ModifiedFiles.ps1 script. The *If* statement is exactly the same in the Get-ModifiedFilesUsePipeline.ps1 script, with the exception of the change to using *$_* instead of *$file*. The ForEach-Object section of the Get-ModifiedFilesUsePipeline.ps1 script is shown here:

```
ForEach-Object {
  if($_.LastWriteTime -ge $dteModified)
    { $changedFiles ++ }
}
```

The user message is the same as that shown in the Get-ModifiedFiles.ps1 script. The completed Get-ModifiedFilesUsePipeline.ps1 script is shown here.

```
Get-ModifiedFilesUsePipeline.ps1

Param(
    $path = "D:",
    $days = 30
) #end param


$dteModified= (Get-Date).AddDays(-$days)
Get-ChildItem -path $path -recurse |
ForEach-Object {
  if($_.LastWriteTime -ge $dteModified)
    { $changedFiles ++ }
}

"The $path has $changedFiles modified files since $dteModified"
```

## Comparing the speed of two scripts

When the Get-ModifiedFilesUsePipeline.ps1 script is run, it seems a little faster, but it might be hard to tell. Was the modification to the script worth the trouble? To determine whether a change to a script makes an improvement in the performance of the script, you can use the Measure-Command cmdlet. You will want to first measure the performance of the original script and then measure the performance of the revised script. To measure the performance of the original script, you supply the path to the Get-ModifiedFiles.ps1 script to the *Expression* parameter of the Measure-Command cmdlet.

In the command line that follows, the error stream is redirected by using the 2> redirection operator. Because I know that doing a recursive directory listing of the C drive generates errors, I am not concerned with seeing them. Therefore, I redirect the errors to the $null variable, and am treated to a clean output.

```
Measure-Command {C:\ScriptFolder\Get-ModifiedFiles.ps1 -path c:} 2>$null
```

The Measure-Command cmdlet returns a *System.TimeSpan* .NET Framework class, which is used to measure the difference between two *System.DateTime* classes. It has a number of properties that report days, hours, minutes, seconds, and milliseconds, and these properties report the time span in units of these divisions. In Figure 13-2, you see that the Get-ModifiedFiles.ps1 script ran for 8 seconds and 828 milliseconds. The *System.TimeSpan* object also reports the time span in total units. The same time span is reported as five different units. For example, the Get-ModifiedFiles.ps1 script run time of 8 seconds and 828 milliseconds translates into 8.8280876 total seconds or 0.147134793333333 total minutes. When expressed in milliseconds, this value is 8828.0876.

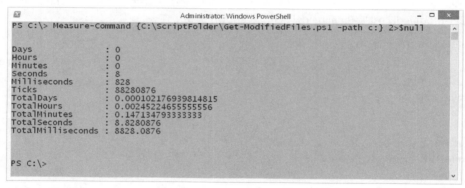

**FIGURE 13-2** The Measure-Command cmdlet returns a *TimeSpan* object.

The double display of time breakdown into days, hours, minutes, seconds, and milliseconds can be confusing to people who are not used to working with the *System.TimeSpan* .NET Framework class. In general, you can probably examine only the *TotalSeconds* property when testing your scripts.

It is now time to see whether the use of the pipeline makes any difference in the performance of the script. To measure the performance of the Get-ModifiedFilesUsePipeline.ps1 script, the path to the Get-ModifiedFilesUsePipeline.ps1 script is passed to the *Expression* parameter of the Measure-Command cmdlet, which results in the command line shown here:

```
PS C:\> Measure-Command {C:\ScriptFolder\Get-ModifiedFilesUsePipeline.ps1 -path c:} 2
>$null
```

After the command has run, the *TimeSpan* object shown in Figure 13-3 is displayed.

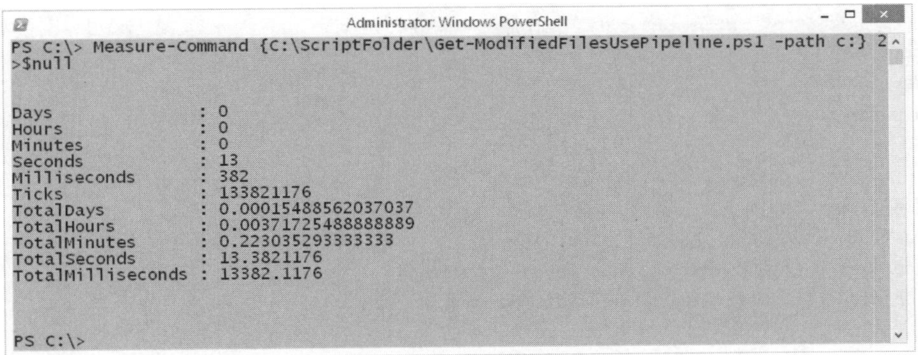

**FIGURE 13-3** *TimeSpan* object displaying improvement in script speed when using the pipeline.

As shown in Figure 13-3, the Get-ModifiedFilesUsePipeline.ps1 script completed in 13.3821176 total seconds. When compared to the original 8.8280876 total seconds, we see the speed of the script declined. This points out the importance of performance testing because, at times, the results are actually counter-intuitive, and you can invest time in trying to improve a script's performance and actually go in the opposite direction.

## Reducing code complexity

Further changes can be made to the Get-ModifiedFilesUsePipeline.ps1 script. This is a more radical modification to the script because it requires removing the ForEach-Object cmdlet and the *If* statement. The following section of code is ripped out:

```
ForEach-Object {
  if($_.LastWriteTime -ge $dteModified)
    { $changedFiles ++ }
}
```

By removing the ForEach-Object cmdlet and the *If* statement, you can get rid of the *$changedFiles* ++ statement and take advantage of the fact that Windows PowerShell automatically returns objects from the cmdlets. The use of the single Where-Object cmdlet should be faster than the more convoluted ForEach-Object cmdlet when combined with the *If* statement. However, you will determine whether the modification is effective when you test the script with the Measure-Object cmdlet. By using a single Where-Object cmdlet, you arrive at the following filter:

```
where-object { $_.LastWriteTime -ge $dteModified }
```

The result of the pipeline operation is stored in the *$changedFiles* variable, which has a *count* property associated with it. Directly reading the *count* property should be faster than incrementing the *$changedFiles* variable as was done in the Get-ModifiedFilesUsePipeline.ps1 script. The entire Get-ModifiedFilesUsePipeline2.ps1 script is shown here.

```
Get-ModifiedFilesUsePipeline2.ps1

Param(
    $path = "D:\",
    $days = 30
) #end param


$changedFiles = $null
$dteModified= (Get-Date).AddDays(-$days)
$changedFiles = Get-ChildItem -path $path -recurse |
where-object { $_.LastWriteTime -ge $dteModified }

"The $path has $($changedFiles.count) modified files since $dteModified"
```

When the Get-ModifiedFilesUsePipeline2.ps1 script is run, the script completes in 12.3324077seconds, which is another decrease in the performance of the script. The *TimeSpan* object that is created by running the Get-ModifiedFilesUsePipeline2.ps1 script is shown in Figure 13-4.

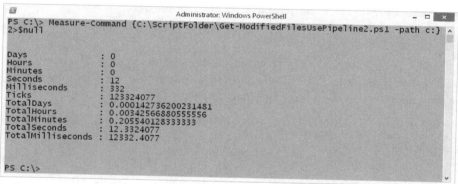

**FIGURE 13-4** *TimeSpan* object indicating that changes were not an improvement to the script.

# Evaluating the performance of different versions of a script

It is relatively simple to use the Measure-Command cmdlet to check the performance of a script and monitor for moderate changes. For more extensive changes to a script, you will want to create different versions of the script. To simplify the testing scenario, it makes sense to create a script that will test the performance of two different scripts. To take into account the difference in performance between run times of the scripts that can be attributed to computer loading, resource contention, and the like, you might want the ability to run the tests multiple times and create a report on the average run time of the scripts.

The Test-TwoScripts.ps1 script allows you to run the performance test of the script multiple times. It also produces a report that details the time that was taken for each run and produces a summary evaluation of the two scripts.

## Command-line parameters

The Test-TwoScripts.ps1 script creates the following command-line parameters:

- The first parameter, *baseLineScript*, is the path to the script that will be the baseline for comparison. Typically, this is the script that you used before you modified it.
- The second parameter is *modifiedScript*, and it is used to reference the script whose changes you want to evaluate. These two scripts do not need to be related to one another.
- The third parameter is the *numberOfTests* parameter. This number controls how many times the scripts will be run. By running the scripts several times and averaging the results, a more accurate picture of the performance of the scripts can be gained.

   When testing, a script might run faster or slower on any given run. This might be due to file caching or to other performance enhancements offered by the operating system, but it might also be due to resource contention or other anomalies.
- The last parameter is the *–log* switched parameter. When the *–log* parameter is present, it causes the script to write the performance information to a temporary text file that is displayed at the end of the completion of the script.

The *Param* section of the script is shown here:

```
Param(
  [string]$baseLineScript,
  [string]$modifiedScript,
  [int]$numberOfTests = 20,
  [switch]$log
) #end param
```

## Functions

The *Test-Scripts* function is used to call the Measure-Command cmdlet for each of the two scripts to be tested. The *Param* section of the function receives two inputs: the *baseLineScript* parameter and the *modifiedScript* parameter. These parameters are cut and pasted from the *Param* section to the script because it is easier than typing everything a second time. Cutting and pasting the parameters also ensures that you avoid typing errors, as shown here:

```
Function Test-Scripts
{
  Param(
  [string]$baseLineScript,
  [string]$modifiedScript
) #end param
```

After the parameters for the *Test-Scripts* function are created, it is time to call the Measure-Command cmdlet, which is called twice. During the first call, the baseline script is passed to the *Expression* parameter of the Measure-Command cmdlet. The string that is passed to the *$baseLineScript* parameter includes the full path to the script as well as all parameters that the script requires to successfully execute. The second Measure-Command cmdlet is called to evaluate the performance of the modified script. The path to the modified script as well as the parameters required to set up the command are passed to the *Expression* parameter of the Measure-Command cmdlet.

```
Measure-Command -Expression { $baseLineScript }
Measure-Command -Expression { $modifiedScript }
} #end Test-Scripts function
```

The *Get-Change* function is used to calculate the percentage increase or decrease in total running time between the baseline script and the modified script. The *baseline* parameter contains the total number of seconds that the baseline script requires to execute. The *modified* parameter contains the total number of seconds that the modified script requires to execute. If the *Test-Scripts* function is called several times (due to the script performing multiple tests), the *$baseLine* variable and the *$modified* variable will contain the cumulative number of seconds of running time from the entire series of tests. To calculate the percentage increase or decrease in total running time, the total number of seconds contained in the *$modified* variable is subtracted from the total number of seconds contained in the *$baseLine* variable, and this number is then divided by the total number of seconds contained in the *$baseLine* variable. The result of this computation is then multiplied by 100. The *Get-Change* function is shown here:

```
Function Get-Change($baseLine, $modified)
{
 (($baseLine - $modified)/$baseLine)*100
} #end Get-Change function
```

After the *Get-Change* function is created, the *Get-TempFile* function is created. The *Get-TempFile* function calls the static *GetTempFileName* method from the *IO.Path* .NET Framework class. The *Get-TempFile* function is shown here:

```
Function Get-TempFile
{
 [io.path]::GetTempFileName()
} #end Get-TempFile function
```

After all of the functions are created, you arrive at the entry point to the script. You must first determine whether the Test-TwoScripts.ps1 script was run with the *–log* switched parameter. If it was launched with the *–log* switched parameter, the *$log* variable will exist. If the *$log* variable exists, the *Get-TempFile* function is called and the resulting temporary file name is stored in the *$logFile* variable.

```
if($log) { $logFile = Get-TempFile }
```

A *for* loop is used to count the number of tests to perform on the scripts. The number of tests is stored in the *$numberOfTests* variable. A status message is displayed to the Windows PowerShell console that indicates the test loop number. This section of the code is shown here:

```
For($i = 0 ; $i -le $numberOfTests ; $i++)
{
 "Test $i of $numberOfTests" ; start-sleep -m 50 ; cls
```

After the loop progress message is displayed, the *Test-Scripts* function is called. The *Test-Scripts* function returns two *System.TimeSpan* objects, which are stored in the *$results* variable.

```
$results= Test-Scripts -baseLineScript $baseLineScript -modifiedScript $modifiedScript
```

Because the *$results* variable contains an array of two *TimeSpan* objects, you can index directly into the array and retrieve the value of the *$TotalSeconds* variable. Use [0] to retrieve the first *TimeSpan* object and [1] to retrieve the second *TimeSpan* object. The total seconds from the current test run is added to the total seconds that are stored in the *$baseLine* and *$modified* variables.

```
$baseLine += $results[0].TotalSeconds
$modified += $results[1].TotalSeconds
```

If the script is run with the *–log* switched parameter, the name of the script, the test number, and the results are written to the log file. The code that performs this action is shown here:

```
If($log)
  {
     "$baseLineScript run $i of $numberOfTests $(get-date)" >> $logFile
     $results[0] >> $logFile
     "$modifiedScript run $i of $numberOfTests $(get-date)" >> $logFile
     $results[1] >> $logFile
  } #if $log
} #for $i
```

The complete Test-TwoScripts.ps1 script is shown here.

```
Test-TwoScripts.ps1

Param(
  [string]$baseLineScript,
  [string]$modifiedScript,
  [int]$numberOfTests = 20,
  [switch]$log
) #end param

Function Test-Scripts
{
  Param(
```

```
    [string]$baseLineScript,
    [string]$modifiedScript,
    [int]$numberOfTests,
    [switch]$log
) #end param
 Measure-Command -Expression { $baseLineScript }
 Measure-Command -Expression { $modifiedScript }
} #end Test-Scripts function


Function Get-Change($baseLine, $modified)
{
   (($baseLine - $modified)/$baseLine)*100
} #end Get-Change function


Function Get-TempFile
{
 [io.path]::GetTempFileName()
} #end Get-TempFile function

# *** Entry Point To Script
if($log) { $logFile = Get-TempFile }
For($i = 0 ; $i -le $numberOfTests ; $i++)
{
 "Test $i of $numberOfTests" ; start-sleep -m 50 ; cls
 $results= Test-Scripts -baseLineScript $baseLineScript -modifiedScript $modifedScript
 $baseLine += $results[0].TotalSeconds
 $modified += $results[1].TotalSeconds
 If($log)
  {
     "$baseLineScript run $i of $numberOfTests $(get-date)" >> $logFile
     $results[0] >> $logFile
     "$modifiedScript run $i of $numberOfTests $(get-date)" >> $logFile
     $results[1] >> $logFile
  } #if $log
} #for $i

"Average change over $numberOfTests tests"
"BaseLine: $baseLineScript average Total Seconds: $($baseLine/$numberOfTests)"
"Modified: $modifiedScript average Total Seconds: $($modified/$numberOfTests)"
"Percent Change: " + "{0:N2}" -f (Get-Change -baseLine $baseLine -modified $modified)
if($log)
{
 "Average change over $numberOfTests tests" >> $logFile
 "BaseLine: $baseLineScript average Total Seconds: $($baseLine/$numberOfTests)" >>
$logFile
```

```
 "Modified: $modifiedScript average Total Seconds: $($modified/$numberOfTests)" >>
$logFile
 "Percent Change: " + "{0:N2}" -f (Get-Change -baseLine $baseLine -modified $modified)
>> $logFile
} #if $log
if($log) { Notepad $logFile }
```

## Testing APIs, web services, SOAP, and REST with Windows PowerShell

**James Brundage and Ibrahim Abdul Rahim, Software Development Engineers**
*Microsoft Corporation*

It's probably easier to test APIs in Windows PowerShell than in any other language because you can use the APIs interactively. When testing APIs, the task normally involves checking both the results from an API and the things that the API should have done within the system. You can easily create objects, run their methods, and get their results in Windows PowerShell. To create an existing .NET class, use the New-Object cmdlet. To load a type from disk, you can use *[Reflection. Assembly]::LoadFrom($FullPath)* to load an assembly. To run a static method or get a static property, use *[Type]::PropertyOrMethod*.

Beginning with Windows PowerShell 2.0, it is easier than ever to test web services. Web service testing is similar to API testing in that you are usually simply running some method and checking the results. However, web tests might pay more attention to timing. To add timing to your tests, use the Measure-Command cmdlet to execute the core of the test and use the *Throw* statement or the Write-Error cmdlet to fail the test if the command takes too long to complete.

Windows PowerShell 2.0 and newer versions make testing Simple Object Access Protocol (SOAP) a snap because you can use SOAP's autodiscovery to create a type to use the web service in PowerShell with the New-WebServiceProxy cmdlet. Because SOAP web services use many different types, I recommend using New-WebServiceProxy in a command that is similar to the one shown here:

```
$webService =New-WebServiceProxy Url –Namespace WebServiceName
```

After you create a proxy of the web service, test it interactively just like any other API by trying different actions and validating the results and side effects.

Because Representational State Transfer (REST) web services are not discoverable, they also are not as easy to test as SOAP web services. However, because REST web services are straightforward to query, you can generally simply query the web service and check the XML that it returns. Most REST web services use a long GET query (like the one you can see in your address bar when you search via a search engine) to provide the parameters to the web service.

To test REST in Windows PowerShell, you should first write a function to wrap the REST web service. For example, this means that if the service takes a topic string, a count of articles to retrieve, and an offset, then you should write a function with a signature that matches the web service (that is, `function Get-RestService([string]$Topic, [int]$count = 20, [int]$offset =0) {} `).

The function used to wrap REST is simple. Typically, all you need to do is use New-Object to create a *webclient*, use the *DownloadString* method to get the results, and then turn the results into an XML object by casting.

```
($client  = New-Object NET.Webclient; $client.DownloadString($url) -as
[xml])
```

When done, you will be able to use the `Select-Xml` cmdlet to query the data returned from the web service to determine whether you should have received this data.

## Displaying the results and creating the log file

After writing to the log file, it is time to display information to the Windows PowerShell console. The number of tests and the average time for each test run is displayed to the console for both the baseline and the modified scripts. The portion of the script that performs this action is shown here:

```
"Average change over $numberOfTests tests"
"BaseLine: $baseLineScript average Total Seconds: $($baseLine/$numberOfTests)"
"Modified: $modifiedScript average Total Seconds: $($modified/$numberOfTests)"
```

The percentage of change between the two scripts is calculated by using the *Get-Change* function. A .NET format specifier is used to display the percentage of change to two decimal places. The *{0:N2}* format specifier indicates two decimal places.

```
"Percent Change: " + "{0:N2}" -f (Get-Change -baseLine $baseLine
-modified $modified)
```

The same information that was just displayed to the console is written to the log file if the script is launched with the –log switched parameter.

```
if($log)
{
 "Average change over $numberOfTests tests" >> $logFile
 "BaseLine: $baseLineScript average Total Seconds:
$($baseLine/$numberOfTests)" >> $logFile
 "Modified: $modifiedScript average Total Seconds:
$($modified/$numberOfTests)" >> $logFile
 "Percent Change: " + "{0:N2}" -f (Get-Change -baseLine $baseLine
-modified $modified) >> $logFile
} #if $log
```

After the log file is updated, it is displayed by using Notepad. The code that displays the log file in Notepad is shown here:

```
if($log) { Notepad $logFile }
```

The log that is produced by running the Test-TwoScripts.ps1 script is shown in Figure 13-5.

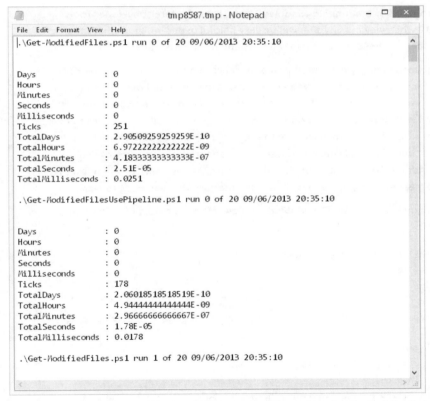

**FIGURE 13-5** Log reporting performance changes over 20 tests by using the Test-TwoScripts.ps1 script.

## Testing graphical applications with Windows PowerShell

James Brundage and Ibrahim Abdul Rahim, Software Development Engineers
*Microsoft Corporation*

The easiest way to test websites in Windows PowerShell is to try scripting Windows Internet Explorer. The incredible amount of data that you can view about a Website can help you determine whether the content is correct. To automate the web, the main object with which you should interact is the Component Object Model (COM) *Shell.Application* object ($Shell = New-Object –ComObject Shell.Application). You can use the *ShellExecute* method of *Shell.Application* to create brand-new windows, and you can use the *Shell.Windows()* method to get (and change) all of the running windows. The Internet Explorer Developer Tools (press F12 when viewing any site) will be very helpful in determining where the content that you need to automate can be found on the webpage.

Webpage testing has two additional areas of special concern, one of which I can be of some help in explaining. Webpages often take one period of time to load the page and another period of time to render individual controls, which can result in the need for multiple waiting periods. In the following example, I wait once to load *Bing.com* and wait again to make sure that the search dialog box is ready for input. The other area of special concern that the web can throw at you involves dealing with Adobe Flash or Microsoft Silverlight pages. At this point, it is significantly easier to treat the webpage as any other user interface that you want to test.

Here is a quick web test written in Windows PowerShell to search for a term on Bing.com:

```
$shell.ShellExecute("http://www.bing.com")
$timeout = New-TimeSpan -Seconds 15
$startTime = Get-Date
do {
    $window = $shell.Windows() | ? { $_.LocationUrl -eq "http://www.bing
.com/" }
} while (-not $window -and
    ($startTime + $timeout) -gt (Get-Date))
if (-not $window) {
    throw "Timed out waiting for Window to load"
}
$timeout = New-TimeSpan -Seconds 5
$startTime = Get-Date
do {
    $searchQuery = $window.Document.getElementById("sb_form_q")
```

```
} while (-not $searchQuery -and
    ($startTime + $timeout) -gt (Get-Date))
if (-not $searchQuery) {
    throw "Timed out waiting for search query box to be available"
}
$searchQuery.InnerText = "foobar"
$window.Document.getElementById("sb_form_go").Click()
```

Windows PowerShell has easy access to console applications and APIs. However, when dealing with GUI applications, Windows PowerShell needs to go through several layers before it can access information about the GUI (such as Text Box text or whether a check box is checked) and execute GUI commands, such as send keys and click buttons.

As in testing webpages, the trick is locating the item with which you want to interact and then interacting with it. Because user interface technologies can use different underlying implementations, the tricks that work for some user interface types will not work for others. The APIs that you can use to access the pages include Microsoft Active Accessibility (MSAA), User Interface Automation (UIA), and C Windows APIs. C Windows APIs require Interop (Add-Type and P/Invoke), while MSAA and UIA have .NET and COM APIs. The Windows Automation Snap-in for Windows PowerShell (*http://www.codeplex.com/WASP*) can help you get started with user interface testing and is based on C Windows API windows.

The trick to automating the majority of tests in user interfaces is to consider most interactions in terms of the keyboard when possible. By using the keyboard, you can use the *SendKeys* API (it's on New-Object –ComObject WScript.Shell) to send the sequence of actions as keys that you can type. You can then validate the user interface changes by pulling out screen positions and text in the Web Application Services Platform (WASP).

If you choose not to actually automate testing, another common approach to testing websites is to keep a store of manual test cases. In this scenario, Windows PowerShell still possesses all that is required to be your testing framework. Windows PowerShell contains two common cmdlets that make this process easy: Read-Host and Write-Host. Read-Host returns what the user provided, and Write-Host writes out prompts for the user. By writing out the steps of a test case using Write-Host and checking for a fixed result from Read-Host, you can effectively write manual test cases for someone else to run in Windows PowerShell.

# Using standard parameters

Windows PowerShell defines two standard parameters that are useful when testing scripts: *debug* and *–whatif*. When the *debug* parameter is implemented in a script, detailed debugging information is displayed to the Windows PowerShell console via the `Write-Debug` cmdlet. When you implement the *–whatif* parameter in a script, the parameters that are supplied to a function are displayed to the console. Both of these features provide you with useful information when testing the functionality of a script.

## Using the *debug* parameter

In Windows PowerShell 4.0, the *debug* parameter is automatically available to you because it is a standard parameter. To use the *debug* parameter, you need to use only [cmdletbinding()] in your function. There is no need to hard-wire checks and the like.

When *$DebugPreference* is set to *Continue*, it means that using the `Write-Debug` cmdlet will cause the string to be displayed on the Windows PowerShell console. If *$DebugPreference* is set to *SilentlyContinue*, which is the default value, the `Write-Debug` cmdlet is ignored unless cmdlet binding is used, and the function is called with the *–Debug* parameter. This variety provides a flexible way of displaying detailed information about the progress of the script without the need to create a debug build and a release build. As a best practice, you should use a `Write-Debug` statement before each method that you call, during value assignment, and before you call a function.

```
New-LocalUserFunction.ps1

Function New-LocalUser
{
  <#
   .Synopsis
    This function creates a local user
   .Description
    This function creates a local user
   .Example
    New-LocalUser -userName "ed" -description "cool Scripting Guy" '
       -password "password"
    Creates a new local user named ed with a description of cool scripting guy
    and a password of password.
   .Parameter ComputerName
    The name of the computer upon which to create the user
   .Parameter UserName
    The name of the user to create
   .Parameter password
    The password for the newly created user
   .Parameter description
    The description for the newly created user
```

```
   .Notes
    NAME:  New-LocalUser
    AUTHOR: ed wilson, msft
    LASTEDIT: 09/6/2013 10:07:42
    KEYWORDS: Local Account Management, Users
    HSG: Based upon HSG-06-30-11
    Requires Admin rights
   .Link
     Http://www.ScriptingGuys.com/blog
#>
[CmdletBinding()]
Param(
 [Parameter(Position=0,
     Mandatory=$True,
     ValueFromPipeline=$True)]
 [string]$userName,
 [Parameter(Position=1,
     Mandatory=$True,
     ValueFromPipeline=$True)]
 [string]$password,
 [string]$computerName = $env:ComputerName,
 [string]$description = "Created by PowerShell"
)
Write-Debug "Connecting to ADSI on $computerName"
$computer = [ADSI]"WinNT://$computerName"
Write-Debug "Calling Create method to create user: $userName"
$user = $computer.Create("User", $userName)
$user.setpassword($password)
$user.put("description",$description)
Write-Debug "Calling SetInfo"
$user.SetInfo()
} #end function New-LocalUser
```

When testing the *New-LocalUser* function, you call the function with the *debug* parameter. In addition to displaying the debug information, you are prompted to confirm the action, which enables you to skip problematic sections of the code, or to continue with the operation as shown in Figure 13-6.

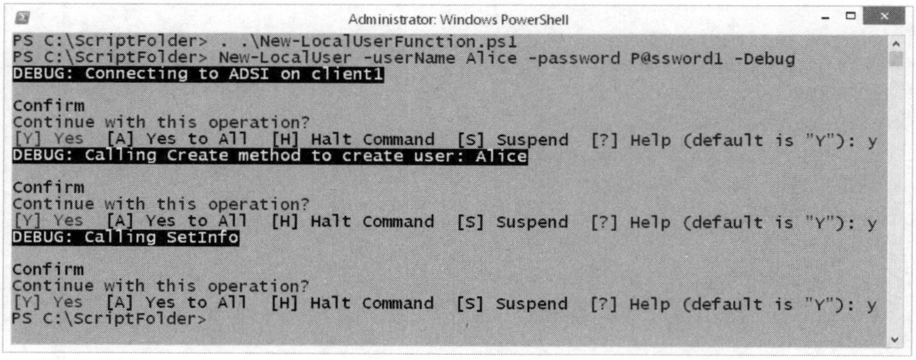

**FIGURE 13-6** Debug information displayed when the script is run with the *debug* switched parameter.

## Using the *Verbose* parameter

When you want to see what a function (or script) is doing in detail, you want verbose output. The difference between verbose and debug output is the purpose of the output. Whereas debug output is specifically designed for debugging purposes, verbose output is designed to inform the user in greater detail about all the steps that are being accomplished. In reality, there is some overlap in the two output streams, but the biggest difference is that running a function with the debug parameter provides you with the opportunity to run or to skip a command. This means that for each *Write-Debug* command you will be prompted for an action. If all you want is more detailed output from the function, you want to use *Write-Verbose* and you want to call the function with the verbose parameter.

The complete Set-LocalGroupFunction.ps1 script appears here.

```
Set-LocalGroupFunction.ps1

Function Set-LocalGroup
{
  <#
    .Synopsis
    This function adds or removes a local user to a local group
    .Description
    This function adds or removes a local user to a local group
    .Example
    Set-LocalGroup -username "ed" -groupname "administrators" -add
    Assigns the local user ed to the local administrators group
    .Example
    Set-LocalGroup -username "ed" -groupname "administrators" -remove
    Removes the local user ed to the local administrators group
    .Parameter username
    The name of the local user
    .Parameter groupname
```

```
   The name of the local group
  .Parameter ComputerName
   The name of the computer
  .Parameter add
   causes function to add the user
  .Parameter remove
   causes the function to remove the user
  .Notes
   NAME:  Set-LocalGroup
   AUTHOR: ed wilson, msft
   LASTEDIT: 09/6/2013 10:23:53
   REQUIRES: admin rights
   KEYWORDS: Local Account Management, Users, Groups
   HSG: HSG-06-30-11
  .Link
    Http://www.ScriptingGuys.com/blog
#Requires -Version 2.0
#>
[CmdletBinding()]
Param(
 [Parameter(Position=0,
     Mandatory=$True,
     ValueFromPipeline=$True)]
 [string]$userName,
 [Parameter(Position=1,
     Mandatory=$True,
     ValueFromPipeline=$True)]
 [string]$GroupName,
 [string]$computerName = $env:ComputerName,
 [Parameter(ParameterSetName='addUser')]
 [switch]$add,
 [Parameter(ParameterSetName='removeuser')]
 [switch]$remove
)
Write-Verbose "Connecting to $GroupName on $computerName"
$group = [ADSI]"WinNT://$ComputerName/$GroupName,group"
if($add)
 {
 Write-Debug "Preparing to add $userName to $groupName"
 Write-Verbose "Preparing to add $userName to $GroupName"
  $group.add("WinNT://$ComputerName/$UserName")
 }
 if($remove)
  {
   Write-Debug "Preparing to remove $userName to $groupName"
```

```
   Write-Verbose "Preparing to remove $userName to $GroupName"
   $group.remove("WinNT://$ComputerName/$UserName")
   }
} #end function Set-LocalGroup
```

When the *Set-LocalGroup* function is called with the *–Verbose* parameter, each of the *Write-Verbose* statements is called during execution and the output appears. This is shown in Figure 13-7.

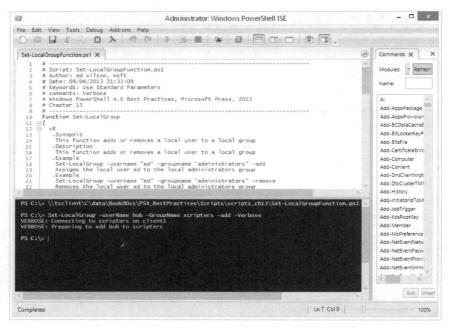

**FIGURE 13-7** Verbose output created when the function implements *Write-Verbose*.

# Using the *whatif* parameter

The *–whatif* parameter is not automatically created. If you want to implement the *–whatif* parameter in your script, you need to create a switched parameter named *–whatif* as well as a function that you can use to display the parameters that are passed to the function. As a best practice, you should implement the *–whatif* parameter whenever the script executes any process that changes system state. Examples of changing system state are deleting files or folders, creating folders or files, and writing values to the registry. If you display information, such as listing the properties of your mouse, this information does not change system state and therefore you should not use the *–whatif* parameter.

The first step in implementing the *–whatif* parameter is to create the switched parameter named *whatif*.

```
[CmdletBinding()]
 Param(
  [Parameter(Position=0,
      Mandatory=$True,
      ValueFromPipeline=$True)]
  [string]$GroupName,
  [string]$computerName = $env:ComputerName,
  [string]$description = "Created by PowerShell",
  [switch]$whatif)
```

You also need to create a statement that accepts all of the parameters that are passed to the function. The easiest way to do this in a simple function is to just use the *If* statement. In the string output, make sure to pick up all the appropriate parameters. You can use the exit statement in your *If* statement, but if you do, the Windows PowerShell console or the Windows PowerShell ISE will close, and you will not be able to actually read the contents of the *What If* statement. Therefore, it is easiest to just use the *Return* statement instead. This appears here:

```
If($whatif)
   {
   "WHATIF: Creating new local group $groupName with description $description on
$computername"
   Return
   } #end Whatif
```

The complete New-LocalGroupFunction.ps1 script is shown here.

```
New-LocalGroupFunction.ps1

Function New-LocalGroup
{

<#
   .Synopsis
    This function creates a local group
   .Description
    This function creates a local group
   .Example
    New-LocalGroup -GroupName "mygroup" -description "cool local users"
    Creates a new local group named mygroup with a description of cool local users.
   .Parameter ComputerName
    The name of the computer upon which to create the group
   .Parameter GroupName
    The name of the Group to create
   .Parameter description
    The description for the newly created group
   .Notes
```

```
    NAME:  New-LocalGroup
    AUTHOR: ed wilson, msft
    LASTEDIT: 09/6/2013 10:07:42
    REQUIRES: Admin rights
    KEYWORDS: Local Account Management, Groups
    HSG: Based upon HSG-06-30-11
   .Link
     Http://www.ScriptingGuys.com/blog
#>
[CmdletBinding()]
Param(
 [Parameter(Position=0,
     Mandatory=$True,
     ValueFromPipeline=$True)]
 [string]$GroupName,
 [string]$computerName = $env:ComputerName,
 [string]$description = "Created by PowerShell",
 [switch]$whatif
)
 If($whatif)
 {
  "WHATIF: Creating new local group $groupName with description $description on
$computername"
  Return
 } #end Whatif
 $adsi = [ADSI]"WinNT://$computerName"
 $objgroup = $adsi.Create("Group", $groupName)
 $objgroup.SetInfo()
 $objgroup.description = $description
 $objgroup.SetInfo()

} #end function New-LocalGroup
```

When the script is run with the *–whatif* parameter, the output shown in Figure 13-8 is
displayed.

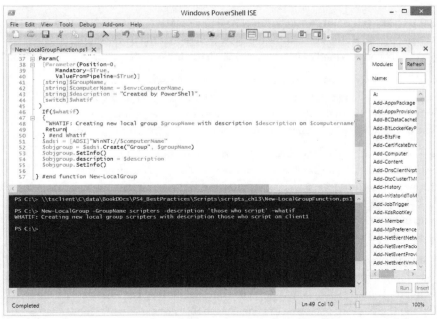

**FIGURE 13-8** The *–whatif* parameter displays a script action but does not execute.

**NOTES FROM THE FIELD**

## Testing scripts

**Enrique Cedeno, MCSE**
*Senior Network Administrator*

As a senior network administrator for a large service provider, I spend a great deal of time writing scripts that are used in our server build processes. The first thing I do when testing a script is to break down the script into functions and test each function individually.

For example, if a script will be connecting to a database, I have set up a test database that has known data inside it. Each function is treated as if it were an individual script. In this way, it is easy to isolate the problem and pinpoint any issues that might arise.

A cohort on our team once wrote a script that connected to a database, but a problem emerged in one of the SQL statements. Although there was no error handling in the script, the script appeared to run okay. However, when I ran the script against the test database, I immediately noticed that the script was returning bogus data. The script was a masterpiece of spaghetti code, and it took the team three days to debug the script. This points to the value of having a database that contains known data. When you run a query and know the type of data that the query should return, you will know immediately whether your script is working properly.

In our production scripts, we trap the output of the script and write it to a log file. We use the `Write-Debug` cmdlet to provide our detailed logging for troubleshooting purposes. When we need to troubleshoot a script, we use a switch that changes the value of the *$DebugPreference* variable to turn on the `Write-Debug` cmdlet.

If we are confronted with a logic error in a script, we run the script in a known test environment and watch the data that is returned very carefully to make sure that the information makes sense. Because we know the test environment, we can tell whether the script is accurate or bogus. If multiple functions are involved and we are doing unit testing, we use the `Write-Debug` cmdlet to display a message that states when the function is being entered and when it is being exited.

One of our golden rules when writing scripts is to write a ton of comments. We do this because we might not touch the script for more than six months after writing it. The comments should explain anything that is unusual, or they can even explain the logic behind the purpose of a piece of code. You should not explain the things that anyone who works with Windows PowerShell will already know how to do. Never include a comment that explains what a cmdlet does. However, always include a comment in a script that explains a particular bug that you discovered and the workaround that you put in place.

For logging errors from the script, we place code in the script that writes all errors to a log file. We use this script during development because you cannot always rely on being able to read error messages from the screen. An added bonus of writing errors to a log file is that this process makes it easy to do automated testing. When we shift the script into production, we turn off the detailed error logging but keep the code in place so that we can enable the detailed error logging via a switch.

## Using *Start-Transcript* to produce a log

An easy way to document the results of a script is to call the *Start-Transcript* function. Although this action will produce limited information, it is an easy way to test your scripts and provide documentation. To use this technique, use the `Start-Transcript` cmdlet to create the transcript log file. By default, the `Start-Transcript` cmdlet overwrites any log files that have the same name as the one specified by the *–path* parameter. To prevent the overwriting behavior, you can use the *Noclobber* parameter when calling the Start-Transcript cmdlet. In the TranscriptBios.ps1 script, the line that calls the Start-Transcript cmdlet is shown here:

```
Start-Transcript -path $path
```

Because the transcript log file will not contain the script name, the *$myInvocation* *.InvocationName* variable is used to obtain the script name. The Start-Transcript cmdlet copies everything that appears on the Windows PowerShell console to the log file. An easy way to get the script name in the log file is to display it to the Windows PowerShell console. Because the time when the script starts might be important, the Get-Date cmdlet is used to display a time stamp that will be written to the transcript log. A subexpression is used with both the *$myInvocation.InvocationName* variable and the Get-Date cmdlet to force the evaluation of the command and return the value to the string.

```
"Starting $($myInvocation.InvocationName) at $(Get-Date)"
```

Next, the *Get-Bios* function is called, which is a standard WMI command using the Get-WmiObject cmdlet. However, the *$myInvocation.InvocationName* variable is used to display the name of the function. The technique of obtaining the called function name provides useful information about the results of the script.

```
Function Get-Bios($computer)
{
 "Calling function $($myInvocation.InvocationName)"
 Get-WmiObject -class win32_bios -computer $computer
}#end function Get-Bios
```

Last, you must stop the transcript by using the Stop-Transcript cmdlet. No additional parameters are needed to stop the transcript.

```
Stop-Transcript
```

The complete TranscriptBios.ps1 script is shown here.

```
TranscriptBios.ps1

Param(
 [Parameter(Mandatory=$true)]
 [string]$path,
 [string]$computer = $env:computername
)#end param


# *** Functions ***


Function Get-Bios($computer)
{
 "Calling function $($myInvocation.InvocationName)"
 Get-WmiObject -class win32_bios -computer $computer
}#end function Get-Bios
```

```
# *** Entry point to script ***

Start-Transcript -path $path
"Starting $($myInvocation.InvocationName) at $(Get-Date)"

Get-Bios -computer $computer
Stop-Transcript
```

When the TranscriptBios.ps1 script is run, it creates a log in the path that is supplied when the script is run. The transcript log is shown in Figure 13-9.

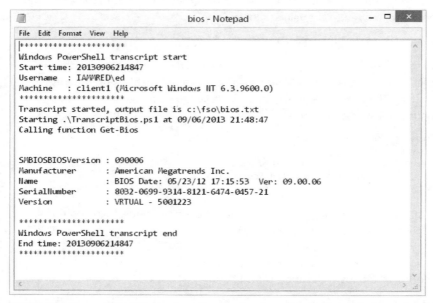

**FIGURE 13-9** Transcript log file documenting results of running the TranscriptBios.ps1 script.

# Advanced script testing

Although running a script and looking for errors will spot syntax problems, missing curly brackets, and even rights and permissions issues, it does not ensure that the script will perform the task it is intended to complete when the script is moved to production. To ensure that the script will work as expected in the production environment, you must test the script in a similar lab environment. The best lab environment is a complete duplication of the production network—down to the same physical infrastructure, including server models with the same BIOS revisions. Some companies maintain a duplicate infrastructure for disaster recovery purposes. If this is the case, the duplicate infrastructure can often be used for application testing.

If you do not have the luxury of working at a company that maintains a duplicate network infrastructure, you can often duplicate the existing hierarchy in virtual machines.

In most cases, it is not a requirement to duplicate the entire network—certainly not all of the client machines. Depending on what the script actually accomplishes, it is often sufficient to re-create the domain controller and a few servers.

## LESSONS LEARNED

### Testing scripts against known data

**Enrique Cedeno, MCSE**
*Senior Network Administrator*

Our team once wrote a script to determine whether a person was a member of a particular group. If the person was a member of this group, they had to change their password every 30 days. When we were writing the script, it was returning bogus names of people. When we investigated the situation, we realized that we needed to address the way in which we were changing the date and instead subtract the date first. If we had not already known who was supposed to be in this particular group, we would not have caught the date manipulation error, which could have created a big problem and made us look ridiculous.

It is possible to write a script to create the users, groups, and organizational units that make up a typical Active Directory implementation, but it is not a requirement to do so. Every enterprise network creates backups of their domain controllers on a regular basis. It is possible to restore the domain into the test machine. As long as the test machines are isolated from the production environment, there will be no problem with the restoration. Of course, depending on how the backup tapes are made and how the files are restored, you might run into issues with hardware incompatibility; however, these issues can generally be resolved. The advantage of using the restore-from-tape method is that passwords, security identifiers (SIDs), relative identifiers (RIDs)—everything—will be exactly the same as the production environment. The disadvantages are the hardware requirements and the amount of time it takes to perform the backup and restore.

A faster solution is to use built-in tools to export only the portion of the Active Directory in which you are interested in working. Two tools can export portions of the Active Directory: the first is CSVDE, and the second is LDIFDE. (For additional information, refer to the Knowledge Base article at *http://support.microsoft.com/kb/237677*.) Of the two, I prefer to use CSVDE because it exports a comma-separated value file that is easy to clean up by using Microsoft Office Excel.

The cleanup process becomes an issue when using either of the two export tools because the data is not exported in the format that will be required for a later import. Therefore, cleanup operations become a necessity, and the tool that makes it the easiest to do the cleanup is the tool that will be the most useful.

Using the CSVDE utility, you can specify the organizational unit that you want to export.

```
PS C:\fso> csvde -f testou.csv -d "ou=testou,dc=nwtraders,dc=com"
Connecting to "(null)"
Logging in as current user using SSPI
Exporting directory to file testou.csv
Searching for entries...
Writing out entries
...
Export Completed. Post-processing in progress...
3 entries exported

The command has completed successfully
```

After the data is exported, it must be cleaned up prior to being imported into another server because a number of the properties that are exported are read-only properties that are controlled by the system.

When the CSV file is cleaned up, you can import it into your test environment. To perform the import, you use the *i* parameter. (Export is the default behavior of CSVDE, and there is no export parameter.)

```
PS C:\fso> csvde -f testou.csv -i
Connecting to "(null)"
Logging in as current user using SSPI
Importing directory from file "testou.csv"
Loading entries....
3 entries modified successfully.

The command has completed successfully
```

### Handling passwords inside a virtual machine

Neither CSVDE nor LDIFDE has the ability to export passwords from Active Directory. If your script tests passwords or authentication mechanisms, you need to use the backup and restore technique discussed earlier. If your test scenario involves noting what happens to specific users and groups, the CSVDE technique will work for that particular application. Because the users are exported with no passwords, you have two choices. The first choice is to import all of the users in a disabled state and then use another script to enable the users and set them with the same password. However, this process seems to be a lot of work for very little value. A better approach is to change the password policy inside the virtual machine to allow empty passwords, which then allows the CSVDE scripts to work fine.

# Additional resources

- The TechNet Script Center at *http://www.microsoft.com/technet/scriptcenter* contains many examples of Windows PowerShell scripts.
- For more information about CSVDE and LDIFDE, see the Knowledge Base article at *http://support.microsoft.com/kb/237677*.
- All scripts from this chapter are available via the TechNet Script Center Script Repository at *http://gallery.technet.microsoft.com/scriptcenter/PowerShell-40 -Best-d9e16039*.

# Documenting scripts

- Gathering documentation from help
- Getting documentation from comments
- Using the AST parser
- Additional resources

One of the great things about Windows PowerShell is the way that it provides the ability to document scripts. In this chapter, we look at different ways of obtaining documentation. We begin with examining documentation from help, and then we move to different ways of getting documentation from the scripts themselves.

## Getting documentation from help

There are many reasons for documenting scripts. It might be due to compliance requirements, for ease of use, or for change control. The easiest way to provide script documentation is to obtain it from the script itself. While there are several different ways of incorporating help into a script, the most robust is to use comment-based help. If your scripts implement comment-based help and if they use a standard set of tags, you might be able to easily meet your documentation needs via standardized help content. Of course, this works only if your scripting guidelines incorporate comment-based help in the checklist of requirements for all production scripts.

The Get-ScriptHelp.ps1 script parses a directory containing scripts, calls Get-Help on each script, and writes the results out to a log file. The complete Get-ScriptHelp.ps1 script appears here.

```
Get-ScriptHelp.ps1

function New-Underline
{
<#
.Synopsis
 Creates an underline the length of the input string
.Example
 New-Underline -strIN "Hello world"
```

```
.Example
 New-Underline -strIn "Morgen welt" -char "-" -sColor "blue" -uColor "yellow"
.Example
 "this is a string" | New-Underline
.Notes
 NAME: New-Underline
 AUTHOR: Ed Wilson
 LASTEDIT: 9/9/2013
 KEYWORDS: Utility
.Link
 Http://www.ScriptingGuys.com
#>
[CmdletBinding()]
param(
     [Parameter(Mandatory = $true,Position = 0,valueFromPipeline=$true)]
     [string]
     $strIN,
     [string]
     $char = "-",
     [string]
     $sColor = "Green",
     [string]
     $uColor = "darkGreen",
     [switch]
     $pipe
) #end param
$strLine= $char * $strIn.length
if(-not $pipe)
  {
   Write-Host -ForegroundColor $sColor $strIN
   Write-Host -ForegroundColor $uColor $strLine
  }
 Else
  {
  $strIn
  $strLine
  }
} #end New-Underline function

Function Get-ScriptHelp
{
 [cmdletbinding()]
 Param ($scriptPath,$filePath)
 Get-ChildItem -Path $scriptPath -filter *.ps1 -Recurse |
 ForEach-Object {
```

```
  If(-not($_.psIsContainer))
    {
      New-Underline "$_" -pipe | Out-File -FilePath $filepath -Append
      Write-Verbose "Getting help for $_.fullName"
      Get-Help $_.fullname -detailed | Out-File -FilePath $filepath -Append
    } #end if
  } #end foreach-object
} #end function get-Scripthelp


# *** Entry Point to Script ***
$ErrorActionPreference = "continue"
$filepath = "C:\fso\BestPracticeScripts.txt"
$Scriptpath = "C:\ScriptFolder"
if(Test-Path $filepath) {Remove-Item $filepath}
Get-ScriptHelp -filepath $filepath -scriptpath $scriptpath -Verbose
Notepad $filepath
```

When the Get-ScriptHelp.ps1 script runs, it parses a folder containing scripts. A filter limits the search to files that have a *ps1* file extension. By default, if an error occurs during the run, the error is ignored and the script continues to process scripts. In a situation where the documentation is critical, you might want to change the value of *$ErrorActionPreference* to *stop* instead of *continue*. To make the script easier to use, any existing log file is automatically deleted, and therefore it is possible to run the script multiple times without worrying about appending results.

This approach relies on comment-based help being one of the first elements in the ps1 script file. If a comment block, which the majority of the scripts from this book contain, precedes the comment-based help, the approach does not work. If using comment-based help is the documentation approach you want to use, you might want to change all of your traditional comment block style of header information into comment-based help. The traditional comment block type of header appears here:

```
# -------------------------------------------------------------------
# Script: Untitled1.ps1
# Author: ed wilson, msft
# Date: 09/08/2013 13:47:33
# Keywords: documentation
# comments: Get-Help
# Windows PowerShell 4.0 Best Practices, Microsoft Press, 2013
# Chapter 14
# -------------------------------------------------------------------
```

Making the change to using comment-based help to produce your script headers means a simple change of technique—instead of using numerous pound signs, use the <# and the #>

hash signs. If you use a few of the standard tags, you can get the documentation easily via Get-Help. The following illustrates a comment-based header block:

```
<#
   .Synopsis
   This is a comment-based block
   .Description
   This illustrates comment-based help used as
   script header
   .Notes
   NAME:  Comment-BasedHeader.ps1
   AUTHOR: ed wilson, msft
   LASTEDIT: 09/08/2013 13:49:40
   KEYWORDS: Documentation, help
   Book: Windows PowerShell 4.0 Best Practices, Microsoft Press, 2013
   Chapter: 14
   .Link
      Http://www.ScriptingGuys.com
 #Requires -Version 4.0
 #>
```

When the Get-ScriptHelp.ps1 script runs, a report similar to the one shown in Figure 14-1 appears.

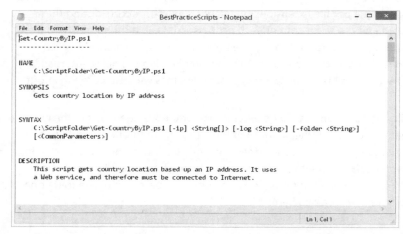

**FIGURE 14-1** By using comment-based header blocks on your scripts, documentation is produced easily.

Documenting scripts is about more than compliance. It is also a good way to examine a script prior to actually running it. This becomes a vital safety check, especially when downloading scripts from places like the Scripting Guys Script Repository. For more information about script safety in this regard, see the sidebar written by Windows PowerShell MVP Jeffery Hicks.

Jeffery Hicks, Windows PowerShell MVP
*Author of PowerShell in Depth: An administrator's guide*

There is no question that the Windows PowerShell community continues to grow by leaps and bounds, including an ever-expanding collection of scripts from sites such as PoshCode.org, TechNet, and a number of Windows PowerShell-related blogs. However, not all scripts are written to the same level of quality you would prefer. How can you tell what the script is going to do? Is it safe to run? Or perhaps you have developed your own script that someone else will be using. Can you trust that it will be executed correctly? For example, you might have the following concerns:

- How does the script handle missing parameters?
- How does the script handle different operating systems?
- How does the script handle a wide range of values for the inputs?
- How does the script handle the different combinations of parameters?

Frankly, some of these issues can be handled during script development. At the beginning of your script or at the start of your function, add the following command:

```
Set-StrictMode -version latest
```

This will ensure that your command doesn't "break the rules." For example, Windows PowerShell will complain if you attempt to use an undefined variable. This is terrific for catching typos. In addition, I always recommend providing default values for script or function parameters as well as casting the parameter to the necessary type. That way, if the user passes the wrong type of object as a parameter, Windows PowerShell will complain. You should also take advantage of the validation attributes to further ensure that users are entering correct parameters. Here's an example that will work in Windows PowerShell 3 or newer versions:

```
Param (
[Parameter(Position=0,ValueFromPipeline,
 HelpMessage="What is the name of the computer to backup?")]
[ValidateScript({ Test-Connection $_ -quiet -count 1})]
[ValidatePattern("^CHI-\w{2}\d{2}$")]
[string]$Computername=$env:computername,
)
```

With this parameter, if an admin enters a computer name, it must start with CHI followed by a dash, 2 characters, and then 2 numbers—for example, CHI-DC02. In addition, the computer must respond to a single ping. If either of these conditions is not met, Windows PowerShell will throw an exception and the command will fail to run, which is better than completing halfway and then failing.

And of course you need to test *everything* in a non-production environment. Your script should follow the same code development process that an internally developed application would follow. I always try to think of the most ridiculous way someone might run the script, plan for it, and test accordingly. I want robustness, and I bet you do too.

Now, what about a script that you've downloaded? How can you tell if it is safe to run? You could blindly run it in a test environment, such as in a virtual machine. But you should look at it first. I realize that you might still be learning Windows PowerShell and perhaps don't fully understand everything you might see. So I have something to help.

In the previous version of this book, I had a Windows PowerShell script that would "profile" a script. That is, it gave you an idea of what commands it would run and identified any potentially dangerous commands. Frankly, the previous version was not very well written. Fortunately, Windows PowerShell 3.0 introduced a new way of parsing script files using an Abstract Syntax Tree (AST). Don't worry too much about what it means. On the companion media or through a download, you should be able to find my script called Get-ASTScriptProfile.ps1.

The script takes the name of a script to profile. You can specify a .ps1 or .psm1 file name. Using the AST, the script will prepare a text report showing you any script requirements, script parameters, commands, and type names. You will see all commands used, including those that can't be resolved and those that I thought might be considered potentially dangerous, such as cmdlets that use the verbs Remove or Stop. Because some people might invoke methods from .NET classes directly, I've also captured all type names. Most of them will probably be related to parameters, but at least you'll know what to look for. The entire report is turned into a "help about" topic stored in your Documents folder and displayed with Get-Help and the awesome *–ShowWindow* parameter.

The report won't detail parameters from nested functions, but you'll still see what commands they will use. The script uses Get-Command to identify commands that might entail loading a module. Most of the time, this shouldn't be an issue, but you still might want to profile the script in a virtualized or test environment. Any unresolved command that you see is either from a module that couldn't be loaded or perhaps an internally defined command. When you know what to look for, you can open the script in your favorite editor and search for the mystery commands.

Practicing safe Windows PowerShell is a habit that you have to cultivate, not only in the scripts and tools that you write but also when using code written by someone else.

# Getting documentation from comments

If scripts do not provide for comment-based help, it might still be possible to obtain documentation from the script based on how well commented the scripts are. The GetCommentsFromScript.ps1 script accepts a path to a script and returns all comments that begin lines from within the script. It does not pick up inline comments but only comments that begin the line. This would include the traditional comment block discussed in the preceding section, as well as any sectional comments. The complete GetCommentsFromScript.ps1 script appears here.

```
GetCommentsFromScript.ps1

Function Get-FileName
{
 Param ($Script)
 $OutPutPath = [io.path]::GetTempPath()
 Join-Path -path $OutPutPath -child "$(Split-Path $script -leaf).txt"
} #end Get-FileName

Function Remove-OutPutFile($OutPutFile)
{
  if(Test-Path -path $OutPutFile)
    {
      $Response = Read-Host -Prompt "$OutPutFile already exists. Do you wish to
delete it <y / n>?"
      if($Response -eq "y")
        { Remove-Item $OutPutFile | Out-Null }
      ELSE
        {
          if(Test-Path -path "$OutPutFile.old") { Remove-Item -Path "$OutPutFile.old"
}
          Rename-Item -path $OutPutFile -newname  "$(Split-Path $OutPutFile -leaf).
old" -Force
        }
    }
} #end Remove-OutPutFile

Function Get-Comments
{
 Param ($Script, $OutPutFile)
 Get-Content -path $Script |
 Foreach-Object {
   If($_ -match '^\#')
     { $_ |
      Out-File -FilePath $OutPutFile -append }
```

```
  } #end Foreach
} #end Get-Comments


Function Get-OutPutFile($OutPutFile)
{
 Notepad $OutPutFile
} #end Get-OutPutFile


# *** Entry point to script ***

$script = 'C:\scriptfolder\Get-ModifiedFilesUsePipeline.ps1'
$OutPutFile = Get-FileName($script)
Remove-OutPutFile($OutPutFile)
Get-Comments -script $script -outputfile $OutPutFile
Get-OutPutFile($OutPutFile)
```

One of the things that the script does is create a documentation file for the script, and it uses the file name and appends a *txt* extension to the file name. In addition, the file is created in the temporary working directory of the user who runs the script. This path always exists on the system. This is accomplished by using the *Get-FileName* function shown here:

```
Function Get-FileName
{
 Param ($Script)
 $OutPutPath = [io.path]::GetTempPath()
 Join-Path -path $OutPutPath -child "$(Split-Path $script -leaf).txt"
} #end Get-FileName
```

The *Get-Comments* function reads the script and uses a simple regular expression pattern to retrieve each line from the script. This function is shown here:

```
Function Get-Comments
{
 Param ($Script, $OutPutFile)
 Get-Content -path $Script |
 Foreach-Object {
    If($_ -match '^\#')
      { $_ |
       Out-File -FilePath $OutPutFile -append }
   } #end Foreach
} #end Get-Comments
```

After the script runs, a file similar to the one shown in Figure 14-2 appears.

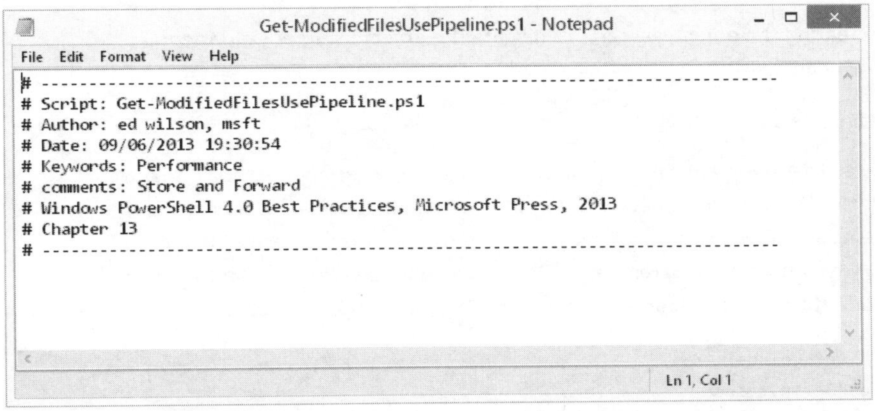

```
# -------------------------------------------------------------------------
# Script: Get-ModifiedFilesUsePipeline.ps1
# Author: ed wilson, msft
# Date: 09/06/2013 19:30:54
# Keywords: Performance
# comments: Store and Forward
# Windows PowerShell 4.0 Best Practices, Microsoft Press, 2013
# Chapter 13
# -------------------------------------------------------------------------
```

**FIGURE 14-2** Comments parsed from a script by using the GetCommentsFromScript.ps1 script.

---

**INSIDE TRACK**

**Chris Bellee, Premier Field Engineer**
*Microsoft Corporation, Australia*

Windows PowerShell cmdlets are the main administrative commands in PowerShell. Cmdlets are compiled programs that encapsulate .NET Framework classes. As progressive versions of Windows PowerShell have been released, many new cmdlets have been added to expand its functionality. For example, Windows PowerShell 1 shipped with 126 default cmdlets, whereas Windows PowerShell 4 (running on Windows 8) has 510 cmdlets available out of the box.

Even with such a large increase in the number of cmdlets, only a small fraction of the .NET framework has been exposed through cmdlets. This is where the New-Object cmdlet comes in very handy, because it allows you to create new instances of .NET classes (known as *objects*), which can then be used within Windows PowerShell.

For example, let's say that I need to test whether a remote machine is listening on port 80. What cmdlet would allow me to do this? The answer (as of Windows PowerShell 4) is that there isn't one, but we can tap directly into the .NET framework and create an object designed just for this purpose. To do this, we use the New-Object cmdlet, specifying the fully qualified class path as the argument to the *–TypeName* parameter. The syntax is very straightforward; in fact, the trickiest part is actually discovering the correct class name in the first place!

```
$tcpClient = New-Object –TypeName System.Net.Sockets.TcpClient
```

After creating the object, we can interrogate the object using our old friend, *Get-Member*.

```
$tcpClient | Get-Member
```

You'll see that there are a number of members (properties and methods) that we could use. The *Connect()* method looks like the one that will allow a connection to a remote machine, but how do we use it? A nice trick is to specify the method name, without its usual parentheses. This forces Windows PowerShell to display the method's different overloads—its number and type of input arguments.

```
$tcpClient.Connect
OverloadDefinitions
-------------------
void Connect(string hostname, int port)
void Connect(ipaddress address, int port)
void Connect(System.Net.IPEndPoint remoteEP)
void Connect(ipaddress[] ipAddresses, int port)
```

There are actually four different sets of input arguments for the *Connect()* method. For this example, we will use the first overload, which accepts a string for the remote machine name and an integer, which represents the remote port number on which to connect.

```
$tcpClient.Connect("Server-01",80)
```

We can now check whether the connection succeeded by querying the object's *Connected* property, which returns a Boolean (true or false) data type.

```
$tcpClient.Connected
```

Put the preceding code into a function or a loop, and you have a simple way to verify remote port availability and to troubleshoot connectivity.

# Using the AST parser

A more powerful means of documenting a script is by using the *PSParser* class from the *System.Management.Automation* .NET Framework namespace. The tokenizer becomes available when using the static *Tokenize* method from the *PSParser* class. The *tokenizer* is used to break a Windows PowerShell script into pieces of code called *tokens*. Using the tokenizer, you can find commands or variables in a Windows PowerShell script. The powerful aspect of using the tokenizer is that it does not matter where within the text that the command appears. In addition, it is easier to use than complex regular expressions.

The ParseScriptCommands.ps1 illustrates parsing a script.

```
ParseScriptCommands.ps1

$errors = $null
$logpath = "C:\fso\commandlog.txt"
$path = 'C:\ScriptFolder'
Get-ChildItem -Path $path -Include *.ps1 -Recurse |
ForEach-Object {
  $script = $_.fullname
  $scriptText = get-content -Path $script
  [system.management.automation.psparser]::Tokenize($scriptText, [ref]$errors) |
  Foreach-object -Begin {
    "Processing $script" | Out-File -FilePath $logPath -Append } '
  -process { if($_.type -eq "command")
    { "'t $($_.content)" | Out-File -FilePath $logpath -Append } }
}
notepad $logpath
```

The first thing that the ParseScriptCommands.ps1 script does is initialize three variables. The first one is used to collect any errors generated by the tokenizer. The second variable is used for the log file, and the last one specifies the directory that contains the Windows PowerShell scripts that need to be parsed. These commands are shown here:

```
$errors = $null
$logpath = "C:\logs\commandlog.txt"
$path = "C:\data\PSExtras"
```

The next four commands are standard Windows PowerShell cmdlets. The Get-ChildItem cmdlet retrieves only Windows PowerShell scripts (that have the .ps1 extension) from the script directory specified earlier. The *–recurse* parameter is required when retrieving the files from the folder. The resulting *fileinfo* objects are pipelined to the ForEach-Object cmdlet, where the full path to each script is stored in the *$script* variable. Next, the Get-Content cmdlet reads each Windows PowerShell script and stores the content of the file in the *$scriptText* variable. This section of the script is shown here:

```
Get-ChildItem -Path $path -Include *.ps1 -Recurse |
ForEach-Object {
  $script = $_.fullname
  $scriptText = get-content -Path $script
```

The *psparser* .NET Framework class in the *System.Management.Automation* namespace has the *Tokenize* static method. The first parameter is a variable containing the contents of a Windows PowerShell script, and the second parameter is a reference variable to hold the errors. The second parameter must be supplied when calling the *Tokenize* method. The tokens are then pipelined to the next section of the script. This command is shown here:

```
[system.management.automation.psparser]::Tokenize($scriptText, [ref]$errors)
```

Use the `Foreach-Object` cmdlet to process each token. The first thing to do is to write the full path to the script to the log file. Next, check to see whether the type property of the token object is a command—if it is, write the command to the log file as well. When finished processing all of the scripts in the folder, display the contents of the log file. This section of the script is seen here:

```
Foreach-object -Begin {
  "Processing $script" | Out-File -FilePath $logPath -Append } '
-process { if($_.type -eq "command")
  { "`t $($_.content)" | Out-File -FilePath $logpath -Append } }
}
notepad $logpath
```

When the script runs, a text file similar to the one seen in Figure 14-3 appears.

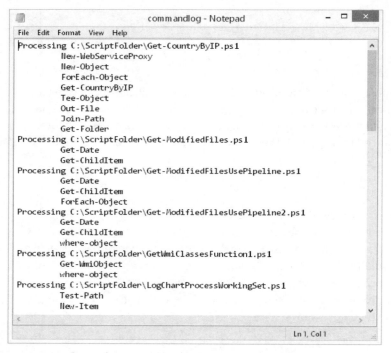

**FIGURE 14-3** Output log created by the ParseScriptCommands.ps1 script.

When you know how to use the Windows PowerShell tokenizer to parse script syntax, it is possible to create a tool that will analyze the script and report on various aspects of the script.

# Additional resources

- The TechNet Script Center at *http://www.microsoft.com/technet/scriptcenter* contains numerous script examples.

- All scripts from this chapter are available via the TechNet Script Center Script Repository at *http://gallery.technet.microsoft.com/scriptcenter/PowerShell -40-Best-d9e16039.*

- The *PSParser* class is documented on MSDN at *http://msdn.microsoft.com/en-us /library/windows/desktop/system.management.automation.psparser(v=vs.85).aspx.*

- The *CommandAST* class is documented on MSDN at *http://msdn.microsoft.com /en-us/library/windows/desktop/system.management.automation.language .commandast(v=vs.85).aspx.*

- You can read more about validation attributes in Windows PowerShell help, or grab a help module written by Jeffery Hicks at *http://jdhitsolutions.com/blog/2012/05 /introducing-the-scriptinghelp-powershell-module/.*

# Deploying the script

# CHAPTER 15

# Managing the execution policy

- Selecting the appropriate script execution policy
- Deploying the script execution policy
- Understanding code signing
- Additional resources

Before you can run a Windows PowerShell script, you must choose the appropriate script execution policy. After you choose the script execution policy, you need to decide how to deploy it to the computers on your network. Because script signing can become an issue with several of the execution policies, in this chapter we will examine the techniques involved with signing scripts. We will then move on to specialized types of scripts and different techniques for maintaining version control.

## Selecting the appropriate script execution policy

Choosing the right level of script support for your environment is an essential first step when it comes to deploying and using Windows PowerShell scripts. The first decision to be made involves whether to allow the use of Windows PowerShell scripts on a particular desktop or server. By default, when Windows PowerShell is installed, scripting is turned off. This action provides an additional level of protection not only from malware but also from careless users and untrained network administrators who are unfamiliar with Windows PowerShell. To allow for the running of scripts, you must make a decision to enable script support. When you enable support for Windows PowerShell scripting, you gain several advantages, including the following:

- The ability to run Windows PowerShell scripts as logon scripts (Windows Server 2008 R2 domain controller (or above) required).
- The ability to remotely administer desktops and servers through both fan-out and fan-in scenarios.
- The ability to quickly apply consistent configuration changes to desktops and servers.
- The ability to save a series of commands for reuse at a later point in time.

- The ability to fine-tune a series of commands and optimize the performance of those commands.
- The ability to use a Windows PowerShell profile.
- The ability to use modules.

## The purpose of script execution policies

Windows PowerShell script execution policies are not a security feature—they are a convenience feature. Script execution policies are designed to raise awareness surrounding the process of running Windows PowerShell scripts. Even if you sign all of your scripts, you cannot guarantee that the script will not wreak havoc on your network. All that you can guarantee is that the script has not been tampered with since you signed it. Anyone can obtain a code-signing certificate—even people who write malware. Therefore, a certificate is not a security panacea. You still need to ensure that both the IT staff and the users are trained to pay attention to their computing environment. Even if you have the script execution policy set to restrict the execution of Windows PowerShell scripts, it is still possible to bypass the execution policy by using the *bypass* switch.

> **NOTE** On Windows Server 2012 R2, the script execution policy is automatically set to Remote Signed. On Windows 8.1, however, the default script execution policy is set to restricted.

## Understanding the different script execution policies

Several levels of scripting support are defined in Windows PowerShell. Each of these levels can potentially alter the ability to run scripts on a local or remote computer. In addition, some of the levels might alter the way in which scripts are written and tested. The five different execution policies and their associated policy settings are shown in Table 15-1.

**TABLE 15-1** Script execution policy settings

| Policy Setting | Changes |
| --- | --- |
| Restricted | <ul><li>Default script execution policy setting</li><li>Runs commands interactively from the Windows PowerShell console</li><li>Pipeline commands permitted</li><li>Creating functions in the Windows PowerShell console permitted</li><li>Use of script blocks in commands allowed</li><li>All files with the extension of (.ps1) are blocked from executing, including all six of the various Windows PowerShell profiles</li><li>Modules are blocked (.psm1 file extension)</li><li>Windows PowerShell configuration files are blocked (.ps1 xml)</li></ul> |

| Policy Setting | Changes |
|---|---|
| AllSigned | ■ Scripts, profiles, modules, and configuration files run when signed by a trusted publisher |
| | ■ Requires all scripts to be signed, including scripts written on local computer |
| | ■ Prompts before running scripts signed by publishers that are not trusted |
| | ■ Prompts before running scripts from trusted publishers the first time the script is run |
| RemoteSigned | ■ Local scripts, profiles, modules, and configuration files run when not signed |
| | ■ Scripts received from the Internet zone must be signed by a trusted publisher prior to running |
| | ■ Prompts before running scripts downloaded from the Internet zone from trusted publishers |
| Unrestricted | ■ All unsigned scripts, profiles, modules, and configuration files run when not signed |
| | ■ Prompts before running scripts received from the Internet zone |
| Bypass | ■ Nothing is blocked and no warning prompts |

## Understanding the Internet zone

Windows PowerShell script execution policies rely on the Internet zone settings from
Windows Internet Explorer. Certain applications, such as Microsoft Office Outlook, also use
and honor the Internet Explorer Internet zone settings. The Internet Explorer security zones
are shown in Figure 15-1.

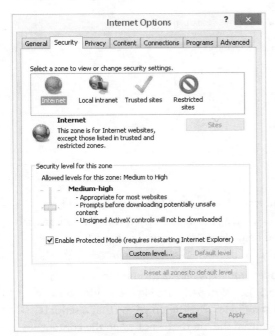

**FIGURE 15-1** Windows PowerShell uses the Internet Explorer security zone settings to determine whether
a script came from a local or remote location.

Internet Explorer adds a tag to the alternate file stream of the script file. When a script is received via Office Outlook (assuming that the antivirus software does not remove the file), a tag is also added to the alternate data stream of the script file. Any application can choose to honor the Internet Explorer definition of Internet zone settings and either add the tag or read the tag that is placed on the file. To view the alternate data stream of the file, you can use the Streams.exe Windows SysInternals utility, which has the ability to both read and delete the Internet zone tag. To search for files with alternate data streams, you can use the –s switch and specify the path to a folder. All files in the specified folder that contain alternate data streams will be returned.

```
PS C:\data\streams> .\streams.exe -s c:\fso

Streams v1.5 - Enumerate alternate NTFS data streams
Copyright (C) 1999-2003 Mark Russinovich
Sysinternals - www.sysinternals.com

c:\fso\InternetScript.ps1:
   :Zone.Identifier:$DATA        26
```

The Zone.Identifier tag is used to indicate that the file was downloaded from the Internet. Attempts to run the InternetScript.ps1 script will be blocked. However, by using the –d switch from the Streams.exe utility, the Internet zone tag is removed. When using the Streams.exe utility to remove the alternate data stream from the file, you must supply the path to the script by name.

```
PS C:\data\streams> .\streams.exe -d C:\fso\InternetScript.ps1

Streams v1.5 - Enumerate alternate NTFS data streams
Copyright (C) 1999-2003 Mark Russinovich
Sysinternals - www.sysinternals.com

C:\fso\InternetScript.ps1:
   :Zone.Identifier:$DATA        26
PS C:\data\streams> .\streams.exe -s c:\fso

Streams v1.5 - Enumerate alternate NTFS data streams
Copyright (C) 1999-2003 Mark Russinovich
Sysinternals - www.sysinternals.com
```

When the alternate data stream is removed from the file, the file is considered to have originated from the local computer and will no longer be blocked. This technique can be used to remove the Internet location from compiled help files (CHM) as well as from scripts and other files that are routinely blocked when they are downloaded from the Internet zone.

If a script is copied from a webpage and saved into a .ps1 file (by using the Windows PowerShell Integrated Scripting Environment [ISE] or Notepad), the file is considered to be in the local Trusted zone because the file was created locally. The only time that a script is tagged as remote is if it is actually downloaded from the Internet—not when the content is cut and pasted from the Internet. This can affect files other than Windows PowerShell files. When Windows PowerShell scripts (that are compressed by certain file compression utilities) are downloaded from the Internet zone as a compressed file, the script is tagged as remote when it is expanded. This is a function of the compression software honoring the Internet Explorer zone settings and therefore does not occur with all compressed files. If the Windows PowerShell script files are packaged by using an executable software installer, the scripts will not pick up the remote location setting because the scripts are considered local after they are installed.

When changing the Windows PowerShell script execution policy to RemoteSigned, scripts that are determined to have come from the Internet zone must be signed prior to executing. Internet Explorer is very aggressive in determining the boundaries for the Internet zone. By default, Universal Naming Convention (UNC) shares are determined to be in the Internet zone, which means that scripts downloaded from an internal share will not execute unless they are signed. Because many companies store their script repositories on an internal file share, a major problem is created. The solution is to add the script share to the Trusted Sites zone in Internet Explorer. To do this, you can directly add the site by using Internet Explorer, adding the location to the registry, or using Group Policy to make the change. In a corporate enterprise, using Group Policy is obviously the best approach.

# Deploying the script execution policy

When deploying the script execution policy, you have several choices. While it is possible to edit the registry to modify the script execution policy, this is generally not the best approach due to the potential for making mistakes and corrupting the registry. Additionally, in most cases it is simply too much unnecessary work. If you want to modify the script execution policy on a local computer, it is a best practice to use the Set-ExecutionPolicy cmdlet to make the change because it is easy to use and you can be assured that it will make the change correctly.

If you have more than a few computers, it is a best practice to use Group Policy to modify the Windows PowerShell script execution policy. Using Group Policy has the advantage of being easily reversible as well as centrally controlled. If you do not use Group Policy, you can use a logon script to make the changes.

## Modifying the registry

It is possible to modify the registry to enable or disable the script execution policy. You might want to take this approach if you are working in an environment that does not have Group Policy deployed. If the Windows PowerShell script execution policy is not modified to enable the use of PowerShell scripts, you might think you are limited to using VBScript or a batch (.bat) file to deploy the registry modification. Because Windows PowerShell includes the *bypass* switch, you will be able to run a Windows PowerShell script in bypass mode and make the requisite changes to the registry. The registry key, HKEY_LocalMachine\ Software\Microsoft\PowerShell\1\ShellIDs\Microsoft.PowerShell\ExecutionPolicy, is shown in Figure 15-2.

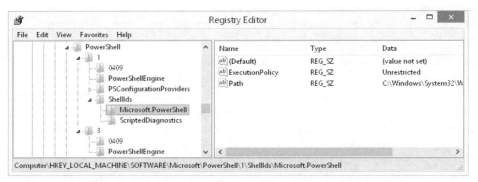

**FIGURE 15-2** Windows PowerShell script execution policy is shown in the registry.

If you are creating a Microsoft Installer (MSI) package to deploy a standardized profile to your computers, you might also want to modify the registry via the MSI package. Such a scenario is more likely to be the exception rather than the rule, and you should generally avoid directly editing the registry.

## Using the Set-ExecutionPolicy cmdlet

The Set-ExecutionPolicy cmdlet can be used to set the Windows PowerShell script execution policy. This cmdlet must be executed from an elevated Windows PowerShell prompt because it modifies the registry. Modifying the registry or using the Set-ExecutionPolicy cmdlet both perform the same task: they change the value of the registry key. When Windows is first installed, the registry keys that control the Windows PowerShell script execution policy do not exist. The default value of the script execution policy is Restricted, but this value is not shown in the registry unless it has been changed. To properly modify the registry entails checking for the existence of the registry key, creating it if it does not exist, or modifying the value if it does exist. The checking and modifying process is a bit tedious and in most cases presents unnecessary work. It is far better to use the Set-ExecutionPolicy cmdlet and avoid the manual registry work.

### Using the Set-ExecutionPolicy cmdlet on a local computer

To modify the Windows PowerShell script execution policy on a local computer, you must run the PowerShell console as an administrator if your operating system is Windows Vista or a later version. (See Figure 15-3.)

Tasks

Run as Administrator

Run ISE as Administrator

Windows PowerShell ISE

Windows PowerShell

Unpin this program from taskbar

Close window

**FIGURE 15-3** To run the Set-ExecutionPolicy cmdlet, Windows PowerShell must be launched with admin rights.

If the user does not have admin rights, the command will generate an error.

```
PS C:\Users\edwils> Set-ExecutionPolicy -ExecutionPolicy remotesigned

Execution Policy Change
The execution policy helps protect you from scripts that you do not trust. Changing the
execution policy might expose you to the security risks described in the about_
Execution_
Policies help topic. Do you want to change the execution policy?
[Y] Yes  [N] No  [S] Suspend  [?] Help (default is "Y"): y
Set-ExecutionPolicy : Access to the registry key 'HKEY_LOCAL_MACHINE\SOFTWARE\Microsoft
\PowerShell\1\ShellIds\Microsoft.PowerShell'
is denied. At line:1 char:20
+ Set-ExecutionPolicy <<<<  -ExecutionPolicy remotesigned
    + CategoryInfo          : NotSpecified: (:) [Set-ExecutionPolicy],
  UnauthorizedAccessException
    + FullyQualifiedErrorId : System.UnauthorizedAccessException,Microsoft.PowerShell
.Commands.SetExecutionPolicyCommand
```

When the command completes successfully, nothing is displayed.

```
PS C:\> Set-ExecutionPolicy -ExecutionPolicy unrestricted
PS C:\>
```

The changes take effect immediately. You can therefore test the script execution policy by attempting to run a script or by using the Get-ExecutionPolicy cmdlet. The Test-Script.ps1 script combines both approaches.

Test-Script.ps1

```
"This test script displays the script execution policy."
Get-ScriptExecutionPolicy
```

## Using the Set-ExecutionPolicy cmdlet via a logon script

If your network does not use Group Policy and you do not relish the idea of editing the registry, you can still set the Windows PowerShell script execution policy. The easiest way to do this is to add a command to your logon script. Because the logon script is being run anyway, you already have the necessary infrastructure in place to configure the script execution policy. To set the script execution policy to RemoteSigned from within a logon script, use the following command:

```
powershell -command &{Set-ExecutionPolicy remotesigned}
```

If the logon script is a batch file, the preceding command works directly. However, if the logon script is a VBScript file, you need to do a bit more work. You can use the *run* method from the *WshShell* object to use the Set-ExecutionPolicy cmdlet to set the Windows PowerShell script execution policy on all of the workstations. The SetScriptExecutionPolicy .vbs script sets the script execution policy to RemoteSigned, but it can easily be modified to set any other policy that is required. Keep in mind that this script must run with admin rights because the Set-ExecutionPolicy cmdlet modifies the registry.

---

**SetScriptExecutionPolicy.vbs**

```
Set WshShell = CreateObject("WScript.Shell")
WshShell.Run("powershell -Noninteractive -command &{Set-ExecutionPolicy
remotesigned}")
```

---

**NOTES FROM THE FIELD**

## Working with Windows PowerShell security

**Richard Siddaway, Microsoft PowerShell MVP**
*UK PowerShell User Group Chairman*

"Windows PowerShell doesn't work. I can't run scripts."

I can't remember the number of times I have seen this sentiment on the forums. It's a question that comes up so often that I always cover it when speaking publicly. The answer is "Yes, it does work" and "You need to change the execution policy."

Scripting has had bad press in certain quarters since the "I Love You" virus of 2000. This virus enticed the user to open an attachment, which sent a copy of the virus using VBScript to all members of the user's address list as well as doing other damage. Strictly speaking, this is a social engineering issue rather than a scripting issue, but Windows PowerShell is designed to counter these threats.

When Windows PowerShell is first installed, it can be used interactively, but it won't run scripts because the execution policy is set to the default of Restricted. We can view the execution policy with the Get-ExecutionPolicy cmdlet. Accounts with administrator privileges can modify the policy with the following code.

```
Set-ExecutionPolicy -ExecutionPolicy RemoteSigned
```

This is a good compromise because it allows local scripts to run, but it blocks scripts from the Internet or UNC mapped drives unless they are signed with a code-signing certificate that the system can accept. Other options include AllSigned (all scripts must be signed) and Unrestricted (any script can run, but a warning is generated if scripts are running from the Internet). AllSigned should be used if you have a code-signing infrastructure. Unrestricted is not recommended. Windows PowerShell 2.0 introduced Bypass, which does not block any scripts and does not issue warnings. You can use Bypass when Windows PowerShell is built into an application or when there is another security model in place for the programs.

Another cause for complaint is that Windows PowerShell scripts cannot be run by double-clicking. If this operation is attempted, the scripts are opened in the default editor. Again, this process occurs by design to help prevent rogue scripts from damaging your systems.

The final "speed bump" to running scripts is that the current folder is not on the path. If you type a script name, Windows PowerShell will not search in the current folder. You need to force access to the local folder using the following command:

```
./myscript.ps1
```

So, do these settings make Windows PowerShell totally secure? Of course not. It is always possible for the Windows PowerShell settings to be changed by human intervention. On the forums, numerous people have asked how to make Windows PowerShell run by double-clicking a script. Just because you *can* do it doesn't mean that you should! My advice is to set the script execution policy to the setting that best fits your organization—AllSigned ideally, but RemoteSigned is the next best choice. Don't change the other settings.

There are a lot of people out there who want to compromise your system. Don't help them. Leave the settings as they are. A great deal of thought went into the Windows PowerShell configuration, and these settings exist for a reason, as we have seen. Enjoy Windows PowerShell, but keep it secure.

## Using Group Policy to deploy the script execution policy

The best way to define the Windows PowerShell script execution policy is to use Group Policy. In Windows Server 2008 R2, a Group Policy object (GPO) for Windows PowerShell contains a setting named Turn On Script Execution. This GPO can be applied to the computer or to the user. As shown in Figure 15-4, there is only one option—the execution policy. Three values can be selected in the Turn On Script Execution GPO, and these three values correspond to the `Set-ExecutionPolicy` settings of Signed, RemoteSigned, and Unrestricted. You are not allowed to set the Bypass policy from within Group Policy.

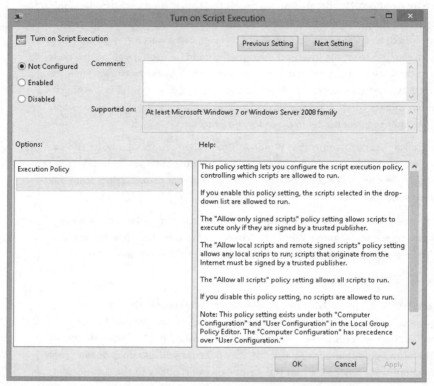

**FIGURE 15-4** Group Policy settings to control Windows PowerShell script execution allow you to choose the execution policy.

When a Group Policy setting is in effect, you are not allowed to override the setting. This is true even if you want to configure a stricter policy or if you launch the Windows PowerShell console with admin rights. If you attempt to modify the execution policy and the script execution policy GPO is currently in effect, an error is displayed to the Windows PowerShell console. This error is somewhat misleading because it begins by stating that the command completed successfully. (See Figure 15-5.)

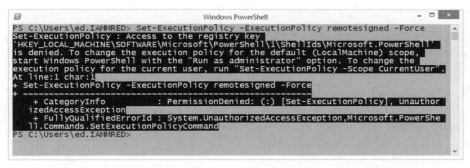

**FIGURE 15-5** Attempts to change the script execution policy when it is managed via a GPO generate an error.

## Working with script execution

**Daniele Muscetta, Program Manager**
*Microsoft Corporation*

Scripting is a powerful tool that allows you to do amazing things, such as integrate and automate, in new ways. Yet, with great power comes great responsibilities.

We have seen abuse of scripting power before—VBScript viruses. Someone sends an email message, the user clicks on it, and it is already too late. Microsoft did not want to make the same mistakes. That's why, for example, .ps1 files are not executed by default, unlike .vbs files.

Also by default, Windows PowerShell scripts are not executed even if you intentionally call them from within the shell. This behavior is determined by a feature called the execution policy. The execution policy should not be considered to be a security feature that will prevent all evils. In fact, the administrator or a user can decide to disable it. The script execution policy is more like a convenience, such as the seatbelts in your car—it is better to keep them fastened at all times, but you always have the option to take them off.

The Windows PowerShell installer configures the execution policy to Restricted as a safe default because most users will never run a PowerShell script in their life. Restricted means that absolutely no script is allowed to run. It is therefore a safe default but not a very useful default if you actually want to run scripts on your machines (and you do, or you would not be reading this).

Therefore, you can use the other commonly used options:

- RemoteSigned means that all scripts and configuration files that are down-loaded from the Internet must be signed by a trusted publisher.
- Unrestricted means that the shell is allowed to load all configuration files and run all scripts. If you run an unsigned script that was downloaded from the Internet, you are prompted for permission before it runs.

Scripters and system administrators are usually very careful when running scripts that they did not personally write, and they either deeply trust the author or have reviewed the script itself. Therefore, they usually relax the execution policy for their machine to either RemoteSigned or Unrestricted. This action might be okay on their development or testing machines, where the script can be checked to determine that it is not harmful. But what do you do about using scripts in a production environment—that is, on your servers and clients?

If you administered Windows XP, Windows PowerShell might not have been on the system if you did not install it, so the possibilities for management were limited. With Windows Server 2008, Windows PowerShell 1.0 is available in the operating system. With Windows 8.1 and Windows Server 2012 R2, you even get Windows PowerShell 4.0 by default. Windows PowerShell allows for a great deal of flexibility in using the shell for your automations and administrative tasks, but it also means that you need to consider a safe way to prevent users from running untrusted scripts.

The AllSigned execution policy is the setting that most people consider to be the safe option. AllSigned requires that all scripts and configuration files are signed by a trusted publisher, including scripts that you write on the local computer. If you are a system administrator, you might want to set the execution policy to AllSigned for your nontechnical users so that they are allowed to run a subset of safe scripts. Nontechnical users who are administered by you will then be allowed to execute only the scripts that you have signed for them (just like keeping them buckled in their seatbelt). However, you will be able to operate with a more relaxed execution policy while writing and testing your own scripts before actually releasing them to production.

At the end of the day, an administrator can use any of the execution policy options to configure her own computer by using the Set-ExecutionPolicy cmdlet, which ultimately stores the execution policy setting in a registry value under HKEY_LOCAL_MACHINE\SOFTWARE\Microsoft\PowerShell\1\ShellIds\Microsoft.PowerShell\Executionpolicy. Now that the execution policy has a registry setting, the setting can also be applied to client workstations centrally by using some handy Group Policy templates (ADM files) that set the registry value for you en masse.

These ADM files have already been written for you by the Windows team and are available on the Microsoft Download Center.

You have even more execution policy options with Windows PowerShell 3.0 and above compared to the options just described for PowerShell 1.0. First, Windows PowerShell 2.0 introduces the concept of scopes, in which you can set an execution policy that is effective only in a particular scope. The valid scopes are Process, CurrentUser, and LocalMachine.

LocalMachine is the default when setting an execution policy. However, an administrator can change her execution policy just for the purpose of testing a script without changing the entire policy on the machine for all users. She can simply change the policy for her scope for the current process (the current session in the current Windows PowerShell process). This setting can be volatile and will stop its effect when the session in which the policy is set is finally closed. Alternatively, she can set a policy that affects only her own user profile by using CurrentUser and having the policy setting stored under her HKEY_CURRENT_USER registry hive. You can even execute different policies for different users on the same computer by using scopes.

Second, Windows PowerShell 2.0 and above has a few brand-new execution policy settings:

- Undefined is used when an execution policy is not defined at all in one or more scopes. If that is the case, the execution policy that you apply depends on the policies set in other scopes. (For example, if no execution policy is defined for CurrentUser but a policy is defined for LocalMachine, the execution policy for LocalMachine takes precedence.) Of course, if there are no policies set for any scopes, the execution policy always defaults to Restricted.

- Bypass is an even more relaxed policy than Unrestricted in that nothing is blocked, and no warnings or prompts are presented to the user when trying to run a script. This execution policy is designed for configurations in which a Windows PowerShell script is built into a larger application or for configurations in which Windows PowerShell is the foundation for a program that has its own security model.

With all of these available options, an administrator can truly choose what is safest/best for his clients/users while still being allowed the flexibility to test and debug his own scripts with ease.

# Understanding code signing

Working with signed scripts in Windows PowerShell is relatively easy and pain free because there are two cmdlets that allow you to sign scripts and verify the script signature. The two cmdlets are Get-AuthenticodeSignature and Set-AuthenticodeSignature. To use the Set-AuthenticodeSignature cmdlet, you must have a code-signing certificate. You can use the Certificate Manager utility, shown in Figure 15-6, to ensure that you have the proper code-signing certificate.

**FIGURE 15-6** The Certificate Manager utility provides a view into the user's certificate stores.

To request a code-signing certificate from the enterprise certification authority (CA), you can use the Certificate Manager utility to submit the request. The Certificate Enrollment Wizard from the Certificate Manager utility is shown in Figure 15-7.

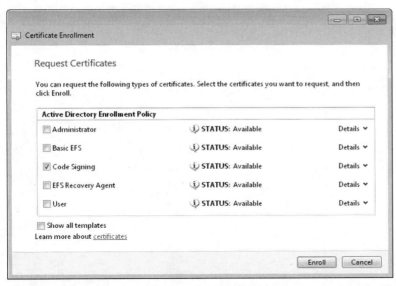

**FIGURE 15-7** The Certificate Manager utility can be used to request certificates if automatic enrollment is not enabled for the domain.

## Additional resources

- The TechNet Script Center at *http://www.microsoft.com/technet/scriptcenter* contains numerous script examples.
- A history of the .NET Framework versions can be found at *http://blogs.msdn.com /dougste/archive/2007/09/06/version-history-of-the-clr-2-0.aspx*.
- You can find help about how to determine which version of the .NET Framework is installed at *http://msdn.microsoft.com/en-us/library/hh925568.aspx*.
- The entry point to the MSDN website is found at *http://msdn.microsoft.com*.

# CHAPTER 16

# Running scripts

- Logon scripts
- Script folder
- Stand-alone scripts
- Help desk scripts
- Additional resources

When it comes to running scripts in Windows PowerShell, all scripts are not equal. You are likely to have many different types of scripts within your environment. Some scripts—written quickly for a one-time use—are little more than a collection of commands that might be typed at the Windows PowerShell console. Other scripts more closely resemble applications and should be treated as such. These are the scripts that are used to perform mission-critical configuration tasks and automated deployment and that are used by the help desk to aid in troubleshooting problems.

## Logon scripts

In Windows PowerShell 4.0, you can use a PowerShell script as a logon script as long as the domain controller is at least running Windows Server 2008 R2. You can use a Windows PowerShell script as a logon script, a logoff script, a startup script, or a shutdown script. Legacy logon scripts are specified via the user object in Active Directory Users and Computers; to specify a Windows PowerShell logon script requires using Group Policy.

To specify either a logon or a logoff script, configure a Group Policy Object setting on the User Configuration/ Policies/ Windows Settings/ Scripts (Logon/Logoff) node. Startup and shutdown scripts are specified in the Computer Configuration node under Policies / Windows Settings / Scripts (Startup / Shutdown). You can configure multiple GPOs containing different scripts and settings and, for performance, disable processing of the configuration settings not specified. You can link the GPOs to the domain or organizational unit, and you can even filter based on group memberships. All of these script options can be configured using Group Policy from within an Active Directory domain, as shown in Figure 16-1, but they can also be configured by using the local Group Policy editor.

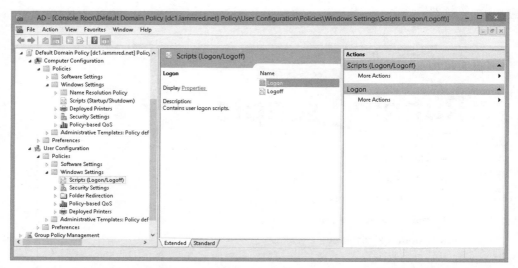

**FIGURE 16-1** Group Policy provides the ability to manage startup, shutdown, logon, and logoff scripts.

By default, logon scripts reside in the NetLogon\Sysvol\Domain\Policies folder. The script editor automatically populates scripts from this location, as shown in Figure 16-2.

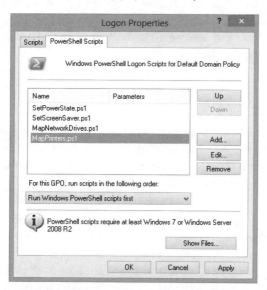

**FIGURE 16-2** Scripts run in the order in which they populate the script property box.

# What to include in logon scripts

Because many of the configuration items that were traditionally performed in logon scripts have migrated to Group Policy preferences, many network administrators run their networks without logon scripts. If you can use Group Policy and avoid the hassle of creating and maintaining logon scripts, you remove one source of potential errors. Most networks are sufficiently complex and have enough legacy applications that they cannot avoid the use of logon scripts. In the past, it was common to use logon scripts for the following purposes:

- Map user drives
- Set default printers

With the ability to use Windows PowerShell for logon scripts, many new and exciting opportunities present themselves within this area of scripting. Simple auditing can be done as well as logging to facilitate the ability to track potential errors. An example is shown in Logon .ps1, in which a new registry key is created to record the user name and the time that the user logs on to the computer. The newly created registry key is shown in Figure 16-3.

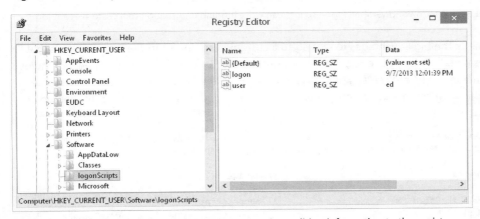

**FIGURE 16-3** Windows PowerShell logon scripts can write auditing information to the registry.

Another useful item accomplished by the Logon.ps1 script is creating a new event log named Logonscripts. The script then writes the full path to the logon script and the time it was executed, which is vital information when troubleshooting logon scripts. One of the key problems is trying to identify which logon script is executing. The Logonscripts event log is shown in Figure 16-4. The full UNC logon script path is stored as a hyperlink. By clicking the hyperlink in the event log details pane, the actual logon script is opened, providing you with the ability to make changes to the logon script if modifications are required. The ability to view the text of the logon script from within the event log makes it easy to troubleshoot logon scripts.

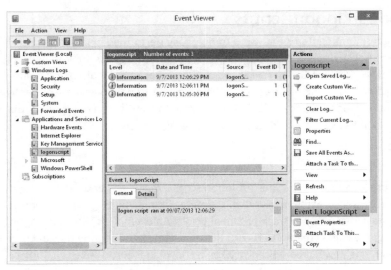

**FIGURE 16-4** Windows PowerShell logon scripts can write logging information to a custom event log.

One of the big advantages to writing to a custom event log from the logon script is that it makes it really easy to query, either locally or remotely. By using the `Invoke-Command` cmdlet, and running the *Get-EventLog* query via a script block, the information is easily obtainable. The following command and output illustrates connecting to a remote computer named client1:

```
PS C:\> invoke-command -ComputerName client1 -ScriptBlock {Get-EventLog -LogName
logonscript} | format-table timewritten, message -wrap

TimeWritten                          Message
-----------                          -------
9/7/2013 12:06:29 PM                 logon script  ran at 09/07/2013 12:06:29
9/7/2013 12:06:11 PM                 logon script \\tsclient\C\data\BookDOcs\P
                                     S4_BestPractices\Scripts\scripts_ch16\Log
                                     on.ps1 ran at 09/07/2013 12:06:11
9/7/2013 12:05:30 PM                 logon script \\tsclient\C\data\BookDOcs\P
                                     S4_BestPractices\Scripts\scripts_ch16\Log
                                     on.ps1 ran at 09/07/2013 12:05:30
```

The complete Logon.ps1 logon script is shown here.

```
Logon.ps1

$ErrorActionPreference = "SilentlyContinue"
if(-not(Test-path -path HKCU:\Software\logonScripts))
 {
  new-Item -path HKCU:\Software\logonScripts
  new-Itemproperty -path HKCU:\Software\logonScripts -name logon `
   -Value $(get-date).tostring() -Force
```

```
  new-Itemproperty -path HKCU:\Software\logonScripts -name user `
   -Value $env:USERNAME -Force
 }
else
 {
  set-Itemproperty -path HKCU:\Software\logonScripts -name logon `
   -Value $(get-date).tostring() -Force
  set-Itemproperty -path HKCU:\Software\logonScripts -name user `
   -Value $env:USERNAME -Force
 }

try
{
 New-EventLog –source logonscript -logname logonscript
}
Catch{ [System.Exception] }
Finally
{
 Write-EventLog -LogName logonscript -Source logonScript `
  -EntryType information `
  -EventId 1 `
  -Message "logon script $($myinvocation.invocationName) ran at $(get-date)"
}
$ErrorActionPreference = "Continue"
```

**Wes Stahler**
*President, Central Ohio PowerShell Users Group*

A request came in to provide metrics on one of our larger shared drives. The specific request was to display the size for all the directories one level below the supplied root. Simple enough, but this particular drive is huge, and running Get-ChildItem against it could potentially take hours.

We have a few options:

- Writing a script that runs Get-ChildItem against the root path
- Potentially utilizing PowerShell Workflow
- Using background jobs

The plan here is to create a new background job for each subfolder. Additionally, we will ensure that we don't consume all the memory by running only a maximum set of jobs at a time. The following code walks through the process:

```
# Root folder
$Path = '\\dfs-p01\dfs\Shared\COM\'

# Grab the folders one level down from the "root" folder
$Folders = Get-ChildItem -Path $path -Directory | Sort-Object Name

# Our scriptblock used in the loop that gets the size of each
subfolder
$sb = {
    param([string]$path)
    $sum = (Get-ChildItem -Path $path -Recurse -Force -ErrorAction
SilentlyContinue| Measure-Object -Property Length -Sum).Sum
    $dt = Get-Date -Format yyyyMMdd
    "{0},{1},{2:##.##}" -f $dt,$path,([long]$sum/1GB)
}

<# Iterate through the subfolders,
    Creating a job for each one until we hit a threshold.
    If we hit a threshold, we wait 10 seconds and try again #>

Foreach ($Folder in $Folders) {
    While ($(Get-Job -state running).count -ge 5){
        "{0}: wait 10 seconds..." -f $folder
        Start-Sleep -Seconds 10
    }

    $name = $Folder.FullName
    Start-Job -ScriptBlock $sb -ArgumentList $name
}

# Save the results to a variable for further analysis
$jobs = Get-Job | Wait-Job | Receive-Job
```

Running this as a set of throttled background jobs resulted in a substantial reduction in runtime as compared to iterating over all the folders sequentially via Get-ChildItem.

## Methods of calling the logon scripts

Logon scripts are commonly called during the logon process. In the past, logon scripts were assigned to the user via Active Directory Users And Computers; however, logon scripts assigned via Active Directory Users And Computers do not understand how to run Windows PowerShell scripts.

You should assign scripts from within Group Policy. You can assign logon, logoff, startup, and shutdown scripts. The great thing about using either a logoff or a shutdown script is that it can be used to unmap drives and printers, which can significantly improve the performance of a computer when it starts up and is unable to find the default printer or some remote share.

---

**NOTES FROM THE FIELD**

**Niklas Goude, Windows PowerShell MVP**
*Product Owner, ZervicePoint, Enfo Zipper*

"Wow, you can do pretty much anything in Windows PowerShell with simple one-line commands, is this really safe?"

This is one of the most common questions that I get from customers. I try to explain that users are restricted by permissions and point out that if a user has a lot of permissions on a system, the user can perform administrative tasks, with or without Windows PowerShell. I also explain that a good practice is to limit a user's privileges on systems.

Of course, there are cases when users, to perform their daily work, need more privileges, such as a company's helpdesk staff. One way of allowing the helpdesk staff to perform their daily tasks without granting them administrative rights on a system is by setting up a restricted endpoint.

A restricted endpoint allows you to control which cmdlets, functions, or scripts a user is permitted to run when using the endpoint. It's also possible to configure the endpoint so that it runs with the permissions of a different account, such as a service account.

Let's say we want our helpdesk staff to manage Active Directory users, computers, and groups by using Windows PowerShell.

First let's take a look at the restricted endpoint configuration. Windows PowerShell includes the New-PSSessionConfigurationFile cmdlet. The cmdlet generates a file containing settings that define a session configuration. Because we want to restrict our helpdesk staff to managing only users, groups, and computers in Active Directory, we could run the following command to generate a configuration file:

```
New-PSSessionConfigurationFile -Path C:\HelpDesk.pssc -SessionType
RestrictedRemoteServer -ModulesToImport ActiveDirectory -VisibleCmdlets
Get-ADUser,Set-ADUser,Get-ADComputer,Set-ADComputer,Get-ADGroup,
Set-ADGroup
```

In the preceding example, we create a new configuration file that restricts the user to the following cmdlets: Get-ADUser, Set-ADUser, Get-ADComputer, Set-ADComputer, Get-ADGroup, and Set-ADGroup. We also use the *ModulesToImport* parameter and set it to *ActiveDirectory*.

Because the helpdesk staff doesn't have permissions to manage users, computers, and groups in Active Directory, we need to configure the endpoint so that it runs with the permissions of an account that has the appropriate permissions.

We can use the Get-Credential cmdlet to store the account credentials in a *PSCredential* object, as follows:

```
$runAsCred = Get-Credential domain\serviceaccount
```

With the configuration file and the credentials in place, we can use the Register-PSSessionConfiguration cmdlet to create a new session configuration. This technique appears here.

```
Register-PSSessionConfiguration -Name HelpDesk -Path C:\HelpDesk.pssc
-Force -RunAsCredential $runAsCred
```

In the preceding example, we use the *PSCredential* object as input to the *RunAsCredential* parameter. We also add the path to the configuration file generated earlier.

In a standard session configuration, you have to be a member of either the builtin \administrators group or the builtin\remote management users group to use it. Because we don't want to add our helpdesk staff to any of these groups, we'll use the Set-PSSessionConfiguration cmdlet to allow additional groups access to the session configuration, as shown here:

```
Set-PSSessionConfiguration -Name HelpDesk -ShowSecurityDescriptorUI
```

In the preceding example, we grant an additional group permissions to use the session configuration.

Now, any user who is a member of the group added in the preceding step can use the restricted endpoint and run the cmdlets exposed by the endpoint.

```
Enter-PSSession -ComputerName SRV01 -ConfigurationName HelpDesk
```

The preceding example demonstrates how a helpdesk staff member connects to the restricted endpoint.

# Script folder

Windows PowerShell scripts can be stored in any folder. They can be stored locally or on a remote file share. If they are stored on a remote file share, the file share should be added to the Trusted Internet zone to enable you to run the scripts without interruption to the scripting environment. If you do not add your remote file share to the Trusted Internet zone, you will be prompted to do so the first time you open the script. If you choose to trust the script, you will then be permitted to work with the script. You can also choose to set the script execution policy to Bypass, which suppresses Internet zone warning messages.

## Deploy locally

One way to avoid the issue of network trusted zones is to store the scripts in a local folder on local workstations. This is also an important consideration if you want to use logon and logoff scripts that might not be available if the scripts are stored remotely. One additional consideration for storing the scripts locally is to improve performance by avoiding the network copy operation that occurs when you attempt to launch the script across the network. The problem with maintaining a local store of scripts is ensuring that the collection of scripts is kept up to date. You can keep the scripts up to date by maintaining version identification for the script collection. You can store the version of the script collection in the registry and check the collection version during the logon process. If the version has been superseded, new scripts can then be copied to the local workstation.

## Deploy an MSI package locally

If scripts are copied from a network share and the share is not added to the Trusted Internet zone, the scripts will not be able to run unless the Windows PowerShell script execution policy is set to Bypass or Unrestricted. If the scripts are installed on the local computer, the scripts will be placed into the local Internet zone. An easy way to deploy the scripts is to create an MSI package that creates the script folder and copies the scripts to the folder. You can then use Group Policy to deploy the MSI package.

# Stand-alone scripts

Stand-alone scripts do not have any external dependencies. They will always run because they do not rely on modules that might or might not be loaded or deployed. They do not use include files because the included file might not always be available. Stand-alone scripts tend to be longer than other types of scripts because they must include all functions, constants, variables, and aliases that the script requires to run without errors.

In an enterprise environment where you have total control over the desktop, you have the ability to ensure that requisite modules, constants, variables, and aliases will be present for the script. You can check for the presence of the module, and if it is missing, you have the option of copying it from a network share and installing or writing an error to a log file. Additionally, you can send an email to the help desk and report the missing dependencies.

## Diagnostics

Diagnostic scripts are written for the purpose of troubleshooting a particular error condition. Often, diagnostic scripts make use of the Windows Management Instrumentation (WMI) performance counter classes and the appropriate Windows PowerShell cmdlets. These types of scripts are typically run only on demand and can be run either remotely or locally, as the situation dictates.

## Reporting and auditing

Reporting scripts gather information from the target computer. These scripts are often launched in a fan-out type of configuration, and they write to a centralized database. These scripts can be called from within logon scripts or from logoff scripts as the need arises, but they can also be launched directly from the Windows PowerShell console and use the fan-out type technology.

---

### NOTES FROM THE FIELD

**Don Jones**
*President, PowerShell.Org*

Just because Workflow is an exciting and (still somewhat) new feature, don't jump to the conclusion that it's the right tool for every job. Workflow is an external technology, and your Windows PowerShell code gets translated over to it. That means that you have to code in a somewhat different style, and things like debugging can be a lot harder. That is, Workflow has some expensive mental overhead. It has advantages, true, but make sure you're actually getting good use of those advantages before you pay that higher cost. For example, a workflow can target remote computers—but so can the much-simpler Windows PowerShell Remoting feature. A workflow can run tasks in parallel—but, in some situations, you might be able to achieve that same parallelization by using jobs.

If you do decide to go with a workflow, you'll run into fewer snags if you start by building a normal, non-workflow function. Pay attention to best practices like spelling out command and parameter names, because in workflow those practices become mandatory (especially in Windows PowerShell 3.0). Get your function working against the local computer, where you have access to all of the shell's debugging and error handling features. Then start converting it into a function. If you run into a snag, rerun your script as a normal function so that you can figure out whether the problem is in your code or whether it's something connected to the workflow environment.

# Help desk scripts

Help desk scripts are a special class of stand-alone scripts because they often need to be able to perform multiple tasks from a single script. At a minimum, help desk scripts must be able to target different computers when they are run. While many scripts write to databases, text files, comma-separated variable (CSV) files, or webpages, most help desk scripts display information to the Windows PowerShell console because the information that is generated must be used during the resolution of the help desk call. As such, the data is not persisted to other formats.

## Avoid editing

A well-designed help desk script should expose all essential functionality through command-line parameters. It is a best practice to avoid editing help desk scripts due to the potential for introducing errors or changing the designed functionality of the script. Help desk scripts should be seen as utilities that provide custom diagnostic information and remediation to localized problems. One way to ensure that the scripts remain unaltered is to sign help desk scripts. When a script is signed, any alteration to the script invalidates the signature of the script. The script will need to be re-signed after it is modified.

To provide the functionality to troubleshoot remote computers, help desk scripts should expose a *–computer* parameter as well as other parameters that improve the functionality of the script.

## Provide a good level of help interaction

Because the help desk script might expose multiple command-line parameters, it is imperative that the help desk script provides help that explains each parameter, the allowed range of values, and a sample of the required syntax. The DisplayProcessor.ps1 script uses help tags to display the synopsis, description, examples, and other information about the script and its use. The DisplayProcessor.ps1 script is fully integrated with the Get-Help cmdlet and supports the standard parameters shown here:

```
Get-Help DisplayProcessor.ps1
Get-Help DisplayProcessor.ps1 –full
Get-Help DisplayProcessor.ps1 –detailed
Get-Help DisplayProcessor.ps1 –examples
```

The complete DisplayProcessor.ps1 script is shown here.

```
DisplayProcessor.ps1

<#
    .Synopsis
     Displays Processor information for the computer processor.
    .Description
     This script displays processor information for the local or
```

```
        remote computer. This includes Processor utilization, processor
        speed, L2 cache size, number of cores, and architecture.
      .Example
      DisplayProcessor.ps1
      Displays processor information for the local computer.
      .Example
      DisplayProcessor.ps1 -computer berlin
      Displays Processor information for a remote computer named berlin.
      .Inputs
       [string]
      .OutPuts
       [string]
      .Notes
       NAME:  Windows PowerShell Best Practices
       AUTHOR: Ed Wilson
       LASTEDIT: 9/7/2013
       VERSION: 1.0.1
       KEYWORDS:
      .Link
        Http://www.ScriptingGuys.com
#Requires -Version 2.0
#>
param(
  [Parameter(position=0)]
  [string]
  [alias("CN")]
  $computer=$env:computername
) #end param


# Begin Functions
function New-Underline
{
<#
.Synopsis
 Creates an underline the length of the input string
.Example
 New-Underline -strIN "Hello world"
.Example
 New-Underline -strIn "Morgen welt" -char "-" -sColor "blue" -uColor "yellow"
.Example
 "this is a string" | New-Underline
.Notes
 NAME:
 AUTHOR: Ed Wilson
 LASTEDIT: 5/20/2009
```

```
VERSION: 1.0.0
KEYWORDS:
.Link
Http://www.ScriptingGuys.com
#>
[CmdletBinding()]
param(
      [Parameter(Mandatory = $true,Position = 0,valueFromPipeline=$true)]
      [string]
      $strIN,
      [string]
      $char = "=",
      [string]
      $sColor = "Green",
      [string]
      $uColor = "darkGreen",
      [switch]
      $pipe
) #end param
$strLine= $char * $strIn.length
if(-not $pipe)
  {
   Write-Host -ForegroundColor $sColor $strIN
   Write-Host -ForegroundColor $uColor $strLine
  }
  Else
  {
  $strIn
  $strLine
  }
} #end New-Underline function

Function Get-Processor
{
 Param ([string]$computer)
 get-wmiobject -class win32_processor -computername $computer |
 foreach-object `
  {
   New-Underline("Processor details for $computer")
   $_.psobject.properties |
   foreach-object `
    {
     If($_.value)
       {
        if ($_.name -match "__"){}
```

```
      ELSE
       {
        $Processor +=@{ $($_.name) = $($_.value) }
       } #end else
     } #end if
   } #end foreach property
   $Processor   ; $Processor.clear()
  } #end foreach Processor
 Return
} #end Get-Processor
# Entry Point

Get-Processor -computer $computer
```

## Additional resources

- The TechNet Script Center at *http://www.microsoft.com/technet/scriptcenter* contains numerous examples of logon scripts and help desk scripts.
- All scripts from this chapter are available via the TechNet Script Center Script Repository at *http://gallery.technet.microsoft.com/scriptcenter/PowerShell-40 -Best-d9e16039.*

# CHAPTER 17

# Versioning scripts

- Why version control?
- Version control software
- Additional resources

When it comes to versioning scripts in Windows PowerShell, there is likely to be a wide divergence of opinion. At every TechEd conference in North America for the last four consecutive years, Windows PowerShell script versioning has come up in the "Birds of a Feather" session.

## Why version control?

Version control involves tracking changes made to production scripts. There are several reasons for maintaining version control of production scripts, including the following:

- Avoids introducing errors into existing production scripts
- Enables accurate troubleshooting of production scripts
- Tracks changes in production scripts
- Maintains a master listing of production scripts
- Maintains compatibility with other scripts

### NOTES FROM THE FIELD

#### Control your source

Don Jones, Microsoft PowerShell MVP
*ConcentratedTech.com*

Unfortunately, some people don't take their scripts seriously. For me, a script is the result of long work at the command line and becomes something that I want to save forever. I don't want the script ruined because a coworker mangled the code or because I lost the only copy of the script that I had. Software developers discovered a solution years ago and named it *source control*. If you take your scripts seriously, you should avail yourself of source control; if you don't take your scripts seriously enough to protect them in this fashion, why are you scripting at all?

Source control repositories keep *every* past version of your script so that you can revert to a previous version at any time. Most source control repositories require that you check out scripts if you want to change them, although some simply keep every version you save, thereby eliminating messy "check-in" and "check-out" steps. Ideally, you have already found yourself a quality script editor—and a *quality* script editor includes source control connectivity, which means that it will interact with popular source control systems.

If your company already has a source control repository, that's great. It's probably based on Microsoft Visual SourceSafe, Microsoft Team Server, or CSV/Subversion, which are open-source solutions. Use your company's source control repository— simply set yourself up with a Windows PowerShell project and check all of your scripts into it. If your company does not have a source control solution, consider something a little simpler to set up and use than those big-iron, developer-oriented solutions. For example, SAPIEN Technologies offers ChangeVue, and a web search for "easy source control" will turn up several source control solutions, including some with fun names, such as FileHamster, Git, and History Explorer. There are also online source control hosting services, such as BeanstalkApp.com and Unfuddle .com as well as hundreds of others, that require only a Subversion client (and that functionality might be included in higher-end script development environments).

If your data is important enough to save in a .ps1 file, that .ps1 file is important enough to save in a source control repository. Scripting in Windows PowerShell *without* version control is like driving without a seatbelt. You can do it—and plenty of people don't regret it—but when you do regret it, you regret it a lot.

## Avoid introducing errors

It is unlikely that a person can make a change to a script without introducing an error. The process of writing scripts is often reduced to making changes to the code and looking for errors. Whether making minor or major changes to an existing script, the potential for break-ing a working production script is great. If the change is substantial and the error is major, it is possible that the script will never work again. By maintaining version control, you work on a copy of the existing script. When the script modifications are completed and tested, the new version of the script becomes the production model of the script. If subsequent use of the script reveals an unexpected problem, you can revert to the previous version of the script. At no time is the production version of the script altered. All changes are tracked, and the changes are made on copies of the script.

# Enable accurate troubleshooting

If you track your scripts by file name only, it quickly becomes impossible to tell one version of a script from another version. If a problem is discovered with a particular script and there is no version control, you must carefully read and compare one version of the script with another version. You cannot be certain which version is the most recent or which script to actually deploy. By maintaining file versions, you can quickly discern that you want to deploy one particular version of the script instead of another version.

If a user of the script files reports a problem with the script and you are maintaining version control, you need only to ask the user which version of the script is being used to detect whether the user has an out-of-date copy of the script or whether the user discovered a new bug in the production version of the code.

# Track changes

Unfortunately, not all changes that are made to production scripts improve the reliability, performance, security, and ease of use of the script. It is a sad fact of the scripting life that some changes introduce errors, diminish performance, and complicate previously easy-to-use scripts. If a particular modification to a script is serious, the changes must be backed out and removed from the production code.

If version control is being maintained, the solution to backing out suboptimal script changes is to revert to the most recent working version of the script. If version control is not being maintained, the solution is to edit the production script and attempt to remove all of the changed lines in the script. If the modifications were not properly commented, your only choice is to try to find a previous version of the script in the backup software or the previous version's utility.

# Maintain a master listing

If you maintain proper version control of your production scripts, you will be able to produce a report that details which scripts are released to production and which scripts are still in progress. If you find a script that is not on the released-to-production list, you will know that the script is not yet authorized for release.

# Maintain compatibility with other scripts

As your script library grows, it is likely that you will begin to develop dependencies on other scripts. This can occur because functions contained in the script are used by other scripts or because the script produces output that is used by another script. In either case, if a script is used either directly or indirectly by other scripts, changes must be tracked carefully and testing must be thorough to ensure that breaking changes are not introduced into multiple scripts.

**Ian Farr, Premier Field Engineer**
*Microsoft Corporation*

As you write more and more scripts, the maintenance and storage of them can be a problem. Being able to easily find code that you wrote a couple of years ago will save you time and frustration! I recommend giving some thought to the location and structure of your script repository.

In the enterprise, if you don't want to use an application as a script repository, you should store your scripts on a network share. Data recovery, data security, and data integrity are important. Let's consider each option:

- For recovery, if you place your repository on a network file share, it is likely that data stored will be replicated and automatically backed up.

- For security, because, in the wrong hands, some scripts can make significant changes to your environment, a network share can secure the data via NTFS permissions and Access Based Enumeration.

- For integrity, you might have access to an Enterprise Certificate Authority or a Commercial Certificate Authority that can issue certificates for signing your scripts. This prevents Windows PowerShell from running a script that has been changed and not resigned.

For a personal script repository, the data could be stored on your computer, on an external drive, or in the cloud by using a technology such as SkyDrive. Whatever option you choose, you still need to think about data recovery, data security, and data integrity:

- For recovery, there's Windows Backup. What about writing a script to back up your scripts? Using cloud storage will provide resilience, but wherever the repository is located, it makes sense to have that data backed-up to a couple of locations.

- For security, you might not care about what happens to your scripts, but I'm guessing you do, so consider physical security, complex passwords, and BitLocker.

- For integrity, you can create your own self-signed certificate for use on your computer. It could be argued that this isn't a necessary for a personal repository, but the option is there for you.

Whether for the enterprise or for private use, the best repositories have a logical structure, such as the following:

- Script Type (for example, PS1, VBS)
- Technology (for example, AD, DHCP)

- Topic (for example, Replication, Scope Management)
- Script Function (for example, Check Replication, Add Scope Option)

For my own repository, the names of my scripts reflect the script function. I also include keywords/tags in the here-string that contain the script description. It's then easy to find scripts from within the repository by using Search. You might even go a step further—a former colleague put in extra effort and wrote a script to parse his repository, because he liked his data presented in a very specific way.

There are a number of points to consider when creating and maintaining a script repository. Ultimately, you'll know what works best for you or your organization.

## Internal version number in the comments

One simple way to maintain version control is to add a version number of the script into the comments. In this way, you can examine the comments of the script to reveal the version of the script. This technique relies on the person who modifies the internal version number of the script when changes are made.

Two challenges are present with this approach to version control. Maintaining an internal version number is a manual approach to versioning and relies on the editor of the script to make a version number change for each modification to the script. There is a real temptation to not tamper with modifying the version number when making minor changes to the script, such as updating comments.

The second challenge with manual version control is that the previous version of the script needs to be renamed so that the current version of the script can be stored. This challenge can be overcome by keeping each version of the script in its own folder. The most recent version of the script is the one in the most recent folder. The Get-ScriptVersion.ps1 script retrieves the version of the script and the last date that the script was edited. It relies on both the version and the last-edit information being stored in the header of the script as shown here:

```
.Notes
NAME:  Windows PowerShell Best Practices
AUTHOR: Ed Wilson
LASTEDIT: 5/20/2009
VERSION: 1.0.0
KEYWORDS:
.Link
Http://www.ScriptingGuys.com
```

The complete Get-ScriptVersion.ps1 script is shown here.

```
Get-ScriptVersion.ps1

function get-ScriptVersion ([string]$path)
{
 $scripts = Get-ChildItem -Path $path -recurse
 ForEach($script in $scripts)
 {
  $info = New-Object psobject
  $scriptText = Get-Content $script.fullname
  $info |
  Add-Member -Name "name" -Value $script.name -MemberType noteproperty
  $lastedit = $scriptText |
  Select-String -Pattern "\s\d{1,1}/\d{1,2}/\d{1,4}"

  if($lastedit.count -gt 1)
   {
     $info |
     Add-Member -Name "LastEdit" -Value $lastedit[0].matches[0].value '
     -membertype noteproperty
   }
  if($lastedit.matches.count -gt 0)
   {
    $info |
    Add-Member -Name "LastEdit" -Value $lastedit.matches[0].value '
    -membertype noteproperty -Force
   }
 $version = $scriptText |
 Select-String -Pattern "\s\d\.\d\.\d"

  if($version.count -gt 1)
   {
    $info |
    Add-Member -Name version -Value $version[0].matches[0].value '
    -membertype noteproperty -Force
   }
  if($version.matches.count -gt 0)
   {
    $info |
    Add-Member -Name version -Value $version.matches[0].value '
    -membertype noteproperty -Force
   }
  $info
  $version = $lastedit = $scriptText = $null
} #end foreach
```

```
} #end function get-ScriptVersion

# *** Entry Point ***

Get-ScriptVersion -path C:\data\BookDOcs\PS4_BestPractices\Scripts |
Format-Table -Property * -AutoSize
```

## Incrementing version numbers

When adding version identification numbers to scripts, it is not typically necessary to go beyond three decimal places. The first number usually represents the major version of the script. A 1.0.0 version number denotes the first release of the script, with no minor versions and no revisions. A major version change is one that involves a number of substantial changes to the script. Typically, these changes create new functionality that requires a major rewrite of the script. A minor version change, such as version 1.1.0, involves less drastic changes and improvements to the script, such as a change that involves performance tuning of the script or that improves the flow of the script. If you are correcting misspelled words, fixing bugs, or improving error handling to the script, you might change the version to 1.1.1.

---

*LESSONS LEARNED*

### Deleting the wrong version of the script

Keep in mind that every change you make to the script should involve a version change. I constantly come across multiple versions of the same script with no easy way to differentiate between the two copies. You should keep the working copy of the script, and rename the previous versions of the script in a manner that is readily identifiable. Inside the script, you should maintain a version table and list what has changed between version numbers. In this manner, you can avoid accidentally deleting the wrong edition of the script.

---

## Tracking changes

When making version changes to your script, you should include a comment indicating the changes that were made to the script. This comment can be included in the Notes section of the header portion of the script. As shown in the Get-WindowsEdition.ps1 script, each version of the script is listed, the date that it was current, and the change that was made that caused the version to be modified. The version table of the script is shown here:

```
.Notes
    NAME:  Get-WindowsEdition.ps1
    AUTHOR: Ed Wilson
```

```
       LASTEDIT: 5/20/2009
       VERSION: 1.2.0 Added Help tags
                   1.1.1 4/2/1009 Added link to http://www.ScriptingGuys.com
                   1.1.0 4/1/2009 Modified to use regex pattern
       KEYWORDS: Windows PowerShell Best Practices
```

The complete Get-WindowsEdition.ps1 script is shown here.

**Get-WindowsEdition.ps1**

```
<#
   .Synopsis
   Gets the version of Windows that is installed on the local computer
   .Description
   Gets the version of Windows that is installed on the local computer. This
   is information such as Windows 7 Enterprise.
   .Example
   Get-WindowsEdition.ps1
   Displays version of windows on local computer.
   .Inputs
   none
   .OutPuts
   [string]
   .Notes
   NAME:  Get-WindowsEdition.ps1
   AUTHOR: Ed Wilson
   LASTEDIT: 9/20/2013
   VERSION: 1.2.0 Added Help tags
               1.1.1 4/2/2009 Added link to http://www.ScriptingGuys.com
               1.1.0 4/1/2009 Modified to use regex pattern
   KEYWORDS: Windows PowerShell Best Practices
   .Link
     Http://www.ScriptingGuys.com
#Requires -Version 4.0
#>


$strPattern = "version"
$text = net config workstation

switch -regex ($text)
{
  $strPattern { Write-Host $switch.current }
}
```

# Version control software

The easiest way to perform Windows PowerShell version control is to use a version control software package. Previous versions of Microsoft Visual Studio contained a source control software package named Visual SourceSafe (VSS). However, for many scripters, VSS was too complicated for a scripting environment. At any rate, VSS is no longer supplied with Visual Studio and is no longer an option.

Third-party version control software packages are available, but most target commercial software developers and are not a good fit for enterprise scripters. The Microsoft SharePoint Server can be used to maintain a master repository for scripts, and it does have checkout and versioning features that will work; however, it needs to be modified to allow Windows PowerShell and VBScripts to be natively stored on the SharePoint site. A better solution is one that integrates directly with the script editor and provides automatic versioning.

**NOTES FROM THE FIELD**

### Using version control software

Alexander Riedel, Vice President
*SAPIEN Technologies*

Ever since Microsoft introduced the Script Encoder for the Windows Script Host and SAPIEN Technologies added the ability to package scripts into executable files within PrimalScript, one question has become quite commonplace on our support forums: "Can you please help me retrieve my script?"

While some of the causes for this usually panic-stricken request have been the lack of backup combined with a failed hard drive, an exploding laptop battery, or a teenager causing a virus infection on Dad's work computer, much more common are the following comments:

- A previous employee here wrote the script, and I don't know where the original is.
- It used to work but now it doesn't. The only thing that still works is the script in the .exe file.
- Somebody changed it, and I don't know what they did to it.

Quite obviously, a simple backup won't help with these types of problems. You need to find out what actually changed. For a software developer, none of these reasons are usually a very big deal. Over the past several decades, the software development industry has created tools and adopted best practices that prevent these things from becoming a disaster. However, because script developers very often don't see themselves as "developers," they sometimes miss out on observing best practices.

From experience, we also know that even the best intentions don't always help; for example, just consider this question: When did *your* last backup happen?

That is why SAPIEN has created a new product called VersionRecall. This product was specifically created for administrators working alone with a need for backup and version control.

Without all the setup and configuration required by traditional version controls systems, it can be installed and ready for use in minutes.

A very important aspect of VersionRecall is that it works without a specific API that would tie it to specific editors or IDEs. Because administrators very often change tools during the course of the day, jumping from the Windows PowerShell ISE to PowerShell Studio, Notepad, and other editing tools, a tool-agnostic approach was a major design requirement.

You can manually submit changes from the software's main application or its command-line tool. But most commonly, you will leave this job to VersionRecall's automatic service, which will automatically detect changed files in designated folders and submit those changes, no matter what software you used to modify a file.

You notice that the operative word here was *automatically*. Set up your environment to automatically back up and track changes to your vital files, and you won't have to call anyone with panic in your voice.

## Additional resources

- The TechNet Script Center at *http://www.microsoft.com/technet/scriptcenter* contains numerous examples of logon scripts and help desk scripts.
- All scripts from this chapter are available via the TechNet Script Center Script Repository at *http://gallery.technet.microsoft.com/scriptcenter/PowerShell -40-Best-d9e16039*.

# CHAPTER 18

# Logging results

- Logging to a text file
- Logging to the event log
- Logging to the registry
- Additional resources

After your scripts are written, deployed, and executed on a system, you need to know whether the scripts ran successfully. The best way to make this determination is to log the results of the scripts. There are many options for logging script results, and we'll look at them in this chapter.

Logging results from scripts is a basic technique. Quite often, you will want to store the results of a script. While there are many options for data storage that range in complexity from writing to a database to creating webpages, three techniques are used so often that they should be part and parcel of the IT professional's scripting toolkit. These techniques are so critical that Windows PowerShell 4.0 has designed cmdlets to simplify the task of logging from the script. The three main logging tools at your disposal are the text file, the event log, and the registry. In this chapter, we will cover best practices that govern choosing one technique over another.

## Logging to a text file

Despite the advances in XML documents, HTML documents, Microsoft Office documents, and other storage mechanisms, the plain text file remains an often-used format for logging purposes. The text file is simple to use, compact, portable, and causes no compatibility issues. The easiest way to write logging information to a text file is to use the redirection operators, of which there are two—the single and the double. The single redirection operator writes to a text file. If the file does not exist, it will be created and the data will be written to it. If the file already exists, the file will be overwritten.

```
PS C:\> Get-Process > C:\data\FSO\process.txt
```

The double redirection operator will create a file if it does not exist. If the file does exist, it will append to the file.

```
PS C:\> Get-Process >> C:\data\FSO\process.txt
```

# Designing a logging approach

One of the design decisions that you will make when implementing logging to a text file is whether you will append to the log file or whether you will overwrite the file. There are several decision points that govern the use of overwriting or appending to the log file, as covered in Table 18-1.

**TABLE 18-1** Logging to text file decision guide

| Mode | Need | Example |
|------|------|---------|
| Append | Maintain history | Log multiple changes made by script |
| Append | Maintain audit | A logon script that documents when a user logged on |
| Append | Maintain tracing | A script that writes error information to a file for each operation it performs |
| Overwrite | Capture return code | A script that writes the success or error returns code from the script to a file |
| Overwrite | Display information that is too wide to fit in the Windows PowerShell console | A script that displays the members of an object |
| Overwrite | Display information that the user might need to scroll or search | A script that displays a detailed log file in which a user might want to use Notepad or some other tool to search for keywords or to scroll through the file contents |

## Overwriting the log

You might decide to overwrite the log file on each occasion if your logging goal is to know whether a particular operation succeeded or failed. This one-time logging approach is useful from a troubleshooting perspective in which historical data is not important and the maintenance of a change log is not desired.

A typical use for a one-time log is the logon script. After the user successfully logs on to the system, there is little need for the log file. However, if the user has problems with his system and is unable to print to his network printer or to access files from his network share, the log becomes an important troubleshooting device.

An example of a logon script with built-in logging is the LogonScriptWithLogging.ps1 script. First, the LogonScriptWithLogging.ps1 script uses the *$errorActionPreference* variable to configure Windows PowerShell to not display any errors to the console while the script is running. Hiding errors from the user during the logon process is generally a best practice because it avoids confusing the user and reduces help desk calls. Next, the script clears the error object; as a result, the only errors that will be present on the error object are errors generated from the logon script. Several variables are initialized to null to avoid possible pollution from the scripting environment.

```
$errorActionPreference = "SilentlyContinue"
$error.Clear()
$startTime ,$endTime , $Message, $logResults = $null
```

The `Test-Path` cmdlet is used to ensure that the logging directory is present on the computer. If the logging directory is not present, it is created by using the `New-Item` cmdlet. The `Join-Path` cmdlet is used to build the complete path to the log file.

```
$logDir = "c:\fso"
if(-not(Test-Path -path $logdir))
  { New-Item -Path $logdir -ItemType directory | Out-Null }
$logonLog = Join-Path -Path $logDir -ChildPath "logonlog.txt"
```

An important item in any log file is a time stamp that informs you of the time that the operation ran. In general, it is a best practice to log the start time of the script as well as the end time to give you an indication of how long it takes the script to run. If a script that normally completes in 3 seconds suddenly takes 35 seconds, it can indicate a problem. The LogonScriptWithLogging.ps1 script uses the *WshNetwork* object to map network drives and set the default printer. After each operation in the script completes, the operation and any resulting errors are written to the *$message* variable.

```
$startTime = (Get-Date).tostring()
$WshNetwork = New-Object -ComObject wscript.network
$WshNetwork.MapNetworkDrive("f:","\\berlin\studentShare")
$message += "'r'nMapping drive f to \\berlin\student share 'r'n$($error[0])"
$WshNetwork.SetDefaultPrinter("berlinPrinter")
$message += "'r'nSetting default printer to berlinPrinter 'r'n$($error[0])"
```

When all actions defined in the script are performed, the script end time is obtained from the `Get-Date` cmdlet and the output message is formatted. Because all of the errors, operations, and time stamps are collected into variables, a single output message can easily be created. The collecting of messages during script operation is a best practice because a single I/O (input/output) operation can be undertaken to create the log file, which is much more efficient than writing to the log file multiple times during the script's progress. A here-string is used to create the log results message, and the single redirection operator writes to the log file.

```
$endTime = (Get-Date).tostring()
$logResults = @"
**Starting script: $($MyInvocation.InvocationName) $startTime.
  $message
**Ending logon script $endTime.
**Total script time was $((New-TimeSpan -Start $startTime '
  -End $endTime).totalSeconds) seconds.
"@
$logResults > $logonLog
```

The complete LogonScriptWithLogging.ps1 script is shown here.

---

**LogonScriptWithLogging.ps1**

```
$errorActionPreference = "SilentlyContinue"
$error.Clear()
$startTime = $endTime = $Message = $logResults = $null
```

```
$logDir = "c:\fso"
if(-not(Test-Path -path $logdir))
  { New-Item -Path $logdir -ItemType directory | Out-Null }
$logonLog = Join-Path -Path $logDir -ChildPath "logonlog.txt"

$startTime = (Get-Date).tostring()
$WshNetwork = New-Object -ComObject wscript.network
$WshNetwork.MapNetworkDrive("f:","\\berlin\studentShare")
$message += "'r'nMapping drive f to \\berlin\student share 'r'n$($error[0])"
$WshNetwork.SetDefaultPrinter("berlinPrinter")
$message += "'r'nSetting default printer to berlinPrinter 'r'n$($error[0])"

$endTime = (Get-Date).tostring()
$logResults = @"
**Starting script: $($MyInvocation.InvocationName) $startTime.
 $message
**Ending logon script $endTime.
**Total script time was $((New-TimeSpan -Start $startTime '
  -End $endTime).totalSeconds) seconds.
"@
$logResults > $logonLog
```

When the LogonScriptWithLogging.ps1 script is run, the log shown in Figure 18-1 is created in the C:\fso directory.

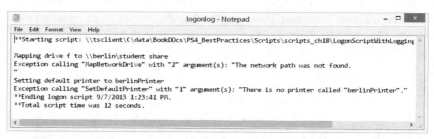

**FIGURE 18-1** Script log showing logon time and status of operation.

## Leveraging CSV files

**Mike Pfeiffer, Premier Field Engineer**
*Microsoft Corporation*

One of the greatest strengths of Windows PowerShell is the ease it gives administrators in building detailed reports. I've always been a big fan of the `Export-Csv` and `ConvertTo-Html` cmdlets, and to this day, I'll still use them all the time. When you're just getting started, the object-based nature of Windows PowerShell makes it pretty straightforward to export structured data to external files using these cmdlets. However, you'll quickly realize that sometimes you need to tweak things to get the data that you're really interested in.

Let me show you how to solve a common problem when it comes to generating your own reports. Suppose you want to export a list of services to a CSV file. You're interested only in services that have dependencies. You begin with a command such as the following:

```
Get-Service |
    Where-Object DependentServices |
        Select-Object DisplayName,DependentServices
```

This looks good in the Windows PowerShell console. You see two columns for each service, as expected. Naturally, you tack on another pipe and export your report to a CSV file.

```
Get-Service |
    Where-Object DependentServices |
        Select-Object DisplayName,DependentServices |
            Export-Csv c:\myservices.csv -NoTypeInformation
```

Now you open your CSV file in Excel, and you're ready to save your report as an Excel spreadsheet, after adding some borders and cell formatting, of course. Your boss and coworkers will be so proud. But don't get too excited just yet. Your *DependentServices* column isn't happy.

| DisplayName | DependentServices |
| --- | --- |
| Windows Audio Endpoint Builder | System.ServiceProcess.ServiceController[] |
| Base Filtering Engine | System.ServiceProcess.ServiceController[] |
| Cryptographic Services | System.ServiceProcess.ServiceController[] |

Notice that the *DependentServices* column is showing the .NET framework type name for each property instead of the actual property values. This is because the value for *DependentServices* is made up of a collection of services that have dependencies on the parent service.

The `Export-CSV` cmdlet is expecting "flat" property values. Think of it like the Windows *Path* variable. The *Path* variable is a single item, but all of the paths within it are separated by a semicolon. This is essentially what you need to do with your report. Your *DependentServices* column values should each be a single string composed of semicolon delimited values. An easy way to accomplish this is by using a custom property. This will give you the ability to fix up the property value with your own expression. Here's how you can fix it:

```
Get-Service |
    Where-Object DependentServices |
        Select-Object DisplayName,@{n='DependentServices';e={$_.
DependentServices -join ';'}} |
            Export-Csv c:\myservices.csv -NoTypeInformation
```

The only difference here is that we've customized the *DependentServices* property. Notice that inside the expression we've used the *-Join* operator. The job of the *-Join* operator is to take multiple strings and combine them into one. Within the expression, we're saying that all of the service objects within the *DependentServices* property should be joined together. Fortunately, the *.ToString()* method will be called on each dependent service for you automatically, and the entire list will be joined to a semicolon-delimited string, giving you readable output in the file.

This is a classic issue that most people run into. In fact, I've been asked about it twice this week, which provided the inspiration for this tip. Remember this technique because you're bound to run into this when you start generating your own reports.

## Appending to the log

If your logging scenario needs to maintain historical data from either a security perspective or from a long-term troubleshooting stance, you will append to your log. You might also decide to append to the log if the script completes a number of discrete operations and you want to maintain a log of each operation's results. Appending might be an important technique if it is possible for the operation to fail midway through the script.

When working with a more complex script, you might want to instrument the script to provide detailed logging information. The LogChartProcessWorkingSet.ps1 script is an example of instrumenting a script. The script uses the *Param* keyword to create a switched command-line parameter named *trace*. When the script is run with the *trace* switch, statements are written to a Tracelog.txt file in the C:\fso directory. The *$errorActionPreference* variable is set to *SilentlyContinue*, and any errors are cleared from the error object. The *$startTime* and *$endTime* variables are set to null. The initialization section of the script is shown here:

```
Param([switch]$trace)
$trace=$true
$errorActionPreference = "SilentlyContinue"
$error.Clear()
$startTime = $endTime = $null
```

The presence of the log directory is checked; if it is not present, it is created. The path to the Tracelog.txt file is created, and the start time of the script is recorded as a string in the *$startTime* variable.

```
$logDir = "c:\fso"
if(-not(Test-Path -path $logdir))
  { New-Item -Path $logdir -ItemType directory | Out-Null }
$traceLog = Join-Path -Path $logDir -ChildPath "Tracelog.txt"
$startTime = (Get-Date).tostring()
```

The script looks for the presence of the *$trace* variable. If the *$trace* variable is found, logging information is written to the Tracelog.txt file. If the *$trace* variable is not found, no logging is done.

```
If($trace)
  {"**Starting script: $($MyInvocation.InvocationName) $startTime" >> $traceLog}
```

When the script completes the creation of the chart, the number of errors that are generated is written to the log file. The *Foreach* statement is used to walk through the collection of errors, and each error is written to the log file.

```
"*** LISTING $($error.count) Errors ***" >> $traceLog
 Foreach ($e in $error) { $e >> $tracelog }
```

> **NOTE** Keep in mind that the *MSGraph.Application* COM object does not exist on a work-station by default. It installs with Microsoft Office.

The completed LogChartProcessWorkingSet.ps1 script is shown here.

```
LogChartProcessWorkingSet.ps1

Param([switch]$trace)
$errorActionPreference = "SilentlyContinue"
$error.Clear()
$startTime = $endTime = $null

$logDir = "c:\fso"
if(-not(Test-Path -path $logdir))
  { New-Item -Path $logdir -ItemType directory | Out-Null }
$traceLog = Join-Path -Path $logDir -ChildPath "Tracelog.txt"
$startTime = (Get-Date).tostring()

If($trace)
  {"**Starting script: $($MyInvocation.InvocationName) $startTime" >> $traceLog}
If($trace)
  {"Creating msgraph.application object" >> $traceLog}
$chart = New-Object -ComObject msgraph.application
$chart.visible = $true
If($trace)
  {"Adding chart column labels" >> $traceLog}
$chart.datasheet.cells.item(1,1) = "Process Name"
$chart.datasheet.cells.item(1,2) = "Working Set"
If($trace)
  {"Adding Data to chart" >> $traceLog}
$r = 2
If($trace)
  {"Obtaining process information" >> $traceLog}
```

```
Get-Process |
ForEach-Object {
  $chart.datasheet.cells.item($r,1) = $_.name
  $chart.datasheet.cells.item($r,2) = $_.workingSet
  $r++
} # end foreach process

$endTime = (Get-Date).tostring()
If($trace)
  {"**ending script $endTime. " >> $traceLog}
If($trace)
  {"**Total script time was $((New-TimeSpan -Start $startTime '
  -End $endTime).totalSeconds) seconds'r'n" >> $traceLog}
"*** LISTING $($error.count) Errors ***" >> $traceLog
 Foreach ($e in $error) { $e >> $tracelog }
```

When the script is run, the log shown in Figure 18-2 is produced.

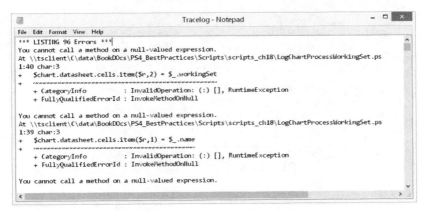

**FIGURE 18-2** Trace log created when running a script with the *trace* switch.

## Using the Out-File cmdlet

In addition to using the redirection operators, you can also use the Out-File cmdlet to create a text file. Both methods create text files, and both methods work in a similar fashion because, inside Windows PowerShell, the redirection operators actually map to Out-File. The difference between the two is that the Out-File cmdlet is configurable and the redirection operators are not. The default values for the redirection operators are as follows:

- The redirection operators use Unicode.

- The redirection operators use the Windows PowerShell console dimensions when writing to files.

Both the redirection operators and the Out-File cmdlet send output through the Windows PowerShell formatter prior to writing to a file. In some cases, the Windows PowerShell formatter can add or change the output in such a way as to cause corruption in certain binary data types.

To change the output encoding of a file, you can use the *Encoding* parameter when creating the file.

```
PS C:\> (Get-Acl -Path C:\fso\access.txt).AccessToString |
Out-File -FilePath C:\fso\outFile.Txt -Encoding ASCII
```

If your output is truncated in the Windows PowerShell console, such as the output shown in Figure 18-3, you can save the output in a text file and use the *width* parameter to capture all of the information.

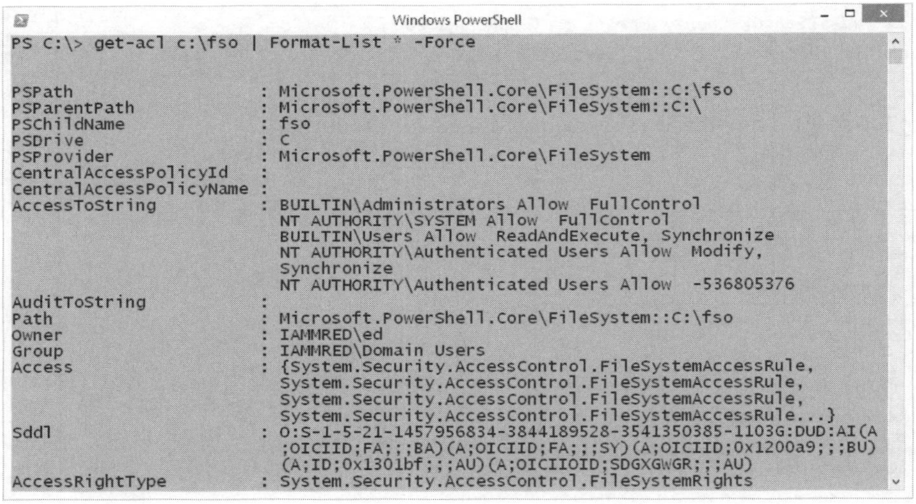

**FIGURE 18-3** Truncated output in the Windows PowerShell console is indicated by three dots.

An example of changing the width in the file by using the *width* parameter is shown here:

```
PS C:\> Get-Acl -Path C:\fso\access.txt |
Out-File -FilePath C:\fso\outFile.Txt -Encoding ASCII -Width 1500
```

If you use a semicolon to separate commands when working at the Windows PowerShell console or in a Windows PowerShell script, you can call Notepad at the same time that you create the file. You can then use the Notepad utility to display all of the information and scroll as required to see the information that is truncated.

By pipelining the results of the process information to the Get-Member cmdlet, the members of the objects are displayed. The content is too wide for the Windows PowerShell console and is truncated. By specifying a width of 200 for the Out-File cmdlet, the member definition will fit on the lines of the file.

```
PS C:\> Get-Process |
Get-Member |
Out-File -FilePath C:\fso\processMembers.txt -Width 200 ;
notepad C:\fso\processMembers.txt
```

The resulting text file is shown in Figure 18-4.

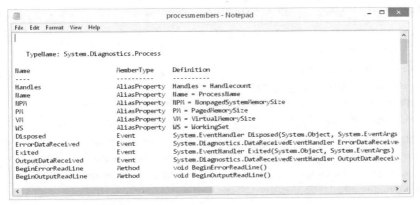

FIGURE 18-4 Notepad allows viewing of wide text files.

## Building maintainable scripts by using logging

Ian Farr, Premier Field Engineer
*Microsoft Corporation, United Kingdom*

Why consider script logging? You'll have to troubleshoot issues with your scripts—I've written scripts for enterprise environments for a number of years and have rarely seen a script that works perfectly with the first draft of code. You'll have to troubleshoot during development, when the script is released into production, and, maybe, others will reuse your hard work. To troubleshoot effectively, you need to understand what it was your script did, and that's where script logging comes in—it's easier to investigate an issue if you can look at logs created by your scripts. Even if you're not troubleshooting, script logging can show you what successful changes were made and can create a valuable audit trail.

What should your script logging capture? That will depend on what the script does. To start, I suggest the following: user name, computer name, script start time, script finish time, tasks completed, and any errors that occur. What file format should be used? That's another one of the many great things about Windows PowerShell—it's very easy to write to a text file, a CSV file, an HTML file, or an XML file. Those aren't your only options though—a colleague of mine created a centralized database for script logging, allowing administrators to analyze logs from many—use your imagination!

How can Windows PowerShell help you out? As you'd expect, there are many features that can assist with script logging, including the following:

- Useful cmdlets for working with logs include Add-Content, Set-Content, Out-File, Tee-Object, Export-CSV, ConvertTo-HTML and Export-CliXML.

- You can use redirection operators (>, >>) to send logging information, from the Success, Error, Warning, Debug, or Verbose streams, to a file. You can even write custom messages for these streams by using cmdlets such as Write-Error, Write-Warning, and Write-Debug, and then redirect that information to a log.

- Invaluable automatic variables for checking the success of operations are $LastExitCode, $Error, and $?. Let's look at $Error—it stores your recent errors as an array of objects, and by selecting properties of the most recent error object, you can refine the information written to your logs.

- A quick and simple form of logging to use in development or troubleshooting is to clear the $Error variable at the start of a script and then export the contents of $Error to a file at the end of the script. You can change the $Error buffer from its default value of 256, by resetting the $MaximumErrorCount automatic variable, to capture a large number of errors.

You'll have to troubleshoot issues with your scripts, so invest time in writing a script logging function—you'll use it again and again!

## Text location

One of the decisions that must be made when working with text files is the location to store the output. This decision is easy if you have a directory in which to store the output, and this is the approach taken in the LogChartProcessWorkingSet.ps1 script. The C:\fso folder is created and used to hold log files. If the user does not have rights to create a folder or to write to the log folder, the logging operation will fail. Another issue encountered when creating a designated log file folder is that the user might not always be available. Because the target folder might not always be available, you must always check for the existence of the folder and create it if it does not exist. An additional problem with using a specific folder is that, in some instances, the system drive is not always C:\. To be safe, you should always check for the system drive and use that location in the script.

All of the potential problems of creating a special log folder can be avoided if you use a folder that always exists on the user's computer. If you use a folder to which the user always has rights to write to, it is even better. Many folders are automatically created on a user's system that can be used to store log files that are created from within a script. The path to special folders is automatically resolved by the system and therefore will always be accurate regardless of the current user name or the drive letter of the system drive. The path to special folders is cumbersome to manually derive; therefore, it is a best practice to use the Microsoft .NET Framework environment class to resolve the path.

In the Get-CountryByIP.ps1 script, the Tee-Object cmdlet is used to display output to the Windows PowerShell console and to also write information to a text file. The Get-CountryByIP.ps1 script uses a web service and the Get-WebServiceProxy cmdlet to resolve an IP address to the country of origin. Besides being fun to play with, the script can be used to automatically detect and configure localization settings.

The Get-CountryByIP.ps1 script begins by using help tags to provide command-line help. In the help section, the synopsis, description, example, inputs, outputs, and notes tags are used to provide detailed help for the script. The help section of the script is shown here:

```
<#
  .Synopsis
   Gets country location by IP address
  .Description
   This script gets country location based upon an IP address. It uses
   a Web service, and therefore must be connected to Internet.
  .Example
   Get-CountryByIP.ps1 -ip 10.1.1.1, 192.168.1.1 -log iplog.txt
   Writes country information to %mydocuments%\iplog.txt and to screen
  .Inputs
   [string]
  .OutPuts
   [PSObject]
  .Notes
   NAME: Get-CountryByIP.ps1
   AUTHOR: Ed Wilson
   VERSION: 1.0.0
   LASTEDIT: 8/20/2009
   KEYWORDS: New-WebServiceProxy, IP, New-Object, PSObject
  .Link
     Http://www.ScriptingGuys.com
#requires -version 2.0
#>
```

The script uses cmdlet binding and creates some command-line parameters. The *ip* parameter is configured as an array of strings and is used to specify the IP address that will be resolved to a country. The *–log* parameter supplies the name of the script. The *folder* parameter designates the special folder to use. The parameter section of the script is shown here:

```
[CmdletBinding()]
Param(
    [Parameter(Mandatory = $true,Position = 0,ValueFromPipeline = $true)]
    [string[]]$ip,
    [string]$log = "ipLogFile.txt",
    [string]$folder = "Personal"
)#end param
```

The main portion of the code is contained in the *Get-CountryByIP* function. The function begins by specifying the Uniform Resource Identifier (URI) that is used to point to the Web Service Definition Language (WSDL) for the web service. The `New-WebServiceProxy` cmdlet is used to create the proxy to the web service. After the web service proxy is created, the object is stored in the variable *$proxy*. The *GetGeoIP* method is called from the object, and the returned data is stored in the *$rtn* variable.

```
Function Get-CountryByIP($IP)
{
 $URI = "http://www.webservicex.net/geoipservice.asmx?wsdl"
 $proxy = New-WebServiceProxy -uri $URI -namespace WebServiceProxy -class IP
 $RTN = $proxy.GetGeoIP($IP)
```

To make it easier to work with the returned data, a new instance of *PSObject* is created by using the `New-Object` cmdlet. The newly returned object is stored in the *$ipReturn* variable. After the *PSObject* instance is created, the `Add-Member` cmdlet is used to add the IP address, country name, and country code to the *PSObject* instance that is stored in the *$ipReturn* variable. When the object is created, it is returned to the calling code.

```
 $ipReturn = New-Object PSObject
 $ipReturn | Add-Member -MemberType noteproperty -Name ip -Value $rtn.ip
 $ipReturn | Add-Member -MemberType noteproperty -Name countryName -Value $rtn
.CountryName
 $ipReturn | Add-Member -MemberType noteproperty -Name countryCode -Value $rtn
.CountryCode
 $ipReturn
} #end Get-CountryByIP
```

The output folder that will be used to store the newly created text file is determined by using the *GetFolderPath* static method from the *Environment* .NET Framework class. The *GetFolderPath* static method must receive an *Environment.SpecialFolder* enumeration value. The *Get-Folder* function is used to return the path to the specified special folder.

```
Function Get-Folder($folderName)
{
 [Environment]::GetFolderPath([environment+SpecialFolder]::$folderName)
} #end function Get-Folder
```

The entry point to the script passes the IP address that is stored in the *$IP* variable and pipelines it to the `Foreach-Object` cmdlet, where the *Get-CountryByIP* function passes the current item on the pipeline to the function via the *ip* parameter. The returned custom *PSObject* instance is then pipelined to the `Tee-Object` cmdlet, and the resulting object is displayed to the Windows PowerShell console and stored in the *$results* variable. The *$results* variable is then pipelined to the `Out-File` cmdlet, and the file path is created by using the `Join-Path` cmdlet that receives the string returned from the *Get-Folder* function. The path to the special folder and the file name are put together to create the path for the output file.

```
$ip |
Foreach-Object { Get-CountryByIP -ip $_ } |
Tee-Object -Variable results
```

```
$results |
Out-File -FilePath '
  (Join-Path -Path (Get-Folder -folderName $folder) -childPath $log)
```

The complete Get-CountryByIP.ps1 script is shown here.

```
Get-CountryByIP.ps1

<#
   .Synopsis
   Gets country location by IP address
   .Description
   This script gets country location based up an IP address. It uses
   a web service, and therefore must be connected to Internet.
   .Example
   Get-CountryByIP.ps1 -ip 10.1.1.1, 192.168.1.1 -log iplog.txt
   Writes country information to %mydocuments%\iplog.txt and to screen
   .Inputs
   [string]
   .OutPuts
   [PSObject]
   .Notes
   NAME: Get-CountryByIP.ps1
   AUTHOR: Ed Wilson
   VERSION: 1.0.0
   LASTEDIT: 8/20/2009
   KEYWORDS: New-WebServiceProxy, IP, New-Object, PSObject
   .Link
     Http://www.ScriptingGuys.com
#requires -version 2.0
#>
[CmdletBinding()]
Param(
   [Parameter(Mandatory = $true,Position = 0,ValueFromPipeline = $true)]
   [string[]]$ip,
   [string]$log = "ipLogFile.txt",
   [string]$folder = "Personal"
)#end param

# *** Function below ***
Function Get-CountryByIP($IP)
{
 $URI = "http://www.webservicex.net/geoipservice.asmx?wsdl"
 $Proxy = New-WebServiceProxy -uri $URI -namespace WebServiceProxy -class IP
 $RTN = $proxy.GetGeoIP($IP)
```

```
$ipReturn = New-Object PSObject -Property @{
    'ip' = $rtn.ip;
    'CountryName' = $rtn.countryname;
    'CountryCode'=$rtn.countrycode}

 $ipReturn
} #end Get-CountryByIP

Function Get-Folder($folderName)
{
 [Environment]::GetFolderPath([environment+SpecialFolder]::$folderName)
} #end function Get-Folder

# *** Entry Point to Script ***

$ip |
ForEach-Object { Get-CountryByIP -ip $_ } |
Tee-Object -Variable results

$results |
Out-File -FilePath '
  (Join-Path -Path (Get-Folder -folderName $folder) -childPath $log)
```

### INSIDE TRACK

## Storing scripts—script repository

**Ian Farr, Premier Field Engineer**
*Microsoft Corporation, United Kingdom*

As you write more and more scripts, the maintenance and storage of them can be a problem. Being able to easily find code you wrote a couple of years ago will save you time and frustration! I recommend giving some thought to the location and structure of your script repository.

In the enterprise, if you don't want to use an application as a script repository, you should store your scripts on a network share. Data recovery, data security, and data integrity are important. Let's consider each option:

- For recovery, if you place your repository on a network file share, it is likely that data stored will be replicated and automatically backed up.

- For security, because some scripts, in the wrong hands, can make significant changes to your environment, a network share can secure the data via NTFS permissions and Access Based Enumeration.

- For integrity, you might have access to an Enterprise Certificate Authority or a Commercial Certificate Authority that can issue certificates for signing your scripts. This prevents Windows PowerShell from running a script that has been changed and not re-signed.

For a personal script repository, the data could be stored on your computer, on an external drive, or in the cloud, using a technology such as SkyDrive. Whatever option you choose, you still need to think about data recovery, data security, and data integrity:

- For recovery, there's Windows Backup. What about writing a script to back up your scripts? Using cloud storage will provide resilience, but wherever the repository is located, it makes sense to have that data backed up to a couple of locations.

- For security, you might not care about what happens to your scripts, but I'm guessing that you do, so consider physical security, complex passwords, and BitLocker.

- For integrity, you can create your own self-signed certificate for use on your computer. It could be argued that this isn't necessary for a personal repository, but the option is there for you.

Whether for the enterprise or for private use, the best repositories have a logical structure. For example:

Script type (for example, PS1, VBS)

   Technology (for example, AD, DHCP)

      Topic (for example, Replication, Scope Management)

         Script function (for example, Check Replication, Add Scope Option)

For my own repository, the names of my scripts reflect the script function. I also include keywords/tags in the here-string that contain the script description. It's then easy to find scripts from within the repository by using Search. You might even go a step further—a former colleague put in extra effort and wrote a script to parse his repository, because he liked his data presented in a very specific way.

There are a number of points to consider when creating and maintaining a script repository. Ultimately, you'll know what works best for you or your organization.

# Networked log files

At times, it might be more convenient to store the logs in a central shared folder instead of storing them on a local computer. This approach can solve many of the problems identified earlier in this chapter that are associated with creating and maintaining a folder on each computer. There are two methods of handling networked log files. The first method is to write directly to the file, and the second is to write to a temporary file on the local host machine and copy the file to the network location. As a best practice, any file that is very large or that might potentially involve large amounts of data should be created locally first and then copied to the network location. In this section, you will examine both approaches.

## Writing directly to the file

The simplest approach to working with networked log files is to write directly to the file. The Out-File cmdlet is able to use a Universal Naming Convention (UNC) path or a mapped network drive path. The UNC path is the most convenient approach because it does not require the creation and maintenance of mapped network drives.

```
Get-Process | Out-File -FilePath \\berlin\netshare\processes.txt
```

For small amounts of data on a well-connected network, the writing directly approach works fine. For larger amounts of data or when working on a network that might have unreliable or limited connectivity, a different approach is required.

## Writing to the local file and copying to the network

Because the creation and the writing to files on a network share is not an optimized operation, you can experience performance problems when writing directly to a networked file share. Writing to local files is an optimized scenario, and copying files to a network share is also a performance operation. Because of the different caveats involved in working with local files and folders, it is a best practice to write to a temporary file in the temporary directory and then copy the temporary file to the networked share. This is not a difficult process, and it will greatly improve the performance of networked logging.

The easiest way to write to a temporary file is to use the *getTempFileName* method from the *Io.Path* .NET Framework class. The *getTempFileName* method creates a temporary file name in the user's temporary directory in a location that looks similar to the one shown here:

```
C:\Users\edwilson\AppData\Local\Temp\tmpE7C6.tmp
```

The New-TempFile.ps1 script illustrates using a local temporary file for output and displaying the results of the operation in Notepad. The New-TempFile.ps1 script creates a function named *New-TempFile* that uses *CmdletBinding* and creates a single input parameter that accepts an array of *PSObjects* in the *$inputObject* variable. The script then calls the *getTempFileName* static method from the *Io.Path* .NET Framework class. The temporary file name is stored in the *$tmpFile* variable. The data contained in the *$inputObject* variable is pipelined to the Out-File cmdlet and then to the temporary file specified in the *$tmpFile* variable. The file path to the temporary file is then returned to the calling code.

```
Function New-TempFile
{
 [CmdletBinding()]
 Param(
  [Parameter(Position=0,ValueFromPipeline=$true)]
  [PSObject[]]$inputObject
 )#end param
  $tmpFile = [Io.Path]::getTempFileName()
  $inputObject | Out-File -filepath $tmpFile
  $tmpFile
} #end function New-TempFile
```

The entry point to the script illustrates how you might interact with this function. It calls the *New-TempFile* function and passes the results of the Get-Service cmdlet to the function via the *inputObject* parameter. The returned file path is stored in the *$rtn* variable. After the temporary file is created, inside the *New-TempFile* function, the file is moved to a file share on a remote server and renamed by using the Move-Item cmdlet.

```
$destination = "\\berlin\fileshare\services.txt"
$rtn = New-TempFile  -inputObject (Get-Service)
Move-Item -path $rtn -destination $destination
```

The complete New-TempFile.ps1 script is shown here.

```
New-TempFile.ps1

Function New-TempFile
{
 [CmdletBinding()]
 Param(
  [Parameter(Position=0,ValueFromPipeline=$true)]
  [PSObject[]]$inputObject
 )#end param
  $tmpFile = [Io.Path]::getTempFileName()
  $inputObject | Out-File -filepath $tmpFile
  $tmpFile
} #end function New-TempFile

# *** Entry Point to Script ***
  $destination = "\\berlin\fileshare\services.txt"
  $rtn = New-TempFile  -inputObject (Get-Service)
  Move-Item -path $rtn -destination $destination
```

## Logging in Windows PowerShell

**Andrew Willett, Systems Architect**
*Unitrans Logistics, Steinhoff Group*

You have written a Windows PowerShell script, tested it on your PC, and deployed it to run on your network—except that something is wrong. But what?

Logging—or as our developer friends call it, *instrumentation*—is both an invaluable tool for testing and debugging your scripts as well as a key part of their life cycle. Logging can tell you when a script succeeds or fails to run as expected, what causes an exception to occur, or it can tell you more detailed information, such as how long it takes a script to execute and why.

Implementing a basic form of logging is simple and is similar to what you might do at the command line. Similar to using > to send the console output to a text file, you can use the Tee-Object cmdlet to store the output in a variable as well as in a text file.

```
Get-Service | Tee-Object -filepath c:\services.txt
```

Using the Tee-Object cmdlet might be easy for individual commands, but it does not work very well for entire scripts. The next logical step is to use Tee-Object where necessary and append the output to the file. Unfortunately, while Tee-Object is able to only overwrite a file, Windows PowerShell encapsulates this functionality and a whole lot more in the Start-Transcript cmdlet. Using the transcript functionality requires two lines of code—one at the start and one at the end—that turn logging on and off, respectively.

```
Start-Transcript -path c:\scriptoutput.txt
    (...)
Stop-Transcript
```

A few useful parameters for Start-Transcript are *–append*, which appends the log to the existing file, and *Noclobber*, which prevents the default behavior of overwriting an existing file. (UNIX admins might recognize this behavior.) The call to the Stop-Transcript cmdlet is implicit, so if you forget to use the command or your code exits through a different path or exception, the script will still close correctly.

Both of these logging cmdlets can be very useful when diagnosing the root cause of a problem with your script in the field or for debugging your script while you are developing and testing it. However, digging through a verbose log of your script is not very helpful when you want to know at a glance whether the script succeeded or whether a failure was simply due to a time-out.

While developing your script, you will be aware of a subset of reasons that it might fail, such as connectivity or a lack of system resources or permissions, as well as how to determine whether it succeeded in its desired function. In addition, your script might look up or determine certain parameters at run time rather than being hard-coded, such as the available network bandwidth, whether the user is running with administrator privileges, or whether the computer is on battery power. Diagnosing a problem after the event can be difficult if you can only *assume* what parameters the script was running at the time. Calling out some of this key information, perhaps appended by the full verbose log, will save you a great deal of time—something I know that many people desire when digging through Windowsupdate.log!

Viewing instrumentation as an entire collection of technology means thinking about the storage and delivery of this information—a text file sitting on the hard disk collecting dust is not very helpful! When you know which pieces are salient pieces of output information, you should decide what to do with this information based on the effects that a failure might cause, whether action needs to be taken and by whom, and how time-critical the issue might be. If the log output is to be used for archive purposes, you should consider where to store the data—such as in the file system, the event log, or on the network—based on the write permissions of the user and your need for a retention period.

The following are some tricks of the trade that you might find useful, along with some examples with which to get started:

■ Sending logging information via email back to the administrator can proactively tell you when a problem has occurred and why—you can even email logging information to your help desk software and have the software set up an incident.

```
$to = "helpdesk@contoso.com"
$from = "scripts@contoso.com"
$subject = "Permissions Error in Script"
$body = "The script could not run as user " + (Get-Content
env:username) +
" was not a member of the required security group."
$server = "smtp.contoso.com"
$smtp = New-Object Net.Mail.SmtpClient($server)
$smtp.Send($from, $to, $subject, $body)
```

■ Outputting the text file to a network file share is a useful way to collate diag-nostic information in a central store, especially when you want to view a list of computers and determine when the script was last executed. When a file name is composed of the computer name and date/time in seconds, you can be assured that the file name will always be unique and that a file name–based sort in File Explorer, albeit crude, will sort the files chronologically.

```
$path = "\\fileserver\logs\script1\" + (Get-Content env:computername)
+
" " + (Get-Date -f "yyyy-MM-dd HHmmss") + ".txt"
Start-Transcript -path $path
```

- Calling out specific errors in the event log is a great way to bubble instrumentation data to the surface, for this is often the first place that technicians will look when diagnosing a problem. The event log can also be monitored by tools commonplace in larger IT shops, such as Microsoft System Center Operations Manager or the Event Collector service.

You can set the log level to Information, Warning, or Error, depending on the severity (or lack of severity) attached to the data, and you can even assign granular error codes based on the root cause of the issue. The only caveat is that administrator privileges are required to set up your own event log source. If you need to use an event log in these scenarios, you must either ensure that the event log is created in advance or commandeer one of the pre-existing Windows sources for your needs.

```
$source = "MyScript"
$log = "Application"
$message = "The script could not run as user " + (Get-Content
env:username) +
" was not a member of the required security group."
$type = "Error"
$id = 1

if (![System.Diagnostics.EventLog]::SourceExists($source)) { [System
.Diagnostics.EventLog]::CreateEventSource($source, $log) }

$eventLog = New-Object System.Diagnostics.EventLog
$eventLog.Log = $log
$eventLog.Source = $source
$eventLog.WriteEntry($message, $type, $id)
```

# Logging to the event log

Windows event logs provide a convenient place to store short status and diagnostic information. You can use the .NET Framework classes directly to create event sources, event logs, and event log entries, or you can use cmdlets. The New-EventLog cmdlet can be used to create a new event log and event log source. To write to an event log, you must supply both a log name and a log source.

To create a new event log and event source requires administrative rights. The error shown here will be generated if administrative rights are not present:

```
PS C:\> New-EventLog -LogName scripting -Source processAudit
New-EventLog : Access is denied. Please try with an elevated user permission.
At line:1 char:13
+ New-EventLog <<<<  -LogName scripting -Source processAudit
    + CategoryInfo          : InvalidOperation: (:) [New-EventLog], Exception
    + FullyQualifiedErrorId : AccessIsDenied,Microsoft.PowerShell.Commands
.NewEventLogCommand
```

To start either the Windows PowerShell console or the Windows PowerShell Integrated Scripting Environment (ISE), you right-click the icon and choose Run As Administrator from the action menu. In a script, you want to use a function, such as *Test-IsAdministrator*, to determine rights prior to attempting to create a new event log. The TestAdminCreateEventLog.ps1 script contains the *Test-IsAdministrator* function. This function begins by creating a minimal amount of help: the synopsis, description, and an example of using the function.

```
function Test-IsAdministrator
{
    <#
    .Synopsis
        Tests if the user is an administrator
    .Description
        Returns true if a user is an administrator,
        false if the user is not an administrator
    .Example
        Test-IsAdministrator
    #>
```

The function uses the *GetCurrent* static method from the *Security.Principal.WindowsIdentity* .NET Framework class. This method returns a *WindowsIdentity* object that represents the current user. The *WindowsIdentity* object is passed to the *System.Principal.WindowsPrincipal* .NET Framework class where it is used to generate an instance of a *WindowsPrincipal* class. The *IsInRole* method receives a *WindowsBuiltinRole* enumeration value that is used to determine whether the user is in the Administrator role.

```
    $currentUser = [Security.Principal.WindowsIdentity]::GetCurrent()
    (New-Object Security.Principal.WindowsPrincipal $currentUser).IsInRole '
    ([Security.Principal.WindowsBuiltinRole]::Administrator)
} #end function Test-IsAdministrator
```

The *Test-IsAdministrator* function returns a Boolean value. If the function is true, the user is in the Administrator role; if it is false, the user is not elevated and the script will exit. If the user is in the Administrator role, the script creates a new event log and source.

```
If(-not (Test-IsAdministrator)) { "Admin rights are required for this script" ; exit }
New-EventLog -LogName scripting -Source processAudit
```

The complete TestAdminCreateEventLog.ps1 script is shown here.

```
TestAdminCreateEventLog.ps1

function Test-IsAdministrator
{
    <#
    .Synopsis
        Tests if the user is an administrator
    .Description
        Returns true if a user is an administrator,
        false if the user is not an administrator
    .Example
        Test-IsAdministrator
    #>
    param()
    $currentUser = [Security.Principal.WindowsIdentity]::GetCurrent()
    (New-Object Security.Principal.WindowsPrincipal $currentUser).IsInRole([Security
.Principal.WindowsBuiltinRole]::Administrator)
} #end function Test-IsAdministrator


# *** Entry Point to Script ***
If(-not (Test-IsAdministrator)) { "Admin rights are required for this script" ; exit }
New-EventLog -LogName scripting -Source processAudit
```

## Using the Application log

The easiest log to use is the Application log because it is always present on the system and because administrative rights are not required. A source must exist in the event log. If you choose a source that exists but an event ID that does not exist, no error will be generated, but the event details will contain a message about a missing source description.

```
PS C:\> Write-EventLog -LogName application -Source certenroll -EntryType information '
-EventId 0 -Message "test"
PS C:\> Get-WinEvent -LogName application -MaxEvents 1 | format-list *

EventID           : 0
MachineName       : EDWILSON.microsoft.com
Data              : {}
Index             : 6130
Category          : (1)
CategoryNumber    : 1
EntryType         : Information
Message           : The description for Event ID '0' in Source 'certenroll' cannot be
found. The local computer may not have the necessary registry information or message
DLL files to display the message or you may not have permission to access them. The
following information is part of the event:'test'
Source            : certenroll
ReplacementStrings : {test}
```

```
InstanceId      : 0
TimeGenerated   : 8/17/2009 12:03:52 PM
TimeWritten     : 8/17/2009 12:03:52 PM
UserName        :
Site            :
Container       :
```

## Creating a custom event log

The best way to use event log logging is to create your own custom event log with its own custom sources. Because the Application log is heavily used by numerous sources, retrieving events involves sorting through thousands of entries. With a custom event log, you are in complete control of how many events are written, the number of sources that are defined, and the level of logging that is done. This means that it is generally easier to retrieve event log entries from a custom event log than from System or Application logs. To create a new event log, use the New-EventLog cmdlet to specify the log name and the source for the events.

**NOTE** If you are following along in the book, running the commands as you read along, the following command will fail because the scripting event source was created in an earlier scenario.

```
New-EventLog -LogName ForScripting -Source scripting
```

The error is due to the scripting source being previously registered on the computer. You need to back up a step and remove the event source. To do this use the following code:

```
Remove-EventLog -Source scripting
PS C:\> New-EventLog -LogName ForScripting -Source scripting
```

To write to the event log, use the Write-EventLog cmdlet. You need to specify the log name, the source, the type of entry, and the event ID and message, which can all be accomplished on a single line.

```
PS C:\> Write-EventLog -LogName ForScripting -Source scripting -EntryType information '
-EventId 0 -Message test
```

To retrieve event log entries, you can use the Get-EventLog cmdlet and specify the event log name.

```
PS C:\> Get-WinEvent-LogName ForScripting
```

```
Index Time          EntryType    Source      InstanceID Message
----- ----          ---------    ------      ---------- -------
    1 Aug 17 12:42  Information  scripting             0 test
```

# Logging to the registry

The registry is an ideal location to store small pieces of information, such as exit codes and time stamps. Due to the nature of the registry, you do not want to store large amounts of data here. In addition, you will need to remove the object-oriented nature of the objects when you write to the registry by pipelining the object to the Out-String cmdlet or by calling one of the *ToString* methods.

The best place to write to the registry is in the Hkey_Current_User hive because the current user has rights to write to the Current_User registry hive, and you therefore avoid rights and permissions issues. This process is illustrated in the CreateRegistryKey.ps1 script, which is used to create a registry key named ForScripting in the Hkey_Current_User hive. A property named *forscripting* is created with the value of *test* assigned to it.

The CreateRegistryKey.ps1 script contains a function named *Add-RegistryValue* that accepts two parameters—the *$key* and the *$value* variables. The function can be further expanded to include the registry root as well. The value of the *$scriptRoot* variable is used to determine where the registry key value will be created. If the path to the *$scriptRoot* registry key does not exist, it will be created, and the registry property value will be added as well. The Test-Path cmdlet is used to ensure that the path to the *$scriptRoot* registry key exists. The New-Item cmdlet is used to create the registry key, and the New-ItemProperty cmdlet is used to create the new registry property and assign its value. The Out-Null cmdlet is used to keep the results of creating the registry key and value from cluttering the Windows PowerShell console.

```
Function Add-RegistryValue($key,$value)
{
 $scriptRoot = "HKCU:\software\ForScripting"
 if(-not (Test-Path -path $scriptRoot))
    {
     New-Item -Path HKCU:\Software\ForScripting | Out-Null
     New-ItemProperty -Path $scriptRoot -Name $key -Value $value '
     -PropertyType String | Out-Null
    }
```

If the registry key does exist, the Set-ItemProperty cmdlet is used to either create the registry property value or change its value. Once again, the results of the cmdlet are pipelined to the Out-Null cmdlet.

```
Else
   {
    Set-ItemProperty -Path $scriptRoot -Name $key -Value $value | '
    Out-Null
   }
```

The entry point to the script calls the *Add-RegistryValue* function and passes the registry key name and the value to modify.

```
Add-RegistryValue -key forscripting -value test
```

The complete CreateRegistryKey.ps1 script is shown here.

```
CreateRegistryKey.ps1

Function Add-RegistryValue
{
 Param ($key,$value)
 $scriptRoot = "HKCU:\software\ForScripting"
 if(-not (Test-Path -path $scriptRoot))
   {
    New-Item -Path HKCU:\Software\ForScripting | Out-Null
    New-ItemProperty -Path $scriptRoot -Name $key -Value $value '
    -PropertyType String | Out-Null
   }
  Else
  {
   Set-ItemProperty -Path $scriptRoot -Name $key -Value $value | '
   Out-Null
  }

} #end function Add-RegistryValue

# *** Entry Point to Script ***
Add-RegistryValue -key forscripting -value test
```

When the CreateRegistryKey.ps1 script is run, nothing is displayed on the screen. The ForScripting registry key is created with the *forscripting* registry property, which is set to a value of *test*, as shown in Figure 18-5.

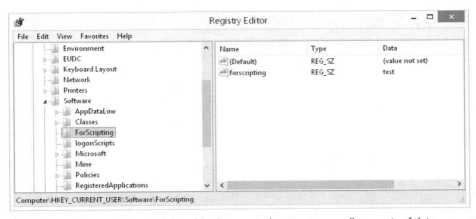

FIGURE 18-5 The Current_User registry hive is a great place to store small amounts of data.

# Additional resources

- The TechNet Script Center at *http://www.microsoft.com/technet/scriptcenter* contains numerous examples of writing to files, the event log, and the registry.

- Take a look at Chapter 3 in *Windows PowerShell™ Scripting Guide* (Microsoft Press, 2008) for more information about how to log script results.

- All scripts from this chapter are available via the TechNet Script Center Script Repository at *http://gallery.technet.microsoft.com/scriptcenter/PowerShell-40 -Best-d9e16039.*

# Troubleshooting scripts

- Understanding debugging in Windows PowerShell
- Using the Set-PSDebug cmdlet
- Debugging scripts
- Additional resources

A well-designed, well-written script rarely needs troubleshooting. This is not to say that all scripts are perfect or that all scripts run without errors the first time they are executed—or even the second time. Yet, a good script should be organized in a manner that makes it easy to read and easy to understand. By default, the two best practices of readability and understandability reduce the amount of troubleshooting necessary to fix errors in a script because they make errors easier to spot. However, when problems do crop up, you will want to know how to debug your script. In this chapter, we will look at the commands to produce a trace of your script, to step through the commands of the script, and to debug the script, and we will examine the best practices involved in choosing tracing, stepping, or debugging commands for identifying errors in scripts. Windows PowerShell 4.0 contains extremely powerful and flexible tools to facilitate troubleshooting when or if it ever becomes a necessity.

## Understanding debugging in Windows PowerShell

If you can read and understand your Windows PowerShell code, chances are, you will need to do very little debugging. But what if you do need to do some debugging? Well, just as excellent golfers spend many hours practicing chipping out of the sand trap in hopes that they will never need to use the skill, so too must a competent Windows PowerShell scripter practice debugging skills in hopes that they will never need to apply the knowledge. Understanding the color coding of the Windows PowerShell ISE, detecting when closing quotation marks are missing, and knowing which pair of braces correspond to which command can greatly reduce the debugging that might be needed later.

Debugging is a skill used to track down, and to eliminate errors from a Windows PowerShell script. There are three different types of errors that coders make. These errors are syntax errors, run-time errors, and logic errors.

# Working with syntax errors

Syntax errors are the easiest to spot, and you usually correct them at design —that is, while you have the Windows PowerShell ISE open and you are writing your script. The reason that syntax errors generally get corrected at design time is because the language parser runs in the background of the Windows PowerShell ISE, and when it detects a syntax error, it marks it with a squiggly line (thus indicating that the command requires additional parameters, decoration, or other attention). This process of correcting syntax errors becomes second nature to seasoned scripters who do not usually view the process as correcting syntax errors but as simply completing commands so that the script runs properly. The most seasoned scripters learn to pay attention to the syntax parser, and they fix errors indicated by the red squiggly lines prior to actually running the code. When not corrected, the error message generated often provides good guidance towards correcting the offending command. Figure 19-1 illustrates a syntax error.

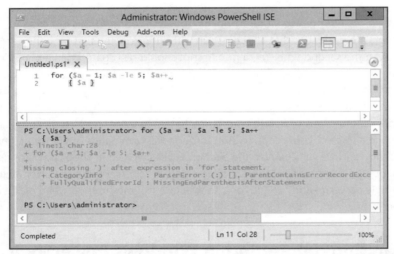

**FIGURE 19-1** The Windows PowerShell ISE highlights potential errors with a red squiggly line. The error message states the offending command and often provides clarification for required changes.

# Working with runtime errors

The syntax parser often does not detect runtime errors. Rather, runtime errors are problems that manifest themselves only when the script runs. Examples of these types of errors include a resource not available (such as a drive or a file), permissions problems (such as a non-elevated user not having the rights to perform an operation), misspelled words, and code dependencies that are not met (such as access to a required module). The good thing is that many of these runtime errors are detectable from within the Windows PowerShell ISE due to the more robust tab expansion mechanism in Windows PowerShell 4.0. For example, it is possible, virtually, to eliminate the resource not available runtime error if you use tab expansion.

This is possible because tab expansion works even across UNC shares. Figure 19-2 illustrates this feature when attempting to use the Get-Content cmdlet to read the contents of the AD_Doc.txt file from the Data share on a server named hyperv1.

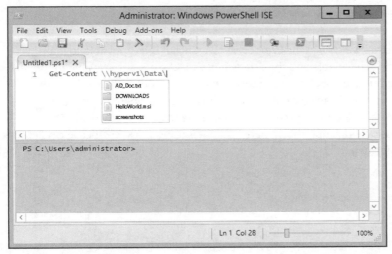

**FIGURE 19-2** Improved tab expansion makes it possible to avoid certain runtime errors.

Unfortunately, tab expansion does not help when it comes to dealing with permissions issues. However, paying attention to the returned error message will help identify that you are dealing with a permission issue. Generally, you receive an Access Is Denied error message. Such an error message appears here when bogususer attempts to access the DC1 server to perform a Windows Management Instrumentation query.

```
PS C:\> Get-WmiObject win32_bios -cn dc1 -Credential iammred\bogususer
Get-WmiObject : Access is denied. (Exception from HRESULT: 0x80070005
(E_ACCESSDENIED))
At line:1 char:1
+ Get-WmiObject win32_bios -cn dc1 -Credential iammred\bogususer
+ ~~~~~~~~~~~~~~~~~~~~~~~~~~~~~~~~~~~~~~~~~~~~~~~~~~~~~~~~~~~~~~~~~
    + CategoryInfo          : NotSpecified: (:) [Get-WmiObject], UnauthorizedA
   ccessException
    + FullyQualifiedErrorId : System.UnauthorizedAccessException,Microsoft.
   PowerShell.Commands.GetWmiObjectCommand
```

One way to detect runtime errors is to use the Write-Debug cmdlet to display the contents of variables that are most likely to contain erroneous data. By moving from a one-line command to a simple script containing variables and a variety of Write-Debug commands, the most common troubleshooting techniques automatically occur. For example, in the RemoteWMISessionNoDebug.ps1 script shown here, there are two main sources of runtime errors: the availability of the target computer, and the credentials used to perform the connection.

```
RemoteWMISessionNoDebug.ps1

$credential = Get-Credential
$cn = Read-Host -Prompt "enter a computer name"
Get-WmiObject win32_bios -cn $cn -Credential $credential
```

By using the immediate window in the Windows PowerShell ISE, it is possible to inter-rogate the values of the *$cn* variable and the *$credential* variable. It is also possible to use the Test-Connection cmdlet to check on the status of the *$cn* computer. By anticipating these typical debugging steps in advance, the script displays the pertinent information and therefore shortcuts any debugging required to make the script properly work. The DebugRemoteWMISession.ps1 script, shown here, illustrates using the Write-Debug cmdlet to provide debugging information.

```
The DebugRemoteWMISession.ps1

$oldDebugPreference = $DebugPreference
$DebugPreference = "continue"
$credential = Get-Credential
$cn = Read-Host -Prompt "enter a computer name"
Write-Debug "user name: $($credential.UserName)"
Write-Debug "password: $($credential.GetNetworkCredential().Password)"
Write-Debug "$cn is up:
  $(Test-Connection -Computername $cn -Count 1 -BufferSize 16 -quiet)"
Get-WmiObject win32_bios -cn $cn -Credential $credential
$DebugPreference = $oldDebugPreference
```

Figure 19-3 illustrates running the DebugRemoteWMISession.ps1 script inside the Windows PowerShell ISE to determine why the script fails. According to the output, the remote server, DC1, is available, but the user Bogus User with the password of BogusPassword is receiving access denied. It might be that the user, Bogus User, does not have an account, does not have access rights, or that the password really is not BogusPassword. The detailed debugging information should help to clarify the situation.

A better way to use the Write-Debug cmdlet is to combine it with the *[CmdletBinding()]* attribute at the beginning of the script (or function). For the *[CmdletBinding()]* attribute to work requires a couple of things. First, the script or function must use at least one parameter. This means that the *param* keyword will be present in the script. Second, the *[CmdletBinding()]* attribute must appear prior to the *param* keyword. When implemented, this change permits use of the common *debug* parameter. When calling the script or the function, use of the *debug* switched parameter causes the debug stream from the Write-Debug cmdlets in the code to appear in the output. This simple change also means that your code no longer needs to change the value of the *$DebugPreference* variable. It also means that you do not need to create your own switched *debug* parameter and include code such as the following at the beginning of your script:

```
Param([switch]$debug)
If($debug) {$DebugPreference = "continue"}
```

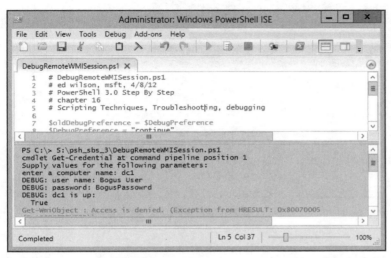

**FIGURE 19-3** Detailed debugging makes solving runtime errors more manageable.

The revised and simplified DebugRemoteWMISession.ps1 script appears here as Switch_DebugRemoteWMISession.ps1. The changes to the script include adding *the [CmdletBinding()]* attribute, creating a parameter named *cn*, and setting the default value to the name of the local computer. The other changes involve removing the toggling of the *$DebugPreference* variable. The complete script appears here.

---

**Switch_DebugRemoteWMISession.ps1**

```
[CmdletBinding()]
Param($cn = $env:computername)
$credential = Get-Credential
Write-Debug "user name: $($credential.UserName)"
Write-Debug "password: $($credential.GetNetworkCredential().Password)"
Write-Debug "$cn is up:
   $(Test-Connection -Computername $cn -Count 1 -BufferSize 16 -quiet)"
Get-WmiObject win32_bios -cn $cn -Credential $credential
```

---

When the Switch_DebugRemoteWMISession.ps1 script runs with the *debug* switch from the Windows PowerShell console, in addition to displaying the debug stream, it also prompts to continue the script. This permits halting execution upon reaching an unexpected value. Figure 19-4 illustrates this technique, when a user named Bogus User, who wants to connect to a remote server named DC1, unexpectedly discovers that he is connecting to a workstation named W8Client6.

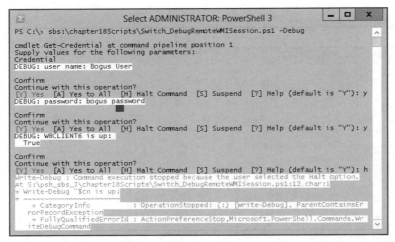

**FIGURE 19-4** Using the *debug* switched parameter to step through potential problems in a script.

## Working with logic errors

Logic errors can be very difficult to detect, because the script appears to work correctly. In fact, in some cases, the script might work perfectly fine. But when things go wrong, they can be difficult to fix. Most of the time, just examining the values of variables does not solve the problem because the code itself works fine. The problem often lies in what is called the *business rules* of the script. These are decisions the code makes that have nothing to do with the correct operation of, for example, a *switch* statement. At times, it might appear that the *switch* statement is not working correctly because the wrong value displays at the end of the code, but quite often, it is the business rules themselves causing the problem.

For a simple example of a logic error, consider the function called *My-Function* in the My-Function.ps1 script shown here.

```
My-Function.ps1

Function my-function
{
 Param(
   [int]$a,
   [int]$b)
   "$a plus $b equals four"
}
```

The *My-Function* function accepts two command-line parameters: *a* and *b*. It then combines the two values and outputs a string stating that the value is four. The tester performs four different tests, and each time the function performs as expected. These tests and the associated output are shown here:

```
PS C:\> S:\psh_sbs_4\chapter19\scripts\my-function.ps1

PS C:\> my-function -a 2 -b 2
2 plus 2 equals four

PS C:\> my-function -a 1 -b 3
1 plus 3 equals four

PS C:\> my-function -a 0 -b 4
0 plus 4 equals four

PS C:\> my-function -a 3 -b 1
3 plus 1 equals four
```

However, when the function goes into production, users begin to complain. Most of the time, the function displays incorrect output. However, the users also report that no errors generate when the function runs. What is the best way to solve the logic problem? Simply adding a couple of `Write-Debug` commands to display the values of the variables *a* and *b* will more than likely not lead to the correct solution. A better way is to step through the code one line at a time and examine the associated output. The easy way to do this is to use the `Set-PSDebug` cmdlet—the topic of the next section in this chapter.

---

**NOTES FROM THE FIELD**

**Luc Dekens, Systems Engineer, Windows PowerShell MVP**
*Eurocontrol*

Sometimes beauty is in the small things. And the [ordered] tag that was introduced in Windows PowerShell version 3 is no different.

Before the introduction of this new tag, the order in which properties of a hash table would be displayed could not be controlled. The issue was easy to fix by adding a `Select-Object` cmdlet. But for me, that didn't support the theory that Windows PowerShell had to be intuitive.

Let me show you with an example.

One of my kids needed to produce for school a table that would demonstrate the Pythagorean Theorem. Easy, because he knew a bit of Windows PowerShell and he was aware he could call the .Net functions from PowerShell.

```
$table = @()
for($i = 0; $i -le 90; $i += 10){
    $rad = $i*[Math]::PI/180
    $cos = [math]::Cos($rad)
```

```
        $sin = [math]::Sin($rad)
        $row = @{
            Angle = $i
            Cosine = "{0:n2}" -f $cos
            Sine = "{0:n2}" -f $sin
            Pythagoras = [math]::Pow($cos,2) + [math]::Pow($sin,2)
        }
        $table += New-Object PSObject -Property $row
}
$table | Export-Csv pyth.csv -NoTypeInformation -UseCulture
```

I leave the details of the script as an exercise for the reader.

My son opened the produced CSV file, and needless to say he was somewhat disappointed.

The script worked; the values were there to prove the theorem. But the columns in the CSV file didn't appear in the order he expected. It just didn't look right to him.

With the arrival of Windows PowerShell V3, I could provide him a solution, without an additional Select-Object line before creating the CSV file.

The new version of his script needed only a small change: the addition of the [ordered] tag on the line where the hash table is created.

```
$table = @()
for($i = 0; $i -le 90; $i += 10){
    $rad = $i*[Math]::PI/180
    $cos = [math]::Cos($rad)
    $sin = [math]::Sin($rad)
    $row = [ordered]@{
        Angle = $i
        Cosine = "{0:n2}" -f $cos
        Sine = "{0:n2}" -f $sin
        Pythagoras = [math]::Pow($cos,2) + [math]::Pow($sin,2)
    }
    $table += New-Object PSObject -Property $row
}
$table | Export-Csv pyth-v3.csv -NoTypeInformation -UseCulture
```

The [ordered] tag doesn't actually introduce anything new to Windows PowerShell; the ordered hash table was already there.

```
$object1 = New-Object System.Collections.Specialized.OrderedDictionary
```

But the V3 way makes it a lot easier to write and read.

```
$object2 = [ordered]@{}
```

With the [ordered] tag came another great new feature in Windows PowerShell V3: *[PSCustomObject]*, a new class specifically designed to create custom objects from a hash table. Two of the advantages of this new class are that it preserves the order and it is blazingly fast compared to some of the other methods used to create custom objects.

```
Function Get-Pythagoras {
    param($angle)

    $rad = $angle*[Math]::PI/180
    $cos = [math]::Cos($rad)
    $sin = [math]::Sin($rad)

    [PSCustomObject]@{
        Angle = $angle
        Cosine = "{0:n2}" -f $cos
        Sine = "{0:n2}" -f $sin
        Pythagoras = [math]::Pow($cos,2) + [math]::Pow($sin,2)
    }
}

for($i = 0; $i -le 90; $i += 10){
    Get-Pythagoras -Angle $i
}
```

# Using the Set-PSDebug cmdlet

The Set-PSDebug cmdlet was available in Windows PowerShell 1.0, and it remains the same in Windows PowerShell 4.0. This does not mean it is a neglected feature, but rather it does what it needs to do. To perform basic debugging in a quick and easy fashion, you cannot beat the combination of features that are available. There are three things that you can do with the Set-PSDebug cmdlet. You can trace script execution in an automated fashion, step through the script in an interactive fashion, and you can enable strict mode. Each of these features will be examined in this section. The Set-PSDebug cmdlet is not designed to do heavy debugging; it is a light weight tool that is useful when you want to produce a quick trace or rapidly step through the script.

# Tracing the script

One of the simplest ways to debug a script is to turn on script-level tracing. When you turn on script-level tracing, each command that is executed is displayed to the Windows PowerShell console. By watching the commands as they are displayed to the Windows PowerShell console, you can determine whether a line of code in your script executes or whether it is being skipped. To enable script tracing, you use the Set-PSDebug cmdlet and specify one of three levels for the trace parameter. The three levels of tracing are described in Table 19-1.

**TABLE 19-1** Tracing levels

| Trace level | Meaning |
| --- | --- |
| 0 | Turns script tracing off. |
| 1 | Traces each line of the script as it is executed. Lines in the script that are not executed are not traced. Does not display variable assignments, function calls, or external scripts. |
| 2 | Traces each line of the script as it is executed. Displays variable assignments, function calls, and external scripts. Lines in the script that are not executed are not traced. |

To illustrate the process of tracing a script and the differences between the different trace levels, look at the CreateRegistryKey.ps1 script. The CreateRegistryKey.ps1 script contains a single function called the *Add-RegistryValue* function. In the *Add-RegistryValue* function, the Test-Path cmdlet is used to determine whether the registry key exists. If the registry key exists, a property value is set. If the registry key does not exist, the registry key is created and a property value is set. The *Add-RegistryValue* function is called when the script executes. The complete CreateRegistryKey.ps1 script is shown here.

```
CreateRegistryKey.ps1

Function Add-RegistryValue($key,$value)
{
 $scriptRoot = "HKCU:\software\ForScripting"
 if(-not (Test-Path -path $scriptRoot))
   {
    New-Item -Path HKCU:\Software\ForScripting | Out-null
    New-ItemProperty -Path $scriptRoot -Name $key -Value $value '
    -PropertyType String | Out-Null
   }
 Else
   {
```

```
   Set-ItemProperty -Path $scriptRoot -Name $key -Value $value | '
   Out-Null
  }

} #end function Add-RegistryValue

# *** Entry Point to Script ***
Add-RegistryValue -key forscripting -value test
```

## Working with trace level 1

When the trace level is set to 1, each line in the script that executes is displayed to the Windows PowerShell console. To set the trace level to 1, you use the Set-PSDebug cmdlet, using the *trace* parameter with the value of 1 assigned to it. When you press Enter, you are immediately presented with a new line, as shown here:

```
Windows PowerShell
Copyright (C) 2013 Microsoft Corporation. All rights reserved.

PS C:\Users\ed.IAMMRED> Set-PSDebug -Trace 1
PS C:\Users\ed.IAMMRED>
```

After the trace level has been set, it applies to everything that is typed in the Windows PowerShell console. If you run an interactive command, run a cmdlet, or execute a script, it will be traced. When the CreateRegistryKey.ps1 script is run and there is no registry key present, the first command debug line displays the path to the script that is being executed. Because Windows PowerShell parses from the top down, the next line that is executed is the line that creates the *Add-RegistryValue* function. This command is on line 10 of the script, because the actual script that executed contains 9 lines that are commented out. When you add the status bar to Notepad (View/Status Bar), the status bar at the lower right corner of Notepad will display the line number. This is shown in Figure 19-5.

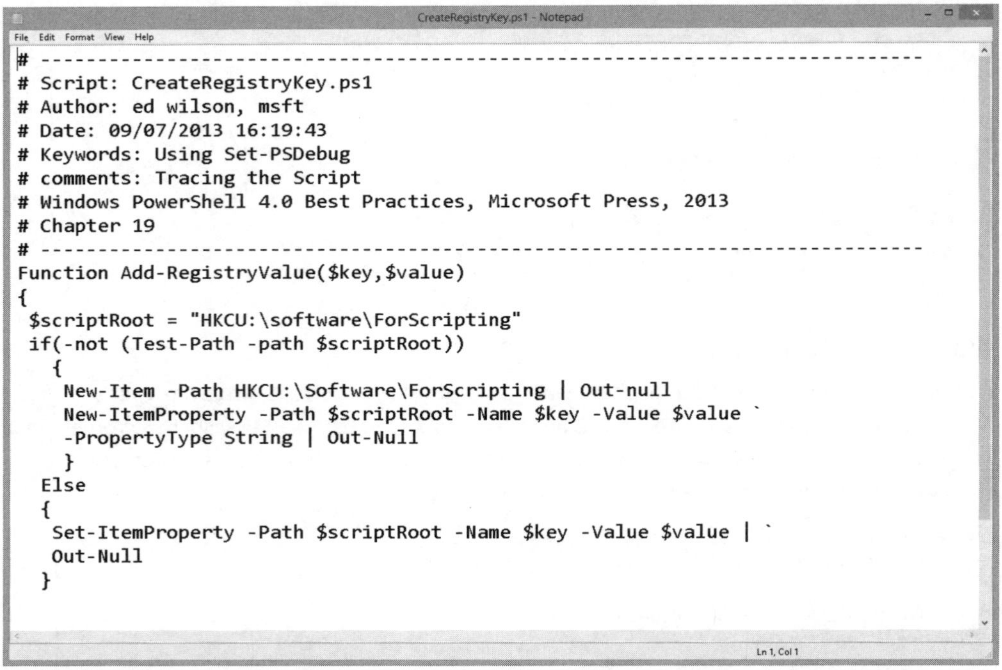



```
# -----------------------------------------------------------------------------
# Script: CreateRegistryKey.ps1
# Author: ed wilson, msft
# Date: 09/07/2013 16:19:43
# Keywords: Using Set-PSDebug
# comments: Tracing the Script
# Windows PowerShell 4.0 Best Practices, Microsoft Press, 2013
# Chapter 19
# -----------------------------------------------------------------------------
Function Add-RegistryValue($key,$value)
{
 $scriptRoot = "HKCU:\software\ForScripting"
 if(-not (Test-Path -path $scriptRoot))
   {
    New-Item -Path HKCU:\Software\ForScripting | Out-null
    New-ItemProperty -Path $scriptRoot -Name $key -Value $value `
    -PropertyType String | Out-Null
    }
  Else
  {
   Set-ItemProperty -Path $scriptRoot -Name $key -Value $value | `
   Out-Null
  }
```

**FIGURE 19-5** The Notepad status bar, at the lower-right corner of Notepad, displays line numbers.

After creating the function, the next line of the script that executes is line 25. Line 25 of the CreateRegistryKey.ps1 script follows the comment that points to the entry point to the script (this last line is seen in Figure 19-5) and calls the *Add-RegistryValue* function by passing two values for the *key* and *value* parameters, as shown here:

```
PS C:\> E:\Data\BookDOcs\PS4_BestPractices\Scripts\scripts_ch19\CreateRegistryKey.ps1
DEBUG:    1+  >>>>
E:\Data\BookDOcs\PS4_BestPractices\Scripts\scripts_ch19\CreateRegistryKey.ps1
DEBUG:   28+  >>>> Add-RegistryValue -key forscripting -value test
DEBUG:   11+  >>>> {
DEBUG:   12+   >>>> $scriptRoot = "HKCU:\software\ForScripting"
DEBUG:   13+  if( >>>> -not (Test-Path -path $scriptRoot))
DEBUG:   15+      >>>> New-Item -Path HKCU:\Software\ForScripting | Out-null
DEBUG:   16+      >>>> New-ItemProperty -Path $scriptRoot -Name $key -Value $value
`
DEBUG:   25+  >>>> } #end function Add-RegistryValue
```

When inside the *Add-RegistryValue* function, the `HKCU:\software\ForScripting` string is assigned to the *$scriptRoot* variable, as shown here:

```
DEBUG:   12+   >>>> $scriptRoot = "HKCU:\software\ForScripting"
```

The *if* statement is now evaluated. If the `Test-Path` cmdlet cannot find the *$scriptRoot* location in the registry, the *if* statement is entered and the commands inside the associated script block will be executed. In this example, *$scriptRoot* is not located, and the commands inside the script block are executed, as shown here:

```
DEBUG:   13+   if( >>>> -not (Test-Path -path $scriptRoot))
```

The New-Item and the New-ItemProperty cmdlets are called on line 15 and 16 of the CreateRegistryKey.ps1 script.

```
DEBUG:   15+       >>>> New-Item -Path HKCU:\Software\ForScripting | Out-null`DEBUG:
16+       >>>> New-ItemProperty -Path $scriptRoot -Name $key -Value $value
```

When the script ends, the Windows PowerShell console parser returns to the default prompt.

By setting the debug trace level to 1, a basic outline of the execution plan of the script is produced. This technique is good for quickly determining the outcome of branching statements (such as the *if* statement) to see whether a script block is being entered. This is illustrated in Figure 19-6.

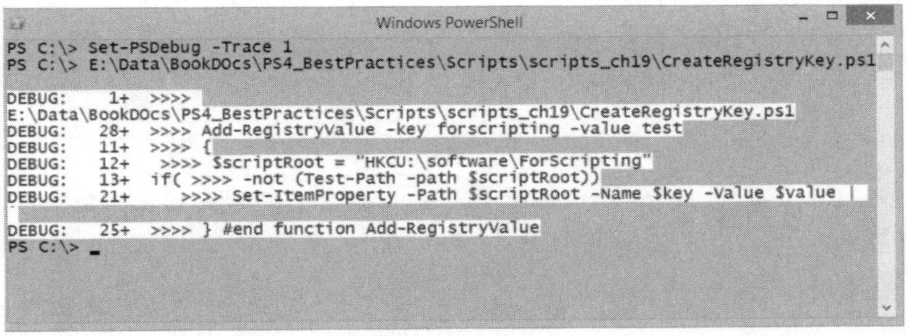

**FIGURE 19-6** Script level 1 tracing displays each executing line of the script.

## Working with trace level 2

When the trace level is set to 2, each line in the script that executes is displayed to the Windows PowerShell console. In addition, each variable assignment, function call, and outside script call is displayed. These additional tracing details are all prefixed with an exclamation mark to make them easier to spot. When the Set-PSDebug *trace* parameter is set to 2, an extra line is displayed indicating a variable assignment, as shown here:

```
PS C:\> Set-PSDebug -Trace 2
DEBUG:   1+  <<<< Set-PSDebug -Trace 2
DEBUG:   2+          $foundSuggestion = <<<<  $false
DEBUG:   ! SET $foundSuggestion = 'False'.
DEBUG:   4+          if <<<< ($lastError -and
DEBUG:   15+         $foundSuggestion <<<<
```

When the CreateRegistryKey.ps1 script is run, the function trace points first to the script, stating it is calling a function called *CreateRegistryKey.ps1*. Calls to functions are prefixed with *! CALL*, making them easy to spot. Windows PowerShell treats scripts as functions. The next function that is called is the *Add-RegistryValue* function. The trace also states where the function is defined by indicating the path to the file, as shown here:

```
PS C:\> y:\CreateRegistryKey.ps1
DEBUG:    1+  <<<< y:\CreateRegistryKey.ps1
DEBUG:     ! CALL function 'CreateRegistryKey.ps1'  (defined in file
'y:\CreateRegistryKey.ps1')
DEBUG:    7+ Function Add-RegistryValue <<<< ($key,$value)
DEBUG:    25+  <<<< Add-RegistryValue -key forscripting -value test
DEBUG:     ! CALL function 'Add-RegistryValue'  (defined in file
'y:\CreateRegistryKey.ps1')
```

The *! SET* keyword is used to preface variable assignments. The first variable that is assigned is the *$scriptRoot* variable.

```
DEBUG:    9+  $scriptRoot = <<<<  "HKCU:\software\ForScripting"
DEBUG:     ! SET $scriptRoot = 'HKCU:\software\ForScripting'.
DEBUG:    10+  if <<<< (-not (Test-Path -path $scriptRoot))
DEBUG:    18+     <<<< Set-ItemProperty -Path $scriptRoot -Name $key -Value
$value | '
DEBUG:    2+         $foundSuggestion = <<<<  $false
DEBUG:     ! SET $foundSuggestion = 'False'.
DEBUG:    4+         if <<<< ($lastError -and
DEBUG:    15+         $foundSuggestion <<<<
PS C:\>
```

When the CreateRegistryKey.ps1 script is run with tracing level 2, the detailed tracing seen in Figure 19-7 is displayed.

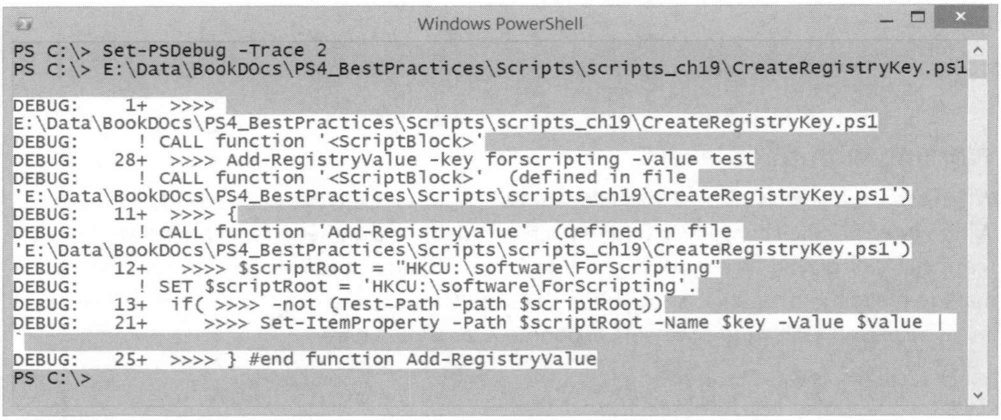

**FIGURE 19-7** Script level 2 tracing adds variable assignments, function calls, and external script calls.

# Stepping through the script

Watching the script trace the execution of the lines of code in the script can often provide useful insight that can lead to a solution to a misbehaving script. If a script is more complicated and is composed of a script with several functions, a simple trace might not be a workable solution. For the occasions when your script is more complex and comprises multiple functions, you will want the ability to step through the script. When you step through a script, debug prompts you before each line of the script runs. A script you might want to step through is the BadScript.ps1 script shown here.

```
BadScript.ps1

Function AddOne([int]$num)
{
  $num+1
} #end function AddOne

Function AddTwo([int]$num)
{
  $num+2
} #end function AddTwo

Function SubOne([int]$num)
{
  $num-1
} #end function SubOne

Function TimesOne([int]$num)
{
   $num*2
} #end function TimesOne

Function TimesTwo([int]$num)
{
  $num*2
} #end function TimesTwo

Function DivideNum([int]$num)
{
  12/$num
} #end function DivideNum

# *** Entry Point to Script ***

$num = 0
SubOne($num) | DivideNum($num)
AddOne($num) | AddTwo($num)
```

The BadScript.ps1 script contains a number of functions that are used to add numbers, subtract numbers, multiply numbers, and divide numbers. There are some problems with the way the script runs because it contains several errors. It would be possible for you to set the trace level to 2 and examine the trace of the script, but with the large number of functions and the types of errors that are contained in the script, it might be difficult to spot the problems with the script. By default, the trace level is set to level 1 when stepping is enabled, and in nearly all cases, it is the best solution for the trace level.

You might prefer to be able to step through the script as each line executes. There are two benefits to using the *step* parameter from the Set-PSDebug cmdlet. The first benefit is that you can watch what happens when each line of the script executes. This allows you to very carefully walk through the script. With the trace feature of Set-PSDebug, it is possible to miss important clues to help solve troubleshooting problems because everything is displayed on the Windows PowerShell console. With the prompt feature, you are asked to choose a response before each line in the script executes. The default choice is *Y*, for "Yes, continue the operation," but you have other choices. When you respond *Y*, the debug line is displayed to the Windows PowerShell console. This is the same debug statement you saw in the trace output, and it is governed by your debug trace level settings. The step prompting is shown here:

```
PS C:\> Set-PSDebug -Step
PS C:\> E:\Data\BookDOcs\PS4_BestPractices\Scripts\scripts_ch19\BadScript.ps1

Continue with this operation?
   1+  >>>> E:\Data\BookDOcs\PS4_BestPractices\Scripts\scripts_ch19\BadScript.ps1
[Y] Yes  [A] Yes to All  [N] No  [L] No to All  [S] Suspend  [?] Help
(default is "Y"):y
DEBUG:   1+  >>>>
E:\Data\BookDOcs\PS4_BestPractices\Scripts\scripts_ch19\BadScript.ps1

Continue with this operation?
  42+  >>>> $num = 0
[Y] Yes  [A] Yes to All  [N] No  [L] No to All  [S] Suspend  [?] Help
(default is "Y"):y
DEBUG:   42+  >>>> $num = 0

Continue with this operation?
  43+  >>>> SubOne($num) | DivideNum($num)
[Y] Yes  [A] Yes to All  [N] No  [L] No to All  [S] Suspend  [?] Help
(default is "Y"):y
DEBUG:   43+  >>>> SubOne($num) | DivideNum($num)

Continue with this operation?
  21+  >>>> {
[Y] Yes  [A] Yes to All  [N] No  [L] No to All  [S] Suspend  [?] Help
(default is "Y"):y
DEBUG:   21+  >>>> {

Continue with this operation?
  22+  >>>> $num-1
[Y] Yes  [A] Yes to All  [N] No  [L] No to All  [S] Suspend  [?] Help
(default is "Y"):y
DEBUG:   22+   >>>> $num-1

Continue with this operation?
  23+  >>>> } #end function SubOne
```

```
[Y] Yes  [A] Yes to All  [N] No  [L] No to All  [S] Suspend  [?] Help
(default is "Y"):y
DEBUG:   23+  >>>> } #end function SubOne

Continue with this operation?
  36+  >>>> {
[Y] Yes  [A] Yes to All  [N] No  [L] No to All  [S] Suspend  [?] Help
(default is "Y"):y
DEBUG:   36+  >>>> {

Continue with this operation?
  37+  >>>> 12/$num
[Y] Yes  [A] Yes to All  [N] No  [L] No to All  [S] Suspend  [?] Help
(default is "Y"):y
DEBUG:   37+   >>>> 12/$num

Continue with this operation?
  19+                                    if ( &  >>>> { Set-StrictMode -Version
 1; $_.PSMessageDetails } ) {
[Y] Yes  [A] Yes to All  [N] No  [L] No to All  [S] Suspend  [?] Help
(default is "Y"):y
DEBUG:   19+                                  if ( &  >>>> { Set-StrictMode
-Version 1; $_.PSMessageDetails } ) {

Continue with this operation?
  19+                                    if ( & {  >>>> Set-StrictMode -Version
 1; $_.PSMessageDetails } ) {
[Y] Yes  [A] Yes to All  [N] No  [L] No to All  [S] Suspend  [?] Help
(default is "Y"):y
DEBUG:   19+                                  if ( & {  >>>> Set-StrictMode
-Version 1; $_.PSMessageDetails } ) {

Continue with this operation?
  19+                                    if ( & { Set-StrictMode -Version 1;
 >>>> $_.PSMessageDetails } ) {
[Y] Yes  [A] Yes to All  [N] No  [L] No to All  [S] Suspend  [?] Help
(default is "Y"):y
DEBUG:   19+                                  if ( & { Set-StrictMode
-Version 1;  >>>> $_.PSMessageDetails } ) {

Continue with this operation?
  1+ &  >>>> { Set-StrictMode -Version 1;
$this.Exception.InnerException.PSMessageDetails }
[Y] Yes  [A] Yes to All  [N] No  [L] No to All  [S] Suspend  [?] Help
(default is "Y"):y
DEBUG:    1+ &  >>>> { Set-StrictMode -Version 1;
$this.Exception.InnerException.PSMessageDetails }

Continue with this operation?
  1+ & {  >>>> Set-StrictMode -Version 1;
$this.Exception.InnerException.PSMessageDetails }
[Y] Yes  [A] Yes to All  [N] No  [L] No to All  [S] Suspend  [?] Help
(default is "Y"):y
```

```
DEBUG:    1+ & {  >>>> Set-StrictMode -Version 1;
$this.Exception.InnerException.PSMessageDetails }

Continue with this operation?
  1+ & { Set-StrictMode -Version 1;  >>>>
$this.Exception.InnerException.PSMessageDetails }
[Y] Yes  [A] Yes to All  [N] No  [L] No to All  [S] Suspend  [?] Help
(default is "Y"):y
DEBUG:    1+ & { Set-StrictMode -Version 1;  >>>>
$this.Exception.InnerException.PSMessageDetails }

Continue with this operation?
  1+ & { Set-StrictMode -Version 1; $this.Exception.InnerException.PSMessageDetails
  >>>> }
[Y] Yes  [A] Yes to All  [N] No  [L] No to All  [S] Suspend  [?] Help
(default is "Y"):y
DEBUG:    1+ & { Set-StrictMode -Version 1;
$this.Exception.InnerException.PSMessageDetails  >>>> }

Continue with this operation?
  19+                                 if ( & { Set-StrictMode -Version 1;
$_.PSMessageDetails  >>>> } ) {
[Y] Yes  [A] Yes to All  [N] No  [L] No to All  [S] Suspend  [?] Help
(default is "Y"):y
DEBUG:  19+                                       if ( & { Set-StrictMode
-Version 1; $_.PSMessageDetails  >>>> } ) {

Continue with this operation?
  26+                                    $errorCategoryMsg = &  >>>> {
Set-StrictMode -Version 1; $_.ErrorCategory_Message }
[Y] Yes  [A] Yes to All  [N] No  [L] No to All  [S] Suspend  [?] Help
(default is "Y"):y
DEBUG:  26+                                      $errorCategoryMsg = &  >>>> {
Set-StrictMode -Version 1; $_.ErrorCategory_Message }

Continue with this operation?
  26+                                    $errorCategoryMsg = & {  >>>>
Set-StrictMode -Version 1; $_.ErrorCategory_Message }
[Y] Yes  [A] Yes to All  [N] No  [L] No to All  [S] Suspend  [?] Help
(default is "Y"):y
DEBUG:  26+                                      $errorCategoryMsg = & {  >>>>
Set-StrictMode -Version 1; $_.ErrorCategory_Message }

Continue with this operation?
  26+                                    $errorCategoryMsg = & { Set-StrictMode
  -Version 1;  >>>> $_.ErrorCategory_Message }
[Y] Yes  [A] Yes to All  [N] No  [L] No to All  [S] Suspend  [?] Help
(default is "Y"):y
DEBUG:  26+                                      $errorCategoryMsg = & {
Set-StrictMode -Version 1;  >>>> $_.ErrorCategory_Message }

Continue with this operation?
  26+                                    $errorCategoryMsg = & { Set-StrictMode
  -Version 1; $_.ErrorCategory_Message  >>>> }
[Y] Yes  [A] Yes to All  [N] No  [L] No to All  [S] Suspend  [?] Help
```

```
(default is "Y"):y
DEBUG:   26+                                    $errorCategoryMsg = & {
Set-StrictMode -Version 1; $_.ErrorCategory_Message  >>>> }


Continue with this operation?
  42+                                      $originInfo = &  >>>> { Set-StrictMode
 -Version 1; $_.OriginInfo }
[Y] Yes  [A] Yes to All  [N] No  [L] No to All  [S] Suspend  [?] Help
(default is "Y"):y
DEBUG:   42+                                      $originInfo = &  >>>> {
Set-StrictMode -Version 1; $_.OriginInfo }


Continue with this operation?
  42+                                      $originInfo = & {  >>>> Set-StrictMode
 -Version 1; $_.OriginInfo }
[Y] Yes  [A] Yes to All  [N] No  [L] No to All  [S] Suspend  [?] Help
(default is "Y"):y
DEBUG:   42+                                      $originInfo = & {  >>>>
Set-StrictMode -Version 1; $_.OriginInfo }


Continue with this operation?
  42+                                      $originInfo = & { Set-StrictMode
-Version 1;  >>>> $_.OriginInfo }
[Y] Yes  [A] Yes to All  [N] No  [L] No to All  [S] Suspend  [?] Help
(default is "Y"):y
DEBUG:   42+                                      $originInfo = & {
Set-StrictMode -Version 1;  >>>> $_.OriginInfo }


Continue with this operation?
  42+                                      $originInfo = & { Set-StrictMode
-Version 1; $_.OriginInfo  >>>> }
[Y] Yes  [A] Yes to All  [N] No  [L] No to All  [S] Suspend  [?] Help
(default is "Y"):y
DEBUG:   42+                                      $originInfo = & {
Set-StrictMode -Version 1; $_.OriginInfo  >>>> }
Attempted to divide by zero.
At E:\Data\BookDOcs\PS4_BestPractices\Scripts\scripts_ch19\BadScript.ps1:37 char:2
+   12/$num
+   ~~~~~~~
    + CategoryInfo          : NotSpecified: (:) [], RuntimeException
    + FullyQualifiedErrorId : RuntimeException


Continue with this operation?
  38+  >>>> } #end function DivideNum
[Y] Yes  [A] Yes to All  [N] No  [L] No to All  [S] Suspend  [?] Help
(default is "Y"):y
DEBUG:   38+  >>>> } #end function DivideNum


Continue with this operation?
  44+  >>>> AddOne($num) | AddTwo($num)
[Y] Yes  [A] Yes to All  [N] No  [L] No to All  [S] Suspend  [?] Help
(default is "Y"):y
DEBUG:   44+  >>>> AddOne($num) | AddTwo($num)
```

```
Continue with this operation?
   11+  >>>> {
[Y] Yes  [A] Yes to All  [N] No  [L] No to All  [S] Suspend  [?] Help
(default is "Y"):y
DEBUG:    11+  >>>> {

Continue with this operation?
   12+  >>>> $num+1
[Y] Yes  [A] Yes to All  [N] No  [L] No to All  [S] Suspend  [?] Help
(default is "Y"):y
DEBUG:    12+   >>>> $num+1

Continue with this operation?
   13+  >>>> } #end function AddOne
[Y] Yes  [A] Yes to All  [N] No  [L] No to All  [S] Suspend  [?] Help
(default is "Y"):y
DEBUG:    13+  >>>> } #end function AddOne

Continue with this operation?
   16+  >>>> {
[Y] Yes  [A] Yes to All  [N] No  [L] No to All  [S] Suspend  [?] Help
(default is "Y"):y
DEBUG:    16+  >>>> {

Continue with this operation?
   17+   >>>> $num+2
[Y] Yes  [A] Yes to All  [N] No  [L] No to All  [S] Suspend  [?] Help
(default is "Y"):y
DEBUG:    17+   >>>> $num+2
2

Continue with this operation?
   18+  >>>> } #end function AddTwo
[Y] Yes  [A] Yes to All  [N] No  [L] No to All  [S] Suspend  [?] Help
(default is "Y"):y
DEBUG:    18+  >>>> } #end function AddTwo
PS C:\>
```

The second benefit to using the *step* parameter with the Set-PSDebug cmdlet is the ability to suspend script execution, run additional Windows PowerShell commands, and then return to the script execution. The ability to return the value of a variable from within the Windows PowerShell console can offer important clues to the problem of what the script is doing. You choose *S* (for suspend) at the prompt, and you are dropped into a nested Windows PowerShell prompt. From there, you retrieve the variable value the same way you do when working at a regular Windows PowerShell console, by typing the name of the variable—tab expansion even works. When you are finished retrieving the value of the variable, you type **exit** to return to the stepping trace.

```
Continue with this operation?
   1+  >>>> E:\Data\BookDOcs\PS4_BestPractices\Scripts\scripts_ch19\BadScript.ps1
[Y] Yes  [A] Yes to All  [N] No  [L] No to All  [S] Suspend  [?] Help
(default is "Y"):y
```

```
DEBUG:    1+  >>>>
E:\Data\BookDOcs\PS4_BestPractices\Scripts\scripts_ch19\BadScript.ps1

Continue with this operation?
  42+  >>>> $num = 0
[Y] Yes  [A] Yes to All  [N] No  [L] No to All  [S] Suspend  [?] Help
(default is "Y"):y
DEBUG:    42+  >>>> $num = 0

Continue with this operation?
  43+  >>>> SubOne($num) | DivideNum($num)
[Y] Yes  [A] Yes to All  [N] No  [L] No to All  [S] Suspend  [?] Help
(default is "Y"):s
PS C:\>> $num
0
PS C:\>> exit
```

If you decide that you would like to see what happens if you run continuously from the point that you just inspected, you can choose *A* (for yes to all) and the script will run to completion without further prompting. If this is the case, you have found the problem. It is also possible, that you will see an error, such as the one that is shown here, when the script attempts to divide by zero.

```
Continue with this operation?
  50+  >>>> AddOne($num) | AddTwo($num)
[Y] Yes  [A] Yes to All  [N] No  [L] No to All  [S] Suspend  [?] Help
(default is "Y"):A
DEBUG:    50+  >>>> AddOne($num) | AddTwo($num)
2
PS C:\>
```

After you have found a specific error, you might want to change the value of a variable from within the suspended Windows PowerShell console to see whether it corrects the remaining logic. To do this, you run the script again, and choose *S* (for suspend) at the line that caused the error. This is where some careful reading of the error messages comes into play. When you chose *A* (yes to all) in the preceding example, the script ran until it came to line 37. The line number indicator follows a colon after the script name. The plus (+) sign indicates the command, which is 12/ $num. The four left arrows indicate that it is the value of the *$num* variable that is causing the problem, as shown here:

```
Attempted to divide by zero.

At E:\Data\BookDOcs\PS4_BestPractices\Scripts\scripts_ch19\BadScript.ps1:37 char:2
+   12/$num
+   ~~~~~~~
    + CategoryInfo          : NotSpecified: (:) [], RuntimeException
    + FullyQualifiedErrorId : RuntimeException
```

You will need to step through the code, until you come to the prompt for line 37. This will be seen as 43+ 12/ <<<< $num, which means that you are at line 37 and that the operation (+) will be to divide 12 by the value of the number contained in the *$num* variable. At this point, you will want to press *S* (for suspend) to drop into a nested Windows PowerShell prompt. Inside there, you can query the value contained in the *$num* variable and change it to a number such as 2. You exit the nested Windows PowerShell prompt and are returned to the stepping. At this point, you should continue to step through the code to see whether any other problems arise. If they do not, you know that you have located the source of the problem.

```
Continue with this operation?
  37+   >>>> 12/$num
[Y] Yes   [A] Yes to All   [N] No   [L] No to All   [S] Suspend   [?] Help
(default is "Y"):s
PS C:\>> $num
0
PS C:\>> $num = 2
PS C:\>> exit

Continue with this operation?
  37+   >>>> 12/$num
[Y] Yes   [A] Yes to All   [N] No   [L] No to All   [S] Suspend   [?] Help
(default is "Y"):y
DEBUG:    37+    >>>> 12/$num
6
```

Of course, locating the source of the problem is not the same as solving the problem, but the previous example points to a problem with the value of *$num*. Your next step would be to look at how *$num* is being assigned its values.

There are a couple of annoyances when working with the Set-PSDebug tracing features. The first problem is stepping through the extra lines of output created by the debugging features. The prompts and output will use half of the Windows PowerShell console window. If you use *Clear-Host* to attempt to clear the host window, you will spend several minutes attempting to step through all the commands used by *Clear-Host*. This is also true if you attempt to change the debug tracing level in midstream. By default, the trace level is set to 1 by the Set-PSDebug *step* parameter. The second problem with the Set-PSDebug *step* parameter occurs when you attempt to bypass a command in the script. You are not allowed to step over a command. Instead, the stepping session ends with an error displayed to the Windows PowerShell console. This is shown in Figure 19-8.

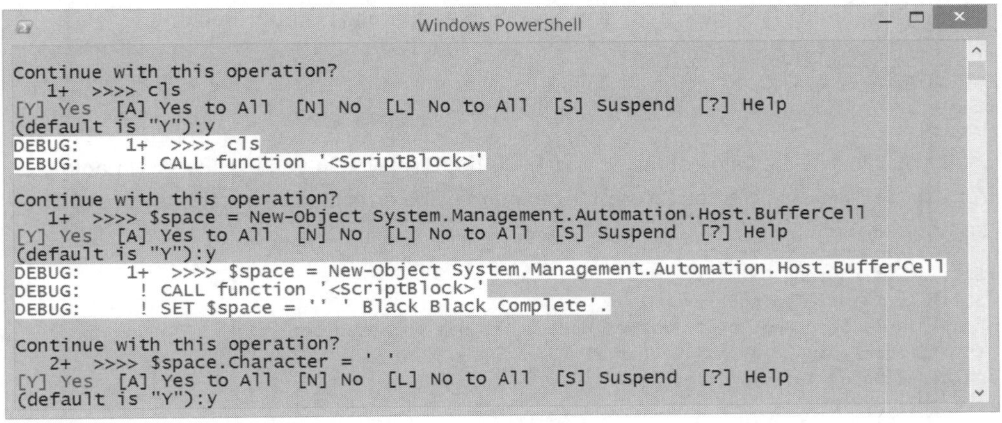

**FIGURE 19-8** Set-PSDebug –*step* does not allow you to step over functions or commands.

To turn off stepping you use the *off* parameter. You will be prompted to step through this command as well.

```
PS C:\> Set-PSDebug -Off
Continue with this operation?
   1+ Set-PSDebug -Off
[Y] Yes  [A] Yes to All  [N] No  [L] No to All  [S] Suspend  [?] Help
(default is "Y"):y
DEBUG:    1+ Set-PSDebug -Off
PS C:\>
```

# Enabling strict mode

One easily correctable problem that can cause debugging nightmares in a script is variables. Variables are often used incorrectly, are non-existent, or initialized improperly. An easy mistake to make is a simple typing error. Simple typing errors can also cause problems when contained in a large complex script.

## Using Set-PSDebug -*strict*

An example of a simple typing error in a script is seen in the SimpleTypingError.ps1 script.

---

**SimpleTypingError.ps1**

```
$a = 2
$b = 5
$d = $a + $b
'The value of $c is: ' + $c
```

---

When the SimpleTypingError.ps1 script is run, the following output is seen:

```
PS C:\> y:\SimpleTypingError.ps1
The value of $c is:
PS C:\>
```

As you can see, the value of the *$c* variable is not displayed. If you use the *strict* parameter from the Set-PSDebug cmdlet, an error is generated. The error tells you that the value of *$c* has not been set.

```
PS C:\> Set-PSDebug -Strict
PS C:\> y:\SimpleTypingError.ps1
The variable $c cannot be retrieved because it has not been set yet.
At y:\SimpleTypingError.ps1:4 char:27
+ 'The value of $c is: ' + $c <<<<
PS C:\>
```

When you go back to the SimpleTypingError.ps1 script and examine it, you will see that the sum of *$a* and *$b* was assigned to *$d* and not assigned to *$c*. The way to correct the problem is to assign the sum of *$a* and *$b* to *$c* and not to *$d* (which was probably the original intention). It is possible to include the Set-PSDebug *–strict* command in your scripts to provide a quick check for uninitialized variables while you are actually writing the script, and you can therefore avoid the error completely.

If you routinely use an expanding string to display the value of your variables, you need to be aware that an uninitialized variable is not reported as an error. The SimpleTypingErrorNotReported.ps1 script uses an expanding string to display the value of the *$c* variable. The first instance of the *$c* variable is escaped by using the backtick character. This causes the variable name to be displayed and does not expand its value. The second occurrence of the *$c* variable is expanded. The actual line of code that does this is shown here:

```
"The value of '$c is: $c"
```

When the SimpleTypingErrorNotReported.ps1 script is run, the following is displayed:

```
PS C:\> Set-PSDebug -Strict
PS C:\> y:\SimpleTypingErrorNotReported.ps1
The value of $c is:
PS C:\>
```

The complete SimpleTypingErrorNotReported.ps1 script is shown here.

---

**SimpleTypingErrorNotReported.ps1**

```
$a = 2
$b = 5
$d = $a + $b
"The value of '$c is: $c"
```

---

To disable strict mode, you use the Set-PSDebug *–off* command.

## Using the Set-StrictMode cmdlet

The Set-StrictMode cmdlet can also be used to enable strict mode. It has the advantage of being scope aware. Where the Set-PSDebug cmdlet applies globally, if the Set-StrictMode cmdlet is used inside a function, it enables strict mode for only the function. There are two modes of operation that can be defined when using the Set-StrictMode cmdlet. The first is version 1, which behaves the same as the Set-PSDebug *–strict* command (except that scope awareness is enforced). This is shown here:

```
PS C:\> Set-StrictMode -Version 1
PS C:\> y:\SimpleTypingError.ps1
The variable '$c' cannot be retrieved because it has not been set.
At y:\SimpleTypingError.ps1:4 char:28
+ 'The value of $c is: ' + $c <<<<
    + CategoryInfo          : InvalidOperation: (c:Token) [], RuntimeException
    + FullyQualifiedErrorId : VariableIsUndefined
PS C:\>
```

The Set-StrictMode cmdlet cannot detect the uninitialized variable contained in the expanding string that is seen in the SimpleTypingErrorNotDetected.ps1 script.

When version 2 mode is enacted, the technique of calling a function like a method is enforced. The AddTwoError.ps1 script passes two values to the *add-two* function by using method notation. Because method notation is allowed when calling functions, no error is normally generated. But method notation of passing parameters for functions works only when there is a single value to pass to the function. To pass multiple parameters, the function notation must be used as shown here:

```
add-two 1 2
```

Another way to call the *add-two* function correctly is to use the parameter names when passing the values, as shown here:

```
add-two –a 1 –b 2
```

Either of the two syntaxes would produce the correct result. The method notation of calling the function displays incorrect information but does not generate an error. An incorrect value being returned from a function with no error being generated can take a significant amount of time to debug. The method notation of calling the *add-two* function is used in the AddTwoError.ps1 script and is shown here:

```
add-two(1,2)
```

When the script is run and the Set-StrictMode *–version 2* command has not been enabled, no error is generated. The output seems to be confusing, because the results of adding the two variables *$a* and *$b* is not displayed. This is shown here:

```
PS C:\> y:\AddTwoError.ps1
1
2
PS C:\>
```

After the `Set-StrictMode` *–version 2* command has been entered and the AddTwoError .ps1 script is run, an error is generated. The error that is generated states that the function was called as if it were a method. The error points to the exact line where the error occurred, as well as showing the function call that caused the error. The function call is preceded with a + sign followed by the name of the function and then four arrows that indicate what was passed to the function. The error message is shown here:

```
PS C:\> Set-StrictMode -Version 2
PS C:\> y:\AddTwoError.ps1
The function or command was called as if it were a method. Parameters should be
separated by spaces. For information about parameters, see the about_Parameters Help
topic.
At Y:\AddTwoError.ps1:7 char:8
+ add-two <<<< (1,2)
    + CategoryInfo          : InvalidOperation: (:) [], RuntimeException
    + FullyQualifiedErrorId : StrictModeFunctionCallWithParens
PS C:\>
```

The complete AddTwoError.ps1 script is shown here.

```
AddTwoError.ps1

Function add-two ($a,$b)
{
 $a + $b
}


add-two(1,2)
```

When you specify `Set-StrictMode` for version 2.0, it checks the following items:

1.  References to uninitialized variables, both directly and from within strings

2.  References to non-existent properties of an object

3.  Calling a function like a method

4.  Variables without a name

If you set strict mode for version 1.0, it checks only for references to uninitialized variables.

If you are not sure whether you want to use strict mode version 2, 3, or 4 (there are no changes), an easy way to solve the problem is to use the value *latest*. This technique is shown here:

```
Set-StrictMode -version latest
```

One issue that can arise with using *latest* is that you do not know what the latest changes might do to your script. Therefore, it is generally safer to use version 1, 2, 3, or 4 when looking for specific types of protection.

### Microsoft Windows PowerShell MVP

Don Jones, Microsoft Windows PowerShell MVP
*CEO, Concentrated Technologies*

In class, I see students struggle with debugging all the time. There are really two simple tricks that make it easier. First, I like to assume from the outset that I'm going to make a mistake, and I build debugging in right from the get-go. For me, that means adding *Write-Debug* calls anytime my script is making a decision (so that I can see what decision it made), anytime I'm changing a variable's contents, and anytime I'm relying on the contents of a property. You might use *Write-Verbose* instead, and I've even seen some folks add a function to their script that automatically adds *PSBreakpoints*. Whatever you choose, that debug output is designed to do one thing and one thing only: validate your assumptions. You see, logic errors—bugs—almost always happen because you've assumed that a variable or property contains something, when in fact it contains something different. Provided that you can state what you *think* they contain, debug output can let you validate that assumption—or correct it. For example, if you're querying *Win32_LogicalDisk* from WMI and you *assume* that the *DriveType* property contains something like "Fixed" or "Removable," debug output would let you realize that it actually contains something like 2 or 3. When I start debugging a script, especially if it's one someone else wrote, I'll often print it out and start walking through it with a pencil. I'll write down what I *expect* variables and properties to contain and then add some *Write-Debug* statements to see whether my expectations were accurate. Usually, my bug can be found wherever my expectations were wrong.

## Debugging scripts

The debugging features of Windows PowerShell 4.0 make the use of the `Set-PSDebug` cmdlet seem rudimentary, or even cumbersome. After you are more familiar with the debugging features of Windows PowerShell 4.0, you might decide to look no longer at the `Set-PSDebug` cmdlet. Several cmdlets enable debugging from both the Windows PowerShell console and from the Windows PowerShell ISE.

The debugging cmdlets are listed in Table 19-2.

**TABLE 19-2** Windows PowerShell debugging cmdlets

| Cmdlet Name | Cmdlet Function |
| --- | --- |
| Set-PSBreakpoint | Sets breakpoints on lines, variables, and commands. |
| Get-PSBreakpoint | Gets breakpoints in the current session. |
| Disable-PSBreakpoint | Turns off breakpoints in the current session. |
| Enable-PSBreakpoint | Re-enables breakpoints in the current session. |
| Remove-PSBreakpoint | Deletes breakpoints from the current session. |
| Get-PSCallStack | Displays the current call stack. |

**NOTES FROM THE FIELD**

## Debugging in Windows PowerShell

**Andy Schneider, Systems Engineer**
*Author of* Get-PowerShell *blog*

I have always found the origin of words to be fascinating. Apparently, the terms *bug* and *debugging* in regard to computers are attributed to Admiral Grace Hopper in the 1940s.

> *While she was working on a Mark II Computer at Harvard University, her associates discovered a moth stuck in a relay and thereby impeding operation, whereupon she remarked that they were "debugging" the system. –Wikipedia*

When I first started scripting and writing a little code, the concept of debugging something seemed to be a very daunting task. However, I have found that by using a few simple steps and thinking through the code, I can debug most of my scripts fairly quickly.

Ninety-nine percent of the time, debugging scripts requires the ability to watch a variable at some point in a script or a function. Have you ever written a function and thought, "If only I knew what *x* was before *y* started messing with it?" A former boss of mine used to tell me to "be the bit" when I was troubleshooting network issues. You have to know exactly where you came from and exactly what your next hop is. Debugging code is similar, but you have to "be the variable."

Windows PowerShell 4.0 offers some great tools for watching variables: the breakpoints. Breakpoints allow you to pause running code in the middle of execution and poke around to see what's happening. The Windows PowerShell ISE makes using breakpoints even easier. You can set a breakpoint on any line in the ISE by using the Debug menu and choosing Toggle Breakpoint or by using the F9 shortcut key.

One thing to be aware of that wasn't immediately intuitive to me is that, when you set a breakpoint in the ISE, it highlights the line on which you set the breakpoint. However, the script will run up to the beginning of that line, but the line itself will not be executed. Remember that you must add the breakpoint after the last line you want to execute. From that point, you can use the Step Into function in the ISE and walk through the rest of your code.

Another feature that I have used is setting a breakpoint based on a variable. Rather than specifying a breakpoint on line 45 column 1, you can create a breakpoint that is triggered any time that a particular variable is accessed. You can do this by using the Set-PSBreakpoint cmdlet and the *variable* parameter. Be sure that when you specify the variable, such as *$var*, that you use only the name of the variable (*var*) and not the dollar sign (*$var*).

One last bit of information that I didn't notice right away was how to navigate within the nested prompt after I hit a breakpoint. If you type **?** or **h**, you will see some usage information that explains how to navigate within this "mini shell." It is interesting that the "nested>" prompt displays this usage information when you press **?**. Under typical circumstances, **?** is an alias for the Where-Object cmdlet, as shown when you type **?** at a normal prompt. Within the nested prompt, there are shortcuts to all of the items in the ISE Debug menu.

The bottom line is that you should not be intimidated by debugging code. With a methodical approach and the tools offered by Windows PowerShell 4.0, the line of code that is causing you grief will bubble up to the top fairly quickly.

## Setting breakpoints

The debugging features in Windows PowerShell use breakpoints. A breakpoint is something that is very familiar to developers who have used products such as Microsoft Visual Studio in the past. But for many IT Pros without a programming background, the concept of a breakpoint is somewhat foreign. A breakpoint is a spot in the script where you would like the execution of the script to pause. Because the script pauses, it is like the stepping functionality that was seen earlier. But because you control where the breakpoint will occur, instead of halting on each line of the script, the stepping experience is much faster. In addition, because you have many different methods to use to set the breakpoint (instead of merely stepping through the script line by line) the breakpoint can be tailored to reveal precisely the information you are looking for.

## Setting a breakpoint on a line number

To set a breakpoint, you use the Set-PSBreakpoint cmdlet. The easiest way to set a break-point is to set it on line 1 of the script. To set a breakpoint on the first line of the script, you use the *line* parameter and *–script* parameter. When you set a breakpoint, an instance of the *System.Management.Automation.LineBreak* Microsoft .NET Framework class is returned and lists the *ID*, *Script*, and *Line* properties that were assigned when the breakpoint was created.

```
PS C:\> Set-PSBreakpoint -line 1 -script Y:\BadScript.ps1
  ID Script              Line Command          Variable         Action
  -- ------              ---- -------          --------         ------
   0 BadScript.ps1          1
```

This breakpoint causes the script to break immediately. You can then step through the function in the same way as when using the Set-PSDebug cmdlet with the *step* parameter. When you run the script, it hits the breakpoint that is set on the first line of the script, and Windows PowerShell enters the script debugger. Windows PowerShell enters the debugger every time that the BadScript.ps1 script is run from the Y drive. When Windows PowerShell enters the debugger, the Windows PowerShell prompt changes to [DBG]: PS C:\>>> to visually alert you that you are inside the Windows PowerShell debugger. To step to the next line in the script, you type **s**. To quit the debugging session, you type **q**. The debugging commands are not case sensitive.

```
PS C:\> Y:\BadScript.ps1
Hit Line breakpoint on 'Y:\BadScript.ps1:1'

BadScript.ps1:1   #
----------------------------------------------------------------------
[DBG]: PS C:\>>> s
BadScript.ps1:16  Function AddOne([int]$num)
[DBG]: PS C:\>>> s
BadScript.ps1:21  Function AddTwo([int]$num)
[DBG]: PS C:\>>> s
BadScript.ps1:26  Function SubOne([int]$num)
[DBG]: PS C:\>>> s
BadScript.ps1:31  Function TimesOne([int]$num)
[DBG]: PS C:\>>> s
BadScript.ps1:36  Function TimesTwo([int]$num)
[DBG]: PS C:\>>> s
BadScript.ps1:41  Function DivideNum([int]$num)
[DBG]: PS C:\>>> s
BadScript.ps1:48  $num = 0
[DBG]: PS C:\>>> s
BadScript.ps1:49  SubOne($num) | DivideNum($num)
[DBG]: PS C:\>>> s
BadScript.ps1:28     $num-1
[DBG]: PS C:\>>> s
BadScript.ps1:43    12/$num
[DBG]: PS C:\>>> s
                                if ($_.FullyQualifiedErrorId -ne
"NativeCommandErrorMessage" -and $ErrorView -ne "CategoryView")
{[DBG]: PS C:\>>> q
PS C:\>
```

Wㅤhen you specify a breakpoint on a script, keep in mind that breakpoints are dependent on the location of the specific script. When you create a breakpoint for a script, you specify the location of the script for which you want to set a breakpoint. I often have several copies of a script that I keep in different locations (for version control). I sometimes become confused when in a long debugging session and open up the wrong version of the script to debug it. This doesn't work. If the script is identical in all respects except for the path to the script, the script will not break. If you want to use a single breakpoint that applies to a specific script that is stored in multiple locations, you can set the breakpoint for the condition inside the Windows PowerShell console, and you do not use the –*script* parameter.

## Setting a breakpoint on a variable

Setting a breakpoint on line 1 of the script is useful for easily entering a debug session, but setting a breakpoint on a variable can often make a problem with a script easy to detect. Of course, this is especially true when you have already determined that the problem pertains to a variable that is either being assigned a value or is being ignored. Three modes can be configured when the breakpoint is specified for a variable, and the modes are specified by using the *mode* parameter. The three modes of operation are listed in Table 19-3.

**TABLE 19-3** Variable breakpoint access modes

| Access Mode | Meaning |
| --- | --- |
| Write | Stops execution immediately before a new value is written to the variable. |
| Read | Stops execution when the variable is read—that is, when its value is accessed to be assigned, displayed, or used. In read mode, execution does not stop when the value of the variable changes. |
| Readwrite | Stops execution when the variable is read or written. |

ㅤㅤTo determine when the BadScript.ps1 script writes to the *$num* variable, you can use the write mode. When you specify the value for the *variable* parameter, do not include the dollar sign in front of the variable name. To set a breakpoint on a variable, you need only to supply the path to the script, the name of the variable, and the access mode. When a variable breakpoint is set, the *System.Management.Automation.LineBreak* .NET Framework class object that is returned does not include the access mode value. This is true even if you use the Get-PSBreakpoint cmdlet to directly access the breakpoint. If you pipeline the *System.Management.Automation.LineBreak* .NET Framework class object to the Format-List cmdlet, you will be able to see that the access mode property is available. In this example, we set a breakpoint when the *$num* variable is written to in the Y:\BadScript.ps1 script.

```
PS C:\> Set-PSBreakpoint -Variable num -Mode write -Script Y:\BadScript.ps1
   ID Script               Line Command          Variable          Action
   -- ------               ---- -------          --------          ------
    3 BadScript.ps1                              num

PS C:\> Get-PSBreakpoint
   ID Script               Line Command          Variable          Action
   -- ------               ---- -------          --------          ------
    3 BadScript.ps1                              num

PS C:\> Get-PSBreakpoint  | Format-List * -Force
AccessMode : Write
Variable   : num
Action     :
Enabled    : True
HitCount   : 0
Id         : 3
Script     : Y:\BadScript.ps1
```

When you run the script after setting the breakpoint (if the other breakpoints have been removed or deactivated, which will be discussed later), the script will enter the Windows PowerShell debugger when the breakpoint is hit—that is, when the value of the *$num* variable is written to. If you step through the script by using the *s* command, you will be able to follow the sequence of operations. Only one breakpoint is hit when the script is run, which is on line 48 when the value is set to 0.

```
PS C:\> Y:\BadScript.ps1
Hit Variable breakpoint on 'Y:\BadScript.ps1:$num' (Write access)

BadScript.ps1:48  $num = 0
[DBG]: PS C:\>>> $num
[DBG]: PS C:\>>> Write-Host $num

[DBG]: PS C:\>>> s
BadScript.ps1:49  SubOne($num) | DivideNum($num)
[DBG]: PS C:\>>> $num
0
```

To set a breakpoint on a read operation for the variable, specify the *variable* parameter and the name of the variable, specify the *–script* parameter with the path to the script, and set *read* as the value for the *mode* parameter.

```
PS C:\> Set-PSBreakpoint -Variable num -Script Y:\BadScript.ps1 -Mode read

   ID Script               Line Command          Variable          Action
   -- ------               ---- -------          --------          ------
    4 BadScript.ps1                              num
```

When you run the script, a breakpoint is displayed each time you hit a read operation on the variable. Each breakpoint is displayed in the Windows PowerShell console as Hit Variable breakpoint followed by the path to the script and the access mode of the variable. In the

BadScript.ps1 script, the value of the *$num* variable is read several times. The truncated output is shown here:

```
PS C:\> Y:\BadScript.ps1
Hit Variable breakpoint on 'Y:\BadScript.ps1:$num' (Read access)

BadScript.ps1:49  SubOne($num) | DivideNum($num)
[DBG]: PS C:\>>> s
Hit Variable breakpoint on 'Y:\BadScript.ps1:$num' (Read access)

BadScript.ps1:49  SubOne($num) | DivideNum($num)
[DBG]: PS C:\>>> s
BadScript.ps1:28    $num-1
[DBG]: PS C:\>>> s
Hit Variable breakpoint on 'Y:\BadScript.ps1:$num' (Read access)

BadScript.ps1:28    $num-1
[DBG]: PS C:\>>> s
```

If you set readwrite as the access mode for the *mode* parameter for the variable *$num* for the BadScript.ps1 script, you receive the feedback shown here:

```
PS C:\> Set-PSBreakpoint -Variable num -Mode readwrite -Script Y:\BadScript.ps1
```

| ID Script        | Line Command | Variable | Action |
| -- ------        | ---- ------- | -------- | ------ |
| 6 BadScript.ps1  |              | num      |        |

When you run the script (assuming that you have disabled the other breakpoints), you will hit a breakpoint each time that the *$num* variable is read to or written to. If you get tired of typing **s** and pressing Enter while you are in the debugging session, you can press Enter to repeat your previous *s* command as you continue to step through the breakpoints. When the script has stepped through the code and hit the error in the BadScript.ps1 script, **q** is typed to exit the debugger.

```
PS C:\> Y:\BadScript.ps1
Hit Variable breakpoint on 'Y:\BadScript.ps1:$num' (ReadWrite access)

BadScript.ps1:48   $num = 0
[DBG]: PS C:\>>> s
BadScript.ps1:49  SubOne($num) | DivideNum($num)
[DBG]: PS C:\>>>
Hit Variable breakpoint on 'Y:\BadScript.ps1:$num' (ReadWrite access)

BadScript.ps1:49  SubOne($num) | DivideNum($num)
[DBG]: PS C:\>>>
Hit Variable breakpoint on 'Y:\BadScript.ps1:$num' (ReadWrite access)

BadScript.ps1:49  SubOne($num) | DivideNum($num)
[DBG]: PS C:\>>>
BadScript.ps1:28    $num-1
[DBG]: PS C:\>>>
Hit Variable breakpoint on 'Y:\BadScript.ps1:$num' (ReadWrite access)
```

```
BadScript.ps1:28    $num-1
[DBG]: PS C:\>>>
BadScript.ps1:43    12/$num
[DBG]: PS C:\>>>
Hit Variable breakpoint on 'Y:\BadScript.ps1:$num' (ReadWrite access)

BadScript.ps1:43    12/$num
[DBG]: PS C:\>>>
                                    if ($_.FullyQualifiedErrorId -ne
"NativeCommandErrorMessage" -and $ErrorView -ne "CategoryView") {
[DBG]: PS C:\>>> q
PS C:\>
```

When using the readwrite access mode of the *mode* parameter for breaking on variables, the breakpoint does not tell you whether the operation is a read operation or a write operation. You must look at the code that is being executed to determine whether the value of the variable is being written or read.

By specifying a value for the *–action* parameter, you can include regular Windows PowerShell code that executes when the breakpoint is hit. For example, if you are trying to follow the value of a variable within the script and you want to display the value of the variable each time the breakpoint is hit, you might want to specify an *–action* parameter that uses the Write-Host cmdlet to display the value of the variable. By using the Write-Host cmdlet, you can also include a string that indicates the value of the variable being displayed. This process is crucial for detecting variables that never initialize because it is easier to notice the displayed value than it is to spot a blank line. The technique of using the Write-Host cmdlet in an *–action* parameter is shown here.

```
PS C:\> Set-PSBreakpoint -Variable num -Action { write-host "num = $num" ;
Break } -Mode readwrite -script Y:\BadScript.ps1

  ID Script            Line Command       Variable       Action
  -- ------            ---- -------       --------       ------
   5 BadScript.ps1                        num            write-host "...
```

When you run Y:\BadScript.ps1 with the breakpoint set, you receive the following output inside the Windows PowerShell debugger:

```
PS C:\> Y:\BadScript.ps1
num =
Hit Variable breakpoint on 'Y:\BadScript.ps1:$num' (ReadWrite access)

BadScript.ps1:48   $num = 0
[DBG]: PS C:\>>> s
BadScript.ps1:49   SubOne($num) | DivideNum($num)
[DBG]: PS C:\>>> s
Set-PSBreakpoint -Variable num -Action { write-host "num = $num" ; break }
-Mode readwrite -script Y:\BadScript.ps1
[DBG]: PS C:\>>> s
num = 0
```

```
Set-PSBreakpoint -Variable num -Action { write-host "num = $num" ; break }
-Mode readwrite -script Y:\BadScript.ps1
[DBG]: PS C:\>>> c
Hit Variable breakpoint on 'Y:\BadScript.ps1:$num' (ReadWrite access)

BadScript.ps1:49  SubOne($num) | DivideNum($num)
[DBG]: PS C:\>>>
```

## Setting a breakpoint on a command

To set the breakpoint on a command, you use the −*command* parameter. You can break on
a call to a Windows PowerShell cmdlet, function, or external script. You can use aliases when
setting breakpoints. When you create a breakpoint for a cmdlet on an alias, the debugger
will hit on the use of the alias only and not the actual command name. In addition, you do
not have to specify a script for the debugger to break. If you do not type a path to a script,
the debugger will be active for any scripts within the Windows PowerShell console session. Every occurrence of the *Foreach* command will cause the debugger to break. Because
*Foreach* is a language statement as well as an alias for the `Foreach-Object` cmdlet, you might
wonder whether the Windows PowerShell debugger will break on both the language statement and the use of the alias for the cmdlet—the answer is no. You can set breakpoints
on language statements, but the debugger will not break on a language statement. As
shown here, the debugger breaks on the use of the *Foreach* alias but not on the use of the
`Foreach-Object` cmdlet:

```
PS C:\> Set-PSBreakpoint -Command foreach

 ID Script            Line Command        Variable        Action
 -- ------            ---- -------        --------        ------
 10                        foreach

PS C:\> 1..3 | Foreach-Object { $_}
1
2
3
PS C:\> 1..3 | foreach { $_ }
Hit Command breakpoint on 'foreach'

1..3 | foreach { $_ }
[DBG]: PS C:\>>> c
1
Hit Command breakpoint on 'foreach'

1..3 | foreach { $_ }
[DBG]: PS C:\>>> c
2
Hit Command breakpoint on 'foreach'

1..3 | foreach { $_ }
[DBG]: PS C:\>>> c
3
```

When creating a breakpoint for the *DivideNum* function used by the Y:\BadScript.ps1 script, you can omit the path to the script because it is the only script that uses the *DivideNum* function. Although doing this makes the command easier to type, it might become confusing when looking through a collection of breakpoints. If you are debugging multiple scripts in a single Windows PowerShell console session, it might become confusing if you do not specify the script to which the breakpoint applies—unless, of course, you are specifically debugging the function because it is used in multiple scripts. Creating a command breakpoint for the *DivideNum* function is shown here:

```
PS C:\> Set-PSBreakpoint -Command DivideNum

 ID Script           Line Command         Variable         Action
 -- ------           ---- -------         --------         ------
 7                        DivideNum
```

When you run the script, it hits a breakpoint when the *DivideNum* function is called. When BadScript.ps1 hits the *DivideNum* function, the value of *$num* is 0. As you step through the *DivideNum* function, you assign the value of 2 to the *$num* variable; the result of 6 is displayed, and then the 12/$num operation is carried out. Next, the *AddOne* function is called, and the value of *$num* is once again 0. When the *AddTwo* function is called, the value of *$num* is also 0.

```
PS C:\> Y:\BadScript.ps1
Hit Command breakpoint on 'DivideNum'

BadScript.ps1:49  SubOne($num) | DivideNum($num)
[DBG]: PS C:\>>> s
BadScript.ps1:43    12/$num
[DBG]: PS C:\>>> $num
0
[DBG]: PS C:\>>> $num =2
[DBG]: PS C:\>>> s
6
BadScript.ps1:50  AddOne($num) | AddTwo($num)
[DBG]: PS C:\>>> s
BadScript.ps1:18    $num+1
[DBG]: PS C:\>>> $num
0
[DBG]: PS C:\>>> s
```

```
BadScript.ps1:23    $num+2
[DBG]: PS C:\>>> $num
0
[DBG]: PS C:\>>> s
2
PS C:\>
```

### INSIDE TRACK

## The best debugging

**Juan Carlos Ruiz Lopez, Senior Premier Field Engineer**
*Microsoft Corporation Spain*

Fortunately (or unfortunately, depending on your perspective), my experience with the Windows PowerShell debugger is a bit limited. Because the Windows PowerShell scripting language is really powerful, most of the loops required by other scripting languages are not needed. In many cases, each cmdlet silently performs the needed looping. These automatic looping features result in less-complicated scripts that often translate into less debugging.

In previous scripting languages, a condition such as an out-of-range loop often necessitated extensive debugging to track down. With Windows PowerShell, you are not immediately faced with these looping problems when running scripts. The best debugging occurs when you don't need debugging. Of course, there are still some classical situations when debugging is a necessity, such as when you call *SomeFunction(Param1,param2)* with the wrong syntax. For most of these situations, adding a `Write-Debug` statement and showing the received variables or parameters will generally suffice. Even better, you can create your own *MyDebug* function so that you can control the colors and formatting that are displayed when you print the information.

I still recommend that you spend some time playing with breakpoints because they really are easy to use and should be learned. You might not need to use them often, but the minimal effort put forth to learn debugging skills is worth it. Even if you never use the Windows PowerShell debugger, you will gain more insight into how Windows PowerShell works.

My favorite Windows PowerShell debugging command is the *k* command, which calls the `Get-PSCallStack` cmdlet. I like to use the *k* command because it is very nice to see who is calling the commands, which is especially important when you have a constantly changing script library and the function you just called seems to be in the wrong module.

# Responding to breakpoints

When the script reaches a breakpoint, control of the Windows PowerShell console is turned over to you. Inside the debugger, you can type any legal Windows PowerShell command and even run cmdlets, such as Get-Process or Get-Service. In addition, several new debugging commands can be typed into the Windows PowerShell console when a breakpoint is reached. The available debug commands are listed in Table 19-4.

**TABLE 19-4** Windows PowerShell debugger commands

| Keyboard Shortcut | Command Name | Command Meaning |
|---|---|---|
| s | Step-into | Executes the next statement and then stops. |
| v | Step-over | Executes the next statement but skips functions and invocations. The skipped statements are executed but not stepped through. |
| o | Step-out | Steps out of the current function and up one level if nested. If the command occurs in the main body, it continues to the end of the script or the next breakpoint. The skipped statements are executed but not stepped through. |
| c | Continue | Continues to run until the script is complete or until the next breakpoint is reached. The skipped statements are executed but not stepped through. |
| l | List | Displays the part of the script that is executing. By default, it displays the current line, five previous lines, and 10 subsequent lines. To continue listing the script, press Enter. |
| l <m> | List | Displays 16 lines of the script beginning with the line number specified by <m>. |
| l <m> <n> | List | Displays <n> lines of the script beginning with the line number specified by <m>. |
| q | Stop | Stops executing the script and exits the debugger. |
| k | Get-PSCallStack | Displays the current call stack. |
| <Enter> | Repeat | Repeats the last command if it was Step-into (s), Step-over (v), or List (l). Otherwise, it represents a submit action. |
| h or ? | Help | Displays the debugger command Help. |

Using the *DivideNum* function as a breakpoint, when the BadScript.ps1 script is run, the script breaks on line 49 when the *DivideNum* function is called. The *s* debugging command is used to step into the next statement and to stop prior to actually executing the command. The *l* debugging command is used to list the five previous lines of code from the BadScript.ps1 script and the 10 lines of code that follow the current line in the script.

```
PS C:\> Y:\BadScript.ps1
Hit Command breakpoint on 'Y:\BadScript.ps1:dividenum'

BadScript.ps1:49  SubOne($num) | DivideNum($num)
[DBG]: PS C:\>>> s
BadScript.ps1:43    12/$num
[DBG]: PS C:\>>> l
```

```
38:    $num*2
39:  } #end function TimesTwo
40:
41:  Function DivideNum([int]$num)
42:  {
43:*   12/$num
44:  } #end function DivideNum
45:
46:  # *** Entry Point to Script ***
47:
48:  $num = 0
49:  SubOne($num) | DivideNum($num)
50:  AddOne($num) | AddTwo($num)
51:
```

After reviewing the code, the *o* debugging command is used to step out of the *DivideNum* function. The remaining code in the *DivideNum* function is still executed, and therefore the divide-by-zero error is displayed. There are no more prompts until the next line of executing code is met. The *v* debugging statement is used to step over the remaining functions in the script, which are still executed. The results are displayed at the Windows PowerShell console.

```
[DBG]: PS C:\>>> o
Attempted to divide by zero.
At Y:\BadScript.ps1:43 char:5
+    12/ <<<< $num
    + CategoryInfo          : NotSpecified: (:) [], RuntimeException
    + FullyQualifiedErrorId : RuntimeException

BadScript.ps1:50  AddOne($num) | AddTwo($num)
[DBG]: PS C:\>>> v
2
PS C:\>
```

## Listing breakpoints

After you set several breakpoints, you might want to know where they are created. One thing to keep in mind is that breakpoints are stored in the Windows PowerShell environment and not in the individual script. Using the debugging features does not involve editing the script or modifying your source code, and the debugging features enable you to debug any script without worrying about corrupting the code. However, because you might have set several breakpoints in the Windows PowerShell environment during a typical debugging session, you might want to know what breakpoints have already been defined. To find out this information, you can use the Get-PSBreakpoint cmdlet.

```
PS C:\> Get-PSBreakpoint
  ID Script          Line Command      Variable      Action
  -- ------          ---- -------      --------      ------
  11 BadScript.ps1        dividenum
  13 BadScript.ps1        if
   3 BadScript.ps1                     num
   5 BadScript.ps1                     num
```

```
 6 BadScript.ps1                              num
 7                        DivideNum
 8                        foreach
 9                        gps
10                        foreach
PS C:\>
```

If you are interested in which breakpoints are currently enabled, you need to use the Where-Object cmdlet and pipeline the results of the Get-PSBreakpoint cmdlet.

```
PS C:\> Get-PSBreakpoint | where { $_.enabled }

 ID Script          Line Command          Variable       Action
 -- ------          ---- -------          --------       ------
 11 BadScript.ps1        dividenum

PS C:\>
```

You can also pipeline the results of Get-PSBreakpoint to a Format-Table cmdlet.

```
PS C:\> Get-PSBreakpoint |
Format-Table -Property id, script, command, variable, enabled -AutoSize

Id Script           Command     variable Enabled
-- ------           -------     -------- -------
11 Y:\BadScript.ps1 dividenum               True
13 Y:\BadScript.ps1 if                     False
 3 Y:\BadScript.ps1             num        False
 5 Y:\BadScript.ps1             num        False
 6 Y:\BadScript.ps1             num        False
 7                  DivideNum              False
 8                  foreach                False
 9                  gps                    False
10                  foreach                False
```

Because the creation of the custom-formatted breakpoint table requires a bit of typing and because the display is extremely helpful, you might consider placing the code into a function that can be included in your profile or in a custom debugging module. Such a function is shown here, stored in the Get-EnabledBreakpointsFunction.ps1 script.

---

**Get-EnabledBreakpointsFunction.ps1**

```
Function Get-EnabledBreakpoints
{
  Get-PSBreakpoint |
  Format-Table -Property id, script, command, variable, enabled -AutoSize
}


# *** Entry Point to Script ***

Get-EnabledBreakpoints
```

---

# Enabling and disabling breakpoints

While you are debugging a script, you might need to disable a particular breakpoint to see how the script runs. To do this, you can use the `Disable-PSBreakpoint` cmdlet.

```
Disable-PSBreakpoint -id 0
```

However, you might also need to enable a breakpoint. To do this, you can use the `Enable-PSBreakpoint` cmdlet.

```
Enable-PSBreakpoint -id 1
```

As a best practice while in a debugging session, you can selectively enable and disable breakpoints to see how the script is running in an attempt to troubleshoot the script. To keep track of the status of breakpoints, you can use the `Get-PSBreakpoint` cmdlet as illustrated in the preceding section.

---

## NOTES FROM THE FIELD

### Debugging scripts

**Vasily Gusev, Systems Administrator, MCSE: Security/Messaging, MCITP: Enterprise/Server Administrator, Microsoft MVP: Windows PowerShell**
*Microsoft Corporation*

In Windows PowerShell 4.0, you have access to really useful debugging features. First, take a look at the `Set-PSBreakpoint` cmdlet, which you can use to assign breakpoints to selected lines of scripts and execute cmdlets, functions, or variables.

For example, when I do Windows PowerShell debugging, instead of modifying the body of my script commands to include a number of *Write-Debug* commands that will output a value of *$var* to the console, I simply assign a breakpoint to the event of its value change. This is a much simpler process and does not require additional cleanup of the script afterward to remove all of the additional commands.

```
Set-PSBreakpoint -Variable var -Mode write
```

After I set the breakpoint inside the Windows PowerShell console and before each change in the value of the *$var* variable, PowerShell stops the execution of commands and enters into debug mode. I can distinguish when I am in debug mode because the prompt changes to include [DBG] at the beginning of each line. In this mode, I can execute all of the usual Windows PowerShell commands as well as view and change variable values.

However, the main advantage of debug mode is that special debugging commands are available, such as *Step-into*, *Step-over*, and *Step-out*, that allow me to move through the executing code without ever leaving debug mode. The *Continue* command exits from debug mode and executes all of the remaining code. The *Quit* command exits the debugger and halts the execution of the script.

Also in the arsenal of Windows PowerShell debugging commands is one that I find very useful while doing command-line debugging—the *List* command. The *List* command displays the current position of the debugger and, by default, also displays the five lines of code before the active line and 10 lines of code after it.

The Enter key feature simplifies working from the command line when debugging because it repeats the last command entered into the debugger. I can execute a *Step-into* command, and the *Step-into* command will execute again each time I press Enter.

I can obtain a list of all debugger commands and their descriptions by typing the letter **h** or using the question mark **?** symbol. This list is useful when I need to quickly refresh myself on the available commands.

The same breakpoints can be set to the event of calling specific commands and functions by using the *–command* switch when creating the breakpoint via the Set-PSBreakpoint cmdlet. You might have guessed that parameters such as *line* and *column* are used for setting breakpoints in the body of a script. Of course, they will work only if you also specify a script to debug by using the *–script* parameter.

Instead of pausing a script and entering the debugger, I can associate almost any action with a breakpoint. For example, if I need to debug a long-running script and cannot sit near the console at all times waiting for errors to occur, I can order the debugger to dump all variables into an XML file and continue running the script.

```
Set-PSBreakpoint -Variable var -Mode write -Action {Get-Variable |
Export-Clixml C:\dump.clixml}
```

Later, I can load this XML to perform variable analysis, as shown here:

```
$Variables = Import-Clixml c:\dump.clixml
```

I can also specify a conditional expression when creating a breakpoint that will take an action if a certain condition is true. For example, the following command will set up a breakpoint that works only if the value of the *$DebugIsOn* variable is set to *$true*:

```
Set-PSBreakpoint -Variable var -Mode write -Action '
{if ($DebugIsOn){break}}
```

It is possible to manage breakpoints after they are created by using other cmdlets that contain the PSBreakpoint noun. The names of these cmdlets are very intuitive. For example, the following command removes all breakpoints from the current session:

```
Get-PSBreakpoint | Remove-PSBreakpoint
```

You can also disable and enable breakpoints without removing the breakpoints by using the Disable-PSBreakpoint and Enable-PSBreakpoint cmdlets, respectively.

## Deleting breakpoints

When you are finished debugging the script, you will want to remove all of the breakpoints that were created during the Windows PowerShell session. There are two ways to do this. The first is to close the Windows PowerShell console. Although this is a good way to clean up the environment, you might not want to do this because you might have remote Windows PowerShell sessions defined or variables that are populated with the results of certain queries. To delete all of the breakpoints, you can use the Remove-PSBreakpoint cmdlet. Unfortunately, there is no *all* switch for the Remove-PSBreakpoint cmdlet. When deleting a breakpoint, the Remove-PSBreakpoint cmdlet requires the breakpoint ID number. To remove a single breakpoint, specify the ID number for the *–id* parameter.

```
Remove-PSBreakpoint –id 3
```

If you want to remove all of the breakpoints, pipeline the results from Get-PSBreakpoint to Remove-PSBreakpoint.

```
Get-PSBreakpoint | Remove-PSBreakpoint
```

If you want to remove only the breakpoints from a specific script, you can pipeline the results through the Where-Object cmdlet.

```
(Get-PSBreakpoint | Where-Object Script – eq "C:\Scripts\Test.ps1")) |
Remove-PSBreakpoint
```

## Debugging scripts with the Windows PowerShell ISE

Osama Sajid, Program Manager: Windows Manageability
*Microsoft Corporation*

The Windows PowerShell ISE is a complete script editor and debugger. If you have a script file (.ps1) loaded in an ISE, you can set a breakpoint on a line by using F9. When the script is run, the execution will stop at that line, and the ISE will allow you to perform one of the following common debugging tasks:

- Execute the line—Step Over (F10)
- Go inside a function—Step Into (F11)
- Execute the rest of the function and come out (Shift-F11)

Pressing F5 continues the execution of the script until the next breakpoint or until the end. These debug commands are also available through the Debug menu.

When the debugger is stopped at a breakpoint, you can view the value assigned to a variable by hovering the cursor on the variable. There is also a debugger prompt (>>>) in the command pane that allows you to execute commands. For example, you can get/set the value of a variable or execute a cmdlet.

Setting a breakpoint on a line is the simplest and most common way of debugging; however, complex situations can arise when you want to stop executing a script if the value of a variable changes or a particular command is executed. Although there is no direct way to halt the execution from the Windows PowerShell ISE user interface, the following cmdlet allows you to perform this action:

```
Set-PSBreakpoint  -variable val -Mode ReadWrite
```

The preceding command sets a breakpoint on the variable named *val* and uses the *mode* parameter with a value of *ReadWrite* to stop execution when the value of the variable is read and just before the value changes.

The following command sets a breakpoint on the execution of the `Get-Process` cmdlet. Whenever Windows PowerShell executes the cmdlet, it will give control to the debugger.

```
Set-PSBreakpoint -command Get-Process
```

Another interesting thing about the Windows PowerShell debugger is its capability to execute a script block when a breakpoint is hit.

```
Set-PSBreakpoint -Variable val -Mode Read -Action '
{Write-Host "Alert: Value of X = $x"; if($val-eq 5){break}}
```

Use of the Windows PowerShell ISE makes debugging very easy. However, all Windows PowerShell debugging can be done from the command line without ISE menus and shortcuts. For example, you can obtain a list of all breakpoints by running `Get-PSBreakpoint` or by disabling a breakpoint using `Disable-PSBreakpoint`. When the script execution stops on a breakpoint, you can use the following debugger commands in Windows PowerShell:

- *s*, Step-into
- *v*, Step-over
- *o*, Step-out
- *c*, Continue
- *q*, Stop

For more information about debugger commands, you can read "about_debuggers" in Windows PowerShell help.

# Additional resources

- The TechNet Script Center at *http://www.microsoft.com/technet/scriptcenter* contains numerous examples of debugging Windows PowerShell scripts.
- All scripts from this chapter are available via the TechNet Script Center Script Repository at *http://gallery.technet.microsoft.com/scriptcenter/PowerShell-40 -Best-d9e16039*.

# CHAPTER 20

# Using the Windows PowerShell ISE

- Running the Windows PowerShell ISE
- Working with Windows PowerShell ISE snippets
- Additional resources

The Windows PowerShell ISE is an integrated scripting environment. It offers superb tab completion, automatic member expansion, and the ability to incorporate script snippets to facilitate the creation of scripts. In this chapter, we will examine these features to see how they are best utilized.

## Running the Windows PowerShell ISE

On Windows 8.1, the Windows PowerShell ISE appears to be a bit hidden. In fact, on Windows Server 2012 R2, it also is a bit hidden. On Windows Server 2012 R2, a Windows PowerShell shortcut automatically appears on the desktop taskbar. Pinning Windows PowerShell to the Windows 8 desktop taskbar is also a Windows PowerShell best practice.

To start the Windows PowerShell ISE, you have a couple of choices. On the Start page of Windows Server 2012 R2, you can type **PowerShell** and both Windows PowerShell and the Windows PowerShell ISE appear as search results. However, on Windows 8, this is not the case. You must type **PowerShell_ISE** to find the Windows PowerShell ISE. Additional ways to launch the Windows PowerShell ISE are to right-click the Windows PowerShell icon and choose either Windows PowerShell ISE or Run ISE As Administrator from the task menu. This task menu appears in Figure 20-1.

Inside the Windows PowerShell console, you need only to type **ise** and it will launch the Windows PowerShell ISE. This shortcut permits quick access to the Windows PowerShell ISE when you need to type more than a few interactive commands.

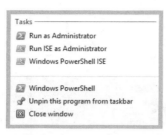

**FIGURE 20-1** Right-clicking the Windows PowerShell icon on the desktop taskbar brings up a task menu permitting you to select the Windows PowerShell ISE.

## Navigating the Windows PowerShell ISE

After the Windows PowerShell ISE launches, two panes appear. On the left side of the screen is an interactive Windows PowerShell console. On the right side of the screen is the command add-on. The command is really a Windows PowerShell command explorer window. When using the Windows PowerShell ISE in an interactive fashion, the command add-on enables you to build a command by using the mouse. After you have built the command, clicking the run button copies the command to the console window and executes the command. This view of the Windows PowerShell ISE is shown in Figure 20-2.

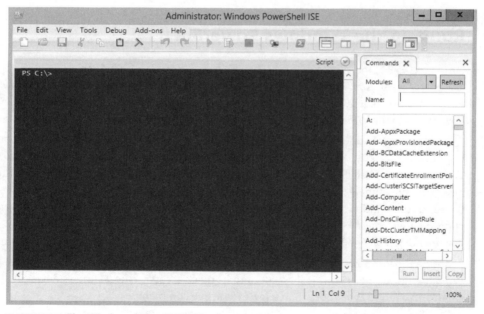

**FIGURE 20-2** The Windows PowerShell ISE presents a Windows PowerShell console on the left and a command add-on on the right side of the screen.

Typing into the Name input box causes the command add-on to search through all Windows PowerShell modules to retrieve a matching command. This is a great way to find and to locate commands. By default, the command add-on uses a wildcard search pattern. Therefore, typing **wmi** returns five cmdlets that include that letter pattern. This is shown in Figure 20-3.

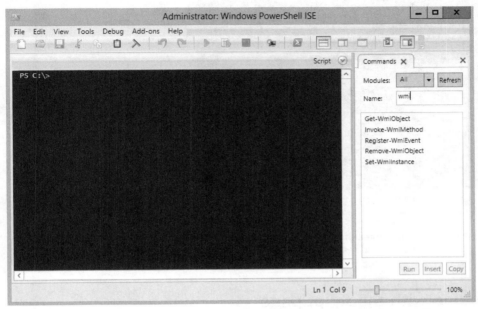

**FIGURE 20-3** The Command add-on uses a wildcard search pattern to find matching cmdlets.

When you find the cmdlet that interests you, select it from the filter list of cmdlet names. Upon selection, the Commands pane changes to the parameters for the selected cmdlet. Each parameter set appears on a different tab. Screen resolution really affects the usability of this feature. The greater the screen resolution, the more usable this feature becomes. With a small resolution, you have to scroll back and forth to see the parameter sets, and you have to scroll up and down to see the available parameters for a particular parameter set. In this view, it is easy to miss important parameters. In Figure 20-4, the Get-WmiObject cmdlet queries the *Win32_Bios* Windows Management Instrumentation class. Upon entering the Windows Management Instrumentation class name in the *class* box, the run button executes the command. The console pane displays first the command and then displays the output from running the command.

> **NOTE** Using the Insert button inserts the command to the console but does not execute the command. This is great for occasions when you want to look over the command prior to actually executing it. It also provides you with the chance to edit the command prior to execution.

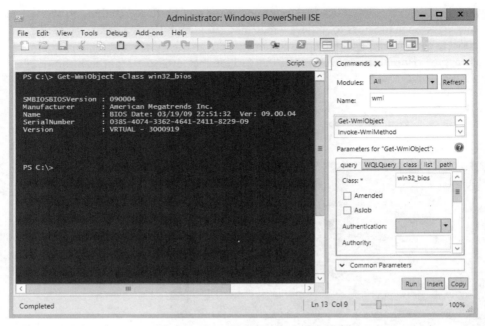

**FIGURE 20-4** Select the command to run from the Command add-on, fill out the required parameters, and click Run to execute Windows PowerShell cmdlets inside the Windows PowerShell ISE.

## Working with the script pane

Clicking the down arrow beside the word *Script* in the upper-right corner of the console pane reveals a fresh script pane. You can also obtain a fresh script pane by selecting New from the File menu or clicking the small white piece of paper icon in the upper-left corner of the Windows PowerShell ISE. You can also use the keyboard shortcut Ctrl-N.

Just because it is called the script pane does not mean that you have to enable script support to use it. As long as the file is not saved, you can enter commands as complex as you like into the script pane with script support restricted. However, after the file is saved, it becomes a script and you will need to deal with the script execution policy at that point.

You can still use the Command add-on with the script pane, but it requires an extra step. Use the Command add-on as described in the preceding section, but instead of using the Run or the Insert button, use the Copy button. Navigate to the appropriate section in the script pane, and then use the paste command (from the right-click menu, or use the Paste command from the Edit menu by clicking the Paste icon on the tool bar or by simply pressing Ctrl-V).

To run commands present in the script pane, click the green triangle in the middle of the tool bar, press F-5, or choose Run from the File menu. The commands from the script pane transfer to the console pane and then execute. Any output associated with the commands appears under the transferred commands. When saved as a script, the commands no longer transfer to the command pane. Rather, the path to the script appears in the console pane along with any associated output.

You can continue to use the Command add-on to build your commands as you pipeline the output from one cmdlet to another. In Figure 20-5, the output from the Get-WmiObject cmdlet pipes to the Format-Table cmdlet. The properties chosen in the Format-Table cmdlet as well as the implementation of the *wrap* switch are configured via the Command add-on.

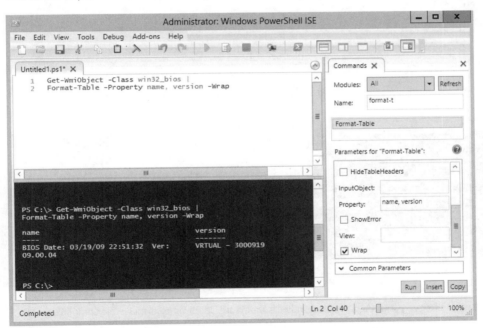

**FIGURE 20-5** Use of the Command add-on permits easy building of commands.

# Tab expansion and IntelliSense

Most advanced scripters will not use the Command add-on because it consumes valuable screen real estate and it requires the use of the mouse to find and to create commands. For advanced scripters, tab expansion and IntelliSense are the keys to productivity. To turn off the Command add-on, either click the x in the upper-right corner of the Command add-on or deselect Show Command Add-on from the View menu. When deselected, the Windows PowerShell ISE remembers your preference and will not display the Command add-on again until you re-select it.

IntelliSense provides pop-up help and options permitting rapid command development without requiring complete syntax knowledge. When you type a cmdlet name, IntelliSense supplies possible matches to the cmdlet names. After you select the cmdlet, IntelliSense displays the complete syntax of the cmdlet. This is shown in Figure 20-6.

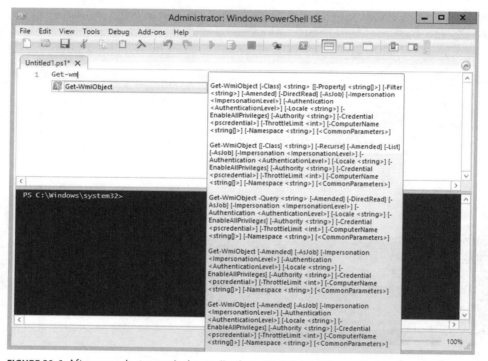

**FIGURE 20-6** After you select a particular cmdlet from the list, IntelliSense displays the complete syntax.

Upon selecting a particular cmdlet, as you come to parameters, IntelliSense displays the applicable parameters in a list. After IntelliSense appears, use the Up or Down arrows to navigate within the list. Press Enter to insert the highlighted option. You can then fill in required values for parameters and go to the next parameter. Once again, as you approach a parameter position, IntelliSense displays the appropriate options in a list. This process continues until you complete the command. Figure 20-7 illustrates selecting the property parameter from the IntelliSense list of optional parameters.

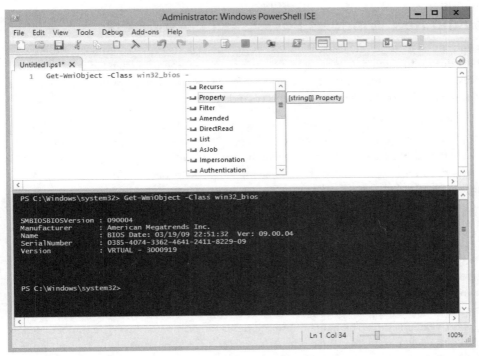

**FIGURE 20-7** IntelliSense displays parameters in a drop-down list. When you select a particular parameter, the data type of the property appears.

# Working with Windows PowerShell ISE snippets

Even experienced scripters love to use the Windows PowerShell ISE snippets because they are a great time saver. It takes just a little bit of familiarity with the snippets themselves, along with a bit of experience with the Windows PowerShell syntax. After you have the requirements under your belt, you will be able to use the Windows PowerShell ISE snippets and create code faster than you previously believed was possible.

## Using Windows PowerShell ISE snippets to create code

To start the Windows PowerShell ISE snippets, use the Ctrl-J keystroke combination. (You can also use the mouse to choose Start Snippets from the Edit menu.) When the snippets appear, type the first letter of the snippet name to quickly jump to the appropriate portion of the snippets. (You can also use the mouse to navigate up and down the snippet list.) When you have identified the snippet you want to use, press Enter to place the snippet at the current insertion point in your Windows PowerShell script pane.

## Creating new Windows PowerShell ISE snippets

After you spend a bit of time using Windows PowerShell ISE snippets, you will wonder how you ever did without them. In that same instant, you will also begin to think in terms of new snippets. Luckily, it is very easy to create a new Windows PowerShell ISE snippet. In fact, there is even a cmdlet to do this: the `New-IseSnippet` cmdlet.

> **NOTE** To create or to use a user-defined Windows PowerShell ISE snippet, you must change the script execution policy to permit the execution of scripts. This is because user-defined snippets load from XML files and reading and loading files requires the script execution policy to permit running scripts. To verify your script execution policy, use the `Get-ExecutionPolicy` cmdlet. To set the script execution policy, use the `Set-ExecutionPolicy` cmdlet.

Use the `New-IseSnippet` cmdlet to create a new Windows PowerShell ISE snippet. After you create the snippet, it becomes immediately available in the Windows PowerShell ISE when you start the Windows PowerShell ISE snippets. The command syntax is simple, but the command takes a large amount of space to complete. Only three parameters are required: *Description*, *Text*, and *Title*. The name of the snippet is the *Title* parameter. The snippet itself is typed into the *Text* parameter. When you want your code to appear on multiple lines, use the `r special character. Of course, to do this means that your *Text* parameter must appear inside double quotation marks and not single quotes. The following code creates a new Windows PowerShell ISE snippet that is a simplified *switch* syntax. It is a single logical line of code.

```
New-IseSnippet -Title SimpleSwitch -Description "A simple switch statemet" -Author "ed
wilson" -Text "Switch () `r{'param1' {  }`r}" -CaretOffset 9
```

When you execute the `New-IseSnippet` command, it creates a new snippets.xml file in the snippets directory within your WindowsPowerShell folder in your documents folder. The simple *switch* snippet XML file is shown in Figure 20-8.

User defined snippets are permanent—that is, they survive closing and re-opening the Windows PowerShell ISE. They also survive reboots because they reside as XML files in your Windows PowerShell folder.

**FIGURE 20-8** Windows PowerShell snippets stored in a snippets.xml file in your Windows PowerShell folder.

## Removing user-defined Windows PowerShell ISE snippets

While there is a New-IseSnippet cmdlet and a Get-IseSnippet cmdlet, there is no Remove-IseSnippet cmdlet. There is no need really, because you have Remove-Item. To delete all of your custom Windows PowerShell ISE snippets, use the Get-IseSnippet cmdlet to retrieve the snippets, and use the Remove-Item cmdlet to delete them. The command is shown here:

```
Get-IseSnippet | Remove-Item
```

If you do not want to delete all of your custom Windows PowerShell ISE snippets, use the Where-Object cmdlet to filter only the ones you do want to delete. The following example uses the Get-IseSnippet cmdlet to list all the user-defined Windows PowerShell ISE snippets on the system:

```
PS C:\Windows\system32> Get-IseSnippet


    Directory: C:\Users\administrator.IAMMRED\Documents\WindowsPowerShell\Snippets


Mode                LastWriteTime     Length Name
----                -------------     ------ ----
-a---         7/1/2012   1:03 AM        653 bogus.snippets.ps1xml
-a---         7/1/2012   1:02 AM        653 mysnip.snippets.ps1xml
-a---         7/1/2012   1:02 AM        671 simpleswitch.snippets.ps1xml
```

Next, use the `Where-Object` cmdlet (? Is an alias for `Where-Object`) to return all of the user-defined Windows PowerShell ISE snippets except the ones that contain the word *switch* within the name. The snippets that make it through the filter are pipelined to the `Remove-Item` cmdlet. In the following code, the *whatif* switch shows which snippets would be removed by the command:

```
PS C:\Windows\system32> Get-IseSnippet | ? name -NotMatch 'switch' | Remove-Item -WhatIf
What if: Performing operation "Remove file" on Target "C:\Users\administrator.IAMMRED\
Documents\WindowsPowerShell\Snippets\bogus.snippets.ps1xml".
What if: Performing operation "Remove file" on Target "C:\Users\administrator.IAMMRED\
Documents\WindowsPowerShell\Snippets\mysnip.snippets.ps1xml".
```

After you have confirmed that only the snippets that you do not want keep will be deleted, remove the *whatif* switch from the `Remove-Item` cmdlet and run the command a second time. To confirm which snippets remain, use the `Get-IseSnippet` cmdlet to see which Windows PowerShell ISE snippets are left on the system.

```
PS C:\Windows\system32> Get-IseSnippet | ? name -NotMatch 'switch' | Remove-Item

PS C:\Windows\system32> Get-IseSnippet


    Directory: C:\Users\administrator.IAMMRED\Documents\WindowsPowerShell\Snippets


Mode                LastWriteTime     Length Name
----                -------------     ------ ----
-a---          7/1/2012   1:02 AM        671 simpleswitch.snippets.ps1xml
```

# Additional resources

- The TechNet Script Center at *http://www.microsoft.com/technet/scriptcenter* contains numerous script examples.
- A history of the .NET Framework versions can be found at *http://msdn.microsoft.com /en-us/library/bb822049.aspx*.
- You can find help about how to determine which version of the .NET Framework is installed, at *http://msdn.microsoft.com/en-us/library/hh925568.aspx*.
- The entry point to the MSDN website is found at *http://msdn.microsoft.com*.

# CHAPTER 21

# Using Windows PowerShell remoting and jobs

- Understanding Windows PowerShell remoting
- Using Windows PowerShell jobs
- Additional resources

Windows PowerShell remoting is the key that transforms Windows PowerShell from an interesting experiment running a few commands to a full-fledged enterprise management solution. In this chapter, we look at how Windows PowerShell remoting works and how it differs from classic remoting. We also explore several scenarios involving the use of remoting for management purposes, and we conclude with a discussion of Windows PowerShell jobs.

## Understanding Windows PowerShell remoting

One of the great improvements in Windows PowerShell 4.0 is the change surrounding remoting. The configuration is easier than it was in Windows PowerShell 2.0, and in many cases, Windows PowerShell remoting "just works." When talking about Windows PowerShell remoting, a bit of confusion can arise because there are several different ways of running commands against remote servers. Depending on your particular network configuration and security needs, one or more methods of remoting might not be appropriate.

## Classic remoting

Classic remoting relies on protocols such as DCOM and RPC to make connections to remote machines. Traditionally, these techniques require opening many ports in the firewall and starting various services that the different cmdlets use. To find the Windows PowerShell cmdlets that natively support remoting, use the Get-Help cmdlet. Specify a value of *computername* for the parameter of the Get-Help cmdlet. This command produces a nice list of all cmdlets that have native support for remoting. The command and associated output are shown here:

```
PS C:\> get-help * -Parameter computername | sort name | ft name, synopsis -auto -wrap
```

```
Name                              Synopsis
----                              --------
Add-Computer                      Add the local computer to a domain or workgroup.
Add-Printer                       Adds a printer to the specified computer.
Add-PrinterDriver                 Installs a printer driver on the specified
                                  computer.
Add-PrinterPort                   Installs a printer port on the specified computer.
Clear-EventLog                    Deletes all entries from specified event logs on
                                  the local or remote computers.
Connect-PSSession                 Reconnects to disconnected sessions.
Connect-WSMan                     Connects to the WinRM service on a remote
                                  computer.
Disconnect-PSSession              Disconnects from a session.
Disconnect-WSMan                  Disconnects the client from the WinRM service on
                                  a remote computer.
Enter-PSSession                   Starts an interactive session with a remote
                                  computer.
Get-CimAssociatedInstance
                                  Get-CimAssociatedInstance [-InputObject]
                                  <ciminstance> [[-Association] <string>]
                                  [-ResultClassName <string>] [-Namespace <string>]
                                  [-OperationTimeoutSec <uint32>] [-ResourceUri
                                  <uri>] [-ComputerName <string[]>] [-KeyOnly]
                                  [<CommonParameters>]

                                  Get-CimAssociatedInstance [-InputObject]
                                  <ciminstance> [[-Association] <string>]
                                  -CimSession <CimSession[]> [-ResultClassName
                                  <string>] [-Namespace <string>]
                                  [-OperationTimeoutSec <uint32>] [-ResourceUri
                                  <uri>] [-KeyOnly] [<CommonParameters>]

Get-CimClass
                                  Get-CimClass [[-ClassName] <string>]
                                  [[-Namespace] <string>] [-OperationTimeoutSec
                                  <uint32>] [-ComputerName <string[]>] [-MethodName
                                  <string>] [-PropertyName <string>]
                                  [-QualifierName <string>] [<CommonParameters>]

                                  Get-CimClass [[-ClassName] <string>]
                                  [[-Namespace] <string>] -CimSession
                                  <CimSession[]> [-OperationTimeoutSec <uint32>]
                                  [-MethodName <string>] [-PropertyName <string>]
                                  [-QualifierName <string>] [<CommonParameters>]

Get-CimInstance
                                  Get-CimInstance [-ClassName] <string>
                                  [-ComputerName <string[]>] [-KeyOnly] [-Namespace
                                  <string>] [-OperationTimeoutSec <uint32>]
                                  [-QueryDialect <string>] [-Shallow] [-Filter
                                  <string>] [-Property <string[]>]
                                  [<CommonParameters>]

                                  Get-CimInstance [-InputObject] <ciminstance>
                                  -CimSession <CimSession[]> [-ResourceUri <uri>]
```

```
                          [-OperationTimeoutSec <uint32>]
                          [<CommonParameters>]

                          Get-CimInstance -CimSession <CimSession[]>
                          -ResourceUri <uri> [-KeyOnly] [-Namespace
                          <string>] [-OperationTimeoutSec <uint32>]
                          [-Shallow] [-Filter <string>] [-Property
                          <string[]>] [<CommonParameters>]

                          Get-CimInstance -CimSession <CimSession[]> -Query
                          <string> [-ResourceUri <uri>] [-Namespace
                          <string>] [-OperationTimeoutSec <uint32>]
                          [-QueryDialect <string>] [-Shallow]
                          [<CommonParameters>]

                          Get-CimInstance [-ClassName] <string> -CimSession
                          <CimSession[]> [-KeyOnly] [-Namespace <string>]
                          [-OperationTimeoutSec <uint32>] [-QueryDialect
                          <string>] [-Shallow] [-Filter <string>]
                          [-Property <string[]>] [<CommonParameters>]

                          Get-CimInstance -ResourceUri <uri> [-ComputerName
                          <string[]>] [-KeyOnly] [-Namespace <string>]
                          [-OperationTimeoutSec <uint32>] [-Shallow]
                          [-Filter <string>] [-Property <string[]>]
                          [<CommonParameters>]

                          Get-CimInstance [-InputObject] <ciminstance>
                          [-ResourceUri <uri>] [-ComputerName <string[]>]
                          [-OperationTimeoutSec <uint32>]
                          [<CommonParameters>]

                          Get-CimInstance -Query <string> [-ResourceUri
                          <uri>] [-ComputerName <string[]>] [-Namespace
                          <string>] [-OperationTimeoutSec <uint32>]
                          [-QueryDialect <string>] [-Shallow]
                          [<CommonParameters>]

Get-CimSession
                          Get-CimSession [[-ComputerName] <string[]>]
                          [<CommonParameters>]

                          Get-CimSession [-Id] <uint32[]>
                          [<CommonParameters>]

                          Get-CimSession -InstanceId <guid[]>
                          [<CommonParameters>]

                          Get-CimSession -Name <string[]>
                          [<CommonParameters>]

Get-Counter               Gets performance counter data from local and
                          remote computers.
Get-EventLog              Gets the events in an event log, or a list of the
                          event logs, on the local or remote computers.
```

| | |
|---|---|
| Get-HotFix | Gets the hotfixes that have been applied to the local and remote computers. |
| Get-PrintConfiguration | Gets the configuration information of a printer. |
| Get-Printer | Retrieves a list of printers installed on a computer. |
| Get-PrinterDriver | Retrieves the list of printer drivers installed on the specified computer. |
| Get-PrinterPort | Retrieves a list of printer ports installed on the specified computer. |
| Get-PrinterProperty | Retrieves printer properties for the specified printer. |
| Get-PrintJob | Retrieves a list of print jobs in the specified printer. |
| Get-Process | Gets the processes that are running on the local computer or a remote computer. |
| Get-PSSession | Gets the Windows PowerShell sessions on local and remote computers. |
| Get-Service | Gets the services on a local or remote computer. |
| Get-WinEvent | Gets events from event logs and event tracing log files on local and remote computers. |
| Get-WmiObject | Gets instances of Windows Management Instrumentation (WMI) classes or information about the available classes. |
| Get-WSManInstance | Displays management information for a resource instance specified by a Resource URI. |

Invoke-CimMethod

```
Invoke-CimMethod [-ClassName] <string>
[[-Arguments] <IDictionary>] [-MethodName]
<string> [-ComputerName <string[]>] [-Namespace
<string>] [-OperationTimeoutSec <uint32>]
[-WhatIf] [-Confirm] [<CommonParameters>]

Invoke-CimMethod [-ClassName] <string>
[[-Arguments] <IDictionary>] [-MethodName]
<string> -CimSession <CimSession[]> [-Namespace
<string>] [-OperationTimeoutSec <uint32>]
[-WhatIf] [-Confirm] [<CommonParameters>]

Invoke-CimMethod [[-Arguments] <IDictionary>]
[-MethodName] <string> -ResourceUri <uri>
-CimSession <CimSession[]> [-Namespace <string>]
[-OperationTimeoutSec <uint32>] [-WhatIf]
[-Confirm] [<CommonParameters>]

Invoke-CimMethod [[-Arguments] <IDictionary>]
[-MethodName] <string> -ResourceUri <uri>
[-ComputerName <string[]>] [-Namespace <string>]
[-OperationTimeoutSec <uint32>] [-WhatIf]
[-Confirm] [<CommonParameters>]

Invoke-CimMethod [-InputObject] <ciminstance>
[[-Arguments] <IDictionary>] [-MethodName]
<string> [-ResourceUri <uri>] [-ComputerName
<string[]>] [-OperationTimeoutSec <uint32>]
[-WhatIf] [-Confirm] [<CommonParameters>]
```

```
                              Invoke-CimMethod [-InputObject] <ciminstance>
                              [[-Arguments] <IDictionary>] [-MethodName]
                              <string> -CimSession <CimSession[]> [-ResourceUri
                              <uri>] [-OperationTimeoutSec <uint32>] [-WhatIf]
                              [-Confirm] [<CommonParameters>]

                              Invoke-CimMethod [-CimClass] <CimClass>
                              [[-Arguments] <IDictionary>] [-MethodName]
                              <string> -CimSession <CimSession[]>
                              [-OperationTimeoutSec <uint32>] [-WhatIf]
                              [-Confirm] [<CommonParameters>]

                              Invoke-CimMethod [-CimClass] <CimClass>
                              [[-Arguments] <IDictionary>] [-MethodName]
                              <string> [-ComputerName <string[]>]
                              [-OperationTimeoutSec <uint32>] [-WhatIf]
                              [-Confirm] [<CommonParameters>]

                              Invoke-CimMethod [[-Arguments] <IDictionary>]
                              [-MethodName] <string> -Query <string>
                              -CimSession <CimSession[]> [-QueryDialect
                              <string>] [-Namespace <string>]
                              [-OperationTimeoutSec <uint32>] [-WhatIf]
                              [-Confirm] [<CommonParameters>]

                              Invoke-CimMethod [[-Arguments] <IDictionary>]
                              [-MethodName] <string> -Query <string>
                              [-QueryDialect <string>] [-ComputerName
                              <string[]>] [-Namespace <string>]
                              [-OperationTimeoutSec <uint32>] [-WhatIf]
                              [-Confirm] [<CommonParameters>]
```

| | |
|---|---|
| Invoke-Command | Runs commands on local and remote computers. |
| Invoke-WmiMethod | Calls Windows Management Instrumentation (WMI) methods. |
| Invoke-WSManAction | Invokes an action on the object that is specified by the Resource URI and by the selectors. |
| Join-DtcDiagnosticResourceManager | |

```
                              Join-DtcDiagnosticResourceManager [-Transaction]
                              <DtcDiagnosticTransaction> [[-ComputerName]
                              <string>] [[-Port] <int>] [-Volatile]
                              [<CommonParameters>]
```

| | |
|---|---|
| Limit-EventLog | Sets the event log properties that limit the size of the event log and the age of its entries. |
| New-CimInstance | |

```
                              New-CimInstance [-ClassName] <string>
                              [[-Property] <IDictionary>] [-Key <string[]>]
                              [-Namespace <string>] [-OperationTimeoutSec
                              <uint32>] [-ComputerName <string[]>]
                              [-ClientOnly] [-WhatIf] [-Confirm]
                              [<CommonParameters>]

                              New-CimInstance [-ClassName] <string>
                              [[-Property] <IDictionary>] -CimSession
```

```
                              <CimSession[]> [-Key <string[]>] [-Namespace
                              <string>] [-OperationTimeoutSec <uint32>]
                              [-ClientOnly] [-WhatIf] [-Confirm]
                              [<CommonParameters>]

                              New-CimInstance [[-Property] <IDictionary>]
                              -ResourceUri <uri> -CimSession <CimSession[]>
                              [-Key <string[]>] [-Namespace <string>]
                              [-OperationTimeoutSec <uint32>] [-WhatIf]
                              [-Confirm] [<CommonParameters>]

                              New-CimInstance [[-Property] <IDictionary>]
                              -ResourceUri <uri> [-Key <string[]>] [-Namespace
                              <string>] [-OperationTimeoutSec <uint32>]
                              [-ComputerName <string[]>] [-WhatIf] [-Confirm]
                              [<CommonParameters>]

                              New-CimInstance [-CimClass] <CimClass>
                              [[-Property] <IDictionary>] [-OperationTimeoutSec
                              <uint32>] [-ComputerName <string[]>]
                              [-ClientOnly] [-WhatIf] [-Confirm]
                              [<CommonParameters>]

                              New-CimInstance [-CimClass] <CimClass>
                              [[-Property] <IDictionary>] -CimSession
                              <CimSession[]> [-OperationTimeoutSec <uint32>]
                              [-ClientOnly] [-WhatIf] [-Confirm]
                              [<CommonParameters>]

New-CimSession

                              New-CimSession [[-ComputerName] <string[]>]
                              [[-Credential] <pscredential>] [-Authentication
                              <PasswordAuthenticationMechanism>] [-Name
                              <string>] [-OperationTimeoutSec <uint32>]
                              [-SkipTestConnection] [-Port <uint32>]
                              [-SessionOption <CimSessionOptions>]
                              [<CommonParameters>]

                              New-CimSession [[-ComputerName] <string[]>]
                              [-CertificateThumbprint <string>] [-Name
                              <string>] [-OperationTimeoutSec <uint32>]
                              [-SkipTestConnection] [-Port <uint32>]
                              [-SessionOption <CimSessionOptions>]
                              [<CommonParameters>]
```

New-EventLog                  Creates a new event log and a new event source on
                              a local or remote computer.
New-PSSession                 Creates a persistent connection to a local or
                              remote computer.
New-PSWorkflowSession         Creates a workflow session.
New-WSManInstance             Creates a new instance of a management resource.
Receive-DtcDiagnosticTransaction

```
                              Receive-DtcDiagnosticTransaction [[-ComputerName]
                              <string>] [[-Port] <int>] [[-PropagationMethod]
                              <DtcTransactionPropagation>] [<CommonParameters>]
```

```
Receive-Job                          Gets the results of the Windows PowerShell
                                     background jobs in the current session.
Receive-PSSession                    Gets results of commands in disconnected sessions.
Register-CimIndicationEvent

                                     Register-CimIndicationEvent [-ClassName] <string>
                                     [[-SourceIdentifier] <string>] [[-Action]
                                     <scriptblock>] [-Namespace <string>]
                                     [-OperationTimeoutSec <uint32>] [-ComputerName
                                     <string>] [-MessageData <psobject>]
                                     [-SupportEvent] [-Forward] [-MaxTriggerCount
                                     <int>] [<CommonParameters>]

                                     Register-CimIndicationEvent [-ClassName] <string>
                                     [[-SourceIdentifier] <string>] [[-Action]
                                     <scriptblock>] -CimSession <CimSession>
                                     [-Namespace <string>] [-OperationTimeoutSec
                                     <uint32>] [-MessageData <psobject>]
                                     [-SupportEvent] [-Forward] [-MaxTriggerCount
                                     <int>] [<CommonParameters>]

                                     Register-CimIndicationEvent [-Query] <string>
                                     [[-SourceIdentifier] <string>] [[-Action]
                                     <scriptblock>] [-Namespace <string>]
                                     [-QueryDialect <string>] [-OperationTimeoutSec
                                     <uint32>] [-ComputerName <string>] [-MessageData
                                     <psobject>] [-SupportEvent] [-Forward]
                                     [-MaxTriggerCount <int>] [<CommonParameters>]

                                     Register-CimIndicationEvent [-Query] <string>
                                     [[-SourceIdentifier] <string>] [[-Action]
                                     <scriptblock>] -CimSession <CimSession>
                                     [-Namespace <string>] [-QueryDialect <string>]
                                     [-OperationTimeoutSec <uint32>] [-MessageData
                                     <psobject>] [-SupportEvent] [-Forward]
                                     [-MaxTriggerCount <int>] [<CommonParameters>]

Register-WmiEvent                    Subscribes to a Windows Management
                                     Instrumentation (WMI) event.

Remove-CimInstance
                                     Remove-CimInstance [-InputObject] <ciminstance>
                                     [-ResourceUri <uri>] [-ComputerName <string[]>]
                                     [-OperationTimeoutSec <uint32>] [-WhatIf]
                                     [-Confirm] [<CommonParameters>]

                                     Remove-CimInstance [-InputObject] <ciminstance>
                                     -CimSession <CimSession[]> [-ResourceUri <uri>]
                                     [-OperationTimeoutSec <uint32>] [-WhatIf]
                                     [-Confirm] [<CommonParameters>]

                                     Remove-CimInstance [-Query] <string>
                                     [[-Namespace] <string>] -CimSession
                                     <CimSession[]> [-OperationTimeoutSec <uint32>]
                                     [-QueryDialect <string>] [-WhatIf] [-Confirm]
                                     [<CommonParameters>]
```

```
                                    Remove-CimInstance [-Query] <string>
                                    [[-Namespace] <string>] [-ComputerName
                                    <string[]>] [-OperationTimeoutSec <uint32>]
                                    [-QueryDialect <string>] [-WhatIf] [-Confirm]
                                    [<CommonParameters>]

Remove-CimSession

                                    Remove-CimSession [-CimSession] <CimSession[]>
                                    [-WhatIf] [-Confirm] [<CommonParameters>]

                                    Remove-CimSession [-ComputerName] <string[]>
                                    [-WhatIf] [-Confirm] [<CommonParameters>]

                                    Remove-CimSession [-Id] <uint32[]> [-WhatIf]
                                    [-Confirm] [<CommonParameters>]

                                    Remove-CimSession -InstanceId <guid[]> [-WhatIf]
                                    [-Confirm] [<CommonParameters>]

                                    Remove-CimSession -Name <string[]> [-WhatIf]
                                    [-Confirm] [<CommonParameters>]
```

| | |
|---|---|
| Remove-Computer | Removes the local computer from its domain. |
| Remove-EventLog | Deletes an event log or unregisters an event source. |
| Remove-Printer | Removes a printer from the specified computer. |
| Remove-PrinterDriver | Deletes printer driver from the specified computer. |
| Remove-PrinterPort | Removes the specified printer port from the specified computer. |
| Remove-PrintJob | Removes a print job on the specified printer. |
| Remove-PSSession | Closes one or more Windows PowerShell sessions (PSSessions). |
| Remove-WmiObject | Deletes an instance of an existing Windows Management Instrumentation (WMI) class. |
| Remove-WSManInstance | Deletes a management resource instance. |
| Rename-Computer | Renames a computer. |
| Restart-Computer | Restarts ("reboots") the operating system on local and remote computers. |
| Restart-PrintJob | Restarts a print job on the specified printer. |
| Resume-PrintJob | Resumes a suspended print job. |

```
Send-DtcDiagnosticTransaction

                                    Send-DtcDiagnosticTransaction [-Transaction]
                                    <DtcDiagnosticTransaction> [[-ComputerName]
                                    <string>] [[-Port] <int>] [[-PropagationMethod]
                                    <DtcTransactionPropagation>] [<CommonParameters>]

Set-CimInstance

                                    Set-CimInstance [-InputObject] <ciminstance>
                                    [-ComputerName <string[]>] [-ResourceUri <uri>]
                                    [-OperationTimeoutSec <uint32>] [-Property
                                    <IDictionary>] [-PassThru] [-WhatIf] [-Confirm]
                                    [<CommonParameters>]
```

```
Set-CimInstance [-InputObject] <ciminstance>
-CimSession <CimSession[]> [-ResourceUri <uri>]
[-OperationTimeoutSec <uint32>] [-Property
<IDictionary>] [-PassThru] [-WhatIf] [-Confirm]
[<CommonParameters>]

Set-CimInstance [-Query] <string> -CimSession
<CimSession[]> -Property <IDictionary>
[-Namespace <string>] [-OperationTimeoutSec
<uint32>] [-QueryDialect <string>] [-PassThru]
[-WhatIf] [-Confirm] [<CommonParameters>]

Set-CimInstance [-Query] <string> -Property
<IDictionary> [-ComputerName <string[]>]
[-Namespace <string>] [-OperationTimeoutSec
<uint32>] [-QueryDialect <string>] [-PassThru]
[-WhatIf] [-Confirm] [<CommonParameters>]
```

| | |
|---|---|
| Set-PrintConfiguration | Sets the configuration information for the specified printer. |
| Set-Printer | Updates the configuration of an existing printer. |
| Set-PrinterProperty | Modifies the printer properties for the specified printer. |
| Set-Service | Starts, stops, and suspends a service, and changes its properties. |
| Set-WmiInstance | Creates or updates an instance of an existing Windows Management Instrumentation (WMI) class. |
| Set-WSManInstance | Modifies the management information that is related to a resource. |
| Show-EventLog | Displays the event logs of the local or a remote computer in Event Viewer. |
| Stop-Computer | Stops (shuts down) local and remote computers. |
| Suspend-PrintJob | Suspends a print job on the specified printer. |
| Test-Connection | Sends ICMP echo request packets ("pings") to one or more computers. |
| Test-WSMan | Tests whether the WinRM service is running on a local or remote computer. |
| Write-EventLog | Writes an event to an event log. |

As you can see, many of the Windows PowerShell cmdlets that have the *computername* parameter relate to WSMAN, CIM, or sessions. To remove these cmdlets from the list, modify the command a bit to include a Where-Object cmdlet. (? is an alias for Where-Object.) The revised command and associated output are shown here:

```
PS C:\> Get-Help * -Parameter computername -Category cmdlet | ? modulename -match
'PowerShell.Management' | sort name | ft name, synopsis -AutoSize -Wrap
```

```
Name           Synopsis
----           --------
Add-Computer   Add the local computer to a domain or workgroup.
Clear-EventLog Deletes all entries from specified event logs on the local or
               remote computers.
Get-EventLog   Gets the events in an event log, or a list of the event logs, on
               the local or remote computers.
```

| | |
|---|---|
| Get-HotFix | Gets the hotfixes that have been applied to the local and remote computers. |
| Get-Process | Gets the processes that are running on the local computer or a remote computer. |
| Get-Service | Gets the services on a local or remote computer. |
| Get-WmiObject | Gets instances of Windows Management Instrumentation (WMI) classes or information about the available classes. |
| Invoke-WmiMethod | Calls Windows Management Instrumentation (WMI) methods. |
| Limit-EventLog | Sets the event log properties that limit the size of the event log and the age of its entries. |
| New-EventLog | Creates a new event log and a new event source on a local or remote computer. |
| Register-WmiEvent | Subscribes to a Windows Management Instrumentation (WMI) event. |
| Remove-Computer | Removes the local computer from its domain. |
| Remove-EventLog | Deletes an event log or unregisters an event source. |
| Remove-WmiObject | Deletes an instance of an existing Windows Management Instrumentation (WMI) class. |
| Rename-Computer | Renames a computer. |
| Restart-Computer | Restarts ("reboots") the operating system on local and remote computers. |
| Set-Service | Starts, stops, and suspends a service, and changes its properties. |
| Set-WmiInstance | Creates or updates an instance of an existing Windows Management Instrumentation (WMI) class. |
| Show-EventLog | Displays the event logs of the local or a remote computer in Event Viewer. |
| Stop-Computer | Stops (shuts down) local and remote computers. |
| Test-Connection | Sends ICMP echo request packets ("pings") to one or more computers. |
| Write-EventLog | Writes an event to an event log. |

Some of the cmdlets provide the ability to specify credentials. This allows you to use a different user account to make the connection and to retrieve the data. Figure 21-1 displays the credential dialog box that appears when the cmdlet runs.

**FIGURE 21-1** Cmdlets that support the *credential* parameter prompt for credentials when supplied with a user name.

This technique of using the *computername* and the *credential* parameters in a cmdlet is shown here:

```
PS C:\> Get-WinEvent -LogName application -MaxEvents 1 -ComputerName ex1 -Credential
nwtraders\administrator

TimeCreated              ProviderName                        Id Message
-----------              ------------                        -- -------
7/1/2012 11:54:14 AM MSExchange ADAccess                   2080 Process MAD.EXE (...
```

However, as mentioned earlier, use of these cmdlets often requires opening holes in the firewall or starting specific services. By default, these types of cmdlets fail when run against remote machines that have not relaxed access rules. An example of this type of error is shown here:

```
PS C:\> Get-WinEvent -LogName application -MaxEvents 1 -ComputerName dc1 -Credential
nwtraders\administrator
Get-WinEvent : The RPC server is unavailable
At line:1 char:1
+ Get-WinEvent -LogName application -MaxEvents 1 -ComputerName dc1 -Credential iam...
+ ~~~~~~~~~~~~~~~~~~~~~~~~~~~~~~~~~~~~~~~~~~~~~~~~~~~~~~~~~~~~~~~~~~~~~~~~~~~~~~~~~~~
    + CategoryInfo          : NotSpecified: (:) [Get-WinEvent], EventLogException
    + FullyQualifiedErrorId : System.Diagnostics.Eventing.Reader.EventLogException,
   Microsoft.PowerShell.Commands.GetWinEventCommand
```

Other cmdlets, such as Get-Service or Get-Process do not have a *credential* parameter, and therefore the command impersonates the logged on user. This command is shown here:

```
PS C:\> Get-Service -ComputerName hyperv -Name bits

Status  Name      DisplayName
------  ----      -----------
Running bits      Background Intelligent Transfer Ser...


PS C:\>
```

Just because the cmdlet does not support alternate credentials does not mean that the cmdlet must impersonate the logged on user. Holding down the Shift key and right-clicking the Windows PowerShell icon brings up an action menu, shown in Figure 21-2, which allows you to run the program as a different user.

**FIGURE 21-2** The action menu from the Windows PowerShell console permits running with different security credentials.

The credential dialog box is shown in Figure 21-3.

**FIGURE 21-3** The credential dialog box permits entering a different user context.

By using the Run As Different User dialog box, alternative credentials are available for Windows PowerShell cmdlets that do not support the *credential* parameter.

## WinRM—Windows Remote Management

Windows Server 2012 R2 installs with WinRm configured and running to support remote Windows PowerShell commands. WinRm is Microsoft's implementation of the industry standard WS-Management Protocol. As such, WinRM provides a firewall-friendly method of accessing remote systems in an interoperable manner. It is the remoting mechanism used by the new CIM cmdlets. As soon as the Windows Server 2012 R2 is up and running, you can make a remote connection and run commands, or you can open an interactive Windows

PowerShell console. However, Windows 8.1 client ships with WinRm locked down. Therefore, the first step is to use the *Enable-PSRemoting* function to configure. When running the *Enable-PSRemoting* function, the following steps occur:

1. Starts or restarts the WinRM service.

2. Sets the WinRM service startup type to Automatic.

3. Creates a listener to accept requests from any Internet Protocol address.

4. Enables inbound firewall exceptions for WS-Man traffic.

5. Sets a target listener named Microsoft.powershell.

6. Sets a target listener named Microsoft.powershell.workflow.

7. Sets a target listener named Microsoft.powershell32.

During each step of this process, the function prompts you to agree (or not) to performing the specified action. If you are familiar with the steps that the function performs and you do not make any changes from the defaults, you can run the command with the *force* switched parameter and it will not prompt prior to making the changes. The syntax of this command is shown here:

```
Enable-PSRemoting -Force
```

The use of the *Enable-PSRemoting* function in interactive mode is shown here, along with all associated output from the command:

```
PS C:\> Enable-PSRemoting

WinRM Quick Configuration
Running command "Set-WSManQuickConfig" to enable remote management of this computer
by using the Windows Remote Management (WinRM) service.
 This includes:
    1. Starting or restarting (if already started) the WinRM service
    2. Setting the WinRM service startup type to Automatic
    3. Creating a listener to accept requests on any IP address
    4. Enabling Windows Firewall inbound rule exceptions for WS-Management traffic
(for http only).

Do you want to continue?
[Y] Yes  [A] Yes to All  [N] No  [L] No to All  [S] Suspend  [?] Help
(default is "Y"):y
WinRM has been updated to receive requests.
WinRM service type changed successfully.
WinRM service started.

WinRM has been updated for remote management.
Created a WinRM listener on HTTP://* to accept WS-Man requests to any IP on this
machine.
WinRM firewall exception enabled.
```

```
Confirm
Are you sure you want to perform this action?
Performing operation "Set-PSSessionConfiguration" on Target "Name:
microsoft.powershell SDDL:
O:NSG:BAD:P(A;;GA;;;BA)(A;;GA;;;RM)S:P(AU;FA;GA;;;WD)(AU;SA;GXGW;;;WD). This will
allow selected users to remotely run Windows PowerShell commands on this computer".
[Y] Yes  [A] Yes to All  [N] No  [L] No to All  [S] Suspend  [?] Help
(default is "Y"):y

Confirm
Are you sure you want to perform this action?
Performing operation "Set-PSSessionConfiguration" on Target "Name:
microsoft.powershell.workflow SDDL:
O:NSG:BAD:P(A;;GA;;;BA)(A;;GA;;;RM)S:P(AU;FA;GA;;;WD)(AU;SA;GXGW;;;WD). This will
allow selected users to remotely run Windows PowerShell commands on this computer".
[Y] Yes  [A] Yes to All  [N] No  [L] No to All  [S] Suspend  [?] Help
(default is "Y"):y

Confirm
Are you sure you want to perform this action?
Performing operation "Set-PSSessionConfiguration" on Target "Name:
microsoft.powershell32 SDDL:
O:NSG:BAD:P(A;;GA;;;BA)(A;;GA;;;RM)S:P(AU;FA;GA;;;WD)(AU;SA;GXGW;;;WD). This will
allow selected users to remotely run Windows PowerShell commands on this computer".
[Y] Yes  [A] Yes to All  [N] No  [L] No to All  [S] Suspend  [?] Help
(default is "Y"):y
PS C:\>
```

When configured, use the Test-WSMan cmdlet to ensure that the WinRM remoting is
properly configured and is accepting requests. A properly configured system replies with the
following information:

```
PS C:\> Test-WSMan -ComputerName w8c504


wsmid           : http://schemas.dmtf.org/wbem/wsman/identity/1/wsmanidentity.xsd
ProtocolVersion : http://schemas.dmtf.org/wbem/wsman/1/wsman.xsd
ProductVendor   : Microsoft Corporation
ProductVersion  : OS: 0.0.0 SP: 0.0 Stack: 3.0
```

This cmdlet works with Windows PowerShell 2.0 remoting as well. The following output is
from a domain controller running Windows 2008 with Windows PowerShell 2.0 installed and
WinRM configured for remote access:

```
PS C:\> Test-WSMan -ComputerName dc1
wsmid           : http://schemas.dmtf.org/wbem/wsman/identity/1/wsmanidentity.xsd
ProtocolVersion : http://schemas.dmtf.org/wbem/wsman/1/wsman.xsd
ProductVendor   : Microsoft Corporation
ProductVersion  : OS: 0.0.0 SP: 0.0 Stack: 2.0
```

If WinRM is not configured, an error returns from the system. Such an error from a
Windows 8.1 client is shown here:

```
PS C:\> Test-WSMan -ComputerName w8c10
Test-WSMan : <f:WSManFault
```

```
xmlns:f="http://schemas.microsoft.com/wbem/wsman/1/wsmanfault" Code="2150859046"
Machine="w8c504.iammred.net"><f:Message>WinRM cannot complete the operation. Verify
that the specified computer name is valid, that the computer is accessible over the
network, and that a firewall exception for the WinRM service is enabled and allows
access from this computer. By default, the WinRM firewall exception for public
profiles limits access to remote computers within the same local subnet.
</f:Message></f:WSManFault>
At line:1 char:1
+ Test-WSMan -ComputerName w8c10
+ ~~~~~~~~~~~~~~~~~~~~~~~~~~~~~~~
    + CategoryInfo          : InvalidOperation: (w8c10:String) [Test-WSMan], Invalid
    OperationException
    + FullyQualifiedErrorId : WsManError,Microsoft.WSMan.Management.TestWSManCommand
```

Keep in mind that configuring WinRM via the *Enable-PSRemoting* function does not enable the Remote Management firewall exception, and therefore PING commands will not work by default when pinging to a Windows 8-based client system.

```
PS C:\> ping w8c504

Pinging w8c504.iammred.net [192.168.0.56] with 32 bytes of data:
Request timed out.
Request timed out.
Request timed out.
Request timed out.

Ping statistics for 192.168.0.56:
    Packets: Sent = 4, Received = 0, Lost = 4 (100% loss).
```

However, as shown here, pings to a Windows 2012 R2 Server do work:

```
PS C:\> ping Server1

Pinging Server1.iammred.net [192.168.0.57] with 32 bytes of data:
Reply from 192.168.0.57: bytes=32 time<1ms TTL=128
Reply from 192.168.0.57: bytes=32 time<1ms TTL=128
Reply from 192.168.0.57: bytes=32 time<1ms TTL=128
Reply from 192.168.0.57: bytes=32 time<1ms TTL=128

Ping statistics for 192.168.0.57:
    Packets: Sent = 4, Received = 4, Lost = 0 (0% loss),
Approximate round trip times in milli-seconds:
    Minimum = 0ms, Maximum = 0ms, Average = 0ms
```

## Create a remote Windows PowerShell session

For simple configuration on a single remote machine, entering a remote Windows PowerShell session is the answer. To enter a remote Windows PowerShell session, use the Enter-PSSession cmdlet to create an interactive remote Windows PowerShell session on a target machine. If you do not supply credentials, the remote session impersonates your current logon. The following output illustrates connecting to a remote computer named dc1. When established, the Windows PowerShell prompt changes to include the name of the remote system. The Set-Location cmdlet (sl is an alias) changes the working directory on the remote system to c:\. Next, the Get-WmiObject cmdlet retrieves the BIOS information on the remote system. The *exit* command exits the remote session, and the Windows PowerShell prompt returns to the default.

```
PS C:\> Enter-PSSession -ComputerName dc1
[dc1]: PS C:\Users\Administrator\Documents> sl c:\
[dc1]: PS C:\> gwmi win32_bios


SMBIOSBIOSVersion : A01
Manufacturer      : Dell Computer Corporation
Name              : Default System BIOS
SerialNumber      : 9HQ1S21
Version           : DELL   - 6



[dc1]: PS C:\> exit
PS C:\>
```

The good thing is that when using the Windows PowerShell transcript tool via Start-Transcript, the transcript tool captures output from the remote Windows PowerShell session as well as output from the local session. Indeed, all commands typed appear in the transcript. The following commands illustrate beginning a transcript, entering a remote Windows PowerShell session, typing a command, exiting the session, and stopping the transcript:

```
PS C:\> Start-Transcript
Transcript started, output file is C:\Users\administrator.IAMMRED\Documents\PowerShell
_transcript.20120701124414.txt
PS C:\> Enter-PSSession -ComputerName dc1
[dc1]: PS C:\Users\Administrator\Documents> gwmi win32_bios


SMBIOSBIOSVersion : A01
Manufacturer      : Dell Computer Corporation
Name              : Default System BIOS
SerialNumber      : 9HQ1S21
Version           : DELL   - 6



[dc1]: PS C:\Users\Administrator\Documents> exit
PS C:\> Stop-Transcript
Transcript stopped, output file is C:\Users\administrator.IAMMRED\Documents\PowerShell
_transcript.20120701124414.txt
PS C:\>
```

Figure 21-4 displays a copy of the transcript from the previous session.

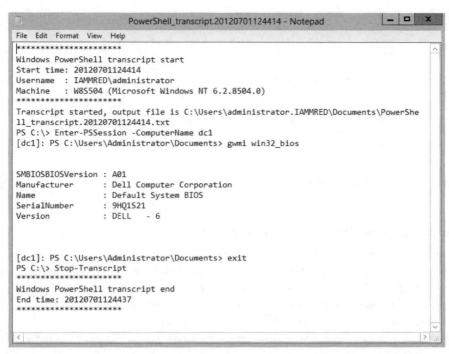

**FIGURE 21-4** The Windows PowerShell transcript tool records commands and output received from a remote Windows PowerShell session.

If you anticipate making multiple connections to a remote system, use the New-PSSession cmdlet to create a remote Windows PowerShell session. The New-PSSession cmdlet permits you to store the remote session in a variable and provides you with the ability to enter and to leave the remote session as often as required—without the additional overhead of creating and destroying remote sessions. In the commands that follow, a new Windows PowerShell session is created via the New-PSSession cmdlet. The newly created session is stored in the *$dc1* variable. Next, the Enter-PSSession cmdlet is used to enter the remote session by using the stored session. A command retrieves the remote host name, and the remote session is exited via the *exit* command. Next, the session is reentered, and the last process retrieved. The session is exited once again. Finally, the Get-PSSession cmdlet retrieves Windows PowerShell sessions on the system, and all sessions are removed via the Remove-PSSession cmdlet.

```
PS C:\> $dc1 = New-PSSession -ComputerName dc1 -Credential iammred\administrator
PS C:\> Enter-PSSession $dc1
[dc1]: PS C:\Users\Administrator\Documents> hostname
dc1
[dc1]: PS C:\Users\Administrator\Documents> exit
PS C:\> Enter-PSSession $dc1
[dc1]: PS C:\Users\Administrator\Documents> gps | select -Last 1
```

```
Handles  NPM(K)    PM(K)     WS(K) VM(M)   CPU(s)     Id ProcessName
-------  ------    -----     ----- -----   ------     -- -----------
    292       9    39536     50412   158     1.97   2332 wsmprovhost


[dc1]: PS C:\Users\Administrator\Documents> exit
PS C:\> Get-PSSession

 Id Name           ComputerName    State    ConfigurationName    Availability
 -- ----           ------------    -----    -----------------    ------------
  8 Session8       dc1             Opened   Microsoft.PowerShell    Available


PS C:\> Get-PSSession | Remove-PSSession
PS C:\>
```

## Run a single Windows PowerShell command

When you have a single command to run, it does not make sense to go through all the trouble of building and entering an interactive remote Windows PowerShell session. Instead of creating a remote Windows PowerShell console session, you can run a single command by using the Invoke-Command cmdlet. If you have a single command to run, use the cmdlet directly and specify the computer name as well as any credentials required for the connection. This technique is shown here, where the last process running on the Ex1 remote server appears:

```
PS C:\> Invoke-Command -ComputerName ex1 -ScriptBlock {gps | select -Last 1}

Handles  NPM(K)    PM(K)     WS(K) VM(M)   CPU(s)     Id ProcessName  PSComputerName
-------  ------    -----     ----- -----   ------     -- -----------  --------------
    224      34    47164     51080   532     0.58  10164 wsmprovhost  ex1
```

If you have several commands or if you anticipate making multiple connections, the Invoke-Command cmdlet accepts a session parameter in the same manner as the Enter-PSSession cmdlet does. In the following output, a new *PSSession* object is created to a remote computer named dc1. The remote session is used to retrieve two different pieces of information. When completed, the session stored in the *$dc1* variable is explicitly remoted.

```
PS C:\> $dc1 = New-PSSession -ComputerName dc1 -Credential iammred\administrator
PS C:\> Invoke-Command -Session $dc1 -ScriptBlock {hostname}
dc1
PS C:\> Invoke-Command -Session $dc1 -ScriptBlock {Get-EventLog application -Newest 1}

 Index Time           EntryType   Source          InstanceID Message PSCompu
                                                                     terName
 ----- ----           ---------   ------          ---------- ------- -------
 17702 Jul 01 12:59   Information ESENT                  701 DFSR... dc1


PS C:\> Remove-PSSession $dc1
```

Use of the `Invoke-Command` cmdlet exposes one of the more powerful aspects of Windows PowerShell remoting: running the same command against a large number of remote systems. The secret behind this power is that the *computername* parameter from the `Invoke-Command` cmdlet accepts an array of computer names. In the following output, an array of computer names is stored in the variable *$cn*. Next, the *$cred* variable holds the credential object for the remote connections. Finally, the `Invoke-Command` cmdlet is used to make connections to all of the remote machines and to return the BIOS information from the systems. The nice thing about this technique is that an additional parameter, *PSComputerName*, is added to the returning object, permitting easy identification of which BIOS is associated with which computer system. The commands and associated output are shown here:

```
PS C:\> $cn = "dc1","dc3","ex1","sql1","wsus1","wds1","hyperv1","hyperv2","hyperv3"
PS C:\> $cred = get-credential iammred\administrator
PS C:\> Invoke-Command -cn $cn -cred $cred -ScriptBlock {gwmi win32_bios}
```

```
SMBIOSBIOSVersion : BAP6710H.86A.0072.2011.0927.1425
Manufacturer      : Intel Corp.
Name              : BIOS Date: 09/27/11 14:25:42 Ver: 04.06.04
SerialNumber      :
Version           : INTEL  - 1072009
PSComputerName    : hyperv3

SMBIOSBIOSVersion : A11
Manufacturer      : Dell Inc.
Name              : Phoenix ROM BIOS PLUS Version 1.10 A11
SerialNumber      : BDY91L1
Version           : DELL   - 15
PSComputerName    : hyperv2

SMBIOSBIOSVersion : A01
Manufacturer      : Dell Computer Corporation
Name              : Default System BIOS
SerialNumber      : 9HQ1S21
Version           : DELL   - 6
PSComputerName    : dc1

SMBIOSBIOSVersion : 090004
Manufacturer      : American Megatrends Inc.
Name              : BIOS Date: 03/19/09 22:51:32  Ver: 09.00.04
SerialNumber      : 3692-0963-10421-7503-9631-2546-83
Version           : VRTUAL - 3000919
PSComputerName    : wsus1

SMBIOSBIOSVersion : V1.6
Manufacturer      : American Megatrends Inc.
Name              : Default System BIOS
SerialNumber      : To Be Filled By O.E.M.
Version           : 7583MS - 20091228
PSComputerName    : hyperv1
```

```
SMBIOSBIOSVersion : 080015
Manufacturer      : American Megatrends Inc.
Name              : Default System BIOS
SerialNumber      : None
Version           : 091709 - 20090917
PSComputerName    : sql1

SMBIOSBIOSVersion : 080015
Manufacturer      : American Megatrends Inc.
Name              : Default System BIOS
SerialNumber      : None
Version           : 091709 - 20090917
PSComputerName    : wds1

SMBIOSBIOSVersion : 090004
Manufacturer      : American Megatrends Inc.
Name              : BIOS Date: 03/19/09 22:51:32  Ver: 09.00.04
SerialNumber      : 89921-9999-0865-2542-2186-80421-69
Version           : VRTUAL - 3000919
PSComputerName    : dc3

SMBIOSBIOSVersion : 090004
Manufacturer      : American Megatrends Inc.
Name              : BIOS Date: 03/19/09 22:51:32  Ver: 09.00.04
SerialNumber      : 2301-9053-4386-9162-8072-56621-16
Version           : VRTUAL - 3000919
PSComputerName    : ex1


PS C:\>
```

# Using Windows PowerShell jobs

You can begin a new Windows PowerShell job by using the Start-Job cmdlet. The command to run as a job is placed in a script block, and the jobs are sequentially named Job1, Job2, and so on. This sequencing is shown here with the new Job10:

```
PS C:\> Start-Job -ScriptBlock {get-process}

Id   Name    PSJobTypeName   State     HasMoreData   Location
--   ----    -------------   -----     -----------   --------
10   Job10   BackgroundJob   Running   True          localhost


PS C:\>
```

The jobs receive job IDs that are also sequentially numbered. The first job created in a Windows PowerShell console is always job ID 1. You can use either the job ID or the job name to obtain information about the job, as shown here:

```
PS C:\> Get-Job -Name job10

Id    Name      PSJobTypeName   State      HasMoreData   Location
--    ----      -------------   -----      -----------   --------
10    Job10     BackgroundJob   Completed  True          localhost

PS C:\> Get-Job -Id 10

Id    Name      PSJobTypeName   State      HasMoreData   Location
--    ----      -------------   -----      -----------   --------
10    Job10     BackgroundJob   Completed  True          localhost


PS C:\>
```

When you see that the job has completed, you can receive the job. The Receive-Job cmdlet returns the same information that returns if a job is not used. The Job1 output is shown here (truncated to save space):

```
PS C:\> Receive-Job -Name job10

Handles  NPM(K)   PM(K)    WS(K)  VM(M)   CPU(s)     Id ProcessName
-------  ------   -----    -----  -----   ------     -- -----------
     62       9    1672     6032     80     0.00   1408 apdproxy
    132       9    2316     5632     62            1364 atieclxx
    122       7    1716     4232     32             948 atiesrxx
    114       9   14664    15372     48            1492 audiodg
    556      62   53928     5368    616     3.17   3408 CCC
     58       8    2960     7068     70     0.19    928 conhost
     32       5    1468     3468     52     0.00   5068 conhost
    784      14    3284     5092     56             416 csrss
    529      27    2928    17260    145             496 csrss
    182      13    8184    11152     96     0.50   2956 DCPSysMgr
    135      11    2880     7552     56            2056 DCPSysMgrSvc
... (truncated output)
```

After a job has been received, that is it—the data is gone, unless you save it to a variable. The following code illustrates this concept:

```
PS C:\> Receive-Job -Name job10
PS C:\>
```

What can be confusing about this is that the job still exists, and the Get-Job cmdlet continues to retrieve information about the job, as shown here:

```
PS C:\> Get-Job -Id 10

Id    Name      PSJobTypeName   State      HasMoreData   Location
--    ----      -------------   -----      -----------   --------
10    Job10     BackgroundJob   Completed  False         localhost
```

As a best practice, use the Remove-Job cmdlet to delete remnants of completed jobs when you are finished using the job object. This will avoid confusion regarding active jobs, completed jobs, and jobs waiting to be processed. After a job has been removed, the Get-Job cmdlet returns an error if you attempt to retrieve information about the job—because it no longer exists. This is illustrated here:

```
PS C:\> Remove-Job -Name job10
PS C:\> Get-Job -Id 10
Get-Job : The command cannot find a job with the job ID 10. Verify the value of the
Id parameter and then try the command again.
At line:1 char:1
+ Get-Job -Id 10
+ ~~~~~~~~~~~~~~~
    + CategoryInfo          : ObjectNotFound: (10:Int32) [Get-Job], PSArgumentException
    + FullyQualifiedErrorId : JobWithSpecifiedSessionNotFound,Microsoft.PowerShell
    .Commands.GetJobCommand
```

When working with the job cmdlets, I like to give the jobs their own name. A job that returns process objects via the Get-Process cmdlet might be called *getProc*. A contextual naming scheme works better than trying to keep track of names such as *Job1* or *Job2*. Do not worry about making your job names too long, because you can use wildcard characters to simplify the typing requirement. When you receive the job, make sure that you store the returned objects in a variable, as shown here:

```
PS C:\> Start-Job -Name getProc -ScriptBlock {get-process}

Id      Name       PSJobTypeName   State       HasMoreData   Location
--      ----       -------------   -----       -----------   --------
12      getProc    BackgroundJob   Running     True          localhost


PS C:\> Get-Job -Name get*

Id      Name       PSJobTypeName   State       HasMoreData   Location
--      ----       -------------   -----       -----------   --------
12      getProc    BackgroundJob   Completed   True          localhost


PS C:\> $procObj = Receive-Job -Name get*
PS C:\>
```

After you have the returned object in a variable, you can use the object with other Windows PowerShell cmdlets. One thing to keep in mind is that the object is deserialized. This is shown here, where I use gm as an alias for the Get-Member cmdlet:

```
PS C:\> $procObj | gm


   TypeName: Deserialized.System.Diagnostics.Process
```

This means that not all the normal members from the *System.Diagnostics.Process* .NET Framework object are available. The normal methods are shown here. (gps is an alias for the Get-Process cmdlet, gm an alias for Get-Member, and *–m* is enough of the *–membertype* parameter to distinguish it on the Windows PowerShell console line.)

```
PS C:\> gps | gm -m method


   TypeName: System.Diagnostics.Process

Name                      MemberType Definition
----                      ---------- ----------
BeginErrorReadLine        Method     System.Void BeginErrorReadLine()
BeginOutputReadLine       Method     System.Void BeginOutputReadLine()
CancelErrorRead           Method     System.Void CancelErrorRead()
CancelOutputRead          Method     System.Void CancelOutputRead()
Close                     Method     System.Void Close()
CloseMainWindow           Method     bool CloseMainWindow()
CreateObjRef              Method     System.Runtime.Remoting.ObjRef CreateObjRef(type
                                     requestedType)
Dispose                   Method     System.Void Dispose()
Equals                    Method     bool Equals(System.Object obj)
GetHashCode               Method     int GetHashCode()
GetLifetimeService        Method     System.Object GetLifetimeService()
GetType                   Method     type GetType()
InitializeLifetimeService Method     System.Object InitializeLifetimeService()
Kill                      Method     System.Void Kill()
Refresh                   Method     System.Void Refresh()
Start                     Method     bool Start()
ToString                  Method     string ToString()
WaitForExit               Method     bool WaitForExit(int milliseconds), System.Void
WaitForExit()
WaitForInputIdle          Method     bool WaitForInputIdle(int milliseconds), bool
WaitForInputIdle()
```

Methods from the deserialized object are shown here, where I use the same command I used previously:

```
PS C:\> $procObj | gm -m method


   TypeName: Deserialized.System.Diagnostics.Process

Name    MemberType Definition
----    ---------- ----------
ToString Method    string ToString(), string ToString(string format, System
.IFormatProvider formatProvider)


PS C:\>
```

A listing of the cmdlets that use the noun job is shown here:

```
PS C:\> Get-Command -Noun job | select name

Name
----
Get-Job
Receive-Job
Remove-Job
Resume-Job
Start-Job
Stop-Job
Suspend-Job
Wait-Job
```

When starting a Windows PowerShell job via the Start-Job cmdlet, you can assign a name to hold the returned job object. You can also assign the returned job object in a variable by using a straightforward value assignment. If you do both, you end up with two copies of the returned job object, as shown here:

```
PS C:\> $rtn = Start-Job -Name net -ScriptBlock {Get-Net6to4Configuration}
PS C:\> Get-Job -Name net

Id   Name   PSJobTypeName   State       HasMoreData   Location
--   ----   -------------   -----       -----------   --------
18   net    BackgroundJob   Completed   True          localhost


PS C:\> $rtn

Id   Name   PSJobTypeName   State       HasMoreData   Location
--   ----   -------------   -----       -----------   --------
18   net    BackgroundJob   Completed   True          localhost
```

Retrieving the job, via the Receive-Job cmdlet, consumes the data. You cannot come back and retrieve the returned data again. This code shown here illustrates this concept:

```
PS C:\> Receive-Job $rtn

Description                 : 6to4 Configuration
State                       : Default
AutoSharing                 : Default
RelayName                   : 6to4.ipv6.microsoft.com.
RelayState                  : Default
ResolutionIntervalSeconds   : 1440


PS C:\> Receive-Job $rtn
```

The preceding example also shows what happens when a script block returns an error. When you use the Receive-Job cmdlet, the error message displays. To find additional information about the code that triggered the error, use the *Job* object stored in either the *$rtn* variable or the *net* named job. You might prefer using the job object stored in the *$rtn* variable, as shown here:

```
PS C:\> $rtn.Command
Get-Net6to4Configuration
```

To clean up first, remove the leftover job objects by getting the jobs and removing the jobs, as shown here:

```
PS C:\> Get-Job | Remove-Job
PS C:\> Get-Job
PS C:\>
```

When you create a new Windows PowerShell job, it runs in the background. There is no indication of whether the job ended in an error or whether it was successful. Indeed, you do not have any idea when the job even completes, other than to use the Get-Job cmdlet several times to see when the job state changes from running to completed. For many jobs, this might be perfectly acceptable. In fact, it might even be preferable when you want to regain control of the Windows PowerShell console as soon as the job begins executing. On other occasions, you might want to be notified when the Windows PowerShell job completes. To do this, you can use the Wait-Job cmdlet. You need to give the Wait-Job cmdlet either a job name or a job ID. After you have done this, the Windows PowerShell console will pause until the job completes. The job, with its completed status, displays on the console. You can then use the Retrieve-Job cmdlet to receive the deserialized objects and store them in a variable.

```
PS C:\> $rtn = Start-Job -ScriptBlock {gwmi win32_product -cn hyperv1}
PS C:\> $rtn
```

| Id | Name  | PSJobTypeName | State   | HasMoreData | Location  |
|----|-------|---------------|---------|-------------|-----------|
| 22 | Job22 | BackgroundJob | Running | True        | localhost |

```
PS C:\> Wait-Job -id 22
```

| Id | Name  | PSJobTypeName | State     | HasMoreData | Location  |
|----|-------|---------------|-----------|-------------|-----------|
| 22 | Job22 | BackgroundJob | Completed | True        | localhost |

```
PS C:\> $prod = Receive-Job -id 22
PS C:\> $prod.Count
2
```

In a newly opened Windows PowerShell console, the Start-Job cmdlet is used to start a new job. The returned job object is stored in the *$rtn* variable. You can pipeline the job object contained in the *$rtn* variable to the Stop-Job cmdlet to stop the execution of the job. If you try to use the job object in the *$rtn* variable directly, to get job information, an error will be generated, as shown here:

```
PS C:\> $rtn = Start-Job -ScriptBlock {gwmi win32_product -cn hyperv1}
PS C:\> $rtn | Stop-Job
PS C:\> Get-Job $rtn
```

```
Get-Job : The command cannot find the job because the job name
System.Management.Automation.PSRemotingJob was not found. Verify the value of the
Name parameter, and then try the command again.
At line:1 char:1
+ Get-Job $rtn
+ ~~~~~~~~~~~~
    + CategoryInfo          : ObjectNotFound: (System.Manageme...n.PSRemotingJob:
   String) [Get-Job], PSArgumentException
    + FullyQualifiedErrorId : JobWithSpecifiedNameNotFound,Microsoft.PowerShell
   .Commands.GetJobCommand
```

You can pipeline the job object to the Get-Job cmdlet and see that the job is in a stopped state. Use the Receive-Job cmdlet to receive the job information, and use the *count* property to see how many software products are included in the variable, as shown here:

```
PS C:\> $rtn | Get-Job

Id    Name      PSJobTypeName   State     HasMoreData   Location
--    ----      -------------   -----     -----------   --------
2     Job2      BackgroundJob   Stopped   False         localhost


PS C:\> $products = Receive-Job -Id 2
PS C:\> $products.count
0
```

In the preceding list, you can see that no software packages were enumerated. This is because the Get-WmiObject command to retrieve information from the *Win32_Product* class did not have time to finish.

If you want to keep the data from your job so that you can use it again later, and you do not want to bother storing it in an intermediate variable, use the *keep* parameter. In the following command, the Get-NetAdapter cmdlet is used to return network adapter information:

```
PS C:\> Start-Job -ScriptBlock {Get-NetAdapter}

Id    Name      PSJobTypeName   State     HasMoreData   Location
--    ----      -------------   -----     -----------   --------
4     Job4      BackgroundJob   Running   True          localhost
```

When checking on the status of a background job and you are monitoring a job that you just created, used the *newest* parameter instead of typing a job number, because it is easier to remember. This technique is shown here:

```
PS C:\> Get-Job -Newest 1

Id    Name      PSJobTypeName   State       HasMoreData   Location
--    ----      -------------   -----       -----------   --------
4     Job4      BackgroundJob   Completed   True          localhost
```

Now, to retrieve the information from the job and to keep the information available, use the *keep* switched parameter as shown here:

```
PS C:\> Receive-Job -Id 4 -Keep
```

```
ifAlias                 : Ethernet
InterfaceAlias          : Ethernet
ifIndex                 : 12
ifDesc                  : Microsoft Hyper-V Network Adapter
ifName                  : Ethernet_7
DriverVersion           : 6.2.8504.0
LinkLayerAddress        : 00-15-5D-00-2D-07
MacAddress              : 00-15-5D-00-2D-07
LinkSpeed               : 10 Gbps
MediaType               : 802.3
PhysicalMediaType       : Unspecified
AdminStatus             : Up
MediaConnectionState    : Connected
DriverInformation       : Driver Date 2006-06-21 Version
                          6.2.8504.0 NDIS 6.30
DriverFileName          : netvsc63.sys
NdisVersion             : 6.30
ifOperStatus            : Up
RunspaceId              : 9ce8f8e6-1a09-4103-a508-c60398527
<output truncated>
```

You can continue to work directly with the output in a normal Windows PowerShell fashion, as shown here:

```
PS C:\> Receive-Job -Id 4 -Keep | select name

name
----
Ethernet


PS C:\> Receive-Job -Id 4 -Keep | select transmitlinksp*

TransmitLinkSpeed
-----------------
      10000000000
```

## Additional resources

- The TechNet Script Center at *http://www.microsoft.com/technet/scriptcenter* contains numerous script examples.
- A history of the .NET Framework versions can be found at *http://msdn.microsoft.com /en-us/library/bb822049.aspx.*

- You can find help about how to determine which version of the .NET Framework is installed, at *http://msdn.microsoft.com/en-us/library/hh925568.aspx*.

- The entry point to the MSDN website is found at *http://msdn.microsoft.com*.

# CHAPTER 22

# Using Windows PowerShell Workflow

- Why use Windows PowerShell Workflow
- Parallel PowerShell
- Workflow activities
- Checkpointing a Windows PowerShell workflow
- Adding a sequence activity to a workflow
- Additional resources

Windows PowerShell Workflow enables IT Pros to solve many common scripting problems. For example, a system requires a reboot to complete configuration before kicking off a second script. Another common scenario is executing a series of commands in either parallel or in series. This chapter begins by looking at the reasons for using a workflow, moves to understanding workflow activities, and then looks at checkpoint and sequencing of workflows.

## Why use Windows PowerShell Workflow

Windows PowerShell workflows are cool because the commands consist of a sequence of related activities. You can use a workflow to run commands that take an extended period of time. A workflow command can survive reboots, disconnected sessions, and even be suspended and resumed without losing the data. This is because the workflow automatically saves state and data at the beginning and at the end of the workflow. In addition, it can use specific points that you specify. These persistence points are like checkpoints or snapshots of the activity. If a failure occurs that is unrecoverable, you can use the persisted data points and resume from the last data point instead of having to begin the entire process anew.

> **NOTE**  Windows PowerShell Workflow is Windows Workflow Foundation. Instead of having to write the workflow in XAML, I can write the workflow using Windows Power-Shell syntax. I can also package the workflow in a Windows PowerShell module if I prefer.

The two main reasons for using Windows PowerShell Workflow are reliability and performance when performing large-scale or long-running commands. These two reasons break down into the following key points:

1. Parallel task execution

2. Workflow throttling

3. Connection throttling

4. Connection pooling

5. Integration with disconnection sessions

## Workflow requirements

You can run a workflow that uses Windows PowerShell cmdlets if the target (the managed node) runs at least Windows PowerShell 2.0. You do not need Windows PowerShell 2.0 if the workflow does not run Windows PowerShell cmdlets. You can use WMI or CIM commands on computers that do not have Windows PowerShell installed–which means that you can use Windows PowerShell Workflow in a heterogeneous environment.

The computer that runs the workflow is the host (client) computer. It must be running at least Windows PowerShell 3.0 and have Windows PowerShell remoting enabled. In addition, the target (managed node) computer must have at least Windows PowerShell 2.0 with Windows PowerShell remoting enabled if the workflow includes Windows PowerShell cmdlets.

## A simple workflow

Although much of the focus around Windows PowerShell Workflow is on large network management, you can use it on your own local computer. You might want to do this if the task at hand might take a long time to run. Therefore, from a learning standpoint, it makes sense to begin with a workflow that simply works on your local computer. To write a workflow, begin with the *workflow* keyword. Provide a name for the workflow, and inside the curly braces (script block), specify the code that you want to use. The syntax is very much like a Windows PowerShell function. HelloUserworkflow.ps1 demonstrates a basic workflow.

```
HelloUserworkflow.ps1

Workflow HelloUser
{ "Hello $env:USERNAME" }
```

Just like a Windows PowerShell function, you need to run the code and load the workflow prior to using it. In the Windows PowerShell ISE, run the script containing the workflow, and in the immediate window you can use the workflow. This is shown in Figure 22-1.

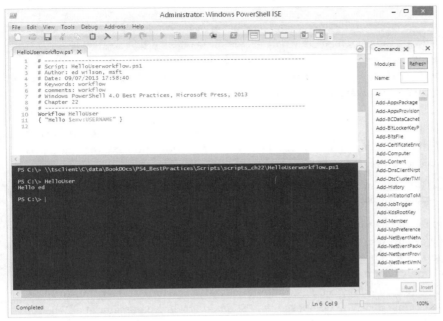

**FIGURE 22-1** Run the workflow from the script pane, and execute the workflow in the script pane of the Windows PowerShell ISE.

You can use normal Windows PowerShell commands and add logic to the workflow if you want. The following workflow uses the Get-Date cmdlet to retrieve the time hour in a 24-hour format. If the hour is less than 12, it displays "good morning." If the hour is between 12 and 18, it displays "good afternoon." Otherwise, it displays "good evening." HelloUserTimeworkflow.ps1 demonstrates the workflow.

```
HelloUserTimeworkflow.ps1

Workflow HelloUserTime
{
 $dateHour = Get-date -UFormat '%H'
 if($dateHour -lt 12) {"good morning"}
 ELSeIF ($dateHour -ge 12 -AND $dateHour -le 18) {"good afternoon"}
 ELSE {"good evening"}
}
```

# Parallel PowerShell

One of the reasons for using a Windows PowerShell workflow is to be able to easily execute commands in parallel. This can result in some significant time savings.

To perform a parallel activity by using a Windows PowerShell workflow, use the *Foreach* keyword with the *–Parallel* parameter. This is followed by the operation and the associated script block. The following example illustrates this technique:

```
Foreach -Parallel ($cn in $computers)
 { Get-CimInstance -PSComputerName $cn -ClassName win32_computersystem }
```

One of the things to keep in mind, here—as in a major source of frustration early on—is that when you call the Get-CimInstance cmdlet from within the script block of my parallel *Foreach*, you have to use the automatically added *PSComputerName* parameter and not the *ComputerName* parameter you would normally use with the cmdlet. This is the way that Windows PowerShell Workflow handles computer names. If you look at the command-line syntax for Get-CimInstance, you do not see the *PSComputerName* parameter at all. The syntax for Get-CimInstance is shown in Figure 22-2.

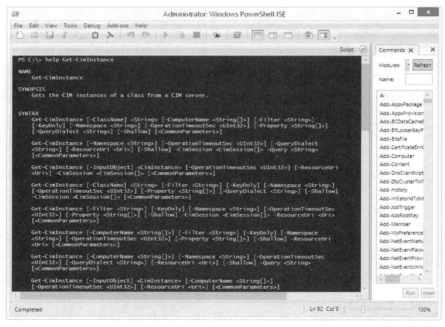

**FIGURE 22-2** The Get-CimInstance cmdlet does not have a *PSComputerName* parameter.

The nice thing is that if you forget to include *–PSComputerName* and try to run a Windows PowerShell workflow, an error arises. The error is detailed enough that it actually tells you the problem, and it tells you what you need to do to solve the problem. This is shown in Figure 22-3.

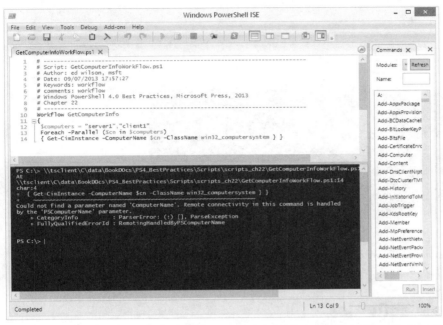

**FIGURE 22-3** Omitting the *PSComputerName* parameter results in an informative error message.

After you rename the parameter in Get-CimInstance, you can run the workflow and it does not generate any errors.

The complete GetComputerInfoWorkFlow.ps1 script appears here.

```
GetComputerInfoWorkFlow.ps1

Workflow GetComputerInfo
{
 $computers = "server1","client1"
 Foreach -Parallel ($cn in $computers)
 { Get-CimInstance -PSComputerName $cn -ClassName win32_computersystem } }
```

You call the workflow, and you are greeted with computer information from each of the servers whose name is stored in the *$computers* variable. The script and the output from the script are shown in Figure 22-4.

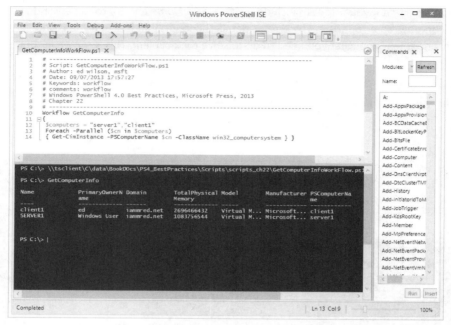

**FIGURE 22-4** Running the workflow produces detailed computer information.

# Workflow activities

A Windows PowerShell workflow is made up of a series of activities. In fact, the basic unit of work in a Windows PowerShell workflow is called an activity. There are five different types of Windows PowerShell Workflow activities that are available for use. Table 22-1 describes the different types of activities.

**TABLE 22-1** Workflow activities and associated descriptions

| Activity | Description |
| --- | --- |
| CheckPoint-Workflow (alias = PSPersist) | Takes a checkpoint. Saves the state and data of a workflow in progress. If the workflow is interrupted or rerun, it can restart from any checkpoint.<br>Use the Checkpoint-Workflow activity along with the *PSPersist* workflow common parameter and the *PSPersistPreference* variable to make your workflow robust and recoverable. |
| ForEach -Parallel | Runs the statements in the script block once for each item in a collection. The items are processed in parallel. The statements in the script block run sequentially. |
| Parallel | All statements in the script block can run at the same time. The order of execution is undefined. |

| Sequence | Creates a block of sequential statements within a parallel script block. The Sequence script block runs in parallel with other activities in the Parallel script block. However, the statements in the Sequence script block run in the order in which they appear. This activity is valid only within a Parallel script block. |
|---|---|
| Suspend-Workflow | Stops a workflow temporarily. To resume the workflow, use the Resume-Job cmdlet. |

## Windows PowerShell cmdlets as activities

Windows PowerShell cmdlets from the core modules are automatically implemented as activities for use in a Windows PowerShell workflow. These core modules all begin with the name *Microsoft.PowerShell*. To find these cmdlets, you can use the Get-Command cmdlet as shown here:

```
Get-Command -Module microsoft.powershell*
```

The command and the associated output from the Get-Command cmdlet appear in Figure 22-5.

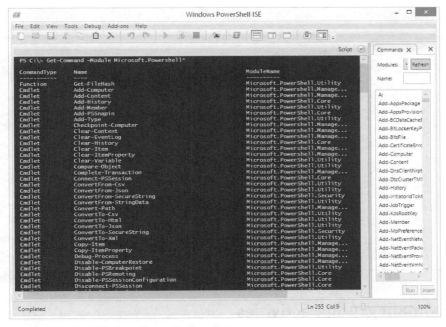

**FIGURE 22-5** Core Windows PowerShell cmdlets.

# Disallowed core cmdlets

Not all of the cmdlets from the Windows PowerShell core modules are permitted as automatic activities for Windows PowerShell workflows. The reason for this is that some of the core cmdlets do not work well in workflows. A quick look at the disallowed list makes this abundantly clear. Table 22-2 lists the disallowed core cmdlets.

**TABLE 22-2** Disallowed core Windows PowerShell cmdlets

| Disallowed cmdlet | Disallowed cmdlet |
| --- | --- |
| Add-History | Invoke-History |
| Add-PSSnapin | New-Alias |
| Clear-History | New-Variable |
| Clear-Variable | Out-GridView |
| Complete-Transaction | Remove-PSBreakpoint |
| Debug-Process | Remove-PSSnapin |
| Disable-PSBreakpoint | Remove-Variable |
| Enable-PSBreakpoint | Set-Alias |
| Enter-PSSession | Set-PSBreakpoint |
| Exit-PSSession | Set-PSDebug |
| Export-Alias | Set-StrictMode |
| Export-Console | Set-TraceMode |
| Get-Alias | Set-Variable |
| Get-History | Start-Transaction |
| Get-PSBreakpoint | Start-Transcript |
| Get-PSCallStack | Stop-Transcript |
| Get-PSSnapin | Trace-Command |
| Get-Transaction | Undo-Transaction |
| Get-Variable | Use-Transaction |
| Import-Alias | Write-Host |

# Non-automatic cmdlet activities

If a cmdlet is not in the Windows PowerShell core modules, it does not mean that it is excluded—in fact, it probably is not excluded. Therefore, when a non-core Windows PowerShell cmdlet is used in a Windows PowerShell workflow, Windows PowerShell will automatically run the cmdlet as an InlineScript activity. An InlineScript activity permits you to run commands in a Windows PowerShell workflow and to share data that would not be otherwise permitted. In the InlineScript script block, you can call all Windows PowerShell commands and expressions and share state and data within the session. This includes imported modules and variable values. For example, the cmdlets from Table 22-2 that are not permitted in a Windows PowerShell workflow could be included in an InlineScript activity.

## Parallel activities

To create a Windows PowerShell workflow that uses a parallel workflow activity, you use the *Parallel* keyword and supply a script block. The workflow in Get-EventLogData.ps1 illustrates this technique.

```
Get-EventLogData.ps1

WorkFlow Get-EventLogData
{
 Parallel
 {
    Get-EventLog -LogName application -Newest 1
    Get-EventLog -LogName system -Newest 1
    Get-EventLog -LogName 'Windows PowerShell' -Newest 1 } }
```

After you run the script containing the *Get-EventLogData* workflow, you go to the execution pane of the Windows PowerShell ISE and execute the workflow. What happens is that the three Get-EventLog cmdlet commands execute in parallel. This results in a powerful and quick way to grab event log data. If you call the workflow with no parameters, it executes on your local computer, as shown in Figure 22-6.

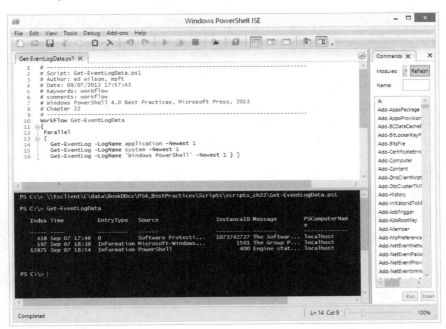

**FIGURE 22-6** Running the workflow with no parameters returns event information.

With a Windows PowerShell workflow, the cool thing is that you automatically gain access to several automatic parameters. One of the automatic parameters is *PSComputerName*. Therefore, with no additional work (this workflow does not exist on Server1 or Server2; it exists only here on my workstation), I can use the automatic *PSComputerName* workflow parameter and run the workflow on two remote servers.

# Checkpointing a Windows PowerShell workflow

If you have a Windows PowerShell workflow and you need to save workflow state or data to disk while the workflow runs, you can configure a checkpoint. In this way, if something interrupts the workflow, it does not need to restart completely. Instead, the workflow resumes from the point of the last checkpoint. Checkpointing of a Windows PowerShell workflow is also sometimes referred to as persistence or persisting a workflow. Because Windows PowerShell workflows run on large distributed networks or control the execution of long-running tasks, it is vital that the workflow can handle interruptions.

## Understanding checkpoints

A checkpoint is a snapshot of the workflow current state. This includes the current values of variables and generated output. Checkpointing persists this data to disk. It is possible to configure multiple checkpoints in a workflow. Windows PowerShell Workflow provides multiple methods for implementing checkpointing. Whatever method you use to generate the checkpoint, Windows PowerShell will use the data in the newest checkpoint for the workflow to recover and to resume the workflow if interrupted. If a workflow runs as a job (such as by using the *AsJob* workflow common parameter), Windows PowerShell retains the workflow checkpoint until job deletion (for example, by using the `Remove-Job` cmdlet).

## Placing checkpoints

You can place checkpoints anywhere in a Windows PowerShell workflow. This includes before and after each command or activity. The counterbalance to this sort of approach is that each checkpoint uses resources, and therefore it interrupts processing of the workflow—often with perceptible results. In addition, every time the workflow runs on a target computer, it checkpoints the workflow.

# Adding checkpoints

There are several levels of checkpoint that you can add to a Windows PowerShell workflow. For example, you can add a workflow at the workflow level or at the activity level. If you add a checkpoint to the workflow level, it will cause a checkpoint to occur at the beginning and at the end of the workflow.

## Workflow checkpoints are free

The absolutely, positively easiest way to add a checkpoint to a Windows PowerShell workflow is to use the *–pspersist* common parameter when calling the workflow.

The workflow in Get-CompInfoWorkflowCheckPointWorkflow.ps1 obtains network adapter, disk, and volume information.

```
Get-CompInfoWorkflowCheckPointWorkflow.ps1

workflow Get-CompInfo
{
   Get-NetAdapter
   Get-Disk
   Get-Volume
}
```

To cause the workflow to checkpoint, call the workflow with the *–PSPersist* parameter and set it to *$true*. The command line appears here:

```
Get-CompInfo -PSComputerName server1, server2 -PSPersist $true
```

When you run the workflow, a progress bar appears. It takes a few seconds due to the checkpoints. This progress bar is shown in Figure 22-7.

After the checkpoints, the workflow completes quickly and displays the gathered information. Figure 22-8 shows the output, as well as the command line used to call the workflow.

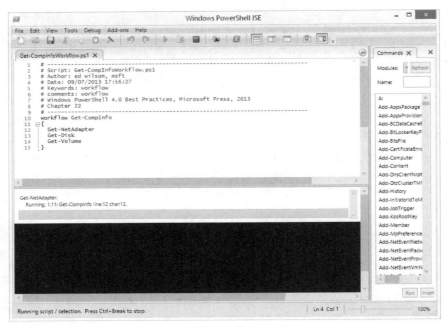

**FIGURE 22-7** Checkpoints cause a workflow to take more time to run.

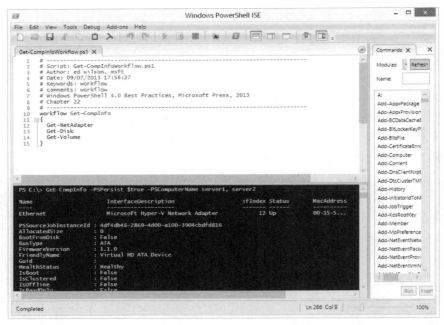

**FIGURE 22-8** After running the script to load the workflow, the command line calls the workflow against two computers and checkpoints the workflow.

## Checkpoint activity

If you use a core Windows PowerShell cmdlet, it picks up an automatic *PSPersist* parameter. You can then checkpoint the workflow at the activity level. Use the *PSPersist* parameter the same way that you do if you use it at the workflow level. To cause a checkpoint, set the value to *$True*. To disable a checkpoint, set it to *$False*.

In the workflow shown in Get-CompInfoWorkflowPersist.ps1, set a checkpoint to occur after the completion of the first and third activity.

```
Get-CompInfoWorkflowPersist.ps1

workflow Get-CompInfo
{
  Get-process -PSPersist $true
  Get-Disk
  Get-service -PSPersist $true
}
```

In the preceding script, the workflow obtains process information and then the workflow takes a checkpoint. Next, disk information and service information appear, and then the final checkpoint occurs.

## Using the CheckPoint-Workflow activity

The CheckPoint-WorkFlow activity causes a workflow to checkpoint immediately. You can place it in any location in the workflow. The big advantage of the Checkpoint-Workflow activity is that you can use it to checkpoint a workflow that does not use the core Windows PowerShell cmdlets as activities. This means, that, for example, you can use a workflow that includes Get-NetAdapter, Get-Disk, and Get-Volume and still be able to checkpoint the activity. You need to use Checkpoint-Workflow because no *–PSPersist* parameter adds automatically to the non-core Windows PowerShell cmdlets. Get-CompInfoWorkflowCheckPointWorkflow .ps1 contains the revised workflow.

```
Get-CompInfoWorkflowCheckPointWorkflow.ps1

workflow Get-CompInfo
{
  Get-NetAdapter
  Get-Disk
  Get-Volume
  Checkpoint-Workflow
}
```

# Adding a sequence activity to a workflow

To add a sequence activity to a Windows PowerShell workflow, all you need to do is use the *Sequence* keyword and specify a script block. When you do this, it causes the commands in the sequence script block to execute sequentially and in the specified order. The key concept here is that a *Sequence* activity occurs within a *Parallel* activity. The *Sequence* activity is required when you want commands to execute in a particular order. This is because commands running inside a *Parallel* activity execute in an undetermined order. The commands in the *Sequence* script block run in parallel with all of the commands in the *Parallel* activity. But the commands within the *Sequence* script block run in the order in which they appear in the script block. The Get-WinFeatureServersWorkflow.ps1 script contains the workflow illustrating this technique.

```
Get-WinFeatureServersWorkflow.ps1

workflow get-winfeatures
{
 Parallel {
    InlineScript {Get-WindowsFeature -Name PowerShell*}
    InlineScript {$env:COMPUTERNAME}
    Sequence {
        Get-date
        $PSVersionTable.PSVersion } }
}
```

In the preceding workflow, the order in which *Get-WindowsFeature*, the inline script, or the *Sequence* activity executes is not determined. The only thing you know for sure is that the Get-Date command runs before you obtain the *PSVersion* value—because this is the order specified in the *Sequence* activity script block.

> **NOTE**  In Windows PowerShell 3.0, it was possible to call a Windows PowerShell cmdlet from a system that did not contain the cmdlet directly within the workflow. In Windows PowerShell 4.0, this type of activity must be inside an InlineScript activity.

To run the workflow, first run the PS1 script that contains the workflow. Next, call the workflow and pass two computer names to it via the *PSComputerName* automatic parameter. Here is a sample command line:

```
get-winfeatures -PSComputerName server1, server2
```

Figure 22-9 shows the Windows PowerShell ISE when calling the workflow. It also illustrates the order in which the commands executed at the time. Note that the commands in the *Sequence* script block executed in the specified order—that is, *Get-Date* executed before

*$PsVersionTable.PSVersion* executed—but that they were in the same *Parallel* stream of execution.

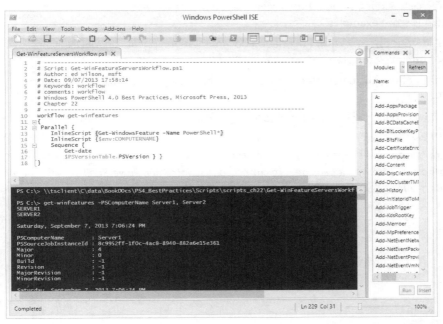

**FIGURE 22-9** The order in which the activities execute is not guaranteed, except for activities identified in the *Sequence*.

## Some workflow coolness

One of the cool things about this workflow is that I executed it from my Windows 8.1-based laptop. What is so cool about that? Well the Get-WindowsFeature cmdlet does not work on desktop operating systems. Therefore, I ran a command from my laptop that does not exist on my laptop—but it does exist on the target Server1 and Server2 computers. All I have to do is place the cmdlet within an InlineScript activity.

Another cool workflow feature is the InlineScript activity. I can access an environmental variable from the remote servers. The InlineScript activity allows me to do things that otherwise would not be permitted in a Windows PowerShell workflow. It adds a lot of flexibility.

# Additional resources

- The TechNet Script Center at *http://www.microsoft.com/technet/scriptcenter* contains numerous script examples.
- Detailed Windows Workflow Foundation documentation appears on MSDN at *http://msdn.microsoft.com/en-us/vstudio/jj684582.*
- Workflow automatic parameters are detailed at *http://technet.microsoft.com/library /jj129719.aspx.*
- Workflow specific parameters are detailed at *http://technet.microsoft.com/en-us /library/jj574194.aspx.*
- All scripts from this chapter are in the file available from the Script Center Script Repository at *http://gallery.technet.microsoft.com/scriptcenter/PowerShell -40-Best-d9e16039.*

# CHAPTER 23

# Using the Windows PowerShell DSC

- Understanding Desired State Configuration
- Controlling configuration drift
- Additional resources

The killer feature of Windows PowerShell 4.0 is Desired State Configuration (DSC). Every presentation at TechEd 2013 in both North America and in Europe that discussed DSC received high marks and numerous comments from audience participants. Clearly, this feature resonates soundly with IT Pros. Therefore, what is Desired State Configuration, how is it used, what are the requirements for implementing it, and how does it help the enterprise administrator?

## Understanding Desired State Configuration

DSC is a set of extensions to Windows PowerShell that permit the management of systems for both the software and the environment on which software services run. Because DSC is part of the Windows Management Framework 4.0 (which includes Windows PowerShell 4.0), it means that it is operating system independent and runs on any computer that can run Windows PowerShell 4.0. DSC ships with the following resource providers:

- Archive
- Environment
- File
- Group
- Log
- Package
- Registry
- Script
- Service

- User
- WindowsFeature
- WindowsProcess

The twelve default resource providers each support a standard set of configuration properties. The providers and supported properties are listed in Table 23-1.

**TABLE 23-1** DSC resource providers and properties

| Provider | Properties |
| --- | --- |
| Archive | Destination, Path, Checksum, DependsOn, Ensure, Force, Validate |
| Environment | Name, DependsOn, Ensure, Path, Value |
| File | DestinationPath, Attributes, Checksum, Contents, Credential, DependsOn, Ensure, Force, MatchSource, Recurse, SourcePath, Type |
| Group | GroupName, Credential, DependsOn, Description, Ensure, Members, MembersToExclude, MembersToInclude |
| Log | Message, DependsOn |
| Package | Name, Path, ProductId, Arguments, Credential, DependsOn, Ensure, LogPath, ReturnCode |
| Registry | Key, ValueName, DependsOn, Ensure, Force, Hex, ValueData, ValueType |
| Script | GetScript, SetScript, TestScript, Credential, DependsOn |
| Service | Name, BuiltInAccount, Credential, DependsOn, StartupType, State |
| User | UserName, DependsOn, Description, Disabled, Ensure, FullName, Password, PasswordChangeNotAllowed, PasswordChangeRequired, PasswordNeverExpires |
| WindowsFeature | Name, Credential, DependsOn, Ensure, IncludeAllSubFeature, LogPath, Source |
| WindowsProcess | Arguments, Path, Credential, DependsOn, Ensure, StandardErrorPath, StandardInputPath, StandardOutputPath, WorkingDirectory |

Because it is possible to extend support for additional resources by creating other providers, you are not limited to configuring only the preceding 12 types of resources.

## The DSC process

To create a configuration by using DSC, you first need a Managed Object Format (MOF) file. MOF is the syntax used by Windows Management Instrumentation (WMI), and therefore it is a standard text type of format. A sample MOF file for a server named Server1 is shown in Figure 23-1.

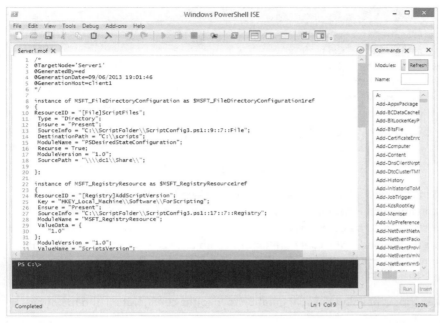

**FIGURE 23-1** A DSC MOF file is a stylized text file in a format the same as used by WMI.

You can easily create your own MOF by creating a DSC configuration script and calling one of the 12 built-in DSC providers or by using a custom provider. To create a configuration script, begin by using the *Configuration* keyword, and provide a name for the configuration. Next open a script block followed by a *node* and a resource provider. The *node* identifies the target of the configuration. In the ScriptFolderConfig.ps1 script, the configuration creates a directory on a target server named Server1. It uses the File resource provider. The source files are copied from a share on the network. *DestinationPath* defines the folder to be created on Server1. *Type* identifies that a directory will be created. *Recurse* specifies that all folders in the source path are copied. The complete ScriptFolderConfig.ps1 script is shown here.

```
ScriptFolderConfig.ps1

#Requires -version 4.0


Configuration ScriptFolder
{
    node 'Server1'
    {
      File ScriptFiles
```

```
    {
        SourcePath = "\\dc1\Share\"
        DestinationPath = "C:\scripts"
        Ensure = "Present"
        Type = "Directory"
        Recurse = $true
    }
    }

}
```

After the ScriptFolderConfig.ps1 script runs inside the Windows PowerShell ISE, the ScriptFolder configuration loads into memory. The configuration is then called in the same way that a function would be called. When the configuration is called, it creates a MOF file for each node that is identified in the configuration. The path to the configuration is used when calling the Start-DscConfiguration cmdlet. There are therefore three distinct phases to this process, as follows:

1. Run the script containing the configuration to load the configuration into memory.

2. Call the configuration, and supply any required parameters to create the MOF file for each identified node.

3. Call the Start-DscConfiguration cmdlet, and supply the path containing the MOF's files created in step 2.

This process appears in Figure 23-2. The configuration appears in the upper script pane, while the command pane shows running the script, calling the configuration, and starting the configuration via the MOF files.

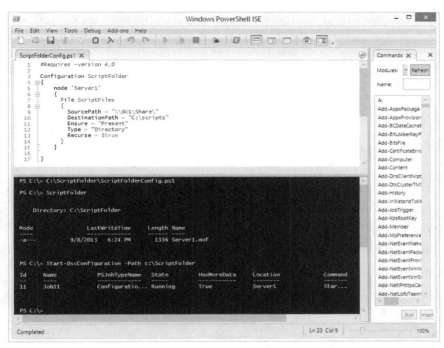

**FIGURE 23-2** To run a configuration against a remote server, use the `Start-DscConfiguration` cmdlet and supply the path to a folder containing the appropriate MOF files.

## Configuration parameters

To create parameters for a configuration, use the *param* keyword in the same manner as you would with functions. The *param* statement goes just after opening the script block for the configuration. As seen in the ScriptFolderVersion.ps1 script, you can even assign default values for the parameters. When a configuration is created, it automatically receives the following three default parameters: *instancename, outputpath* and *configurationdata*. The *instancename* parameter holds the instance name of the configuration. The *instancename* value of a configuration is used to uniquely identify the resource ID used to identify each resource specified in the configuration—normally, the default value for this is good. The *outputpath* parameter holds the destination for storing the configuration MOF file. This permits redirecting the MOF file that is created to a different folder than the one holding the script that is run. The default is to create the MOF files in the same folder that holds the script that creates the configuration. Storing the MOF files in a different location makes it easier to reuse them and to update them. The *configurationdata* parameter accepts a hashtable holding configuration data. In addition, any parameters specified in the *param* statement in the configuration are also available when calling the configuration.

By calling the configuration directly from the script that creates the configuration, you can simplify the process of creating the MOF. The ScriptFolderVersion.ps1 script adds a second resource provider to the configuration. The Registry provider is used to add a registry key, forscripting, to the HKLM\Software registry key. The registry value name is ScriptsVersion, and the data is set to 1.0. The use of the registry provider is shown here:

```
Registry AddScriptVersion
{
  Key = "HKEY_Local_Machine\Software\ForScripting"
  ValueName = "ScriptsVersion"
  ValueData = "1.0"
  Ensure = "Present"
}
```

The additional resource provider call is placed right under the closing brace used to close off the previous call to the File resource provider.

The complete ScriptFolderVersion.ps1 script is shown here.

```
ScriptFolderVersion.ps1

#Requires -Version 4.0

Configuration ScriptFolderVersion
{
 Param ($server = 'server1')
    node $server
    {
      File ScriptFiles
      {
        SourcePath = "\\dc1\Share\"
        DestinationPath = "C:\scripts"
        Ensure = "present"
        Type = "Directory"
        Recurse = $true
      }
      Registry AddScriptVersion
      {
        Key = "HKEY_Local_Machine\Software\ForScripting"
        ValueName = "ScriptsVersion"
        ValueData = "1.0"
        Ensure = "Present"
      }

    }
}

ScriptFolderVersion
```

# Setting dependencies

Everything does not happen at the same time when calling a DSC configuration. Therefore, to ensure that activities occur at the right time, you use the *DependsOn* keyword in the configuration. For example, in the ScriptFolderVersionUnzip.ps1 script, the Archive resource provider is used to unzip a compressed file that is copied down from the shared folder. The script files are copied from the share with the ScriptFiles activity supported by the File resource provider. Because these files must be downloaded from the network share before the zipped folder can be uncompressed, the *DependsOn* keyword is used. Because the File ScriptFiles resource activity creates the folder structure containing the compressed folder, the path used by the Archive resource provider can be hard-coded. The path is local to the server that actually runs the configuration. The Archive activity is shown here:

```
Archive ZippedModule
{
  DependsOn = "[File]ScriptFiles"
  Path = "C:\scripts\PoshModules\PoshModules.zip"
  Destination = $modulePath
  Ensure = "Present"
}
```

The ScriptFolderVersionUnzip.ps1 script parses the *$env:PSModulePath* environmental variable to obtain the path to the Windows PowerShell Modules location in the Program Files directory. Following the configuration, it also calls the configuration and redirects the MOF file to the C:\Server1Config folder. It then calls the `Start-DscConfiguration` cmdlet and provides a specific job name for the job. It then uses the *–verbose* parameter to provide more detailed information about the progress. The complete script is shown here.

```
ScriptFolderVersionUnzip.ps1

#Requires -version 4.0


Configuration ScriptFolderVersionUnzip
{
 Param ($modulePath = ($env:PSModulePath -split ';' |
    ? {$_ -match 'Program Files'}),
    $Server = 'Server1')
    node $Server
    {
      File ScriptFiles
      {
        SourcePath = "\\dc1\Share\"
        DestinationPath = "C:\scripts"
        Ensure = "present"
        Type = "Directory"
        Recurse = $true
      }
```

```
        Registry AddScriptVersion
        {
          Key = "HKEY_Local_Machine\Software\ForScripting"
          ValueName = "ScriptsVersion"
          ValueData = "1.0"
          Ensure = "Present"
        }
        Archive ZippedModule
        {
          DependsOn = "[File]ScriptFiles"
          Path = "C:\scripts\PoshModules\PoshModules.zip"
          Destination = $modulePath
          Ensure = "Present"
        }
      }
   }
}

ScriptFolderVersionUnZip -output C:\server1Config
Start-DscConfiguration -Path C:\server1Config -JobName Server1Config -Verbose
```

## Configuration data

To modify the way a configuration runs, it is necessary to specify configuration data. This
can take the place of a separate file, or it can be added directly via an array of hashtables. To
create a local user, it is necessary to specify PSDscAllowPlainTextPassword = $true in the
configuration data—this is a requirement, even if not directly supplying the password as plain
text. In the DemoUserConfig.ps1 configuration script, the user credentials are supplied to the
configuration via the Get-Credential cmdlet. This produces a secure string. But the error that
generates from running the configuration states that storing an encrypted password as plain
text is supported only if the configuration permits it. This error is shown in Figure 23-3.

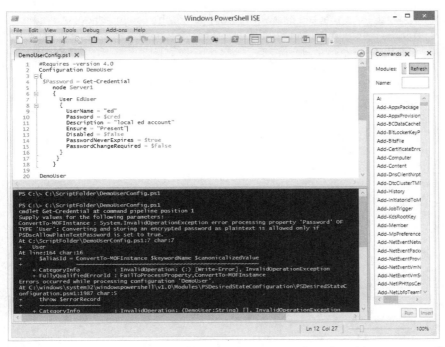

**FIGURE 23-3** An error arises if the configuration does not permit storing plain text passwords.

The complete DemoUserConfig.ps1 configuration script is shown here.

```
DemoUserConfig.ps1

#Requires -version 4.0
Configuration DemoUser
{
 $Password = Get-Credential
    node Server1
    {
      User EdUser
      {
        UserName = "ed"
        Password = $cred
        Description = "local ed account"
        Ensure = "Present"
        Disabled = $false
        PasswordNeverExpires = $true
        PasswordChangeRequired = $false
      }
    }
   }

DemoUser
```

The problem is not the way that the password is supplied to the configuration, but rather what happens after the configuration runs—it decrypts the password and stores it in plain text in the MOF file. This is shown in Figure 23-4.

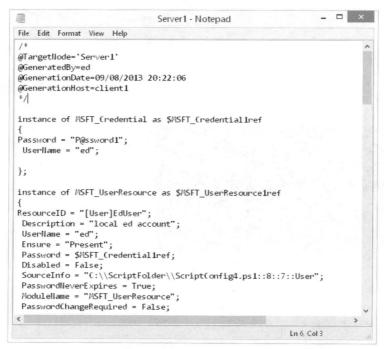

```
/*
@TargetNode='Server1'
@GeneratedBy=ed
@GenerationDate=09/08/2013 20:22:06
@GenerationHost=client1
*/

instance of MSFT_Credential as $MSFT_Credential1ref
{
Password = "P@ssword1";
 UserName = "ed";

};

instance of MSFT_UserResource as $MSFT_UserResource1ref
{
ResourceID = "[User]EdUser";
 Description = "local ed account";
 UserName = "ed";
 Ensure = "Present";
 Password = $MSFT_Credential1ref;
 Disabled = False;
 SourceInfo = "C:\\ScriptFolder\\ScriptConfig4.ps1::8::7::User";
 PasswordNeverExpires = True;
 ModuleName = "MSFT_UserResource";
 PasswordChangeRequired = False;
```

**FIGURE 23-4** After being permitted by the configuration, the password stores in plain text in the MOF file.

Because this stores the password in plain text in the MOF file, the Windows PowerShell team wanted to ensure that you are aware of exactly what you are doing. (By the way, the alternative to storing the password in plain text is to encrypt the password with a certificate.)

After you create the configuration data, you call the configuration and specify the newly created configuration data. This is shown here:

```
$configData = @{
            AllNodes = @(
                    @{
                        NodeName = "Server1";
                        PSDscAllowPlainTextPassword = $true
                        }
                )
        }

ScriptFolder -ConfigurationData $configData
```

## Creating users with the user provider

To create a local user, call the user provider, and specify the user name. The password is passed to the password property as a *PSCredential* object. This is different than just a *SecureString* object, which might be expected. This is because the *PSCredential* object contains both the user name as well as the password (as a *SecureString* object). Next comes the *Description* property and whether or not to enable the user account. It is possible to create disabled user accounts by setting the *Disabled* property to *$True*. The last two things to configure are the *PasswordNeverExpires* property and the *PasswordChangeRequired* property. The following portion of the configuration script illustrates this technique:

```
User EdUser
    {
       UserName = "ed"
       Password = $cred
       Description = "local ed account"
       Ensure = "Present"
       Disabled = $false
       PasswordNeverExpires = $true
       PasswordChangeRequired = $false
    }
```

## Creating groups with the group provider

To create a local group with the local group provider, you need to specify the group name to the *GroupName* property. You also should specify the description for the group. The members themselves are added via an array of user names. Because the users should exist prior to attempting to add them to the group, the *DependsOn* property is used to specify the dependency upon the users. This is illustrated in the following code block:

```
Group Scripters
    {
       GroupName = "Scripters"
       Credential = $cred
       Description = "Scripting Dudes"
       Members = @("ed")
       DependsOn = "[user]Eduser"
    }
```

The complete ScriptFolderVersionUnzipCreateUsersAndProfile.ps1 script is shown here.

```
ScriptFolderVersionUnzipCreateUsersAndProfile.ps1

#Requires -Version 4.0
Configuration ScriptFolder
{
 Param ($modulePath = ($env:PSModulePath -split ';' |
    ? {$_ -match 'Program Files'}))
    node Server1
```

```
{
  User EdUser
  {
    UserName = "ed"
    Password = $cred
    Description = "local ed account"
    Ensure = "Present"
    Disabled = $false
    PasswordNeverExpires = $true
    PasswordChangeRequired = $false
  }
  Group Scripters
  {
    GroupName = "Scripters"
    Credential = $cred
    Description = "Scripting Dudes"
    Members = @("ed")
    DependsOn = "[user]Eduser"
  }
  File ScriptFiles
  {
    SourcePath = "\\dc1\Share\"
    DestinationPath = "C:\scripts"
    Ensure = "present"
    Type = "Directory"
    Recurse = $true
  }
  Registry AddScriptVersion
  {
    Key = "HKEY_Local_Machine\Software\ForScripting"
    ValueName = "ScriptsVersion"
    ValueData = "1.0"
    Ensure = "Present"
  }
  Archive ZippedModule
  {
    DependsOn = "[File]ScriptFiles"
    Path = "C:\scripts\PoshModules\PoshModules.zip"
    Destination = $modulePath
    Ensure = "Present"
  }
  File PoshProfile
  {
    DependsOn = "[File]ScriptFiles"
```

```
        SourcePath = "C:\scripts\PoshProfiles\Microsoft.PowerShell_profile.ps1"
        DestinationPath = "$env:USERPROFILE\WindowsPowerShell\Microsoft.PowerShell_
profile.ps1"
        Ensure = "Present"
        Type = "File"
        Recurse = $true
    }


    }
}

$cred = get-credential
$configData = @{
                AllNodes = @(
                        @{
                            NodeName = "Server1";
                            PSDscAllowPlainTextPassword = $true
                            }
                    )
            }

ScriptFolder -ConfigurationData $configData
Start-DscConfiguration Scriptfolder
```

## Controlling configuration drift

Because Windows PowerShell DSC is idempotent, you can run the same configuration script multiple times without fear of creating multiple resources or generating errors. Therefore, if the same configuration runs multiple times, if the configuration has not drifted, no changes are made. If the configuration has drifted, you can easily bring the server back into the desired state. You do not need to worry about modifying the configuration script to correct only detected errors. In fact, you do not even need to worry about configuration drift—you just run the same configuration, and you can be ensured that the server is brought back into state. In the situation where a server must match the DSM state, you can use the task scheduler to run *Start-DscConfiguration* on a regular interval that matches the specific urgency of the required checks.

Another way to check for configuration drift is to use the *Test-DscConfiguration* function. The way to do this is to create a CIM session to the remote servers whose configuration requires checking. Do this from the same server that was used to create the DSC in the first place so that access to the MOF files is assured. After the CIM session is created, pass it to the *Test-DscConfiguration* function. This technique is shown here:

```
PS C:\> $session = New-CimSession -ComputerName server1, server2 -Credential
iammred\administrator

PS C:\> Test-DscConfiguration -CimSession $session
True
True
```

The SetServicesConfig.ps1 script, shown here, creates two configuration MOF files—one for each server specified in the node array.

```
SetServicesConfig.ps1

Configuration SetServices
{
 node @('Server1', 'Server2')
 {
  Service Bits
  {
   Name = "Bits"
   StartUpType = "Automatic"
   State = "Running"
   BuiltinAccount = 'LocalSystem'
  }
  Service Browser
  {
   Name = "Browser"
   StartUpType = "Disabled"
   State = "Stopped"
   BuiltinAccount = 'LocalSystem'
  }
  Service DHCP
  {
   Name = "DHCP"
   StartUpType = "Automatic"
   State = "Running"
   BuiltinAccount = 'LocalService'
  }
 }
}

SetServices -OutputPath C:\ServerConfig
Start-DscConfiguration -Path C:\ServerConfig
```

Figure 23-5 illustrates running the configuration and using CIM to verify that the configuration is still intact.

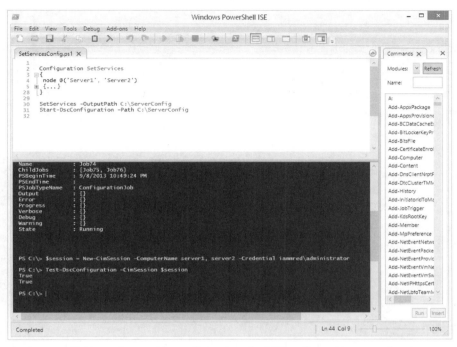

**FIGURE 23-5** CIM is used to test the configuration of a DSC configured target node.

# Additional resources

- The TechNet Script Center at *http://www.microsoft.com/technet/scriptcenter* contains numerous script examples.
- All scripts from this chapter are in the file available from the Script Center Script Repository at *http://gallery.technet.microsoft.com/scriptcenter/PowerShell-40 -Best-d9e16039*.

# Index

## Symbols

## A

## B

# O

# T

# U

# V

# X

# Z

# About the author

 **ED WILSON** is the Microsoft Scripting Guy and a well-known scripting expert. He writes the daily Hey Scripting Guy! blog. He has also spoken at TechEd and at the Microsoft internal TechReady conferences. He is a Microsoft-certified trainer who has delivered a popular Windows PowerShell workshop to Microsoft Premier Customers worldwide. He has written 10 books, including seven on Windows scripting that were published by Microsoft Press. He has also contributed to nearly a dozen other books. His most recent books by Microsoft Press include *Windows PowerShell 3.0 Step by Step* and *Windows PowerShell 3.0 First Steps*. Ed holds more than 20 industry certifications, including Microsoft Certified Systems Engineer (MCSE) and Certified Information Systems Security Professional (CISSP). Prior to coming to work for Microsoft, he was a senior consultant for a Microsoft Gold Certified Partner, where he specialized in Active Directory design and Exchange implementation. In his spare time, he enjoys woodworking, underwater photography, and scuba diving.